Foundations First

SENTENCES AND PARAGRAPHS

WITH READINGS

THIRD EDITION

Laurie G. Kirszner
University of the Sciences in Philadelphia

Stephen R. Mandell
Drexel University

Bedford / St. Martin's
Boston ■ New York

For Bedford/St. Martin's

Developmental Editor: Joelle Hann
Senior Production Editor: Harold Chester
Senior Production Supervisor: Dennis J. Conroy
Marketing Manager: Casey Carroll
Art Director: Lucy Krikorian
Text Design: Linda M. Robertson
Copy Editor: Alice Vigliani
Photo Research: Christine Buese/Photosearch, Inc.
Cover Design: Donna Lee Dennison
Cover Art: Painting, *Market Day* © 2005 Richard H. Fox/Strata-art.com
Composition: Stratford/TexTech
Printing and Binding: R.R. Donnelley & Sons Company

President: Joan E. Feinberg
Editorial Director: Denise B. Wydra
Editor in Chief: Karen S. Henry
Director of Development: Erica T. Appel
Director of Marketing: Karen Melton Soeltz
Director of Editing, Design, and Production: Marcia Cohen
Managing Editor: Shuli Traub

Library of Congress Control Number: 2007928249

Manufactured in the United States of America.

2 1 0
f

For information, write: Bedford/St. Martin's, 75 Arlington Street, Boston, MA 02116 (617-399-4000)

ISBN-10: 0-312-45996-3 (Instructor's Annotated Edition)
ISBN-13: 978-0-312-45996-3 (Instructor's Annotated Edition)

ISBN-10: 0-312-45989-0 (Student Edition with Readings)
ISBN-13: 978-0-312-45989-5 (Student Edition with Readings)

ISBN-10: 0-312-45995-5 (Student Edition)
ISBN-13: 978-0-312-45995-6 (Student Edition)

Acknowledgments
Acknowledgments and copyrights appear at the back of the book on pages 585–86, which constitute an extension of the copyright page.

Preface for Instructors

We believe that in college, writing comes first and that students learn writing skills most meaningfully in the context of their own writing. For this reason, *Foundations First: Sentences and Paragraphs*, like our paragraph-to-essay text *Writing First*, takes a "practice in context" approach, teaching students the skills they need to become better writers by having them practice in the context of their own writing.

Equally important, *Foundations First* offers not just grammar and writing help but also a collection of invaluable resources to prepare developmental students for college work. By providing unique coverage of study skills, vocabulary building, ESL issues, and critical reading, *Foundations First* gives students the support and encouragement they need to build a solid foundation for success in college and beyond.

In *Foundations First*, as in the classroom and in everyday life, writing is essential. For this reason, we begin with thorough coverage of the writing process. Most chapters begin with a writing prompt, and extensive writing practice is also central to the grammar chapters of the text. Throughout the book, students learn to become better writers by applying each chapter's concepts to writing, revising, and editing their own writing.

We wrote this book for adults—our own interested, concerned, and hardworking students—and we tailored the book's approach and content to them. Instead of exercises that reinforce the idea that writing is a dull, pointless, and artificial activity, we chose fresh, contemporary examples (both student and professional) and worked hard to develop interesting exercises and writing assignments. Throughout *Foundations First* we try to talk *to* students, not *at* or *down* to them. We try to be concise without being abrupt, thorough without being repetitive, direct without being rigid, specific without being prescriptive, and flexible without being inconsistent. Our most important goal is simple: to create an engaging text that motivates students to improve their writing and that gives them the tools they need to do so.

Organization

Foundations First: Sentences and Paragraphs has a flexible organization that lets instructors teach various topics in the order that works best for their students. The book opens with Unit One on academic survival skills. This unit includes two chapters of practical advice to help students succeed in college. Unit Two provides a comprehensive discussion of the writing process. Units Three through Six focus on sentence skills, grammar, punctuation, mechanics, and spelling. Unit Seven, which appears only in *Foundations First with Readings,* includes eighteen essays (four by student writers), accompanied by study questions and writing prompts. Finally, two appendixes, "Building Word Power" and "Strategies for Workplace Success," help students to master the vocabulary highlighted in the text and to prepare for real-world job situations.

For instructors wishing to emphasize the patterns of development, an Index of Rhetorical Patterns points to essays and paragraphs that exemplify particular modes. (All of the patterns are covered in Chapters 5–13, and the essays in Unit Seven include at least one example of each pattern.)

Features

When we wrote *Foundations First,* our goal was to create the most complete sentence-to-paragraph text available for developmental writers. In preparing the third edition, we retained all the features that instructors told us contributed to the book's accessibility and effectiveness.

A complete resource for improving student writing. With one comprehensive unit on paragraphs (including coverage of all the major patterns of development and a chapter on moving from paragraphs to essays), two units on sentences, two on grammar, one on reading, and numerous examples of student writing throughout the text, *Foundations First* provides comprehensive coverage of basic writing in a format that gives instructors maximum flexibility in planning their courses.

"Practice in Context" writing activities. A two-step exercise strand in most chapters enables students to write, revise, and edit their own work from the outset. Chapters typically begin with a ***Seeing and Writing*** activity that asks students to write a response to a visual. At the end of the chapter, a ***Revising and Editing*** activity helps students fine-tune their initial response, applying the skills they have learned and practiced in the chapter.

Numerous opportunities for practice and review. *Foundations First* helps students practice grammar in the context of connected-discourse exercises that mirror the kinds of material they are likely to read and write in college. ***Self-Assessment Checklists*** guide students in revising and editing their work. ***Chapter Reviews***—featuring ***Editing Practices***, ***Collaborative Activities***, and ***Review Checklists***—encourage students to think critically about writing. Finally, ***Answers to Odd-Numbered Exercises*** at the end of the book let students check their own work as they practice and review.

A strong visual appeal for basic writing students. More than two dozen visual writing prompts help students generate ideas for writing. Thumbnail photos in the Editing Practices provide cultural context for new vocabulary as well as support for students who are visual learners.

An emphasis on the connection between reading and writing. *Foundations First* presents reading as an integral part of the writing process, offering numerous student and professional examples throughout the text. Chapter 2, "Reading for Academic Success," introduces the basic techniques of active reading and shows students how to get the most out of their academic and professional reading. Eighteen selections (four of them by students) in Chapter 37, "Readings for Writers," provide material for writing assignments and classroom discussion.

An integrated approach to building vocabulary. In every chapter, ***Word Power*** boxes help students learn new words and use them in the context of their own writing. Appendix A, "Building Word Power," gives students additional opportunities for expanding their vocabulary.

Extensive help for ESL students. Chapter 30 addresses concerns of nonnative writers. ***ESL Tips*** throughout the *Instructor's Annotated Edition* provide helpful hints to novice and experienced instructors alike.

Practical help with college and workplace skills. The two chapters in Unit One orient students to key college skills such as note-taking, time management, and academic reading, while Appendix B, "Strategies for Workplace Success," models such real-world skills as writing résumés and cover letters and preparing for job interviews.

Content that respects students as serious writers. The tone and level of the explanatory material and the subject matter of the exercises and examples acknowledge the diverse interests, ages, and experiences of developmental students.

New to This Edition

We have worked hard to make the third edition of *Foundations First* even more useful to developmental writers and their instructors. Recognizing that students often need help not just with grammar and writing but also with staying focused and on task, we streamlined the instructions, examples, exercises, and marginal notes to make the text simpler, cleaner, and more accessible to basic writing students. Additionally, we support our "students first" philosophy with chapters that cover basic study skills and related issues, helping students make a successful transition to college. Other innovative features are designed to make students' writing practice meaningful, productive, and enjoyable.

More coverage of the patterns of paragraph development. Nine new chapters, one on each rhetorical mode, provide annotated student models, a thorough explanation of the writing process, and extra step-by-step guidance that students need to master the fundamentals of paragraph writing. To appeal to visual learners, Chapter Reviews now include a visual writing prompt.

More basic instruction that helps beginning writers master important concepts. Terminology, explanations, and exercises have been simplified to be more accessible to beginning writers. Without diluting important coverage, *Foundations First* is now more accessible than ever to the students who need the most help with basic grammar and rhetorical concepts.

Streamlined design and navigation that keeps students engaged. In-class testing with students and instructors showed that many students are easily distracted as readers. In the third edition of *Foundations First*, marginal elements have been integrated into the body of the main text, and the book has been redesigned to put important information where students will be sure to read it. The easy-to-use, full-color design also helps students locate key information quickly and easily.

More integrated help with grammar throughout the book that helps students apply concepts they are learning to their writing.

- **New *Grammar in Context* boxes in the paragraph chapters.** These boxes help students identify and correct common grammar problems related to the rhetorical pattern they are learning in the paragraph chapters. Cross-references to *Foundations First*'s grammar sections direct students to where they can get more help on the grammar issues they find the most challenging.
- **New *Unit Reviews* that allow students to practice editing in realistic situations.** New five-paragraph, end-of-unit essays contain multiple types of errors, allowing students to identify and correct common errors they are likely to encounter in their own writing. More practice is available online **in extra Unit Reviews in the *Exercise Central* database.**

Updated coverage and additional help that keeps beginning students' needs in mind.

- **New readings and student essays.** Six professional essays in Chapter 37, "Readings for Writers," chosen for their currency and interest are new to this edition. Also, many of the student essays featured in the twenty-one Chapter Reviews are new.
- **Updated ESL coverage and new *ESL Workbook*.** The comprehensive ESL chapter, which addresses concerns of special interest to nonnative writers, has been thoroughly revised to meet the needs of today's ESL students. The new ancillary, *The Bedford/St. Martin's ESL Workbook*, provides even more ESL exercises and coverage for students who need it most.
- **Thoroughly revised and updated exercises that engage student interest.** Hundreds of new exercises throughout the book cover more current events as well as more diverse subjects in the areas of work, academics, historical events, cultural issues, and everyday life.

Ancillaries

Foundations First is accompanied by comprehensive teaching support that includes the following items:

Print Resources

- The *Instructor's Annotated Edition* features numerous teaching tips in the margins, including ESL tips designed especially for instructors teaching nonnative speakers. The book's annotations include answers to all the practice exercises in *Foundations First*.
- *Classroom Resources for Instructors Using* Foundations First, **Third Edition**, offers advice for teaching developmental writing as well as chapter-by-chapter pointers for using *Foundations First* in the classroom, answers to all of the book's practice exercises, sample syllabi, and full chapters on collaborative learning.
- *Teaching Developmental Writing: Background Readings*, **Third Edition**, by Susan Naomi Bernstein, contains professional readings on topics of interest to instructors. Helpful chapter introductions, informative headnotes, suggested classroom activities, pedagogical tips, and questions accompany the readings.
- *Supplemental Exercises to Accompany* Foundations First, **Third Edition**, offers additional grammar exercises plus cross-references to more practice at the online *Exercise Central* exercise collection.
- *Diagnostic and Mastery Tests to Accompany* Foundations First, **Third Edition**, offers diagnostic and mastery tests that complement the topics covered in *Foundations First*.
- *Transparency Masters to Accompany* Foundations First, **Third Edition**, includes numerous models of student writing, and is downloadable from the *Foundations First* Web site.
- *The Bedford/St. Martin's ESL Workbook* includes a broad range of exercises covering grammatical issues for multilingual students of varying language skills and backgrounds. Answers can be found in the back.
- *From Practice to Mastery* (a study guide for the Florida Basic Skills Exit Tests in reading and writing) gives students all the resources they need to practice for—and pass—the Florida tests in reading and writing. It includes pre- and post-tests, abundant practices, and clear instruction in all the skills covered on the exam.

New Media Resources

- **The Book Companion Site at bedfordstmartins.com/foundationsfirst** provides quick access to extensive instructor resources, including downloadable print ancillaries (*Classroom Resources, Diagnostic and Mastery Tests, Transparency Masters*) that accompany *Foundations First*. Student resources include additional exercises on *Exercise Central*, sample annotated student paragraphs and essays, and access to *Re:Writing Basics*.
- *Exercise Central* **at bedfordstmartins.com/foundationsfirst** is the largest collection of interactive grammar and writing exercises available online, tests a wide variety of skills, and provides immediate feedback. Assessment tools allow teachers to track student work.
- **The** *Exercise Central to Go: Writing and Grammar Practices for Basic Writers* **CD-ROM** provides hundreds of practice items to help students build their writing and editing skills. No Internet connection necessary.

- *Re:Writing Basics* **at bedfordstmartins.com/rewritingbasics** is an easy-to-navigate Web site that offers the most popular and widely used free resources from Bedford/St. Martin's, including writing and grammar exercises, model documents, instructor resources, help with the writing process, tips on college success, and more.
- **The** ***Testing Tool Kit: A Writing and Grammar Test Bank*** **CD-ROM** allows instructors to create secure, customized tests and quizzes from nearly two thousand questions covering forty-seven topics. It also includes ten prebuilt diagnostic tests.
- **The** ***Make-a-Paragraph Kit*** is a fun, interactive CD-ROM that includes "Extreme Paragraph Makeover," an animation that teaches students about paragraph development. It also contains exercises to help students build their own paragraphs, audiovisual tutorials on four of the most common serious errors for basic writers, and the content from *Exercise Central to Go: Writing and Grammar Practices for Basic Writers*.
- ***Foundations First*** **content for course management systems** is ready for use in Blackboard, WebCT, and other popular course management systems. For more information about Bedford/St. Martin's course management offerings, visit **bedfordstmartins.com/cms**.

Ordering Information

To order any of the ancillaries for *Foundations First*, contact your local Bedford/St. Martin's sales representative, email **sales_support@bfwpub.com** or visit our Web site at **bedfordstmartins.com**.

Use these ISBNs when ordering the following supplements packaged with your students' book:

Foundations First: Sentences and Paragraphs **with readings**

Supplemental Exercises:
ISBN-10: 0-312-47377-X; ISBN-13: 978-0-312-47377-8
Exercise Central to Go CD-ROM:
ISBN-10: 0-312-47378-8; ISBN-13: 978-0-312-47378-5
Make-a-Paragraph Kit CD-ROM:
ISBN-10: 0-312-47360-5; ISBN-13: 978-0-312-47360-0
From Practice to Mastery (for Florida):
ISBN-10: 0-312-47379-6; ISBN-13: 978-0-312-47379-2
The Bedford/St. Martin's ESL Workbook:
ISBN-10: 0-312-47380-X; ISBN-13: 978-0-312-47380-8

Foundations First: Sentences and Paragraphs **without readings**

Supplemental Exercises:
ISBN-10: 0-312-47383-4; ISBN-13: 978-0-312-47383-9
Exercise Central to Go CD-ROM:
ISBN-10: 0-312-47388-5; ISBN-13: 978-0-312-47388-4
Make-a-Paragraph Kit CD-ROM:
ISBN-10: 0-312-47361-3; ISBN-13: 978-0-312-47361-7
From Practice to Mastery (for Florida):
ISBN-10: 0-312-47386-9; ISBN-13: 978-0-312-47386-0
The Bedford/St. Martin's ESL Workbook:
ISBN-10: 0-312-47387-7; ISBN-13: 978-0-312-47387-7

Acknowledgments

In our work on *Foundations First,* we have benefited from the help of a great many people.

Franklin E. Horowitz of Teachers College, Columbia University, drafted an early version of Chapter 30, "Grammar and Usage Issues for ESL Writers," and his linguist's insight continues to inform that chapter. Linda Stine of Lincoln University devoted energy and vision to the preparation of *Classroom Resources for Instructors Using FOUNDATIONS FIRST*. Linda Mason Austin of McLennan Community College drew on her extensive experience to contribute Teaching Tips and ESL Tips to the *Instructor's Annotated Edition.* Susan Bernstein's work on the compilation and annotation of *Teaching Developmental Writing: Background Readings* reflects her deep commitment to scholarship and teaching. We are very grateful for their contributions.

We thank Kristen Blanco, Stephanie Hopkins, Judith Lechner, Carolyn Lengel, Carol Sullivan, Jessica Carroll, Charlotte Gale, and Pamela Gerth for their contributions to the exercises and writing activities in the text, and Linda Stine for developing the PowerPoint presentation featured on the *Foundations First* Web site.

Foundations First could not exist without our students, whose words appear on almost every page of the book, whether in sample sentences, paragraphs, or essays. We thank all of them, past and present, who allowed us to use their work.

Instructors throughout the country have contributed suggestions and encouragement at various stages of the book's development. For their collegial support, we thank Connie Baumgardner, Cleveland State Community College; Cheyenne M. Bonnell, Copper Mountain College; Lory Conrad, University of Arkansas–Fort Smith; Nissa Dalager, Rasmussen College; Theresa Dolan, Los Angeles Trade-Technical College; Stacey DuVal, University of Arkansas–Fort Smith; Michal Eskayo, St. Augustine College; Debra Justice, Hopkinsville Community College; Joshua Mattern, Waubonsee Community College; Brit Osgood-Treston, Riverside Community College; Catherine Rusco, Muskegon Community College; Shusmita Sen, Spokane Community College; and Denielle True, Manatee Community College.

At Bedford/St. Martin's, we thank founder and former president Chuck Christensen and president Joan Feinberg, who believed in this project and gave us support and encouragement from the outset. We thank Erica Appel, Director of Development, for overseeing this edition, and we also thank Laura King, associate editor, for her work in managing the revision of the book's ancillaries and coordinating the writing of new exercises. We are also grateful to Robin Butterhof and Nina Gantcheva, editorial assistants, for helping with numerous tasks, big and small; Dennis Conroy, senior production supervisor; Irwin Zucker and Harold Chester, senior project editors, for guiding the book ably through production; and Lucy Krikorian, art director, for once again overseeing a beautiful and innovative design. Thanks also go to Casey Carroll, marketing manager, and his team and to our outstanding copyeditor, Alice Vigliani, and excellent proofreader, Roberta Sobotka. And finally, we thank our editor, Joelle Hann, whose hard work and dedication kept the project moving along.

We are grateful, too, for the continued support of our families—Mark, Adam, and Rebecca Kirszner, and Demi, David, and Sarah Mandell. Finally, we are grateful for the survival and growth of the writing partnership we entered into when we were graduate students. We had no idea then of the wonderful places our collaborative efforts would take us. Now, we know.

Laurie G. Kirszner
Stephen R. Mandell

Contents

A Student's Guide to Using *Foundations First*

What *Foundations First* Can Do for You

Whether you write as a student, as an employee, as a parent, or as a concerned citizen, your writing almost always has a specific purpose. When you write an essay, a memo, a letter, or a research paper, you are writing not just to complete an exercise but also to give other people information or to tell them your ideas or opinions. That is why, in this book, we don't ask you simply to do grammar exercises; in each chapter, we also ask you to apply the skills you are learning to your own writing.

As teachers—and former students—we know how demanding college can be and how hard it is to juggle school, work, and family responsibilities. We also know that you don't want to waste your time or money. That is why in *Foundations First* we make information easy to find and use and provide many features to help you become a better writer.

If you take the time now to familiarize yourself with these features, you will be able to use the book more effectively later on. The following sections will help.

How *Foundations First* Makes Information Easy to Find and Use

Brief table of contents. Inside the front cover is a brief table of contents that summarizes the topics covered in this book. The brief contents can help you find a particular chapter quickly.

Parts of speech review. Inside the back cover is a quick review of the eight major parts of speech. Refer to this as needed to review grammar's most basic elements.

Detailed table of contents. The table of contents that starts on page xi provides a detailed breakdown of the book's topics. Use this table of contents to find a specific part of a particular chapter.

Index. The index, which appears at the back of the book starting on page 587, helps you find all the available information about a particular topic.

The topics appear in alphabetical order, so, for example, if you wanted to find out how to use commas, you would find the *C* section and look up the word *comma*. (If the page number following a word is **boldfaced**, it means that on that page you can find a definition of the word.)

List of Self-Assessment Checklists. On page xxviii is a list of checklists designed to help you write, revise, and edit paragraphs and even essays. Use this list to find the checklist that is most useful for the particular writing task you are working on.

Easy-to-use navigational tools. At the tops of most pages of *Foundations First*, you'll find ***quick-reference corner tabs*** consisting of green-and-blue boxes, each containing a number and a letter. This information tells you which chapter you have turned to and which section of that chapter you are looking at. ***Cross-references*** (for example, "see 10B") within instructional boxes like the ***Focus*** and the ***Grammar in Context*** boxes will point you to another section of the book. Together, the tabs and the cross-references help you find information quickly. For example, if a cross-reference in the text suggested, "For more on topic sentences, see 10B," you could use the tabs to quickly locate section 10B.

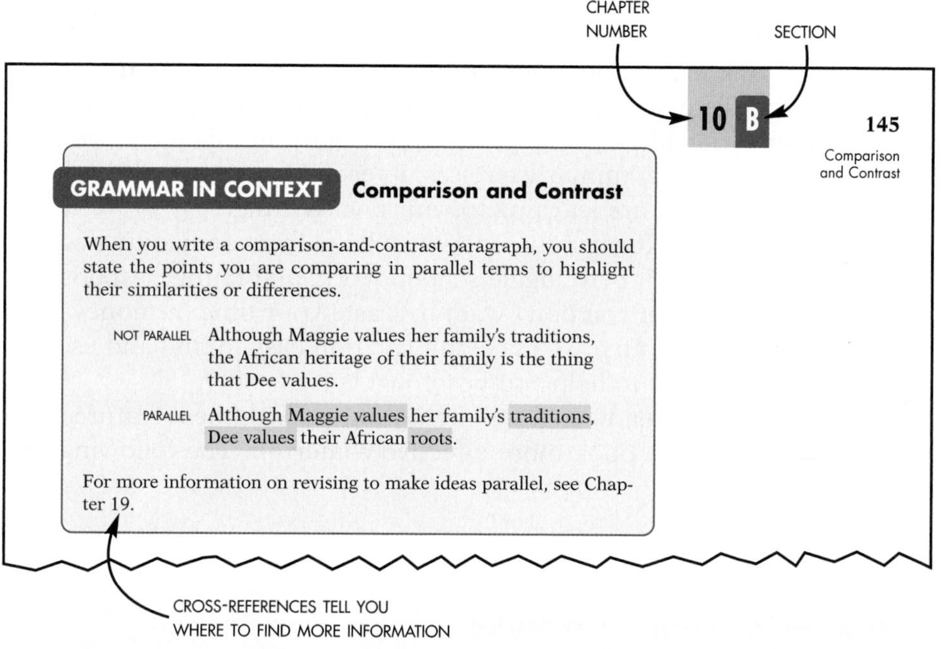

How *Foundations First* Can Help You Become a Better Writer

Preview boxes. Each chapter starts with a list of key concepts that will be discussed in the chapter. Looking at these boxes before you skim the chapter will help you get an overview of the material that will be covered.

Seeing and Writing activities. Most chapters include a two-part writing activity that helps you apply specific skills to your own writing. Each chapter starts with a *Seeing and Writing* exercise, accompanied by a visual, that asks you to write about a particular topic. Later, a ***Revising and Editing*** exercise guides you in fine-tuning your writing.

17
Sentences
PREVIEW
In this chapter, you will learn
• to form complex sentences with subordinating conjunctions (17A)
• to punctuate with subordinating conjunctions (17B)
• to form complex sentences with relative pronouns (17C)
Word Power
estranged separated from someone else by feelings of hostility or indifference
diverge to go in different directions
SEEING AND WRITING
Look at the picture above, which shows a group of childhood friends. Then, write a paragraph about the childhood friends you've lost touch with. Why do you think you don't see these friends anymore? Which, if any, would you like to see again?

Focus boxes. Throughout the book, boxes with the word *Focus* in a dark red banner highlight useful information, identify key points, and explain difficult concepts.

FOCUS ***There is* and *There are***

When a sentence begins with *there is* or *there are*, the word *there* is not the subject of the sentence. The subject comes after the form of the verb *be*.

> There is (V) still one ticket (S) available for the playoffs.
>
> There are (V) still ten tickets (S) available for the playoffs.

Grammar in Context boxes. In Chapters 3–14 you will find boxes that identify key grammar issues in the patterns of paragraph development. Use these boxes to increase your understanding of important issues in your writing.

GRAMMAR IN CONTEXT **Argument**

When you write an argument paragraph, you need to show the relationships among your ideas. You do this by combining simple sentences to create both compound and complex sentences.

COMPOUND SENTENCE The only thing that will work is outlawing sodas completely~~. No~~ *, and no* one is suggesting this.

COMPLEX SENTENCE Recently, some people have suggested taxing soda~~. They~~ *because they* think it is not healthy for young people.

For more information on how to create compound sentences, see Chapter 16. For more information on how to create complex sentences, see Chapter 17.

Self-Assessment Checklists. Chapters 3–14 include Self-Assessment Checklists that give you a handy way to check your work and measure your progress. Use these checklists to help you revise your writing before you hand it in.

SELF-ASSESSMENT CHECKLIST: Writing a Narrative Paragraph

- ☐ Does your topic sentence state your paragraph's main idea?
- ☐ Do your sentences move clearly from one event to another?
- ☐ Have you included enough details to make the events clear to readers?
- ☐ Have you used appropriate transitional words and phrases?
- ☐ Have you avoided run-ons as you connected events in your narrative?
- ☐ Have you included a concluding statement that sums up your paragraph's main idea?

Marginal notes. In the margins of *Foundations First*, you'll find two kinds of notes that give you additional information in an easy-to-read format. ***Word Power*** boxes define words that you may find useful in working with a particular writing assignment or reading selection. For additional practice with specific skills, ***cross-references to Exercise Central,*** an online collection of nearly 9,000 exercises, appear in the margin as well.

> **Word Power**
>
> **institution** a well-known person, place, or thing

> **ON THE WEB**
>
> *For more practice identifying action verbs, visit* Exercise Central *at bedfordstmartins .com/foundationsfirst.*

Review Checklists. All grammar chapters and many of the writing chapters end with a summary of the most important information in the chapter. Use these checklists to review material for quizzes or to remind yourself of the main points in the chapter you've been studying.

> **REVIEW CHECKLIST:**
> **Moving from Paragraph to Essay**
>
> - Many essays have a thesis-and-support structure: the thesis statement presents the main idea, and the body paragraphs support the thesis. (See 14A.)
> - Begin by focusing on your assignment, purpose, and audience. (See 14B.)
> - Narrow your general assignment to a topic you can write about. (See 14B.)
> - Use one or more strategies to find ideas to write about. (See 14C.)

Answers to Odd-Numbered Exercises. Starting on page 575, you'll find answers for some of the Practice items in the book. When you need to study a topic independently, or when your instructor has you complete a Practice but not hand it in, you can consult these answers to see if you're on the right track.

How to Access Additional Exercises and Resources Online

Foundations First's companion Web site is free and open to anyone to use. There you will get access to *Exercise Central*, a database of nearly 9,000 practice exercises, as well as to *Re:Writing Basics*, a resource center with help for many issues that affect your experience in the writing classroom and in college, like how to take good notes and how to avoid plagiarism.

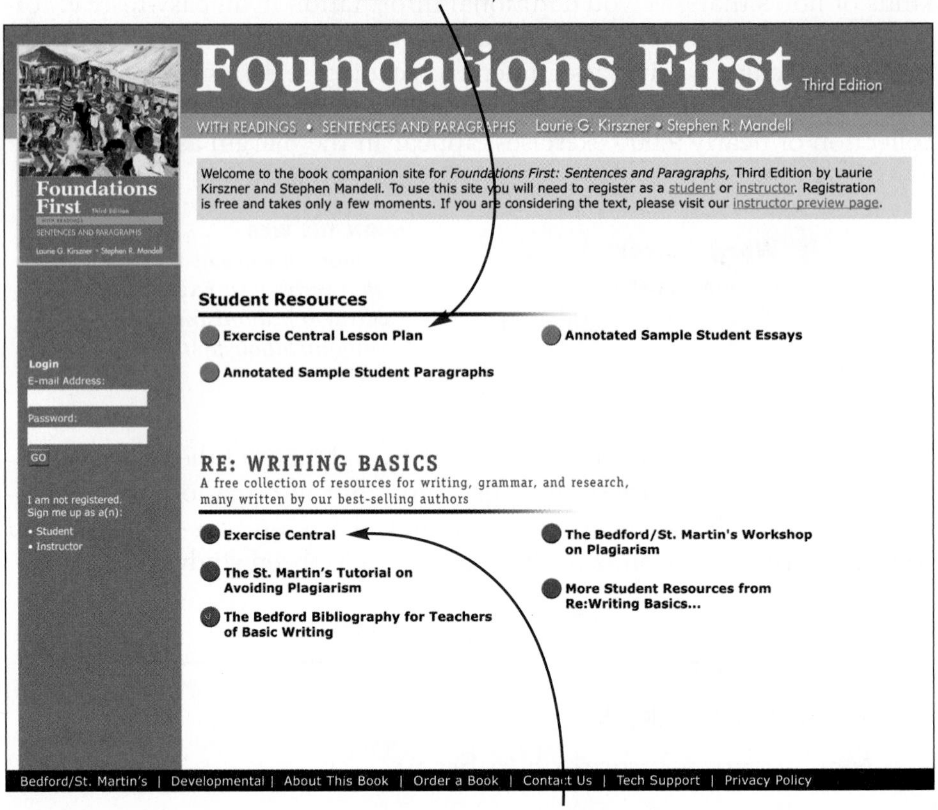

FOR A CUSTOMIZED LESSON PLAN USING EXERCISE CENTRAL, GO HERE

Foundations First Third Edition

WITH READINGS • SENTENCES AND PARAGRAPHS Laurie G. Kirszner • Stephen R. Mandell

Welcome to the book companion site for *Foundations First: Sentences and Paragraphs,* Third Edition by Laurie Kirszner and Stephen Mandell. To use this site you will need to register as a student or instructor. Registration is free and takes only a few moments. If you are considering the text, please visit our instructor preview page.

Student Resources

- **Exercise Central Lesson Plan**
- **Annotated Sample Student Essays**
- **Annotated Sample Student Paragraphs**

ONCE YOU'VE REGISTERED, LOG IN HERE

Login
E-mail Address:
Password:
GO

REGISTER HERE

I am not registered. Sign me up as a(n):
• Student
• Instructor

RE: WRITING BASICS
A free collection of resources for writing, grammar, and research, many written by our best-selling authors

- **Exercise Central**
- **The Bedford/St. Martin's Workshop on Plagiarism**
- **The St. Martin's Tutorial on Avoiding Plagiarism**
- **More Student Resources from Re:Writing Basics...**
- **The Bedford Bibliography for Teachers of Basic Writing**

Bedford/St. Martin's | Developmental | About This Book | Order a Book | Contact Us | Tech Support | Privacy Policy

FOR EXTRA PRACTICE WITH WRITING AND GRAMMAR, GO HERE

Visit **bedfordstmartins.com/foundationsfirst** to register. It's free and you will only have to register once. Keep a record of your username and password so that you can easily sign in on future visits.

When you have finished exploring or using the *Foundations First* Web site, you can close the screen. You may return to the Web site as many times as you like.

How *Foundations First* Can Help You Succeed in Other Courses

In a sense, this whole book is all about succeeding in other courses. After all, as we said earlier, writing is the key to success in college. But *Foundations First* also includes sections that you may find especially useful in courses you take later on in college. We have designed these sections so you can use them either on your own or with your instructor's help.

Chapter 1, "Strategies for College Success." Here you'll find tips for making your semester (and your writing course) as successful as possible. Included are effective strategies for taking notes, completing homework assignments, finding and evaluating Web sources, doing well on exams, and managing your time efficiently.

Chapter 2, "Reading for Academic Success." This chapter will teach you the skills you need to become an active reader. It also offers specific strategies for reading in different situations—in college, in the workplace, and in daily life—and includes advice and examples on how to approach reading textbooks, newspapers, Web sites, inter-office memos, and emails.

Appendix A, "Building Word Power." This practical guide tells you how to get the most out of your dictionary. It also offers tips for building your vocabulary and gives you opportunities to practice using the words you've encountered in the Word Power boxes.

Appendix B, "Strategies for Workplace Success." This step-by-step guide explains how to define your professional goals, find job openings, research companies, and market yourself by writing effective résumés, job-application letters, and follow-up letters, and by preparing for job interviews.

We hope *Foundations First* will help you become a better writer and student. If you have suggestions for improving this book, please send them to: Laurie Kirszner and Stephen Mandell, c/o Bedford/St. Martin's, 33 Irving Place, New York, NY 10003.

Self-Assessment Checklists for Revising and Editing Your Writing

Unit Two of *Foundations First* includes a series of Self-Assessment Checklists to help you write, revise, and edit paragraphs and essays. You can use these checklists in your writing course and in other courses that include written assignments. The page number for each checklist is included here.

UNIT ONE

Learning Practical Success Strategies

Strategies for College Success

CHAPTER

1

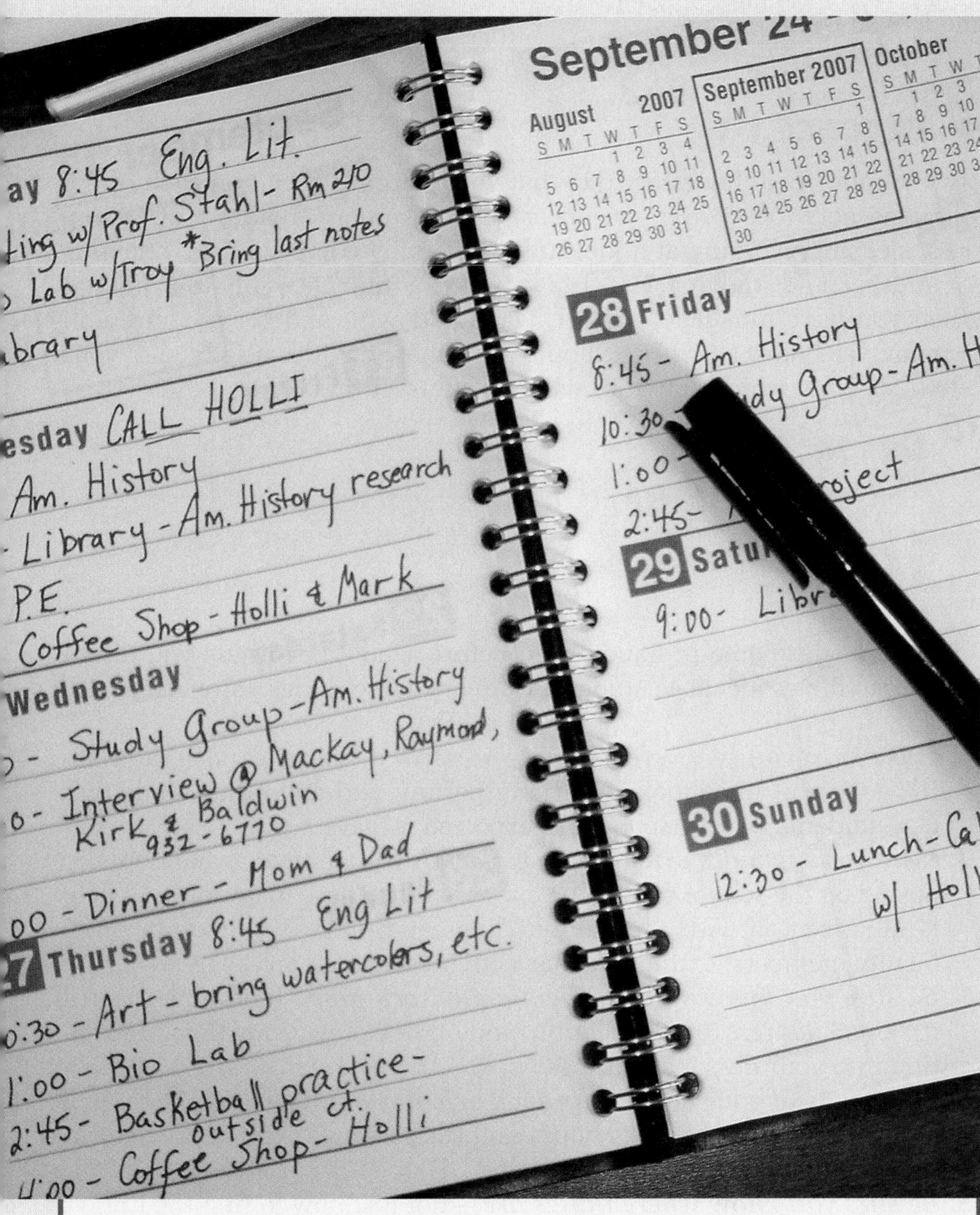

PREVIEW

In this chapter, you will learn

- orientation strategies (1A)
- first-week strategies (1B)
- day-to-day strategies (1C)
- note-taking strategies (1D)
- homework strategies (1E)
- exam-taking strategies (1F)
- time-management strategies (1G)
- public-speaking strategies (1H)
- Internet strategies (1I)

SEEING AND WRITING

The picture above shows two pages of a busy student's organizer. How do you manage to fit everything you need to do into the limited time you have? Look at the picture, and then write a few sentences that answer this question.

By deciding to go to college, you have decided to make some important changes in your life. In the long run, you will find that the changes will be positive, but there will be some challenges as well. One way in which your life will change is that now, perhaps more than ever, you will find yourself short of time. Life will become a balancing act as you juggle classroom time, commuting time, work time, and study time along with family responsibilities and time for yourself. The strategies discussed in this chapter can help make your life as a college student more productive and less stressful.

◆ PRACTICE 1-1

List the number of hours per day that you expect to spend on each of the following activities while you are a college student: reading, attending class, sleeping, working at a job, fulfilling family commitments, relaxing, commuting, and studying. (Be sure you have a total of twenty-four hours.) When you have finished your list, trade lists with another student, and compare your daily activities. Should any other activities be added to your list? If so, from which activities will you subtract time?

A Orientation Strategies

▶ **Word Power**

orientation adjustment to a new environment

orient to adjust

Some strategies come in handy even before school begins, as you orient yourself to life as a college student. Here are some things you need to do.

1. ***Make sure you have everything you need:*** a college catalog, a photo ID, a student handbook, a parking permit, and any other items that new students at your school are expected to have.
2. ***Read your school's orientation materials*** (distributed as handouts or posted on the school Web site) very carefully. These materials will help familiarize you with campus buildings and offices, course offerings, faculty members, extracurricular activities, and so on.
3. ***Be sure you know your academic adviser's name*** (and how to spell it), email address, office location, and office hours. Copy this information into your personal address book.
4. ***Get a copy of your college library's orientation materials.*** These will tell you about the library's hours and services and explain procedures such as how to use an online catalog.
5. ***Be sure you know where things are***—not just how to find the library and the parking lot but also where you can do photocopying or buy a newspaper.

◆ PRACTICE 1-2

Visit your school's Web site. List the three most useful pieces of information you find there. Now, compare your list with those of other students in your class. Did reading their lists lead you to reevaluate your own? Do you still think the three items you listed are the most useful?

1. ______________________________

2. ______________________________

3. ______________________________

◆ PRACTICE 1-3

Working in a group of three or four students, draw a rough map of your school's campus, including the general locations of the following: the library, the financial aid office, the registrar's office, the cashier, the cafeteria, the bookstore, the computer lab, the campus police, the student health office. Now, make up a quiz for another group of students, asking them to locate three additional buildings or offices on their map.

B First-Week Strategies

College can seem like a confusing place at first, but from your first day as a college student, there are steps you can take to help you get your bearings.

1. ***Make yourself at home.*** Find places on campus where you can get something to eat or drink, and find a good place to study or relax before or between classes. As you explore the campus, try to locate all the things you may need—for example, pay phones, ATMs, and rest rooms.
2. ***Know where you're going and when you need to be there.*** Check the building and room number for each of your classes and the days and hours the class meets. Copy this information onto the front cover of the appropriate notebook. Pay particular attention to classes with irregular schedules (for example, a class that meets from 9 a.m. to 10 a.m. on Tuesdays but from 11 a.m. to 12 noon on Thursdays).
3. ***Introduce yourself to other students.*** Networking with other students is an important part of the college experience. Get the name, phone number, and email address of two students in each of your classes. If you miss class, you will need to get in touch with someone to find out what material you missed.
4. ***Familiarize yourself with each course's syllabus.*** At the first meeting of every course, your instructor will hand out a syllabus. (The syllabus may also be posted on the course's Web page.) A syllabus gives you three kinds of useful information.
   - Information that can help you plan a study schedule—for example, when assignments are due and when exams are scheduled
   - Practical information, such as the instructor's office number and email address and the books and supplies you need to buy
   - Information about the instructor's policies on absences, grading, class participation, and so on
5. ***Buy books and supplies with care.*** When you buy your books and supplies, be sure to keep the receipts, and don't write your name in your books until you are certain that you are not going to drop a course. (If you write in a book, you will not be able to return it.) If your

> **Word Power**
> **networking** interacting with others to share information

> **Word Power**
> **syllabus** an outline or summary of a course's main points (the plural form is *syllabi*)

roster of courses is not definite, you should wait a few days to buy your texts. You should, however, buy some items right away: a separate notebook and folder for each course you are taking, a college dictionary, and a pocket organizer. In addition to the books and other items required for a particular course (for example, a lab notebook, a programmable calculator, art supplies), you should buy pens and pencils in different colors, blank computer disks, paper clips or a stapler, Post-it notes, highlighter pens, and so on—and a backpack or bookbag in which to keep all these items.

FOCUS Using a Dictionary

Even though your word-processing program will have a spell checker, you still need to buy a dictionary. A college dictionary tells you not only how to spell words but also what words mean and how to use them. (For more on using a dictionary, see Appendix A.)

6. ***Set up your notebooks.*** Establish a separate notebook (or a separate section of a divided notebook) for each of your classes. (Notebooks with pocket folders can help you keep graded papers, worksheets, handouts, and class syllabi all in one place.) Copy your instructor's name, email address, phone number, and office hours and location onto the inside front cover of the notebook; write your own name, address, and phone number on the outside, along with the class schedule.

◆ PRACTICE 1-4

Set up a notebook for each course you are taking. Then, exchange notebooks with another student, and review each other's notebooks.

C Day-to-Day Strategies

As you get busier and busier, you may find that it's hard to keep everything under control. Here are some strategies to help you as you move through the semester.

1. ***Find a place to study.*** As a college student, you will need your own private place to work and study. Even if it's just a desk in one corner of your dorm room (or, if you are living at home or off-campus, in one corner of your bedroom), you will need a place that is yours alone, a place that will be undisturbed when you leave it. (The kitchen table, which you share with roommates or family members, will not work.) This space should include everything you will need to make your work easier—quiet, good lighting, a comfortable chair, a clean work surface, storage for supplies, and so on.

2. ***Set up a bookshelf.*** Keep your textbooks, dictionary, calculator, supplies, and everything else you use regularly for your coursework in one place—ideally, in your own workspace. That way, when you need something, you will know exactly where it is.
3. ***Set up a study schedule.*** Identify thirty- to forty-five-minute blocks of free time before, between, and after classes. Set aside this time for review. Remember, studying should be part of your regular routine, not something you do only the night before an exam.

FOCUS Skills Check

Don't wait until you have a paper to write to discover that you don't know how to use a computer well enough. Be sure your basic word-processing skills are at the level you need for your work. If you need help, get it right away.

Your school's computer lab should be the first place you turn for help with word processing, but writing center and library staff members may also be able to help you.

4. ***Establish priorities.*** It's important to understand what your priorities are. Before you can establish priorities, however, you have to know which assignments are due first, which ones can be done in steps, and which tasks or steps will be most time consuming. Then, you must decide which tasks are most pressing. (For example, studying for a test to be given the next day is more pressing than reviewing notes for a test scheduled for the following week.) Finally, you have to decide which tasks are more important than others. For example, studying for a midterm is more important than studying for a quiz, and the midterm for a course you are in danger of failing is more important than the midterm for a course in which you are doing well. Remember, you can't do everything at once; you need to know what must be done immediately and what can wait.

> **Word Power**
> **priorities** things considered more important than others

5. ***Check your mail.*** If you have a campus mailbox or email account, check it regularly—if possible, several times a day. If you miss a message, you may miss important information about changes in assignments, canceled classes, or rescheduled quizzes.
6. ***Schedule conferences.*** Try to meet with each of your instructors during the semester even if you are not required to do so. You might schedule one conference during the second or third week of school and another a week or two before a major exam or paper is due. These meetings will help you understand exactly what is expected of you, and your instructors will appreciate and respect your initiative.
7. ***Become familiar with the student services available on your campus.*** College is hard work, and you can't do everything on your own. There is nothing wrong with getting help from your school's writing center or tutoring center or from the center for students with disabilities (which serves students with learning disabilities as well as physical challenges), the office of international students, or the counseling center, as well as from your adviser or course instructors. Think

of yourself as a consumer. You are paying for your education, and you are entitled to—and should take advantage of—all the services available to students.

FOCUS Asking for Help

Despite all your careful planning, you may still run into trouble. For example, you may miss an exam and have to make it up; you may miss several days of classes in a row and fall behind in your work; you may have trouble understanding the material in one of your courses; or a family member may get sick. Don't wait until you are overwhelmed to ask for help. If you have an ongoing personal problem or a family emergency, let your instructors know immediately.

◆ PRACTICE 1-5

Try to figure out how and when you study best. Do you do your best studying in the morning or late at night? Alone or in a busy library? When you have answered these questions, set up a weekly study schedule. Begin by identifying your free time and deciding how you can use it most efficiently. Next, discuss your schedule with a group of three or four other students. How much time does each of you have available? How much time do you think you need? Does the group consider each student's study schedule to be realistic? If not, why not?

D Note-Taking Strategies

Learning to take notes in a college class takes practice, but taking good notes is essential for success in college. Here are some basic guidelines that will help you develop and improve your note-taking skills.

During Class

1. ***Come to class.*** If you miss class, you miss notes—so come to class, and come on time. In class, sit where you can see the board and hear the instructor. Don't feel you have to keep sitting in the same place in each class every day; change your seat until you find a spot that's comfortable for you.
2. ***Date your notes.*** Begin each class by writing the date at the top of the page. Instructors frequently identify material that will be on a test by dates. If you do not date your notes, you may not know what to study.
3. ***Know what to write down.*** You can't possibly write down everything an instructor says. If you try to do this, you will miss a lot of important information. Listen carefully *before* you write, and listen for cues to what's important. For example, sometimes the instructor will tell you that something is important or that a particular piece of information

will be on a test. Sometimes he or she will write key terms and concepts on the board. If the instructor emphasizes an idea or underlines it on the board, you should do the same in your notes. (Of course, if you have done the assigned reading before class, you will recognize important topics and know to take especially careful notes when these topics are introduced in class.)

4. ***Include examples.*** Try to write down an example for each general concept introduced in class—something that will help you remember what the instructor was talking about. (If you don't have time to include examples as you take notes during class, add them when you review your notes.) For instance, if your world history instructor is explaining *nationalism*, you should write down not only a definition but also an example, such as "Germany in 1848."
5. ***Write legibly, and use helpful signals.*** Use dark (blue or black) ink for your note-taking, but keep a red or green pen handy to highlight important information, jot down announcements (such as a change in a test date), note gaps in your notes, or question confusing points. Do not take notes in pencil, which is hard to read and less permanent than ink.
6. ***Ask questions.*** If you do not hear (or do not understand) something your instructor says, or if you need an example to help you understand something, *ask!* But don't immediately turn to another student for clarification. Instead, wait to see if the instructor explains further, or if he or she pauses to ask if anyone has a question. If you're not comfortable asking a question during class, make a note of the question and ask the instructor—or send an email—after class.

After Class

1. ***Review your notes.*** After every class, try to spend ten or fifteen minutes rereading your notes, filling in gaps and examples while the material is still fresh in your mind. When you review, try giving each day's notes a title so you can remember the topic of each class. This will help you locate information when you study.
2. ***Recopy information.*** When you have a break between classes or when you get home, recopy important pieces of information from your notes.
   - Copy announcements (such as quiz dates) onto your calendar.
   - Copy reminders (for example, a note to schedule a conference before your next paper is due) into your organizer.
   - Copy questions you want to ask the instructor onto the top of the next blank page in your notes.

Before the Next Class

1. ***Reread your notes.*** Leave time just before each class to skim the previous class's notes once more. This strategy will get you oriented for the class to come and remind you of anything that needs clarification or further explanation.
2. ***Ask for help.*** Call or e-mail a classmate if you need to fill in missing information; if you still need help, see the instructor during office hours, or come to class early to ask your question before class begins.

◆ PRACTICE 1-6

Compare the notes you took in one of your classes with notes taken by another student in the same class. How are your notes different? Do you think you need to make any changes in the way you take notes?

E Homework Strategies

Doing homework is an important part of learning in college. Homework gives you a chance to practice your skills and measure your progress. If you are having trouble with the homework, chances are you are having trouble with the course. Ask the instructor or teaching assistant for help *now*; don't wait until the day before the exam. Here are some tips for getting the most out of your homework.

1. ***Write down the assignment.*** Don't expect to remember an assignment; copy it down. If you are not sure exactly what you are supposed to do, check with your instructor or with another student.
2. ***Do your homework, and do it on time.*** Teachers assign homework to reinforce classwork, and they expect homework to be done on a regular basis. It is easy to fall behind in college, and trying to do three—or five—nights' worth of homework in one night is not a good idea. If you do several assignments at once, you not only overload yourself but you also miss important day-to-day connections with classwork.
3. ***Be an active reader.*** Get into the habit of highlighting your textbooks and other material as you read. (For specific strategies for active reading, see Chapter 2.)
4. ***Join study groups.*** A study group of three or four students can be a valuable support system for homework as well as for exams. If your schedule permits, do some homework assignments—or at least review your homework—with other students on a regular basis. In addition to learning information, you will learn different strategies for doing assignments.

◆ PRACTICE 1-7

Working in a group of three or four students, list the ways in which a study group might benefit you. How many students should be in the group? How often should they meet? Should the group include students whose study habits are similar or different? What kind of help do you think you would need? What kind of help could you offer to other students?

F Exam-Taking Strategies

Preparation for an exam should begin well before the exam is announced. In a sense, you begin this preparation on the first day of class.

Before the Exam

1. ***Attend every class.*** Regular attendance in class—where you can listen, ask questions, and take notes—is the best possible preparation for exams. If you do have to miss a class, arrange to copy (and read) another student's notes *before the next class* so you will be able to follow the discussion.
2. ***Keep up with the reading.*** Read every assignment, and read it before the class in which it will be discussed. If you don't, you may have trouble understanding what is going on in class.
3. ***Take careful notes.*** Take careful, thorough notes, but be selective. If you can, compare your notes on a regular basis with those of one or two other students in the class; working together, you can fill in gaps or correct errors. Establishing a buddy system will also force you to review your notes regularly instead of just on the night before the exam.
4. ***Study on your own.*** When an exam is announced, adjust your study schedule—and your priorities—so you have time to review everything. (This is especially important if you have more than one exam in a short period of time.) Review all your material (class notes, readings, and so on), and then review it again. Make a note of anything you don't understand, and keep track of topics you need to review. Try to predict the most likely questions, and—if you have time—practice answering them.
5. ***Study with a group.*** If you can, set up a study group. Studying with others can help you understand the material better. However, don't come to group sessions unprepared and expect to get everything from the other students. You must first study on your own.
6. ***Make an appointment with your instructor.*** Make an appointment with the instructor or with the course's teaching assistant a few days before the exam. Bring to this conference any specific questions you have about course content and about the format of the upcoming exam. (Be sure to review all your study material before the conference.)
7. ***Review the material one last time.*** The night before the exam is not the time to begin your studying; it is the time to review. When you have finished your review, get a good night's sleep.

During the Exam

Like an athlete before a big game or a musician before an important concert, you will already have done all you could to get ready for the test by the time you walk into the exam room. Your goal now is to keep the momentum going and not do anything to undermine all your hard work.

> **Word Power**
> **undermine** to weaken support for something

1. ***Read through the entire exam.*** Be sure you understand how much time you have, how many points each question is worth, and exactly what each question is asking you to do. Many exam questions call for just a short answer—*yes* or *no*, *true* or *false*. Others ask you to fill in a blank with a few words, and still others require you to select the best answer from among several choices. If you are not absolutely certain what kind of answer a particular question calls for, ask the instructor or the proctor *before* you begin to write. (Remember, on some tests

there is no penalty for guessing, but on other tests it is best to answer only those questions you have time to read and consider carefully.)

> **FOCUS Writing Essay Exams**
>
> If you are asked to write an essay on an exam, remember that what you are really being asked to do is write a **thesis-and-support essay**. Chapter 14 of this text will tell you how to do this.

2. ***Budget your time.*** Once you understand how much each section of the exam and each question are worth, plan your time and set your priorities, devoting the most time to the most important questions. If you know you tend to rush through exams, or if you find you often run out of time before you get to the end of a test, you might try putting a mark on your paper when about one-third of the allotted time has passed (for a one-hour exam, put a mark on your paper after twenty minutes) to make sure you are pacing yourself appropriately.
3. ***Reread each question.*** Carefully reread each question *before* you start to answer it. Underline the **key words**—the words that give specific information about how to approach the question and how to phrase your answer.

> **FOCUS Key Words**
>
> Here are some helpful key words to look for on exams.
>
> | | | |
> |---|---|---|
> | analyze | explain | suggest results, effects, outcomes |
> | argue | give examples | summarize |
> | compare | identify | support |
> | contrast | illustrate | take a stand |
> | define | recount | trace |
> | demonstrate | suggest causes, origins, contributing factors | |
> | describe | | |
> | evaluate | | |

Remember, even if everything you write is correct, your response is not acceptable if you don't answer the question. If a question asks you to *compare* two novels, *summarizing* one of them will not be acceptable.

4. ***Brainstorm to help yourself recall the material.*** If you are writing a paragraph or an essay, look frequently at the question as you brain-

storm. (You can write your brainstorming notes on the inside cover of the exam book.) Quickly write down all the relevant points you can think of—the textbook's points, your instructor's comments, and so on. The more you can think of now, the more you will have to choose from when you write your answer. (For more on brainstorming, see 3C.)

5. ***Write down the main idea.*** Looking closely at the way the question is worded and at your brainstorming notes, write a sentence that states the main idea of your answer. If you are writing a paragraph, this sentence will be your **topic sentence**; if you are writing an essay, it will be your **thesis statement**.

For more on topic sentences, see 3D. For more on thesis statements, see 14D.

6. ***List your key points.*** You don't want to waste your limited (and valuable) time writing a detailed outline, but an informal outline that lists just your key points is worth the little time it takes. An informal outline will help you plan a clear direction for your paragraph or essay.
7. ***Draft your answer.*** You will spend most of your time actually writing the answers to the questions on the exam. Follow your outline, keep track of time, and consult your brainstorming notes when you need to—but stay focused on your writing.
8. ***Reread, revise, and edit.*** When you have finished drafting your answer, reread it carefully to make sure that it says everything you want it to say—and that it answers the question.

FOCUS Academic Honesty

Academic honesty—the standard for truth and fairness in work and behavior—is very important in college. Understanding academic honesty goes beyond simply knowing that it is dishonest to cheat on a test. To be sure you are conforming to the rules of academic honesty, try to follow these guidelines.

- Don't re-use papers you wrote in high school. The written work you are assigned in college is designed to help you learn, and your instructors expect you to do the work for the course when it is assigned.
- Don't copy information from a book or article or paste material from a Web site directly into your papers. Using someone else's words or ideas without proper acknowledgment constitutes **plagiarism**, a very serious offense.
- Don't ask another student (or your parents) to help you write or revise a paper. If you need help, ask your instructor or a writing center tutor.
- Don't allow another student to copy your work on a test.
- Don't allow another student to turn in a paper you wrote (or one you helped him or her write).
- Don't work with other students on a take-home exam unless your instructor gives you permission to do so.
- Never buy a paper. Even if you edit it, it is still not your own work.

G Time-Management Strategies

Learning to manage your time is important for success in college. Here are some strategies you can adopt to make this task easier.

> **Word Power**
> **consistently** regularly, steadily

1. ***Use an organizer.*** Whether you prefer a print organizer or an electronic one, you should certainly use one—and use it consistently. If you are most comfortable with paper and pencil, purchase a "week-on-two-pages" academic year organizer (one that begins in September, not January). The "week-on-two-pages" format (see p. 15) has two advantages: it gives you more writing room for Monday through Friday than for the weekend, and it also lets you view an entire week at once.

   Carry your organizer with you at all times. At the beginning of the semester, copy down key pieces of information from each course syllabus—for example, the date of every quiz and exam and the due date of every paper. As the semester progresses, continue to write in assignments and deadlines, and also enter information such as days when a class will be canceled or will meet in the computer lab or in the library, reminders to bring a particular book or piece of equipment to class, and appointments with instructors or other college personnel. If you like, you can also jot down reminders and schedule appointments that are not related to school—for example, changes in your work hours, a dentist appointment, or lunch with a friend. (In addition to writing notes on the pages for each date, some students like to keep a separate month-by-month "to do" list. Crossing out completed items can give you a feeling of accomplishment—and make the road ahead look shorter.)

   On the following page, the first sample organizer pages show how you can use an organizer to keep track of deadlines, appointments, and reminders. The second sample organizer pages include not only this information but also a study schedule, with notes about particular tasks to be done each day.
2. ***Use a calendar.*** Buy a large calendar, and post it where you will see it every morning—for example, on your desk, on the refrigerator, or wherever you keep your keys and your student ID. At the beginning of the semester, fill in important dates such as school holidays, work commitments, exam dates, and due dates for papers and projects. When you return from school each day, update the calendar with any new information you have entered into your organizer.
3. ***Plan ahead.*** If you think you will need help from a writing-center tutor to revise a paper that is due in two weeks, don't wait until day thirteen to try to make an appointment; all the time slots may be filled by then. To be safe, make an appointment for help about a week in advance.
4. ***Learn to enjoy downtime.*** One final—and very important—point to remember is that you are entitled to "waste" a little time. When you have a free minute, take time for yourself—and don't feel guilty about it.

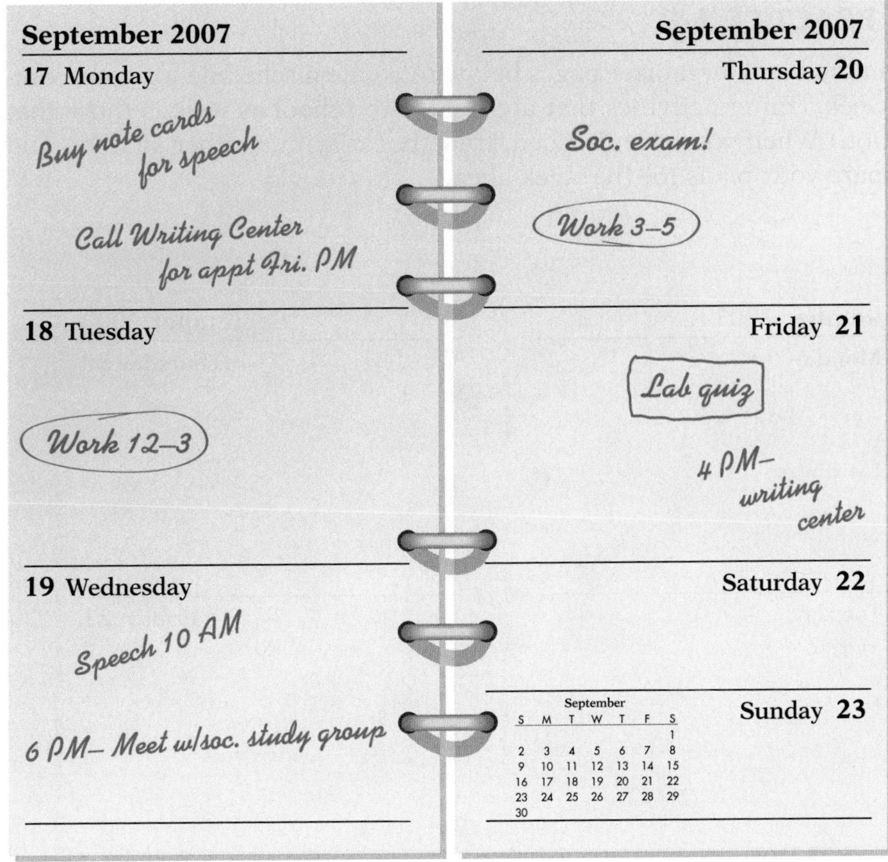

Sample Organizer Pages: Deadlines, Appointments, and Reminders Only

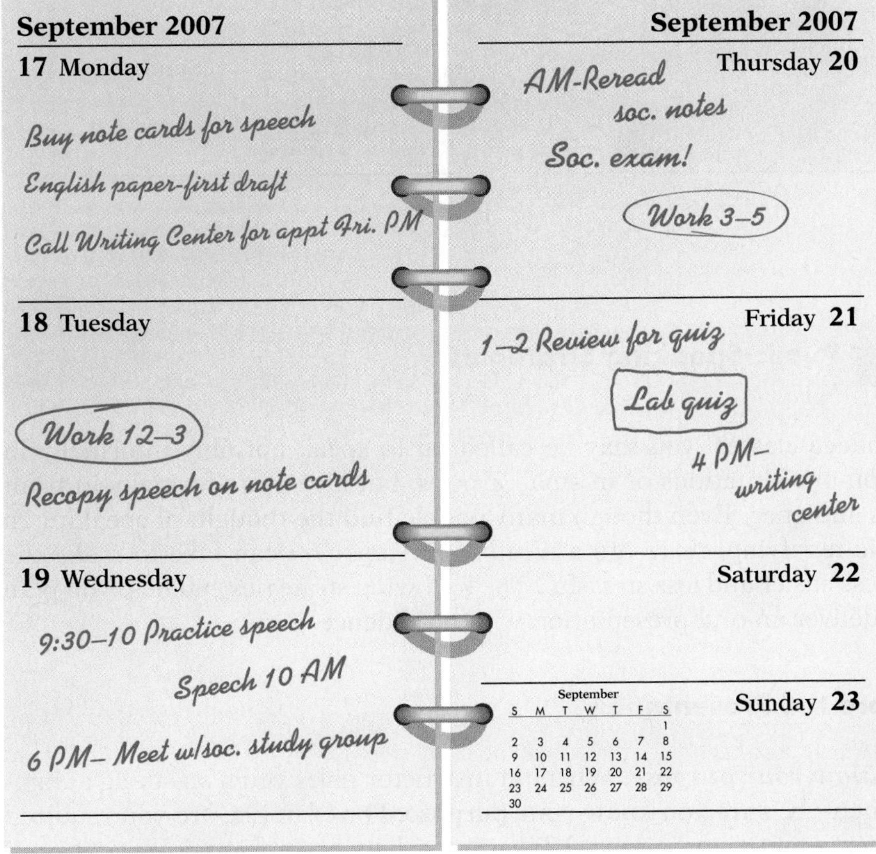

Sample Organizer Pages: Deadlines, Appointments, Reminders, and Study Schedule

◆ PRACTICE 1-8

Fill in the blank organizer pages below to create a schedule for your coming week. (Enter activities that are related to school as well as those that are not.) When you have finished, trade books with another student, and compare your plans for the week ahead.

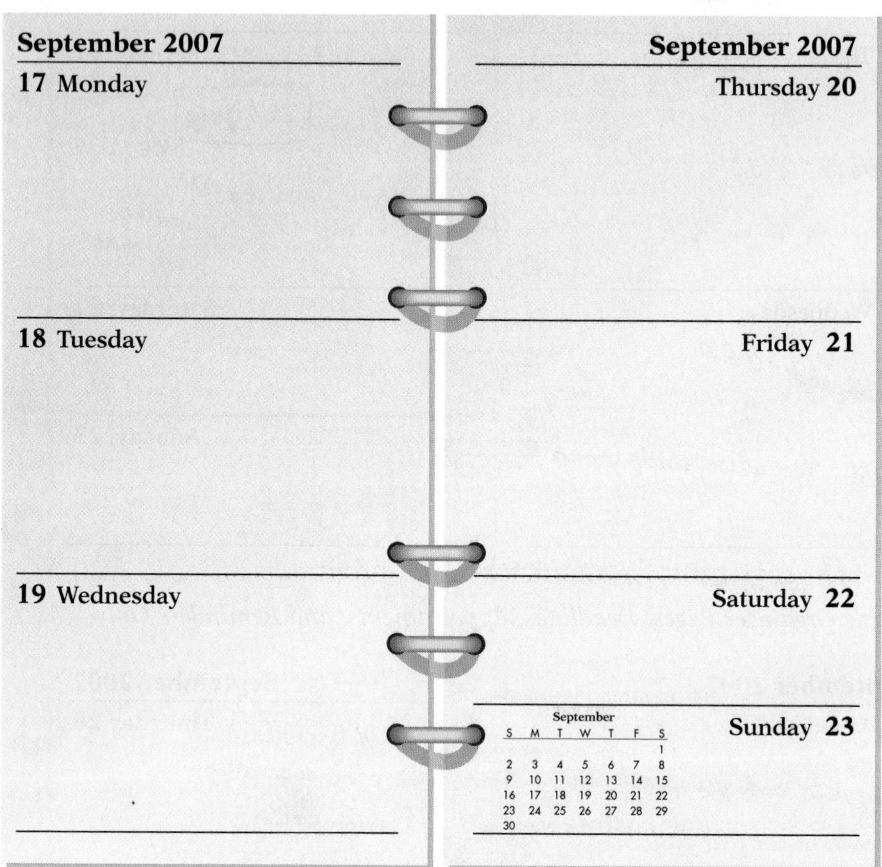

H Public-Speaking Strategies

In college classes, you may be called on to speak not only informally in one-on-one situations or in small groups, but also more formally in front of an audience. Even though many people find the thought of speaking in public terrifying, there are a number of steps you can take to make the process easier and less stressful. The following strategies can help you plan and deliver an oral presentation with confidence.

Before the Presentation

1. ***Know your purpose.*** When an instructor gives you a speaking assignment, be sure you know your purpose. For example, are you required to recount an experience? Take a stand on a controversial issue?

2. ***Know your audience.*** Try to figure out what listeners already know (and how they feel) about the topic of your speech. If some listeners are more knowledgeable and sophisticated than others, you have to figure out how to appeal to both groups without insulting one or confusing the other.
3. ***Identify your main idea.*** The strategies discussed in 3D can help you identify your speech's main idea. Keep this statement clear and simple. Remember, readers can reread a passage they cannot understand; in an oral presentation, you have only one chance to communicate your ideas to your audience.
4. ***Gather support for your main idea.*** Do not expect listeners to accept your main idea without facts, examples, or other details to support it. Even with such support, be prepared for listeners who will challenge you or ask you to explain your ideas in more depth.
5. ***Think of your presentation in three parts.*** A time-tested piece of advice for speakers is "Tell them what you're going to tell them; tell them; tell them what you told them." The point behind this advice is that a speaker needs to state the main idea in simple terms and then to repeat that idea throughout the speech. The speech's main idea should be evident at the beginning of the speech, in the body of the speech, and in the conclusion. An effective speaker figures out how to accomplish this goal and how to help the audience understand the main idea without making the speech monotonous.
6. ***Develop notes for each part.*** Usually, instructors in public-speaking classes want you to give extemporaneous presentations: speeches that you have planned and practiced but that you do not read word for word from a fully written-out essay. These teachers will direct you to prepare notes—usually, on index cards—to keep in front of you as you speak to your audience.
7. ***Use clear signals to guide your listeners.*** Be sure to give listeners cues about where you are in the speech—for example, when you are about to present the main idea, when you will present support for the main idea, and when you are about to finish. Because it is more difficult to follow a speech than a piece of writing, you will need to include more **transitions** from one idea to another than you would in your writing. (For lists of useful transitional words and phrases, see 4C.)
8. ***Prepare visual aids.*** You will not always need visual aids, but sometimes—for example, when you are explaining a process or tracing causes—you will communicate your main idea and supporting points more clearly if you give the audience something to look at. If, for example, you are explaining how an abacus works, you may want to show one to your listeners. If you are talking about a dance, you may want to have someone perform its steps during your presentation. In other cases, you may show photos, drawings, maps, posters, or even a videotape.

   Alternatively, you may use presentation software such as Microsoft PowerPoint to produce graphs, charts, or lists that you can project from your computer. Or, you can print these visuals on acetate sheets and, with an overhead projector, enlarge and display them on a wall or screen.

   The PowerPoint slide on the next page was prepared by a student for a presentation on how he found a job.

> **Word Power**
> **sophisticated** experienced and refined

> **Word Power**
> **extemporaneous** prepared, but performed without the help of notes

> **Word Power**
> **abacus** an ancient instrument used for making mathematical calculations

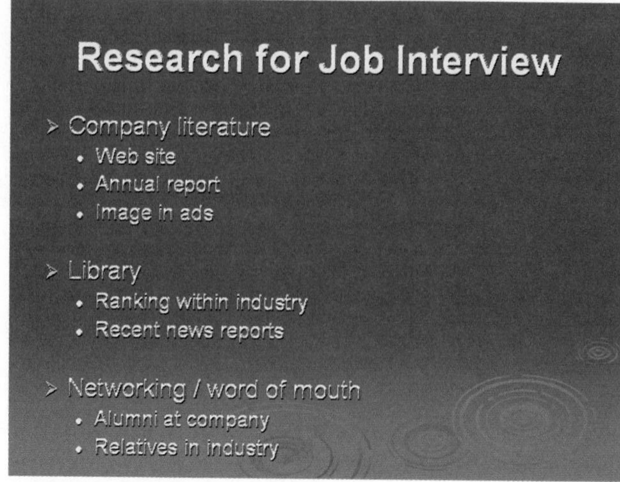

Sample PowerPoint Slide

9. ***Integrate your visuals.*** Don't just show or read the visual to your audience; tell them more than they can see or read for themselves. For example, on a map, you might point out the route of the trip you are reporting on; for a bar graph, you might compare the raw numbers—stating, for example, how much more ice cream is sold in July than in January.
10. ***Practice.*** Be sure to rehearse enough to make sure that you know the order of points in your presentation (including when to show visual aids) and how to move from one point to the next. You should rehearse enough so that even though you have only notes in front of you, you are confident that you can convert the words and phrases to full sentences. Leave time for a trial run with a friend, and ask for feedback on content and delivery; then, take the time to apply the friend's feedback and improve your presentation. Finally, leave time to rehearse more—cutting and adding as necessary—until you know you can stay within the required time limit.

FOCUS Designing and Displaying Visual Aids

- Don't clutter your visuals with pictures (or, in the case of presentation software such as PowerPoint, with special effects).
- Don't use visuals that your audience cannot see clearly. Use images that are large enough for your audience to see and that will reproduce clearly.
- Don't make lettering too small. Use 40- to 50-point type for titles, 25- to 30-point type for major points, and 20- to 25-point type for other points.
- Don't include long sentences or full paragraphs. Use bulleted lists (like this one) instead.

(continued on following page)

(continued from previous page)

- Don't put more than three or four points on one visual.
- Don't use too many colors or too many different styles of type.
- Make sure that there is a clear contrast between the background and the lettering. (See the sample PowerPoint slide on p. 18.)
- Don't distract your audience by showing them the visual before you introduce it or after you finish talking about it.
- Don't talk to the visual. Look at and talk to your audience. Even if you have to point to the visual on the screen, make sure you are looking at your audience when you speak.

During the Presentation

1. ***Accept nervousness as part of the process.*** The trick is to convert this fear into the positive energy that will catch and hold your audience's attention.
2. ***Look at your audience.*** Don't begin speaking while you are still looking at your notes. Look at your audience. Most speech coaches advise speakers to pick a few people in different parts of the room and to alternate eye contact among them during the speech.
3. ***Speak slowly.*** No matter how slowly you think you are speaking, chances are you can slow down further. Take your time.
4. ***Keep movement to a minimum.*** Don't pace as you speak or move your hands erratically. Stand in one spot, and gesture to emphasize a point or to display a visual aid. (Arrange in advance to have someone in the audience perform certain tasks—for example, distributing handouts.) Depending on the topic and level of formality of your speech (and your instructor's guidelines), you may stand directly in front of your audience or behind a lectern.

Word Power

lectern a stand or desk with a slanted top that supports a speaker's notes

FOCUS Dealing with Anxiety

Your goal should not be to eliminate anxiety totally. The complete absence of anxiety in a speaker can lead to overconfidence, which can irritate and even bore an audience. Instead, learn to cope with anxiety by doing enough preparation so that you feel you own your speech. In other words, work on the speech to the point where you are comfortable with your main idea and supporting points. You want to be so familiar with the material that you can relax enough to sound natural, not stiff.

5. ***Don't get flustered if someone asks you to speak louder.*** In addition, do not get upset if some people in your audience look bored; you

might change your pace or volume to get more attention, but remember that a bored person may be overtired, preoccupied, or just a poor listener.

6. ***Leave time for questions.*** Your audience may want to ask questions or challenge what you have said. If someone asks a question that you have already answered in your speech, repeat the information as briefly as possible. And do not be upset if someone begins to argue with you; an appropriate response might be "I never thought of that angle," "I don't agree because . . . ," or "I need to think about that point more."

FOCUS Group Presentations

Sometimes a public-speaking assignment will call for a group presentation that requires you to cooperate with other students. Whether you are participating in a panel discussion about college services or performing a dramatic reading of a one-act play, a group presentation involves intensive behind-the-scenes work.

Be sure you understand your own role as well as everyone else's: Who is in charge? Who sets the pace? Who prepares and displays the visuals? Furthermore, everyone in a group situation must bear responsibility for sticking to a schedule for research and rehearsal. After rehearsals and after the actual presentation, everyone should contribute to evaluating the group effort and figuring out how to improve the next time around.

I Internet Strategies

When people refer to the Internet, they usually mean the **World Wide Web**. The Web relies on **links**—highlighted words and phrases. By clicking on these links, you can move easily from one part of a document to another or from one **Web site** (collection of documents) to another.

Finding Information on the Internet

To use the Internet, you need an Internet **browser**, a tool that enables your computer to display Web pages. The most popular browsers are Netscape Navigator and Internet Explorer. (Most new computers come with one of these browsers already installed.)

Before you can access the Internet, you have to be **online**. Once you are online, you need to connect to a **search engine**, a program that helps you find information by sorting through the millions of documents that are available on the Internet. Among the most popular search engines are Yahoo! (www.yahoo.com) and Google (www.google.com). The Google home page appears on the next page.

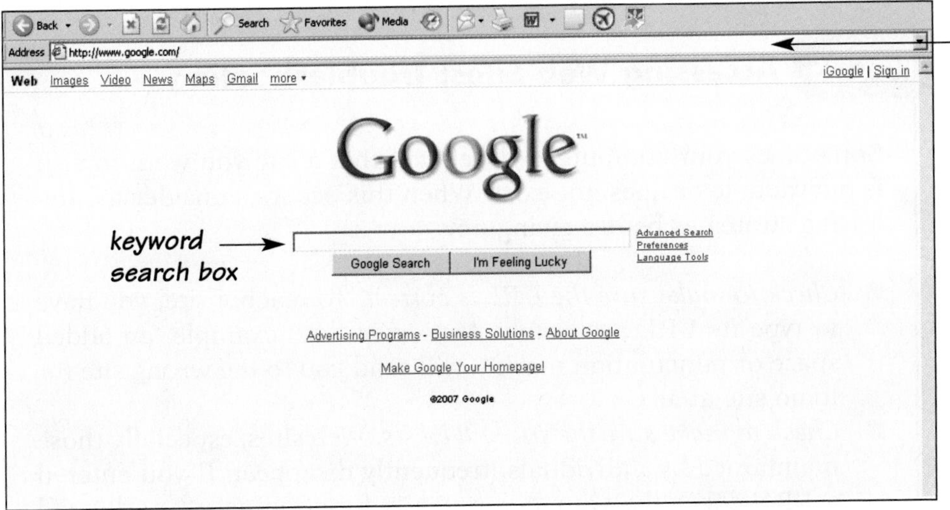

Google Home Page

There are several ways to use a search engine to find information.

- *You can enter a Web site's URL.* All search engines have a URL search box in which you can enter a Web site's **URL** (electronic address). When you click on the URL or hit your computer's Enter key, the search engine connects you to the Web site.
- *You can do a keyword search.* All search engines let you do a **keyword search**: you type a term (or terms) into a keyword search box, and the search engine retrieves documents that contain the term.
- *You can do a subject search.* Some search engines, such as Yahoo!, let you do a **subject search**. First, you choose a broad subject from a list of subjects: *Computers & Internet*, *News & Media*, *Business & Economy*, and so on. Each of these general subjects leads you to more specific subjects, until eventually you get to the subtopic that you want. The Yahoo! subject guide directory appears below.

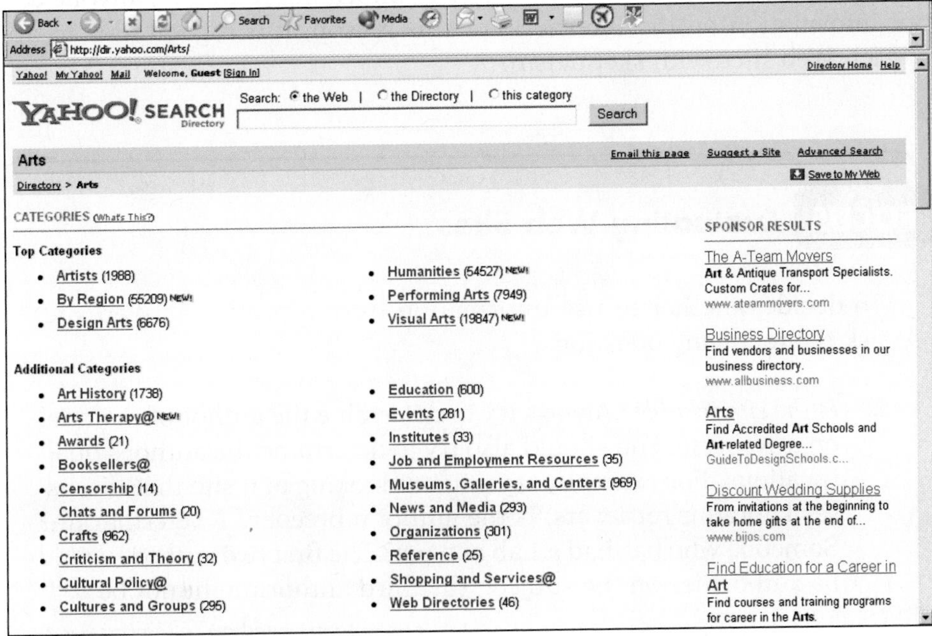

Yahoo! Subject Guide Directory

FOCUS Accessing Web Sites: Troubleshooting

Sometimes your computer will tell you that a site you want to visit is unavailable or does not exist. When this occurs, consider the following strategies before giving up.

- *Check to make sure the URL is correct.* To reach a site, you have to type its URL accurately. Any error—for example, an added space or punctuation mark—will send you to the wrong site (or to no site at all).
- *Check to make sure the site still exists.* Web sites, especially those maintained by individuals, frequently disappear. If you entered a URL correctly, your computer is functioning properly, and you still cannot access a site, chances are that the site no longer exists.
- *Try revisiting the site later.* Sometimes Web sites experience technical problems that prevent them from being accessed. Your computer will tell you if a site is temporarily unreachable.
- *Try deleting parts of the URL.* Begin by deleting the end of the URL up to the first slash: www.lib.Berkeley.edu/teachinglib/guides/internet/~~findinginfo.html~~. Then, try accessing the site again. If this doesn't work, delete the URL up to the next slash. As a last resort, try to reach the site's home page—the first part of the URL: www.lib.Berkeley.edu/. Once you get to the home page, follow the links to the part of the Web site that you want.

Evaluating Web Sites

> **Word Power**
> **skepticism** a doubtful or questioning attitude

Not every Web site is a valuable source of information. In fact, anyone can put information on the Internet. For this reason, it is a good idea to approach Web sites with skepticism.

FOCUS Evaluating Web Sites

To decide whether to use information from a particular Web site, ask the following questions.

- *Is the site reliable?* Always try to determine the author of material on a Web site. You should also try to determine the author's qualifications. For example, say you are looking at a site that discusses Labrador retrievers. Is the author a breeder? A veterinarian? Someone who has had a Lab as a pet? The first two authors would be authorities on the subject; the third author might not be.

(continued on following page)

(continued from previous page)

- *Does the site have a hidden purpose?* When you evaluate a Web site, be sure to consider its purpose. For example, a site discussing the health benefits of herbal medicine would have one purpose if it were sponsored by a university and another purpose if it were sponsored by a company selling herbal remedies.
- *Is the site up-to-date?* If a site has not been recently updated, you should question the information it contains. A discussion of bird flu in China, for example, would be out of date if it were written before the widespread outbreak in 2005. You would have to continue your search until you found a more current discussion.
- *Is the information on the site trustworthy?* A site should include evidence—facts and expert opinions—to support what it says. If it does not contain such evidence, you should consider the information to be unsupported personal opinion.

Word Power

evaluating examining something to judge its value, quality, or importance

Using the Internet to Locate Information

You can use the Internet to find information about the subjects you are studying. Certain sites, such as the following ones, can help you access information related to your courses.

Art History
Art History on the Web
www.witcombe.sbc.edu/ARTHLinks.html

Education
Education World
www.education-world.com

Literature
On-Line Books Page
www.digital.library.upenn.edu/books

Science
Scirus
www.scirus.com

Sociology and Social Work
Social Work and Social Sciences
www.gwbseb.wustl.edu/websites.html

You can also use the Internet for help with your writing. Below are just a few of the many Web sites that you can consult to answer questions that may come up as you write.

Advice on Revision
Paradigm Online Writing Assistant
english.ttu.edu/kairos/3.1/news/paradigm/revision.htm

Help in Writing Paragraphs
Purposes of Paragraphs
www.fas.harvard.edu/~wricntr/para.html

Tips on Grammar
The Online English Grammar
www.edunet.com/English/grammar

Tips on Proofreading
Tips for Effective Proofreading
www.ualr.edu/~owl/tipsforproofreading.html

Finally, you can use the Internet to locate everyday information. For example, you can access news and weather reports, download voter registration information, get directions, obtain consumer information, or even apply for a job. The following sites are just a few of the many resources available on the Internet.

Dictionaries
yourDictionary.com
www.yourdictionary.com

Employment
America's Job Bank
www.ajb.dni.us/

Law and Legal Information
American Law Sources Online
www.lawsource.com/also

Maps and Directions
MapBlast!
www.mapblast.com/myblast/index.mb

Newspapers
Newspapers.Com
www.newspapers.com

Telephone Directories
Switchboard.com
www.switchboard.com

FOCUS Web Sites

For a comprehensive list of Web sites, go to the *Foundations First* Web site: www.bedfordstmartins.com/foundationsfirst.

◆ PRACTICE 1-9

At home or in your school's computer lab, practice entering five of the URLs listed on pages 23–24. Make sure you enter the URLs exactly as they appear on the page. If entering a URL does not take you to the appropriate Web site, check to make sure that you entered the URL correctly. (If the site is no longer active, choose another URL from the list.)

◆ PRACTICE 1-10

Working in a group of four students, select one of the Web sites listed on pages 23–24. At home or in your school's computer lab, access the site, and make a list of three things you like and three things you dislike about it. Then, exchange lists with another student in your group. On what do you agree? On what do you disagree?

◆ PRACTICE 1-11

Use one of the search engines mentioned on page 20 to locate a Web site that focuses on a topic you know a lot about—for example, your hometown, a famous person, or a sport. Evaluate the site according to the guidelines listed on pages 22–23.

REVISING AND EDITING

Look back at your response to the Seeing and Writing exercise on page 3. Now that you have read the information in this chapter, you should have a better idea of how to manage your time in the weeks and months to come. How do you think you will fit everything in? Which of the strategies described in this chapter do you think you will find most helpful? Revise your Seeing and Writing response so that it answers these questions.

REVIEW CHECKLIST: Strategies for College Success

- Some strategies come in handy even before school begins. (See 1A.)
- From your first day as a college student, there are steps you can take to help you get your bearings. (See 1B.)
- Day-to-day strategies can help you move through the semester. (See 1C.)
- Learning to take good notes is essential for success in college. (See 1D.)
- Doing homework gives you a chance to practice your skills and measure your progress. (See 1E.)
- Preparation for an exam should begin well before the exam is announced. (See 1F.)
- Learning to manage your time is important for success in college. (See 1G.)
- Knowing how to make an oral presentation can be a useful skill for college students. (See 1H.)
- Knowing how to use the Internet can help you succeed in college and beyond. (See 1I.)

CHAPTER 2

Reading for Academic Success

PREVIEW

In this chapter, you will learn

- how to become an active reader (2A)
- how to preview, highlight, annotate, outline, and summarize a reading assignment (2B)
- how to read different kinds of texts (2C)

Word Power

highlight to mark a page to emphasize important details

annotate to make explanatory notes on a page

SEEING AND WRITING

The picture above shows a student marking the pages of her textbook to highlight important information. When you read your textbooks, you will understand them better if you highlight and annotate the pages as this student is doing. Marking the pages can also be a useful strategy in other reading situations.

A Becoming an Active Reader

Reading is essential in all your college courses. To get the most out of your college reading, you should be prepared to take a critical stance—commenting on, questioning, evaluating, and even challenging what you read. In other words, you should learn to become an active reader.

In practical terms, being an **active reader** means actively participating in the reading process: approaching a reading assignment with a clear understanding of your purpose, and marking the text to help you understand what you are reading.

You may find it easier to understand the concept of active reading if you see how this strategy applies to "reading" a picture. Like a written text, every **visual text**—a photograph, an advertisement, a chart, or a graph; a work of fine art, such as a painting or a piece of sculpture; and even a Web site—has a message to communicate. Visual texts communicate their messages through the specific words and images they choose and through the way these words and images are arranged on the page.

When you approach a visual, your first step is to identify the words and images you see on the page. Then, you consider how they are arranged and what their relationship is to one another.

In the following ad for Tropicana orange juice, the main idea—that the product's juicier pulp gives it fresh-squeezed taste—is expressed in the heading: "We squeeze the oranges, not the pulp." This message is supported by the large central image, which emphasizes the link among the juice carton, the glass of juice, and the orange. The smaller type also supports the ad's claim, presenting specific information that explains how and why this brand of juice is fresher and tastier than others.

Tropicana Advertisement

In the visual below, a painting by the American artist Winslow Homer, the images are not supported by written text, but the message is still clear. Here, the central image—the man alone in the middle of the ocean, surrounded by open space—clearly conveys the painting's emotions: fear, desperation, hopelessness. The surrounding images—the choppy waves, the threatening sky, the sharks—reinforce and support this impression.

Winslow Homer, The Gulf Stream *(1899)*

When you "read" visuals such as these, at first you get just a general sense of what you see. But as you read more actively, you let your mind take you beyond what is represented on the page. You ask why certain details were selected, why they are arranged as they are, what comes to mind when you see the picture, and whether or not you find the visual effective.

For example, why is the orange in the Tropicana ad on page 27 labeled "Handle with Care"? Why is it placed in front of the juice carton? Will the ad encourage consumers to purchase this brand of juice rather than another? If so, why? If not, why not? In the Winslow Homer painting, what is the man looking at? Does he see anything in the distance? How might he have come to be alone on the ocean? Is the painting frightening? Would it have a different impact if the artist had used lighter colors? If he had added or eliminated any details?

Active reading of a written text, like active reading of a visual text, encourages you to move beyond what is on the page and to "read between the lines." In this way, it gives you a deeper understanding of the material.

The process of actively reading a written text is explained and illustrated in the following section.

B Understanding the Reading Process

Determining Your Purpose

Even before you start reading, you should ask yourself some questions about your purpose—why you are reading. The answers to these questions will help you understand what kind of information you hope to get out of your reading and how you will use this information.

Questions about Your Purpose

- Will you be expected to discuss what you are reading? If so, will you discuss it in class or in a conference with your instructor?
- Will you have to write about what you are reading? If so, will you be expected to write an informal response (for example, a journal entry) or a more formal one (for example, an essay)?
- Will you be tested on the material?

Previewing

When you **preview**, you skim a passage to get a sense of the writer's main idea and key supporting points and, if possible, the general emphasis of the passage. You can begin by focusing on the title, the first paragraph (which often contains a purpose statement or overview), and the last paragraph (which often contains a summary of the writer's points). You should also look for clues to the writer's message in the passage's **visual signals** (headings, boxes, and so on) as well as in its **verbal signals** (the words and phrases the writer uses to convey order and emphasis).

Using Visual Signals

- Look at the title.
- Look at the opening and closing paragraphs.
- Look at each paragraph's first sentence.
- Look at headings.
- Look at *italicized* and **boldfaced** words.
- Look at numbered lists.
- Look at bulleted lists (like this one).
- Look at visuals (graphs, charts, tables, photographs, and so on).
- Look at any information that is boxed.
- Look at any information that is in color.

Using Verbal Signals

- Look for phrases that signal emphasis ("The *primary* reason"; "The *most important* idea").
- Look for repeated words and phrases.
- Look for words that signal addition (*also, in addition, furthermore*).
- Look for words that signal time sequence (*first, after, then, next, finally*).
- Look for words that identify causes and effects (*because, as a result, for this reason*).
- Look for words that introduce examples (*for example, for instance*).
- Look for words that signal comparison (*likewise, similarly*).
- Look for words that signal contrast (*unlike, although, in contrast*).
- Look for words that signal contradiction (*however, on the contrary*).
- Look for words that signal a narrowing of the writer's focus (*in fact, specifically, in other words*).
- Look for words that signal summaries or conclusions (*to sum up, in conclusion*).

When you have finished previewing the passage, you should have a general sense of what the writer wants to communicate.

◆ PRACTICE 2-1

Following is a brief newspaper article by Nathan Black, a Colorado high school student. Preview the article in preparation for class discussion as well as for the other activities that will be assigned throughout section 2B.

As you read, try to identify the writer's main idea and key supporting points, and write that information on the blank lines that follow the article.

After a Shooting

Nathan Black

High school students in Littleton now have a new excuse to get out of class for a few extra minutes: the lockdown drill. My school had its first last year. While most students sat quietly in locked classrooms, a few teachers responded to simulated crises, like a student injury. It's one of many new features of life in Littleton since the Columbine High shootings of 1999. Most people have tried to move on, but some aspects of our lives have changed forever. 1

That reality will soon face the people of Santee, California, where two students were killed on Monday. And the shooting yesterday of a girl by a schoolmate in 2

Pennsylvania, and the arrest this week of two boys in Twentynine Palms, California, after police found a "hit list" of their classmates, suggest that Columbine's experience will become still more common.

Apart from lockdown drills, there have been few changes in security procedures. The greatest change has been the increase of paranoia. For example, a few weeks after the shooting I was working on a graph assignment with a friend. We arranged the points on the graph to spell out a humorous but inappropriate message. 3

A month earlier, my friend would have said, "The teacher's going to be mad." This time he said, "If we turn this in, we'll be expelled." 4

There's the difference. The worst case I've heard of took place in Canada. A boy had written and performed, for class, a dark, vengeful monologue. After his performance, rumors swirled about hit lists, and the boy was arrested. The police said he had made death threats. No hard evidence appears to have been found in the boy's home—just the monologue. His story has now entered the larger tale of Littleton and its aftermath. 5

Only time can ease this paranoia. I wish time would hurry up about it. 6

Yet good changes have also occurred. The killings at Columbine and elsewhere have been a pitiless wake-up call to adults. Last April, 1,500 of my peers gathered at a local college to discuss education. Adults want our perspective. They may want it now because of fear, but they want it. 7

Such conversations have to continue. Violence is still happening, and as long as my school needs a lockdown drill, we need to keep asking: Why do kids kill each other, and how can we stop them? There's no answer yet. But the fact that we're looking makes me feel a little less helpless. 8

Main idea

____

____

Key supporting points

1. ____
   ____

2. ____

____

3. ____

____

4. ____

____

Highlighting

After you have previewed a passage, read it again, this time more carefully. Now, your goals are to identify connections between one point and another and to follow the writer's line of thought.

As you read, keep a pen (or a highlighter pen) handy so you can **highlight**, using underlining and symbols to identify important information. This active reading strategy will reinforce your understanding of the writer's main idea and key supporting points and will help you see the relationships among them. (If you want to highlight material in a book that you do not own, photocopy the passage and then highlight it.)

The number and kinds of highlighting symbols you use when you read are up to you. All that matters is that your symbols are clear, meaningful, and easy to remember.

Highlighting Symbols

- Underline or highlight key ideas.
- Box or circle words or phrases you want to remember.
- Place a check mark (✓) or star (*) next to an important idea.
- Place a double check mark (✓✓) or double star (**) next to an especially significant idea.
- Draw lines or arrows to connect related ideas.
- Put a question mark beside a word or idea that you do not understand.
- Number the writer's key supporting points or examples.

Highlight freely, but try not to highlight too much. Remember, you will eventually be rereading every highlighted word, phrase, and sentence—and your study time is limited. Highlight only the most important, most useful information—for example, definitions, examples, and summaries.

FOCUS Knowing What to Highlight

You want to highlight what's important—but how do you *know* what's important? As a general rule, you should look for the same **visual signals** you looked for when you did your previewing. Many

(continued on following page)

(continued from previous page)

of the ideas you will need to highlight will probably be found in material that is visually set off from the rest of the text—opening and closing paragraphs, lists, and so on. Also, continue to look for **verbal signals**—words and phrases like *however, therefore, another reason*, and *the most important point*—that often introduce key points. Together, these visual and verbal signals will give you clues to the writer's meaning and emphasis.

Here is how a student highlighted a passage from an introductory American history textbook. The passage focuses on the position of African Americans in society in the years immediately following World War II. Because the passage includes no visual signals apart from the title and paragraph divisions, the student looked carefully for verbal signals.

Black Protest and the Politics of Civil Rights

"I spent four years in the army to free a bunch of Frenchmen and Dutchmen," an African-American corporal declared, "and I'm hanged if I'm going to let the Alabama version of the Germans kick me around when ✓ I get home." Black men and women filled 16 percent of military positions in World War II; they as well as civilians resolved that the return to peace would not be a return to the racial injustices of prewar America. Their ✓ political (?) clout had grown with the migration of two million African Americans to northern and western cities, where they could vote and their ballots could make a difference. Even in the South, the proportion of blacks who were allowed to vote inched up from 2 percent to 12 percent in the 1940s. Pursuing civil rights through the courts and Congress, the National Association for the Advancement of Colored People (NAACP) counted half a million members.

In the postwar years, individual African Americans broke through the color barrier, achieving several * "firsts." Jackie Robinson integrated major league baseball when he started at first base for the Brooklyn Dodgers in 1947, braving abuse from fans and players to win the Rookie of the Year Award. In 1950, Ralph J. Bunche received the Nobel Peace Prize for his contributions to the United Nations, and Gwendolyn Brooks earned the Pulitzer Prize for poetry.

** Still, in most respects little had changed, especially in the South, where
violence greeted African Americans' attempts to assert their rights. Armed ①
white men turned back Medgar Evers (who would become a key civil
rights leader in the 1960s) and four other veterans who were trying to vote
in Mississippi. A mob lynched Isaac Nixon for voting in Georgia, and ②
an all-white jury acquitted the men accused of his murder. In the South,
governors, U.S. senators, and other politicians routinely intimidated ③
potential voters with threats of economic retaliation and violence.

—James L. Roark et al., *The American Promise*, Third Edition

The student who highlighted this passage was preparing for a meeting of her study group. Because the class would be taking a midterm the following week, each member of the study group needed to understand the material very well. The student began her highlighting by placing check marks beside two important advances for African Americans cited in paragraph 1 and by drawing arrows to specific examples of blacks' political influence. (Although she thought she knew the meaning of the word *clout*, she circled it anyway and placed a question mark above it to remind herself to check its meaning in a dictionary.)

In paragraph 2, she boxed the names of prominent postwar African Americans and underlined their contributions, circling and starring the key word "firsts." She then underlined and double-starred the entire passage's main idea—the first sentence of paragraph 3—numbering the examples in the paragraph that support this idea.

◆ PRACTICE 2-2

Review the highlighted passage from the history textbook (pp. 33–34). How would your own highlighting of this passage be similar to or different from the sample student highlighting?

◆ PRACTICE 2-3

Reread "After a Shooting" (pp. 30–31). As you read, highlight the passage by underlining and starring main ideas, boxing and circling key words, and checkmarking important points. Also, circle each unfamiliar word, and put a question mark above it.

Annotating

As you highlight, you should also annotate what you are reading. **Annotating** a passage means making notes—of questions, reactions, reminders, and ideas for discussion or writing—in the margins or between the lines. Keeping an informal record of ideas as they occur to you will help prepare you to discuss the reading with your classmates—and, eventually, to write about it.

Asking yourself the following questions as you read will help you write useful annotations.

Questions for Annotating

- What is the writer saying?
- What is the writer's purpose—his or her reason for writing?
- What kind of audience is the writer addressing?
- Is the writer responding to another writer's ideas?
- What is the writer's main idea?
- How does the writer support his or her points? With facts? Opinions? Both facts and opinions? What supporting details and examples does the writer use?
- Does the writer include enough supporting details and examples?
- Do you understand the writer's vocabulary?
- Do you understand the writer's ideas?
- Do you agree with the points the writer is making?
- Do you see any connections between this passage and something else you have read?

The following passage reproduces the student's highlighting of the American history textbook from pages 33–34 and also illustrates her annotations.

Black Protest and the Politics of Civil Rights

"I spent four years in the army to free a bunch of Frenchmen and Dutchmen," an African-American corporal declared, "and I'm hanged if I'm going to let the Alabama version of the Germans kick me around when ✓ I get home." Black men and women filled 16 percent of military positions in World War II; they as well as civilians resolved that the return to peace would not be a return to the racial injustices of prewar America. Their ✓ political (?) clout [= power] had grown with the migration of two million African Americans to northern and western cities, where they could vote and their ballots could make a difference. Even in the South, the proportion of blacks who were allowed to vote inched up from 2 percent to 12 percent in the 1940s. Pursuing civil rights through the courts and Congress, the National Association for the Advancement of Colored People (NAACP) counted half a million members.

Achievements of African Americans:

Military

Politics

In the postwar years, individual African Americans broke through the color barrier, achieving several * "firsts." Jackie Robinson integrated major

Sports, world politics, literature

league baseball when he started at first base for the Brooklyn Dodgers in 1947, braving abuse from fans and players to win the Rookie of the Year Award. In 1950, Ralph J. Bunche received the Nobel Peace Prize for his contributions to the United Nations, and Gwendolyn Brooks earned the Pulitzer Prize for poetry.

In South, voters intimidated * * Still, in most respects little had changed, especially in the South, where violence greeted African Americans' attempts to assert their rights. Armed ① white men turned back Medgar Evers (who would become a key civil rights leader in the 1960s) and four other veterans who were trying to vote in Mississippi. A mob lynched Isaac Nixon for voting in Georgia, and ② an all-white jury acquitted the men accused of his murder. In the South, *Threats of violence* governors, U.S. senators, and other politicians routinely intimidated ③ potential voters with threats of economic retaliation and violence.

—James L. Roark et al., *The American Promise*, Third Edition

In her annotations, this student put some of the writer's key ideas into her own words and recorded ideas she hoped to discuss in her study group.

◆ PRACTICE 2-4

Reread "After a Shooting" (pp. 30–31). As you reread, refer to the Questions for Annotating (p. 35), and use them to guide you in annotating the passage as you write your own ideas and questions in the margins. Note where you agree or disagree with the writer, and briefly explain why. Quickly summarize any points you think are particularly important. Take time to look up any unfamiliar words you have circled, and write brief definitions for them.

◆ PRACTICE 2-5

Trade workbooks with another student, and read over his or her highlighting and annotating of "After a Shooting." How are your written responses similar to the other student's? How are they different? Do your classmate's responses help you see anything new about the article?

Outlining

Another technique you can use to help you understand a reading assignment better is **outlining**. Unlike a **formal outline**, which follows fairly strict conventions, an **informal outline** is easy to make and can be a valuable reading tool: it shows you which ideas are more important than others, and it shows you how ideas are related.

To make an informal outline of a reading assignment, follow these guidelines.

FOCUS Making an Informal Outline

1. Write or type the passage's main idea at the top of a sheet of paper.
2. At the left margin, write down the most important idea of the first paragraph or section of the passage.
3. Indent the next line a few spaces, and list the examples or details that support this idea.
4. As ideas become more specific, indent further. (Ideas that have the same degree of importance are indented the same distance from the left margin.)
5. Repeat this process with each paragraph or section of the passage.

NOTE: Your word-processing program will have an outline function that automatically formats the different levels of your outline.

The student who highlighted and annotated the passage on pages 35–36 made the following informal outline to help her understand its content.

Main idea: Although African Americans had achieved a lot by the end of World War II, they still faced prejudice and violence.

- African Americans as a group had made significant advances.
  - Many had served in the military.
  - Political influence was growing.
    - More African Americans voted.
    - NAACP membership increased.
- Individual African Americans had made significant advances.
  - Sports: Jackie Robinson
  - World politics: Ralph Bunche
  - Literature: Gwendolyn Brooks
- Despite these advances, much remained the same for African Americans, especially in the South.
  - Blacks faced violence and even lynching if they tried to vote.
  - Elected officials threatened potential voters.

◆ PRACTICE 2-6

Working on your own or in a small group, make an informal outline of "After a Shooting" (pp. 30–31). Refer to your highlighting and annotations as you construct the outline. When you have finished, check to make sure your outline shows which ideas the writer is emphasizing and how those ideas are related.

Summarizing

Once you have highlighted and annotated a passage, you may want to try summarizing it. A **summary** retells, *in your own words*, what a passage is about. A summary condenses a passage, so it generally leaves out all but the main idea, key supporting points, and examples. A summary omits minor details and nonessential material, and it does not include your own ideas or opinions.

FOCUS Writing a Summary

1. Review your outline.
2. Consulting your outline, restate the passage's main idea *in your own words*.
3. Consulting your outline, restate the passage's supporting points. Add words and phrases between sentences where necessary to connect ideas.
4. Reread the original passage to make sure you haven't left out anything significant.

The student who highlighted, annotated, and outlined the passage from the history textbook wrote the following summary.

> Although African Americans had achieved a lot by the end of World War II, they still faced prejudice and even violence. As a group, they had made significant advances, which included military service and increased participation in politics, as indicated by voting and NAACP membership. Individual African Americans had also made significant advances in sports, world politics, and literature. Despite these advances, however, much remained the same for African Americans after World War II. Their situation was especially bad in the South. For example, African Americans still faced the threat of violence and even lynching if they tried to vote. Many elected officials also discouraged blacks from voting, often threatening them with violence.

◆ PRACTICE 2-7

On a separate sheet of paper, write a brief summary of "After a Shooting" (pp. 30–31). Use your outline as a guide, and remember to keep your summary short and to the point. (Your summary will probably be about one-quarter to one-third the length of the original passage.)

C Reading in College, in the Community, and in the Workplace

In college, in your life as a citizen of a community, and in the workplace, you will read material in a variety of different formats—for example, textbooks, newspapers, Web sites, and job-related memos, letters, emails, and reports.

Although the active reading process you have just reviewed can be applied to all kinds of material, various kinds of reading often require slightly different strategies during the previewing stage. One reason for this is that different kinds of reading may have different purposes: to present information, to persuade, and so on. Another reason is that the various texts you read are aimed at different audiences, and different audiences require different signals about content and emphasis. For these reasons, you need to look for different kinds of verbal and visual signals when you preview different kinds of reading material.

Reading Textbooks

Much of the reading you do in college is in textbooks (like this one). The purpose of a textbook is to present information, and when you read a textbook, your goal is to understand that information. To do this, you need to figure out which ideas are most important as well as which points support those key ideas and which examples illustrate them.

☑ CHECKLIST: Reading Textbooks

Look for the following features as you preview:

- ☐ **Boldfaced** and *italicized* words, which can indicate terms to be defined
- ☐ Boxed checklists or summaries, which may appear at the ends of sections or chapters
- ☐ Bulleted or numbered lists, which may list key reasons or examples or summarize important material
- ☐ Diagrams, charts, tables, graphs, photographs, and other visuals that illustrate the writer's points

◆ PRACTICE 2-8

The following passage from an introductory psychology textbook defines and illustrates the term *attribution*. Identify the passage's visual and verbal signals, and use them to help you identify the main idea and key supporting points. Then, highlight and annotate the passage.

ATTRIBUTION
Explaining Behavior

Attribution *refers to the process of explaining people's behavior. What are the fundamental attribution error, the actor-observer discrepancy, and the self-serving bias? How do these biases shape the attributions we make?*

As you're studying in the college library, the activities of two workers catch your attention. The two men are trying to lift and move a large file cabinet. "Okay, let's lift it and tip it this way," one guy says with considerable authority. In unison, they heave and tip the file cabinet. When they do, all four file drawers come flying out, bonking the first guy on the head. As the file cabinet goes crashing to the floor, you bite your lip to keep from laughing and think to yourself, "Yeah, they're obviously a pair of 40-watt bulbs."

Why did you arrive at that conclusion? After all, it's completely possible that the workers were not dimwits. Maybe the lock on the file drawers broke. Or maybe there was some other explanation for their mishap.

Attribution is the process of inferring the cause of someone's behavior, including your own. Psychologists also use the word *attribution* to refer to the explanation you make for a particular behavior. The attributions you make have a strong influence on your thoughts and feelings about other people.

If your attribution for the file cabinet incident was that the workers were not very bright, you demonstrated a pattern that occurs consistently in explaining the behavior of other people. *We tend to spontaneously attribute the behavior of others to internal, personal characteristics, while downplaying or underestimating the effects of external, situational factors.* This bias is so common in individualistic cultures that it's called the **fundamental attribution error** (Ross, 1977). Even though it's entirely possible that situational forces are behind another person's behavior, we tend to automatically assume that the cause is an internal, personal characteristic.

The fundamental attribution error plays a role in a common explanatory pattern called **blaming the victim**. The innocent victim of a crime, disaster, or serious illness is blamed for having somehow caused the misfortune or for not having taken steps to prevent it. For example, many people blame the poor for their dire straits, the sick for bringing on their illness, and battered women and rape survivors for somehow "provoking" their attackers. Hindsight makes it seem as if the victim should have been able to predict and prevent what was going to happen (Carli & Leonard, 1989).

Along with the fundamental attribution error, a second bias contributes to unfairly blaming the victim of misfortune. People have a strong need to believe that the world is fair—that "we get what we deserve and deserve what we get." Social psychologist Melvin Lerner (1980) calls this the **just-world hypothesis**. Blaming the victim reflects the belief that, because the world is just, the victim must have done *something* to deserve his or her fate.

Why do we have a psychological need to believe in a just world? Well, if you believe the world is unfair, then no one—including you—is safe from tragic twists of fate and chance, no matter how virtuous, careful, or conscientious you may be (Thornton, 1992). Hence, blaming the victim and believing the just-world hypothesis provide a way to psychologically defend yourself against the threatening thought, "It could just as easily have been me."

—Don H. Hockenbury and Sandra K. Hockenbury, *Psychology*, Third Edition

Reading Newspapers

As a student, as an employee, and as a citizen, you read school, community, local, and national newspapers. Like textbooks, newspapers communicate information. In addition to containing relatively objective news articles, however, newspapers also contain editorials (which aim to persuade) as well as feature articles (which may be designed to entertain as well as to inform).

✓ CHECKLIST: Reading Newspapers

Look for the following features as you preview:

- The name of the section in which the article appears (News, Business, Lifestyle, Sports, and so on)
- Headlines
- Boldfaced headings within articles
- Labels like *editorial*, *commentary*, or *opinion*, which indicate that an article is the writer's opinion
- Brief biographical information at the end of an opinion piece
- Phrases or sentences in boldface that emphasize key points
- The article's first sentence, which often answers the questions *who*, *what*, *why*, *where*, *when*, and *how*
- The **dateline**, which tells you the city the writer is reporting from
- Related articles that appear on the same page—for example, boxed information and **sidebars**, short articles that provide additional background on people and places mentioned in the article
- Photographs

◆ PRACTICE 2-9

Using the checklist above as a guide, preview the following newspaper article. When you have finished, highlight and annotate the article.

Philadelphia students get a scholarship guarantee

All seniors with a financial need and proper grades will qualify.

By Susan Snyder and Kristin E. Holmes
INQUIRER STAFF WRITERS

1 Philadelphia public high school students who want to go to college—and who have the grades—will no longer be held back by lack of money.

2 What could be a dream come true for thousands of the city's 10,700 seniors was announced yesterday—a four-year, $40 million plan to pay up to $3,000 for each eligible student whose freshman-year funds fall short.

3 Mayor Street and the Philadelphia School District pledged the scholarships over the next four years for about 9,600 seniors in public schools and 1,100 more in charter schools. Most of the 4,000 city students who attend college each year require financial aid.

4 District officials could not say how many students could get the promised funds for tuition and room and board—but they estimated that lack of money keeps 2,000 to 3,000 city students from pursuing college each year.

5 "Everyone will have an opportunity to go to college," Street told students at a college-awareness rally at Temple University's Liacouras Center. The so-called "last-dollar scholarships" would cover whatever state and financial aid do not.

6 Amauris Matos-Reyes, 15, was among 2,000 high school students who cheered and applauded the announcement. Matos-Reyes, who attends Thomas A. Edison/John C. Fareira High School, sees help for students from low-income families who may not have the financial means to pay for college.

7 "This gives a chance to everybody," Matos-Reyes said. "It gives them hope that they can become what they want to be."

8 Funding for the program, called CORE Philadelphia (College Opportunity Resources for Education), is subject to approval by both City Council and the School Reform Commission, which oversees the district.

9 The city and district will shoulder the financial burden for the first four years of the program. U.S. Rep. Chaka Fattah said he was trying to create a $150 million endowment fund to cover the scholarships after 2008.

10 The program could grow as more students realize they can afford to attend college, officials said.

11 Could the city and district afford it if all its graduates decide to go to college?

12 "That's a problem we'd like to have," said Debra Kahn, city education secretary.

13 The promise comes with a few strings: Students will be eligible for up to $3,000 each only for their freshman year, and they must be accepted by one of the 14 State System of Higher Education universities, Community College of Philadelphia, or one of the four state-related institutions: Temple and Lincoln Universities, Pennsylvania State University or the University of Pittsburgh. In addition, students must have attended the city's public or charter schools for at least four consecutive years prior to graduation to be eligible.

14 Zuleica Diaz, a Kensington High School freshman, hopes the grant will help her achieve her goal of attending Temple University and becoming a kindergarten teacher.

15 "I don't think [my parents] will pay because it costs too much," said Diaz, 15, "but this is a chance, and I'm happy."

16 Matos-Reyes, who is considering a career in medicine or computer engineering and design, is concerned that his college education would be a financial strain for his family.

17 "That's why I try my hardest in

A promise of aid for college dreams

MICHAEL BRYANT / Inquirer Staff Photographer

Bin Woo (center) and Brandon Walker (right) *of Carver High School of Engineering and Science are among the students cheering the city and school district's announcement of the four-year, $40 million plan.*

school, so that my parents don't have to worry," Matos-Reyes said. "This helps a lot. It takes the weight a little bit off of them."

18 Fattah said the city's students would be encouraged to reach for goals that they might have thought were unattainable.

19 "The whole thrust here is to send kids a signal that college is possible. College is within your reach if you get to your senior year," he said. "Four years from today, we expect Philadelphia to lead the nation in the number of students graduating from high school and going on to college."

20 Fattah already has approached groups, such as the Bill and Melinda Gates Foundation, seeking funding. In addition, the Student Loan Marketing Association (Sallie Mae) will underwrite all administrative operating costs for the program, he said.

21 The financial help comes as national reports warn of tens of thousands of students from low-income families being kept out of college because of money. Last year, the Advisory Committee on Student Financial Assistance reported that 170,000 top high school graduates from low- and moderate-income families could not afford to enroll in college.

The "average unmet need" of an urban student going off to college is $4,000, and that's after receiving aid and loans, according to the Cleveland-based National College Access Network. 22

While many communities have started college-access scholarship programs, Philadelphia's new program appears to be the most extensive, offering aid to everyone, said Tina Millano, executive director. 23

Congress created a similar program in 1999 for students in Washington, and the Washington Post reported this month that it might be paying off: Private surveys show it has spurred significant gains in college attendance. The report says no public agency has attendance figures before and after 2000, when the legislation took effect. 24

CORE at a Glance

Test Scores

Average Scholastic Assessment Test score for the Philadelphia School District for 2001–02: **832**.

Average SAT score for incoming freshmen in the State System of Higher Education for fall 2002: **992**.

Costs

Tuition for the 14 State System of Higher Education schools: **$4,598**.

Room and board: **$4,290** to **$5,390**.

Students

Average number of district seniors who graduate each year: **9,600**.

Estimated number eligible for the new financial-aid program: **4,000**.

Number of seniors in charter schools this year: **1,100**.

Estimated number eligible: Not available.

For More Information

Students and families who want more information on college preparation, choices, financial resources, and other issues may call the district's office of College and Career Awareness at 215-299-7807 or go to the CORE Philadelphia Web site at www.corephilly.org.

25 In Pennsylvania, tuition at the 14 State System of Higher Education institutions is about $4,600; room and board varies among the schools, ranging from $4,290 to $5,390.

26 Tom Gluck, a spokesman for the state system, said city applicants would have to follow normal admission procedures, which are up to each university. The system does not anticipate creating any spaces or special measures for city students.

27 "It's simply making certain that cost is not a barrier to those who are ready and interested and qualified to attend our universities," Gluck said.

28 The number of freshman positions varies each year, depending on enrollment. For fall 2002, the system received 68,786 applications; 47,311 were accepted, and 19,059 enrolled. Of those, 3,613 were Philadelphia public- and private-school students.

29 To start the scholarship fund, the school district will kick in $6 million a year for the first four years if the School Reform Commission approves. Paul Vallas, district chief executive officer, said the district would use federal funds. The city's contribution—$4 million—is subject to approval by City Council. Street said he likely would seek the funds through refinancing.

30 Councilman Michael Nutter and Councilwoman Blondell Reynolds Brown said the program sounded worthy of support. "I care very deeply about college access, and I look forward to details of the program. On its face, it certainly sounds like a great idea," Nutter said.

31 Because only the freshman year would be covered, officials acknowledged that students would have to find other funding sources for the following three years. "We want to get them started," Fattah said.

Reading Web Sites

In schools, businesses, and community settings, people turn to the Web for information. However, because many Web sites have busy, crowded pages, reading one can require you to work hard to distinguish important information from not-so-important material. Some Web sites—particularly those whose **URLs** (electronic addresses) end in .com—may have a persuasive rather than an informative purpose (for example, their purpose may be to sell a product or to promote a political position). Those designated .edu (educational institution) or .org (nonprofit organization) are more likely—although not guaranteed—to present unbiased information. (For more on evaluating Web sites, see 1I.)

☑ CHECKLIST: Reading Web Sites

Look for the following features as you preview:

- URL designation (.com, .org, and so on)
- Links to other sites (underlined in blue)
- Graphics
- Color

(continued on following page)

(continued from previous page)

- Headings
- Boxed material
- Page layout (placement of images and text on the page)
- Type size
- Photographs

◆ PRACTICE 2-10

The following is the home page of the U.S. Environmental Protection Agency. Preview this page, looking closely at the features listed in the checklist above. What information attracts your attention the most? Why? Do you think this page communicates its information effectively? How could its presentation be improved?

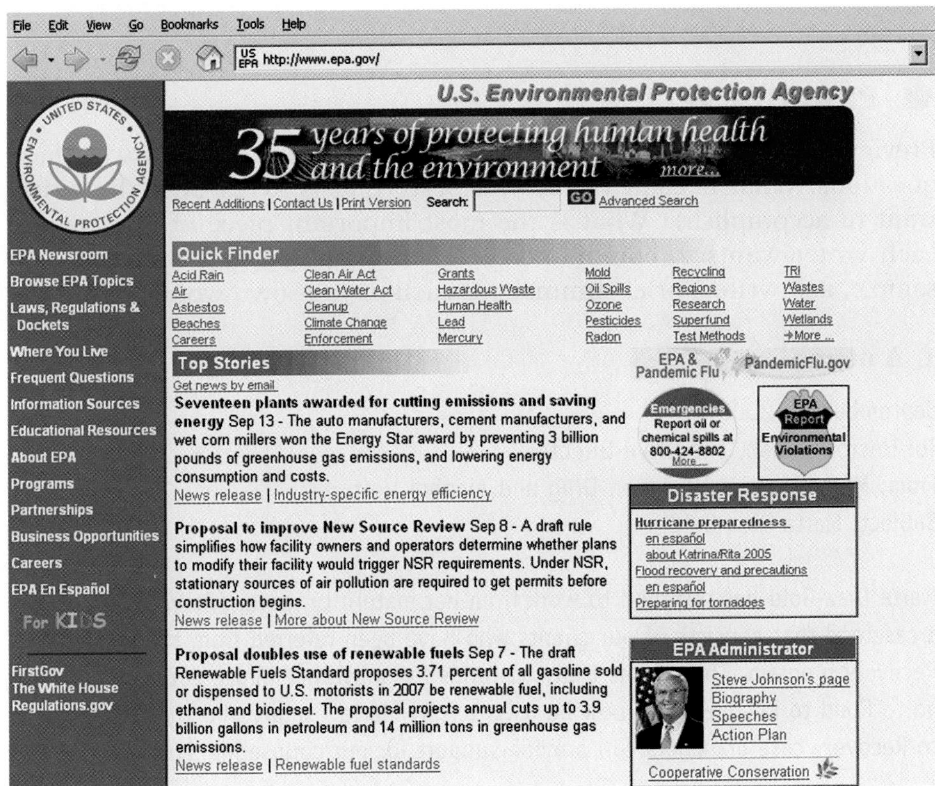

Reading on the Job

In your workplace, you will be called on to read memos, letters, emails, and reports. These documents, which may be designed to convey information or to persuade, are often addressed to a group rather than to a single person. (Note that the most important information is often presented *first*—in a subject line or in the first paragraph.)

CHECKLIST: Reading on the Job

Look for the following features as you preview:

- Numbered or bulleted lists of tasks or problems (numbers indicate the order of the items' importance)
- In an email, links to the Web
- In a memo or an email, the person or persons addressed
- In a memo or an email, the subject line
- In a memo or a report, headings that highlight key topics or points
- The first and last paragraphs and the first sentence of each body paragraph, which often contain key information
- Boldfaced, underlined, or italicized words

◆ PRACTICE 2-11

Preview the following samples of on-the-job writing, and answer these questions: What is each writer's purpose (that is, what does the writer want to accomplish)? What is the most important piece of information each writer wants to communicate? Then, highlight and annotate each sample, and write a brief summary of each in your own words.

1. A memo

September 10, 2006
To: Hector Garzon, Executive Director
From: Marco Morales, Director, Drug and Alcohol Unit
Subject: Marta Diaz-Gold

Marta Diaz-Gold has returned to work from her maternity leave. I have assigned her a caseload that consists of our clients who have been referred from the Road to Recovery program. This means that the funds for substance abuse counseling that go to Road to Recovery can now be used to pay Marta's salary and that the Road to Recovery case managers can provide support for our counseling services.

Marta and I have agreed on the following:

- Regular monthly meetings with Road to Recovery case managers
- Weekly reports to me from Marta regarding progress on the Road to Recovery caseload
- Joint review of Marta's work by Miriam Cabrera and myself after six months

Marta will be meeting with the current counselor and each individual client this week so she can make a smooth transition into her new position. As of next week, she will have full responsibility for all these clients. Because the Road to Recovery clients will not constitute a full caseload, it is understood that Marta will also be getting clients on a regular rotation from our other drug and alcohol programs.

Cc: Miriam Cabrera, Human Resources Director
Marta Diaz-Gold

2. An email

To: University Faculty, Staff, and Students
Re: Emergency Closing

KYW News Radio (1060) has assumed responsibility for coordinating and managing the school closing program in our area. School numbers will be announced twice every hour. The University's radio identification number is **117.** The number for students attending evening classes at the University is **2117.** You may also find information about school closings on the radio station's Web site at **www.kyw1060.com.** In addition, school closings will also be announced *by name* on WTFX-Fox TV (channel 29).

☑ REVIEW CHECKLIST: Reading for Academic Success

- ☐ Become an active reader. (See 2A.)
- ☐ Preview your reading assignment. (See 2B.)
- ☐ Highlight your reading assignment. (See 2B.)
- ☐ Annotate your reading assignment. (See 2B.)
- ☐ Outline your reading assignment. (See 2B.)
- ☐ Summarize your reading assignment. (See 2B.)
- ☐ Learn how to read different kinds of texts. (See 2C.)

UNIT TWO

Writing Effective Paragraphs

Writing a Paragraph

CHAPTER
3

PREVIEW

In this chapter, you will learn

- to understand paragraph structure (3A)
- to focus on your assignment, purpose, and audience (3B)
- to find ideas to write about (3C)
- to identify your main idea and write a topic sentence (3D)
- to choose supporting points (3E)
- to arrange your supporting points (3F)
- to draft your paragraph (3G)
- to revise your paragraph (3H)

SEEING AND WRITING

The picture above shows a college classroom. Look at the picture, and then consider all the reasons you decided to go to college. Think about this question carefully before you read the pages that follow. This is the topic you will be writing about as you move through this chapter.

Word Power

self-esteem pride in oneself; self-respect

It's no secret that writing is essential in most of the courses you will take in college. Whether you write a lab report or an English paper, a midterm or a final, your ability to organize your ideas and express them in writing will affect how well you do. In other words, succeeding at writing is the first step toward succeeding in college. Even more important, writing is a key to success outside the classroom. On the job and in everyday life, if you can express yourself clearly and effectively, you will stand a better chance of achieving your goals and influencing the world around you.

This chapter will guide you through the process of writing a **paragraph**. Because paragraphs play an important part in almost all the writing you do, learning to write a paragraph is central to becoming an effective writer.

A Understanding Paragraph Structure

Before you can begin the process of writing a paragraph, you need to have a basic understanding of paragraph structure.

A **paragraph** is a group of sentences that is unified by a single main idea. The **topic sentence** states the main idea, and the rest of the sentences in the paragraph provide details and examples that support the main idea. At the end of the paragraph, a **concluding statement** summarizes the main idea.

Paragraph

To write a paragraph, you need a main idea and convincing support. The main idea, stated in the topic sentence, unifies the paragraph. After the main idea come sentences that support the topic sentence. These sentences present details and examples that help readers understand the paragraph's main idea. The final sentence is a concluding statement that sums up the main idea. If you follow this general structure, you are on your way to writing an effective paragraph.

NOTE: The first sentence of a paragraph is **indented**, starting about half an inch from the left-hand margin. Every sentence begins with a capital letter, and most end with a period. (Sometimes a sentence ends with a question mark or an exclamation point.)

B Focusing on Your Assignment, Purpose, and Audience

In college, a writing task almost always begins with an assignment. Before you begin to write, stop to ask yourself some questions about this **assignment** (*what* you are expected to write) as well as about your **purpose** (*why* you are writing) and your **audience** (*for whom* you are writing). If you answer these questions now, you will save yourself a lot of time later.

Questions about Assignment, Purpose, and Audience

Assignment

- What is your assignment?
- Do you have a word or page limit?
- When is your assignment due?
- Will you do your writing at home or in class?
- Will you work on your own or with other students?
- Will your instructor return your work so you can revise it?

Purpose

- Are you expected to express your feelings—for example, to tell how you feel about a story in the newspaper?
- Are you expected to give information—for example, to answer an exam question?
- Are you expected to take a position on a controversial issue?

Audience

- Who will read your paper—just your instructor or other students, too?
- Do you have an audience beyond the classroom—for example, your supervisor at work or the readers of your school newspaper?
- How much will your readers already know about your topic?
- Will your readers expect you to use a formal or an informal style? (For example, are you writing a research paper or a personal essay?)

◆ PRACTICE 3-1

Each of the following writing tasks has a different audience and purpose. On the lines following each task, write a few notes about how you would approach the task. (The Questions about Assignment, Purpose, and Audience above can help you decide on the best approach.) When you have finished, discuss your responses with the class or in a group of three or four students.

1. For the other students in your writing class, describe the best or worst class you have ever had.

   ____

   ____

   ____

2. Write a short letter to your school newspaper in which you try to convince readers that a certain course should no longer be offered at your school.

   ____

   ____

   ____

3. Write a letter applying for a job. Explain how the courses you have taken will help you in that job.

____

____

____

____

____

C Finding Ideas to Write About

Once you understand your assignment, purpose, and audience, you can begin to find ideas to write about. This process can be challenging, and it is different for every writer. You may be the kind of person who likes a structured way to find ideas, or you may prefer a looser, more relaxed way to find things to write about. As you gain more experience as a writer, you will learn which of the four strategies discussed in the pages that follow (*freewriting*, *brainstorming*, *clustering*, and *journal writing*) work best for you.

Julia Reyes, a student in an introductory writing course, was given the following assignment.

> **Word Power**
> **dilemma** a situation that requires a choice between two alternatives

ASSIGNMENT Is it better to go to college right after high school or to wait? Write a paragraph in which you answer this question.

Before she could begin her paragraph, Julia needed to find ideas to write about. To help students practice using different ways to find ideas, Julia's instructor required them to try all four strategies. The pages that follow explain each of these strategies and show how Julia used them.

Freewriting

When you **freewrite**, you write whatever comes into your head, and you write for a set period of time without stopping. Grammar and spelling are not important; what is important is to get your ideas down on paper. So even if your words don't seem to be going anywhere, keep on writing. Sometimes you freewrite to find a topic. Most often, however, you freewrite on a specific topic that your instructor gives you. This strategy is called **focused freewriting**.

When you finish freewriting, read what you have written, and try to find an idea you think you might be able to write more about. Underline this idea, and then freewrite again, using the underlined idea as a starting point.

Here is Julia's focused freewriting on the topic "Is it better to go to college right after high school or to wait?"

Which is better? To start college right away? To wait? I waited, but last year was such a waste of time. Such a waste. Every job I had was stupid. Telemarketing — the worst worst job. Why didn't I just quit the first day? (Money.) Waitressing was a hard job. Everybody had an attitude. The customer was always right, blah blah. Another waste of time. Why didn't I just go right to college? I needed money. And I was sick of school. School was hard. I wasn't good at it. But work was boring. But now I hate how all my friends are a year ahead of me. So I guess it's better not to wait.

Freewriting

◆ PRACTICE 3-2

Read Julia's freewriting. What ideas do you think she should write more about? Write your suggestions on the following lines.

____

____

____

____

____

◆ PRACTICE 3-3

Freewrite about the topic "Why did you decide to go to college?" On a blank sheet of lined paper (or on your computer), write for at least five minutes without stopping. If you can't think of anything to write, just write the last word over and over again until something else comes to mind.

◆ PRACTICE 3-4

Reread the freewriting you did for Practice 3-3. Underline the sentence that expresses the most interesting idea. Use this sentence as a starting point for a focused freewriting exercise.

Brainstorming

When you **brainstorm**, you write down all the ideas you can think of about your topic. Brainstorming is different from freewriting, and it looks different on the page. Instead of writing on the lines, you write all over the page. You can star, check, box, or underline words, and you can ask questions, make lists, and draw arrows to connect ideas.

Here are Julia's brainstorming notes on the topic "Is it better to go to college right after high school or to wait?"

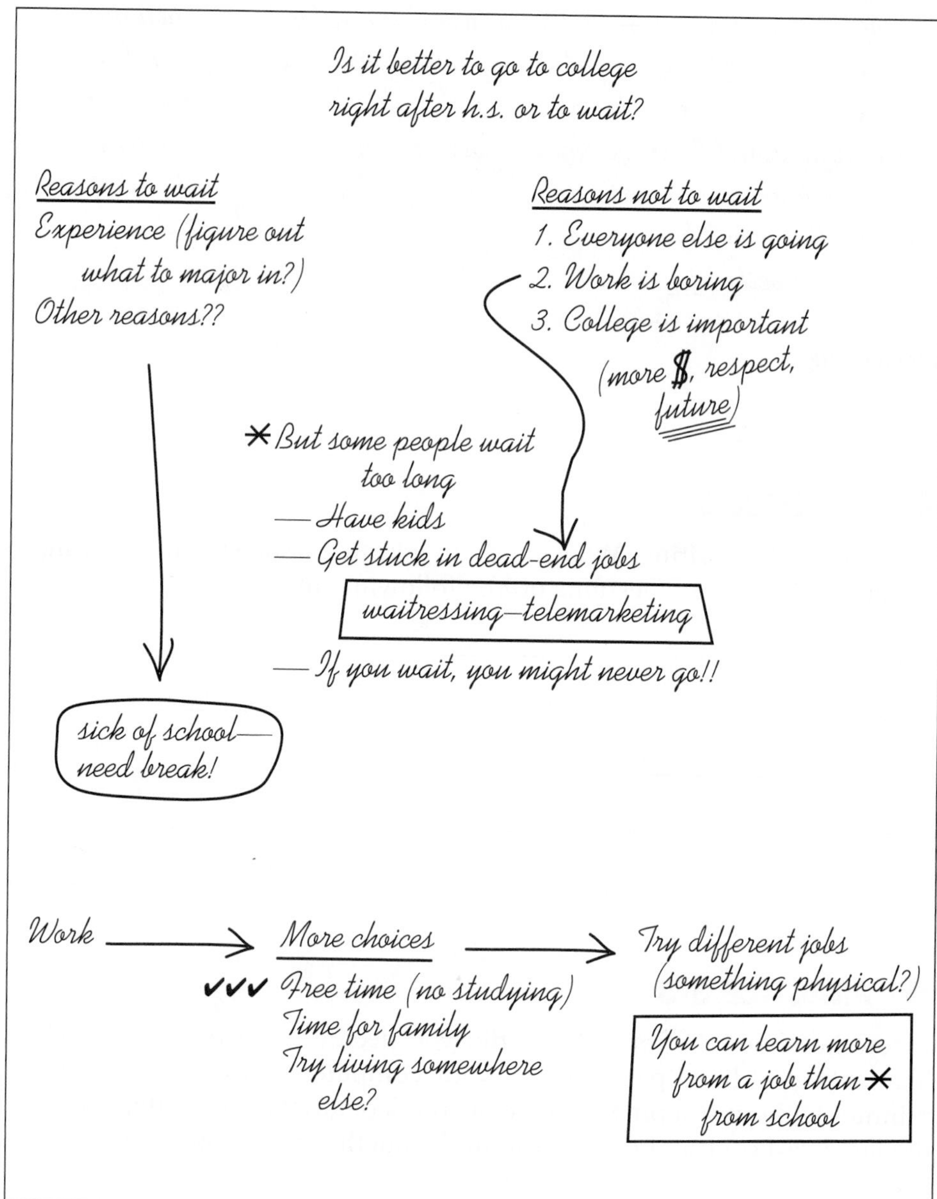

Brainstorming Notes

◆ PRACTICE 3-5

Read Julia's brainstorming notes. How is her brainstorming similar to her freewriting (p. 55)? How is it different? Which ideas do you think she should write more about? Which ones should she cross out? Write your suggestions on the following lines.

____

____

____

◆ PRACTICE 3-6

Practice brainstorming on the topic "Why did you decide to go to college?" Write on a sheet of *unlined* paper. Write quickly, without worrying about being neat or using complete sentences. Experiment with writing on different parts of the page, making lists, drawing arrows to connect related ideas, and starring important ideas. When you have finished, look over what you have written. Which ideas seem most interesting? Did you come up with any new ideas in your brainstorming that you did not think of in your freewriting?

FOCUS Collaborative Brainstorming

You usually brainstorm on your own, but at times you may find it helpful to do **collaborative brainstorming**, working with other students to find ideas. Sometimes, your instructor may ask you and another student to brainstorm together. At other times, the class might brainstorm as a group while your instructor writes ideas on the board. However you brainstorm, your goal is the same: to come up with as much material about your topic as you can.

◆ PRACTICE 3-7

Brainstorm with three or four other students on the topic of why you decided to attend college. First, choose one person to write down ideas on a sheet of paper or on a section of the board. Then, discuss the topic informally. After about fifteen minutes, review all the ideas that have been listed. Has the group come up with any ideas that you can use in your writing? Be sure to keep a list of these ideas so that you can use them later on.

Clustering

If you like brainstorming, you will probably also be comfortable with **clustering**, which is sometimes called *mapping*. When you cluster, you begin by writing your general topic in the center of a sheet of paper. Then, you draw lines from the general topic to related ideas, moving from the center to the corners of the page. (These lines will look like spokes of a wheel or branches of a tree.) Your ideas will get more and more specific as you move from the center to the edges of the page.

When you finish clustering, you can cluster again on a new sheet of paper, this time beginning with a specific idea that you thought of the first time.

Here is Julia's clustering on the topic "Is it better to go to college right after high school or to wait?"

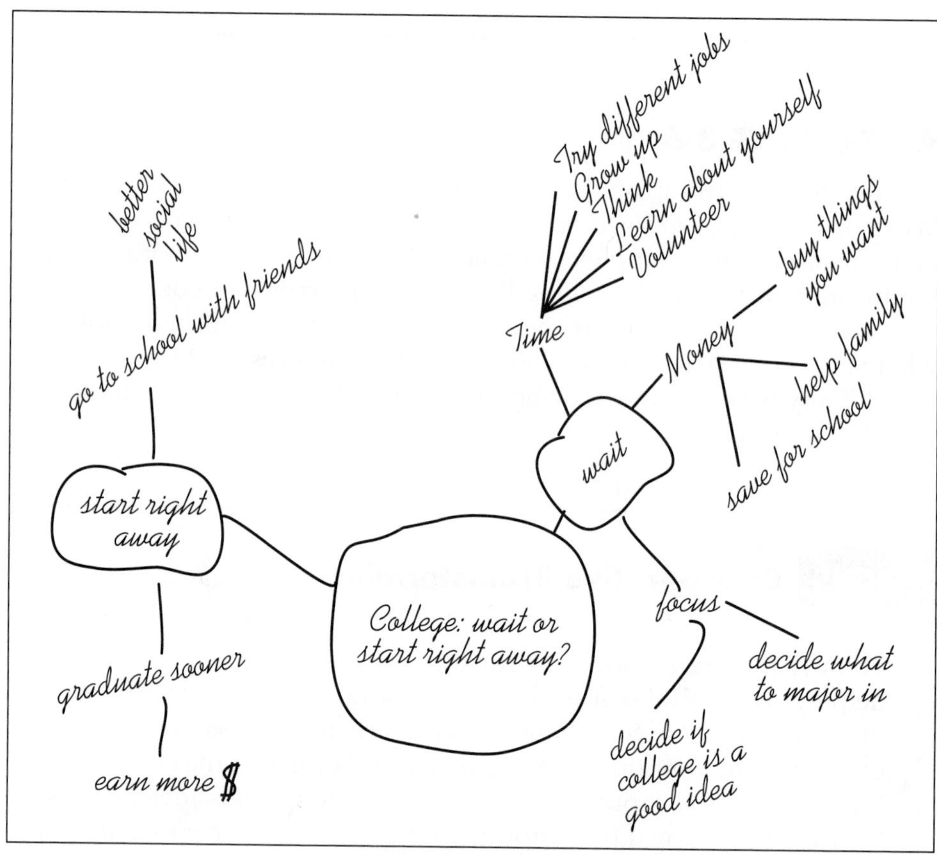

Clustering

◆ PRACTICE 3-8

How is Julia's clustering similar to her brainstorming on the same subject (p. 56)? How is it different? Which branch of her cluster diagram do you think Julia should focus on? Why? Should she add any other branches? Write your suggestions on the following lines. Then, discuss them with the class or in a small group.

____

____

____

____

____

____

____

____

____

◆ PRACTICE 3-9

Practice clustering on the topic "Why did you decide to go to college?" Begin by writing this topic in the center of a sheet of unlined paper. Circle the topic, and then draw branches to connect specific ideas and examples, moving toward the edges of the page. When you have finished, look over what you have written. Which ideas are the most interesting? Which ones do you think you can write more about? Have you come up with any new ideas that your freewriting and brainstorming did not suggest?

Journal Writing

A **journal** is a place to write down your thoughts. It is also a place to jot down ideas that you might be able to write more about and a place to think on paper about your assignments. In your journal, you can do problem solving, try out sentences, keep track of details and examples, and keep a record of interesting things you read or observe.

Once you have started writing regularly in your journal, go back every week or so and reread what you have written. You may find ideas for an assignment you are working on—or just learn more about yourself.

FOCUS Journals

Here are some subjects you can write about in a journal.

- *Your schoolwork* Writing regularly about the topics you are studying in school is one way to become a better student. For example, you can think on paper about what you are learning, write down questions about topics you are having trouble understanding, and examine new ideas.
- *Your job* You can write about the day-to-day triumphs and frustrations of your job. For example, you can write down conversations with coworkers, or you can list problems and remind yourself how you solved them. Rereading your journal may help you understand your strengths and weaknesses as an employee.
- *Your ideas about your community and your world* As you learn more about the social and political world around you, you can explore your reactions to new ideas. For example, you may read an interesting story in the newspaper or see something on television or on the Internet that challenges your beliefs. Even if you are not ready to talk to others about what you are thinking, you can still "talk" to your journal.
- *Your impressions of what you observe* Many writers carry their journals with them and record interesting, unusual, or funny things they notice as they go about their daily business. If you get into the habit of writing down your observations and reactions, you may be able to use them later in your writing.

(continued on following page)

(continued from previous page)

- *Personal thoughts* Although you may not feel comfortable writing about your personal thoughts and experiences—especially if your instructor will read your journal—you should try to be as honest as you can. Writing about relationships with family and friends, personal problems, and hopes and dreams can help you get to know (and understand) yourself better.

Here is Julia's journal entry on the topic "Is it better to go to college right after high school or to wait?"

This is a hard topic for me to write about. When I finished high school, I never wanted to go to school again. High school was hard. I worked hard, but teachers always said I could do better. Studying was boring. I couldn't concentrate. I never seemed to get things right on homework or on tests. Things seemed easier for everyone else. Sometimes I hated school. So I decided I'd work and not go to college right away, or maybe ever. But after a year, here I am. I'm still not sure why. School always felt hard. Work was boring, but it was easy. For the first time, I could do everything right. I got raises and promotions and better hours because I was a good worker. I wasn't judged by how I did on some dumb test. For once, I had some self-esteem. So why am I here? Good question.

Journal Entry

◆ PRACTICE 3-10

Buy a notebook to use as a journal. Make an appointment with yourself to write for fifteen minutes or so—during lunch, for example, or right before you go to bed—every day. Then, write your first journal entry. Being as honest with yourself as possible, try to explain why you really decided to go to college.

D Identifying Your Main Idea and Writing a Topic Sentence

When you think you have enough material to write about, it is time for you to find a main idea to develop in your paragraph.

To find a main idea for your paragraph, begin by looking over what you have already written. As you read through your freewriting, brainstorming, clustering, and journal entries, look for the main idea that your material seems to support. The sentence that states this main idea and gives your writing its focus will be your paragraph's **topic sentence**.

The topic sentence of your paragraph is important because it tells both you and your readers what the focus of your paragraph will be. An effective topic sentence has three characteristics.

1. **A topic sentence is a complete sentence.** There is a difference between a *topic* and a *topic sentence*. The **topic** is what the paragraph is about.

   TOPIC Whether or not to start college right after high school

   A **topic sentence**, however, is a complete sentence that includes a subject and a verb and expresses a complete thought.

   TOPIC SENTENCE Students should not start college right after they finish high school.

2. **A topic sentence is more than just an announcement of what you plan to write about.** A topic sentence makes a point about the topic the paragraph discusses.

   ANNOUNCEMENT In this paragraph, I will explain my ideas about whether or not students should go to college right after high school.

   TOPIC SENTENCE My ideas about when to start college changed when I became a college student.

3. **A topic sentence presents an idea that can be discussed in a single paragraph.** If your topic sentence is too broad, you will not be able to discuss it in just one paragraph. If your topic sentence is too narrow, you will not be able to say much about it.

   TOPIC SENTENCE TOO BROAD Students have many different reasons for deciding whether or not to go to college right after high school.

   TOPIC SENTENCE TOO NARROW Most students begin college right after high school.

   EFFECTIVE TOPIC SENTENCE Students who begin college right after high school may be too immature to do well in school.

When Julia Reyes reviewed her notes, she saw that most of her material supported the idea that it was better to wait instead of starting college right after high school. She stated this idea in a topic sentence.

> I think it's better to wait a few years instead of beginning college right after high school.

When Julia thought about how to express her topic sentence, she knew it had to be a complete sentence, not just a topic, and that it would have to make a point, not just announce what she planned to write about. When she reread the topic sentence she had written, she decided that it did these things and that it was neither too broad nor too narrow, making a statement she could support in a paragraph.

◆ PRACTICE 3-11

Read the following items. Put a check mark next to each one that you think would make an effective topic sentence for a paragraph.

Examples

Raccoons in the suburbs. ______

Raccoons often find food and shelter in the suburbs. __✓__

1. The country's most exciting roller coasters. ______
2. Some of the country's most exciting roller coasters are made of wood. ______
3. It is dangerous to use a cell phone while driving. ______
4. In this paragraph, I am going to write about cell phones and driving. ______
5. Daytime television shows can be addictive. ______
6. Some facts about daytime television shows. ______

◆ PRACTICE 3-12

The following topic sentences are either too broad or too narrow. On the line after each sentence, write *Too broad* if the sentence is too broad and *Too narrow* if the sentence is too narrow. Then, rewrite each sentence—making it more specific or more general—so that it could be an effective topic sentence for a paragraph.

Examples

Eating in a restaurant is interesting.

Too broad. Possible rewrite: Eating in a Mexican restaurant is interesting because there are so many food choices.

I email my friend every day.

Too narrow. Possible rewrite: Email is a good way to keep in touch with friends.

1. The price of textbooks is very high.

____

____

2. At the video store, I can never find the movie I want to rent.

____

____

3. The United States is a beautiful country.

____

____

4. Using a computer is easy.

____

____

5. American workers often wear jeans and sneakers to the office on casual Fridays.

____

____

◆ PRACTICE 3-13

In Practices 3-3, 3-6, and 3-9, you practiced freewriting, brainstorming, and clustering. Now, you are ready to write a paragraph in response to the following assignment.

Why did you decide to go to college?

Your first step is to find a main idea for your paragraph. Look over the work you have done so far, and decide what main idea your material can best support. On the lines below, write a topic sentence that expresses this idea.

Topic sentence: ____

____

____

E Choosing Supporting Points

After you identify your main idea and state it in a topic sentence, review your notes again. Now, you are looking for specific details and examples to support your topic sentence. Write or type your topic sentence at the top of a sheet of paper. As you review your notes and continue to think about your topic, list all the supporting points you think you might be able to use in your paragraph.

Julia listed the following points to support her paragraph's topic sentence. After she read through her list of points, she crossed out two points she did not think would support her topic sentence very well.

TOPIC SENTENCE (MAIN IDEA) I think it's better to wait a few years instead of beginning college right after high school.

- Work experience
- Chance to earn money
- ~~Avoid friends from high school~~
- ~~Develop new hobbies~~
- Chance to develop self-esteem
- Time to grow up
- Chance to decide if college is right for you

◆ PRACTICE 3-14

Now that you have a topic sentence for your paragraph, reread your freewriting, brainstorming, and clustering exercises, and list below all the points you can use to support your topic sentence. You can also list any new points you think of.

Topic sentence: ______________________________

____

Supporting points:

- ______________________________
- ______________________________
- ______________________________
- ______________________________
- ______________________________

F Arranging Your Supporting Points

Once you have listed all the supporting points you want to write about, arrange them in the order in which you plan to discuss them. Julia arranged her supporting points in the following list.

TOPIC SENTENCE I think it's better to wait a few years instead of beginning college right after high school.

1. Waiting gives people time to work and earn money.
2. Waiting gives people time to think about life and grow up.
3. Waiting helps people decide if college is right for them.
4. Waiting gives people a chance to develop self-esteem.

◆ PRACTICE 3-15

Reread the points you listed in Practice 3-14. Does each point support your topic sentence? Cross out any points that do not. On the following lines, arrange the remaining points in the order in which you plan to write about them.

1. ______________________________

2. ______________________________

3. ______________________________

4. ______________________________

G Drafting Your Paragraph

So far, you have found a main idea for your paragraph, written a topic sentence, listed supporting points, and arranged these points in the order in which you will write about them. Now, you are ready to write a first draft.

Begin drafting your paragraph by stating your topic sentence. Then, referring to your list of supporting points, write down your ideas without worrying about correct sentence structure, word choice, spelling, or punctuation. If you think of a good idea that is not on your list, write it down. (Don't worry at this point about where it fits or whether you will keep it.)

You can type your first draft, or you can write it by hand. Remember, though, that your first draft is a rough draft that you will revise. If you plan to revise on your handwritten draft, make things easy for yourself by leaving wide margins and skipping lines so you have room to add ideas. If you type your draft, use large type and leave extra space between lines.

When you have finished your rough draft, don't start correcting it right away. Take a break, and then return to your draft and read it.

Here is the first draft of Julia's paragraph on the topic "Is it better to go to college right after high school or to wait?"

Waiting

I think it's better to wait a few years instead of beginning college right after high school. Many people start college right after high school just because that's what everybody else is doing. But that's

(continued on following page)

(continued from previous page)

not always the right way to go. Different things are right for different people. There are other possible choices. Taking a few years off can be a better choice. During this time, people can work and earn money. They also have time to think and grow up. Waiting can even help people decide if college is right for them. Finally, waiting gives them a chance to develop self-esteem. For all these reasons, waiting a year or two between high school and college is a good idea.

Draft

◆ PRACTICE 3-16

Read Julia's draft paragraph. What do you think she should change in her draft? What should she add? What should she take out? Write your suggestions on the following lines. Then, discuss your suggestions with the class or in a small group.

____

____

____

____

◆ PRACTICE 3-17

Using the material you came up with for Practice 3-14, draft a paragraph on the topic of why you decided to go to college. Be sure to state your main idea in the topic sentence, and support it with specific points. Leave wide margins; if you like, skip lines. (If you type your draft, leave extra space between lines.) When you have finished, give your paragraph a title.

H Revising Your Paragraph

When you revise your work, you "re-see" it. **Revision** means much more than correcting a few commas or crossing out one word and putting another one in its place. Often, it means moving sentences around, adding words and phrases, and even changing the topic sentence. To get the most out of revision, begin by carefully rereading your draft—first aloud, then to yourself. Then, consider each of the questions on the checklist that follows.

SELF-ASSESSMENT CHECKLIST: Revising Your Paragraph

- Does your topic sentence state your main idea?
- Do you have enough points to support your main idea?
- Have you used enough examples and details?
- Are all your examples and details necessary?
- Does every sentence say what you mean?
- Does the order of your sentences make sense?
- Is every word necessary?
- Have you used the right words?
- Does your paragraph have a concluding statement that summarizes your main idea?

After Julia drafted the paragraph on pages 65–66, she used the Self-Assessment Checklist above to help her revise her paragraph.

Waiting

For students who are not getting much out of school, it is often
~~I think it's~~ better to wait a few years instead of beginning college
away
right after high school. Many people start college right ~~after high school~~

(continued on following page)

(continued from previous page)

that is / *However, that is*

just because ~~that's~~ what everybody else is doing. ~~But that's~~ not always

thing to do.

the right ~~way to go.~~ ~~Different things are right for different people.~~

often

~~There are other possible choices.~~ Taking a few years off can be a better

for college. Working at different jobs can help them decide on a career.

choice. During this time, people can work and earn money. ~~They also have~~

Taking a year or two off also gives people

time to think and grow up. Waiting can even help people decide if college

really / *Most important of all,*

is right for them. ~~Finally,~~ waiting gives them a chance to develop self-

me,

esteem. For ~~all these reasons,~~ waiting a year ~~or two~~ between high school

was

and college ~~is~~ a good idea., *and I think it can be a good idea for other students, too.*

I was a poor student in high school. School always felt hard. When I took a year off, everything changed. In high school, I always saw all the things I couldn't do. At work, I learned what I could do. Now, I think I can succeed.

Revised Draft

When she revised her paragraph, Julia crossed out sentences, added sentences, and changed the way she worded her ideas. Her biggest change was adding an explanation of how taking a year off had helped her. She also revised her topic sentence to reflect the broader perspective her personal experience gave her. Here is the final version of her revised paragraph.

Waiting

Topic sentence

For students who are not getting much out of school, it is often better to wait a few years instead of beginning college right after high school. Many people start college right away just because that is what everybody else is doing. However, that is not always the right thing to do. Taking a few years off can often be a better choice. During this time, people can work and earn money for college. Working at different jobs can help them decide on a career. Taking a year or two off also gives people time to think and grow up. Waiting can even help people decide if college is really right for them. Most important of all, waiting gives them a chance to develop self-esteem. I was a poor student in high school. School always felt hard. When I took a year off, everything changed. In high school, I always saw all the things I couldn't do. At work, I learned what I could do. Now, I think I can succeed. For me, waiting a year between high school and college was a good idea, and I think it can be a good idea for other students, too.

Support

Concluding statement

FOCUS Editing

Don't confuse revision with editing, which comes *after* revision. When you **edit**, you check for correct grammar, punctuation, mechanics, and spelling. Then, you proofread your writing carefully for typing errors that a computer spell checker may not identify. You also make sure that you have indented the first sentence of your paragraph and that every sentence begins with a capital letter and ends with a period.

Remember, editing is a vital last step in the writing process. Readers may not take your ideas seriously if you have errors in grammar or spelling.

◆ PRACTICE 3-18

Read the final version of Julia's revised paragraph (p. 68), and compare it with her first draft (pp. 65–66). What specific changes did she make? Which do you think are her best changes? Why? Answer these questions on the following lines. Then, with the class or in a small group, discuss your reaction to the revised paragraph.

____

____

____

____

____

____

◆ PRACTICE 3-19

Use the Self-Assessment Checklist on page 67 to help evaluate the paragraph you drafted for Practice 3-17. What else can you add to support your topic sentence? Should anything be crossed out because it doesn't support your topic sentence? Can anything be stated more clearly? On the following lines, list some of the changes you might make in your draft.

____

____

____

____

____

• REVISING AND EDITING

Revise the draft paragraph that you wrote in this chapter. Begin by crossing out unnecessary material and any material you want to rewrite, and then add new and rewritten material. After you finish your revision, edit the paragraph, checking grammar, punctuation, mechanics, and spelling—and look carefully for typing errors. When you are satisfied with your paragraph, print out a clean copy.

☑ REVIEW CHECKLIST: Writing a Paragraph

- Be sure you understand paragraph structure. (See 3A.)
- Consider your assignment, purpose, and audience. (See 3B.)
- Use different strategies—freewriting, brainstorming, clustering, and journal writing—to help you find ideas to write about. (See 3C.)
- Identify your main idea, and write a topic sentence. (See 3D.)
- Choose supporting points from your notes. (See 3E.)
- Arrange your supporting points in a logical order. (See 3F.)
- Write a draft of your paragraph. (See 3G.)
- Revise and edit your draft. (See 3H.)

Fine-Tuning Your Paragraph

CHAPTER 4

PREVIEW

In this chapter, you will learn

- to write unified paragraphs (4A)
- to write well-developed paragraphs (4B)
- to write coherent paragraphs (4C)

SEEING AND WRITING

The picture above shows the Feast of San Gennaro, a festival held every year in the Little Italy neighborhood of New York City. Look at the picture, and then write a paragraph about an event that you wanted to attend but could not. What was special about the event? What caused you to miss it?

Word Power

spectacle a public performance or show; an unusual sight

A Writing Unified Paragraphs

A paragraph is **unified** when all of its sentences support the main idea stated in the topic sentence. A paragraph is not unified when its sentences do not support the main idea in the topic sentence. When you revise, you can make your paragraphs unified by crossing out sentences that do not support your topic sentence. The following paragraph is not unified.

Paragraph Not Unified

Although applying for a loan can be confusing, the process is not all that difficult. The first step is to determine which bank has the lowest interest rate. There are a lot of banks in my neighborhood, but they aren't very friendly. The last time I went into one, I waited for twenty minutes before anyone bothered to wait on me. Once you have chosen a bank, you have to go to the bank in person and apply, and if the bank isn't friendly, you don't want to go there. This is a real problem when you apply for a loan. If you have any questions about the application, you won't be able to get anyone to answer them. After you have submitted the application comes the hard part—waiting for approval.

After stating that applying for a loan is not difficult, the writer of the paragraph above wanders from his main idea to complain about how unfriendly the banks in his neighborhood are. For this reason, most of the sentences in the paragraph do not support the topic sentence.

The following revised paragraph is unified. When the writer reread his paragraph, he deleted the sentences that did not support his topic sentence. Then, he added sentences that did. The result is a paragraph that supports its main idea: that applying for a loan is easy.

Paragraph Unified

Although applying for a loan can be confusing, the process is not all that difficult. The first step is to determine which bank has the lowest interest rate. ~~There are a lot of banks in my neighborhood, but they aren't very friendly. The last time I went into one, I waited for twenty minutes before anyone bothered to wait on me.~~ Although a half-percent difference in rates may not seem like much, over the course of a four-year loan, the savings can really add up. Once you have chosen a bank, you have to go to the bank in person and apply.~~, and if the bank isn't friendly, you don't want to go there. This is a real problem when you apply for a loan. If you have any questions about the application, you won't be able to get anyone to answer them.~~ Make sure you tell the loan officer exactly what rate you are applying for. Then, take the application home and fill it out, being careful not to omit any important information. If you have any problems with your credit, explain them on the application or in a separate letter. Take the application back to the bank, and ask any questions you might have. (Do not sign the application until all your questions have been answered.) After you have submitted the application comes the hard part—waiting for approval.

Support added

Support added

—Hector de la Paz (student)

◆ PRACTICE 4-1

Underline the topic sentence in each of the following paragraphs. Keep in mind that the topic sentence will not always be the first sentence of the paragraph.

Example

Learning to drive was very difficult. My father wanted to teach me to drive, but he didn't have time. My older brother said he would do it. We used his car, which had a stick shift. This made it a lot harder to learn to drive. He took me to a big, empty parking lot so that I wouldn't crash into anything. I practiced how to start the car. When I got the car started, I had trouble shifting to the next gear. The engine kept stalling again and again. My brother yelled at me, and I felt stupid. After a while, he let me take the car on the road. It was hard to shift and steer at the same time. Whenever I stopped for a red light, the car jerked and stalled. As I practiced, I eventually got the hang of it. Finally, I passed my driving test, and now I am a good driver.

1. The Innocence Project arranges for lawyers and law students to help free innocent people who have been wrongly convicted. Sometimes, a DNA test can prove that these people are innocent, but this testing is often not done. The test is expensive, and prisoners cannot afford it. Unfortunately, they have no other way to prove their innocence, except to hope that the Innocence Project will choose their cases. The lawyers and law students in the Innocence Project study the cases and take those they think they can win. As a result of the Innocence Project, more than one hundred and seventy people in the United States have been released from jail. Fourteen of these people had been sentenced to death. Thousands of other prisoners are waiting and hoping that they will be released from jail as a result of the work of the Innocence Project.

2. Most adults went to public schools when they were young. They sat in rows, listened to the teacher, and went to recess with many other children. At the end of the day, they went home to their families. These days, many children are home-schooled. Instead of going to school, they stay home and learn. Usually, the mother is the teacher. She may order books and materials on the Internet. She teaches all the subjects to her children. Although some people worry that home-schooled children do not interact enough with people outside their family, many of these home-schooled children do well once they get to college.

3. What were your parents thinking when they gave you your name? Did they give you a popular name? If so, other children in your class probably had the same name. Some popular names change over time. Biblical names have been popular for boys for many years. In recent years, for example, the top boys' names have come from the Bible—Jacob, Michael, and Joshua. Girls' names are different. In the past, many girls were named Mary, but recently some of the most popular girls' names have been Emily, Emma, and Madison. Today, girls are often named after characters from books, movies, or television shows. Most likely, your name is a name that was popular when you were born.

◆ PRACTICE 4-2

The following paragraph has no topic sentence. Read it, and then choose the best topic sentence from the list below.

People cheat on taxes, people cheat on their spouses, and people cheat on their insurance claims. People cheat on this, and they cheat on that. They skim a little off the top here and add a little over there. No one seems to be playing by the rules anymore. It's time we started challenging people for their dishonesty. What does all this cheating say about our society? Maybe it says that we're incapable of succeeding honorably. Maybe it suggests that honesty is just for people who don't understand how the world works. When we cheat or accept the fact that someone else cheats, we are really only cheating ourselves. In the long run, we have to live with the guilt that cheating creates and pay the price for our dishonesty.

Put a check mark next to the topic sentence that best expresses the main idea in the paragraph above.

1. Everyone, regardless of age or gender, seems to be cheating. ________
2. Cheating is bad for society. ________
3. Cheating is so widespread that we do not realize the harm it does. ________
4. Lots of people cheat. ________
5. There is nothing we can do to stop the cheating that we see around us. ________

◆ PRACTICE 4-3

The following paragraphs do not have topic sentences. Think of a topic sentence that sums up each paragraph's main idea, and write it on the line above the paragraph.

Example

Books can be banned from schools and libraries for various reasons.
____

____

Each year, the American Library Association puts out a list of the books that people want removed from libraries and classrooms. Books like *The Catcher in the Rye* by J. D. Salinger and *Forever* by Judy Blume have been challenged for sexual content and offensive language. The Harry Potter series by J. K. Rowling is often criticized for supposedly encouraging witchcraft. Books like *Daddy's Roommate* have been challenged for promoting homosexuality. Finally, *The Adventures of Huckleberry Finn* by Mark Twain has been challenged for alleged racism.

1. ____

____

Until the 1960s, wearing a hat was a mark of adulthood. It was a more formal time when many men wore suits and hats even at sports events. For women, dresses, white gloves, and hats were essential for many occasions. By 1960, though, going hatless was more common. Many people resisted the formal look of the past and began to dress much more casually. They abandoned their suits, dresses, white gloves, and hats. Going bareheaded became the rule except on very special occasions. Even though designers have often predicted that hats are coming back in style, this hasn't happened.

2. ____

____

Tupperware, a type of plastic food storage container, was first sold in 1951 at home parties. In a friend's living room, housewives would be invited to check out the various sizes and shapes of the plastic storage containers with the famous "burping" seal. They would pick the ones they wanted and order them from the Tupperware consultant—a housewife like them. Today, you can still find Tupperware parties in some places, but so many women work outside the home that they need other ways to buy Tupperware. Shopping malls may have Tupperware showcases—booths where shoppers can purchase Tupperware. Shoppers can also buy Tupperware online, directly from the company. They may even get an email invitation to an online party, where they can buy Tupperware.

3. ____

____

Do you like to shop? If so, being a mystery shopper could be your dream job. A mystery shopper goes to a store, checks it out, and completes a questionnaire about its prices, customer service, cleanliness, and other things that affect a customer's experience. Typical locations for mystery shopping are department stores, supermarkets, restaurants, and bars. As a result of the shopper's report, the store might improve its staff training or lower its prices to be more competitive. Most mystery shoppers earn between $12 and $20 for a shopping trip of less than an hour. They usually work part-time. It is not a very highly paid job, but for someone who likes to shop, it might be perfect.

◆ PRACTICE 4-4

Read the following paragraphs. Write *unified* after the paragraphs that are unified and *not unified* after the ones that are not unified.

Example

Pet ownership is a big responsibility. Thousands of families adopt dogs and cats every month. Other family activities include taking vacations and playing sports together. In fact, families who spend time together tend to be happier and communicate more. Most people give little thought to the animals' needs for a proper diet, exercise, company, and veterinary care. In fact, few people realize how much time and money they will spend taking care of their pets. not unified

1. Drivers must be careful to avoid road rage incidents. Road rage occurs when a driver loses control over his or her emotions in a stressful situation. Driving in bad weather can be very stressful. A car does not handle as easily on snowy or icy roads as it does on dry ones. Snow tires can make winter driving safer. Even with snow tires, though, driving on slippery roads requires concentration. Road rage can lead to property damage and even injury. Therefore, drivers should always keep their emotions under control. ____________

2. Music can either help or hurt a person's ability to recall information. For example, students who study while listening to loud dance music tend to remember less than those who study in quiet settings. The reason for this is that dance music has a strong rhythm, which tends to distract a person from the material being studied. Classical music, on the other hand, may help improve memory. Research shows that some people remember information more clearly if they listen to quiet classical music while studying. Understanding the link between music and memory can help students make wise choices about listening to music while studying. ____________

3. Georgia O'Keeffe was a bold and influential painter. Her most famous paintings are of flowers and of scenes from the Southwest. Many tourists visit the Southwest to enjoy its beautiful deserts. Taos, New Mexico, is an especially busy tourist spot. O'Keeffe developed a unique painting style. She created dramatic images that went against the artistic fashion of her times. In fact, her rich use of color has inspired many artists. Quite a few artists today work in video and collage as well as in paint. O'Keeffe's work is on display in many of the world's leading museums. ____________

◆ PRACTICE 4-5

Reread the paragraphs in Practice 4-4 that you decided were not unified. First, underline the topic sentence in each paragraph. Then, cross out the sentences in each paragraph that do not belong.

Example

Pet ownership is a big responsibility. Thousands of families adopt dogs and cats every month. ~~Other family activities include taking vacations and playing sports together. In fact, families who spend time together tend to be happier and communicate more.~~ Most people give little thought to the animals' needs for a proper diet, exercise, company, and veterinary care. In fact, few people realize how much time and money they will spend taking care of their pets.

1. Drivers must be careful to avoid road rage incidents. Road rage occurs when a driver loses control over his or her emotions in a stressful situation. Driving in bad weather can be very stressful. A car does not handle

as easily on snowy or icy roads as it does on dry ones. Snow tires can make winter driving safer. Even with snow tires, though, driving on slippery roads requires concentration. Road rage can lead to property damage and even injury. Therefore, drivers should always keep their emotions under control.

2. Music can either help or hurt a person's ability to recall information. For example, students who study while listening to loud dance music tend to remember less than those who study in quiet settings. The reason for this is that dance music has a strong rhythm, which tends to distract a person from the material being studied. Classical music, on the other hand, may help improve memory. Research shows that some people remember information more clearly if they listen to quiet classical music while studying. Understanding the link between music and memory can help students make wise choices about listening to music while studying.

3. Georgia O'Keeffe was a bold and influential painter. Her most famous paintings are of flowers and of scenes from the Southwest. Many tourists visit the Southwest to enjoy its beautiful deserts. Taos, New Mexico, is an especially busy tourist spot. O'Keeffe developed a unique painting style. She created dramatic images that went against the artistic fashion of her times. In fact, her rich use of color has inspired many artists. Quite a few artists today work in video and collage as well as in paint. O'Keeffe's work is on display in many of the world's leading museums.

◆ PRACTICE 4-6

Read the following topic sentences. Then, on the lines that follow, write a paragraph that develops the main idea that is stated in each topic sentence. After you finish, check to make sure that the paragraphs you have written are unified.

1. Many people don't pay their bills on time. ______________________

____
____
____
____
____

2. My neighborhood is an interesting place. ______________________

____
____
____
____
____

3. If I were president of this college, I would make a few changes. ______

______

______

______

______

______

B Writing Well-Developed Paragraphs

A paragraph is **well developed** when it includes the details and examples needed to support the topic sentence. Without this material, readers will have difficulty following your discussion. As you write, imagine your readers asking, "What do you mean?" or "What support do you have for this statement?" Be sure your paragraph answers these questions.

How do you determine how much support you need? The answer to this question depends on how complicated the idea in your topic sentence is. If your topic sentence is relatively simple and straightforward—for example, "My school's registration process is a nightmare"—two or three well-chosen examples will probably be enough. If, however, your statement is more complicated—for example, "The plan that the mayor has presented for building a new stadium is flawed"—you will have to present more support.

FOCUS Developing Paragraphs with Details and Examples

Details and examples can make a paragraph convincing. For example, in a paragraph on a history test, you could say that many soldiers were killed during the American Civil War. Your paragraph would be far more effective, however, if you said that over 500,000 soldiers were killed during the Civil War—more than in all the other wars in U.S. history combined.

When you check your paragraphs to make sure they are well developed, look for unsupported general statements. If you find any, add the details and examples you need to support these statements. The following paragraph is not well developed.

Paragraph Not Well Developed

Special effects now bring to the screen images that never could have been shown before. Computers have created effects that would have been too expensive or too difficult to create years ago. In the future, special effects will become even more realistic. They may even blur the line between what the audience believes to be real and what actually is real.

The paragraph above consists of one topic sentence and three general statements. It does not, however, give readers specific information about how computerized special effects have changed the film industry (which is what the topic sentence promises). In the following revised paragraph, notice how the writer added details and examples that help readers understand the point made by the topic sentence.

Well-Developed Paragraph

Topic sentence

Details and examples

Special effects now bring to the screen images that never could have been shown before. Computers have created effects that would have been too expensive or too difficult to create years ago. For example, in the movie *Titanic*, computerized special effects showed the *Titanic* splitting in half as it sank. Real actors were combined with computer-generated figures to show people falling to their deaths from the upended ship. In *Gladiator*, computerized special effects were used to re-create the ancient city of Rome. In addition, the film was able to show gladiators fighting in a computer-generated re-creation of the Colosseum as it might have appeared two thousand years ago. In the future, special effects will become even more realistic. They may even blur the line between what the audience believes to be real and what actually is real.

—Andrew McGillin (student)

NOTE: Length is no guarantee that a paragraph is well developed. A paragraph that contains one generalization after another can be quite long and still not provide enough support.

◆ PRACTICE 4-7

Some of the following paragraphs are well developed; others are not. On the line after each paragraph, write *well developed* if the paragraph is well developed and *not well developed* if it is not.

Example

The National Spelling Bee has many purposes. It encourages children to improve their spelling, vocabulary, and English usage. As a result, children can read and write better and get higher scores on standardized tests. Spelling bees also encourage friendly competition among children and their schools. *not well developed*

1. PlumpyNut can help starving people survive. PlumpyNut is peanut-based paste that was invented by a French scientist in 1999. It comes in a foil wrapper and does not need to be refrigerated. PlumpyNut is a high-energy, high-protein food that can save people's lives. Before PlumpyNut came into use, the most common nutritious food given to starving people was based on powdered milk. However, this milk-based food needed clean water and careful preparation by medical staff. PlumpyNut is much simpler to use. It can be fed to a child by a parent. The contents of the foil packet can be used after it has been opened. PlumpyNut is truly a lifesaver. ______________

2. Jeans have a long history. They were invented by Levi Strauss in 1873. Strauss had a dry goods store in San Francisco. One of his customers kept ripping his pants, so Strauss made pants that would be stronger. He got a patent on his invention, and blue jeans were born. At first, they were called "waist overalls." In the 1960s, the term "jeans" became popular. Today, there are many kinds of jeans sold by many different companies. ____________

3. Oprah's Book Club has put many new and classic books on the best-seller list. In 1996, Oprah Winfrey started her book club, which recommends books that she has chosen. She chooses books that deal sympathetically with real human problems. She has picked books by Nobel Prize winners as well as new books by previously unknown authors. Most of the books on her list have become very popular with readers. ____________

◆ PRACTICE 4-8

The following paragraphs are not well developed. On the lines below each paragraph, write three questions or suggestions that might help the writer develop his or her ideas more fully.

Example

Adam Sandler is a wonderful comedian. Some of his movies are absolutely hilarious. He is especially good at using funny voices to express his emotions. I never get tired of watching Adam Sandler's movies. I have seen *The Wedding Singer*, *The Waterboy*, and *Click* several times each.

1. *Describe the voices Adam Sandler uses.*
2. *Describe the roles he plays in one of the movies mentioned.*
3. *Tell about the funny way he talks in these movies.*

1. For me, having a regular study routine is important. I need to do the same things at the same times. If I have important school work to do, I stick to my routine. As long as I follow my schedule, everything works out all right.

1. ____________
2. ____________
3. ____________

2. Religion is a deeply personal issue. Attitudes toward religion vary from person to person. One person I know considers religion an essential part of life. Another feels just the opposite. Because of such differences, it is impossible to generalize about religious attitudes.

1. ____________
2. ____________
3. ____________

◆ PRACTICE 4-9

Choose one of the paragraphs from Practice 4-8. Reread it, and review your suggestions for improving it. Then, rewrite the paragraph, adding any details and examples you think are needed to make it well developed.

____

____

____

____

____

____

____

____

C Writing Coherent Paragraphs

A paragraph is **coherent** when all its sentences are arranged in a definite order. Readers should not have to guess why one sentence follows another. You can make a paragraph coherent by arranging details and examples in a logical order and by choosing transitional words and phrases to show the connections between sentences.

In general, you can arrange the ideas in a paragraph in three ways: in *time order*, in *spatial order*, or in *logical order*.

Time Order

You use **time order** to arrange events in the order in which they occurred. News reports, historical accounts, and process explanations are usually arranged like this.

The following paragraph presents events in time order. (Transitional words and phrases are underlined.)

> No other American writer achieved as great a reputation on the basis of a single book as Ralph Ellison did. Ellison was born in 1914 in Oklahoma City, Oklahoma, and grew up in the segregated South. In 1936, he came to New York City to earn money to pay his tuition at Tuskegee Institute, where he was a senior majoring in music. After becoming friends with many writers who were part of the Harlem Renaissance—a flowering of art, music, and literature among African Americans—he decided to remain in New York. During this period, Richard Wright, author of *Native Son* and *Black Boy*, encouraged Ellison to write his first short story. In the years that followed, Ellison published two collections of essays and some short fiction. Eventually, in 1952, he wrote *Invisible Man*, the novel that established him as a major twentieth-century writer.
>
> —Mike Burdin (student)

▶ **Word Power**

renaissance a rebirth or revival

This paragraph moves in time order, tracing events from Ellison's childhood in the South to his arrival in New York to the publication of *Invisible Man*. Notice that throughout the paragraph, the writer uses transitional words and phrases that signal time order—*in 1914, in 1936, after, during this period, in the years that followed,* and *eventually*—to help make the paragraph coherent.

Some Transitional Words and Phrases That Signal Time Order

after	finally	still	dates (for example, "in 1920")
afterward	first . . . next	then	times (for example, "at 8 o'clock," "that night")
at first	later	recently	
before	meanwhile	today	
during	now	until	
earlier	since	when	
eventually	soon	while	

◆ PRACTICE 4-10

Read the following paragraphs, whose sentences are organized in time order. Underline the transitional words and phrases that make each paragraph coherent.

Example

Writing a research paper requires several steps. First, you must choose a topic to write about. The topic should be broad enough to allow for an interesting discussion but narrow enough to cover in a few pages. Next, begin researching your topic. Reference works, books, articles, and Web sites are all good places to look for information. While you are gathering material, you might adjust your topic on the basis of what you are learning about it. When you have finished collecting information, it is time to plan your paper by drafting an outline. Then, it is time to write and to revise. Finally, you will want to add a bibliography or works-cited page and proofread your paper.

1. A job interview is most likely to go well when you are prepared for it. The first step is to determine your strengths. Do you have the right level of education for the job? Are you experienced in the field? What special skills do you have? The next step is to research the company and the kind of business it does. If you have a thorough knowledge of the company, you will make a good impression and be able to answer many questions. Finally, decide what points you want to emphasize in the interview. Although the interviewer will guide the conversation, you should be ready to offer your own thoughts as well.

2. Filmmaker Spike Lee has had a successful career making unusual movies. Before he started making movies professionally, he was a film student at New York University. In 1986, he released his first feature film, *She's Gotta Have It*. Critics praised this low-budget movie for its strong characters and clever dialogue. Then, Lee went on to make such acclaimed

movies as *Do the Right Thing*, *Jungle Fever*, and *Malcolm X*. In these movies, he explored issues of race in America. Recently, he made *When the Levees Broke*, a documentary about Hurricane Katrina, and *Inside Man*, a film about a bank robbery. What many people do not realize is that Lee writes, produces, directs, and acts in many of his films.

◆ PRACTICE 4-11

The following paragraph includes no transitional words and phrases to connect ideas. Read the paragraph carefully. Then, after consulting the list of transitional words and phrases on page 82, add appropriate transitions to connect the paragraph's ideas in time order.

A Killer Disease

The worst pandemic in the history of the world occurred in 1918, when the flu killed between 20 and 40 million people. __________, soldiers in American military camps began to get sick during their training for combat in World War I. __________, as military units moved from one battlefield to another in Europe, the disease spread from soldier to soldier. __________, it started to spread to civilians. __________, the war ended, and as people came together to celebrate, they continued to spread the flu. __________, the flu attacked people all over the world, especially young people who had previously been healthy. __________, doctors were trying desperately to find ways to treat their flu patients, but nothing worked. To stop the spread of the disease, gauze masks and quarantines were tried, but these efforts had little effect. __________, millions of people all over the world were dying. __________, we know a little more about the 1918 flu.

Word Power

pandemic an epidemic that affects many people over a wide area

◆ PRACTICE 4-12

Arrange the following sentences into a coherent paragraph. Be sure you are able to explain why you arranged the sentences the way you did. (Begin by identifying the paragraph's main idea.)

___ 1. During colonial times, public voice votes were common.

___ 2. Soon, individual voters may be able to cast ballots on the Internet.

___ 3. Voting machines, which ensured privacy and accuracy, were common by the early 1900s.

___ 4. Then, voting became a private matter with the use of secret paper ballots around the time of the Revolutionary War.

___ 5. Until the late 1800s, political parties printed and distributed their own ballots.

___ 6. Voting methods in the United States have changed dramatically in the past 250 years.

___ 7. Recently, voting officials have used computers to count votes.

Spatial Order

You use **spatial order** to present details in relation to one another—from top to bottom, from right to left, from far to near, and so on. Spatial order is used most often in paragraphs that describe something—for example, in a lab report describing a piece of equipment or in an art history paper describing a painting.

The following paragraph uses spatial order. (Transitional words and phrases are underlined.)

> When I was fourteen, my family and I traveled to Michigan to visit the town where my great-grandmother had lived. Somerset was hardly a town; in fact, it was just a collection of farms and cow pastures. Scattered through the fields were about twenty buildings. One of them was my great-grandmother's old brick farmhouse that was sold after she died. Next to the house were a rusting silo and a faded barn. In front of the house was a long wooden porch that needed painting. On the porch were a potted plant, two white wooden rocking chairs, and a swing. The house was locked, so all we could do was walk around it and look. The lace curtains that my great-grandmother had made before she died still hung in each window. In back of the house was a small cemetery that contained eight graves. There, off in the corner, on the oldest-looking stone, was the name "Azariel Smith"—the name of my great-grandmother's father.
>
> —Molly Ward (student)

This writer uses spatial order as she describes her great-grandmother's farmhouse. She moves from far to near, beginning by describing the fields around the farmhouse and then moving closer to the house itself. Eventually, she moves behind the farmhouse to the cemetery and then to a specific grave. Notice how transitional words and phrases that signal spatial order—*next to*, *in front*, *on the porch*, *in back*, *there*, and *in the corner*—help make the paragraph coherent.

Some Transitional Words and Phrases That Signal Spatial Order

above	beside	next to	over
along	here	on the bottom	there
around	in back	on the top	under
behind	in front	on/to the left	
below	inside	on/to the right	
beneath	near	outside	

◆ PRACTICE 4-13

Read the following paragraphs, whose details are arranged in spatial order. Underline the transitional words and phrases that make each paragraph coherent.

Example

My childhood home was a typical one-story house. The front door opened into a small foyer. Above the foyer and to the right was a carpeted living room shaped like the letter *L*. The short part of the *L* served as our dining room. Behind the living room was the kitchen. A hallway led from the kitchen to a bathroom on the right and then to two bedrooms. Below the bedrooms was a playroom. At the other end of the first floor, beneath the living room, was a garage.

1. Visitors to the White House in Washington, D.C., tour rooms that are decorated in a variety of styles and that serve a variety of functions. For example, in front of the Visitors' Entrance is the Library, furnished in the style of the Federal period (1800–1820). To the left of the Library is the Vermeil Room, decorated in gold and silver and used occasionally as a women's lounge. To the right and front of the Library is the East Room, traditionally used for large gatherings, such as concerts and press conferences. Next to the East Room is the Green Room, a drawing room decorated in delicate shades of green. Beside the Green Room is the Blue Room, an oval-shaped room used as a reception area. From the Blue Room, visitors enter the Red Room, decorated in the French Empire style. These and other public rooms give visitors a sense of the beauty and history of the White House.

2. My favorite restaurant in New York is in an old firehouse in Greenwich Village. It is located just east of Bleecker Street. In front, where horse-drawn carriages used to enter and leave the building, there is now a large bay window. To the right of the window is the door. Inside, the firehouse is long and narrow, with a bar on the left and a fireplace on the right. Clustered around the fireplace are a few chairs and loveseats. The interior is lighted by candles and gaslights. Small trees covered in tiny white lights are placed along the staircase and in the corners. But the most striking feature of all is the color: it's decorated entirely in rich, romantic red.

◆ PRACTICE 4-14

The following paragraph includes no transitional words and phrases to connect ideas. Read the paragraph carefully. Then, after consulting the list of transitional words and phrases on page 84, add appropriate transitions to connect the paragraph's ideas in spatial order.

Scrapbooking—A Popular Hobby

Many people are now saving, collecting, and arranging their memorabilia in scrapbooks. The scrapbook is usually a hard-surfaced album, which can be 8½ x 11 inches or smaller. ____________, the pages are made of special paper that does not fade or weaken over time. A typical page might have, __________, a person's name in fancy letters. __________ the name might be a group of photographs of that person at some unforgettable life events, such as playing on a winning soccer team or celebrating a special birthday. __________ of a page, a scrapbook might feature glitter or colored tape outlining a high school or college graduation program. __________, there might be some photographs of the graduate in his or her cap and gown. __________ of the page, fancy ribbons might surround prom tickets. Scrapbooks give people a way to collect their valued memories in a creative and long-lasting way.

◆ PRACTICE 4-15

Arrange the following sentences into a coherent paragraph. Be sure you are able to explain why you arranged the sentences the way you did. (Begin by identifying the paragraph's main idea.)

___ 1. Next to the video gallery is a display of celebrity portraits.

___ 2. For example, in front of the museum, on the main lawn, officials have installed a brightly colored fountain.

___ 3. In a small gallery to the left of the entrance hall, videotapes made by artists play on three monitors.

___ 4. The Middletown Museum of Art includes several displays designed to attract younger visitors.

___ 5. Inside the main doors is the large entrance hall, with a dozen large, spinning mobiles hanging from the ceiling.

___ 6. Officials hope young people will wander behind and above the entrance hall toward the rest of the museum's art exhibits.

___ 7. Behind the fountain, a series of small animal sculptures leads toward the main doors.

Logical Order

You use **logical order** to indicate why one idea logically follows another. For example, a paragraph may move from general to specific or from specific to general. In addition, writers may start with the least important idea and end with the most important one, or they may begin with the most important idea and then go on to the less important ones.

The following paragraph presents ideas in logical order. (Transitional words and phrases are underlined.)

As someone who is both a parent and a student, I have had to develop strategies for coping. For example, I try to do my studying at night, after I have put my son to bed. I want to give my son all the attention that he deserves, so after I pick him up from day care, I play with him, read to him, and watch a half hour of TV with him. When I am sure he is asleep, I begin doing my schoolwork. I also try to use every spare moment that I have during the day. For instance, if I have an hour between classes, I go to the computer lab and do some work. While I eat lunch, I get some of my reading out of the way. When I ride home from work on the bus, I review my class notes. Most important, I always keep my priorities in mind. My first priority is my son, my second priority is my schoolwork, and my last priority is keeping my apartment clean.

—Vanessa Scully (student)

The writer of this paragraph moves from her least important to her most important point. Notice how transitional words and phrases that signal logical order—*for example, also, for instance,* and *most important*—help make the paragraph coherent.

Some Transitional Words and Phrases That Signal Logical Order

also	furthermore	not only . . . but also
consequently	in addition	one . . . another
equally important	in conclusion	similarly
first . . . second . . . third	in fact	the least important
for example	last	the most important
for instance	moreover	therefore

◆ PRACTICE 4-16

Read the following paragraphs, whose sentences are organized in logical order. Underline the transitional words and phrases that make each paragraph coherent.

Example

Among the many reasons to support school sports, the most important is the education students get on the playing field. Students in a sports program such as basketball or track learn teamwork, self-confidence, and the value of physical fitness. They also feel a sense of belonging that athletes on a team enjoy. In addition, schools often benefit financially from the sales of tickets to sporting events. Attending a football game may help provide students with new textbooks and other materials. The least important reason to support school sports is the chance that a student athlete might go on to become a famous sports figure. Such success is extremely rare, and young people should be encouraged to pursue other, more practical careers.

1. The negative effects of illegal drug use are as serious now as they have ever been. First, illegal drug users risk arrest every time they buy, sell, or use drugs. Drug enforcement has become more aggressive over time, and

jail sentences are often long. Moreover, drug use is associated with problems such as crime and unemployment. Drug users are more likely to be involved in crimes or to experience periods of unemployment than are people who do not use drugs. But the most important risk to drug users is the physical and mental damage that drugs can cause. Such damage can be life threatening and is often irreversible.

2. I have made some important decisions lately. For example, last year I decided to move from my home in rural Connecticut to an apartment in New York City. This move has had many benefits. For instance, being in the city gave me more career opportunities. It also helped me to meet many more people than I could have in my small Connecticut town. Furthermore, I found plenty of interesting things to do with my time. My new interests include Thai cooking and salsa dancing. In fact, I find the cultural mix in the city interesting and exciting.

◆ PRACTICE 4-17

The following paragraph includes no transitional words and phrases to connect ideas. Read the paragraph carefully. Then, after consulting the list of transitional words and phrases on page 87, add appropriate transitions to connect the paragraph's ideas in logical order.

Showing Support

Wearing an "awareness bracelet" can be a way to show support for a team, a political opinion, or a charitable cause. ___________ use of awareness bracelets is to show support for a sports team. ___________, fans of the Boston Celtics basketball team wear green awareness bracelets. ___________, supporters of the Boston Red Sox baseball team can show their loyalty by wearing red bracelets. Awareness bracelets can ___________ express political views. ___________, there are bracelets for those who support the Democratic and Republican parties. There is even a bracelet for people who oppose global warming. ___________, people can wear awareness bracelets to support a worthy charity. ___________, there are special bracelets for victims of the tsunami in Southeast Asia, of Hurricane Katrina, and of the genocide in Darfur, Sudan. Because awareness bracelets also make a fashion statement, many young people have adopted this method of expressing their views.

◆ PRACTICE 4-18

Arrange the following sentences into a coherent paragraph. Be sure you are able to explain why you arranged the sentences the way you did. (Begin by identifying the paragraph's main idea.)

____ 1. At this time, Rankin became one of the first women in the world elected to a governing body.

____ 2. Jeanette Rankin had one of the most unusual political careers in American history.

____ 3. As a result of this vote, Rankin lost her bid for election to the Senate in 1918, but she remained active in peace issues.

____ 4. Although this constitutional amendment passed the House, it was defeated in the Senate and not enacted until 1919.

____ 5. In 1916, four years before American women had the right to vote, she was elected to Congress.

____ 6. While in Congress, Rankin helped draft a constitutional amendment to give women the right to vote.

____ 7. In 1940, after being reelected to Congress, Rankin cast her vote against U.S. entry into World War II.

____ 8. Perhaps Rankin's most important action was her vote against U.S. entry into World War I.

____ 9. In conclusion, Rankin is remembered as someone who stood by her principles, regardless of the cost to her career.

____ 10. By doing so, Rankin became the only member of Congress to vote against U.S. entry into both world wars.

• REVISING AND EDITING

Look back at your response to the Seeing and Writing exercise on page 71. First, make sure your paragraph has an effective topic sentence. Then, revise the paragraph so that it is unified, well developed, and coherent.

CHAPTER REVIEW

◆ EDITING PRACTICE

Read the following student paragraphs, and evaluate each one in terms of its unity, development, and coherence. First, underline the topic sentence. Next, cross out any sentences that do not support the topic sentence. Then, add transitional words and phrases where needed. Finally, discuss in class what additional details, facts, and examples might be added to each paragraph.

1. At a young age, pirate Anne Bonny traded a life of wealth and privilege for one of adventure and crime. In 1716, she ran away from home to marry

Anne Bonny and Mary Read

a sailor. Sailors passed through the place where she lived, on the East Coast of the United States, on a regular basis. Later, she met a pirate named Calico Jack Rackham. Bonny soon left her husband to join Rackham's crew. She developed a reputation as a fierce fighter. In 1720, Bonny met another female pirate named Mary Read. They were captured by authorities. Bonny, who was pregnant, was not sentenced to death because executing a pregnant woman was against the law. Read received a death sentence. Before it could be carried out, she died of a fever in prison. No one knows what finally became of Bonny.

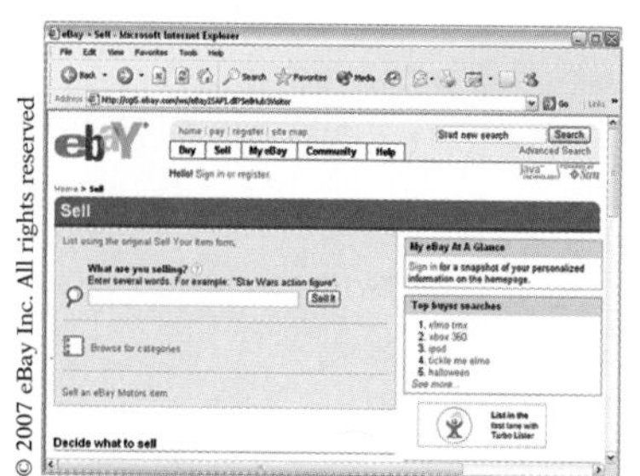

eBay home page

2. People should know certain things before they start to sell anything on eBay. They have to register and open an eBay account. They can sell clothes, furniture, jewelry, electronic devices, cars, toys, or almost anything else. They should fill out a form that describes the item, the price, the shipping cost, and the method of payment. If the sale is successful, the sellers will receive an email from eBay. They will have to pay eBay a fee to sell each item. This fee is based on the item's value. They will have to pay eBay a fee based on the item's selling price. When receipt of payment is confirmed, they can ship the items to the buyers.

Cars at a NASCAR race

3. NASCAR, which stands for the National Association for Stock Car Auto Racing, sponsors one of the most popular sporting events in the United States. Years ago, NASCAR events used to be held mainly in the South. To lower the risks of terrible accidents, NASCAR drivers have to wear special seat belts and restraints for the head and neck. Races take place all over the country, including New Hampshire, Delaware, Nevada, and California. The biggest race of the season is the Daytona 500. In 1979, it was the first stock car race to be televised from start to finish. NASCAR drivers are famous among race fans. Dale Earnhardt Jr. and Jeff Gordon are extremely popular. Fans follow the careers of their favorite drivers and sometimes spend an entire week at the racetrack, cheering on their favorites as they prepare for a big race.

◆ COLLABORATIVE ACTIVITIES

1. Working in a group, list some distractions that make it hard for students to perform well in college. Arrange these distractions from least important to most important. Then, create a topic sentence that states the main idea suggested by your list. Finally, draft a paragraph in which you discuss why some students have difficulty in college.
2. Think of a place you know well. Write a paragraph that describes the place so that readers will be able to imagine it. Decide on a specific spatial order—for example, outside to inside, left to right, or front to back. When you have finished, trade paragraphs with another student. See if you can sketch the place described in your partner's paragraph. If you cannot, offer suggestions that could improve his or her description.
3. Bring to class a paragraph from a newspaper or a magazine. Working in a group of three students, underline each paragraph's topic sentence. Then, decide whether each paragraph is unified, well developed, and coherent. If it is not, work together to make it more effective.

✓ REVIEW CHECKLIST: Fine-Tuning Your Paragraph

- ☐ A paragraph is unified when it focuses on a single main idea, which is stated in the topic sentence. (See 4A.)
- ☐ A paragraph is well developed when it contains enough details and examples to support the main idea. (See 4B.)
- ☐ A paragraph is coherent when its sentences are arranged in a definite order and it includes all necessary transitional words and phrases. (See 4C.)

CHAPTER

5 Exemplification

PREVIEW

In this chapter, you will learn to write an exemplification paragraph.

▶ Word Power

adversity difficulty

improvise to make do, to manage

marooned stranded

● SEEING AND WRITING

The picture above shows the cast members from the classic television show *Gilligan's Island*, a comedy that followed the adventures of seven people stranded on an uninhabited island. Look at the picture, and then write a paragraph in which you discuss what skills you would need to survive on a deserted island.

In Chapters 3 and 4, you learned how to write effective paragraphs. In Chapters 5 through 13, you will learn different ways of organizing your ideas within paragraphs.

A What Is Exemplification?

What do we mean when we say that an instructor is *good* or that a football team is *bad*? What do we mean when we say that a character in a play is *underdeveloped* or that a particular war was *wrong*? To clarify general statements like these, we use **exemplification**—that is, we give **examples**, specific instances that illustrate a general idea.

General Statement	*Specific Examples*
Today is going to be a hard day.	Today is going to be a hard day because I have a history test in the morning and a lab quiz in the afternoon. I also have to go to work an hour earlier than usual.
My car is giving me problems.	My car is burning oil and won't start on cold mornings. In addition, I need a new set of tires.

An **exemplification paragraph** explains or clarifies a general idea—stated in the topic sentence—by providing specific examples. Personal experiences, class discussions, observations, conversations, and reading can all be good sources of examples.

An exemplification paragraph begins with a topic sentence and is followed by examples that support the general statement made in the topic sentence. Examples are arranged in **logical order**—for example, from least important to most important or from general to specific. How many examples you need depends on your topic sentence. A complicated statement might require many examples to support it. A simple, straightforward statement might require fewer examples. The paragraph closes with a concluding statement that sums up its main idea.

> **Word Power**
> **conclusion** the end or the finish

An exemplification paragraph generally has the following structure.

Topic Sentence ______________________________

Example #1 ______________________________

____

Example #2 ______________________________

____

Example #3 ______________________________

____

Concluding Statement ______________________________

____

The following paragraph uses examples to make the point that Philadelphia is an exciting city to visit.

Topic sentence

Transitions introduce examples

Concluding statement

If you know where to go, Philadelphia can be an exciting city to visit. For example, Philadelphia is a city of museums. Within walking distance of each other are the Art Museum, the Rodin Museum, the Academy of Natural Sciences, and the Franklin Institute Science Museum. There are also less well-known museums, such as the Mutter Medical Museum, the Polish American Cultural Center Museum, and the Please Touch Museum. In addition, Philadelphia has a number of world-class sports teams. If you are lucky, you might be able to get tickets to see the Eagles play football at Lincoln Financial Field or the 76ers play basketball at the Wachovia Center. You can also see other professional sports teams, such as the Phillies, the Flyers, and the Wings, Philadelphia's professional lacrosse team. Finally, you can visit some of Philadelphia's historic sites, such as the Betsy Ross House, Independence Hall, the National Constitution Center, and the Liberty Bell. As you can see, it is no wonder that many people who visit Philadelphia for the first time say that they can't wait to come back.

—Jeffrey Smith (student)

When you write an exemplification paragraph, be sure to include appropriate transitional words and phrases. These transitions will help readers follow your discussion by indicating how one example is related to another as well as how each example supports the topic sentence.

Some Transitional Words and Phrases for Exemplification

also
finally
first . . . second . . . (and so on)
for example
for instance
furthermore
in addition
moreover
one example . . . another example
specifically
the most important example
the next example

GRAMMAR IN CONTEXT Exemplification

When you write an exemplification paragraph, always use a comma after the introductory transitional word or phrase that introduces your examples.

(continued on following page)

(continued from previous page)

For example, Philadelphia is a city of museums.

In addition, Philadelphia has a number of world-class sports teams.

Finally, you can visit some of Philadelphia's historic sites.

For information on using commas with introductory transitional words and phrases, see 31B.

B Writing an Exemplification Paragraph

◆ PRACTICE 5-1

Read this exemplification paragraph, and answer the questions that follow it.

Matchbox cars are tiny die-cast models that come in a wide variety of styles. For example, the most common Matchbox models are about 2.5 inches long. These are the model cars most often seen in toy stores. There are also larger cars, called "Major" or "Super Kings." Because Majors are unusual and fairly expensive, collectors often buy them. Matchbox does not restrict itself to making model cars. For instance, the company has made airplanes called "Sky Busters" that it sold in stores and supplied to the major airlines. Matchbox has also made a series of fantasy vehicles called "Ultra Heroes." In addition to these items, Matchbox makes double-decker buses, helicopters, and trucks as well as play sets that include fire stations and car washes. Because of this wide variety of models, people who collect or play with Matchbox cars have no trouble finding new and unusual items to buy.

—Michael Graham (student)

> **Word Power**
> **die-casting** a process of forcing very hot metal into a mold

1. Underline the topic sentence of the paragraph.
2. List the specific examples the writer uses to support the topic sentence. The first example has been listed for you.

   Small cars that are found in toy stores
   ____

   ____

____

____

3. Circle the transitional words and phrases that the writer uses to connect examples in the paragraph.
4. Underline the paragraph's concluding statement.

◆ PRACTICE 5-2

Following are four topic sentences for exemplification paragraphs. After each sentence, list three examples that could support the main idea. For example, if you were writing about the poor quality of food in your school cafeteria, you could give examples of mystery meat, weak coffee, and stale bread.

1. Many of the skills learned by our grandparents are not needed in today's high-tech world.

____

____

____

2. People who want to get their news from the Internet have a variety of options.

____

____

____

3. I have always been very unlucky (or lucky) in love.

____

____

____

4. Although many people criticize television shows as mindless, there are a few important exceptions.

____

____

____

◆ PRACTICE 5-3

Choose one of the following topics.

Why the Internet is important to you	Violence in movies or video games

The importance of family in your life
A memorable book or movie
The benefits of a healthy diet
How not to act at a party
How your school could be improved
The accomplishments of someone you admire
Your favorite city
The demands of being a parent
Drivers who are a menace
Trends on your college campus
Exercise for busy people
The best jobs for a recent graduate
The consequences of putting things off
Problems you overcome daily

◆ PRACTICE 5-4

On a separate sheet of paper, use one or more of the strategies discussed in 3C to help you come up with examples for the topic you have chosen.

◆ PRACTICE 5-5

Review your notes from Practice 5-4, and list below the four or five examples that can best help you develop a paragraph on the topic you have chosen.

- ____
- ____
- ____
- ____
- ____

◆ PRACTICE 5-6

Reread your list of examples from Practice 5-5. Now, write a topic sentence that states the main idea your paragraph will discuss.

Topic sentence: ________________________________

____

◆ PRACTICE 5-7

On the lines below, arrange the examples you listed in Practice 5-5 in a logical order—for example, from least important to most important.

1. ____
2. ____
3. ____

4. ______________________________

5. ______________________________

◆ PRACTICE 5-8

Draft your exemplification paragraph.

◆ PRACTICE 5-9

Using the Self-Assessment Checklist below, revise your exemplification paragraph.

◆ PRACTICE 5-10

Print out a final draft of your exemplification paragraph.

● REVISING AND EDITING

Look back at the Seeing and Writing exercise on page 92, and evaluate the paragraph you wrote for unity, support, and coherence. Then, prepare a final draft of your paragraph.

☑ SELF-ASSESSMENT CHECKLIST: Writing an Exemplification Paragraph

- ☐ Does the topic sentence clearly state the main idea of your paragraph?
- ☐ Do all your examples support your topic sentence?
- ☐ Have you used enough examples?
- ☐ Have you used appropriate transitional words and phrases?
- ☐ Have you put a comma after the transitional words or phrases that introduce your examples?
- ☐ Have you included a concluding statement that sums up your paragraph's main idea?

CHAPTER REVIEW

◆ EDITING PRACTICE

1. The following student exemplification paragraph is missing a topic sentence, transitional words and phrases, and a concluding statement. After reading the paragraph, fill in the missing elements on the appropriate lines below. (Look on p. 94 for a list of transitions.)

____

____________________________. ________________, people should never exaggerate on a résumé. Employees can usually spot exaggerations. They know that "food professional" at a fast-food restaurant means that a person was flipping hamburgers or working at the counter. ________________, people should not be vague about their accomplishments. They shouldn't just say that they saved the company money or that they have management experience. Instead, they should include the exact amount of money they saved or the specific management duties they performed. ________________, people should never attempt to cover up gaps in their employment history. They should not invent jobs or lie about the amount of time they worked. Instead, they should explain any gaps in a cover letter. ____

____

> ▶ **Word Power**
> **exaggerate** to overstate

> ▶ **Word Power**
> **qualifications** skills, knowledge, or experience

2. Create an exemplification paragraph by adding examples that support the topic sentence below. Make sure you connect the examples with appropriate transitions. End the paragraph with a clear concluding statement. Then, add an appropriate title.

____

Shoppers can do a number of things to make sure they get the most for their money. ______________________________

____

____

____

▶ **Word Power**

public service a service performed for the benefit of the public

3. The billboard pictured below shows a Mothers Against Drunk Drivers (MADD) public service advertisement. Look at the picture carefully. Then, write an exemplification paragraph explaining how this advertisement gets its point across to its audience. Begin your paragraph with a topic sentence that states the point you want to make about the ad. Then, give examples to support your topic sentence.

CHAPTER

6

Narration

PREVIEW

In this chapter, you will learn to write a narrative paragraph.

SEEING AND WRITING

The picture above shows a bride and groom with their family after a wedding on a beach. Look at the picture, and then write a paragraph in which you tell the story of how this couple met and how they decided where their wedding should be held.

Word Power

commitment devotion or dedication

sentimental overly romantic

A What Is Narration?

Narration is writing that tells a story. A **narrative paragraph** should have a topic sentence that tells readers the point of the paragraph—that is, why you are telling a particular story. For example, you could be telling how an experience you had as a child changed you, how the life of Helen Keller is inspiring, or how the Battle of Gettysburg was the turning point of the Civil War.

Effective narrative paragraphs should include vivid details that make the events you are discussing come alive for readers. The more specific the details you include, the better your narrative paragraph will be.

A narrative paragraph begins with a topic sentence that is followed by a series of events. An effective narrative paragraph includes only those events that tell the story; it avoids irrelevant information that could distract or confuse readers. In addition, a narrative paragraph presents events in a definite **time order**, usually the order in which events actually occurred. The paragraph ends with a concluding statement that sums up what is stated in the topic sentence.

A narrative paragraph has the following structure.

Topic Sentence ______________________________

Event #1 ______________________________

____

Event #2 ______________________________

____

Event #3 ______________________________

____

Concluding Statement ______________________________

____

The writer of the following paragraph relates events that support the point that the fashion designer Chloe Dao had a difficult life.

Overnight Success

Topic sentence

Chloe Dao traveled a difficult road to become a successful fashion designer. When Dao was a baby, her parents decided to leave her native country, Laos, and come the United States. Unfortunately, the Viet Cong captured her and her family as they tried to cross the border. They were sent to a refugee camp, where they stayed for four years. In 1979, when she was eight, Dao and her family were allowed to come to the United States. Then, they had to earn enough money to live. Dao's mother worked three jobs. On the weekends, the entire family ran the snack bar at a flea market. Finally, they saved enough money to open a successful dry cleaning business. When she was twenty, Dao moved to New York to attend school. After she graduated, she got a job as production manager for designer Melinda Eng. Eventually, she opened a boutique, where she featured clothes that she designed. Her big break came in 2006 when she was chosen as a finalist on the reality show *Project Runway*. Although Chloe Dao may appear to be an "overnight success," she had to struggle to get where she is today.

Transitions link events in time order

Concluding statement

—Christine Clark (student)

As you arrange your ideas in your narrative paragraphs, be sure to use clear transitional words and phrases, as the student writer does in the paragraph above. These signals help readers follow your narrative by indicating the order of the events you discuss.

Some Transitional Words and Phrases for Narration

after	first . . . second . . . third	times (for example, "two days," "five minutes," "ten years")
as	immediately	then
as soon as	later	when
before	later on	while
by this time	meanwhile	
dates (for example, "in 2006")	next	
earlier	now	
eventually	soon	
finally	suddenly	

GRAMMAR IN CONTEXT **Narration**

When you write a narrative paragraph, you tell a story. As you become involved in your story, you might begin to string events together without proper punctuation. If you do, you will create a **run-on**.

INCORRECT (RUN-ON) Dao's mother worked three jobs on the weekends, the entire family ran the snack bar at a flea market.

(continued on following page)

(continued from previous page)

CORRECT Dao's mother worked three jobs. On the weekends, the entire family ran the snack bar at a flea market.

For information on how to recognize and correct run-ons, see Chapter 20.

B Writing a Narrative Paragraph

◆ PRACTICE 6-1

Read this narrative paragraph, and answer the questions that follow it.

When I first came to live in a dormitory at college, I was homesick. Before I came to college, I had thought that living with lots of other students would be fun and exciting. It was, but not at first. When my parents left me at school, I looked around at my dorm room and was depressed. It looked cramped and empty. I couldn't see how two people could live in such a tiny space, and I missed my room at home. When my roommate burst through the door, smiling and joking, I felt better. We talked about our high schools and our families. Later on, we made plans to fix up the room with some posters. When it was time to eat, we went to the cafeteria for dinner. I was used to meat and potatoes; however, the cafeteria was serving salads and veggie burgers. Suddenly, I wanted to be home, eating with my family. I even missed my little sister. When we went to bed that night, I thought about the changes that I would have to adapt to. Now, I realized that living away from home would be very challenging.

—Melinda Deni (student)

1. Underline the topic sentence of the paragraph.
2. List the major events of the narrative. The first event has been listed for you.

My new dorm room seemed very small.

____

____

____

3. Circle the transitional words and phrases that the writer uses to link events in time.
4. Underline the paragraph's concluding statement.

◆ PRACTICE 6-2

Following are four topic sentences for narrative paragraphs. After each topic sentence, list four events you could include in a narrative paragraph to support the main idea. For example, if you were telling about a dinner that turned out to be a disaster, you could tell about how the meat burned, the vegetables were overcooked, and the guests arrived late.

1. The day started out normally enough, but before it was over, my life had changed forever.
2. When I was young, my grandmother told me a story about her childhood.
3. I'll never forget my first "best friend."
4. It was a difficult decision for me to make.

◆ PRACTICE 6-3

Choose one of the following topics (or a topic of your own).

A happy time
Your proudest moment
A frightening event
A family story
A conflict with authority
A new experience
An injustice you experienced
An embarrassing moment
A favorite holiday memory
A challenge you faced and overcame
A risk you took
A coincidence
An unexpected gift
A great loss
A lesson you learned
An experience that caused you to grow up

◆ PRACTICE 6-4

On a separate sheet of paper, use one of the strategies in 3C to help you recall events and details for the topic you have chosen in Practice 6-3.

◆ PRACTICE 6-5

Review your notes from Practice 6-4, and list below four or five events that could help you develop a narrative paragraph on the topic you have chosen.

- ____________________
- ____________________
- ____________________
- ____________________
- ____________________

◆ PRACTICE 6-6

Reread your list of events from Practice 6-5. Then, draft a topic sentence that states the main idea your paragraph will discuss.

Topic sentence: ____________________

____

◆ PRACTICE 6-7

On the lines below, arrange the events you listed in Practice 6-5 in the order in which they occurred.

1. ____________________
2. ____________________

3. ______________________________

4. ______________________________

5. ______________________________

◆ PRACTICE 6-8

Draft your narrative paragraph.

◆ PRACTICE 6-9

Using the Self-Assessment Checklist below, revise your narrative paragraph.

◆ PRACTICE 6-10

Print out a final draft of your narrative paragraph.

● REVISING AND EDITING

Look back at the Seeing and Writing exercise on page 101, and evaluate the paragraph you wrote for unity, support, and coherence. Then, prepare a final draft of your paragraph.

☑ SELF-ASSESSMENT CHECKLIST: Writing a Narrative Paragraph

- ☐ Does your topic sentence state your paragraph's main idea?
- ☐ Do your sentences move clearly from one event to another?
- ☐ Have you included enough details to make the events clear to readers?
- ☐ Have you used appropriate transitional words and phrases?
- ☐ Have you avoided run-ons as you connected events in your narrative?
- ☐ Have you included a concluding statement that sums up your paragraph's main idea?

CHAPTER REVIEW

◆ EDITING PRACTICE

1. The following student narration paragraph is missing a topic sentence, transitional words and phrases, and a concluding statement. After reading the paragraph, fill in the missing elements on the appropriate lines below. (See p. 103 for a list of transitions.)

____

____

The date started well enough. I picked Tracy up at her apartment. __________ we left, I had to get the approval of her roommates. Apparently, I passed the test. Next, we drove to a small Italian restaurant that I like. __________ the owner tried to seat us, Tracy said that she didn't like the table. __________, she found a table she liked. __________, we sat down and ordered. When the food came, Tracy sent it back because she said it wasn't what she had expected. When the waiter brought her another platter, she sent it back because she said it was too cold. __________, dinner was over, and we went back to her apartment to talk. We didn't agree about anything. I told her I liked a certain movie, and she said she didn't. I told her who I voted for in the last election, but she voted for another person. If I had an opinion about anything, she had the opposite opinion. __________, I had had enough. I told Tracy that I had to get up early the next morning, and I went home. ______________________________

____

____

2. Create a narrative paragraph by adding events to support the topic sentence on the next page. Make sure you connect the events with appropriate transitions. End the paragraph with a clear concluding statement that sums up the main idea. Then, add an appropriate title.

____

When I was young, I had a very unusual ambition. ____________

____

____

____

____

____

____

____

____

____

3. The picture below shows two people, surrounded by various objects, standing in front of a house. Look at the picture carefully, and then write a narrative paragraph that tells the story of the people in the picture. Begin your paragraph with a topic sentence that states the main point of the story. In the rest of the paragraph, present the events that develop your topic sentence. Make sure the events you present are arranged in clear chronological order.

CHAPTER

7

Description

PREVIEW

In this chapter, you will learn to write a descriptive paragraph.

▶ **Word Power**

grate a framework of metal bars

quaint old-fashioned

exotic foreign, unusual

SEEING AND WRITING

The picture above shows a scene in the French quarter of New Orleans. Study the picture carefully, and then write a paragraph that describes what you see. Include enough specific details so that readers will be able to "see" the scene you are describing without looking at the picture.

A What Is Description?

In a personal email, you may describe a new boyfriend or girlfriend. You also use description in your college writing. In a biology lab manual, for example, you may describe the structure of a cell, and in a report for a nursing class, you may describe a patient you treated.

When you write a **description**, you use words to help paint a picture for your readers. You use language that creates a vivid impression of what you have seen, heard, smelled, tasted, or touched. The more specific details you include, the better your description will be.

The following description is flat because it includes no specific details.

Flat description

Today I saw a beautiful sunrise.

In contrast, the description below is full of details that convey the writer's experience to readers.

Rich description

Early this morning, as I walked along the sandy beach, I saw the sun rise slowly out of the ocean. At first, the ocean looked red. Then, it turned slowly to pink, to aqua, and finally to blue. As I stood watching the sun, I heard the waves hit the shore, and I felt the cold water swirl around my toes. For a moment, even the small grey and white birds that hurried along the shore seemed to stop and watch the dazzling sight.

The revised description relies on sight (*saw the sun rise slowly out of the ocean*; *looked red*; *turned slowly to pink, to aqua, and finally to blue*), touch (*the sandy beach*; *felt the cold water*), and sound (*heard the waves hit the shore*).

FOCUS Description

Vague, overused words—such as *good*, *nice*, *bad*, and *beautiful*—do not help readers see what you are describing. When you write a descriptive paragraph, try to use specific words and phrases that make your writing come alive.

A **descriptive paragraph** should have a topic sentence that states the main point you want to make in your paragraph ("My sister's room is a pig sty"; "The wooden roller coaster in Coney Island is a work of art"). This topic sentence should be followed by the details that support the topic sentence. These details are arranged in a definite **spatial order**, the order in which you observed the scene you are describing—for example, from near to far or from top to bottom. The paragraph ends with a concluding statement that sums up the main idea stated in the topic sentence.

A descriptive paragraph generally has the following structure.

Topic Sentence ______________________________

Detail #1 ______________________________

____

Detail #2 ______________________________

____

Detail #3 ______________________________

____

Concluding Statement ______________________________

____

The student writer of the following paragraph uses descriptive details to support the idea that the Lincoln Memorial is a monument to American democracy.

The Lincoln Memorial

Topic sentence

Transitions link details in spatial order

Concluding statement

The Lincoln Memorial was built to celebrate American democracy. In front of the monument is a long marble staircase that leads from a reflecting pool to the Memorial's entrance. Thirty-six columns surround the building. Inside the building are three rooms. The first room contains the nineteen-foot-tall statue of Lincoln. Seated in a chair, Lincoln looks exhausted after the long Civil War. One of Lincoln's hands is a fist, showing his strength, and the other is open, showing his kindness. On either side of the first room are two other rooms. On the wall of one room is the Gettysburg Address. On the wall of the other room is the Second Inaugural Address. Above the Gettysburg Address is a mural that shows an angel freeing the slaves. Above the Second Inaugural Address is another mural. It shows the people of the North and the South coming back together. As its design shows, the Lincoln Memorial was built to celebrate both the sixteenth president and the nation's struggle for democracy.

—Nicole Lentz (student)

As you arrange your ideas in a descriptive paragraph, be sure to use appropriate transitional words and phrases. These signals will lead readers from one detail to another and will indicate the order in which you are discussing them.

Some Transitional Words and Phrases for Description

above	in front of	on top of
behind	inside	outside
below	nearby	the first . . . the second
between	next to	the next
beyond	on	under
in	on one side . . .	
in back of	on the other side . . .	

GRAMMAR IN CONTEXT **Description**

When you write a descriptive paragraph, you sometimes use **modifiers**—words and phrases that describe another word or group of words. A modifier should be placed as close as possible to the word it is supposed to modify. If you place modifying words or phrases too far from the words they modify, you create a **misplaced modifier** that will confuse readers.

CONFUSING Seated in a chair, the long Civil War has clearly exhausted Lincoln. (Was the Civil War seated in a chair?)

CLEAR Seated in a chair, Lincoln is clearly exhausted by the long Civil War.

For information on how to identify and correct misplaced modifiers, see Chapter 24.

B Writing a Descriptive Paragraph

◆ PRACTICE 7-1

Read this descriptive paragraph, and answer the questions that follow it.

This morning, the people on the bus were strangely quiet. When the doors to the bus opened, I saw that it was almost empty. Inside the bus, way in the back, two people who were coming home from a night of clubbing were sleeping. Nearby,

I saw a small woman dressed in a black and white waitress uniform. She held a paper container of coffee in both hands and looked out the window into the dim light. At the next stop, several people came onto the bus. They slumped down in their seats, closed their eyes, and tried to catch a few more minutes of sleep. In the front of the bus, a short, unshaven man took out a newspaper, folded it so that only a small bit was showing, and tried to read. As I watched, I realized that he was reading the same page again and again. The only sounds were the engine and the screeching of the brakes as the bus came to a stop. No one was really awake yet. It was as if everyone was quietly waiting for the day to start.

—Caitlin McNally (student)

1. Underline the topic sentence of the paragraph.
2. What are some of the details the writer uses to describe the people on the bus? The first detail has been listed for you.

   Two people coming home

   ______

   ______

   ______

3. List some of the transitions the writer uses to lead readers from one detail to another.

   ______

   ______

   ______

4. Underline the paragraph's concluding statement.

◆ PRACTICE 7-2

Following are four topic sentences for descriptive paragraphs. After each topic sentence, list three details that could help convey why you are writing the description. For example, to describe an interesting person, you could tell what the person looked like, how he or she behaved, and what he or she said.

1. It was a long hike, but when we finally got to the top of the mountain, the view was incredible.

   ______

   ______

   ______

2. Every community has one house that all the kids think is haunted.

____

____

____

3. In every living situation, there is one person who is an unbelievable slob.

____

____

____

4. I'll never forget the first time I did something really dangerous.

____

____

____

◆ PRACTICE 7-3

Choose one of the following topics (or a topic of your own) as the subject of a descriptive paragraph.

A favorite place	A favorite article of clothing
A place you dislike	A souvenir from a trip
A private spot on campus	Someone you see every day
An unusual person	A building you find interesting
Your dream house	Your car or truck
A friend or family member	Something you would like to have
A work of art	A statue or monument
A valued possession	Someone you admire
Your workplace	A fashion disaster

◆ PRACTICE 7-4

On a separate sheet of paper, use one or more of the strategies discussed in 3C to help you come up with specific details about the topic you have chosen. If you can, observe your subject directly, and list your observations.

◆ PRACTICE 7-5

Review your notes from Practice 7-4, and list below some details that could help you develop a descriptive paragraph on the topic you have chosen.

- ____
- ____

- ____________________
- ____________________
- ____________________
- ____________________

◆ PRACTICE 7-6

Reread your list of details from Practice 7-5. Then, draft a topic sentence that summarizes the main point you want to make in your paragraph.

Topic sentence: ____________________

____

◆ PRACTICE 7-7

On the lines below, arrange the details you listed in Practice 7-5. You might arrange them in the order in which you look at the subject—for example, from left to right, near to far, or top to bottom.

1. ____________________
2. ____________________
3. ____________________
4. ____________________
5. ____________________
6. ____________________

◆ PRACTICE 7-8

Draft your descriptive paragraph.

◆ PRACTICE 7-9

Using the Self-Assessment Checklist on page 117, revise your descriptive paragraph.

◆ PRACTICE 7-10

Print out a final, edited draft of your descriptive paragraph.

REVISING AND EDITING

Look back at the Seeing and Writing exercise on page 110, and evaluate the paragraph you wrote for unity, support, and coherence. Then, prepare a final, edited draft of your paragraph.

SELF-ASSESSMENT CHECKLIST: Writing a Descriptive Paragraph

- ☐ Does your topic sentence state the paragraph's main idea?
- ☐ Do all your details support your topic sentence?
- ☐ Are your details specific enough to give readers a picture of your subject?
- ☐ Have you used appropriate transitional words and phrases?
- ☐ Have you been careful to place modifying words and phrases clearly?
- ☐ Have you included a concluding statement that sums up your paragraph's main idea?

CHAPTER REVIEW

EDITING PRACTICE

1. The following student descriptive paragraph is missing a topic sentence, transitional words and phrases, and a concluding statement. After reading the paragraph, fill in the missing elements on the appropriate lines below. (See p. 113 for a list of transitions.)

Disaster Area

____

____

When I open the door to her room, the clutter is overwhelming. Directly ________ the room, under the windows, is my sister's desk. Interestingly, this is the neatest, most organized part of her room. ____________ side of her desk is a large blue dictionary. Next to that are two large white loose-leaf binders. __________ side of the desk are two stacks of CDs and a small television set. On another wall is my sister's bed. It is almost always unmade and covered with CDs, clothes, books, magazines, an empty bag of potato chips, a half-eaten sandwich, and three or four stuffed animals. __________ the bed is her dresser. Usually, the drawers are open, and their contents are draped over the front of the drawers. If she has had a particularly bad time deciding what to wear, the floor will be covered with clothes. __________ of the dresser is a jumbled collection of make-up, perfume bottles, hair spray, brushes, cotton balls, at least one hairdryer, and several empty soda cans. ____

____

2. Create a descriptive paragraph by adding details to support the following topic sentence. Make sure you connect details with appropriate transitions. End the paragraph with a clear concluding statement that sums up the main idea. Then, add an appropriate title.

____

My picture in my high school yearbook reveals a lot about me.

____

____

____

____

____

____

____

____

____

____

____

____

3. The picture below shows a beachfront hotel in South Beach, a resort area in Miami Beach, Florida. Look at the picture carefully, and write a descriptive paragraph for a brochure that advertises the hotel. Begin with a topic sentence that states the main point of your paragraph. Then, in the rest of the paragraph, supply specific details about the hotel's location and facilities. Your goal is to persuade prospective customers to stay at the hotel.

CHAPTER

8 Process

PREVIEW

In this chapter, you will learn to write a process paragraph.

SEEING AND WRITING

The picture above shows someone trying to fix a burst water pipe. Look at the picture, and then write a paragraph explaining how to fix a problem that commonly occurs in a house or apartment.

Word Power

cautious careful

concern a reason to worry

unanticipated not expected

A What Is Process?

When you describe a **process**, you tell readers how something works or how to do something. For example, you could explain how the optical scanner at the checkout counter of a food store works, how to hem a pair of pants, how to send a fax, how to make a bed, how to prepare a healthy meal, or how to send a text message.

A **process paragraph** should begin with a topic sentence that identifies the process. It should also identify the point you want to make about it (for example, "Parallel parking is easy once you know the secret," or "By following a few steps, you can design an effective résumé"). The rest of the paragraph should clearly describe the steps in the process, one at a time. These steps should be presented in strict **time order**—in the order in which they occur or are to be performed. The paragraph should end with a concluding statement that sums up the process.

A process paragraph generally has the following structure.

Topic Sentence ______________________________

Step #1 ______________________________
____

Step #2 ______________________________
____

Step #3 ______________________________
____

Concluding Statement ______________________________
____

There are two types of process paragraphs: **process explanations** and **instructions**.

Process Explanations

In a **process explanation**, your purpose is to help readers understand how something works or how something happens—for example, how a cell phone operates or how to write a computer program. In this case, you do not expect readers to perform the process. The student writer of the following paragraph, a volunteer firefighter, explains how a fire extinguisher works.

Even though many people have fire extinguishers in their homes, most people do not know how they work. A fire extinguisher is a metal cylinder

Topic sentence

filled with a material that will put out a fire. All extinguishers operate the same way. First, the material inside the cylinder is put under pressure. Next, when an operating lever on top of the metal cylinder is squeezed, a valve is opened. The pressure inside the fire extinguisher is released. As the compressed gas in the cylinder rushes out, it carries the material in the fire extinguisher along with it. Then, a nozzle at the top of the cylinder concentrates the stream of liquid, gas, or powder coming from the fire extinguisher so it can be aimed at a fire. Finally, the material comes in contact with the fire and puts it out. Every home should have at least one fire extinguisher located where it can be easily reached when it is needed. Most important, everyone should know how to use a fire extinguisher.

Transitions introduce steps in process

Concluding statement

—David Turner (student)

Instructions

When you write **instructions**, your purpose is to give readers the information they need to actually perform a task or activity—for example, to fill out an application, to operate a piece of machinery, or to cook a meal. Because you expect readers to follow your instructions, you address them directly, using **commands** to tell them what to do (*check the gauge . . . pull the valve*). In the following paragraph, the writer gives humorous instructions on how to get food out of a vending machine.

Man vs. Machine

Long ago, the first food machines were the servants of people. Now, these machines have turned against their creators. The result is a generation of machines that will take a little girl's allowance and keep her Cheetos, too. Luckily, there is a foolproof method of getting a vending machine to give up its food.

Topic sentence

1. First, approach the vending machine coolly. Make sure that you don't seem frightened or angry. The machine will sense these emotions and steal your money.
2. Second, be polite. Say hello, compliment the machine on its selection of goodies, and smile. Be careful. If the machine thinks you are trying to take advantage of it, it will steal your money.
3. Third, if the machine steals your money, remain calm. Ask nicely to get the food you paid for.

Transitions introduce steps in process

4. Finally, it is time to get serious. Hit the side of the vending machine with your fist. If this doesn't work, lower your shoulder and throw yourself at the machine. (A good kick or two might also help.) When the machine has had enough, it will drop your snack, and you can grab it.

If you follow these few simple steps, you should have no trouble walking away from vending machines with the food you paid for.

Concluding statement

—Adam Cooper (student)

Transitions are very important in process paragraphs like the two you have just read. They enable readers to clearly identify each step—for example, *first, second, third,* and so on. In addition, they establish a sequence that helps readers move easily through the process you are describing.

Some Transitional Words and Phrases for Process

after that	first	soon
as	immediately	the first (second, third) step
as soon as	later	the last step
at the same time	meanwhile	then
at this point	next	the next step
before	now	when
finally	once	while

GRAMMAR IN CONTEXT Process

When you write a process paragraph, you may find yourself making **illogical shifts** in tense, person, number, and voice. If you shift from one tense, person, number, or voice to another without good reason, you may confuse your reader.

CONFUSING First, the vending machine should be approached coolly. Make sure that you don't seem frightened or angry. (illogical shift from passive to active voice)

CLEAR First, approach the vending machine coolly. Make sure that you don't seem frightened or angry. (consistent use of active voice)

For information on how to avoid illogical shifts in tense, person, number, and voice, see Chapter 23.

B Writing a Process Paragraph

◆ PRACTICE 8-1

Read this process paragraph, and answer the questions that follow it.

In October 2003, engineers, scientists, and National Park Service employees worked together to move a 2,000-pound bell. The Liberty Bell, a symbol of freedom and justice around the world, was moved from a small pavilion on Market Street in Philadelphia to a larger home in the new Constitution Center. But because the bell is so fragile, it took months of careful planning before the experts felt ready to undertake the task. First, a Vermont company, with help from the National Science Foundation, designed small sensors to attach to the bell. During the move, these sensors would sound an alarm on a nearby computer if the bell experienced stress. Next, experts x-rayed the bell to determine what impurities the metal contained and what the various thicknesses were. After they made sure the bell was ready, the experts loaded it onto a specially designed cart for the 200-yard trip to its new home. The actual trip — over a distance of about two football fields — took four hours to complete.

—Sean Camburn (student)

1. Underline the topic sentence of the paragraph.
2. List the transitions that tell you that the writer is moving on to another step in the process. The first transition has been listed for you.

   First
   ____
   ____
   ____

3. How many steps did it take to move the bell?

   ____

4. List the steps on the lines below.

   ____
   ____
   ____

5. Underline the paragraph's concluding statement.

◆ PRACTICE 8-2

Following are four topic sentences for process paragraphs. List three steps or stages that might occur in each process.

1. Registering for college courses can be a frustrating process.

   ____
   ____
   ____

2. Balancing a checkbook is not as complicated as it may seem.

____

____

____

3. Parallel parking is not difficult if you follow a few simple steps.

____

____

____

4. Buying products online can save you time and money.

____

____

____

◆ PRACTICE 8-3

Choose one of the topics below (or a topic of your own) as the subject of a process paragraph.

Preparing a holiday meal
Writing a letter of complaint
Getting out of debt
Planning a party
Deciding on a gym to join
Succeeding at a job interview
Studying for a test
Taking care of a pet
Living on a budget
Meeting new people
Dressing well
Breaking up with someone

◆ PRACTICE 8-4

Use one or more of the strategies described in 3C to help you come up with as many steps as you can for the topic you have chosen. List these steps on a separate sheet of paper.

◆ PRACTICE 8-5

Review the steps you listed in Practice 8-4, and decide whether to write a process explanation or a set of instructions. Then, choose the steps you want to include from the list you made in Practice 8-4, and list them below.

- ______________________________
- ______________________________
- ______________________________
- ______________________________
- ______________________________
- ______________________________
- ______________________________
- ______________________________

◆ PRACTICE 8-6

Reread your list of steps from Practice 8-5. Then, write a topic sentence that identifies the process you will discuss and communicates the point you will make about it.

Topic sentence: ____

____

____

◆ PRACTICE 8-7

Review the steps you listed in Practice 8-5. Then, write them down in time order, moving from the first step to the last.

1. ______________________
2. ______________________
3. ______________________
4. ______________________
5. ______________________
6. ______________________
7. ______________________
8. ______________________

◆ PRACTICE 8-8

Draft your process paragraph.

◆ PRACTICE 8-9

Using the Self-Assessment Checklist on page 127, revise your process paragraph.

◆ PRACTICE 8-10

Print out a final draft of your process paragraph.

● REVISING AND EDITING

Look back at the Seeing and Writing exercise on page 120, and evaluate the paragraph you wrote for unity, support, and coherence. Then, prepare a final draft of your paragraph.

✓ SELF-ASSESSMENT CHECKLIST: Writing a Process Paragraph

- Does the topic sentence identify the process your paragraph will discuss?
- Does the topic sentence indicate whether you are giving instructions or explaining how something works?
- Do you include all the steps in the process?
- Do you present the steps in the order in which they occur?
- Have you included the transitions that readers will need to follow the process?
- Have you avoided illogical shifts in tense, person, number, and voice?
- Have you included a concluding statement that sums up your paragraph's main idea?

CHAPTER REVIEW

◆ EDITING PRACTICE

1. The following student process paragraph is missing a topic sentence, transitional words and phrases, and a concluding statement. After reading the paragraph, fill in the missing elements on the appropriate lines below. (See p. 123 for a list of transitions.)

Starting Over

____

____

Before you begin dating, keep in mind that as a single parent, you should date only when you are ready. _______________, once you decide to go out on a date, is to take things slowly. Both you and your children need to get used to the fact that you are dating. _______________, make sure that your children are cared for when you are on a date. Parents or close friends are best because your children will feel safe with them. _______________, talk to your children. Explain that you would like to spend time with someone you like. Do not talk about marriage or getting them a "new parent." ____________, if you decide you would like to introduce the person you are dating to your children, keep the first visit short, and schedule additional visits far apart. Also, do not show your date too much affection in front of your children. ____________, be patient. It may take a long time for both you and your children to be comfortable with your new life. ____________________

____

2. Create a process paragraph by adding details to support the following topic sentence. Make sure you connect the steps in the process with appropriate transitions. End the paragraph with a clear concluding statement that sums up the main idea. Then, add an appropriate title.

____

A chat room can be a good place to meet new friends, if you follow a few simple steps. ____________________

____

____

____

____

____

____

____

____

____

____

____

____

____

____

____

3. The picture below shows a supermarket employee. Look at the picture carefully, and write a process paragraph in which you explain how to do a job you've held. Begin your paragraph with a topic sentence that identifies the process you are describing. Then, in the rest of the paragraph, present the steps of the process in clear chronological order.

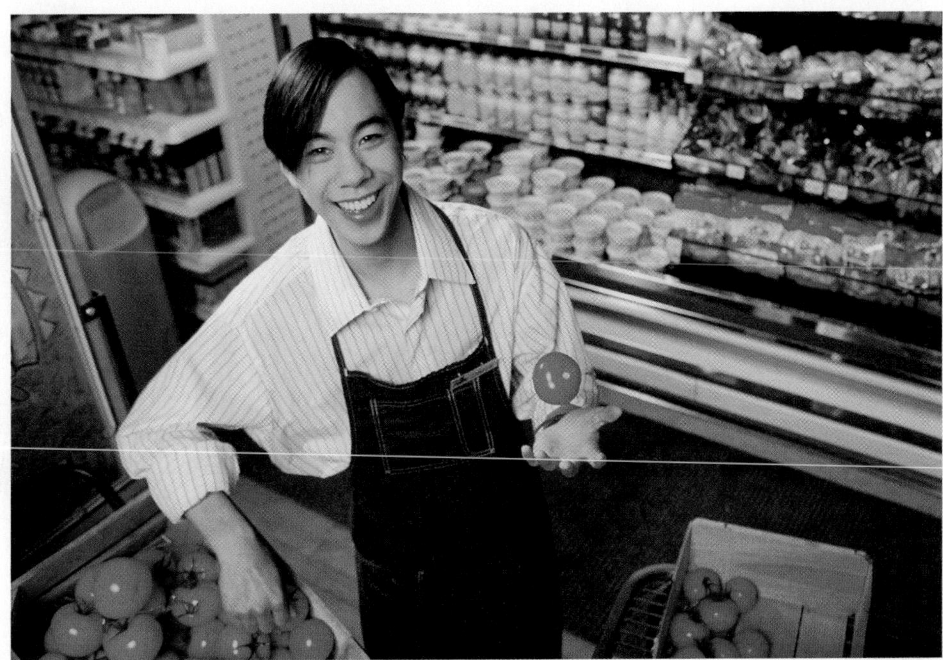

CHAPTER

9 Cause and Effect

PREVIEW

In this chapter, you will learn to write a cause-and-effect paragraph.

Word Power

conceited self-important

humble modest

empower to give power or confidence

self-esteem self-worth

SEEING AND WRITING

The picture above shows Taylor Hicks, *American Idol* winner. Look at the picture, and imagine how your life would change if you won this competition. Then, write a paragraph in which you discuss how winning *American Idol* would affect you and the people you know.

A What Is Cause and Effect?

What is causing global warming? Why is the cost of college so high? How does smoking affect a person's health? What would happen if the city increased its sales tax? How dangerous is the avian flu? All these questions have one thing in common: they try to determine the causes or effects of an action, event, or situation. A **cause** is something or someone that makes something happen. An **effect** is something brought about by a particular cause.

Cause		*Effect*
Increased airport security	→	Long lines at airports
Weight gain	→	Exercise program
Seatbelt laws passed	→	Increased use of seatbelts

A **cause-and-effect paragraph** helps readers understand why something happened or is happening, or shows readers how one thing affects something else. A cause-and-effect paragraph begins with a topic sentence that tells readers whether the paragraph is focusing on causes or on effects (for example, "There several reasons why the cost of gas is so high" or "Going to the writing center has given me confidence as well as skills"). The rest of the paragraph should discuss the causes or the effects, one at a time. The causes or effects are arranged in some kind of **logical order**—for example, from least important to most important. The paragraph ends with a concluding statement that restates the main idea.

A cause-and-effect paragraph generally has the following structure:

Topic Sentence ______________________________

Cause (or effect) #1 ______________________________

____

Cause (or effect) #2 ______________________________

____

Cause (or effect) #3 ______________________________

____

Concluding Statement ______________________________

____

The following paragraph focuses on causes.

Health Alert

Topic sentence

Transitions introduce causes of weight gain

Concluding statement

For a number of reasons, Americans are gaining weight at a frightening rate. First, many Americans do not eat healthy foods. They eat a lot of food that is high in salt and that contains a lot of saturated fat. Also, many Americans eat on the run, grabbing a doughnut or muffin on the way to work and eating fast food for lunch or dinner. Another reason Americans are gaining weight is that they eat too much. They take too much food and think they must eat everything on their plates. They do not stop eating when they are full, and they often have second helpings and dessert. The most important reason for this alarming weight gain is that Americans do not exercise. They sit on the couch and watch hours of television and get up only to have a snack or a soda. The effect of this unhealthy lifestyle is easy to predict. Unless Americans begin eating better, many will develop severe health problems in the future.

—Jen Toll (student)

The paragraph below focuses on effects.

Second Thoughts

Topic sentence

Transitions introduce effects of dropping out

When I dropped out of high school before my senior year, I had no idea how this action would affect my life. My parents told me that I was making a big mistake. It didn't take long for me to realize that they were right. Dropping out had some negative effects on my life. The first effect was that I became a social outcast. At the beginning, my friends called and asked me to go out with them. Gradually, school activities took up more and more of their time. Eventually, they had no time for me. Another effect was that I realized that my job wasn't good. When I was in school, working part time at a bookstore didn't seem bad. Once it became my full-time job, however, I knew that I was going nowhere. Without a diploma or some college education, I couldn't get a better job. The most important effect was that my girlfriend broke up with me. One day she told me that she didn't like dating a dropout. She said I had no goals and no future. I had to agree with her. When I heard that she had started dating a sophomore in college, something clicked. I went to school at night and got my GED and then applied to community college. Now that I am taking college classes, I realize how wrong I was to drop out of high school and how lucky I am lucky to have a second chance.

— Dan Tarr (student)

Concluding statement

Transitions in cause-and-effect paragraphs, as illustrated in the two paragraphs above, show the connections between a cause and its effects or between an effect and its causes. In addition, they identify the relationship between various causes or effects—for example, which cause or effect is more important than another or which comes before another.

Some Transitional Words and Phrases for Cause and Effect

another cause	one cause (effect, reason)	the first (second, third, final) reason
another effect	since	the most important cause
as a result	so	the most important effect
because	the first (second, third, final) cause	the most important reason
consequently	the first (second, third, final) effect	therefore
finally		
for		
for this reason		
moreover		

GRAMMAR IN CONTEXT Cause and Effect

When you write a cause-and-effect paragraph, be careful not to confuse the words *affect* and *effect*. *Affect* is a verb meaning "to influence." *Effect* is a noun meaning "result."

> The ~~affect~~ effect of this unhealthy lifestyle is easy to predict. (*effect* is a noun)
>
> When I dropped out of high school before my senior year, I had no idea how this action would ~~effect~~ affect my life. (*affect* is a verb)

For more information on *effect* and *affect*, see Chapter 36.

B Writing a Cause-and-Effect Paragraph

◆ PRACTICE 9-1

Read this cause-and-effect paragraph, and answer the questions that follow it.

It's hard to imagine why someone would go to all the trouble and expense of moving, but I had some very good reasons for packing my things and moving to another apartment. My first reason for moving was that I had noisy neighbors. When I looked at the apartment, the rental agent promised me that it would be quiet. He didn't bother to tell me that the apartment across the hall was rented by two guys who came and went at all hours of the day and night. Every weekend, and most nights, they had friends over, and this made it impossible for me to sleep or to study. Another reason that I moved was that the landlord never fixed things. The stove never worked right, and I never could be sure if I would get heat or hot water. My most disturbing reason for moving was that the landlord made a habit of coming into my apartment without telling me. As soon as I moved in, I began to notice that things weren't right. I would come home from classes and notice that the door wasn't locked—even though I remembered locking it. Once I noticed that my DVD player had been disconnected and that a drawer that I had closed was open. Later, a neighbor told me that the landlord came around and inspected all the apartments once a month. When I told the rental agent that the landlord shouldn't come into my apartment anytime he felt like it, he told me to read my lease. By the end of the year, I decided that I had had enough, and I moved.

—Jean Wong (student)

1. Underline the topic sentence of the paragraph.
2. Does the paragraph focus on causes or effects? How do you know?

   ____

   ____

   ____

3. List the transitions that tell you the writer is moving from one cause to another.

   ____

   ____

   ____

4. List the causes on the lines below.

   ____

   ____

   ____

5. Underline the paragraph's concluding statement.

◆ PRACTICE 9-2

Following are four topic sentences for cause-and-effect paragraphs. List three causes or effects for each sentence.

1. Indoor air pollution is caused by a number of items we use every day.

 ____

 ____

2. Indoor air pollution can have harmful effects on our health.

 ____

 ____

3. Cell phones are popular for many reasons.

 ____

 ____

4. Cell phones have changed our society.

 ____

 ____

◆ PRACTICE 9-3

Choose one of the topics below (or a topic of your own) as the subject of a cause-and-effect paragraph.

Causes of problems falling asleep
Effects of lack of communication on a relationship
Causes of road rage
Effects of Internet chat rooms
Why you attend the college you do
Effects of excessive drinking
Causes of obesity among young adults
The possible effects of global warming
Why you belong to a particular organization
The effects of divorce on children
Why certain students succeed
The effects of a positive (or negative) attitude
The reasons students cheat
Causes of low voter turnout

◆ PRACTICE 9-4

Freewrite or brainstorm (described in 3C) to help you think of as many causes or effects as you can for the topic you have chosen.

◆ PRACTICE 9-5

Review your notes for Practice 9-4, and create a cluster diagram. Write the topic in the center of the page, and draw arrows branching out to specific causes or effects.

◆ PRACTICE 9-6

Choose the most important causes or effects from your notes from Practices 9-4 and 9-5. List them on the lines below.

- ______________________________
- ______________________________
- ______________________________
- ______________________________
- ______________________________
- ______________________________

◆ PRACTICE 9-7

Reread your list of causes or effects from Practice 9-6. Then, draft a topic sentence that introduces your topic and communicates the point you want to make about it.

____

____

____

◆ PRACTICE 9-8

List the causes or effects you will discuss in your paragraph, arranging them in an effective order—for example, from least important to most important.

1. ______________________________
2. ______________________________
3. ______________________________
4. ______________________________
5. ______________________________
6. ______________________________

◆ PRACTICE 9-9

Now, draft your cause-and-effect paragraph.

◆ PRACTICE 9-10

Using the Self-Assessment Checklist on page 137, revise your cause-and-effect paragraph.

◆ PRACTICE 9-11

Print out a final draft of your cause-and-effect paragraph.

● REVISING AND EDITING

Look back at the Seeing and Writing exercise on page 130, and evaluate the paragraph you wrote for unity, support, and coherence. Then, prepare a final draft of your paragraph.

☑ SELF-ASSESSMENT CHECKLIST: Writing a Cause-and-Effect Paragraph

- ☐ Does your topic sentence clearly state your paragraph's main idea?
- ☐ Does the topic sentence indicate whether the focus of the paragraph is on causes or effects?
- ☐ Are the causes and effects clearly identified?
- ☐ Do transitional words and phrases signal a shift from one cause or effect to another?
- ☐ Have you used *affect* and *effect* correctly?
- ☐ Have you included a concluding statement that sums up your paragraph's main idea?

CHAPTER REVIEW

◆ EDITING PRACTICE

1. The following student cause-and-effect paragraph is missing a topic sentence, transitional words and phrases, and a concluding statement. After reading the paragraph, fill in the missing elements on the appropriate lines below. (See p. 133 for a list of transitions.)

Doing My Part

____

____

_______________ is that now I recycle. I try to separate bottles, cans, and paper.

I even recycle used cooking oil and old batteries that I replaced. Our township requires us to separate trash, but many people just put everything into a big plastic bag and throw it away. I choose to recycle. ________________ is that now I take public transportation. When I go to school, I take the train. That way, I use less gas and oil. If hundreds of people took the train, we would all help to cut down on the pollution in the world. Also, when I leave my car at home, I save money. I don't have to pay for gas, parking, or bridge tolls. ________________ is that now I buy items that can be reused before they are thrown away. For example, instead of using paper towels, I use cloth towels that I wash. I even refill the empty ink cartridges from my printer so that I can use them again. ______________________________

____

2. Create a cause-and-effect paragraph by adding effects to support the following topic sentence. Make sure you connect the effects with appropriate transitions. End the paragraph with a clear concluding statement that sums up the main idea. Then, add an appropriate title.

____

Too much television viewing can have harmful effects on young children. ____

____

____

____

____

____

____

____

____

____

____

____

____

3. The picture below shows a scene from the video game *Mortal Kombat*. Look at the picture carefully, and write a cause-and-effect paragraph that tells how violent video games affect the people who play them. Do you think they are dangerous, or do you think they are just harmless entertainment? Begin with a topic sentence that states the main idea of your paragraph. In the rest of the paragraph, discuss the effects that are relevant to your topic sentence.

CHAPTER

10

Comparison and Contrast

PREVIEW

In this chapter, you will learn to write a comparison-and-contrast essay.

SEEING AND WRITING

The picture above shows a big dog and a little dog. Look at the picture, and then write a paragraph in which you compare these two dogs. Tell how they are alike, and then tell how they are different.

Word Power

affectionate loving

ferocious fierce

intimidating threatening

timid shy, nervous

A What Is Comparison and Contrast?

When you buy something—for example, an air conditioner, a car, a hair dryer, or a computer—you often comparison-shop. You look at various models to determine how they are alike and how they are different. Eventually, you decide which one you want to buy. In other words, you *compare and contrast*. When you **compare**, you look at how two things are similar. When you **contrast**, you look at how they are different.

Comparison-and-contrast paragraphs can examine just similarities or just differences, or they can examine both. A comparison-and-contrast paragraph begins with a topic sentence that tells readers whether the paragraph is going to discuss similarities or differences. The topic sentence should also make clear the focus of the comparison (for example, "Toni Morrison and Maya Angelou have similar ideas about the effects of discrimination" or "My parents and I have different definitions of success"). The rest of the paragraph should discuss the same or similar points for both subjects. Points should be arranged in **logical order**—for example, from least important to most important. A comparison-and-contrast paragraph ends with a concluding statement that reinforces the main point of the comparison.

There are two kinds of comparison-and-contrast paragraphs: *subject-by-subject comparisons* and *point-by-point comparisons*.

Subject-by-Subject Comparisons

In a **subject-by-subject comparison**, you divide your comparison into two parts and discuss one subject at a time. In the first part of the paragraph, you discuss all your points about one subject. Then, in the second part, you discuss all your points about the other subject. (In each part of the paragraph, you discuss the points in the same order.)

A subject-by-subject comparison is best for short paragraphs in which you do not discuss too many points. Readers will have little difficulty remembering the points you discuss for your first subject as you move on to discuss the second subject.

A subject-by-subject comparison generally has the following structure.

Topic Sentence ______________________________

____

Subject A ______________________________

Point 1 ______________________________

____

Point 2 ______________________________

____

Point 3 ______________________________

____

Subject B ______________________________

Point 1 ______________________________

____

Point 2 ______________________________

____

Point 3 ______________________________

____

Concluding Statement ______________________________

____

The writer of the following paragraph uses a subject-by-subject comparison to compare two ways of traveling to Boston.

Getting to Boston

Topic sentence

Subject A: Going to Boston by car

Transitions emphasize differences

Subject B: Going to Boston by train

When I visited my sister in Boston last year, I realized that taking the train was better than traveling by car. Driving to Boston from Philadelphia takes about six-and-a-half hours. I often drive alone with only my car radio or iPod for company. By the third hour, I am bored and tired. Traffic is also a problem. The interstate roads are crowded and dangerous. Trucks often drive above the speed limit, and cars weave in and out of lanes without warning. If my attention wanders, I can get into serious trouble. If there is an accident, I might have to wait for over an hour until the police clear the highway. Going by train, however, is much better. When I went last year, I met other students and had some interesting conversations. In contrast to when I drove, on the train I took a nap when I got tired, and snacked when I got hungry. I was even able to plug my laptop into an outlet on the train and work on some assignments. When I finished, I leaned back and read a book. Best of all, unlike when I drove, I never got stuck in traffic. As a result, when I finally got to Boston, I was rested and ready for a visit with my sister.

This experience showed me that going to Boston by train is much better than driving.

Concluding statement

—Forrest Williams (student)

Point-by-Point Comparisons

When you write a **point-by-point comparison**, you discuss a point about one subject and then discuss the same point about the second subject. You use this alternating pattern throughout the paragraph.

A point-by-point comparison is a good strategy for paragraphs in which you discuss many points. It is also a good choice if the points you are discussing are technical or complicated. Because you compare the two subjects one point at a time, readers will able to see each point of comparison before moving on to the next point.

A point-by-point comparison generally has the following structure.

Topic Sentence ______________________________

____

Point 1 ______________________________

Subject A ______________________________

____

Subject B ______________________________

____

Point 2 ______________________________

Subject A ______________________________

____

Subject B ______________________________

____

Point 3 ______________________________

Subject A ______________________________

____

Subject B ______________________________

____

Concluding Statement ______________________________

____

In the following paragraph, the writer uses a point-by-point comparison to compare two characters in a short story.

Topic sentence

Point 1: Different personalities

Point 2: Different attitudes toward life

Point 3: Different attitudes toward tradition

Transitions emphasize differences between two subjects

Concluding statement

Two Sisters

Although they grew up together, Maggie and Dee, the two sisters in Alice Walker's short story "Everyday Use," are very different. Maggie, who was burned in a fire, is shy and has low self-esteem. When she walks, she shuffles her feet and looks down at the ground. Dee, however, is confident and outgoing. She looks people in the eye when she talks to them and is very opinionated. Maggie seems satisfied with her life. She never complains or asks for anything more than she has, and she has remained at home with her mother in rural Georgia. In contrast, Dee has always wanted nicer things. She has gone away to school and hardly ever visits her mother and Maggie. The biggest difference between Maggie and Dee is their attitude toward tradition. Although Maggie values her family's traditions, Dee values her African roots. Maggie cherishes her family's handmade quilts and furniture, hoping to use them with her own family. Unlike Maggie, Dee sees the handmade objects as things to be displayed, not used. The many differences between Maggie and Dee add conflict and tension to the story.

—Margaret Caracappa (student)

Transitions are important in a comparison-and-contrast paragraph. Transitions tell readers when you are moving from one point (or one subject) to another. Transitions also make your paragraph more coherent by showing readers whether you are focusing on similarities (for example, *likewise* or *similarly*) or on differences (for example, *although* or *in contrast*).

Some Transitional Words and Phrases for Comparison and Contrast

although	one difference . . . another difference
but	one similarity . . . another similarity
even though	on the contrary
however	on the one hand . . . on the other hand
in comparison	similarly
in contrast	though
like	unlike
likewise	whereas
nevertheless	

GRAMMAR IN CONTEXT **Comparison and Contrast**

When you write a comparison-and-contrast paragraph, you should state the points you are comparing in parallel terms to highlight their similarities or differences.

NOT PARALLEL Although Maggie values her family's traditions, the African heritage of their family is the thing that Dee values.

PARALLEL Although Maggie values her family's traditions, Dee values their African roots.

For more information on revising to make ideas parallel, see Chapter 19.

B Writing a Comparison-and-Contrast Paragraph

◆ PRACTICE 10-1

Read this comparison-and-contrast paragraph, and answer the questions that follow it.

Having been both a smoker and a nonsmoker, I feel qualified to compare the two ways of life. When I smoked, I often found myself banished from public places such as offices, restaurants, and stores when I felt the urge to smoke. I would huddle with my fellow smokers outside, in all kinds of weather, just for a cigarette. As more and more people stopped smoking, I found myself banished from private homes, too. I spent a lot of money on cigarettes, and the prices seemed to rise faster and faster. I worried about lung cancer and heart disease. My colds wouldn't go away, and they often turned into bronchitis. Climbing stairs and running left me breathless. Now that I have stopped smoking, my life is different. I can go anywhere and socialize with anyone. The money I have saved in the last year on cigarettes is going to pay for a winter vacation in Florida. After not smoking for only a few weeks, I could breathe more easily. I had more energy for running and climbing stairs. I have also avoided colds so far. I'm not as worried about lung and heart disease. In fact, I've been told that my lungs should be as healthy as those of a nonsmoker within another year or so. Quitting smoking was one of the smartest moves I ever made.

—Margaret Gonzales (student)

1. Underline the topic sentence of the paragraph.
2. Does this paragraph deal mainly with similarities or differences?

____

How do you know?

____

____

3. Is this paragraph a subject-by-subject or a point-by-point comparison? How do you know?

____

____

____

____

____

4. List some of the contrasts the writer describes. The first contrast has been listed for you.

When she was a smoker, she often had to smoke outside of public and private places. As a nonsmoker, she can go anywhere.

____

____

____

____

5. Underline the paragraph's concluding statement.

◆ PRACTICE 10-2

Following are four topic sentences for comparison-and-contrast paragraphs. First, identify the two things being compared. Then, list three similarities or differences for the two subjects. For example, if you were comparing two authors, you could show the similarities and/or differences in the subjects they write about, their styles of writing, and the kinds of readers they attract.

1. My life plan has changed a lot since I was a child.

____

____

____

2. The media's portrayal of young people is often very negative, but the true picture is more positive.

____

____

____

3. These two styles of music are very similar.

____

____

____

4. As soon as I get to my job, I become a different person.

____

____

____

◆ PRACTICE 10-3

Choose one of the following topics (or a topic of your own) as the subject of a comparison-and-contrast paragraph.

Two different regions of the US
The differences between two political candidates
What you thought college would be like before you started and what it actually is like
Two different sports
How people see you and how you really are
The work of two different writers
Two different electronic devices
How you and your best friend are alike (or different)
Two different movie stars
Writing letters and sending email
The music you listen to and the music your parents listen to
Technology today and ten years ago
Differences in the lives of the rich and poor
Two different jobs
Dog owners and cat owners
Small-town life versus big-city life
Two different bosses or teachers

◆ PRACTICE 10-4

Use one or more of the strategies described in 3C to help you think of as many similarities or differences as you can for the topic you have chosen. (If you use clustering, create a separate cluster diagram for each of the two subjects you are comparing.)

◆ PRACTICE 10-5

Review your notes on the topic you chose in Practice 10-3. Decide whether to focus on similarities or differences. On the following lines, list the similarities or differences that can best help you develop a comparison-and-contrast paragraph on the topic you have chosen.

____

____

____

◆ PRACTICE 10-6

Reread your list of similarities or differences from Practice 10-5. Then, draft a topic sentence that introduces your two subjects and indicates whether your paragraph will focus on similarities or differences.

Topic sentence: ______________________________

____

____

◆ PRACTICE 10-7

Decide whether you will write a subject-by-subject or a point-by-point comparison. Then, use the appropriate outline below to help you plan your paragraph. Before you begin, decide on the order in which you will present your points—for example, from least important to most important. (For a subject-by-subject paragraph, begin by deciding which subject you will discuss first.)

Subject-by-Subject Comparison

Subject A ______________________

Point 1 ______________________

Point 2 ______________________

Point 3 ______________________

Subject B ______________________

Point 1 ______________________

Point 2 ______________________

Point 3 ______________________

Point-by-Point Comparison

Point 1 ______________________

Subject A ______________________

Subject B ______________________

Point 2 ______________________

Subject A ______________________

Subject B ______________________

Point 3 ______________________

Subject A ______________________

Subject B ______________________

◆ PRACTICE 10-8

Now, draft your comparison-and-contrast paragraph.

◆ PRACTICE 10-9

Using the Self-Assessment Checklist below, revise your comparison-and-contrast paragraph.

◆ PRACTICE 10-10

Print out a final draft of your comparison-and-contrast paragraph.

• REVISING AND EDITING

Look back at the Seeing and Writing exercise on page 140, and evaluate it for unity, support, and coherence. Then, prepare a final draft of your paragraph.

✓ SELF-ASSESSMENT CHECKLIST: Writing a Comparison-and-Contrast Paragraph

- ☐ Does your topic sentence state your paragraph's main idea?
- ☐ Does your topic sentence indicate the two things you will compare?
- ☐ Have you followed the correct format for a subject-by-subject or a point-by-point comparison?
- ☐ Have you discussed the same or similar points for both subjects?
- ☐ Have you used appropriate transitional words and phrases?
- ☐ Have you stated your points in parallel terms?
- ☐ Have you included a concluding statement that sums up your paragraph's main idea?

CHAPTER REVIEW

◆ EDITING PRACTICE

1. The following student comparison-and-contrast paragraph is missing a topic sentence, transitional words and phrases, and a concluding statement. After reading the paragraph, fill in the missing elements on the appropriate lines below. (See p. 144 for a list of transitions.)

Commuters versus Dorm Students

____

____

____

Just come to an 8 o'clock class any morning, and the differences are obvious. ________________, commuters are fighting just to keep awake after a one-hour ride to school. ________________, dorm students are wide awake after a brisk ten-minute walk to class. As a result of being sleep deprived, commuters are frequently grumpy, irritable, and unfriendly. Dorm students, ________________, are generally alert and in good spirits. After all, they have probably gotten an extra hour of sleep. The differences between dorm students and commuters do not end in class. Between classes, dorm students can go back to their rooms and grab a nap before the next class. Commuters, ________________, must find something to do or somewhere to go before their next class. Often, this means walking around campus trying to find a quiet place to rest. When classes are finished for the day, dorm students can go back to their rooms and study until dinner, or they can get involved in one of the many activities available on campus. Commuters, ________________, must trudge wearily to the bus stop or subway.

____

____

____

► **Word Power**
trudge to walk with effort, to plod

2. Create a comparison-and-contrast paragraph by adding points that support the topic sentence, contrasting your goals in high school and your goals today. Make sure you connect the points with appropriate transitions. End the paragraph with a clear concluding statement that sums up the main idea. Then, add an appropriate title.

____

When I was in high school, my goals were different from what they are today. ______________________________

3. The pictures below show two portrayals of boxers. Look at the two pictures carefully, and write a paragraph in which you compare them. Begin with a topic sentence that states the main point of your paragraph. Then, in the rest of the paragraph, discuss the points that support the main idea in your topic sentence. End your paragraph with a concluding statement that sums up your paragraph's main idea.

Classification

CHAPTER 11

PREVIEW

In this chapter, you will learn to write a classification paragraph.

SEEING AND WRITING

The picture above shows a small neighborhood store. Look at the picture, and then write a paragraph discussing the kinds of stores in your neighborhood. For example, you could discuss mom-and-pop stores (such as bodegas), convenience stores (such as 7-Elevens), and superstores (such as Wal-Mart).

Word Power

dry goods fabrics and clothing

hardware tools, nails, hinges, and the like

produce fruits and vegetables

bodega small grocery store in urban neighborhood, specializing in Hispanic products

A What Is Classification?

Classification is the act of sorting items (people, things, or ideas) into categories. You classify when you organize your bills into those you have to pay now and those you can pay later or when you sort the clothes in a dresser drawer into piles of socks, T-shirts, and underwear. College assignments often ask you to classify. For example, a question on a history exam may ask you to classify those who fought in the American Revolution. To answer this question, you would have to put these individuals into three groups: colonists, British soldiers, and British sympathizers (Tories).

In a **classification paragraph**, you tell readers how items can be sorted into categories or groups. The topic sentence introduces the subject of the paragraph and identifies the categories you will discuss. (For example, "Animals can be classified as vertebrates or invertebrates" or "Before you go camping, you should put the items you are thinking of packing into three categories: those that are absolutely necessary, those that could be helpful, and those that are not really necessary.")

The rest of the paragraph discusses each of the categories, one at a time. Your discussion of each category should include enough details and examples to show how it is different from the other categories. You should also treat each category in the same way. In other words, you should not discuss features of one category that you do not discuss for the others. The categories should be arranged in **logical order**—for example, from most important to least important or from smallest to largest. Finally, each category should be *distinct*. In other words, none of the items in one category should also fit into another category. For example, you would not classify novels into mysteries, romances, and paperbacks, because both mystery novels and romance novels could also be paperbacks. A classification paragraph should end with a concluding statement that reinforces the main point that was stated in the topic sentence.

A classification paragraph generally has the following structure.

Topic Sentence ______________________________

____

Category #1 ______________________________

____

Category #2 ______________________________

____

Category #3 ______________________________

____

Concluding Statement ______________________________

____

The writer of the following paragraph classifies items into three distinct groups.

Types of Bosses

Basically, I've had three kinds of bosses in my life: the uninterested boss, the supervisor, and the micromanager. The first type is an uninterested boss. This boss doesn't care what workers do as long as they do the job. When I was a counselor at summer camp, my boss fell into this category. As long as no campers (or, worse yet, parents) complained, he left you alone. He never cared if you followed the activity plan for the day or gave the kids an extra snack to keep them quiet. The second type of boss is a supervisor. This kind of boss will check you periodically and give you helpful advice. You'll have a certain amount of freedom but not too much. When I was a salesperson at the Gap, my boss fell into this category. She helped me through the first few weeks of the job and encouraged me to do my best. At the end of the summer, I had learned a lot about the retail business and had good feelings about the job. The last, and worst, type of boss is the micromanager. This kind of boss gets involved in everything. My boss at Taco Bell was this kind of person. No one could do anything right. There was always a better way. If you rolled a burrito one way, he would tell you to do it another way. If you did it the other way, he would tell you to do it the first way. Because of the constant criticism, people quit all the time. This boss never seemed to understand that people need praise every once and a while. Even though the second type of boss—the supervisor—expects a lot and makes you work, it is clear to me that this boss is better than the other types.

—Melissa Burrell (student)

Topic sentence

Transitions introduce three categories of bosses

Concluding statement

Transitions are important in a classification paragraph. They introduce each new category and tell readers when you are moving from one category to another (for example, *the first type*, *the second type*). They can also indicate which categories you think are more important than others (for example, *the most important*, *the least important*).

Some Transitional Phrases for Classification

one kind . . . another kind
one way . . . another way
the first (second, third) category
the first group . . . the last group
the first type . . . the second type
the most (or least) important group
the next part

GRAMMAR IN CONTEXT **Classification**

When you write a classification paragraph, you may list the categories you are going to discuss. If you use a colon to introduce your list, make sure that a complete sentence comes before the colon.

INCORRECT Basically, bosses can be divided into: the uninterested boss, the supervisor, and the micromanager.

CORRECT Basically, I've had three kinds of bosses in my life: the uninterested boss, the supervisor, and the micromanager.

For more information on how to use a colon to introduce a list, see 33B.

B Writing a Classification Paragraph

◆ PRACTICE 11-1

Read the classification paragraph below, and answer the questions that follow.

Because people travel so much, international symbols have been created to help them find what they need when they don't know the language. These symbols show pictures instead of words. One group of symbols is for transportation. For example, airports have easy-to-understand pictures of planes, taxis, buses, and trains to help people get where they need to go. Another group of symbols is for travelers' personal needs. For example, men's and women's toilets have different symbols. There are signs for drinking fountains and baby-changing tables. A final group of symbols helps travelers when they get to their destinations. For example, international travelers often have to change their money in a new country. They can find a currency exchange at a sign that shows an American dollar, a British pound, and a Japanese yen. If they need to find a hotel or a restaurant, they can look for the sign with a bed or a knife and fork. Clearly, these symbols make it much easier for people to travel in countries where they do not speak the language.

—Laurent Fischer (student)

1. Underline the paragraph's topic sentence.
2. List the categories that the writer uses to present the types of international symbols discussed.

   ____

   ____

   ____

3. List the transitional words and phrases that let the reader know that a new category is being introduced.

   ____

   ____

   ____

4. Underline the paragraph's concluding statement.

◆ PRACTICE 11-2

Following are four topic sentences for classification paragraphs. For each sentence, list three or four categories under which information could be discussed.

1. On every road in the United States, motorists encounter three types of drivers.

   ____

   ____

   ____

2. Students can be sorted into a number of distinct categories.

   ____

   ____

   ____

3. Advertisers try to appeal to women in various ways.

   ____

   ____

   ____

4. Reality shows fall into several categories.

   ____

   ____

   ____

◆ PRACTICE 11-3

Choose one of the topics below as the subject for a classification paragraph.

Types of exercises
Kinds of friends
Types of video games
Snack foods
Types of parties you've gone to
Kinds of jobs
Types of drivers
Popular music
Parenting styles
Ways to relieve stress
Methods of arguing
Types of college pressures
Types of sports fans
Kinds of teachers
College courses
Types of shoppers

◆ PRACTICE 11-4

On a separate sheet of paper, use one or more of the strategies described in 3C to help you decide how to classify items in the topic you have chosen. Identify as many categories as you can.

◆ PRACTICE 11-5

Review the list of categories you came up with for the topic you chose in Practice 11-4. On the following lines, list the three or four categories you can best develop in your paragraph.

Category 1 ______________________________

Category 2 ______________________________

Category 3 ______________________________

Category 4 ______________________________

◆ PRACTICE 11-6

On the lines below and on the next page, list as many examples as you can for each category you chose in Practice 11-5.

Category 1 ______________________________

Example 1 ______________________________

Example 2 ______________________________

Example 3 ______________________________

Example 4 ______________________________

Category 2 ______________________________

Example 1 ______________________________

Example 2 ______________________________

Example 3 ______________________________

Example 4 ______________________________

Category 3 ____________________

Example 1 ____________________

Example 2 ____________________

Example 3 ____________________

Example 4 ____________________

Category 4 ____________________

Example 1 ____________________

Example 2 ____________________

Example 3 ____________________

Example 4 ____________________

◆ PRACTICE 11-7

On the lines below, list the categories in the order in which you will discuss them.

Category 1 ____________________

Category 2 ____________________

Category 3 ____________________

Category 4 ____________________

◆ PRACTICE 11-8

Reread the list you made in Practice 11-6. Then, draft a topic sentence that introduces both your subject and the categories you will discuss.

Topic sentence: ____________________

____

◆ PRACTICE 11-9

Now, draft your classification paragraph.

◆ PRACTICE 11-10

Using the Self-Assessment Checklist on page 160, revise your classification paragraph.

◆ PRACTICE 11-11

Print out a final draft of your classification paragraph.

REVISING AND EDITING

Look back at the Seeing and Writing exercise on page 153, and evaluate the paragraph you wrote for unity, support, and coherence. Then, prepare a final draft of your paragraph.

SELF-ASSESSMENT CHECKLIST: Writing a Classification Paragraph

- ☐ Does your topic sentence state your paragraph's main idea?
- ☐ Does your topic sentence introduce your subject as well as the categories you will discuss?
- ☐ Do you clearly identify each category and distinguish it from the others?
- ☐ Are the categories distinct from one another?
- ☐ Do you include enough examples in each category?
- ☐ Do transitional words and phrases signal the shift from one category to another?
- ☐ If you introduce your categories with a colon, do you have a complete sentence before the colon?
- ☐ Have you included a concluding statement that sums up your paragraph's main idea?

CHAPTER REVIEW

EDITING PRACTICE

The following student classification paragraph is missing a topic sentence, transitional words and phrases, and a concluding statement. After reading the paragraph, fill in the missing elements on the appropriate lines below. (See p. 156 for a list of transitions.)

Types of Rocks

____

____

________________, igneous rock, is molten rock that has cooled and solidified.

Igneous rocks, such as pumice and granite, are formed when volcanic eruptions bring molten rock to the earth's surface. Other types of igneous rocks are formed when molten rock solidifies slowly underground. ______________, sedimentary rock, is formed from the sediment that is deposited at the bottom of the ocean. Sedimentary rocks, such as sandstone and shale, are deposited in layers, with the oldest sediments on the bottom and the newest on top. ______________, metamorphic rock, is created by heat and pressure. These rocks are buried deep below the earth's surface for millions of years. The weight and high temperatures that they are exposed to alter their structure and mineral composition. The most common metamorphic rocks are marble, slate, gneiss, and quartzite. __________

____

____

2. Create a classification paragraph by adding information about the three categories to support the following topic sentence. Make sure you connect the categories with appropriate transitions. End the paragraph with a clear concluding statement that sums up the main idea. Then, add an appropriate title.

____

There are three kinds of love: parental love, close personal friendship, and romantic love. ______________________

____

____

____

____

____

____

____

____

____

____

____

3. The pictures below depict scenes from movies about teachers. Look at the pictures carefully, and write a paragraph that classifies the different types of teachers that you have encountered. Begin your paragraph with a topic sentence that identifies your paragraph's subject and the categories you will discuss. Then, in the rest of the paragraph, present examples that show how each category is different from the others. End your paragraph with a concluding statement that sums up the paragraph's main idea.

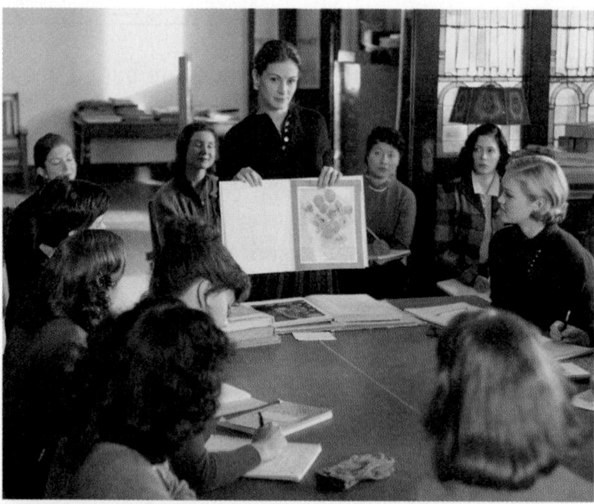

Julia Roberts playing a 1950s art history professor in the 2003 film Mona Lisa Smile

Edward James Olmos as a high school math teacher in the 1988 film Stand and Deliver

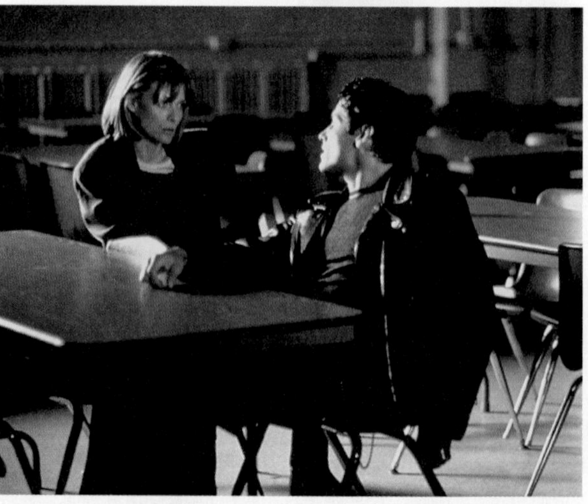

Michelle Pfeiffer as a teacher with a student in the 1995 film Dangerous Minds

CHAPTER 12

Definition

PREVIEW

In this chapter, you will learn to write a definition paragraph.

SEEING AND WRITING

The picture above shows firefighters leaving the rescue area near the World Trade Center after their shift on September 13, 2001. Look at the picture, and then write a paragraph in which you define the term *hero*. What qualities do you think heroes should possess? What people do you consider to be heroes?

Word Power

courageous brave
determined firm, strong-minded
daring bold
invincible unbeatable

A What Is Definition?

During a conversation, you might say that a friend is *stubborn*, that a stream is *polluted*, or that a neighborhood is *dangerous*. Without some explanation, however, these terms mean very little. In order to make yourself clear, you have to define what you mean by *stubborn*, *polluted*, or *dangerous*. Like conversations, academic assignments also may involve definition. In a history paper, for example, you might have to define *imperialism*, and on a biology exam, you might be asked to define *mitosis*.

A **definition** tells what a word means. When you want your readers to know exactly how you are using a specific term, you define it.

When most people think of definitions, they think of the **formal definitions** they see in a dictionary. Formal definitions have a three-part structure that includes the following parts:

- The term to be defined
- The general class to which the term belongs
- The things that make the term different from all other items in the general class to which the term belongs

Term	*Class*	*Differentiation*
Ice hockey	is a game	played on ice by two teams on skates who use curved sticks to try to hit a puck into an opponent's goal.
Spaghetti	is a pasta	made in the shape of long, thin strings, usually served with a sauce.

A single-sentence formal definition is often not enough to define a specialized term (*point of view* or *premeditation*, for example), an abstract concept (*happiness* or *success*, for example), or a complicated subject (*global warming*, for example). In these cases, you may need to expand the basic formal definition by writing a definition paragraph.

A **definition paragraph** is an expanded formal definition. For this reason, its topic sentence often includes a formal definition. Definition paragraphs do not follow any one particular pattern of development; in fact, a definition paragraph may define a term by using any of the patterns discussed in this text. For example, a definition paragraph may explain a concept by *comparing* it to something else or by giving *examples*. A definition paragraph ends with a concluding statement that summarizes the main point of the paragraph.

Here is one possible structure for a definition paragraph. Notice that it uses a combination of **narration** and **exemplification**.

Topic Sentence ______________________________

____

Point #1 ______________________________

Narration ______________________________

Point #2 ______________________________

Example ______________________________

Example ______________________________

Point #3 ______________________________

Example ______________________________

Example ______________________________

Concluding Statement ______________________________

____

The writer of the following paragraph uses several patterns of development—including classification and exemplification—to define the term *happiness*.

Happiness

Although people disagree about what brings happiness, a feeling of contentment or joy, I know exactly what happiness means to me. The first kind of happiness is the result of money. It comes from unexpectedly finding a twenty-dollar bill in my pocket. It comes from hitting the jackpot on a slot machine after putting in just one quarter. The second kind of happiness is about success. It comes from getting an A on a test or being told that my financial aid has been renewed for another year. Of course, I know that happiness is not just about money and success. The most valuable kind of happiness comes from the small things in life that make me feel good. This kind of happiness is taking the time to have a cup of coffee before class or eating lunch at an old-fashioned diner in my neighborhood. It is watching kids play Little League ball in the summer or playing pick-up basketball with my friends. It is finding out that I can still run a couple of miles even though I haven't

Topic sentence includes formal definition

Transitions introduce three kinds of happiness

Concluding statement

exercised in a while or that I can still remember all the state capitals that I had to memorize in school. For me, happiness is more than just money or success; it is the little things that bring joy to my life.

—Edward Fernandez (student)

Transitions are important for definition paragraphs. In the paragraph above, the transitional words and phrases *first kind*, *second kind*, and *most valuable* introduce the categories and tell readers when they are moving from one category to another. The following box lists some of the transitional words and phrases that are used in definition paragraphs. In addition to these transitions, you can also use the transitional words and phrases for the specific pattern (or patterns) that you use to develop your paragraph.

Some Transitional Words and Phrases for Definition

also	one characteristic . . . another characteristic
first (second, third)	one way . . . another way
for example	specifically
in addition	the first kind . . . the second kind
in particular	unlike
like	

GRAMMAR IN CONTEXT **Definition**

A definition paragraph often includes a formal definition of the term or idea you are going to discuss. When you write a formal definition, be careful not to use the phrase *is where* or *is when*.

Happiness is ~~when you have a~~ a feeling of contentment or joy.

◆ PRACTICE 12-1

Read this definition paragraph, and answer the questions that follow.

Bollywood movies are popular films that are made in Mumbai, India. The term *Bollywood* is a combination of the words *Hollywood*, home of the U.S. movie industry, and *Bombay*, the former name for the city of Mumbai. Bollywood movies have several characteristics that Indian audiences want. First, most Bollywood movies are musicals. Song-and-dance scenes are essential. In most cases, the songs are pre-recorded by professional singers, and the actors in the movie lip-synch the lyrics. The dancing may be in classical Indian style, or it may mix classical style with modern Western pop numbers. Second, the plot of a Bollywood movie is likely to be exaggerated, with many surprises and coincidences. Many plots involve star-crossed lovers, angry parents, and love triangles. Third, Indian audiences want to get their money's worth. As a result, Bollywood movies are often over three hours long and offer a mixture of comedy and thrills in addition to the main plot. Because of their popularity, Bollywood movies have made the Indian movie industry the largest in the world.

—Megha Patel (student)

1. Underline the topic sentence of the paragraph.
2. Does the topic sentence include a formal definition of the paragraph's subject? ________
3. List the three characteristics that the writer presents to help readers understand the nature of Bollywood movies.

____

____

____

4. What patterns of development does the writer use in the definition?

____

____

____

5. Underline the paragraph's concluding statement.

◆ PRACTICE 12-2

Following are four topic sentences for definition paragraphs. Each sentence contains an underlined word or phrase. List two ways you could develop an extended definition of the underlined word or phrase.

1. Surveillance cameras help communities to fight crime.

____

____

2. Terrorism is a world-wide problem.

____

____

3. Liquid bandages are a new way to treat cuts and scrapes.

____

____

4. An abridged dictionary contains a limited number of words.

____

____

◆ PRACTICE 12-3

Choose one of the topics below (or a topic of your own) as the subject of a definition paragraph.

A symbol of your religion (for example, a star, a crucifix, or a crescent)
A style of popular music
A technical term
A tool found in most households
A fad
Success
A foreign term
A good day
Sexual harassment
Stress
An ideal mate
Freedom
A concept that is important in a course you are taking

◆ PRACTICE 12-4

Use one of the strategies described in 3C to help you find information about the term you have chosen to define. Your goal is to list the item's features or characteristics. You may also make notes about the item's origin or history or explain how it is like or unlike other similar things.

◆ PRACTICE 12-5

Review your notes from Practice 12-4. On the following lines, list the details that can help you develop a definition paragraph.

- ______________________________
- ______________________________
- ______________________________
- ______________________________
- ______________________________
- ______________________________

◆ PRACTICE 12-6

On the lines below, list the ideas you will discuss in your paragraph, arranging them in an effective order.

1. ______________________________
2. ______________________________
3. ______________________________
4. ______________________________
5. ______________________________

◆ PRACTICE 12-7

Reread your list from Practice 12-5. Then, draft a topic sentence that summarizes the points you want to make about the term you are going to define.

Topic sentence: ______________________________

____

____

◆ PRACTICE 12-8

On a separate sheet of paper, write your definition paragraph.

◆ PRACTICE 12-9

Using the Self-Assessment Checklist on pages 169–170, revise your definition paragraph.

◆ PRACTICE 12-10

Print out a final draft of your definition paragraph.

● REVISING AND EDITING

Look back at the Seeing and Writing exercise on page 163, and evaluate the paragraph you wrote for unity, support, and coherence. Then, prepare a final draft of your paragraph.

☑ SELF-ASSESSMENT CHECKLIST: Writing a Definition Paragraph

- ☐ Does your topic sentence state your paragraph's main idea?
- ☐ Does your topic sentence identify the term to be defined?
- ☐ Does it include a formal definition?
- ☐ Have you developed the rest of the paragraph with one or more of the patterns of development discussed in this text?

(continued on following page)

(continued from previous page)

- Have you used appropriate transitional words and phrases to introduce your points?
- Have you avoided using *is when* and *is where* in your definition?
- Have you included a concluding statement that sums up your paragraph's main idea?

CHAPTER REVIEW

◆ EDITING PRACTICE

1. The following student definition paragraph is missing a topic sentence, transitional words and phrases, and a concluding statement. After reading the paragraph (and possibly consulting a dictionary), fill in the missing elements on the appropriate lines below. (Look on p. 166 for a list of transitions.)

What Are Blogs?

____

____

Blogs first appeared in the 1990s and have since become very popular. Blogs resemble online journals. They may include the thoughts of the blogger about his or her life. ____________, they may comment on what is happening on the Web or in the world. Some of the most popular blogs are *Google Weblog*, *Boing Boing*, and *Joel on Software*. Usually, blog entries are listed in reverse chronological order, with the most recent appearing first. ____________, entries on a blog can be unrelated. At other times, they can focus on a particular topic. ____________ online journals, however, blogs often contain links between entries. ____________, they may contain links to other sites, frequently other blogs. Because anyone with an Internet connection can publish a blog, they vary quite a bit in content and quality. Some blogs have just a few readers. ____________, others, such as those written by popular radio talk-show hosts, may be read by thousands of people each month. ______

2. Create a definition paragraph by adding sentences to support the following topic sentence. Use several different patterns of development, and be sure to include transitional words and phrases to lead readers through your discussion. End the paragraph with a clear concluding statement. When you are finished, add an appropriate title.

______

A parent is more than simply someone who has children. ______

3. The pictures below show Americans from several different backgrounds. Look at the pictures carefully, and then write a paragraph in which you define the term *American*. In what way do the people in the pictures fit (or not fit) your definition? Begin your paragraph with a topic sentence that identifies the term you will define. Then, in the rest of the paragraph, define the term by using any of the patterns of development discussed in this text.

Friends

A mixed-race family

An Indian-American family

Latina girls showing off their dresses

CHAPTER

13

Argument

PREVIEW

In this chapter, you will learn to write an argument paragraph.

SEEING AND WRITING

The picture above shows a scene from the classic 1969 film *Easy Rider*. Except for Colorado, Illinois, Iowa, and New Hampshire, which permit riders and passengers to go helmet free, each state has some type of helmet requirement for motorcycle riders. Look at the picture, and then write a paragraph in which you argue against this (or any other) law that you consider unfair or unjust. Make sure you include the specific reasons why you object to the law you are discussing.

▶ **Word Power**

excessive extreme

foolhardy reckless

indefensible hard to defend

unwarranted unnecessary

A What Is Argument?

When most people hear the word *argument*, they think of the heated exchanges they hear on television interview programs or on talk radio. These discussions, however, are more like shouting matches than arguments. True **argument** involves taking a well-thought-out position on a *debatable topic*—a topic on which reasonable people may disagree. (For example, "Should intelligent design be taught in high school classrooms?" or "Should teenagers who commit felonies be tried as adults?")

In an argument, you attempt to convince people of the strength of your ideas not by shouting but by presenting **evidence**—facts and examples. In the process, you also consider opposing ideas, and if they are strong, you acknowledge their strengths. If your evidence is solid and your logic is sound, you will present a convincing argument.

When you write an **argument paragraph**, your purpose is to persuade readers that your position has merit. To write an effective argument paragraph, follow these guidelines.

- *Write a clear topic sentence that states your position.* Use words like *should, should not*, or *ought to* in your topic sentence to make your position clear to readers.

  The federal government should lower the tax on gasoline.

  The city should not build a new sports stadium.

- *Present points that support your topic sentence.* For example, if your purpose is to argue for placing warning labels on unhealthy snack foods, you should give several reasons why this would be a good idea.
- *Present convincing support.* Support each of your points with evidence (facts and examples).

FOCUS Evidence

There are two kinds of evidence—*facts* and *examples*:

1. A **fact** is a piece of information that can be verified. If you make a point, you should be prepared to support it with facts—for example, statistics, observations, or statements that are accepted as true.
2. An **example** is a specific illustration of a general statement. To be convincing, an example should be clearly related to the point you are making.

- *Address opposing arguments.* Try to imagine what your opponent's arguments might be, and show how they are inaccurate or weak. By addressing these objections in your paragraph, you strengthen your position.

- *Write a strong concluding statement.* A concluding statement reinforces the main idea of your paragraph. In an argument paragraph, it is especially important to summarize the position you introduced in your topic sentence.

An argument paragraph generally has the following structure.

Topic Sentence ______________________

____

Point #1 ______________________

____

Point #2 ______________________

____

Point #3 ______________________

____

Opposing Argument #1 ______________________

____

Opposing Argument #2 ______________________

____

Concluding Statement ______________________

____

The writer of the following argument paragraph presents three reasons to support the position she states in her topic sentence.

Taxing Soda

Recently, some people have suggested taxing soda because they think it is not healthy for young people. I am against this tax because it is unfair, it is unnecessary, and it won't work. The first reason this kind of tax is bad is that it is not fair. The American Medical Association (AMA) thinks the tax will fight obesity in the United States. However, people should be allowed to decide for

Topic sentence

themselves whether they should drink soda. It is not right for a group of doctors or politicians to decide what is best for everybody. Another reason this kind of tax is bad is that it is unnecessary. It would be better to set up educational programs to help children make decisions about what they eat. In addition, the AMA could educate parents so they will stop buying soda for their children. Education will do more to help children than a tax will. Finally, this kind of tax is bad because it won't work. As long as soda is for sale, children will drink it. The only thing that will work is outlawing soda completely, and no one is suggesting this. Of course, some people say that soda should be taxed because it has no nutritional value. This is true, but many snack foods have little nutritional value, and no one is proposing a tax on snack food. In addition, not everyone who drinks soda is overweight, let alone obese. A tax on soda would hurt everyone, including people who are healthy and don't often drink it. The key to helping young people is not to tax them but to teach them what a healthy diet is.

Transitions introduce points that support the topic sentence

Transitions introduce opposing arguments

Concluding statement

—Ashley Hale (student)

Transitions are important for argument paragraphs. In the paragraph above, the transitional words and phrases *the first reason*, *another reason*, and *finally* tell readers they are moving from one point to another. Later in the paragraph, the transitional phrases *of course* and *in addition* introduce two opposing arguments.

Some Transitional Words and Phrases for Argument

accordingly	finally	on the one hand . . .
admittedly	however	on the other hand
although	in addition	since
because	in conclusion	therefore
but	in fact	the first reason . . .
certainly	in summary	another reason
consequently	meanwhile	thus
despite	moreover	to be sure
even so	nevertheless	truly
even though	nonetheless	
first . . . second . . .	of course	

GRAMMAR IN CONTEXT Argument

When you write an argument paragraph, you need to show the relationships among your ideas. You do this by combining simple sentences to create both compound and complex sentences.

COMPOUND SENTENCE The only thing that will work is outlawing sodas completely~~. No~~ *, and no* one is suggesting this.

COMPLEX SENTENCE Recently, some people have suggested taxing soda~~. They~~ *because they* think it is not healthy for young people.

For more information on how to create compound sentences, see Chapter 16. For more information on how to create complex sentences, see Chapter 17.

B Writing an Argument Paragraph

◆ PRACTICE 13-1

Read this argument paragraph, and answer the questions that follow it.

The Importance of Voting

Many American voters never cast a ballot, and voter turnout is often below 50 percent even in presidential elections. It is very sad that people give up this hard-won right. It is in each person's best interest to vote. One reason to vote is that government affects every part of our lives. It is foolish not to have a say about who makes the laws and regulations people have to live with. If a citizen does not vote, he or she loses control over taxes, the educational system, health care, the environment, and even what roads will be built and which bridges repaired. Another reason to vote is to support a particular political party. If a person believes in that party's policies, it is important to vote to elect that party's candidates and keep them in power. A third reason to vote is that voting enables people to influence public policy. Many people seem to think a single vote doesn't matter, but even if a voter's candidate does not win, his or her vote isn't wasted. The voter has expressed an opinion by voting, and the government in power is affected by public opinion. To keep our democracy working and to participate in government, all citizens must exercise their right to vote.

—Lori Wessier (student)

1. Underline the topic sentence of the paragraph. Why do you think the writer places the topic sentence where she does?

____

____

2. What issue is the writer addressing?

What is the writer's position on the issue?

3. List some of the reasons the writer uses to support her position. The first reason has been listed for you.

The most important reason to vote is that government affects every part of our lives.

4. Where does the writer address an opposing argument?

5. Underline the paragraph's concluding statement.

◆ PRACTICE 13-2

Following are four topic sentences for argument paragraphs. For each statement, list three points that could support the statement. For example, if you were arguing in favor of banning smoking in all public places, you could say that smoking is a nuisance, a health risk, and a fire hazard.

1. Employers should offer flexible time schedules to employees.

2. Women's college sports teams should be supported on an equal level with men's teams.

____

____

____

3. Driving under the influence of alcohol is a widespread problem among young people.

____

____

____

4. Congress should act at once to increase the minimum wage.

____

____

____

◆ PRACTICE 13-3

Choose one of the following topics (or a topic of your own) as the subject of an argument paragraph.

Why you would be a good president
Should illegal immigrants be allowed to become citizens?
Is college necessary for success?
Is our right to privacy being lost?
A law that should be changed
Why a particular improvement is needed in your town
A policy or requirement that should be changed at your school
Should student athletes be required to take drug tests?
Why workplaces should offer childcare facilities
An environmental issue
A health-care issue
Safety on your campus
Financial aid policies at your school
Gay marriage

◆ PRACTICE 13-4

Once you have chosen an issue in Practice 13-3, write a journal entry exploring your position on the issue. Consider the following questions.

- What is your position?
- Why do you feel the way you do?
- What specific actions do you think should be taken?
- What objections might be raised against your position?
- How might you respond to these objections?

◆ PRACTICE 13-5

Review your journal entry, and make some additional notes about the issue you have chosen. Then, select the points that best support your position. List the points below. After you have finished, list the strongest objections to your position.

Supporting Points:

- ______________________________
- ______________________________
- ______________________________
- ______________________________

Objections:

- ______________________________
- ______________________________

◆ PRACTICE 13-6

Draft a topic sentence that clearly expresses the position you will take in your paragraph.

Topic sentence: ______________________________

____

◆ PRACTICE 13-7

On the lines below, list the points that support your position, arranging them in an effective order (for example, from least to most important).

1. ______________________________
2. ______________________________
3. ______________________________
4. ______________________________
5. ______________________________

◆ PRACTICE 13-8

On a separate sheet of paper, write your argument paragraph.

◆ PRACTICE 13-9

Using the Self-Assessment Checklist on page 181, revise your argument paragraph.

◆ PRACTICE 13-10

Print out a final draft of your argument paragraph.

● REVISING AND EDITING

Look back at the Seeing and Writing exercise on page 173, and evaluate the paragraph you wrote for unity, support, and coherence. Then, prepare a final draft of your paragraph.

☑ SELF-ASSESSMENT CHECKLIST: Writing an Argument Paragraph

- Does your topic sentence clearly state your position?
- Do you support your points with specific facts and examples?
- Have you addressed possible opposing arguments?
- Have you used appropriate transitional words and phrases to introduce your points and to identify opposing arguments?
- Have you combined sentences to create compound and complex sentences that show how your ideas are related?
- Have you included a concluding statement that summarizes your position?

CHAPTER REVIEW

◆ EDITING PRACTICE

1. The following student argument paragraph is missing a topic sentence, transitional words and phrases, and a concluding statement. After reading the paragraph, fill in the missing elements on the appropriate lines below. (Look on p. 176 for a list of transitions.)

Stop Animal Experimentation

____

____

The work many scientists have already done on animal behavior suggests that animals feel, think, and even communicate with each other. ______________, work with whales and dolphins shows how smart these animals are. Not only can they be trained, but they can also think. ______________, it seems that the gap between human beings and the rest of the animal kingdom is getting smaller. ______________, wild chimpanzees have been seen using tools to pry termites out of termite mounds. In the laboratory, some chimps have been taught to use sign language. These developments are making it more and more difficult to justify animal experiments. ______________, some people will say that animal experimentation is necessary to save human lives. But the fact is that many experiments done on animals are not necessary, and even those that are necessary could be done in ways that would cut down on or eliminate suffering and death.

____

____

2. Create an argument paragraph by adding several points to support the following topic sentence. Be sure to include transitional words and phrases to introduce your points. If possible, try to address at least one argument against your position. End the paragraph with a clear concluding statement. When you are finished, add an appropriate title.

____

Hitting children is never a good way to discipline them. ________

____

____

____

____

____

____

____

____

____

____

____

3. The picture below shows a 2006 pro-immigration rally. Since then, several states have passed laws restricting the rights of undocumented immigrants. Look at the picture carefully, and write a paragraph in which you argue either that these restrictions are a good idea or that they violate rights that all people should have, regardless of their immigration status. Begin your paragraph with a topic sentence that states your position. Then, in the rest of the paragraph, present and support the points that support your position.

CHAPTER 14

Moving from Paragraph to Essay

PREVIEW

In this chapter, you will learn

- to understand essay structure (14A)
- to focus on your assignment, purpose, and audience (14B)
- to find ideas to write about (14C)
- to identify your main idea and state your thesis (14D)
- to choose your supporting points (14E)
- to draft your essay (14F)
- to revise and edit your essay (14G)

Word Power

brawl a noisy fight

conflict a disagreement or clash

altercation a quarrel

SEEING AND WRITING

Look at the picture above, which shows a brawl among players on two baseball teams. Then, write a paragraph in which you consider whether or not there is too much violence in some sports.

A Understanding Essay Structure

In the previous chapters, we have been discussing paragraphs. Now, we will focus on essays. An **essay** is a group of paragraphs about one subject. In this chapter, you will see how the strategies you learned for writing paragraphs can help you write essays.

In some ways, essays and paragraphs are similar. For example, both paragraphs and essays have a single **main idea**. In a paragraph, the main idea is presented in a **topic sentence**, and the rest of the paragraph supports this main idea. The paragraph often ends with a concluding statement that sums up the main idea.

Paragraph

The **topic sentence** states the main idea of the paragraph.

Support develops the main idea with details and examples.

The **concluding statement** sums up the main idea.

In an essay, the main idea is presented in a **thesis statement**. The first paragraph—the **introduction**—presents the thesis statement. The main part of the essay consists of several **body paragraphs** that support the thesis statement. (Each of these body paragraphs contains a topic sentence that states the paragraph's main idea, one point in support of the essay's thesis.) The essay ends with a **conclusion** that restates the thesis statement (in different words) and brings the essay to a close. This essay structure is called **thesis and support**.

Thesis-and-Support Essay

Opening remarks introduce the subject to be discussed.

Introduction

The **thesis statement** presents the main idea of the essay in the last sentence of the first paragraph.

Topic sentence (first point)

Support (details and examples)

Topic sentence (second point)

Support (details and examples)

Body paragraphs

Topic sentence (third point)

Support (details and examples)

The **restatement of the thesis** summarizes the essay's main idea.

Closing remarks present the writer's last thoughts on the subject.

Conclusion

The rest of this chapter explains the process of writing a **thesis-and-support essay**.

B Focusing on Your Assignment, Purpose, and Audience

Most of the essays you write in college will be in response to assignments that your instructors give you. Before you can begin to write about these assignments, you should to determine why you are expected to write (your **purpose**) and for whom you will be writing (your **audience**). Once you understand your audience and purpose, you are ready to address your assignment.

In your writing class, you may be given general assignments such as the following ones.

- Discuss something your school could do to improve the lives of returning older students.
- Examine a decision you made that changed your life.
- Write about someone you admire.

Before you can respond to these general assignments, you will need to ask yourself some questions. Exactly what could your school do to improve the lives of older students? What decision did you make that changed your life? What person do you admire? By asking yourself questions like these, you can narrow these general assignments to specific **topics** that you can write about.

- Free day care for students who have children
- The effects of my giving up smoking
- My grandfather

◆ PRACTICE 14-1

The following topics are too general for a short essay. In the line that follows each assignment topic, narrow the topic down so it is suitable for a brief essay.

Example: A personal problem

How I learned to deal with stress

1. A problem at your school

____

2. Blended families

____

3. Unwanted presents

____

4. Current styles

____

5. Censorship

____

C Finding Ideas to Write About

Once you have a topic, you need to find something to say about it. You do this by using *freewriting*, *brainstorming*, *clustering*, or *journal writing*—just as you do when you write a paragraph.

◆ PRACTICE 14-2

Reread the Seeing and Writing exercise on page 184, and review section 3C of this text. Then, on a separate sheet of paper, use whatever strategies you like—such as *freewriting* or *brainstorming*—to help you come up with material for your essay on violence in sports. If your instructor gives you permission, you may discuss your ideas with other students.

D Identifying Your Main Idea and Stating Your Thesis

Once you have gathered information about your topic, you need to decide what specific points you want to make about it. You begin doing this by looking through your material to see what main idea it can support. You express this main idea in a **thesis statement**: a single sentence that clearly states the main idea that you will discuss in the rest of your essay.

Topic	*Thesis Statement*
Free day care for students	Free day care on campus would improve the lives of the many students who are also parents.
The effects of my giving up smoking	Giving up smoking saved me money and gave me self-respect.
My grandfather	Even though he is over sixty years older than I am, my grandfather is my role model.

Like a topic sentence, a thesis statement tells readers what to expect. An effective thesis statement must do two things.

- *An effective thesis statement must make a point about your topic.* For this reason, it must do more than simply state a fact or announce what you plan to write about.

  STATEMENT OF FACT Free day care is not available on our campus.

  ANNOUNCEMENT In this essay, I will discuss free day care on campus.

  EFFECTIVE THESIS STATEMENT Free day care on campus would improve the lives of the many students who are also parents.

  Neither a statement of fact nor an announcement of what you will discuss makes a point about your topic. For this reason, these kinds of statements give you nothing to discuss in your essay. However, an effective thesis statement indicates the position you will take on your topic and thus tells you what to write about in your essay.

- *An effective thesis statement must be specific and clearly worded.*

  VAGUE THESIS STATEMENT Giving up smoking helped me a lot.

  EFFECTIVE THESIS STATEMENT Giving up smoking saved me money and gave me self-respect.

The effective thesis statement on the previous page is focused and clearly signals what points the essay will develop. In contrast, the vague thesis statement gives no idea of what the essay will discuss. (For example, how has giving up smoking helped?)

FOCUS Stating Your Thesis

At this stage of the writing process, your thesis is **tentative**, not definite. As you write and revise, you are likely to change it—possibly several times.

◆ PRACTICE 14-3

In the space provided, indicate whether each of the following items is a fact (*F*), an announcement (*A*), a vague statement (*VS*), or an effective thesis (*ET*). If your instructor gives you permission, you can break into groups and do this exercise collaboratively.

Examples

Domestic violence is a problem. VS

The federal government should provide more funding for programs that help victims of domestic violence. ET

1. Americans have a life expectancy of more than seventy-seven years. ______
2. There are several reasons why life expectancy has risen in the past century. ______
3. Slavery was a bad practice. ______
4. The minimum wage is below six dollars an hour in many states. ______
5. An increase in the federal minimum wage is necessary. ______
6. In this essay, I will describe some funny incidents when my father and I were confused with each other. ______
7. Most Americans say they believe in God. ______
8. Churches can help drug addicts in three ways. ______
9. Sending letters by means of the post office is really slow. ______
10. Email has some clear advantages over regular mail. ______

◆ PRACTICE 14-4

Carefully review the material you have gathered for your essay about violence in sports. Then, write a tentative thesis statement for your essay on the following lines.

Tentative thesis statement: ______________________________

____

E Choosing Your Supporting Points

After you have decided on a tentative thesis statement, your next step is to decide on the individual points you will use to support it. When you have identified the points you will discuss, list them in the order in which you intend to write about them. For example, you might arrange the points from most general to most specific or from least important to most important. You can use this list of points as a rough outline for your essay. (For a discussion of choosing and arranging points, see 3E and 3F.)

◆ PRACTICE 14-5

Review the tentative thesis statement you wrote in Practice 14-4. Then, review the material you came up with in Practice 14-2, and decide which points you will use to support your thesis statement. List those points on the lines below.

____

____

____

____

____

____

Now, arrange these points in the order in which you plan to write about them. Cross out any points that do not support your thesis statement.

1. ______________________________
2. ______________________________
3. ______________________________
4. ______________________________
5. ______________________________

F Drafting Your Essay

Once you have decided on a thesis and have arranged your points in the order in which you will present them, you are ready to draft your essay. Each paragraph should include a topic sentence that states a point in support of the thesis. It should also include the details and examples readers will need to understand the point.

Keep in mind that you are writing a rough draft, one that you will revise and edit later. Your goal at this point is simply to get your ideas down so that you can react to them. Even so, your draft should have a thesis-and-support structure.

Here is the first draft of an essay by David Weaver, a student in an introductory writing class. Before he wrote his essay, David went through the process discussed in this chapter: he chose a topic, brainstormed and wrote a journal entry, decided on a tentative thesis, and selected and arranged his supporting points.

My Grandfather's Lessons

My grandfather, Richard Weaver, is seventy years old and lives in Leola, a small town outside Lancaster, Pennsylvania. When I was eight, I lived with my grandparents for almost a year. During that time, my grandfather became my role model.

When I lived with my grandparents, there was never a dull moment. My grandfather always had interesting and unusual ideas. He showed me that you don't have to spend money or go places to have a good time. An afternoon in his workshop was more than enough to keep me entertained. Working next to my grandfather, I learned the value of having patience and of doing a job right the first time.

If there ever is a problem, you can always count on my grandfather because he is a very caring and understanding person. He not only cares about his family, but he also cares about the whole community. He is known in the community as a caring and sharing person. Whenever anyone needs help, he is always there — whatever the cost or personal inconvenience.

One major thing that my grandfather taught me is always to be honest. He told me that in the long run, honesty will be its own reward. He taught me that if you find something that is not yours, you should make an effort to find the person who it belongs to so that the person will not suffer from the loss. This also shows how caring of other people my grandfather is.

These characteristics — doing a job right, caring, and being honest — describe my grandfather. Now that I have grown up, I have adopted these special and important characteristics of his.

◆ PRACTICE 14-6

Reread David Weaver's first draft. What changes would you suggest he make? What might he add? What might he delete? Write your suggestions on the following lines. If your instructor gives you permission, you can break into groups and do this exercise collaboratively.

◆ PRACTICE 14-7

On a separate sheet of paper, write a draft of your essay about violence in sports. Be sure to include the thesis statement you drafted in Practice 14-4 as well as the points you listed in the last part of Practice 14-5.

G Revising and Editing Your Essay

When you **revise** your essay, you reconsider the choices you made when you wrote your first draft. As a result, you rethink (and frequently rewrite) parts of your essay. Some of your changes will be major—for example, deleting several sentences or even crossing out or adding whole paragraphs. Other changes will be minor—for example, crossing out a sentence or adding or deleting a word or phrase.

Before you begin to revise, try to put your essay aside for at least an hour or two. Time away from your essay will help you distance yourself from your writing so you can see it critically. When you do start to revise, keep in mind that revision is not a neat process. Don't be afraid to revise directly on your first draft, marking it up with lines, arrows, and cross-outs as well as writing between the lines and in the margins.

When you are finished revising, **edit** your essay, concentrating on grammar, punctuation, mechanics, and spelling.

To make your revision and editing more orderly and more efficient, you may want to use the following checklists to guide you.

☑ SELF-ASSESSMENT CHECKLIST: Revising Your Essay

- ☐ Does your essay have an introduction, a body, and a conclusion?
- ☐ Does your essay have a specific clearly worded thesis statement?
- ☐ Does your thesis statement make a point about your topic?
- ☐ Does each body paragraph have a topic sentence?
- ☐ Does each body paragraph focus on one point that supports the thesis statement?
- ☐ Are the body paragraphs unified, well developed, and coherent?
- ☐ Does your conclusion restate your thesis?

✓ SELF-ASSESSMENT CHECKLIST: Editing Your Essay

Editing for Common Sentence Problems

- ☐ Have you avoided run-ons? (See Chapter 20.)
- ☐ Have you avoided sentence fragments? (See Chapter 21.)
- ☐ Do your subjects and verbs agree? (See Chapter 22.)
- ☐ Have you avoided illogical shifts? (See Chapter 23.)
- ☐ Have you avoided dangling and misplaced modifiers? (See Chapter 24.)

Editing for Grammar

- ☐ Are your verb forms and verb tenses correct? (See Chapters 25 and 26.)
- ☐ Have you used nouns and pronouns correctly? (See Chapters 27 and 28.)
- ☐ Have you used adjectives and adverbs correctly? (See Chapter 29.)

Editing for Punctuation, Mechanics, and Spelling

- ☐ Have you used commas correctly? (See Chapter 31.)
- ☐ Have you used apostrophes correctly? (See Chapter 32.)
- ☐ Have you used other punctuation correctly? (See Chapter 33.)
- ☐ Have you used capital letters where they are required? (See Chapter 34.)
- ☐ Have you used quotation marks correctly where they are needed? (See Chapter 34.)
- ☐ Have you spelled every word correctly? (See Chapter 35.)

When David Weaver revised his essay about his grandfather, he decided to change his tentative thesis statement so that it reflected what he had actually written. In addition, he added topic sentences to help readers see how his body paragraphs related to his thesis statement. To do this, he added transitional words and phrases (*one thing*; *another thing*; *the most important thing*). He also added examples to clarify several generalizations that he had made in his body paragraphs. (He took some of these examples from his journal.) Finally, he expanded his introduction and conclusion.

After he finished revising and editing his essay, David proofread it to make sure that he had not missed any errors. Finally, he checked to see that his essay followed his instructor's guidelines.

FOCUS Guidelines for Submitting Your Papers

Always follow the requirements that your instructor gives you for submitting papers.

- Unless your instructor tells you otherwise, type your name, your instructor's name, the course name and number, and the date (day, month, year) in the upper left-hand corner, one-half inch from the top.
- Type on one side of each sheet of paper.
- Double-space your work.
- Leave one-inch margins on all sides of the page.
- Type your last name and the page number in the upper right-hand corner of each page (including the first page).

Here is the final draft of David's essay.

David Weaver Weaver 1

Professor Yanella

Composition 101

18 Oct. 2007

My Grandfather's Lessons

Introduction — Opening remarks; Thesis statement

My grandfather, Richard Weaver, is seventy years old and lives in Leola, a small town outside of Lancaster, Pennsylvania. He has lived there his entire life. As a young man, he apprenticed as a stone mason and eventually started his own business. He worked as a stone mason until he got silicosis and had to retire. He now works part time for the local water department. When I was eight, my mother was very sick, and I lived with my grandparents for almost a year. During that time, my grandfather taught me some important lessons about life.

First body paragraph — Topic sentence; Support

One thing my grandfather taught me was that I did not have to spend money or go places to have a good time. An afternoon in his workshop was more than enough to keep me entertained. We spent many hours together working on small projects, such as building a wagon, and large projects, such as building a tree house. My grandfather even designed a pulley system that carried me from the roof of his house to the tree house. Working next to my

Weaver 2

grandfather, I also learned the value of patience and of hard work. He never cut corners or compromised. He taught me that it was easier to do the job right the first time than to do it twice.

Another thing my grandfather taught me was the importance of helping others. Whenever anyone needs help, my grandfather is always there—whatever the cost or personal inconvenience. One afternoon a year ago, a friend called him from work and asked him to help fix a broken water pipe. My grandfather immediately canceled his plans and went to help. When he was a member of the volunteer fire department, my grandfather refused to quit even though my grandmother thought the job was too dangerous. His answer was typical of him: he said that because people depended on him, he could not let them down.

Topic sentence

Support

Second body paragraph

The most important thing my grandfather taught me was that honesty is its own reward. One day, when my grandfather and I were in a mall, I found a wallet. I held it up and proudly showed it to my grandfather. When I opened it up and saw the money inside, I couldn't believe it. I had wanted a mountain bike for the longest time, but every time I had asked my grandfather for one, he had told me to be thankful for what I already had. So when I saw the money, I thought that my prayers had been answered. My grandfather, however, had other ideas. He told me that we would have to call the owner of the wallet and tell him that we had found it. Later that night, we called the owner (his name was on his driver's license inside the wallet), and he came over to pick up his money. As soon as I saw him, I knew that my grandfather was right. The man looked as if he really needed the money. When he offered me a reward, I told him no. After he left, my grandfather told me how proud of me he was.

Topic sentence

Support

Third body paragraph

The lessons I learned from my grandfather—doing a job right, helping others, and being honest—were important. Now that I have grown up, I have adopted these special qualities of his. I only hope that someday I can pass them on to my own children and grandchildren the way my grandfather passed them on to me.

Restatement of thesis

Closing remarks

Conclusion

◆ PRACTICE 14-8

What did David add to his draft? What did he delete? What other changes could David have made? Write your suggestions on the following lines.

● REVISING AND EDITING

- Using the Self-Assessment Checklist for revising your essay on page 192 as a guide, evaluate the essay on violence in sports that you wrote in this chapter. Can you support your points more fully? What points can you delete? Can any ideas be stated more clearly? (You may want to get feedback by exchanging essays with another student.) On the following lines, describe any changes you think you should make to your draft.

- Revise and edit the draft of your essay, writing any new material between the lines or in the margins. Then, edit this revised draft, using the Self-Assessment Checklist for editing your essay on page 193 to find errors in grammar, punctuation, mechanics, and spelling.

CHAPTER REVIEW

◆ EDITING PRACTICE

After reading the following incomplete student essay, write an appropriate thesis statement on the lines provided. (Make sure your thesis statement clearly communicates the essay's main idea.) Next, fill in the topic sentences for the second, third, and fourth paragraphs. Finally, restate the thesis (in different words) in your conclusion.

To Praise or Not to Praise

When I was growing up, praise was something children had to earn. It was not handed out lightly. Because I felt that more praise would have meant greater self-esteem, I promised myself I would praise my own children every chance I got. However, ten years of experience as a parent has changed my views. I have come to realize that too much praise, given too easily, is not good.

A father teaching his son to ride a bike.

[Thesis statement] ______________________________

____

____

[Topic sentence for the second paragraph] ______________________________

____

____

____

When children feel they are valued, they learn more easily and work harder when the going gets tough. Self-doubt makes children too frightened of failure to take risks and overcome obstacles. When my older son, Tim, was a preschooler, I gave him lots of praise to build his self-esteem. My strategy worked. He is now a confident fifth-grader who does well in school and has many friends. I did the same for Zachary, who is six, with the same good results.

[Topic sentence for the third paragraph] ______________________________

____

____

____

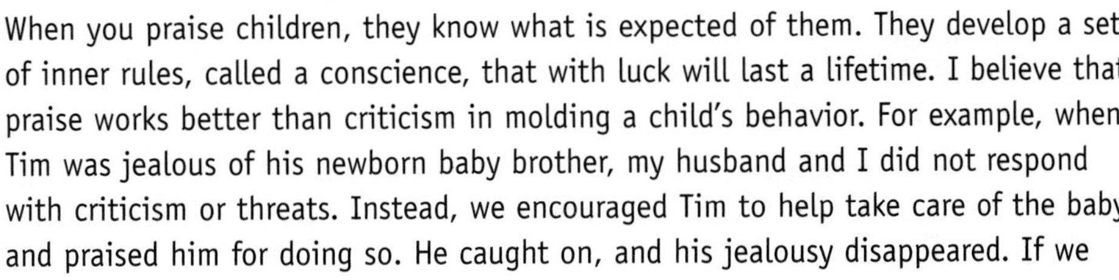

When you praise children, they know what is expected of them. They develop a set of inner rules, called a conscience, that with luck will last a lifetime. I believe that praise works better than criticism in molding a child's behavior. For example, when Tim was jealous of his newborn baby brother, my husband and I did not respond with criticism or threats. Instead, we encouraged Tim to help take care of the baby and praised him for doing so. He caught on, and his jealousy disappeared. If we had criticized or threatened him, I am sure his natural jealousy of the baby would have gotten worse.

[Topic sentence for the fourth paragraph] ______________________

____

____

One of the harmful effects of praising my children too much was that they did not continue working on anything once they were praised for it. If I told them a first draft of a report or a drawing or a kite they were making was good, they put it aside and stopped working on it. Then they would get angry if I tried to get them to improve their work. I finally learned not to praise things that needed more effort. I learned to say things like, "Tell me more about the topic of this report. It's interesting. What else do you know about it?" It took a while before I learned how to say things so that I was not criticizing the children but also was not over-praising them.

[Restatement of thesis in conclusion] ______________________

____

____

____

My children seem to be less dependent on praise than they used to be, and they work harder at getting things right. I hope to use these new techniques in my future career as a preschool teacher and also teach them to other parents.

◆ COLLABORATIVE ACTIVITIES

1. Working with another student, find an article in a magazine or a newspaper about a controversial issue that interests both of you. Then, identify the thesis statement of the article and the main points used to support that thesis. Underline topic sentences that state these points, and make a list of the details and examples that support each topic sentence. How does the article use the thesis-and-support structure to discuss the issue? How could the article be improved?
2. Working in a small group, develop thesis statements suitable for essays on two of the following topics.

   True friendship
   Professional athletes' salaries
   Censoring the Internet
   The value of volunteer work
   A course I will always remember
   Improving the public schools
   A favorite electronic gadget
   A community problem
3. Choose one of the thesis statements you wrote for activity 2. Working with another student, make a list of at least three points that could be used to support the thesis.

✓ REVIEW CHECKLIST: Moving from Paragraph to Essay

- Many essays have a thesis-and-support structure: the thesis statement presents the main idea, and the body paragraphs support the thesis. (See 14A.)
- Begin by focusing on your assignment, purpose, and audience. (See 14B.)
- Narrow your general assignment to a topic you can write about. (See 14B.)
- Use one or more strategies to find ideas to write about. (See 14C.)
- State your main idea in a thesis statement. (See 14D.)
- List the points that best support your thesis, and arrange them in the order in which you plan to discuss them. (See 14E.)
- As you write your first draft, make sure your essay has a thesis-and-support structure. (See 14F.)
- Revise your essay. (See 14G.)
- Edit the final draft of your essay. (See 14G.)

UNIT THREE

Writing Effective Sentences

Writing Simple Sentences

CHAPTER 15

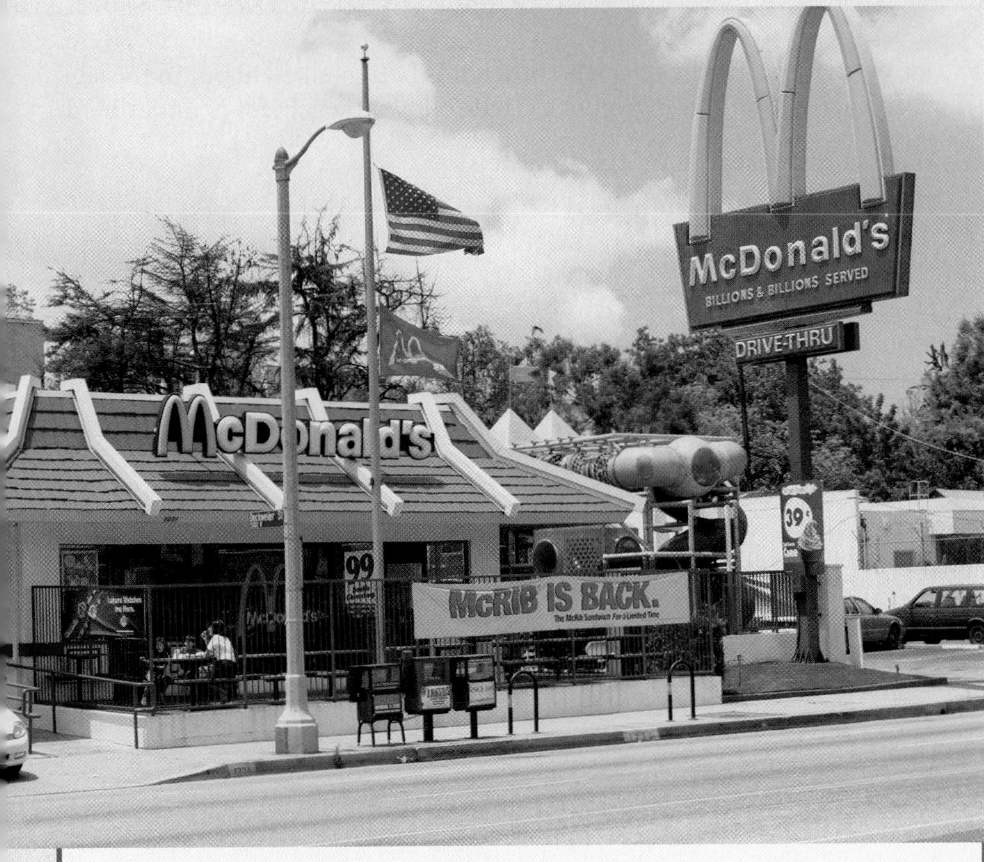

• SEEING AND WRITING

If you met a person who had never been to McDonald's, what would you tell him or her about this fast-food restaurant? The picture above shows a typical McDonald's restaurant. Look at the picture, and then write a paragraph that answers this question.

PREVIEW

In this chapter, you will learn

- to identify a sentence's subject (15A)
- to recognize singular and plural subjects (15B)
- to identify prepositions and prepositional phrases (15C)
- to distinguish a prepositional phrase from a subject (15C)
- to identify action verbs (15D)
- to identify linking verbs (15E)
- to identify helping verbs (15F)

Word Power

institution a well-known person, place, or thing

A **sentence** is a group of words that expresses a complete thought. Every sentence includes both a subject and a verb. A **simple sentence** consists of a single **independent clause**: one subject and one verb.

McDonald's is an American institution.

A Identifying Subjects

The **subject** of a sentence tells who or what is being talked about in the sentence. In each of the three sentences that follow, the subject is underlined.

Marissa did research on the Internet.

The research librarian helped her find a topic for her paper.

It was due in March.

The subject of a sentence can be a noun or a pronoun. A **noun** names a person, place, or thing—*Marissa, librarian*. A **pronoun** takes the place of a noun—*I, you, he, she, it, we, they*.

◆ PRACTICE 15-1

On the lines below, write in a subject (a noun or pronoun) that tells *who* or *what* is being talked about in the sentence.

Example: The ___wind___ howled.

1. __________ was terrified.
2. The fierce __________ was very loud.
3. __________ banged on the roof.
4. A wild __________ barked in the distance.
5. Suddenly, a __________ rapped on the window.
6. __________ screamed and ran to the door.
7. Opening the door, __________ saw a frightening sight.
8. __________ closed the door immediately.
9. Outside, the howling __________ grew stronger.
10. Finally, __________ and __________ arrived.

FOCUS Simple and Complete Subjects

A sentence's **simple subject** is just a noun or a pronoun.

Marissa librarian it

(continued on following page)

(continued from previous page)

A sentence's **complete subject** is the simple subject along with all the words that describe it.

the research librarian

NOTE: A two-word name, such as *Marissa Johnson*, is a simple subject.

◆ PRACTICE 15-2

Underline each sentence's simple subject—the noun or pronoun that tells who or what the sentence is about. Then, put brackets around the complete subject.

✣ **ON THE WEB**
For more practice identifying subjects, visit Exercise Central *at bedfordstmartins.com/ foundationsfirst.*

Example: [Most people]need help waking up in the morning.

(1) Alarm clocks have changed a lot in recent years. (2) A loud, buzzing noise used to be the only option. (3) Now, consumers have many more models to choose from. (4) For example, they can choose to wake up to nature sounds or to light. (5) Heavy sleepers can buy clocks that will go off over and over again. (6) People can also set their alarms for a different time each day. (7) Times have changed since the days of the simple wind-up alarm clock. (8) Alarm clocks can now give weather reports and even monitor a person's sleep stages. (9) Few people use these fancy models, however. (10) In most cases, we still wake up to the radio or to a simple beep.

◆ PRACTICE 15-3

The following sentences have no subjects. Fill in each line below with a complete subject—a simple subject along with all the words that describe it. Remember to begin each sentence with a capital letter.

Example: ___My energetic sister___ runs a small business.

1. ______________ crashed through the picture window.
2. ______________ is my least favorite food.
3. ______________ gave the players a pep talk during halftime.
4. ______________ fell from the sky.
5. ______________ placed the glass slipper on Cinderella's foot.
6. ______________ always makes me cry.

7. ______________________ disappeared into a black hole.

8. ______________________ really meant a lot to me.

9. ______________________ ate five pounds of chocolate-covered cherries.

10. ______________________ lived happily ever after in a big house at the top of a hill.

B Recognizing Singular and Plural Subjects

The subject of a sentence can be *singular* or *plural*. A **singular subject** is one person, place, or thing.

Marissa did research on the Internet.

A **plural subject** is more than one person, place, or thing.

Students often do research on the Internet.

A plural subject that joins two subjects with *and* is called a **compound subject**.

Marissa and Jason did research on the Internet.

◆ PRACTICE 15-4

Each item listed here could be the subject of a sentence. Write *S* after each item that could be a singular subject, and write *P* after each item that could be a plural subject.

Examples

Joey Ramone __S__

The Ramones __P__

Joey and Johnny Ramone __P__

1. hot-fudge sundaes ______
2. the USS *Enterprise* ______
3. life and death ______
4. the McCaughey septuplets ______
5. my Web site ______
6. three blind mice ______
7. Betty and Barney Rubble ______

ON THE WEB
For more practice recognizing singular and plural subjects, visit Exercise Central *at bedfordstmartins.com/ foundationsfirst.*

8. her two children ______

9. Texas ______

10. Ruben Blades ______

◆ PRACTICE 15-5

First, underline the simple subject in each sentence. Then, label each singular subject *S*, and label each plural subject *P*. (Remember that a compound subject is plural.)

Example: The Vietnam Veterans Memorial opened to the public on November 11, 1982.

1. The memorial honors men and women killed or missing in the Vietnam War.
2. More than 58,000 names appear on the black granite wall.
3. More than two and a half million people visit the Memorial each year.
4. Visitors leave mementoes at the site.
5. Some men and women, for example, leave letters and photographs.
6. Other people leave items like combat boots, stuffed animals, rosaries, and dog tags.
7. One man leaves a six-pack of beer each year.
8. Visitors also leave cigarettes, flowers, canned food, and clothing.
9. Spouses, children, parents, and friends leave offerings for men and women lost in the war.
10. A Persian Gulf War veteran left his medal for his father.

C Identifying Prepositional Phrases

As you have seen, every sentence includes a subject and a verb. As you try to identify sentence subjects, you may be confused by prepositional phrases, which include nouns or pronouns.

A **prepositional phrase** is made up of a **preposition** (a word like *on*, *to*, *in*, or *with*) and its **object** (the noun or pronoun it introduces).

Preposition	+	*Object*	=	*Prepositional Phrase*
on		the roof		on the roof
to		Leah's apartment		to Leah's apartment
in		my Spanish class		in my Spanish class
with		her		with her

Because the object of a preposition is a noun or a pronoun, it may look like the subject of a sentence. However, the object of a preposition can never be a subject. To identify a sentence's subject, cross out every prepositional phrase.

SUBJECT — PREPOSITIONAL PHRASE

The price ~~of a new home in the San Francisco Bay area~~ is very high.

After you cross out the prepositional phrases, you will easily be able to identify the sentence's subject. Remember, every prepositional phrase is introduced by a preposition.

Frequently Used Prepositions

about	behind	for	off	toward
above	below	from	on	under
across	beneath	in	onto	underneath
after	beside	including	out	until
against	between	inside	outside	up
along	beyond	into	over	upon
among	by	like	through	with
around	despite	near	throughout	within
at	during	of	to	without
before	except			

◆ PRACTICE 15-6

ON THE WEB
For more practice identifying prepositional phrases, visit **Exercise Central** *at bedford stmartins.com/foundations first.*

Each of the sentences in the following paragraph includes at least one prepositional phrase. To identify each sentence's subject—the noun or pronoun that the sentence is about—first cross out every prepositional phrase. Then, underline the simple subject.

Example: Sudoku puzzles are popular ~~around the world~~.

(1) People are wild about these puzzles. (2) They can be full of challenges. (3) Each puzzle consists of nine 3x3 squares. (4) The player must write numbers in the squares. (5) However, each number may only appear once in each column, each row, and each 3x3 square. (6) The level of difficulty of each puzzle is determined by the "givens." (7) The "givens" of an individual puzzle make that puzzle unique. (8) Mathematicians with an interest in sudoku have discovered over five billion unique grids. (9) However, solvers of these puzzles are not usually mathematicians. (10) In fact, sudoku does not require an expert knowledge of math.

D Identifying Action Verbs

An **action verb** tells what the subject does, did, or will do. In the sentences below, the action verbs are underlined twice.

Tiger Woods plays golf.

Columbus sailed across the ocean.

Andrea will go to Houston next month.

Action verbs can also show mental or emotional action.

Nirav often thinks about his future.

Wendy loves backpacking.

When the subject of a sentence performs more than one action, the sentence includes two or more action verbs.

Lois left work, drove to Somerville, and met Carmen for dinner.

◆ PRACTICE 15-7

In each of the following sentences, underline each action verb twice. Some sentences include more than one action verb.

Example: Many nineteenth-century Americans left their homes and journeyed to unfamiliar places.

(1) During the 1840s, thousands of Americans traveled west to places like Oregon, Nevada, and California. (2) Many travelers began their journey in Independence, Missouri. (3) In towns all around Missouri, travelers advertised in newspapers for strong young companions for the journey west. (4) Thousands of wagons eventually departed from Independence on the dangerous four-month trip to California. (5) Whole families packed their bags and joined wagon trains. (6) The wagons carried food, supplies, and weapons. (7) Some travelers wrote letters to friends and relatives back east. (8) Others wrote in journals. (9) In these letters and journals, we see the travelers' fear and misery. (10) Traveling 2,500 miles west across plains, deserts, and mountains, many people suffered and died.

✣ **ON THE WEB**
For more practice identifying action verbs, visit Exercise Central *at bedfordstmartins .com/foundationsfirst.*

◆ PRACTICE 15-8

Insert an action verb in each space to show what action the subject is, was, or will be performing.

Example: I __drove__ my car to the grocery store.

1. Good athletes sometimes _________ but often _________.
2. After opening the letter, Michele _________.
3. The little boat _________ and _________ on top of the waves.
4. Thousands of people _________ in the rain.
5. The computer _________, _________, and died.
6. The hurricane _________ the residents and _________ the town.
7. Smoke _________ out of the windows.
8. The Doberman _________.
9. A voice _________ from the balcony.
10. Wanda _________ the door.

E Identifying Linking Verbs

A **linking verb** does not show action. Instead, it connects the subject to a word or words that describe or rename the subject. In the following sentence, the linking verb is underlined twice.

Calculus is a difficult course.

In this sentence, the linking verb (*is*) links the subject (*calculus*) to the words that describe it (*a difficult course*).

Many linking verbs, such as *is*, are forms of the verb *be*. Other linking verbs refer to the senses (*look, feel, seem*, and so on).

Tremaine looks very handsome today.

Time seemed to pass quickly.

Frequently Used Linking Verbs

act	become	look	sound
appear	feel	remain	taste
be (am, is, are, was, were)	get	seem	turn
	grow	smell	

◆ PRACTICE 15-9

Underline the verb in each of the following sentences twice. Then, in the blank, indicate whether the verb is an action verb (*AV*) or a linking verb (*LV*).

Example: Many celebrities use their fame to sell products. *AV*

1. Consumers are more likely to buy a product endorsed by a familiar person. ______

2. Some companies even name their products for celebrities. ______

3. In the beauty industry, there are more "celebrity perfumes" than ever before. ______

4. Performers like Jennifer Lopez and Britney Spears now have their own perfumes. ______

5. These fragrances appeal to the star's fans. ______

6. Fans seem ready to spend money in order to smell like their idols. ______

7. Men appear to be part of this trend as well. ______

8. For example, businessman Donald Trump represents a successful men's cologne. ______

9. These popular celebrity scents are clearly very profitable. ______

10. Our fascination with celebrities provides fragrance companies with plenty of marketing opportunities. ______

ON THE WEB
For more practice identifying linking verbs, visit Exercise Central *at bedfordstmartins .com/foundationsfirst.*

◆ PRACTICE 15-10

In the following sentences, underline each linking verb twice. Then, circle the complete subject and the word or words that describe or rename it.

Example: (The juice) tasted (sour).

1. The night grew cold.
2. The song seems very familiar.
3. In 2000, George W. Bush became the forty-third president of the United States.
4. College students feel pressured by their families, their instructors, and their peers.
5. Many people were outraged at the mayor's announcement.
6. The cheese smelled peculiar.
7. The fans appeared upset by their team's defeat.
8. After the game, the crowd turned ugly.
9. Charlie got sick after eating six corn dogs.
10. A mother's love remains strong and true.

F Identifying Helping Verbs

Many verbs are made up of more than one word. For example, the verb in the following sentence is made up of two words.

Andrew must make a choice.

In this sentence, *make* is the **main verb**, and *must* is a **helping verb**. A sentence's complete verb is made up of the main verb plus all the helping verbs that accompany it.

Helping verbs include forms of *be*, *have*, and *do* as well as the words *must*, *will*, *can*, *could*, *may*, *might*, *should*, and *would*.

- Some helping verbs, like forms of *be* and *have*, combine with main verbs to give information about when the action occurs.

  Ana has worked at the diner for two years.

- Forms of *do* combine with main verbs to form questions and negative statements.

  Does Ana still work at the diner?

  Ana does not work on Saturdays.

- Other helping verbs indicate ability (*can*), possibility (*may*), necessity (*should*), obligation (*must*), and so on.

  Ana can choose her own hours.

  Ana may work this Saturday.

  Ana should take a vacation this summer.

  Ana must work hard to earn money for college.

Frequently Used Helping Verbs

am	did	has	might	were
are	do	have	must	will
can	does	is	should	would
could	had	may	was	

◆ **PRACTICE 15-11**

Each of these sentences includes one or more helping verbs as well as a main verb. Underline the complete verb (the main verb and all the helping verbs) in each sentence twice. Then, put a check mark above the main verb.

Example: Elizabeth II has been✓ Queen of England since 1952.

1. Obese adolescents may risk serious health problems as adults.
2. The candidates will name their running mates within two weeks.
3. Henry has been thinking about his decision for a long time.

ON THE WEB
For more practice identifying main verbs and helping verbs, visit Exercise Central *at bedfordstmartins.com/foundationsfirst.*

4. Do you want breakfast now?
5. I could have been a French major.
6. This must be the place.
7. I have often wondered about my family's history.
8. You should have remembered the mustard.
9. Jenelle has always loved animals.
10. Research really does take a long time.

• REVISING AND EDITING

Look back at your response to the Seeing and Writing exercise on page 203. Reread it carefully, and then complete the following tasks.

- Underline the simple subject of every sentence once.
- Underline the complete verb (the main verb plus all the helping verbs) of every sentence twice.
- Circle all the helping verbs in each sentence, and put a check mark above the main verb.

CHAPTER REVIEW

◆ EDITING PRACTICE

Read the following paragraph. Underline the simple subject of each sentence once, and underline the verb twice. To help you locate the subject, cross out the prepositional phrases. The first sentence has been done for you.

The Triangle Shirtwaist Company fire

The Triangle Shirtwaist Company Fire

~~On March 25, 1911~~, a terrible event revealed the unsafe conditions ~~in factories across the United States~~. On that day, a fire at the Triangle Shirtwaist Company killed 146 workers, mainly young immigrant women. These women could not leave the building during working hours. In fact, the factory owners locked most of the exit doors during the day. On the day of the fire, flames spread quickly through the ten-story building. Workers were trapped behind locked doors. Fire engine ladders could not reach the upper floors. In their terror, some people leaped to their deaths from the burning building. After this tragedy, American labor unions

Woman (left) wearing a shirtwaist

grew stronger. Workers eventually gained the right to a shorter workweek and better working conditions. Today, fire safety is very important at most workplaces. For this reason, a tragedy like the one at the Triangle Shirtwaist Company should never happen again.

◆ COLLABORATIVE ACTIVITIES

1. Working in a group of three or four students, write a subject on a slip of paper. On another slip, write a prepositional phrase; on a third, write an action verb. Fold up the slips, keeping subjects, prepositional phrases, and action verbs in separate piles. Choose one slip from each pile, and use them to create an interesting sentence, adding whatever other words are necessary.
2. Working in a group of three students, have each person list three nouns on a blank sheet of paper and pass the paper to the next student, who should add a verb beside each noun. Then, have the third person add a prepositional phrase that can complete each sentence. Each student should then label the subject, verb, and prepositional phrase in the three sentences he or she has completed.
3. ***Composing original sentences*** Working in a group, create five simple sentences on a topic of your choice. Make sure each sentence contains a subject and a verb. When you have finished, check your sentences to make sure each sentence begins with a capital letter and ends with a period.

REVIEW CHECKLIST: Writing Simple Sentences

- The subject tells who or what is being talked about in the sentence. (See 15A.)
- A subject can be singular or plural. (See 15B.)
- The object of a preposition cannot be the subject of a sentence. (See 15C.)
- An action verb tells what the subject does, did, or will do. (See 15D.)
- A linking verb connects the subject to a word or words that describe or rename the subject. (See 15E.)
- Many verbs are made up of more than one word: a main verb and one or more helping verbs. (See 15F.)

Writing Compound Sentences

CHAPTER 16

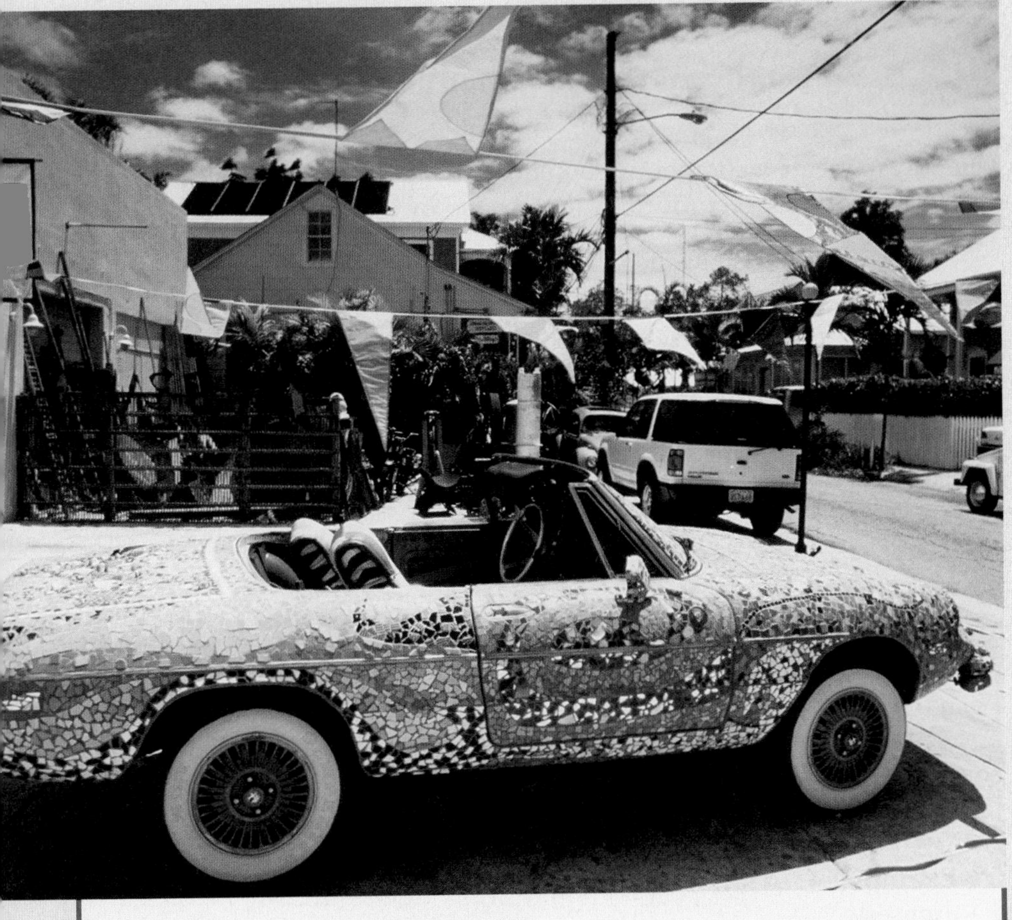

PREVIEW

In this chapter, you will learn

- to form compound sentences with coordinating conjunctions (16A)
- to form compound sentences with semicolons (16B)
- to form compound sentences with transitional words and phrases (16C)

SEEING AND WRITING

The picture above shows a car that is truly one of a kind. Suppose you wanted to sell this car. Study the picture carefully, and then write a paragraph in which you describe the car in a way that would make someone want to buy it.

Word Power

unique the only one; one of a kind

classic something typical; an outstanding example of its kind

The most basic kind of sentence, a **simple sentence**, consists of a single **independent clause**: one subject and one verb.

Many college students major in psychology.

Many other students major in business.

A **compound sentence** is made up of two or more simple sentences (independent clauses).

A Using Coordinating Conjunctions

One way to create a compound sentence is by joining two simple sentences with a **coordinating conjunction** preceded by a comma.

Many college students major in psychology, but many other students major in business.

Coordinating Conjunctions

and	nor	so
but	or	yet
for		

◆ PRACTICE 16-1

Each of the following compound sentences is made up of two simple sentences joined by a coordinating conjunction. Underline the coordinating conjunction in each compound sentence. Then, bracket the two simple sentences. Remember that each simple sentence includes a subject and a verb.

Example: [I do not like unnecessary delays], nor [do I like lame excuses].

✣ **ON THE WEB**
For more practice forming compound sentences with coordinating conjunctions, visit Exercise Central *at bedfordstmartins.com/foundationsfirst.*

1. Speech is silver, but silence is golden.
2. I fought the law, and the law won.
3. The house was dark, so he didn't ring the doorbell.
4. He decided to sign a long-term contract, for he did not want to lose the job.
5. They will not surrender, and they will not agree to a cease-fire.
6. I could order the chicken fajitas, or I could have chili.
7. She has lived in California for years, yet she remembers her childhood in Kansas very clearly.
8. Professor Blakemore was interesting, but Professor Salazar was inspiring.

9. Melody dropped French, and then she added Italian.

10. Give me liberty, or give me death.

Coordinating conjunctions join ideas that are of equal importance.

Idea (Simple Sentence)	+	*Coordinating Conjunction*	+	*Idea (Simple Sentence)*	=	*Compound Sentence*
Brenda is a vegetarian	+	but	+	Larry eats everything	=	Brenda is a vegetarian, but Larry eats everything.

Coordinating conjunctions describe the relationship between the two ideas, showing how and why the ideas are connected. Different coordinating conjunctions have different meanings.

Word Power

coordinating being equal in importance, rank, or degree

- To indicate addition, use *and*.

  Edgar Allan Poe wrote horror fiction in the nineteenth century, and Stephen King writes horror fiction today.

- To indicate contrast or contradiction, use *but* or *yet*.

  Poe wrote short stories, but King writes both stories and novels.

  Poe died young, yet his stories live on.

- To indicate a cause-and-effect connection, use *so* or *for*.

  I liked *Carrie*, so I decided to read King's other novels.

  Poe's "The Tell-Tale Heart" is a chilling tale, for it is about a horrible murder.

- To present alternatives, use *or*.

  I have to finish *Cujo*, or I won't be able to sleep.

- To eliminate alternatives, use *nor*.

  I have not read *The Green Mile*, nor have I seen the movie.

FOCUS Using Commas with Coordinating Conjunctions

When you use a coordinating conjunction to join two simple sentences into a compound sentence, always place a comma before the coordinating conjunction.

We can see a movie, or we can go to a club.

◆ PRACTICE 16-2

Fill in the coordinating conjunction—*and, but, for, nor, or, so,* or *yet*—that most logically links the two parts of each of the following compound sentences.

Example: Marcus bought a used car instead of a new one, ___for___ he wanted to save money.

1. The restaurant did not have a children's menu, ______ did it have a menu for seniors.
2. On my birthday, I want to visit my boyfriend, ______ I want him to visit me.
3. She enjoyed studying in Costa Rica, ______ she decided to stay for an extra semester.
4. Some companies offer their employees health insurance, ______ many workers cannot afford to pay for it.
5. I will wait for Megan outside, ______ you can find our seats.
6. Caitlyn buys her textbooks online, ______ the prices are lower there than in the campus bookstore.
7. Every Memorial Day, my family goes camping, ______ we always bring our two dogs.
8. Truman Capote needed to do research for his book *In Cold Blood*, ______ he traveled to Holcomb, Kansas.
9. Kyle wants to be an actor, ______ he doesn't want to move to Hollywood.
10. Tom Cruise may decide to make a fourth *Mission Impossible* movie, ______ he may not.

◆ PRACTICE 16-3

Fill in the coordinating conjunction—*and, but, for, nor, or, so,* or *yet*—that most logically links the two parts of each of the following compound sentences.

Example: Three doctors met as teenagers in Newark, New Jersey, ___and___ they made a pact to beat the odds.

(1) George Jenkins, Sampson Davis, and Rameck Hunt agreed to go to college and become doctors, ______ they promised to help each other

succeed. (2) The odds were against them, _______ they lived in inner-city neighborhoods devastated by drugs and violence. (3) They had not had many opportunities, _______ had they had many positive role models. (4) Two of them had been involved in crime, _______ one of them had spent time in jail. (5) Fortunately, all three were accepted at University High, a school for gifted students, _______ they would never have met. (6) They did not make a big deal of their pact, _______ they all took it seriously. (7) None of them wanted to disappoint the others, _______ they all worked very hard to make their dream a reality. (8) The young men's success can be seen as a result of their intelligence and determination, _______ it was also a result of their loyal friendship. (9) Jenkins, Davis, and Hunt hoped their story would inspire others, _______ they wrote a book called *The Pact* about the promise they made. (10) They have also started The Three Doctors Foundation, _______ they hope to create real opportunities for other minority youths in inner-city communities.

◆ PRACTICE 16-4

Using the coordinating conjunctions provided, add a complete independent clause to each of the following pairs of sentences to create two different compound sentences. Remember that each coordinating conjunction establishes a different relationship between ideas.

Example

They married at age eighteen, and *they had ten children*.

They married at age eighteen, so *they had to grow up together*.

1. Date rape is a complex and emotional issue, so _______________________________.

   Date rape is a complex and emotional issue, but _______________________________.

2. Drunk drivers should lose their licenses, for _______________________________.

   Drunk drivers should lose their licenses, or _______________________________.

3. A smoke-free environment has many advantages, and ______________________________.

   A smoke-free environment has many advantages, but ______________________________.

4. Female pilots have successfully flown combat missions, yet ______________________________.

   Female pilots have successfully flown combat missions, so ______________________________.

5. The death penalty can be abolished, or ______________________________.

   The death penalty cannot be abolished, nor ______________________________.

◆ PRACTICE 16-5

Add coordinating conjunctions to combine these sentences where necessary to relate one idea to another. Remember to put a comma before each coordinating conjunction you add.

Example: Drive-in movies were a popular form of entertainment in the 1950s, but today, ~~. Today,~~ only a few drive-ins remain.

(1) Americans love the freedom and independence of driving a car. (2) They also love movies. (3) Not surprisingly, the United States was the home of the very first drive-in movie theater. (4) The first drive-in opened in New Jersey in 1934. (5) The second one, Shankweiler's Drive-In in Orefield, Pennsylvania, opened the same year. (6) Today, the very first drive-in no longer exists. (7) There is not a single drive-in theater remaining in the entire state of New Jersey. (8) However, Shankweiler's is still open for business. (9) Fans of drive-ins can still go there. (10) Shankweiler's Drive-In still has the in-car speakers that moviegoers used to hang in their car windows. (11) They are rarely used. (12) Instead, drive-in visitors simply turn on the car radio to hear the movie sound. (13) Shankweiler's broadcasts movie soundtracks on FM stereo.

(14) Anyone with a car, a love of movies, and a sense of history should make a trip to Shankweiler's Drive-In.

◆ PRACTICE 16-6

Add coordinating conjunctions to combine sentences where necessary to relate one idea to another. Remember to put a comma before each coordinating conjunction you add.

Example: Young children want their own cell phones~~.~~ , but parents ~~Parents~~ do not always see this as a good idea.

(1) Many young children want their own cell phones. (2) It can be difficult for them to convince their parents that a cell phone is a necessity. (3) Some parents think cell phones are too expensive. (4) They do not want to pay the bills. (5) Other parents feel that cell phones are just status symbols. (6) Meanwhile, wireless companies are designing more cell phones with young children and teens in mind. (7) They see the youth market as very important. (8) More and more parents are giving in. (9) They are buying cell phones for their children. (10) After all, parents want the security of knowing their children can be reached. (11) Cell phone companies realize that parents are anxious about their children's safety. (12) They are beginning to add features that allow parents to track a child's location. (13) Children do not like this invasion of their privacy. (14) Parents find such features hard to resist. (15) The cell phone conflict may seem new. (16) It is just another example of the age-old battle between protective parents and their independent children.

◆ PRACTICE 16-7

Write an original compound sentence on each of the following topics. Use the coordinating conjunction provided, and remember to put a comma before the coordinating conjunction in each compound sentence.

Example: *Topic:* course requirements
Coordinating conjunction: but

Composition is a required course for all first-year students, but biology is not required.

1. *Topic:* the high cost of textbooks
   Coordinating conjunction: so

   ____

   ____

   ____

2. *Topic:* interracial dating
   Coordinating conjunction: but

   ____

   ____

   ____

3. *Topic:* two things you hate to do
   Coordinating conjunction: and

   ____

   ____

4. *Topic:* why you made a certain decision
   Coordinating conjunction: for

   ____

   ____

5. *Topic:* something you regret
   Coordinating conjunction: yet

   ____

   ____

6. *Topic:* two possible career choices
   Coordinating conjunction: or

   ____

   ____

7. *Topic:* two chores you would rather not do
   Coordinating conjunction: nor

   ____

   ____

B Using Semicolons

Another way to create a compound sentence is by joining two simple sentences (independent clauses) with a **semicolon**.

> The Democrats held their convention in Boston; the Republicans held their convention in New York.

FOCUS Avoiding Sentence Fragments

A semicolon can only join two complete sentences. It cannot join a sentence and a fragment.

INCORRECT [FRAGMENT: Because New York City has excellent public transportation]; it was a good choice for the convention.

CORRECT New York City has excellent public transportation; it was a good choice for the convention.

For more on avoiding sentence fragments, see Chapter 21.

◆ PRACTICE 16-8

Each of the following items consists of a simple sentence followed by a semicolon. For each item, add another simple sentence to create a compound sentence.

Example: Some people love to watch sports on television; *others would rather play a game than watch one*.

1. Baseball is known as "America's pastime"; ______________________.
2. The most-played sport in the United States is probably basketball; ______________________.
3. Soccer has gained popularity in recent years; ______________________.
4. American football requires size and strength; ______________________.
5. Professional sports teams usually give their fans something to cheer about; ______________________.
6. The Olympic Games honor athletes from around the world; ______________________.
7. Individual athletes compete in sports such as track and field; ______________________.
8. Some athletes are models of good sportsmanship; ______________________.

ON THE WEB
For more practice forming compound sentences with semicolons, visit **Exercise Central** *at bedfordstmartins .com/foundationsfirst.*

9. A good coach knows how to encourage an athlete; ____________________

____.

10. Many children admire sports heroes; ____________________________

____.

C Using Transitional Words and Phrases

Another way to create a compound sentence is by joining two simple sentences with a **transitional word or phrase**. When a transitional word or phrase joins two sentences, a semicolon always comes *before* the transitional word or phrase, and a comma always comes *after* it.

> Women's pro basketball games are often sold out; however, not many people watch the games on television.
>
> Soccer has become very popular in the United States; in fact, more American children play soccer than any other sport.

Frequently Used Transitional Words

also	however	still
besides	instead	subsequently
consequently	meanwhile	then
eventually	moreover	therefore
finally	nevertheless	thus
furthermore	otherwise	

Frequently Used Transitional Phrases

after all	in addition	of course
as a result	in comparison	on the contrary
at the same time	in contrast	that is
for example	in fact	
for instance	in other words	

Although you can use just a semicolon to link similar or contrasting ideas, adding a transitional word or phrase shows the exact relationship between the ideas. Different transitional words and phrases convey different meanings.

- Some transitional words and phrases signal addition: *also, besides, furthermore, in addition, moreover,* and so on.

> Golf can be an expensive sport; besides, it can be hard to find a public golf course.

- Some transitional words and phrases show a cause-and-effect connection: *as a result, therefore, consequently, thus,* and so on.

  Professional baseball players are bigger and stronger than ever before; therefore, home runs have become more common.

- Some transitional words and phrases indicate contradiction or contrast: *nevertheless, however, in contrast, still,* and so on.

  Some of the world's best athletes are track stars; nevertheless, few of their names are widely known.

- Some transitional words and phrases present alternatives: *instead, on the contrary, otherwise,* and so on.

  Shawn got a football scholarship; otherwise, he could not have gone to college.

  He didn't make the first team; instead, he backed up other players.

- Some transitional words and phrases indicate time sequence: *at the same time, eventually, finally, later, meanwhile, subsequently, then,* and so on.

  The popularity of women's tennis has been growing; meanwhile, the popularity of men's tennis has been declining.

◆ PRACTICE 16-9

Each item below consists of a simple sentence followed by a semicolon and a transitional word or phrase. For each item, add an independent clause to create a complete compound sentence.

Example: Shopping malls have spread throughout the country; in fact, *they have replaced many main streets*.

ON THE WEB
For more practice forming compound sentences with transitional words and phrases, visit Exercise Central *at bedfordstmartins.com/foundationsfirst.*

1. Nearly every community is near one or more shopping malls; as a result, ______________________________.
2. Some malls include hundreds of stores; moreover, ______________________________.
3. Malls include restaurants as well as stores; therefore, ______________________________.
4. Some malls serve as social centers; in fact, ______________________________.

5. Shopping at malls offers many advantages over traditional shopping; however, ____.

6. Malls offer many employment opportunities; for example, ____.

7. Malls provide a safe, climate-controlled atmosphere; nevertheless, ____.

8. Many stores seem to have similar merchandise; in addition, ____.

9. The Mall of America, in Minnesota, even includes an amusement park; therefore, ____.

10. Some people think malls are wonderful; still, ____.

◆ PRACTICE 16-10

In each of the following sentences, underline the transitional word or phrase that joins the two independent clauses. Then, add a semicolon and a comma to set off each transitional word or phrase.

Example: Most Americans see the one-room schoolhouse as a thing of the past; however, about 400 one-room schools still operate in the United States.

1. Most of these tiny schools are in isolated rural areas that is they exist in places far from towns with larger school systems.
2. Montana and Nebraska still have some one-room schools in contrast more densely populated states do not have any.
3. Most one-room schools have only one teacher and a few students therefore one room is all they need.

4. The addition of just a few children can cause a school to outgrow its one room as a result the town may have to build a larger school.
5. These days, declining population is the reason most one-room schools close in other words the town does not have enough students to make operating the school worthwhile.
6. Running a one-room school can be expensive consequently many rural communities share a larger school with nearby towns.
7. Supporters of one-room schools see many benefits for example students in these schools get more individual attention from their teachers.
8. One-room schools tend to produce confident, thoughtful students moreover these students tend to do well on state-wide tests.
9. One-room schools also give a town's residents a sense of community and tradition therefore many towns fight hard to keep their schools.
10. So far, the Croydon Village School in New Hampshire has managed to keep its doors open still residents do not take their school for granted.

◆ PRACTICE 16-11

Consulting the lists of transitional words and phrases on page 224, choose a word or expression that logically connects each pair of sentences below into one compound sentence. Be sure to punctuate appropriately.

Example: Temporary shrines along roadways are a familiar sight these days; however, some ~~. Some~~ people find them distracting and even dangerous.

1. Most of these shrines honor the victims of car accidents. It makes sense to have memorials along the roadways.
2. Some shrines are nearly invisible. Some are almost impossible to miss.
3. A shrine is sometimes just a simple white cross. People often add flowers, photos, toys, or teddy bears.
4. No one wants victims to be forgotten. These memorials can cause problems.
5. The shrines can create obstacles for snowplows and lawnmowers. They can distract curious drivers.

▶ Word Power

shrine a place at which respects are paid to a person who has died

6. Delaware is one state taking steps to limit the number of shrines on its roads. Officials want mourners to use an established memorial park.
7. This seems to be a sensible compromise. It does not address one essential issue.
8. The exact location of the victim's death is important to mourners. Mourners will even put themselves in danger to reach the right spot.
9. Most states do not enforce their regulations about temporary memorials. some memorials remain beside roads for many months.
10. Some kind of public outlet for people's grief is clearly needed. This debate is likely to continue.

◆ PRACTICE 16-12

Using the specified topics and transitional words or phrases, create five compound sentences. Be sure to punctuate correctly.

Example: *Topic:* popular music
Transitional word: nevertheless

Many popular singing groups today seem to have been put together by a committee; nevertheless, many of these groups sell millions of records.

1. *Topic:* finding a job
   Transitional phrase: for example

   ____

   ____

2. *Topic:* gun safety
   Transitional word: otherwise

   ____

   ____

3. *Topic:* teenage pregnancy
   Transitional phrase: as a result

   ____

   ____

4. *Topic:* credit card debt
   Transitional word: still

   ____

   ____

5. *Topic:* watching television
   Transitional word: however

____

____

• REVISING AND EDITING

Look back at your response to the Seeing and Writing exercise on page 215. Underline every compound sentence. Have you used the coordinating conjunction or transitional word or phrase that best communicates your meaning? Have you punctuated these sentences correctly? Make any necessary revisions.

Now, look for a pair of short simple sentences in your writing that you could combine, and use one of the three methods discussed in this chapter to join them into one compound sentence.

CHAPTER REVIEW

◆ EDITING PRACTICE

The following student paragraph contains many short, choppy, simple sentences. To revise it, link pairs of sentences by adding an appropriate coordinating conjunction, by adding a semicolon, or by adding an appropriate transitional word or phrase. (There are many different correct ways to revise the paragraph.) Remember to put commas before coordinating conjunctions that join two simple sentences and to use semicolons and commas correctly with transitional words and phrases. The first two sentences have been combined for you.

Murderball Slays Stereotypes

The 2005 documentary *Murderball* introduced many people to an unfamiliar sport~~. It~~ ; at the same time, it helped change people's views of disabled athletes. Most audiences had never heard of quadriplegic rugby. They were not prepared for the full-contact nature of the sport. In quad rugby, players in wheelchairs smash into each other. They often fall out of their chairs. For many viewers, this is difficult to watch. Physically disabled people are usually seen as fragile. *Murderball* tells a different story. The players clearly love the roughness of the game. They refuse to wear

A man playing quad rugby

Quad rugby players

pads, helmets, or other protective gear. The audience is not allowed to pity these men. The audience is encouraged to admire the players and their fast-paced, demanding sport. Quad rugby is exciting to watch. Spectators are easily caught up in the game. The players are also highly competitive, strong, and even arrogant. They resemble many able-bodied professional athletes. For player Mark Zupan, this resemblance is key. He does not want the emphasis to be on the players' disabilities. He wants people to recognize their abilities. The movie *Murderball* makes people do just that.

◆ COLLABORATIVE ACTIVITIES

1. Working in a small group, use a coordinating conjunction to join each sentence in the left-hand column below with a sentence in the right-hand column to create ten compound sentences. Use as many different coordinating conjunctions as you can to connect ideas. Be sure each coordinating conjunction you choose conveys a logical relationship between ideas, and remember to put a comma before each one. You may use some of the listed sentences more than once. (Many different combinations—some serious and factually accurate, some humorous—are possible.)

   Miniskirts get shorter every year.
   Those shoes are an ugly color.
   Berries usually ripen in the summer.
   Wild mushrooms grow all over the world.
   I bought seven pairs of earrings.
   His pants are dragging on the ground.
   Everyone at work has to wear a uniform.
   The yard is full of dandelions.
   Ostrich eggs are enormous.
   Cherry tomatoes make excellent snacks.

   Some come with a belt.
   They are torn and dirty.
   My mother hates them.
   Some kinds are edible.
   The silver ones are my favorites.
   Only experts should pick them.
   Digging them up is my job.
   I will not try them on.
   I love to throw them in salads.
   Each one could make several omelettes.

2. Working in a group of three or four students, invent a new sport. Begin by writing one rule of the game in the form of a simple sentence. Then, pass the paper to the person on your right. That person should expand the rule into a compound sentence.

   Example

   ORIGINAL RULE The ball must not touch the ground.

   CHANGED RULE The ball must not touch the ground; moreover, the players can only move the ball with their elbows.

Keep going until you have five complete rules. Then, work together to write additional sentences describing the playing area, teams, uniforms, or anything else about the game that you like. Use compound sentences whenever possible.

3. ***Composing original sentences*** Working in a group, create six compound sentences. Make sure that each compound sentence includes two simple sentences, each with a subject and a verb. Two of your sentences should join clauses with coordinating conjunctions, two with semicolons, and two with transitional words or phrases. When you have finished, check your sentences to make sure you have punctuated them correctly.

✓ REVIEW CHECKLIST: Writing Compound Sentences

- A compound sentence is made up of two simple sentences (independent clauses).
- A coordinating conjunction—*and, but, for, nor, or, so,* or *yet*—can join two simple sentences into one compound sentence. A comma always comes before the coordinating conjunction. (See 16A.)
- A semicolon can join two simple sentences into one compound sentence. (See 16B.)
- A transitional word or phrase can join two simple sentences into one compound sentence. When it joins two sentences, a transitional word or phrase is always preceded by a semicolon and followed by a comma. (See 16C.)

CHAPTER 17

Writing Complex Sentences

PREVIEW

In this chapter, you will learn

- to form complex sentences with subordinating conjunctions (17A)
- to punctuate with subordinating conjunctions (17B)
- to form complex sentences with relative pronouns (17C)

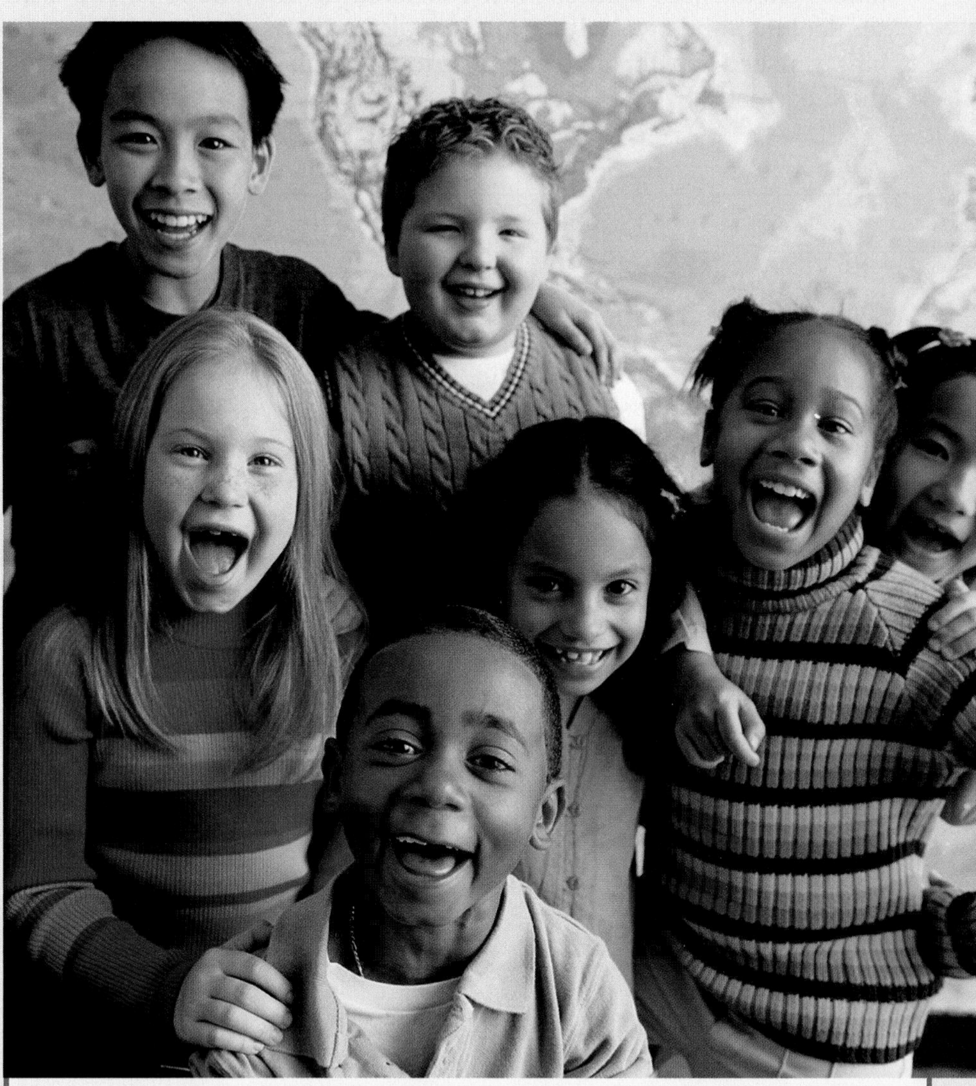

▶ Word Power

estranged separated from someone else by feelings of hostility or indifference

diverge to go in different directions

● SEEING AND WRITING

Look at the picture above, which shows a group of childhood friends. Then, write a paragraph about the childhood friends you've lost touch with. Why do you think you don't see these friends anymore? Which, if any, would you like to see again?

In this chapter, you will learn to combine dependent and independent clauses to create complex sentences. A **complex sentence** is made up of one independent clause and one or more dependent clauses. A **clause** is a group of words that contains both a subject and a verb.

An **independent clause** can stand alone as a sentence.

INDEPENDENT CLAUSE Tanya was sick yesterday.

A **dependent clause** cannot stand alone as a sentence. It needs other words to complete its meaning.

DEPENDENT CLAUSE Because Tanya was sick yesterday

What happened because Tanya was sick yesterday? To answer this question, you need to add an independent clause that completes the idea in the dependent clause. Combining these two clauses creates a single **complex sentence**.

COMPLEX SENTENCE [DEPENDENT CLAUSE: Because Tanya was sick yesterday,] [INDEPENDENT CLAUSE: I had to work a double shift.]

NOTE: Sometimes the independent clause comes first in a complex sentence: *I had to work a double shift because Tanya was sick yesterday.*

Word Power

independent free from the influence of others

dependent relying on another for support

A Using Subordinating Conjunctions

One way to create a complex sentence is to join two simple sentences (independent clauses) with a dependent word called a **subordinating conjunction**—a word like *although* or *because*. The subordinating conjunction signals the relationship between the two simple sentences. For example, look at the following two sentences.

TWO SENTENCES The election was close. The state supreme court did not order a recount.

What is the connection between the close election and the action of the court? By adding a subordinating conjunction, you can make the relationship between these two ideas clear.

COMPLEX SENTENCE Although the election was close, the state supreme court did not order a recount.

Here, the subordinating conjunction *although* indicates that one event happened even though the other event occurred.

Frequently Used Subordinating Conjunctions

after	if only	till
although	in order that	unless
as	now that	until
as if	once	when
as though	provided	whenever
because	rather than	where
before	since	whereas
even if	so that	wherever
even though	than	whether
if	though	while

Different subordinating conjunctions express different relationships between dependent and independent clauses.

Relationship between Clauses	*Subordinating Conjunction*	*Example*
Time	after, before, since, until, when, whenever, while	Before the storm hit land, the people evacuated the town.
Reason or cause	as, because, since	The senator suggested raising the retirement age because the Social Security program was running out of money.
Result or effect	in order that, so that	We need to put computers in all public libraries so that everyone can have access to the Internet.
Condition	even if, if, unless	Global warming will get worse unless we do something now.
Contrast	although, even though, though, whereas	Even though he dropped out of college, Bill Gates was able to start Microsoft.
Location	where, wherever	Where there's smoke, there's fire.

◆ PRACTICE 17-1

ON THE WEB
For more practice forming complex sentences with subordinating conjunctions, visit Exercise Central *at* ***bedfordstmartins.com/foundationsfirst.***

Write an appropriate subordinating conjunction on each blank line below. Consult the list of subordinating conjunctions above to make sure you choose one that establishes a logical relationship between ideas. (The required punctuation has been provided.)

Example: ___If___ you were alive in the early part of the twentieth century, you probably saw a vaudeville show.

(1) ______ there was film, radio, or television, people needed other forms of entertainment. (2) Vaudeville shows were a popular choice in

the late nineteenth and early twentieth centuries ______ you lived in a city. (3) ______ vaudeville shows were variety shows with many different acts, there was usually something for everyone. (4) You could often see comedians, mind readers, and escape artists as well as singers and dancers ______ you went to a vaudeville show. (5) The "headliner," the biggest star, usually went next to last, ______ a less popular performer went last. (6) ______ it is difficult to imagine, all the performers had to do several shows a day. (7) ____________ this was exhausting for the entertainers, it was convenient for audiences. (8) ______ you wanted to see a show, there was usually one playing. (9) ______ no one is certain why the vaudeville boom ended in the 1920s, there are several possible reasons. (10) ______ the Depression began and radio was invented, most vaudeville theaters went out of business.

◆ PRACTICE 17-2

Complete each of the following complex sentences by finishing the dependent clause on the line provided. Make sure each dependent clause includes both a subject and a verb.

Example: Some students succeed in school because *they have good study habits*.

1. After ____________________, these students review their lecture notes and reread the assignment.
2. They memorize facts from their notes even though ____________________.
3. Sometimes these students copy key facts from lectures onto note cards so that ____________________.
4. Teachers sometimes give surprise quizzes because ____________________.
5. Students might do poorly on these quizzes unless ____________________.
6. Even if ____________________, they are prepared for the unexpected.

7. Whenever __________________________, good students ask questions to be sure they understand the assignment.

8. When __________________________, good students begin their research early.

9. They narrow the topic and develop a tentative thesis before __________________________________.

10. Since __________________________, good students are always prepared.

B Punctuating with Subordinating Conjunctions

To punctuate a complex sentence that contains a subordinating conjunction, follow these rules:

- Use a comma after the dependent clause.

  DEPENDENT CLAUSE: Although they had no formal training as engineers, INDEPENDENT CLAUSE: Orville and Wilber Wright built the first airplane.

  Although they had no formal training as engineers, Orville and Wilber Wright built the first airplane.

- Do not use a comma after the independent clause.

  INDEPENDENT CLAUSE: Orville and Wilber Wright built the first airplane DEPENDENT CLAUSE: although they had no formal training as engineers.

  Orville and Wilber Wright built the first airplane although they had no formal training as engineers.

◆ PRACTICE 17-3

Some of the following complex sentences are punctuated correctly, and some are not. Put a *C* next to every sentence that is punctuated correctly. If the punctuation is not correct, edit the sentence to correct it.

Example: When the movie *Lords of Dogtown* came out in 2005, interest in skateboarding was already at an all-time high. C

1. Skateboarding has come a long way since the first commercial boards became available in the 1950s. ____

2. Teenagers used to skateboard wherever they could find exciting terrain. ____

3. They could practice their moves, because they were not afraid to break the law. ____

❖ **ON THE WEB**
For more practice punctuating with subordinating conjunctions, visit Exercise Central *at bedfordstmartins.com/foundationsfirst.*

4. As skateparks became more common, the sport lost some of its bad-boy character. _____
5. Now that skateboarding is more popular skating gear has become very fashionable. _____
6. Millions of people wear skating gear, whether they own a skateboard or not. _____
7. Sporting goods stores make much more money selling skateboarding shoes and T-shirts than they make selling skateboards. _____
8. Some of the old-school skateboarders are disappointed, now that their sport is more mainstream. _____
9. They prefer the old approach of "skate and destroy" whereas newcomers tend to obey the law and wear helmets. _____
10. Other skateboarding veterans are happy about the change because they own stores selling skateboarding gear. _____

◆ PRACTICE 17-4

Combine each of the following pairs of sentences to form one complex sentence, using the subordinating conjunction that follows each pair. Make sure you include a comma where one is required.

Example: ~~People~~ *Although people* fear dreadful viruses such as Ebola~~.~~*, not* ~~Not~~ enough has been done to give medical supplies to health-care workers in Africa. (although)

1. Many Westerners rarely think about problems in Africa. The lack of money for medical supplies should concern everyone. (although)
2. Diseases in African countries often spread. Hospitals and medical personnel there do not have basic equipment. (because)
3. An outbreak of Ebola virus appeared in northern Uganda in 2000. Doctors and nurses did not have disinfectants and latex gloves. (when)
4. Ebola spreads. Bodily fluids from an infected person come into contact with the skin of a healthy person. (whenever)
5. The Ebola virus makes a patient bleed heavily. Medical workers without gloves are in danger. (because)

6. Health-care workers must be careful in an Ebola outbreak. Their skin never touches the skin of their patients. (so that)
7. The virus is named for the Ebola River in Zaire. It first appeared there in human beings. (because)
8. The Ugandan outbreak raged. Doctors and nurses did their best to stop it. (while)
9. A doctor and several nurses died of the Ebola virus. More than half of the patients survived. (even though)
10. Wealthier nations should help poor countries get basic medical supplies. Medical workers can stop infections like Ebola from spreading. (so that)

◆ PRACTICE 17-5

Use each of the subordinating conjunctions below in an original complex sentence. Make sure you punctuate your sentences correctly.

Example

subordinating conjunction: even though

My little sister finally agreed to go to kindergarten even though she was afraid.

1. *subordinating conjunction:* because

____

____

2. *subordinating conjunction:* after

____

____

3. *subordinating conjunction:* even if

____

____

4. *subordinating conjunction:* until

____

____

5. *subordinating conjunction:* whenever

____

____

C Using Relative Pronouns

Another way to create a complex sentence is to join two simple sentences (independent clauses) with a dependent word called a **relative pronoun** (*who, which, that,* and so on). For example, look at the following pair of sentences.

TWO SENTENCES Tiger Woods had won every major golf tournament by the year 2000. He was only twenty-four years old at the time.

Adding a relative pronoun creates a dependent clause that describes a noun or a pronoun in the independent clause.

COMPLEX SENTENCE Tiger Woods, who was only twenty-four years old at the time, had won every major golf tournament by the year 2000.

NOTE: The relative pronoun always refers to a word in the independent clause. *Who* and *whom* always refers to people. *Which* and *that* refer to things.

Relative Pronouns

that	which	whoever	whomever
what	who	whom	whose

◆ PRACTICE 17-6

In each of the following complex sentences, underline the dependent clause, and circle the relative pronoun. Then, draw an arrow from the relative pronoun to the noun or pronoun it describes.

Example: Indian Americans who wish to maintain their heritage celebrate Diwali, the Festival of Lights.

1. This holiday, which lasts five days, involves special foods, candles, prayers, and presents.
2. The roots of this celebration are in Hinduism, which is one of the oldest religions in the world.

ON THE WEB
For more practice forming complex sentences with relative pronouns, visit Exercise Central *at bedfordstmartins.com/foundationsfirst.*

3. Among the special sweets baked for this holiday are cakes that contain saffron, almonds, butter, and milk.
4. Offerings are made to Krishna, who is one of the three main gods of Hinduism.
5. In the evenings, families light candles that stand for the banishing of ignorance and darkness.
6. On the first day of the celebration, people who want good fortune during the coming year decorate their houses with rice flour and red footprints.
7. The second day celebrates a legend about Krishna, who is said to have rescued sixteen thousand daughters of gods and saints from a demon king.
8. The third and most important day consists of feasts, gifts, pilgrimages to temples, and visits to friends whom the family wishes to see.
9. The fourth day, which is associated with legends about mountains, is considered a good day to start a new project.
10. On the last day, families, who meet to exchange gifts, express their love for one another.

◆ PRACTICE 17-7

Combine each of the following pairs of sentences into one complex sentence, using the relative pronoun that follows each pair.

, which inspired the great American novel Moby Dick,

Example: Whaling ^ was once a part of American culture. ~~Whaling inspired the great American novel *Moby Dick*.~~ (which)

1. In the nineteenth century, American whalers sailed around the world to hunt whales. Their jobs were very dangerous. (who)
2. Whale oil provided light in many American homes. It burns very brightly. (which)
3. Today, U.S. laws protect several whale species. They are considered to be in danger of extinction. (that)
4. Most Americans approve of the U.S. ban on whaling. They no longer need whale oil for lighting. (who)

5. Whale hunting is the focus of a disagreement between the United States and Japan. The two countries have different ideas about whaling. (which)
6. In 2000, Japanese whalers doubled the number of whales they killed. Japanese whalers had been killing some whales every year for research. (who)
7. Some of the whales killed in the Japanese hunt are considered by the U.S. government to be endangered. They include minke whales, Bryde's whales, and sperm whales. (which)
8. Whale meat is a special treat to some Japanese. They consider eating whale to be a part of their culture. (who)
9. The U.S. government argues that the Japanese whale hunt is not for research, but for businesses. The businesses want whale meat to sell to restaurants. (that)
10. Many Japanese do not want the United States to tell them what to do. They may not think the Japanese whale hunt is a good idea. (who)

◆ PRACTICE 17-8

Complete each of the following items by creating a complex sentence. Make sure that each clause of the complex sentence contains a subject and a verb.

Example: A hamburger that *has been barbecued on a grill is one of my favorite things*.

1. When my mother ____.
2. My best friend, who ____.
3. If you ever ____.
4. Although most people ____.
5. My dream job, which ____.

• REVISING AND EDITING

Look back at your response to the Seeing and Writing exercise on page 232. Underline every complex sentence, and circle the subordinating conjunction or relative pronoun.

Now, look at your other sentences. Do you have a pair of simple sentences that could be combined with a subordinating conjunction or a relative pronoun? Would combining sentences make the connection between them clearer? If so, revise the sentence pair to create a complex sentence.

CHAPTER REVIEW

◆ EDITING PRACTICE

Read the following paragraph, and then revise it by using subordinating conjunctions or relative pronouns to combine pairs of short sentences. Be sure to punctuate correctly. The first revision has been done for you.

El Día de los Niños

In 1996, young Latinos held a national summit in Texas, where they established El Día de los Niños. Nine hundred people from twenty-two states came to the summit~~. They came to~~ *so that they could* consider the challenges facing young Latinos. At the summit, parents agreed to be involved with their children. They agreed to teach them about their culture. They also agreed to inspire them with goals and dreams. The community wanted the children to succeed. They said they would set up programs to address issues these young people faced. The National Latino Children's Institute (NLCI) agreed to sponsor El Día de los Niños. They decided that communities should celebrate the day on April 30th. Each city would pass a resolution recognizing the day. The day is supposed to follow principles outlined in the NLCI handbook. In addition to El Día de los Niños, the NLCI sponsors many other programs for Latinos. Each year they choose outstanding community programs. These programs are called La Promesa (The Promise). An example of a Promesa program is the Latino Dollars for Scholars of Rhode Island. It raises money for scholarships. Latino parents also want to support programs like El Día de los Niños. These programs help their young people to honor their cultural background while also succeeding in American society.

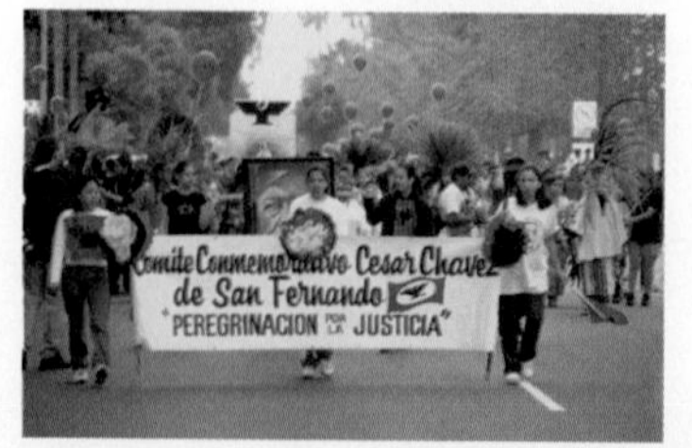

◆ COLLABORATIVE ACTIVITIES

1. Working in a group of four students, develop a list of four well-known actors. Now, working in pairs, write a simple sentence about each actor on the list. Following each sentence, write a subordinating conjunction or relative pronoun in parentheses. When both pairs of students have finished, trade papers. Then, turn each simple sentence into a complex sentence by using the subordinating conjunction or relative pronoun suggested. Finally, get back together with your group, and compare sentences.

   Example
   Samuel L. Jackson was relatively unknown before *Pulp Fiction*. (although)

   Although Samuel L. Jackson was relatively unknown before *Pulp Fiction*, he is now a very popular actor.

2. As a group, decide on the plot for a film starring all the people on the list of actors your group developed in activity 1. Then, write a series of sentences that explain what part each actor plays. Use a subordinating conjunction or relative pronoun in each sentence you write.
3. Using only simple sentences, write a paragraph to a Hollywood studio explaining one reason why the studio should make the film your group created in activity 2. Then, exchange paragraphs with another member of your group so he or she can create complex sentences from the simple sentences you wrote. Work together to edit all four paragraphs, and then turn the best reasons in the paragraphs into a letter arguing for the production of your film.
4. ***Composing original sentences*** Working in a small group, write five complex sentences. Make sure each one contains (1) a dependent clause with a subordinating conjunction, a subject, and a verb, and (2) an independent clause with a subject and a verb. When you have finished, check your sentences to make sure you have punctuated them correctly.

☑ REVIEW CHECKLIST: Writing Complex Sentences

- A complex sentence consists of one independent clause and one or more dependent clauses.
- Subordinating conjunctions—such as *after*, *although*, *because*, *when*, and *while*—are dependent words that can join two simple sentences into one complex sentence. (See 17A.)
- Always use a comma after a dependent clause. Do not use a comma after an independent clause. (See 17B.)
- Relative pronouns are dependent words that can join two simple sentences into one complex sentence. Adding a relative pronoun creates a dependent clause that describes a noun or a pronoun in the independent clause. (See 17C.)

CHAPTER 18

Fine-Tuning Your Sentences

PREVIEW

In this chapter, you will learn

- to vary sentence openings (18A)
- to combine sentences (18B)
- to choose exact words (18C)
- to use concise language (18D)
- to avoid clichés (18E)

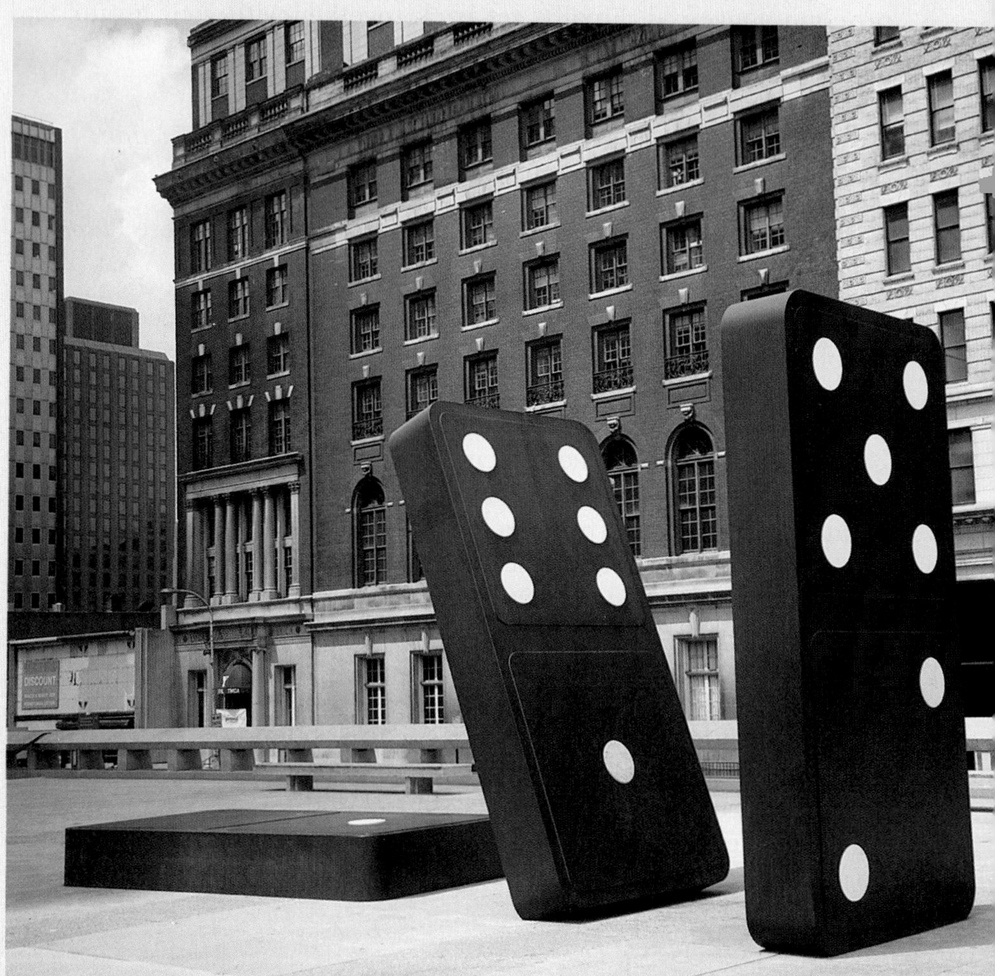

Word Power

subsidize to give financial support to a project

priority an important or urgent goal

commission to place an order for something

SEEING AND WRITING

The picture above shows a large sculpture of three dominoes in downtown Philadelphia. Do you think publicly funded artworks like this one enrich our cities, or do you think the money they cost could be put to better use elsewhere? Look at the picture, and then write a paragraph in which you explain your position.

A Varying Sentence Openings

When all the sentences in a paragraph begin in the same way, the paragraph may seem dull and repetitive. In the following paragraph, for example, every sentence begins with the subject.

> The AIDS quilt contains thousands of panels. Each panel represents a death from AIDS. One panel is for a young college student. Another panel is for an eight-year-old boy. This panel displays his baseball cap. A third panel displays a large picture of a young man. This panel includes a quotation: "Blood saved his life, and it took it away."

Beginning every sentence with the subject makes the paragraph above choppy and monotonous. You can make your paragraphs more interesting by varying your sentence openings.

Beginning with Adverbs

Instead of beginning every sentence with the subject, you can begin some sentences with **adverbs**.

> The AIDS quilt contains thousands of panels. Sadly, each panel represents a death from AIDS. One panel is for a young college student. Another panel is for an eight-year-old boy. This panel displays his baseball cap. Finally, a third panel displays a large picture of a young man. This panel includes a quotation: "Blood saved his life, and it took it away."

Adding the adverbs *sadly* and *finally* makes the paragraph's sentences flow more smoothly.

Beginning with Prepositional Phrases

You can also begin some sentences with **prepositional phrases**. A prepositional phrase is a preposition (*of*, *by*, *along*, and so on) and all the words that go along with it (*of the people*, *by the curb*, *along the road*).

> The AIDS quilt contains thousands of panels. Sadly, each panel represents a death from AIDS. One panel is for a young college student. Another panel is for an eight-year-old boy. In the center, this panel displays his baseball cap. Finally, a third panel displays a large picture of a young man. Under the picture, this panel includes a quotation: "Blood saved his life, and it took it away."

◆ PRACTICE 18-1

Several sentences in the following paragraph contain adverbs and prepositional phrases that could be moved to the beginnings of the sentences. Revise the passage to vary the sentence openings by moving adverbs to the beginnings of two sentences and moving prepositional phrases to the beginnings of three other sentences. Be sure to place a comma after these adverbs and prepositional phrases.

Example: ~~Stock~~ car racing has grown very popular ~~in recent years.~~ [inserted: In recent years, stock]

(1) Stock car racing has grown into a multibillion-dollar sport since the 1940s. (2) NASCAR, the National Association of Stock Car Auto Racing, was formed in 1949. (3) The association originally raced "stock cars"—unmodified Fords and Chevys. (4) The Daytona 500 was the first stock car race televised in 1960. (5) The deaths of three drivers in 1964 led to safety modifications in the stock cars. (6) Only the stock car body remains the same today. (7) Stock cars are still inspected according to strict rules, however. (8) Stock car racing entered a new era in the 1980s after President Reagan came to watch driver Richard Petty's 200th and final win. (9) The death of racing legend Dale Earnhardt in 2000 brought wide attention to the sport. (10) NASCAR jackets, NASCAR books, and other NASCAR merchandise add to the sport's revenues today.

ON THE WEB
For more practice varying sentence openings, visit Exercise Central *at bedford stmartins.com/foundations first.*

◆ PRACTICE 18-2

Listed below are three adverbs and three prepositional phrases. To vary sentence openings in the paragraph that follows, add each of these words or phrases to the beginning of one sentence. Be sure your additions connect the passage's ideas clearly and logically. Remember to add commas where they are needed.

Adverbs	*Prepositional Phrases*
Surprisingly	In one recent study
Unfortunately	For security reasons
Often	In fact

Example: ~~People~~ choose computer passwords that are fairly obvious. [inserted: Often, people]

(1) The most popular computer passwords are the names of family members, sports teams, and pets. (2) These may be easy for users to remember, but they are also easy for others to guess. (3) Experts recommend using a combination of letters and numbers. (4) Few people do this. (5) Most people use the same password over and over, and few keep their passwords secret. (6) Researchers discovered that most people are willing to tell others their passwords. (7) Seventy-one percent told theirs to the interviewer in exchange for a chocolate bar. (8) Many even explained what the passwords meant. (9) The most popular password of

all is not a familiar name like "Jenny" or "Lakers" or "Spot." (10) "Admin" is the most common, but this is not because people choose it. (11) Many computer programs come with this password already installed. (12) People just do not bother to change it.

B Combining Sentences

You can also create sentence variety by experimenting with different ways to combine short simple sentences.

Creating Compound and Complex Sentences

Two simple sentences can be combined into one **compound sentence**.

TWO SIMPLE SENTENCES Many young adults do not vote. They have no right to complain about politicians.

COMBINED (COMPOUND SENTENCE) Many young adults do not vote, so they have no right to complain about politicians.

Two simple sentences can also be combined into one **complex sentence**.

TWO SIMPLE SENTENCES Many young adults do not vote. They do not trust politicians.

COMBINED (COMPLEX SENTENCE) Many young adults do not vote because they do not trust politicians.

Paragraphs like the following one, which consists entirely of short simple sentences, can be very boring.

> Many young adults do not vote. They do not trust politicians. Maybe they are too lazy to vote. Maybe they don't think their votes will do any good. Some vote in national elections. They don't vote in local elections. Others don't vote at all. They have no right to complain about politicians. Voter turnout in the United States is low. It is much higher in many other countries. Citizens of other countries vote in high numbers. They know how important their votes are. Americans should follow their example.

Combining some of the short simple sentences into compound and complex sentences creates a more interesting paragraph.

COMPLEX
Many young adults do not vote because they don't trust politicians.
COMPOUND
Maybe they are too lazy to vote, or maybe they don't think their votes will
COMPOUND
do any good. Some vote in national elections, but they don't vote in local

COMPOUND elections. Others don't vote at all, so they have no right to complain about politicians. COMPLEX Although voter turnout in the United States is low, it is much higher in many other countries. COMPLEX Citizens of these countries vote because they know how important their votes are. Americans should follow their example.

◆ PRACTICE 18-3

The paragraph below consists entirely of short sentences. Add variety to the paragraph by combining several sentences to create compound or complex sentences.

Example: Meetup.com is a popular Web site~~.~~ , and millions ~~Millions~~ of people visit it.

(1) The founder of Meetup.com wanted more people to meet in person. (2) He wanted people to really get to know one another. (3) People were not meeting other people face-to-face. (4) They were spending all their time on the Internet. (5) Meetup.com was designed to solve this problem. (6) People can search for groups by interest. (7) They can browse groups located nearby. (8) Any group can schedule meetings. (9) Groups may list contact information to allow members to meet in person. (10) The site became very popular during the 2004 presidential election. (11) Political groups used it to coordinate rallies. (12) Today, some groups attract people with very specific interests. (13) For example, there is a group for almost every breed of dog. (14) Other groups welcome people with varied interests. (15) Meetup.com provides ways for all kinds of people to meet.

Expanding Simple Sentences

Another way to create sentence variety is by expanding a pair of short simple sentences into one longer simple sentence. You can do this by turning one of the short sentences into a phrase that describes the sentence's subject.

TWO SENTENCES Public libraries provide essential services. They are often underfunded.

COMBINED Often underfunded, public libraries provide essential services. (The phrase *often underfunded* describes *libraries*.)

TWO SENTENCES Gas prices are rising. They are getting higher every day.

COMBINED Gas prices are rising, getting higher every day. (The phrase *getting higher every day* describes *gas prices*.)

TWO SENTENCES William Shakespeare was a great playwright. He wrote comedies, tragedies, and history plays.

COMBINED William Shakespeare, a great playwright, wrote comedies, tragedies, and history plays. (The phrase *a great playwright* describes *William Shakespeare*.)

◆ PRACTICE 18-4

Combine each pair of short sentences into a single longer sentence.

Example: Hummingbirds seem to hover in the air. They flap their wings fifty-five times per second.

Flapping their wings fifty-five times per second, hummingbirds seem to hover in the air.

1. Stephen Colbert is a comedian. He hosts *The Colbert Report*.

____

2. The house needs major repairs. It has been neglected for years.

____

3. Duke basketball games are loud and exciting. They are always sold out.

____

4. The survivors were stranded on a desert island. They considered their options.

____

5. The ten coworkers won the lottery. They were holding the winning ticket.

____

Creating a Series

Another way to vary your sentences is to combine a group of simple sentences into one sentence that includes a **series** of words. This strategy can eliminate a boring string of similar sentences and repetitive phrases.

GROUP OF SENTENCES Consumers are buying more iPods. They are also buying more cell phones. They are buying more bottled water, too.

COMBINED (SERIES OF NOUNS) Consumers are buying more iPods, cell phones, and bottled water.

GROUP OF SENTENCES Samantha registered for fall classes. She bought her books. After that, she went back to work.

COMBINED (SERIES OF VERBS) Samantha registered for fall classes, bought her books, and went back to work.

GROUP OF SENTENCES On his graduation day, Alex was excited. He was also proud. He was a little nervous as well.

COMBINED (SERIES OF ADJECTIVES) On his graduation day, Alex was excited, proud, and a little nervous.

◆ PRACTICE 18-5

Combine each group of simple sentences into a single sentence that uses a series of words.

Example: *Lost* is a popular ABC show. *Desperate Housewives* is another popular ABC program. A third popular show on ABC is *Grey's Anatomy*.

Lost, Desperate Housewives, and Grey's Anatomy are popular ABC shows.

1. Rebecca fed the elephants. She also watered the lemurs. Then, she talked to the children.

____

____

2. College work is interesting. It is also challenging. College work is important too.

____

3. One of America's favorite sports is basketball. Baseball is another favorite sport. Football is also a favorite.

____

4. Reading the newspaper keeps readers informed. The paper can give readers advice. It can entertain them, too.

____

____

5. A ripe cantaloupe smells sweet. It looks orange. It sounds hollow.

____

C Choosing Exact Words

When you revise your writing, check to make sure you have used words that clearly express your ideas. Try to avoid vague, overused words like *good, nice, great, terrific, bad,* and *interesting*. Whenever possible, replace general words like these with more specific ones.

Specific words refer to particular people, places, and things. **General** words refer to entire classes of things. Sentences that contain specific words create a clearer picture for readers than sentences containing only general ones.

In each of the following pairs of sentences, the sentence that includes specific words is clearer and more interesting than the one that does not.

GENERAL The old car went down the street.

SPECIFIC The pink 1959 Cadillac convertible glided smoothly down Main Street.

GENERAL I would like to apply for the job you advertised.

SPECIFIC I would like to apply for the assistant manager's job you advertised in the Sunday *Inquirer*.

ON THE WEB
For more practice choosing exact words, visit Exercise Central *at bedfordstmartins .com/foundationsfirst.*

◆ PRACTICE 18-6

In the following paragraph, underline the specific words that help you picture the scene the writer describes. The first sentence has been done for you.

(1) *Anna in the Tropics*, a Pulitzer Prize–winning play by Nilo Cruz, brings audiences into the simmering heat of a Cuban cigar factory. (2) The story is set in 1929 in Ybor City, a lively immigrant community in Tampa, Florida. (3) This was a time before the rumbling and buzzing of machinery filled most factories. (4) In this hot, humid world, a whirring ceiling fan was sometimes the only sound workers heard as they hunched over their sticky, repetitive work. (5) The play's main action begins when Juan Julian, an elegant man in a sharply pressed white linen suit, arrives to fill the silence. (6) The calm and romantic Julian sits on a wooden platform in the center of the hollow room and reads aloud as the workers roll the moist, brown tobacco leaves with their stained fingers. (7) However, Julian does not read a local newspaper or an instructive textbook; instead, he reads *Anna Karenina*, Tolstoy's novel about doomed

Russian lovers. (8) Thus, he brings Anna to the steamy, tropical coast of Florida. (9) At the same time, he also brings his eager listeners to the harsh, frozen landscape of nineteenth-century Russia. (10) The play *Anna in the Tropics* connects these two worlds.

◆ PRACTICE 18-7

Below are five general words. In the blank beside each, write a more specific word related to the general word. Then, use the more specific word in a sentence of your own.

Example

tool *claw hammer*

Melanie pried the rusty nails out of each weather-beaten board with a claw hammer.

1. game

2. house

3. job

4. exercise

5. car

◆ PRACTICE 18-8

The following paragraph is a vaguely worded job-application letter. On a separate page, rewrite the paragraph, substituting specific words for the general words of the original and adding details where necessary. Start by making the first sentence, which identifies the applicant and the job, more specific. Then, add specific information about the applicant's background and qualifications, expanding the original paragraph into a three-paragraph letter.

I am currently attending college and would like to apply for the position advertised. I have a strong interest in that field. My background includes high school and college coursework that relates to this position. I also have personal experience that would make me a good choice. I am qualified for this job, and I would appreciate the opportunity to be considered. Thank you for your consideration.

D Using Concise Language

Wordy constructions get in the way of clear communication. **Concise language**, however, says what it has to say in as few words as possible. When you revise, cross out words that add nothing to your meaning, and substitute more concise language where necessary.

WORDY In spite of the fact that the British troops outnumbered them, the colonists fought on.

CONCISE Although the British troops outnumbered them, the colonists fought on.

WORDY There are many people who have serious allergies.

CONCISE Many people have serious allergies.

WORDY It is my opinion that everyone should have good health care.

CONCISE Everyone should have good health care.

WORDY During the period of the Great Depression, many people were out of work.

CONCISE During the Great Depression, many people were out of work.

WORDY In the newspaper article, it said the situation was serious.

CONCISE The newspaper article said the situation was serious.

FOCUS Using Concise Language

The wordy phrases listed below add nothing to a sentence. If you spot them in your writing, see if you can delete them or substitute a more concise phrase.

Wordy	*Concise*
It is clear that	(delete)
It is a fact that	(delete)

(continued on following page)

(continued from previous page)

The reason is that	Because
It is my opinion that	(delete)
Due to the fact that	Because
Despite the fact that	Although
At the present time	Today/Now
At that time	Then
In most cases	Usually
In order to	To

Unnecessary repetition—saying the same thing twice for no reason—can also make your writing wordy. When you revise, delete repetition that adds nothing to your sentences.

WORDY Seeing the ocean for the first time was the most exciting and thrilling experience of my life.

CONCISE Seeing the ocean for the first time was the most exciting experience of my life.

WORDY Some people can't make their own decisions by themselves.

CONCISE Some people can't make their own decisions.

WORDY They were repeatedly told time and time again to follow safety procedures.

CONCISE They were repeatedly told to follow safety procedures.

◆ PRACTICE 18-9

✣ **ON THE WEB**
For more practice using concise language, visit Exercise Central *at bedfordstmartins .com/foundationsfirst.*

To make the following sentences more concise, cross out wordy expressions and unnecessary repetition, substituting more concise expressions where necessary.

Example: ~~It is a fact that in~~ *In* April 2006, over a million people marched in support of immigrant rights.

1. Immigrants and their supporters stayed away from work, school, and shopping in order to send a message to Washington.
2. The reason that they were demonstrating was because the federal government wanted to pass new anti-immigration laws.
3. The proposed laws that the government was suggesting would make it much harder for illegal immigrants to live in the United States.
4. Protesters wanted to call attention to immigrants' valuable and useful contributions to the American economy.

5. Participation in the protest varied from state to state and was not the same everywhere.
6. However, some companies did have to close for the day due to the fact that their employees were demonstrating.
7. There were some groups who organized counter-demonstrations.
8. Despite the fact that marchers on both sides were angry, the gatherings remained peaceful and nonviolent.
9. We do not yet know how or in what way these protests will affect future immigration laws in years to come.
10. It is my opinion that at the very least, the "Day Without Immigrants" made Americans think about the valuable contributions their immigrants make.

◆ PRACTICE 18-10

The following passage is wordy. Cross out unnecessary words, and make any revisions that may be needed.

Example: Soap and water can clean hands just as well as antibacterial ~~germ-fighting~~ products can.

(1) A few years ago, antibacterial cleaning products were introduced throughout the American market all across the country. (2) These products are now promoted in commercial advertisements. (3) The ads try to make people afraid and fearful of the germs in their homes. (4) Mothers of children are often the targets of these scary commercials. (5) When the ads first appeared, frightened people immediately began buying antibacterial soap to kill off the invisible germs they could not see.

(6) It is a fact that ordinary soap does not kill every household germ. (7) However, new research suggests that antibacterial products may actually kill good germs that are helpful to human beings. (8) These products may also strengthen dangerous bacteria due to the fact that the strongest germs will still survive. (9) Scientists have warned that children who grow up in germ-free homes may get sick from normally harmless bacteria that do not usually hurt people. (10) Therefore, in the final analysis, antibacterial products may do more harm than good.

E Avoiding Clichés

Clichés are phrases—like *raining cats and dogs* and *hard as a rock*—that have been used so often that people no longer pay attention to them. Clichés do nothing to improve writing; in fact, they may even get in the way of clear communication.

To make your point effectively, try to replace a cliché with a direct statement or a fresh expression.

CLICHÉ After a year of college, I learned that what goes around comes around.

REVISED After a year of college, I learned that if I don't study, I won't do well.

CLICHÉ With the pressures of working and going to school, I feel like a rat in a maze.

REVISED With the pressures of working and going to school, I feel as if I never know where to turn next.

◆ PRACTICE 18-11

Cross out any clichés in the following sentences. Then, either substitute a fresher expression, or restate the idea in more direct language.

Example: A cup of coffee is a needed ~~shot in the arm~~ boost for many hard-working Americans.

(1) Many Americans get their get up and go from a morning cup of coffee. (2) Today, many find that designer coffees go down smooth as silk. (3) In fact, there are more designer coffees than you can shake a stick at. (4) Some coffees are made from beans imported from the four corners of the globe, from such places as Hawaii, Sumatra, and Kenya. (5) Others have flavors that melt in your mouth, such as hazelnut, vanilla, and raspberry. (6) Still other coffee drinks, such as cappuccino, lattes, and frappuccino, include lots of milk straight from the cow. (7) Some designer coffees even combine all three elements—exotic beans, strong flavors, and milk—to create a taste that is out of this world. (8) Consumers pay an arm and a leg for these designer coffees. (9) In fact, Seattle, the home of the Starbucks chain, even went out on a limb and tried to tax designer coffees. (10) Although the Starbucks chain

❖ **ON THE WEB**
For more practice avoiding clichés, visit Exercise Central *at bedfordstmartins.com/foundationsfirst.*

is top dog in the designer coffee business today, other chains and individual coffee shops offer just as much bang for the buck.

• REVISING AND EDITING

Look back at your response to the Seeing and Writing exercise on page 244. Are your sentence openings varied? Have you combined sentences wherever possible? Revise them if necessary. Then, make sure that your language is as exact and concise as possible. Finally, make sure you have not used any clichés in your writing.

CHAPTER REVIEW

◆ EDITING PRACTICE

Read the following paragraph, and then revise it by moving at least two adverbs and at least two prepositional phrases to the beginnings of sentences. Combine sentences wherever possible. Then, revise the paragraph's sentences so that they use exact words and concise language and do not include clichés. The first sentence has been revised for you.

A student searches for a library book

A man does computer research at a library

The Public Library

~~It goes without saying that many~~ ^Many of us cannot imagine living ~~somewhere~~ without a good library. However, it is a fact that libraries were not always as widespread as they are in this day and age. The number and scope of public libraries in America has grown by leaps and bounds over the last two centuries. It all began with Benjamin Franklin. When Franklin helped start The Library Company of Philadelphia in 1731, opportunities to get books were few and far between. In those days, books were very expensive and in short supply. We are fortunately not in the same boat today due to the fact that books are now more widely available. In fact, we rely and depend on libraries more than ever. These days, libraries have more extensive offerings. In addition to books, libraries provide the public with many other things. For example, many public libraries lend DVDs and Books on Tape to borrowers. Some even offer classes for children and adults. Free computer access has recently become one of the libraries' most valued services. It is beyond a shadow of a doubt that our lives would be far less rich without our terrific network of public libraries.

◆ COLLABORATIVE ACTIVITIES

1. Working in a group of three or four students, make a list of every cliché you can think of. Then, working on your own, write new, fresh expressions to replace the clichés on your list. Finally, discuss the new expressions with the rest of the group, and choose your favorites.
2. Working in the same group, write a paragraph containing two or three of the fresh expressions you listed for activity 1. When you have finished, trade paragraphs with another group. Make any revisions in the paragraph that you think are necessary to vary the paragraph's sentences or to eliminate vague language or wordiness. Finally, discuss the changes in your paragraph and the other group's paragraph with the other group.
3. Bring in a paragraph from a newspaper or magazine that you think contains clichés or wordy or vague language. Working in a group, look through the articles everyone has contributed, and choose the paragraph that most needs revision. Then, revise the paragraph to eliminate the problems.
4. ***Composing original sentences*** Working in a group, write five sentences. Be sure to vary your sentence openings, choose exact words, use concise language, and avoid clichés. When you have finished, check your sentences to make sure you have no errors in grammar, punctuation, or spelling.

☑ REVIEW CHECKLIST: Fine-Tuning Your Sentences

- ☐ You can make your sentences more interesting by varying your sentence openings. (See 18A.)
- ☐ Try combining sentences to add variety to your writing. (See 18B.)
- ☐ Try to replace general words with specific ones. (See 18C.)
- ☐ Delete wordy expressions, substituting concise language where necessary. (See 18D.)
- ☐ Avoid clichés (overused expressions). (See 18E.)

CHAPTER

19

Using Parallelism

PREVIEW

In this chapter, you will learn

- to recognize parallel structure (19A)
- to use parallel structure (19B)

SEEING AND WRITING

Look at the picture above, which shows a group of high school seniors at graduation. Then, write a paragraph in which you discuss how you have changed since you graduated from high school.

Word Power

mature full-grown

mellow to gain wisdom and tolerance with age

perspective a view or outlook; the ability to see things as they are

A Recognizing Parallel Structure

Parallelism means using the same kinds of words, phrases, or clauses to express similar ideas.

Paul Robeson was an actor and a singer. (two nouns)

When my brother comes home from college, he eats, sleeps, and watches television. (three verbs)

Elephants are big, strong, and intelligent. (three adjectives)

Jan likes to run, to do aerobics, and to lift weights. (three phrases)

Faulty parallelism occurs when different kinds of words, phrases, or clauses are used to express similar ideas.

NOT PARALLEL I like composition, history, and taking math.

PARALLEL I like composition, history, and math. (All three items in the series are nouns.)

NOT PARALLEL The wedding guests danced, ate, and were drinking toasts.

PARALLEL The wedding guests danced, ate, and drank toasts. (All three verbs are in the past tense.)

NOT PARALLEL The Manayunk bike race is long and climbs steeply and is difficult.

PARALLEL The Manayunk bike race is long, steep, and difficult. (All words in the series are adjectives.)

NOT PARALLEL We can go to the movies, or playing miniature golf is an option.

PARALLEL We can go to the movies, or we can play miniature golf. (Both independent clauses have the same structure.)

◆ PRACTICE 19-1

In each of the following sentences, underline the words, phrases, and clauses that are parallel.

Example: The pitcher threw a tantrum in the dugout, threatened his teammates in the locker room, and called a press conference to criticize the coaches.

1. The tornado was sudden, unexpected, and destructive.
2. Petra ordered an egg-white omelet, a green salad with no dressing, and two slices of cheesecake.
3. After the test, I wanted to lie down and take a nap.

ON THE WEB
For more practice recognizing parallel structure, visit Exercise Central *at bedfordstmartins.com/foundationsfirst.*

4. Chloe had a giant tattoo, a pierced nose, and perfect manners.
5. The store's new owners expanded the parking lot and added a deli counter.
6. The vandals broke the windows, painted graffiti on the walls, and threw garbage on the floor.
7. Before she goes to bed, my niece likes a bath, a story, and a lullaby.
8. The almanac predicted a long, cold, and snowy winter.
9. A beautiful voice and acting ability are important for an opera singer.
10. Maria bought a bicycle, Terence bought a bus pass, and Sheila bought a pair of hiking boots.

◆ PRACTICE 19-2

In each of the following sentences, decide whether the underlined words are parallel. If so, write *P* in the blank. If not, edit the sentence to make the words parallel.

Examples

The contestants argued, sunbathed, and ~~they~~ watched each other suspiciously. ______

A retired Navy SEAL, a river guide, and a corporate trainer were the last players on the island. __P__

1. Hundreds of people wanted to be on a game show that required them to live on an island, catch their own food, and they could not have contact with the outside world. ______
2. The contestants had to be resourceful and healthy. ______
3. The last person on the island would win a car and a million dollars. ______
4. *Survivor* was modeled on a Swedish game show that had forty-eight contestants and a thirty-thousand-dollar prize. ______
5. The contestants held their breath underwater, rowed a canoe, and rats and caterpillars were eaten by them. ______
6. Many viewers decided that it was much more fun to watch *Survivor* than watching summer reruns. ______

7. Each week, the television audience saw one person win a contest and another person would get voted off the island. ______

8. The corporate trainer was manipulative, argumentative, and he often schemed. ______

9. Some viewers loved him, some viewers hated him, but all of them talked about his victory. ______

10. The show became so popular that the contestants came home to endorsements, acting roles, and becoming famous. ______

B Using Parallel Structure

Parallel structure is especially important in *paired items, comparisons*, and *items in a series*.

Paired Items

Use parallel structure for paired items connected by a **coordinating conjunction**—*and, but, for, nor, or, so*, or *yet*.

Jemera takes Alex to day care *and* then goes to work.

You can register to vote now, *or* you can register next week.

Also use parallel structure for paired items joined by **correlative conjunctions**.

Correlative Conjunctions

both . . . and	neither . . . nor	rather . . . than
either . . . or	not only . . . but also	

Darryl is good *both* in English *and* in math.

The movie was *not only* long *but also* boring.

I would *rather* take classes in the morning *than* take them in the afternoon.

Comparisons

Use parallel structure for comparisons formed with *than* or *as*.

It often costs less to rent a house *than* to buy one.

In basketball, natural talent is *as* important *as* hard work.

Items in a Series

Use parallel structure for a series of three or more items.

At the zoo, we saw the penguins walk, swim, and fish.

Unemployment is low because of a healthy economy, low inflation, and high consumer demand.

To do well in school, you should attend class regularly, take careful notes, and set aside time to study.

NOTE: Use commas to separate three or more items in a series. See 31A.

Items in a List

Use parallel structure for items in a numbered or bulleted list.

There are three reasons to go to college:

1. To learn
2. To increase self-esteem
3. To get a better job

ON THE WEB
For more practice using parallel structure, visit **Exercise Central** *at bedfordstmartins.com/foundationsfirst.*

◆ PRACTICE 19-3

In each of the following sentences, underline the parts of the sentence that should be parallel. Then, edit each sentence to make it parallel.

Example: In Spain, people greet each other with two kisses and always ~~starting~~ start with the right cheek.

1. Most countries have a standard greeting: a handshake, a series of kisses, a hug, a bow, or they nod their heads.
2. In the United States, there is no established custom, so often it can get confusing.
3. Most Americans greet each other with a handshake, a cheek kiss, by waving, or a hug.
4. However, greetings vary widely, and predicting them can be difficult.
5. A greeting often depends on people's ages, what their genders are, and the situation.
6. For instance, a man might greet a woman with a kiss but a slap on the back might be his choice for a man.
7. Businesspeople are often more comfortable shaking hands with each other than to kiss each other.

8. In general, most people would rather stick out a hand than they would risk a kiss.
9. An unexpected kiss can result not only in bumped noses but also it can be really embarrassing.
10. For the time being, how to greet others will continue to puzzle people both in their jobs and when they socialize.

◆ PRACTICE 19-4

In each of the following sentences, fill in the blanks with parallel words, phrases, or clauses of your own that make sense in context.

Example: When I am at school, my favorite things to do are *hang out with friends*, *go to the cafeteria*, and *play Frisbee*.

1. My favorite classes are ______________ and ______________.
2. If I could take any class at school, it would be ______________ or ______________.
3. To graduate from school, I will need to be able to ______________, ______________, and ______________.
4. The fields I am most interested in are ______________, ______________, and ______________.
5. Fields that do not interest me at all are ______________ and ______________.
6. When I'm not at school, I enjoy ______________, ______________, and ______________.
7. These activities are [or are not] related to my schoolwork because they are ______________ and ______________.
8. Although these are considered leisure activities, I still learn something from them, such as ______________ and ______________.
9. Next year, I will either ______________ or ______________.
10. After I graduate, I hope to ______________ or ______________.

● **REVISING AND EDITING**

Look back at your response to the Seeing and Writing exercise on page 259. First, underline every pair or series of words, phrases, or clauses. Then, revise your work to make sure you have used parallel words where necessary.

CHAPTER REVIEW

◆ EDITING PRACTICE

Read the following paragraph, which contains examples of faulty parallelism. Then, identify the sentences you think need to be corrected, and make the changes necessary to create parallelism. The first sentence has been edited for you.

The Strangest Instrument

Many people think that electronic musical instruments are a recent invention and ~~produced by~~ a product of modern technology. This is not exactly true, however. In 1919, Leon Theremin, a Russian electronics genius, created an instrument that looked strange and was also strange sounding. Today, this instrument is called a theremin. A theremin looks like a metal box with two antennas. One antenna controls volume, and pitch is controlled by the other. A theremin player simply moves his or her hands over the antennas to change the pitch. Only a very few players are able to make the theremin play the right note and also play it at the right time. Because of its weird outer-space sound, the theremin is used in science fiction movies, horror movies, and movies that involve suspense. Rock bands also use the theremin to get particular sound effects. One of the unusual uses and it was also memorable was in the Beach Boys' 1966 hit song "Good Vibrations." Today, theremin collectors buy early theremins, purchase new theremins, and kits are used to build theremins.

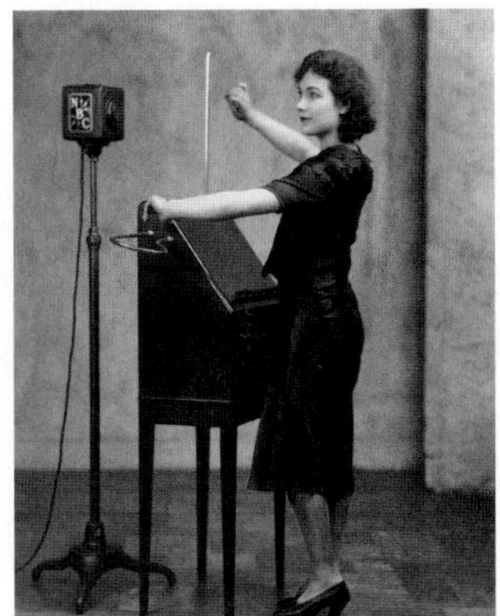

A woman playing a theremin during the 1920s

A theremin

◆ COLLABORATIVE ACTIVITIES

1. Working on your own, write a simple sentence. Then, working in a group of three students, pass the paper to another person in the group, who should add a parallel noun, verb, adjective, phrase, or clause to your sentence. Next, pass the paper to the third person in the group to

check for correct parallelism. Finally, as a group, compare the finished sentences to the originals and discuss the changes.

2. Working on your own, make a list of at least three points to support one of these topics:

   Why I like a particular recording artist

   Why I chose this college

   The most serious problems in my community

   Next, write a sentence that includes all the points on your list. Then, working in a group, read aloud the sentence you wrote. Finally, discuss the parallelism in the finished sentence.

3. Working with three other students, decide on a topic for a paragraph. Next, have each student write a topic sentence for a paragraph on that topic. This sentence should contain parallel words, phrases, or clauses. As a group, choose the topic sentence you like best. Then, support it with additional sentences that include parallel items.

4. ***Composing original sentences*** Working in a group, create five sentences illustrating effective parallelism. When you have finished, check your sentences to correct any errors in grammar, punctuation, or spelling.

✓ REVIEW CHECKLIST: Using Parallelism

- Use the same kinds of words, phrases, and clauses to express similar ideas. (See 19A.)
- Use parallel structure with paired items. (See 19B.)
- Use parallel structure in comparisons formed with *than* or *as*. (See 19B.)
- Use parallel structure for items in a series or in a numbered or bulleted list. (See 19B.)

UNIT REVIEW

Read the following student essay, which contains some sentences that are not as clear or forceful as they could be. Revise the sentences whenever possible by moving prepositional phrases or adverbs to the beginnings of sentences; combining short, choppy sentences; using more exact words; editing out wordy expressions and clichés; and correcting faulty parallelism. The first editing change has been made for you.

A College Bargain

Community colleges have changed since they started at the beginning of the twentieth century. These public colleges began when ~~people involved in education~~ educators decided that some students would benefit from two years of schooling after high school. Veterans began attending community colleges after World War II. There are many students since then who have gone to community colleges to save money. Community colleges today are a big part of the higher education system in the United States.

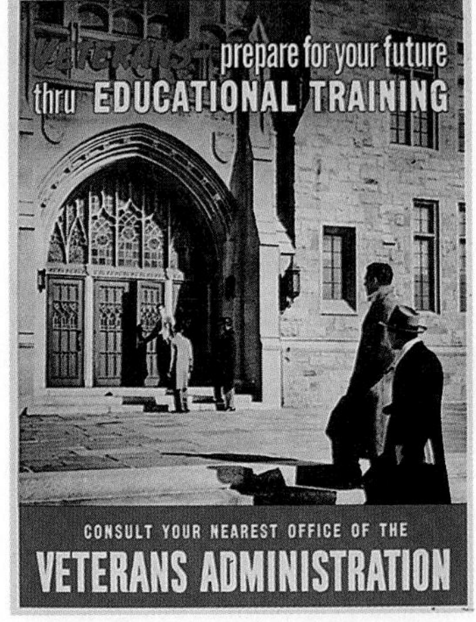

Advertisement for post–World War II college

The first community colleges were often called "junior colleges." They started when it was not enough for some students to get a high school education. Still, some students were not right for four-year colleges. Some students, for example, were preparing for technical jobs. These students needed practical training. They didn't need a four-year diploma. They went to community college for one or two years. Then, jobs were found by them. For example, they might repair radios, or they could become barbers. Many community colleges were "normal schools." Normal schools trained new teachers. There were many people who were out of a job during the Great Depression of the 1930s. Community colleges at that time stressed job preparation.

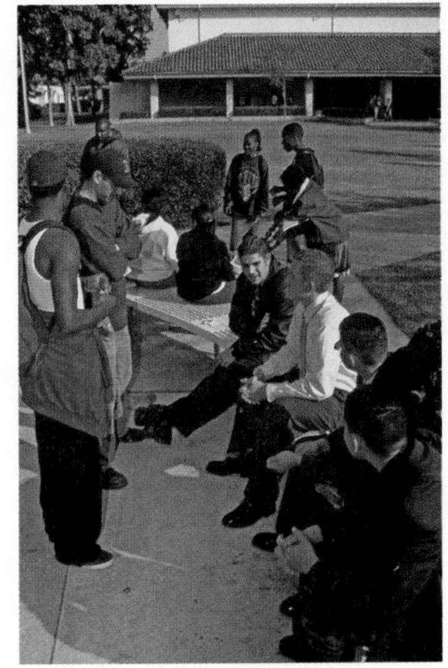

Students at an urban community college.

The next period of community college development began after World War II ended in 1945. Many veterans went to college on the GI Bill. The U.S. government paid $500 for college tuition and fees. This money also covered the cost of books. Veterans often used their GI Bill benefits to go to community colleges. They lived at home while they went to school. Adult education was growing rapidly at this time. Community colleges were good places for adults to continue their education. Most adults wanted to live at home and commute to school. The cost was low for students. The cost was also low for the taxpayers who paid for community colleges.

Community colleges eventually became a way for college students to get a good education, and saving money could be done at the same time. Low cost has always been an important factor for community college students. They can save money by living at home for two years. Tuition is lower there than at four-year colleges. Students who attend community college spend much less on their education than students who choose to attend four-year colleges. Students can transfer to four-year colleges after two years. Community colleges work with four-year colleges to make sure that their students' college credits can be transferred.

Suburban community college

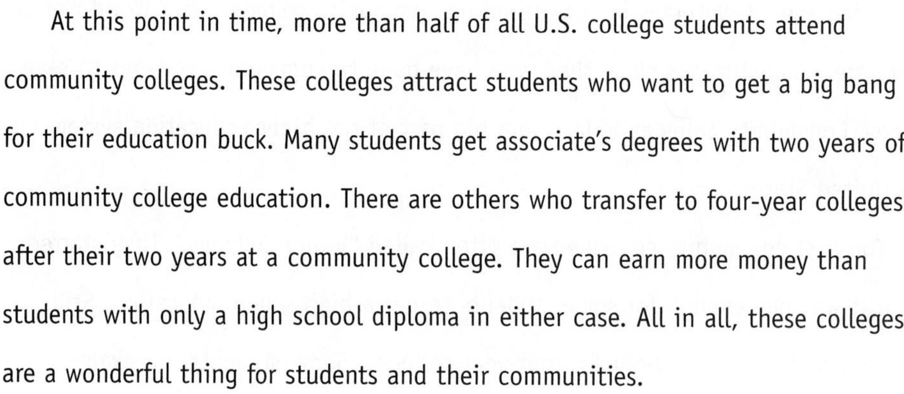

At this point in time, more than half of all U.S. college students attend community colleges. These colleges attract students who want to get a big bang for their education buck. Many students get associate's degrees with two years of community college education. There are others who transfer to four-year colleges after their two years at a community college. They can earn more money than students with only a high school diploma in either case. All in all, these colleges are a wonderful thing for students and their communities.

UNIT FOUR

Solving Common Sentence Problems

CHAPTER

20

Run-Ons

PREVIEW

In this chapter, you will learn

- to recognize two kinds of run-ons: fused sentences and comma splices (20A)
- to correct run-ons in five different ways (20B)

SEEING AND WRITING

The picture above shows Barbie dolls dressed for playing basketball. Do you think Barbie is a positive role model for young girls? Why or why not? Look at the picture, and then write a paragraph in which you answer these questions.

Word Power

role model a person who serves as a model of behavior

A Recognizing Run-Ons

A sentence consists of at least one independent clause—one subject and one verb.

The economy has improved.

A **run-on** is an error that occurs when two sentences (independent clauses) are joined incorrectly. There are two kinds of run-ons: *fused sentences* and *comma splices*.

A **fused sentence** occurs when two sentences are incorrectly joined without any punctuation.

FUSED SENTENCE [The economy has improved] [many people still do not have jobs.]

A **comma splice** occurs when two sentences are incorrectly joined with just a comma.

COMMA SPLICE [The economy has improved], [many people still do not have jobs.]

Word Power

fused melded together

splice a connection made by joining two ends

ON THE WEB

For more practice recognizing fused sentences and comma splices, visit Exercise Central *at bedfordstmartins.com/foundationsfirst.*

◆ PRACTICE 20-1

Some of the sentences below are correct, but others are run-ons (fused sentences or comma splices). In the blank after each sentence, write *C* if the sentence is correct and *RO* if it is a run-on.

Example: Why did we have to leave the game, it was only drizzling? RO

1. San Francisco is a very friendly city it has great restaurants too. ______
2. The Chicago Cubs have not won a World Series since 1908, some people say they are cursed because of a goat. ______
3. Cartoons used to be created with pen and ink today most cartoons are created by computers. ______
4. In his spare time, my brother enjoys designing Web sites. ______
5. I really want to download that song, it sounds like my favorite band. ______
6. Last night's episode of *CSI* was really good it kept me guessing for the entire hour. ______

7. We plan to get to the airport two hours early everyone says the lines are long right before Thanksgiving. ______
8. Yesterday she interviewed for a job with Google, it is the largest search engine on the Internet. ______
9. For years, soccer has been getting more and more popular in the United States. ______
10. I get most of my news from *The Daily Show*, Jon Stewart is informative as well as funny. ______

◆ PRACTICE 20-2

Some of the sentences in the following passage are correct, but others are run-ons (fused sentences or comma splices). In the blank after each sentence, write *C* if the sentence is correct, *FS* if it is a fused sentence, and *CS* if it is a comma splice.

Example: After immigrating to the United States, Cesar Millan lived on the streets for a month, now he has his own TV show. CS

(1) Cesar Millan has earned the name "The Dog Whisperer" because he is able to communicate with dogs. ______ (2) He takes on the most difficult cases, he trains the dogs who pull, bite, jump, and attack. ______ (3) Every week on his TV program *The Dog Whisperer*, Millan shows owners how to behave he also shows them how not to behave. ______ (4) Millan is always calm but firm, and he does not raise his voice. ______ (5) Millan is critical of American dog owners they give their dogs too much power. ______ (6) According to Millan, humans should lead, dogs should follow. ______ (7) Millan grew up in Mexico, and his ideas about dogs come from his childhood experiences there. ______ (8) In Mexico, dogs are dogs humans are humans. ______ (9) Obviously, his methods make sense to Americans, his popularity is growing. ______ (10) Millan used to run his business out of the back of a van, now he owns the Dog Psychology Center and hosts a popular TV show. ______

B Correcting Run-Ons

FOCUS Correcting Run-Ons

You can correct run-ons in five ways.

1. Use a period to create two separate sentences.

   The economy has improved. Many people still do not have jobs.

2. Use a coordinating conjunction (*and, but, or, nor, for, so, yet*) to connect ideas.

   The economy has improved, but many people still do not have jobs.

3. Use a semicolon to connect ideas.

   The economy has improved; many people still do not have jobs.

4. Use a semicolon followed by a transitional word or phrase to connect ideas.

   The economy has improved; however, many people still do not have jobs.

5. Use a dependent word (*although, because, when*, and so on) to connect ideas.

   Although the economy has improved, many people still do not have jobs.

1. Use a period to create two separate sentences. Be sure each sentence begins with a capital letter and ends with a period.

INCORRECT (FUSED SENTENCE) Frances Perkins was the first female cabinet member she was President Franklin D. Roosevelt's secretary of labor.

INCORRECT (COMMA SPLICE) Frances Perkins was the first female cabinet member, she was President Franklin D. Roosevelt's secretary of labor.

CORRECT (TWO SEPARATE SENTENCES) Frances Perkins was the first female cabinet member. She was President Franklin D. Roosevelt's secretary of labor.

◆ PRACTICE 20-3

Correct each of the following run-ons by using a period to create two separate sentences. Be sure both sentences begin with a capital letter and end with a period.

Example: In 1933, Charles Darrow began selling the board game Monopoly~~,~~ . He ~~he~~ adapted this game from several others on the market.

1. Parker Brothers turned down Darrow's first offer to sell Monopoly, the company has now sold over 200 million games.
2. The race car was voted America's favorite token, other Monopoly tokens include the dog, hat, and thimble.
3. Monopoly was recently updated the company asked the public to vote on possible new settings for the game.
4. The original game used locations in Atlantic City the updated version uses landmarks from cities across the country.
5. The old version of Monopoly had railroads on the board, the new version of the game has airports instead.

2. Use a coordinating conjunction to connect ideas. If you want to indicate a particular relationship between ideas—for example, a cause-and-effect link or a contrast—use a coordinating conjunction (*and, but, or, nor, for, so,* or *yet*) to connect the ideas. Always place a comma before the coordinating conjunction.

INCORRECT (FUSED SENTENCE)	"Strange Fruit" is best known as a song performed by Billie Holiday it was originally a poem.
INCORRECT (COMMA SPLICE)	"Strange Fruit" is best known as a song performed by Billie Holiday, it was originally a poem.
CORRECT	"Strange Fruit" is best known as a song performed by Billie Holiday, but it was originally a poem. (ideas are connected with the coordinating conjunction *but*)

◆ PRACTICE 20-4

Correct each of the following run-ons by using a coordinating conjunction (*and, but, or, nor, for, so,* or *yet*) to connect ideas. Be sure to put a comma before each coordinating conjunction.

Example: Most advertisements are found in commercials , but some advertisers use product placement in TV shows and movies.

1. A company pays a fee, a TV or movie character uses its product onscreen.
2. For example, E.T. ate Reese's Pieces the candy company paid the movie's producers.
3. Car companies want to show off a new model, how do they reach their audience?
4. The automaker paid a fee Will Smith drove an Audi in *I, Robot*.
5. Many people ignore commercials, with product placement, advertisers' messages are hard to miss.

3. Use a semicolon to connect ideas. If you want to indicate a close connection—or a strong contrast—between two ideas, use a semicolon.

INCORRECT (FUSED SENTENCE) Jhumpa Lahiri is the daughter of immigrants from Calcutta she won the Pulitzer Prize for her first book.

INCORRECT (COMMA SPLICE) Jhumpa Lahiri is the daughter of immigrants from Calcutta, she won the Pulitzer Prize for her first book.

CORRECT Jhumpa Lahiri is the daughter of immigrants from Calcutta; she won the Pulitzer Prize for her first book. (ideas are connected with a semicolon)

◆ PRACTICE 20-5

Correct each of the following run-ons by using a semicolon to connect ideas. Do not use a capital letter after the semicolon unless the word that follows is a proper noun.

Example: Energy drinks have become popular among teenagers and young adults~~,~~; the high levels of caffeine and various additives give them a boost of energy.

1. Caffeine is the primary ingredient in most energy drinks this chemical stimulates the central nervous system and increases alertness.
2. Energy drinks appeal to students and professionals, they need a quick and easy way to fight mental and physical fatigue.
3. Advertisements for energy drinks stress this boost of energy, Red Bull uses the slogan "Red Bull gives you wings."
4. Red Bull owns approximately 70 percent of the energy drink market, large corporations and many smaller companies also sell energy drinks.

5. Some scientists worry about the dangers of consuming energy drinks studies have so far not shown any serious negative effects.

4. Use a semicolon followed by a transitional word or phrase to connect ideas. To show a specific relationship between two closely related ideas, add a transitional word or phrase after the semicolon.

Some Frequently Used Transitional Words and Phrases

as a result	moreover
finally	nevertheless
for example	now
however	still
in addition	therefore
in fact	thus

INCORRECT (FUSED SENTENCE) The human genome project is very important it may be the most important scientific research of the last hundred years.

INCORRECT (COMMA SPLICE) The human genome project is very important, it may be the most important scientific research of the last hundred years.

CORRECT The human genome project is very important; in fact, it may be the most important scientific research of the last hundred years. (ideas are connected with a semicolon and the transitional phrase *in fact*)

Word Power

genome a complete set of chromosomes and its associated genes

◆ PRACTICE 20-6

Correct each of the following run-ons by using a semicolon, followed by the transitional word or phrase in parentheses, to connect ideas. Be sure to put a comma after the transitional word or phrase.

Example: Author Theodor Seuss Geisel never received his doctorate, ; *however,* the world knows him by his pen name "Dr. Seuss." (however)

1. Geisel wrote many of his books as poetry, he illustrated most of his own books. (in addition)
2. He used a small number of words to encourage children to read his publisher made lists of words for Geisel to use. (in fact)
3. *The Cat in the Hat* uses about 220 different words *Green Eggs and Ham* uses only 50 words. (in contrast)
4. Political issues were very important to Geisel, *The Lorax* warns readers about the dangers facing the environment. (for example)

5. Geisel died in 1991, "Dr. Seuss" lives on in books, in movies, in cartoons, and even in a Broadway musical called *Seussical*. (however)

FOCUS Connecting Ideas with Transitional Words and Phrases

A run-on often occurs when you use a transitional word or phrase to join two sentences but do not include the required punctuation.

INCORRECT (FUSED SENTENCE) It is easy to download information from the Internet however it is not always easy to evaluate the information.

INCORRECT (COMMA SPLICE) It is easy to download information from the Internet, however it is not always easy to evaluate the information.

To correct this kind of run-on, put a semicolon before the transitional word or phrase, and put a comma after it.

CORRECT It is easy to download information from the Internet; however, it is not always easy to evaluate the information.

5. Use a dependent word to connect ideas. When one idea is dependent on another, you can connect the two ideas by adding a dependent word.

Some Frequently Used Dependent Words

after	eventually	when
although	if	which
as	then	who
because	unless	
even though	until	

INCORRECT (FUSED SENTENCE) J. K. Rowling is now the best-selling author of the Harry Potter books not long ago she was an unemployed single mother.

INCORRECT (COMMA SPLICE) J. K. Rowling is now the best-selling author of the Harry Potter books, not long ago she was an unemployed single mother.

CORRECT Although J. K. Rowling is now the best-selling author of the Harry Potter books, not long ago she was an unemployed single mother. (ideas are connected with the dependent word *although*)

INCORRECT (FUSED SENTENCE) Harry Potter is an orphan he is also a wizard with magical powers.

INCORRECT (COMMA SPLICE) Harry Potter is an orphan, he is also a wizard with magical powers.

CORRECT Harry Potter, who is an orphan, is also a wizard with magical powers. (ideas are connected with the dependent word *who*)

◆ PRACTICE 20-7

Correct each of the run-ons below in one of the following ways: by creating two separate sentences, by connecting ideas with a comma followed by a coordinating conjunction, by connecting ideas with a semicolon, or by connecting ideas with a semicolon and a transitional word or phrase. Be sure the punctuation is correct. Remember to put a semicolon before, and a comma after, each conjunctive adverb or transitional expression.

ON THE WEB
For more practice correcting run-ons, visit **Exercise Central** *at bedfordstmartins.com/foundationsfirst.*

Example: All over the world, people eat flatbreads, ^and different countries have different kinds.

1. Flatbread is bread that is flat usually it does not contain yeast.
2. An example of a flatbread in the United States is the pancake, many Americans eat pancakes with maple syrup.
3. The tortilla is a Mexican flatbread tortillas are made of corn or wheat.
4. A favorite flatbread in the Middle East is the pita, it may have a pocket that can be filled with vegetables or meat.
5. Italians eat focaccia, when they put cheese on a focaccia, it becomes a pizza.
6. Crackers are another kind of flatbread the dough is baked until it is crisp.
7. Indian cooking has several kinds of flatbreads, all of them are delicious.
8. Matzoh resembles a large, square cracker, it is a traditional food for the Jewish holiday of Passover.
9. Fifty years ago, most people ate only the flatbreads from their native lands, today flatbreads are becoming popular all over the world.
10. Many American grocery stores sell tortillas, pita, and other flatbreads Americans love flatbread sandwiches.

◆ PRACTICE 20-8

Correct each of the following run-ons (fused sentences and comma splices) by connecting ideas with a dependent word from the list on page 278.

Examples

, which
Text messaging ^ forces people to use abbreviations, ~~it~~ ^ has helped to create a new vocabulary.

because
For instance, ^ typing on a cell phone is difficult, people use phrases like "cul8r."

1. Text messaging has become more popular, people have found more reasons to text.
2. Advertisers and politicians want to reach as many people as possible, they too are finding ways to use text messages.
3. School administrators need to get in touch with parents quickly they are also using text messaging.
4. Text messaging is slow, it has many advantages.
5. People are not always near a computer they can still send and receive mail on their cell phones.
6. In addition, talking on a cell phone may attract attention, using a cell phone to send a text message may not.
7. In fact, students may text each other during tests, schools are starting to ban cell phones.
8. Ultimately, text messaging allows people to receive all kinds of information quickly and easily this is both useful and distracting.
9. Users subscribe to the appropriate service, they can receive sports scores, weather reports, and stock prices as text messages.
10. However, text messaging grows in popularity, users may also end up with ads, spam, and other unwanted mail.

◆ PRACTICE 20-9

Review the five strategies for correcting run-ons. Then, correct each fused sentence or comma splice below in the way that best indicates the relationship between ideas. Be sure to use appropriate punctuation.

; however,

Example: Wangari Maathai grew up poor and female in rural Kenya ^ she went on to earn a PhD in biology and international recognition as a peace activist.

1. For years, Wangari Maathai has successfully fought for peace, prosperity, and democracy in Kenya, she received the Nobel Peace Prize in 2004.
2. She first became known in 1977, she organized the Green Belt Movement.
3. Kenya was developing fast, the disappearance of the forests was causing many problems for the people.
4. People did not have wood for fuel soil erosion was making farming difficult.
5. Maathai saw poor women suffering because of the reckless development, she encouraged them to plant trees.
6. The movement was a great success it has been copied by women in other developing countries.
7. Maathai is a political activist as well as a biology professor and tree-planter, she has also promoted democracy and human rights in Kenya.
8. She helped remove Kenya's corrupt president from power, she risked her own life in the process.
9. In 2002, she was elected to Kenya's parliament she now serves as an assistant environment minister.
10. Many people worry about the world's problems, Maathai continues to fight for positive change.

• REVISING AND EDITING

Look back at your response to the Seeing and Writing exercise on page 271. Can you spot any run-ons? Correct each run-on you find. If you do not find any in your own writing, work with a classmate to correct his or her writing, or edit the work you did for another assignment.

CHAPTER REVIEW

◆ EDITING PRACTICE

Read the following paragraph. Then, revise it by carefully correcting each run-on. Be sure to use appropriate punctuation. The first error has been corrected for you.

Pigeons

To most people, pigeons are an annoyance. Many city parks are full of pigeons; they are also found on building ledges and monuments. Most people think of pigeons as dirty, disgusting creatures that soil cars, sidewalks, and buildings, others recognize their unique abilities. There are several different types of pigeons one of the most interesting, the passenger pigeon, is now extinct. Passenger pigeons were used during wartime they carried messages in capsules attached to their legs. A pigeon named Cher Ami (French for "dear friend") became famous during World War I for saving two hundred American soldiers lost behind enemy lines, he delivered a message with their location. A pigeon with similar abilities is the homing pigeon, it will travel hundreds of miles to get back home. No one is sure how these birds find their way some people think they follow the lines in the earth's magnetic field. Others think they use the sun and stars still others think they simply use their excellent senses of sight, smell, and hearing. There are many interesting facts about pigeons, most people still consider them a nuisance.

Pigeon

◆ EDITING PRACTICE

Read the following paragraph. Then, revise it by carefully correcting each run-on. Be sure to use appropriate punctuation. The first error has been corrected for you.

Stripes

As old-fashioned ~~Old-fashioned~~ ideas about prison life are becoming popular again the striped prison uniform is making a comeback. Most American prisons stopped requiring prisoners to wear stripes more than fifty years ago, at the time, wearing stripes was seen as humiliating. However, there is a reason for bringing back striped uniforms these uniforms can help people identify escaped prisoners. Most people outside of prisons do not wear jumpsuits with horizontal stripes, other popular prison clothing resembles everyday clothing. Denim is a popular uniform material in prisons, denim blends in too well with clothing worn by people on the street. Orange jumpsuits may be noticeable, they also may look too much like the uniforms worn by sanitation workers. Escaped prisoners in striped suits are easy to spot, even at night, the stripes are highly visible. Some people still object to striped uniforms they argue that these uniforms are designed to humiliate prisoners. However, in states using the old uniforms, the stripes are very popular with voters. Many Americans think prison life is too easy, they want prisoners to be treated more harshly. Only time will tell if striped uniforms will catch on nationwide.

Prisoners in the 1932 movie I Am a Fugitive from a Chain Gang

◆ COLLABORATIVE ACTIVITIES

1. Find two examples of run-ons in papers you have written, in your school newspaper, or online; sometimes, errors like these also appear in national magazines or newspapers. Bring your two examples to class. Then, working with another student, exchange examples, and make corrections to the run-ons your classmate found. Finally, discuss your corrections with each other.
2. Copy down four sentences you hear on a television or radio news program, and bring your sentences to class. Then, working in a group of three or four students, pass your sentences to another person in the group. Check to make sure that the sentences you receive contain no run-ons.
3. Working in a group, rewrite the sentences transcribed for activity 2, turning them into run-ons. Then, exchange the incorrect sentences with another group, and correct their sentences. Finally, compare the original sentences with your corrected sentences, and discuss any differences with the other group.
4. ***Composing original sentences*** Working in a group, collaborate to write five sentences on a topic of the group's choice, being careful to avoid run-ons. When you have finished, check your sentences to correct any errors in grammar, punctuation, or spelling.

✓ REVIEW CHECKLIST: Run-Ons

- A run-on is an error that occurs when two sentences are incorrectly joined. (See 20A.)
- A fused sentence occurs when two sentences are incorrectly joined without any punctuation. A comma splice occurs when two sentences are incorrectly joined with just a comma. (See 20A.)
- You can correct a run-on in one of five ways:
  - by creating two separate sentences;
  - by connecting ideas with a comma followed by a coordinating conjunction;
  - by connecting ideas with a semicolon;
  - by connecting ideas with a semicolon and a transitional word or phrase;
  - by connecting ideas with a dependent word. (See 20B.)

CHAPTER 21

Sentence Fragments

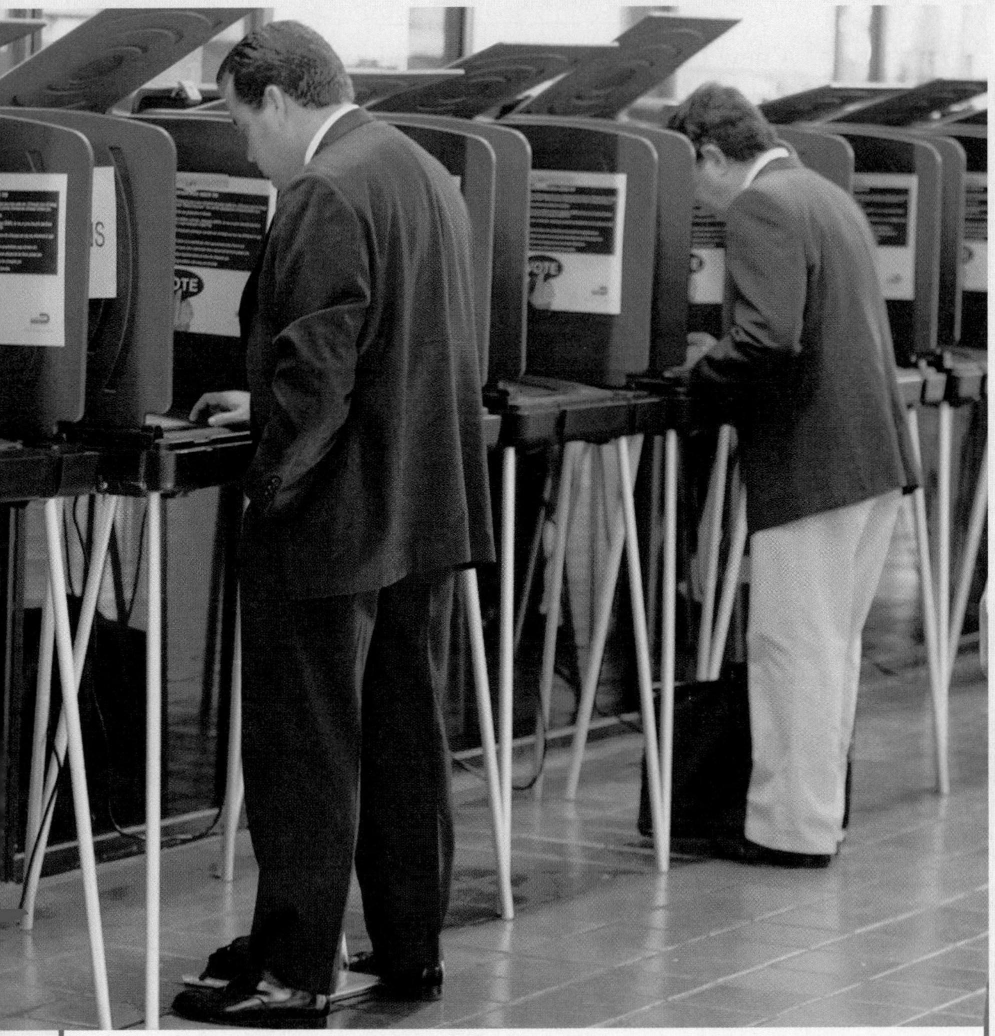

PREVIEW

In this chapter, you will learn

- to recognize sentence fragments (21A)
- to correct phrase fragments (21B)
- to correct incomplete-verb fragments (21C)
- to correct dependent clause fragments (21D)

SEEING AND WRITING

The picture above shows two men at voting machines. Why do you think so many young people don't vote? Look at the picture, and then write a paragraph explaining why you think this situation exists.

Word Power

apathy a lack of interest

apathetic feeling or showing a lack of interest

alienated emotionally withdrawn or unresponsive

A Recognizing Sentence Fragments

A **sentence fragment** is an incomplete sentence. Every sentence must include at least one subject and one verb, and every sentence must express a complete thought. If a group of words does not do *all* these things, it is a fragment and not a sentence—even if it begins with a capital letter and ends with a period. The following is a complete sentence.

SENTENCE A new U.S. president (S) was elected (V). (includes both a subject and a verb and expresses a complete thought)

Because a sentence must have both a subject and a verb and must also express a complete thought, the following groups of words are not sentences.

FRAGMENT (NO VERB) A new U.S. president. (What point is being made about the president?)

FRAGMENT (NO SUBJECT) Was elected. (Who was elected?)

FRAGMENT (INCOMPLETE THOUGHT) When the new U.S. president was elected. (What happened when the new president was elected?)

◆ PRACTICE 21-1

❖ **ON THE WEB**
For more practice recognizing sentence fragments, visit **Exercise Central** *at bedford stmartins.com/foundations first.*

Each of the following items is a fragment because it lacks a subject, a verb, or both. Add any words needed to turn the fragment into a complete sentence.

Example: The sparkling lake.

The sparkling lake reflected the sunlight.

1. Eats sunflower seeds for breakfast.

2. A terrible scream.

3. Ate quickly, hoping to win the pie-eating contest.

4. Answered the question.

5. Wore a purple and pink tutu and waved a magic wand.

6. Harold and Sally, the king and queen of the prom.

7. The old house on the hill, dark and empty.

8. The last two pieces of dental floss.

9. Skidded off the road into a ditch.

10. The leaves with their beautiful fall colors.

FOCUS **Identifying Sentence Fragments**

In paragraphs and in longer pieces of writing, sentence fragments sometimes appear next to complete sentences. You can often correct a sentence fragment by attaching it to a nearby sentence that includes the missing subject or verb. In the following example, a fragment appears right after a complete sentence.

COMPLETE SENTENCE — FRAGMENT

Okera majored in two subjects. English and philosophy.

To correct the fragment, attach it to the complete sentence that contains the missing subject (*Okera*) and verb (*majored*).

Okera majored in two subjects, English and philosophy.

◆ PRACTICE 21-2

In the following passage, some of the numbered groups of words are missing a subject, a verb, or both. First, identify each fragment by labeling it *F*. Next, decide how each fragment could be attached to a nearby word group to create a complete new sentence. Finally, rewrite the entire passage, using complete sentences, on the lines provided.

Example: Some people use lip balm. ____ To keep their lips from drying out. F

Rewrite: Some people use lip balm to keep their lips from drying out.

(1) According to some users of lip balm. ____ (2) This product is addictive. ____ (3) The purpose of lip balm. ____ (4) Is to keep the lips. ____ (5) From getting chapped. ____ (6) Can people become dependent on lip balm? ____ (7) Some users say yes. ____ (8) However, the makers of lip balm. ____ (9) Strongly disagree. ____ (10) They say it is completely safe. ____

Rewrite:

◆ PRACTICE 21-3

In the following paragraph, some of the numbered groups of words are missing a subject, a verb, or both. First, underline each fragment. Then, decide how each fragment could be attached to a nearby word group to create a complete new sentence. Finally, rewrite the entire paragraph, using complete sentences, on the lines provided.

Example: Ray Romano did the voice for Manny the Mammoth in the movie *Ice Age*. And also in the sequel.

Rewrite: Ray Romano did the voice for Manny the Mammoth in the movie Ice Age and also in the sequel.

(1) The main characters in most animated movies nowadays. (2) Have the voices of celebrities. (3) Producers want stars in a film. (4) To bring in a bigger audience. (5) And to increase the movie's chances of success. (6) Generally, famous names do not matter to children. (7) But are

important to adults. (8) For instance, fans of Willem Dafoe and Ellen DeGeneres did not go to see *Finding Nemo* to watch cartoon fish. (9) But to hear their favorite actors' voices. (10) All in all, celebrity voices help make animated films more popular.

Rewrite:

____

____

____

____

____

____

____

B Phrase Fragments

Every sentence must include a subject and a verb. A **phrase** is a group of words that is missing a subject or a verb or both, so it cannot stand alone as a sentence. When you punctuate a phrase as if it is a sentence, you create a fragment.

To correct a phrase fragment, add the words needed to make it a complete sentence. (You will often find these words in a nearby sentence.)

PHRASE FRAGMENT

INCORRECT The horse jumped. Over the fence.

CORRECT The horse jumped over the fence.

PHRASE FRAGMENT

INCORRECT The *Lethal Weapon* movies have two stars. Mel Gibson and Danny Glover.

CORRECT The *Lethal Weapon* movies have two stars, Mel Gibson and Danny Glover.

INCORRECT Sequels have been made for many popular action movies.

PHRASE FRAGMENT

Such as *Lethal Weapon*, *Die Hard*, *Terminator*, and *The Matrix*.

CORRECT Sequels have been made for many popular action movies, such as *Lethal Weapon*, *Die Hard*, *Terminator*, and *The Matrix*.

PHRASE FRAGMENT

INCORRECT He made the decision. To become a paralegal.

CORRECT He made the decision to become a paralegal.

ON THE WEB
For more practice correcting phrase fragments, visit **Exercise Central** *at bedfordstmartins.com/foundationsfirst.*

◆ PRACTICE 21-4

Each of the following phrases is a fragment because it lacks a subject, a verb, or both. Correct each fragment by adding any words needed to turn the fragment into a complete sentence.

Example: With a loud crash.

The bookcase fell to the floor with a loud crash.

1. In a ten-story apartment building.

2. On the ledge outside the window.

3. To borrow a car and drive to Toledo.

4. At the beginning of football season.

5. Such as a bag of pretzels and a giant bottle of Gatorade.

6. During the announcement.

7. Such as a brand-new washing machine.

8. With a pile of books in her arms.

9. To see the first flash of lightning.

____

____

10. Along the banks of the river.

____

____

◆ PRACTICE 21-5

In the following paragraph, some of the numbered groups of words are phrase fragments. First, identify each fragment by labeling it *F*. Then, decide how each fragment could be attached to a nearby word group to create a complete new sentence. Finally, rewrite the entire paragraph, using complete sentences, on the lines provided.

Example: Mexican artist Frida Kahlo lived and painted. ____ In the first half of the twentieth century. __F__

Rewrite: *Mexican artist Frida Kahlo lived and painted in the first half of the twentieth century.*

(1) Frida Kahlo is known to many for her marriage to fellow artist Diego Rivera. ____ (2) A mural painter. ____ (3) She is also famous for her many self-portraits. ____ (4) In these portraits, Kahlo is usually dressed up. ____ (5) In colorful clothes. ____ (6) In her portraits, she is adorned. ____ (7) With jewelry and flowers. ____ (8) The scenes that surround her are often exotic. ____ (9) With a dreamlike atmosphere. ____ (10) Kahlo's paintings express the reality of her own life. ____ (11) A life of great beauty and great pain. ____

Rewrite:

____

____

____

____

____

____

____

◆ PRACTICE 21-6

In the following paragraph, some of the numbered groups of words are phrase fragments. First, underline each fragment. Then, decide how each fragment could be attached to a nearby word group to create a complete new sentence. Finally, rewrite the entire paragraph, using complete sentences, on the lines provided.

Example: In 1883, the volcanic island of Krakatoa erupted. ~~Off~~ off the coast of Java.

Rewrite: *In 1883, the volcanic island of Krakatoa erupted off the coast of Java.*

(1) To this day, the eruption of Krakatoa remains one of the worst disasters. (2) In recorded history. (3) Nearly forty thousand people died. (4) The eruption caused tsunamis. (5) Giant tidal waves one hundred feet high. (6) In addition, the force of the eruption caused changes in climate. (7) Around the world. (8) Writer Simon Winchester researched this disaster. (9) In 2003, he published a best-selling book. (10) *Krakatoa: The Day the World Exploded.*

Rewrite:

____

____

____

____

____

____

C Incomplete-Verb Fragments

Every sentence must include a subject and a verb. If the verb is missing or incomplete, a word group is a fragment, not a sentence. **Participles**—verb forms that function as adjectives—are not complete verbs. They need **helping verbs** to complete them. There are two kinds of participles.

- **Present participles** always end in *-ing*. A present participle, such as *rising*, cannot stand alone in a sentence without a helping verb (is *rising*, was *rising*, were *rising*, and so on). When you use a present participle without a helping verb, you create a fragment.

FRAGMENT

INCORRECT The moon was full and round. Rising over the ocean.

One way to correct the fragment is to attach it to the sentence that comes right before it.

CORRECT The moon was full and round, rising over the ocean.

Another way to correct the fragment is to add a subject and a helping verb.

CORRECT The moon was full and round. It was rising over the ocean.

FOCUS Using Helping Verbs with Present Participles

To serve as the main verb of a sentence, a present participle must be completed by a form of the verb *be*.

Helping Verb	+	*Present Participle*	=	*Complete Verb*
am		rising		am rising
is		rising		is rising
are		rising		are rising
was		rising		was rising
were		rising		were rising
has been		rising		has been rising
have been		rising		have been rising
had been		rising		had been rising

FOCUS Incomplete-Verb Fragments with *Being*

The present participle *being* is often used incorrectly as if it were a complete verb.

INCORRECT I was twenty minutes late for my job interview. The result being that I didn't get the job.

To correct this kind of fragment, substitute a form of the verb *be* that can stand alone in a sentence—for example, *is*, *was*, *are*, or *were*.

CORRECT I was twenty minutes late for my job interview. The result was that I didn't get the job.

- **Past participles** often end in *-ed*, but irregular past participles may have other endings. A past participle, such as *hidden*, cannot stand alone in a sentence without a helping verb (*is hidden*, *was hidden*, *had hidden*, and so on). When you use a past participle without a helping verb, you create a fragment.

FRAGMENT

INCORRECT I saw the sun. Hidden behind the clouds.

One way to correct the fragment is to attach it to the sentence that comes right before it.

CORRECT I saw the sun, hidden behind the clouds.

Another way to correct the fragment is to add a subject and a helping verb.

CORRECT I saw the sun. It was hidden behind the clouds.

FOCUS Using Helping Verbs with Past Participles

To serve as the main verb of a sentence, a past participle must be completed by a form of the verb *be* or *have*.

Helping Verb(s) +	*Past Participle* =	*Complete Verb*
am	hidden	am hidden
is	hidden	is hidden
are	hidden	are hidden
was	hidden	was hidden
were	hidden	were hidden
has	hidden	has hidden
have	hidden	have hidden
had	hidden	had hidden
has been	hidden	has been hidden
have been	hidden	have been hidden
had been	hidden	had been hidden

◆ PRACTICE 21-7

ON THE WEB
For more practice correcting incomplete verbs, visit **Exercise Central** *at bedford stmartins.com/foundations first.*

Each of the following is a fragment because it does not include a complete verb. Correct each fragment by adding a subject and a helping verb.

Example: Driving a new car that runs on hydrogen fuel.

Revised: *My father is now driving a new car that runs on hydrogen fuel.*

1. Watching the season finale of *The Apprentice*. ______________

2. Jogging in the park all morning with her dog. ______________

3. Been in this business for over twenty years. ______________

4. Looking for books in Spanish at the new bookstore. ______________

5. Wearing jeans to school. ______________________________

____

6. Given to me by my grandparents. ______________________

____

7. Gone to San Francisco for the summer. __________________

____

8. Telling me to get a haircut. ___________________________

____

9. Almost forgotten how to ride a bicycle. __________________

____

10. Always complaining about the homework. ________________

____

D Dependent Clause Fragments

Every sentence must include a subject and a verb and express a complete thought. A **dependent clause** is a group of words that is introduced by a dependent word, such as *although*, *because*, or *after*. A dependent clause includes a subject and a verb, but it does not express a complete thought, so it cannot stand alone as a sentence.

The following dependent clause is incorrectly punctuated as if it were a sentence.

FRAGMENT After Jeanette got a full-time job.

This sentence fragment includes a subject (*Jeanette*) and a complete verb (*got*), but it does not express a complete thought. Readers expect the thought to continue, but it stops short. What happened after Jeanette got a full-time job? Was the result positive or negative? To turn this fragment into a sentence, you need to complete the thought.

SENTENCE After Jeanette got a full-time job, she was able to begin paying off her loans.

- Some dependent clauses are introduced by dependent words called **subordinating conjunctions** (*although*, *because*, *if*, and so on).

  The following dependent clause is punctuated as if it were a sentence.

  FRAGMENT Although many students study French in high school.

  This sentence fragment includes a subject (*many students*) and a complete verb (*study*), but it does not express a complete thought.

To correct this fragment, add an **independent clause** (a complete sentence) to complete the thought and finish the sentence.

SENTENCE Although many students study French in high school, Spanish is more popular.

- Other dependent clauses are introduced by dependent words called **relative pronouns** (*who, which, that,* and so on).

The following dependent clauses are punctuated as if they were sentences.

FRAGMENT Marc Anthony, who is Puerto Rican.

FRAGMENT Zimbabwe, which was called Rhodesia at one time.

FRAGMENT One habit that has been observed in many overweight children.

Each of these three sentence fragments includes a subject (*Marc Anthony, Zimbabwe, One habit*) and a complete verb (*is, was called, has been observed*). However, they are not sentences because they do not express complete thoughts.

To correct each of these fragments, add the words needed to complete the thought.

SENTENCE Marc Anthony, who is Puerto Rican, records in both English and Spanish.

SENTENCE Zimbabwe, which was called Rhodesia at one time, is a country in Africa.

SENTENCE One habit that has been observed in many overweight children is excessive television viewing.

◆ PRACTICE 21-8

Turn each of the following dependent clause fragments into a complete sentence by adding a group of words that completes the thought.

Example: Because he wanted to get married.

Revised: *He needed to find a job because he wanted to get married.*

1. This young man, who has a very promising future.

Revised: ______

2. After the music and dancing had stopped.

Revised: ______

ON THE WEB
For more practice correcting dependent clause fragments, visit Exercise Central *at bedfordstmartins.com/foundationsfirst.*

3. A box turtle that was trying to find water.

Revised: ______________________________

____

4. Even though hang gliding is a dangerous sport.

Revised: ______________________________

____

5. Although most people think of themselves as good drivers.

Revised: ______________________________

____

6. Parents who do not set limits for their children.

Revised: ______________________________

____

7. Frequent-flier miles, which can sometimes be traded for products as well as for airline tickets.

Revised: ______________________________

____

8. Whenever Margaret got up late.

Revised: ______________________________

____

9. While she searched the crowd frantically.

Revised: ______________________________

____

10. A politician, who has to raise huge amounts of money to run for office.

Revised: ______________________________

____

◆ PRACTICE 21-9

All of the following are fragments. Turn each fragment into a complete sentence, and write the revised sentence on the line below the fragment. Whenever possible, try creating two different revisions.

Example: When a huge bat flew out of the closet.

Revised: *I was just climbing into bed when a huge bat flew out of the closet.*

Revised: *When a huge bat flew out of the closet, I decided to check out of the hotel.*

1. Finding a twenty-dollar bill on the sidewalk.

   Revised: ______________________________

   Revised: ______________________________

2. Disappeared without a trace.

   Revised: ______________________________

   Revised: ______________________________

3. The tiny plastic ballerina spinning inside the music box.

   Revised: ______________________________

   Revised: ______________________________

4. Anyone who has ever worked for tips.

   Revised: ______________________________

   Revised: ______________________________

5. The basket, which was filled with exotic tropical fruits.

   Revised: ______________________________

   Revised: ______________________________

6. Banned from the sport for life.

   Revised: ______________________________

   Revised: ______________________________

7. Without a hat or coat.

   Revised: ______________________________

   ____

   Revised: ______________________________

   ____

8. Continuing to play with her toys.

   Revised: ______________________________

   ____

   Revised: ______________________________

   ____

9. Returning to the scene of the crime.

   Revised: ______________________________

   ____

   Revised: ______________________________

   ____

10. Below the surface of the muddy brown river.

   Revised: ______________________________

   ____

   Revised: ______________________________

   ____

• REVISING AND EDITING

Look back at your response to the Seeing and Writing exercise on page 285. Is every sentence complete? Check every sentence to be sure that it has a subject and a verb, that the verb is complete, and that the sentence expresses a complete thought.

If you spot a fragment, revise it by adding the words needed to make it a complete sentence. (Remember, you may be able to correct a fragment simply by attaching it to a nearby sentence.) If you do not find any fragments in your own writing, work with a classmate to correct his or her writing, or edit work that you did for another assignment.

CHAPTER REVIEW

◆ EDITING PRACTICE

Read the following paragraph, and underline each fragment. Then, correct the fragment by adding the words necessary to complete it or by attaching the fragment to a nearby sentence. The first error has been corrected for you.

Outsider Art

Over the past few decades~~.~~ , more ~~More~~ and more people have been recognizing the artwork of nonmainstream artists. Some of these works are called "outsider art." This is valuable and unusual art. That is created by untrained or self-taught artists. Because these artists have not attended art school. They are not familiar with artistic styles and traditions. Their work seems almost childlike. But very original. They make up their own techniques and often choose unusual materials. Such as plywood or plastic bottles. Many outsider artists live on the margins of society. Away from cultural influences. Usually, they are not focused. On showing or selling their art. Today, outsider art which is becoming more popular among art collectors. Galleries and Web sites are now dedicated to promoting outsider art. In addition, outsider artists showing their work at major museums.

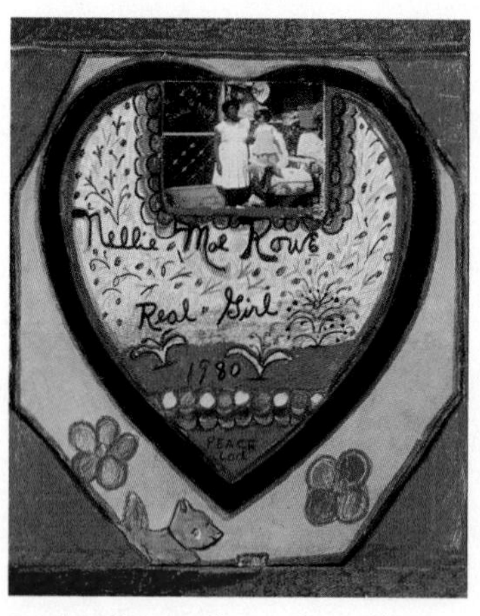

Real Girl, *outsider art by Nellie Mae Rowe, 1980*

◆ EDITING PRACTICE

Read the following paragraph, and underline each fragment. Then, correct the fragment by adding the words necessary to complete it or by attaching the fragment to a nearby sentence. The first error has been corrected for you.

The Americans with Disabilities Act

Many people living in the United States are familiar with the Americans with Disabilities Act (ADA)~~.~~ , which ~~Which~~ protects the rights of people with disabilities. The ADA was created to guarantee disabled people greater access to all parts of society. Including employment, transportation, and telecommunications. The ADA took many years to develop. During the 1970s and 1980s, activism in the disabled community grew. Inspired by the civil rights movement. More people became involved in the fight. For the rights of people with disabilities. When it finally passed in 1990, the ADA was a great victory. For all people with disabilities. The mentally as well as the physically challenged. Although the ADA does not guarantee success for all people with disabilities. It promises them a fair chance. For many, this means an opportunity. To work and to be independent. Ultimately, the ADA benefits everyone. Many accommodations required by the ADA make workspaces and businesses safer for all people. Those with and those without disabilities. Americans also strengthen their communities and their democracy. When they allow everyone to participate.

Disabled student receiving diploma

◆ COLLABORATIVE ACTIVITIES

1. Copy down three fragments that you find in magazine or newspaper advertisements, and bring them to class. Then, exchange fragments with another student. Correct the fragments you receive, and discuss your corrections with your classmate.
2. Bring a newspaper to class. Working in a group of three or four students, find three headlines that are fragments. Then, working on your own, turn each fragment into a complete sentence. Finally, compare your sentences with those written by other students in your group, and choose the best sentence for each headline.
3. Discuss some of the fragments you worked on in activities 1 and 2. Why were fragments used in the advertisements and the headlines? How are these fragments different from the complete sentences you wrote? Which work more effectively? Why?
4. ***Composing original sentences*** Working in a group, collaborate to create five sentences that contain no fragments. Make sure that at least one sentence contains a dependent clause, at least one contains a present participle, and at least one contains a past participle. When you have finished, check your sentences to correct any errors in grammar, punctuation, or spelling.

☑ REVIEW CHECKLIST: Sentence Fragments

- A sentence fragment is an incomplete sentence. Every sentence must include a subject and a verb and must express a complete thought. (See 21A.)
- Phrases cannot stand alone as sentences. (See 21B.)
- Every sentence must include a complete verb. (See 21C.)
- Dependent clauses cannot stand alone as sentences. (See 21D.)

CHAPTER

22 Subject-Verb Agreement

PREVIEW

In this chapter, you will learn

- to understand subject-verb agreement (22A)
- to understand agreement with *be*, *have*, and *do* (22B)
- to understand agreement with compound subjects (22C)
- to understand agreement when words come between the subject and the verb (22D)
- to understand agreement with indefinite pronouns as subjects (22E)
- to understand agreement when the verb comes before the subject (22F)

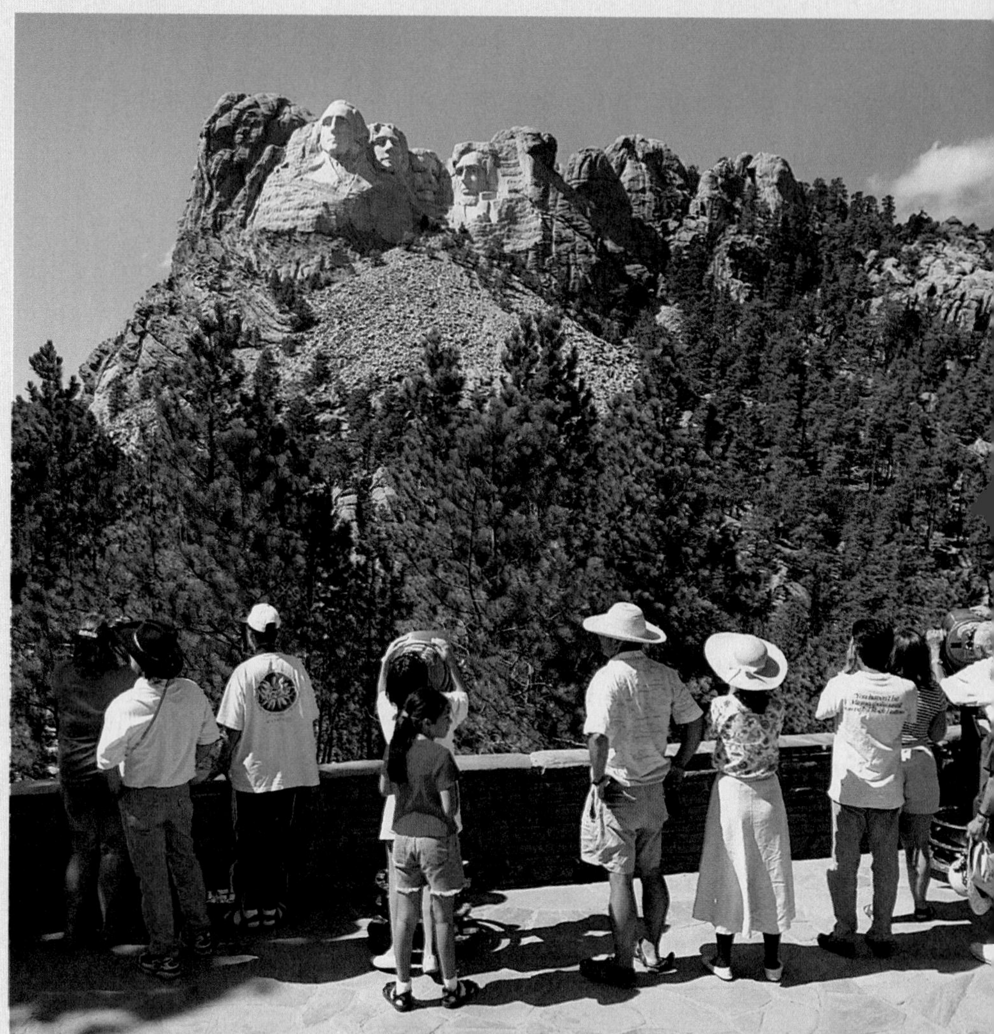

Word Power

monument a structure built as a memorial

observer someone who watches

symbol a thing that represents something else

SEEING AND WRITING

The picture above shows the Mount Rushmore National Memorial in the Black Hills of South Dakota. Look at the picture, and then write a paragraph describing what you see. Use present tense verbs throughout your paragraph.

A Understanding Subject-Verb Agreement

A sentence's subject (a noun or a pronoun) and verb must **agree**: singular subjects take singular verbs, and plural subjects take plural verbs.

Most subject-verb agreement problems occur in the present tense, where third-person singular subjects (*he*, *she*, and *it*) require special verb forms. *Regular verbs* in the *present tense* form the third-person singular by adding *-s* or *-es* to the **base form** of the verb (the present tense form of the verb that is used with *I*).

Subject-Verb Agreement

	Singular	***Plural***
1st person	I walk	Alex and I/we walk
2nd person	you walk	you walk
3rd person	he/she/it walks	they walk
	the woman walks	the women walk
	Alex walks	Alex and Sam walk

◆ PRACTICE 22-1

Underline the correct form of the verb in each of the following sentences. Make sure that the verb agrees with the subject.

Example: Every Valentine's Day, people (buys/buy) millions of little Conversation Hearts for their sweethearts.

(1) Most people (knows/know) the New England Confectionery Company by the name NECCO. (2) This long-established candy company (makes/make) NECCO Wafers, Sweethearts Conversation Hearts, and Sky Bar Candy Bars, as well as many other sweets. (3) The wafers and hearts (remains/remain) NECCO's best-known products. (4) Year after year, the recipe (stays/stay) the same. (5) As a result, the sugary candies (tastes/taste) the same as they did 150 years ago. (6) They also (continues/continue) to come in the same colors. (7) Surprisingly, NECCO still (produces/produce) its candy in Massachusetts, where the company was founded in 1847. (8) NECCO regularly develops new products and (updates/update) the sayings on its Conversation Hearts. (9) The playful

✣ **ON THE WEB**
For more practice understanding subject-verb agreement, visit Exercise Central *at bedfordstmartins .com/foundationsfirst.*

phrases (continues/continue) to be especially popular on Valentine's Day. (10) As long as Valentine's Day (exists/exist), it seems NECCO will exist as well.

◆ PRACTICE 22-2

Fill in the blank with the correct present tense form of the verb in parentheses.

Example: Hiroshima's Peace Memorial Park ___covers___ (cover) a large area of city land.

(1) In many ways, present-day Hiroshima, Japan, ____________ (seem) like any other busy, modern city. (2) Tall buildings, buses, and crowds ____________ (fill) the active downtown. (3) On summer nights, the baseball stadium ____________ (roar) with the sounds of excited Hiroshima Carp fans. (4) However, powerful reminders of the past ____________ (exist) as well. (5) The Peace Memorial Park and Museum now ____________ (stand) where the atomic bomb struck in 1945. (6) The park ____________ (contain) dozens of monuments, statues, ponds, and memorials, including the Children's Peace Monument. (7) This monument ____________ (honor) Sadako, a child who died of leukemia as a result of the bomb's radiation. (8) Every year, schoolchildren ____________ (show) their support for world peace by bringing millions of paper cranes to this statue of Sadako. (9) At the other end of the park, the Peace Memorial Museum ____________ (provide) information about World War II, the development of the atomic bomb, the bomb's effects, and the peace movement. (10) By maintaining this large memorial park, the people of Hiroshima ____________ (hope) to stop a similar event from happening again.

B *Be, Have, and Do*

The verbs *be, have,* and *do* are irregular in the present tense. The best way to avoid problems with these verbs is to memorize their forms.

Subject-Verb Agreement with Be

	Singular	**Plural**
1st person	I am	we are
2nd person	you are	you are
3rd person	he/she/it is	they are
	Tran is	Tran and Ryan are
	the boy is	the boys are

Subject-Verb Agreement with Have

	Singular	**Plural**
1st person	I have	we have
2nd person	you have	you have
3rd person	he/she/it has	they have
	Shana has	Shana and Robert have
	the student has	the students have

Subject-Verb Agreement with Do

	Singular	**Plural**
1st person	I do	we do
2nd person	you do	you do
3rd person	he/she/it does	they do
	Ken does	Ken and Mia do
	the book does	the books do

◆ PRACTICE 22-3

Fill in the blank with the correct present tense form of the verb *be*.

Example: The Tour de France ____is____ a popular bicycle race.

1. Every July, the Tour de France __________ televised all over the world.
2. Lance Armstrong __________ a seven-time winner of the Tour de France.
3. Because of him, many people __________ fans of this event.
4. They __________ proud of him for overcoming cancer.
5. They like to watch him because they know he __________ not a quitter.

ON THE WEB
For more practice avoiding agreement problems with **be, have,** *and* **do,** *visit* **Exercise Central** *at bedfordstmartins .com/foundationsfirst.*

◆ PRACTICE 22-4

Fill in the blank with the correct present tense form of the verb *have*.

Example: You ___have___ to be cautious when shopping for a used car.

1. An educated car shopper __________ a better chance of getting a high-quality vehicle.
2. The car salespeople __________ their own interests in mind.
3. For this reason, buyers __________ to look out for themselves.
4. Fortunately, the Internet __________ a lot to offer people who want to buy a used car.
5. Many sites __________ customer ratings and reviews of the best used cars.

◆ PRACTICE 22-5

Fill in the blank with the correct present tense form of the verb *do*.

Example: Therapy animals ___do___ many different kinds of community-service work.

1. For example, many dogs __________ important work in schools and hospitals.
2. Animals __________ not do their work alone, of course.
3. A person, usually the pet's owner, __________ therapy along with the animal.
4. First, you __________ an evaluation to make sure the animal is a good candidate.
5. Other animals besides dogs __________ therapy as well.

◆ PRACTICE 22-6

Fill in the blank with the correct present tense form of *be*, *have*, or *do*.

Example: All over the world, soccer ___is___ (be) a popular sport.

(1) Everywhere except in the United States, soccer __________ (be) called football. (2) In the United States, however, football __________ (have) a different meaning. (3) American football __________ (have)

many fans, but most of them __________ (be) in the United States. (4) Soccer __________ (have) a much larger audience worldwide than American football. (5) Soccer __________ (do) not have the popularity in the United States that it __________ (have) in most other places. (6) Nevertheless, the World Cup __________ (have) more and more U.S. fans every year.

(7) The World Cup __________ (be) the most important international soccer tournament. (8) Like Olympic events, World Cup matches __________ (be) contests between countries, and fans __________ (have) a patriotic loyalty to their teams. (9) To make its country proud, a team __________ (do) anything to win. (10) The United States __________ (have) men's and women's soccer teams that play in the World Cup. (11) When our teams __________ (do) well, we __________ (be) more interested in the tournament. (12) Fortunately, our teams __________ (be) internationally competitive. (13) The women __________ (do) particularly well. (14) The U.S. women's team __________ (be) almost always one of the top four teams in the world. (15) They __________ (have) first-place trophies from both the 1991 and 1999 World Cups. (16) As a result, players like Mia Hamm __________ (be) famous and __________ (have) the admiration and respect of many young soccer players.

(17) American football __________ (do) a good job of attracting an audience in the United States. (18) Although soccer __________ (be) not yet the spectator sport that football is, many children in the United States __________ (be) soccer players. (19) Because of this, soccer __________ (have) a great future in this country.

C Compound Subjects

The subject of a sentence is not always a single word. It can also be a **compound subject**, which consists of two or more words. To avoid agreement problems with compound subjects, follow these rules.

- When the parts of a compound subject are connected by *and*, use a plural verb.

  Every day, Sarah and Tom drive to school.

- When both parts of a compound subject are connected by *or*, the verb agrees with the word that is closer to it. If the word closer to the verb is singular, use a singular verb. If the word closer to the verb is plural, use a plural verb.

  Every day, Sarah or her friends drive to school.

  Every day, her friends or Sarah drives to school.

◆ PRACTICE 22-7

ON THE WEB
For more practice avoiding agreement problems with compound subjects, visit Exercise Central *at bedford stmartins.com/foundations first.*

Underline the correct verb in each of the following sentences.

Example: My sisters or my mother (mows/mow) the lawn every weekend.

1. Bag lunches and carpools (is/are) good ways to save money.
2. A Republican or a Democrat always (wins/win) the presidential election.
3. Oprah or her advisors (chooses, choose) the topics for her TV shows.
4. Credit counselors or a financial consultant (helps/help) a person get out of debt.
5. Alex and Gabrielle (is/are) able to text-message each other during class by using a high-pitched ringtone their teacher cannot hear.
6. Rosa Parks and Martin Luther King Jr. (continues/continue) to be honored for their roles in the Montgomery bus boycott of 1955–1956.
7. Snacks and water (makes/make) walking long distances more enjoyable.
8. As the experience of Pete Rose illustrates, if a baseball player or a coach (bets/bet) on his own sport, he will be banned from the game.
9. In the documentary *Country Boys*, Appalachian teenagers Chris and Cody (struggles/struggle) to overcome their difficult childhoods.
10. Children and teenagers (does/do) the best job learning how to use new technology.

D Phrases between Subject and Verb

Remember, a verb must always agree with its subject. Do not be confused if a **prepositional phrase** (a phrase that begins with *of*, *in*, *between*, and so on) comes between the sentence's subject and verb. Keep in mind that a noun or pronoun that is part of a prepositional phrase cannot be the subject of the sentence.

A box of chocolates makes a very good gift.

High levels of radon occur in some houses.

An easy way to identify the subject of a sentence is to cross out the prepositional phrase.

A box ~~of chocolates~~ makes a very good gift.

High levels ~~of radon~~ occur in some houses.

FOCUS Phrases between Subject and Verb

Watch out for phrases that begin with expressions such as *as well as*, *in addition to*, or *along with*. A noun or pronoun that is part of such a phrase cannot be the subject of a sentence.

The mayor, as well as members of the city council, supports the pay increase. (*Mayor*, not *members*, is the subject.)

◆ PRACTICE 22-8

In each of the following sentences, cross out the phrase that separates the subject and the verb. Then, underline the simple subject of the sentence once and the verb that agrees with the subject twice.

Example: Some people ~~in China~~ (travels/travel) by bicycle.

1. A resident of one of China's cities (goes/go) a long distance to work.
2. Westerners in China (expects/expect) to see many bicycles.
3. A black bicycle with a huge, heavy frame (has/have) been a common sight in China for many years.
4. The streets in Beijing and other large cities (has/have) bicycle lanes.
5. Today, the economy of China (is/are) booming.
6. Chinese citizens with high-paying jobs (is/are) not likely to commute by bicycle.
7. A worker with a long commute (does/do) not want to spend hours bicycling to work.
8. A bus, as well as private cars, (pollutes/pollute) the air.

ON THE WEB
For more practice avoiding agreement problems when a prepositional phrase comes between the subject and the verb, visit Exercise Central *at bedfordstmartins.com/foundationsfirst.*

9. Many Chinese people under age thirty (does/do) not even know how to ride a bicycle.

10. A Chinese store with a stock of bicycles (rents/rent) the old-fashioned black ones, mainly to tourists.

E Indefinite Pronoun Subjects

Indefinite pronouns—*anybody, everyone*, and so on—do not refer to specific persons or things. Most indefinite pronouns are singular and take singular verbs.

Everyone likes ice cream.

Each of the boys carries a beeper.

Neither of the boys misses class.

Nobody wants to see the team lose.

Singular Indefinite Pronouns

anybody	either	neither	one
anyone	everybody	nobody	somebody
anything	everyone	no one	someone
each	everything	nothing	something

Some indefinite pronouns are plural—*many, several, few, both, others*. Plural indefinite pronouns take plural verbs.

Many watch the nightly news on television.

Few get their news from the Internet.

◆ PRACTICE 22-9

Underline the correct verb in each of the following sentences.

Example: After a year in AmeriCorps, everybody (receives/receive) a small grant to help pay for college or graduate school.

(1) To become an AmeriCorps volunteer, one (has/have) to make a pledge to "get things done" for America. (2) Everyone in this service organization (joins/join) because of a desire to help others. (3) Each of the volunteers (makes/make) a commitment to serve for ten to twelve months. (4) Many (spends/spend) their year of service teaching, tutoring, or mentoring. (5) Others (chooses/choose) to work on improving public health or the environment. (6) Everything (is/are) funded by the govern-

❖ **ON THE WEB**
For more practice avoiding agreement problems, visit Exercise Central *at bedford stmartins.com/foundations first.*

ment's Corporation for National and Community Service. (7) Almost anybody (is/are) eligible to apply to be an AmeriCorps volunteer. (8) To be considered, somebody (needs/need) only to be seventeen or older and a lawful resident of the United States. (9) Something about this organization (inspires/inspire) hope and determination in people. (10) Few (regrets/regret) the decision to become an AmeriCorps volunteer.

F Verbs before Subjects

A verb agrees with its subject even if it comes *before* the subject, as it does in questions.

V S
Where is the ATM?

V S
Where are Zack and Angela?

V S
Why are they running?

If you have trouble identifying the subject, answer the question with a statement.

V S S V
Where is the ATM? The ATM is inside the bank.

FOCUS *There is* and *There are*

When a sentence begins with *there is* or *there are*, the word *there* is not the subject of the sentence. The subject comes after the form of the verb *be*.

V S
There is still one ticket available for the playoffs.

V S
There are still ten tickets available for the playoffs.

◆ PRACTICE 22-10

First, underline the simple subject of each sentence. Then, circle the correct form of the verb.

Example: What (is/are) your reasons for applying to this college?

1. There (is/are) an excellent nursing program here.
2. Where (is/are) you planning to live during the semester?

❖ **ON THE WEB**
For more practice avoiding agreement problems when the verb comes before the subject, visit Exercise Central *at bedfordstmartins.com/foundationsfirst.*

3. There (is/are) an inexpensive dormitory on Third Avenue.
4. What (does/do) the students here usually like best about the school?
5. How difficult (is/are) the placement tests?
6. What (has/have) been the most popular major in the last five years?
7. There (is/are) more people taking business courses today than there were twenty years ago.
8. There (has/have) been few nursing jobs available lately.
9. How many years (does/do) an average student take to graduate?
10. There (is/are) no simple answer to that question.

● REVISING AND EDITING

Look back at your response to the Seeing and Writing exercise on page 302. Make sure every verb agrees with its subject. If you find any incorrect verb forms, cross them out, and write the correct forms above them.

CHAPTER REVIEW

◆ EDITING PRACTICE

Read the following paragraph. If the underlined verb does not agree with its subject, cross out the verb, and write in the correct form. If it does, write *C* above the verb. The first sentence has been done for you.

New mother at airport with child adopted from abroad

Family Leave

Every parent has (C) the right to take time off from work after the birth or adoption of a child. The Family and Medical Leave Act (FMLA) of 1993 promise the same amount of leave to men as it do to women. The law guarantees twelve weeks of unpaid leave to each parent. Although there is several restrictions, anyone who request leave are supposed to receive it. However, many men do not take paternity leave because there are a lot of pressure to keep working. A woman who gives birth are more likely to feel pressure to stay at home with her new baby. Ideally, the law takes pressure off both parents and allow them to spend more time together with their infant.

◆ EDITING PRACTICE

Read the following paragraph. If the underlined verb does not agree with its subject, cross out the verb, and write in the correct form. If it does, write *C* above the verb. The first sentence has been done for you.

Credit Card Debt

Although it C is one of the most expensive ways to be in debt, many people in this country ~~carries~~ carry a large credit-card balance. This kind of debt often develops before we realize it are happening. Despite our best efforts, balances creep upward. The problem is that the companies that issues credit cards make them very easy to get. Once people has credit cards, it is easy for them to spend more than they should. Most companies offers benefits for using their cards. There is companies that gives clients free airfare or merchandise when they spend a certain amount. Either points or a small payment get you the benefits. Sometimes we forget, however, that the credit-card companies wants to keep us in debt. We live in a culture that encourage us to spend. Too many people falls into this trap, but there is ways to prevent this from happening. First, everyone need to learn how credit-card companies makes their money. For example, the minimum payment is often not much more than the interest owed on the balance. By paying just the minimum, users never gets out of debt—even if they pay their bills. If we want to use credit cards, we needs to take the time to read the rules.

Credit cards

An overdue bill

◆ COLLABORATIVE ACTIVITIES

1. Working on your own, write five subjects (people, places, or things) on a sheet of paper. The subjects can be singular or plural. Then, working in a group of three students, pass the paper to another member of the group. On the paper you receive, write a prepositional phrase for each of the five subjects. Then, pass the paper again, and finish the sentences on the paper you receive.

   Example

First Student	*Second Student*	*Third Student*
The pizza	*that has a burned crust*	*tastes funny.*

   Finally, review the paper you started with, and correct any subject-verb agreement errors in the sentences that have been created from your subjects.
2. Each student in the group should write the same five subjects from activity 1 on another sheet of paper. Next, each student should pass his or her paper to another member of the group, who will change each subject to a compound subject. Then, the third member of the

group will complete the sentences. When you get your paper back, check subject-verb agreement.

3. Working in the same group, choose one sentence from activity 1 and one sentence from activity 2. As a group, write a paragraph that contains both sentences. Make sure that at least one additional sentence contains an indefinite pronoun used as a subject. Check the paragraph to be sure there are no errors in subject-verb agreement. When your group is satisfied with its paragraph, have one member read it to the class.
4. ***Composing original sentences*** Working in a group of three students, write four sentences in the present tense. Make sure that one sentence has a compound subject, one has a prepositional phrase between the subject and the verb, one has an indefinite pronoun as a subject, and one has a subject that comes after the verb. Make sure none of the sentences contains errors in subject-verb agreement.

✓ REVIEW CHECKLIST: Subject-Verb Agreement

- Singular subjects (nouns and pronouns) take singular verbs, and plural subjects take plural verbs. (See 22A.)
- The irregular verbs *be*, *have*, and *do* often present problems with subject-verb agreement in the present tense. (See 22B.)
- Compound subjects can cause problems in agreement. (See 22C.)
- Words that come between the subject and the verb do not affect subject-verb agreement. (See 22D.)
- Most indefinite pronouns, such as *no one* and *everyone*, are singular and take a singular verb when they serve as the subject of the sentence. (See 22E.)
- A verb agrees with its subject even if the verb comes before the subject. (See 22F.)

Illogical Shifts

CHAPTER 23

PREVIEW

In this chapter, you will learn

- to avoid illogical shifts in tense (23A)
- to avoid illogical shifts in person (23B)
- to avoid illogical shifts in voice (23C)

SEEING AND WRITING

The picture above shows a female soldier. Look at the picture, and then write a paragraph in which you consider whether or not women should serve as front-line combat troops. Consider both sides of the issue before you write your paragraph.

Word Power

gender sex (male or female)
rigor a hardship or difficulty
parity equality in power or value

A **shift** occurs whenever a writer changes *tense*, *person*, or *voice* in a sentence or a paragraph. As you write and revise, make sure that any shifts you make are **logical**—that is, that they occur for a reason.

A Shifts in Tense

Tense is the form a verb takes to show when an action took place or a situation occurred. The three basic tenses are *past*, *present*, and *future*. An **illogical shift in tense** occurs when a writer shifts from one tense to another for no apparent reason.

ILLOGICAL SHIFT We sat at the table for more than an hour before a server comes and takes our order. (shift from past tense to present tense)

REVISED We sat at the table for more than an hour before a server came and took our order. (consistent use of past tense)

Of course, a shift in tense is often necessary. For example, in the following sentence, a shift in tense shows a change in the writer's attitude from the past to the present.

LOGICAL SHIFT In high school, I just wanted to have fun, but now I want to become a graphic artist. (necessary shift from past tense to present tense)

◆ PRACTICE 23-1

Underline the verbs in the following sentences. Then, correct any illogical shifts in tense by rewriting the verb in the correct tense above the line. If a sentence is correct, write *C* in the blank after the sentence.

❖ **ON THE WEB**
For more practice avoiding illogical shifts in tense, visit Exercise Central *at* bedford stmartins.com/foundations first.

Examples

The actor Ossie Davis died in 2005 when he ~~is~~ was eighty-seven years old. _____

When I started college, I took out several student loans, and now I have to pay them back. C

1. After Eduardo worked on his car, we go on a road trip together. _____
2. People are now able to discuss their hobbies online if they choose. _____
3. We told her not to eat the cookies, but she eats them anyway. _____
4. Anthony and Alexis took a romantic vacation before the baby arrives. _____

5. In 1994, hotel manager Paul Rusesabagina saved over a thousand people when he shelters Tutsi refugees at his hotel in Rwanda. ____
6. Your teacher told me that you receive the highest grade in the class last semester. ____
7. Megan wanted to help disadvantaged people, so she became a public defender. ____
8. Before I called the meeting, I review my notes. ____
9. A small road ran through this town before they build the highway. ____
10. Yesterday, I had biology lab, and today I have play rehearsal. ____

B Shifts in Person

Person is the form a pronoun takes to indicate who is speaking, spoken about, or spoken to.

Person

	Singular	*Plural*
1st person	I	we
2nd person	you	you
3rd person	he, she, it	they

An **illogical shift in person** occurs when a writer shifts from one person to another for no apparent reason.

ILLOGICAL SHIFT Before a person gets a job in the computer industry, you have to take a lot of courses. (shift from third person to second person)

REVISED Before a person gets a job in the computer industry, he or she has to take a lot of courses. (consistent use of third person)

ILLOGICAL SHIFT The students were told that you have to attend a conference each week. (shift from third person to second person)

REVISED The students were told that they had to attend a conference each week. (consistent use of third person plural)

◆ PRACTICE 23-2

Correct any illogical shifts in person in the following sentences. If necessary, change any verbs that do not agree with the new subjects. If a sentence is correct, write *C* in the blank.

> ✣ **ON THE WEB**
> *For more practice avoiding illogical shifts in person, visit* **Exercise Central** *at bedford stmartins.com/foundations first.*

Example: I stopped at the computer store because ~~you~~ I can recycle empty printer cartridges there. _____

1. Some people may decide not to buy a Toyota because you can buy a similar Hyundai for less money. _____
2. Students can learn Spanish by taking a class, but you can also learn Spanish by reading books and listening to CDs. _____
3. Before you buy an airline ticket, you should compare prices by checking several Web sites. _____
4. Kyra worked on an assembly line where you could not spend more than thirty seconds on each task. _____
5. Brian said that he bought all his furniture on eBay. _____
6. When a cook makes a stir-fry, you have to prepare all the ingredients before starting to cook. _____
7. The instructor informed his students that you should proofread carefully. _____
8. Even though Patrick is careful with his personal information, he is still afraid of identity theft. _____
9. Most people know that they can buy inexpensive furniture at the Salvation Army store. _____
10. Scientists tell us that you can suffer bone loss if I do not have enough calcium in your diet. _____

C Shifts in Voice

Voice is the form a verb takes to indicate whether the subject is acting or is acted upon. When a sentence is in the **active voice**, the subject *performs* the action. When a sentence is in the **passive voice**, the subject *receives* the action—that is, it is acted upon.

ACTIVE VOICE Pablo Neruda won the Nobel Prize in Literature in 1971.

PASSIVE VOICE The Nobel Prize in Literature was won by Pablo Neruda in 1971.

An **illogical shift in voice** occurs when a writer shifts from active to passive voice or from passive to active voice for no apparent reason.

ILLOGICAL SHIFT The jazz musician John Coltrane played the tenor sax, and the soprano sax was also played by him. (active to passive)

REVISED The jazz musician John Coltrane played the tenor sax, and he also played the soprano sax. (consistent use of active voice)

ILLOGICAL SHIFT *Fences* was written by August Wilson, and he also wrote *The Piano Lesson*. (passive to active)

REVISED August Wilson wrote *Fences*, and he also wrote *The Piano Lesson*. (consistent use of active voice)

FOCUS Changing from Passive to Active Voice

You should use the active voice in most of your college writing because it is stronger and more direct than the passive voice. To change a sentence from passive to active voice, determine who or what performs the action, and make this noun the subject of this new sentence.

PASSIVE VOICE Three world records in track were set by Jesse Owens in a single day. (Jesse Owens performs the action.)

ACTIVE VOICE Jesse Owens set three world records in track in a single day.

◆ PRACTICE 23-3

Correct any illogical shifts in voice in the following sentences, using active voice wherever possible. Change any verb that does not agree with its new subject. If a sentence is correct, write *C* in the blank.

Example: Whenever that song comes on the radio, ~~I am made~~ *it makes me* happy. ~~by it.~~ ____

1. The sandwich special was ordered by Anna, and Dave ordered the chef's salad. ____
2. Although they all know English, Portuguese is spoken by them at home. ____

ON THE WEB
For more practice avoiding illogical shifts in voice, visit Exercise Central *at* *bedfordstmartins.com/foundationsfirst.*

3. In 1910, Camp Fire Girls was founded by Luther Gulick, and the organization still exists today. _____
4. Because the essay was written by Jeremy, it has few mistakes. _____
5. The Kingdom of Lesotho does have a king, but the country is governed by the prime minister. _____
6. Whenever we give my dad a present, he always pretends he likes it. _____
7. Camouflage is worn by soldiers and hunters so that they blend in with their surroundings. _____
8. The judges could not decide, so the prize was given by them to both skaters. _____
9. A settlement was discussed by the lawyers, but the defendant refused it. _____
10. Many young people do not vote, and most politicians want that to change. _____

> **● REVISING AND EDITING**
>
> Look back at your response to the Seeing and Writing exercise on page 315. Revise any illogical shifts in tense, person, or voice.

CHAPTER REVIEW

◆ EDITING PRACTICE

Read the following paragraph, which contains illogical shifts in tense, person, and voice. Then, edit the paragraph to correct the illogical shifts, making sure subjects and verbs agree. The first sentence has been edited for you.

A panel from the graphic novel Persepolis

Graphic Novels

Today, many people are reading graphic novels, and ^*they* we are taking them more seriously than ever before. Graphic novels are book-length comics, and classic comic techniques are used by graphic novelists. These artists tell all kinds of complex stories through their illustrated panels. For example, in his books *Maus* and *Maus II*, Art Spiegelman writes about the Holocaust and told his father's story of survival. In *Persepolis* and *Persepolis* 2, Marjane Satrapi tells the story of her childhood in Iran in the 1970s and 1980s when the country was gripped by the Islamic Revolution. Although these authors focus on real events, others focused on their own invented worlds. For instance, many people love Frank Miller's *Sin City* series because you feel as if you are in a world of shadowy streets. Another favorite graphic novelist who creates alternate realities is Alan Moore; his books included *Watchmen*, *V for Vendetta*, and the *League of Extraordinary Gentlemen* series. As more and more people read these books and discover that they are not just comics, more attention and respect are gained by graphic novels. And, as readers acknowledge the importance of these books, you are beginning to see graphic novels on required reading lists.

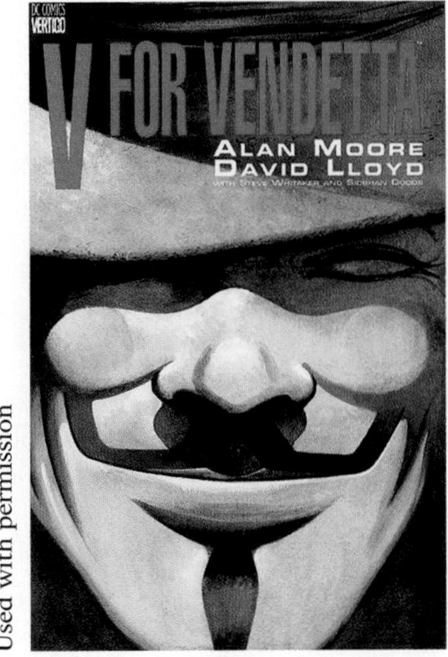

The cover of V for Vendetta

◆ EDITING PRACTICE

Read the following paragraph, which contains illogical shifts in tense, person, and voice. Then, edit the paragraph to correct the illogical shifts, making sure subjects and verbs agree. The first sentence has been edited for you.

A Great Olympic Moment

When Eric Moussambani, a swimmer from Equatorial Guinea, arrived at the 2000 Olympic games in Sydney, Australia, *most swimming fans did not know* his name. ~~was not known by most swimming fans.~~ Moussambani was not famous, his qualifying time was slow, and he is unfamiliar with Olympic-size pools. He trained in the ocean, they had no coach, and his country had no swim team. In other words, no one expects him to win; even Moussambani hoped just to be able to finish the two laps in his qualifying heat. Soon after the race was started by him, he was struggling. However, as he splashed through the water, his efforts were noticed by the crowd. The people in the bleachers rose up and cheered him on because you saw how hard he was trying. In the end, although he did not qualify for the finals, the race was finished by Eric Moussambani, and his determination and spirit earned him the admiration of many. Now, people know his name, and his heroic swim is remembered by them with great respect.

Swimmer Eric Moussambani

◆ COLLABORATIVE ACTIVITIES

1. Working in a group of four students, choose a subject to write sentences about. Each pair of students should write two simple sentences, one using the subject with a present tense verb and the other using the same subject with a past tense verb. Then, work with your partner to combine the two sentences into a single sentence that contains an illogical shift. Finally, exchange sentences with the other pair in your group, and correct the shifts in the other students' sentences.

   Example

SUBJECT	*Three blind mice*
PRESENT TENSE SENTENCE	*Three blind mice hide from the cat.*
PAST TENSE SENTENCE	*Three blind mice ran after the farmer's wife.*
SENTENCE WITH ILLOGICAL SHIFT	*Three blind mice hide from the cat and ran after the farmer's wife.*
CORRECTED SENTENCE	*Three blind mice hid from the cat and ran after the farmer's wife.*

2. Working in a group of three or four students, write a paragraph explaining how to do a simple task. Use *you* as the subject throughout the paragraph. When you have finished, go back and change every other sentence so that the subject is *a person*, *someone*, *people*, *students*, or some other third-person word or phrase. Then, exchange paragraphs with another group. Correct the illogical shifts in person so that the whole paragraph uses the third person.
3. Bring to class five sentences from newspapers, magazines, or textbooks that use the passive voice. Then, revise these sentences by changing them to active voice. In a group of four students, discuss your revisions. If a sentence is awkward in the active voice, or if you cannot change it to the active voice, discuss the reasons why this is so.
4. ***Composing original sentences*** Working in a group of three students, write five sentences in the passive voice. When you have finished, check your sentences to correct any errors in grammar, punctuation, or spelling.

☑ REVIEW CHECKLIST: Illogical Shifts

- An illogical shift in tense occurs when a writer shifts from one verb tense to another for no apparent reason. (See 23A.)
- An illogical shift in person occurs when a writer shifts from one person to another for no apparent reason. (See 23B.)
- An illogical shift in voice occurs when a writer shifts from active to passive voice or from passive to active voice for no apparent reason. (See 23C.)

Dangling and Misplaced Modifiers

CHAPTER 24

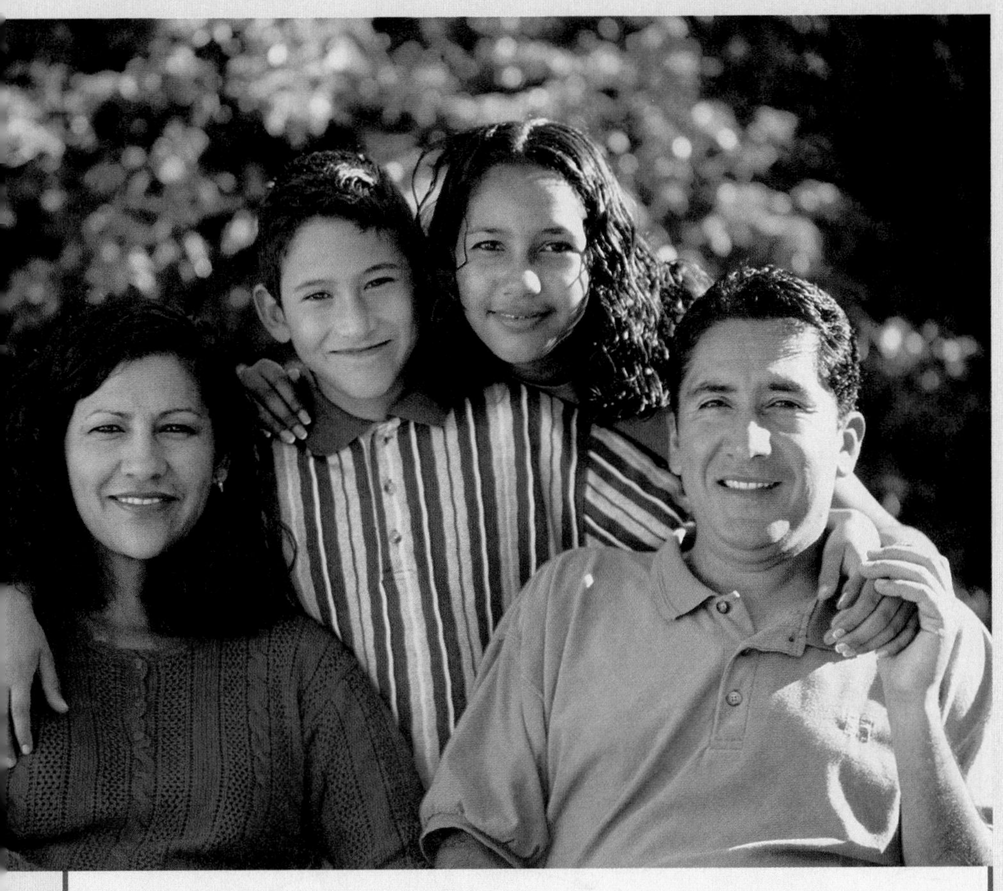

PREVIEW

In this chapter, you will learn

- to identify *-ing* modifiers (24A)
- to identify *-ed* modifiers (24B)
- to recognize and correct dangling modifiers (24C)
- to recognize and correct misplaced modifiers (24D)

SEEING AND WRITING

The picture above shows a family. Look at the picture, and then write a paragraph in which you tell a story from your own family's history. If possible, discuss the significance this story has for your family.

Word Power

generation a group of individuals born and living at about the same time

heritage something passed down from previous generations

migrate to move from one region to another

Word Power

modify to describe, limit, or qualify.

A **modifier** is a word or word group that gives information about another word in a sentence. To avoid confusion, a modifier should be placed as close as possible to the noun or pronoun it modifies—ideally, directly before or directly after it. Many word groups that act as modifiers are introduced by present participles or past participles.

A Identifying *-ing* Modifiers

An *-ing* modifier—also called a **present participle modifier**—consists of the *-ing* form of the verb along with the words it introduces. The modifier provides information about a noun or a pronoun that appears next to it in a sentence.

-ING MODIFIER

Remembering what he had come to do, Robert reached in his pocket for the ring.

-ING MODIFIER

Dancing to the music of Frank Sinatra, Madeline knew she was in love.

FOCUS Placing *-ing* Modifiers

An *-ing* modifier can come at the beginning, in the middle, or at the end of a sentence.

Returning to the streets they had left, many early rock singers were soon forgotten.

Many early rock singers, returning to the streets they had left, were soon forgotten.

Many early rock singers were soon forgotten, returning to the streets they had left.

◆ PRACTICE 24-1

In each of the following sentences, underline the *-ing* modifier. Then, draw an arrow from the modifier to the word it gives information about.

Example: Holding on tightly, the movers lifted the piano.

1. Surfing the Web, Ada found a blog written by a young woman in Sri Lanka.
2. Ali, following the rules, stood in line outside the stadium to meet his favorite player.
3. Sampling the appetizers, I waited for Jake to arrive at the party.

ON THE WEB
For more practice identifying -ing modifiers, visit Exercise Central *at bedfordstmartins .com/foundationsfirst.*

4. Amy bit down, trying to keep a straight face.
5. Wanting to keep some open space downtown, the city planners decided not to sell the park to developers.
6. The tired student, working late into the night, stopped for a snack.
7. Explaining the significance of the architecture at Machu Picchu, the tour guide led us up the trail.
8. Advancing at just the right moment, Roberto was able to score a goal for Spain.
9. Eric's parents, wishing him luck, dropped him off in front of his dorm.
10. The musicians, tuning their instruments, prepared to play the overture.

◆ PRACTICE 24-2

Write five sentences that contain *-ing* modifiers. Then, underline each modifier, and draw an arrow from the modifier to the word it gives information about.

Example: *Wearing her new dress, my sister went to Sunday school.*

1. ______________________________
____
2. ______________________________
____
3. ______________________________
____
4. ______________________________
____
5. ______________________________
____

B Identifying *-ed* Modifiers

An *-ed* modifier—also called a **past participle modifier**—consists of the past participle form of the verb (usually ending in *-d* or *-ed*) along with the words it introduces. Like an *-ing* modifier, an *-ed* modifier provides information about a noun or a pronoun that appears next to it in a sentence.

-ED MODIFIER

Submitted to the Continental Congress on June 7, 1776, the Declaration of Independence was approved on July 4.

-ED MODIFIER

Invited to the White House, Sojourner Truth met President Abraham Lincoln.

FOCUS Placing *-ed* Modifiers

A past participle modifier can come at the beginning, in the middle, or at the end of a sentence.

Shocked by the ruling, the lawyer said she would appeal.

The lawyer, shocked by the ruling, said she would appeal.

"I will appeal," said the lawyer, shocked by the ruling.

◆ PRACTICE 24-3

ON THE WEB
For more practice identifying -ed *modifiers, visit* Exercise Central *at bedfordstmartins .com/foundationsfirst.*

In each of the following sentences, underline the *-ed* modifier. Then, draw an arrow from the modifier to the word it modifies.

Example: Experienced in nursing and in leadership, Major General Gale Pollack was well qualified to head the U.S. Army Nurse Corps.

1. Seated in the fifth row, I had a clear view of the actors' faces.
2. The woman, determined to be polite, stepped outside to answer her cell phone.
3. Georgia, fascinated by bugs, decided to become an entomologist.
4. Warned that criminals had robbed a bank downtown, the Justice League set out to find them.
5. The game, delayed by rain, did not start on time.
6. The Hoover Dam, completed in 1936, created Lake Mead.
7. Forced to increase the price of stamps, the U.S. Postal Service apologized to the public.
8. Changed by their ballroom dancing experiences, the fifth-graders in the documentary *Mad Hot Ballroom* learned to see themselves as graceful.
9. The furniture, produced on an assembly line, looked as if it might fall apart.
10. Protected by plenty of styrofoam, the pottery arrived safely.

◆ PRACTICE 24-4

Write five sentences that contain *-ed* modifiers. Then, underline the modifier, and draw an arrow from the modifier to the word it gives information about.

Example: Frightened by the thunder, the cat hid under the couch.

1. ______________________________

2. ______________________________

3. ______________________________

4. ______________________________

5. ______________________________

C Correcting Dangling Modifiers

A **dangling modifier** "dangles" because the word it is supposed to modify does not appear in the sentence. Often, a dangling modifier comes at the beginning of a sentence and seems to modify the word that follows it. Look at the following sentence.

DANGLING MODIFIER Working overtime, my salary almost doubled.

In the sentence above, the present participle modifier *working overtime* seems to be modifying *salary*. But this makes no sense. How can salary work overtime? The word the present participle modifier should logically modify is missing. To correct this sentence, you need to supply the missing word.

REVISED Working overtime, I almost doubled my salary.

As the example above illustrates, the easiest way to correct a dangling modifier is to supply the word (a noun or pronoun) that the dangling modifier should actually modify.

DANGLING MODIFIER Living in England, his first collection of poems was published. (Did the poetry collection live in England?)

REVISED Living in England, Robert Frost published his first collection of poems.

DANGLING MODIFIER: Distracted by my cell phone, my car almost drove off the road. (Did the phone distract the car?)

REVISED: Distracted by my cell phone, I almost drove my car off the road.

◆ PRACTICE 24-5

Rewrite the following sentences, which contain dangling modifiers, by supplying a word to which each modifier can logically refer.

✣ **ON THE WEB**
For more practice correcting dangling modifiers, visit **Exercise Central** *at bedford stmartins.com/foundations first.*

Example: Watching from the bleachers, my daughter hit a home run.

Watching from the bleachers, I saw my daughter hit a home run.

1. Coming home from a long day of mowing lawns, an ice cream cone sounded perfect.

2. Following the recipe, the cake was easy to make.

3. Convinced by friends to leave her current job, a new job was found in two weeks.

4. Wanting to buy a home in 1935, a Sears mail-order house was thought to be the best choice.

5. Working full-time at the coffee shop, my homework did not always get finished.

6. Taken from their city homes by the Children's Aid Society, trains took them west to be adopted by farming families.

7. Raised in Florida, the winters in Michigan seemed harsh.

____

____

8. Stationed abroad for twelve months, her family was left at home.

____

____

9. Prepared for an afternoon at the game, the rain was unexpected.

____

____

10. Dropping a coin in the fountain, a wish was made.

____

____

D Correcting Misplaced Modifiers

Ideally, a modifier should come right before or right after the word it modifies. A **misplaced modifier** appears to modify the wrong word because it is placed incorrectly in the sentence. To correct this problem, move the modifier so that it is as close as possible to the word it is supposed to modify.

MISPLACED MODIFIER I ran to the window wearing my bathrobe. (Was the window wearing the bathrobe?)

REVISED Wearing my bathrobe, I ran to the window.

MISPLACED MODIFIER The dog ran down the street frightened by the noise. (Was the street frightened by the noise?)

REVISED Frightened by the noise, the dog ran down the street.

FOCUS Misplaced Modifiers

Prepositional phrases can also be misplaced in a sentence.

MISPLACED MODIFIER My sister served cookies to her friends on tiny plates. (Were the friends sitting on tiny plates?)

REVISED My sister served cookies on tiny plates to her friends.

❖ **ON THE WEB**
For more practice correcting misplaced modifiers, visit Exercise Central *at bedford stmartins.com/foundations first.*

◆ PRACTICE 24-6

Rewrite the following sentences, which contain misplaced modifiers, so that each modifier clearly refers to the word it is supposed to modify.

Example: Wallowing in a cool mud bath, Mr. Phelps scratched the back of the prize pig.

Mr. Phelps scratched the back of the prize pig wallowing in a cool mud bath.

1. The angry bull threw every rodeo rider with a ring in his nose.

2. The trick-or-treaters rang every doorbell carrying enormous bags of candy.

3. Blushing furiously, the bathroom door was quickly closed by Henry.

4. Attracted to the bright light, the candles were surrounded by moths.

5. A car is not likely to be damaged by rust kept in a garage.

6. A group of homeless men camped at the edge of the city under a highway overpass.

7. A bartender served strong drinks with enthusiasm.

8. Decorated with a skull and crossbones, she carefully read the warning label.

9. Blowing kisses, a white limousine waited as the director came out of the restaurant.

10. Accidentally tying her shoelaces together, nursery school was a struggle for Amy that morning.

• REVISING AND EDITING

Look back at your response to the Seeing and Writing exercise on page 323. First, underline any *-ing* or *-ed* modifiers you find. Then, revise any dangling or misplaced modifiers. Make sure each modifier clearly refers to a word that it can logically describe.

CHAPTER REVIEW

◆ EDITING PRACTICE

Read the following paragraph. Then, rewrite the sentences to correct dangling and misplaced modifiers. In some cases, you may have to supply a word to which the modifier can logically refer. The first sentence has been corrected for you.

Dyslexia

Learning to read and write, *many people experience* difficulties. ~~are experienced by many people.~~ Diagnosed with dyslexia, this disability frightens some people. Frustrated by their attempts to read and write, these activities are avoided by them. They do not want anyone to know they have trouble fearing embarrassment. Feeling stupid, their attention often turns to other activities. Interpreted by teachers as a lack of interest in learning, serious learning problems can be caused by dyslexia. Inherited from learning-disabled family members, intelligence is not related to dyslexia. Extremely intelligent people can be dyslexic. Fortunately, more educators are making an effort to identify the problem, knowing how to recognize the signs of dyslexia. Focusing on new and inventive methods, dyslexics can be taught successfully by educators.

◆ EDITING PRACTICE

Read the following paragraph. Then, rewrite the sentences to correct dangling and misplaced modifiers. In some cases, you may have to supply a word to which the modifier can logically refer. The first sentence has been corrected for you.

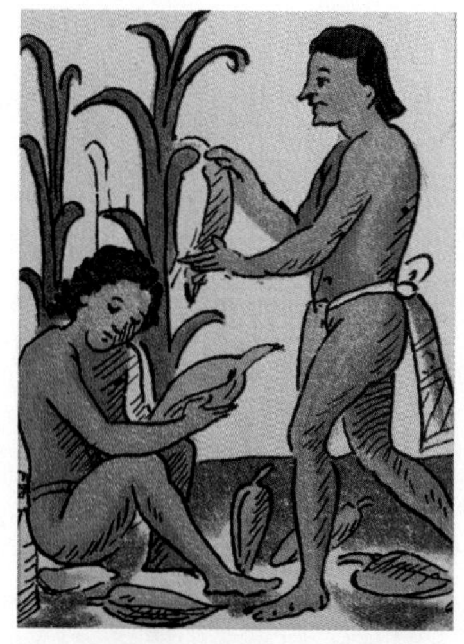

Native people cultivating corn

Eating popcorn at the movies, 1952

E-Z Pop popcorn

The History of Popcorn

~~Usually eaten in a movie theater, most~~ Most Americans do not think much about popcorn, usually eaten in a movie theater. However, popcorn has a long and interesting history. Popcorn is a truly American food. Exploring a cave in New Mexico, ears of popping corn more than five thousand years old were found. Arriving from Europe, native peoples offered to sell popcorn to Columbus and his crew. In addition, brought by the native Americans, the Pilgrims ate popcorn at the first Thanksgiving. Liking this local food, popcorn was eaten as a breakfast food by early English colonists. By the nineteenth century, street vendors sold popcorn from pushcarts. Sold in movie theaters, movies were soon associated with popcorn. The popularity of the fluffy white snack continued through the Great Depression. Arriving in the 1940s, the movie business was hurt by television, and people ate less popcorn. However, things soon changed. Preparing their favorite snack at home, popcorn was made popular again. In the 1950s, people made popcorn in pots on the stove. In the 1960s, popcorn was made in prepackaged foil pans that puffed up as the popcorn popped. Today, popcorn is made in the microwave. Popped in a microwave, in a prepackaged container, or in a pot on the stove, Americans today like to eat popcorn when they watch TV. Wherever they eat it, most Americans are unaware of the long history of popcorn.

◆ COLLABORATIVE ACTIVITIES

1. Work in a group of four or five students. On a sheet of paper, one student should write an *-ing* or *-ed* modifier. The next student should then complete the sentence and pass the sheet to a third student, who should write another modifier to continue the idea begun in the first sentence. Keep passing the paper from student to student until the group has written at least six sentences.
2. Look over the sentences your group wrote in activity 1. Then, discuss the ways you decided to complete the sentences. Check to be sure that no modifiers are dangling or misplaced.
3. Working in a group, write five *-ing* or *-ed* modifiers. Then, trade lists with another group. Work together to complete the sentences, making sure that at least two sentences contain dangling or misplaced modifiers (the sillier, the better). Finally, pass the sentences back to the group that wrote the modifiers, and have them correct the sentences.
4. ***Composing original sentences*** Working together, write five sentences that contain *-ing* or *-ed* modifiers. Make sure that none of the sentences contain a dangling or misplaced modifier. When you have finished, check your sentences to correct any errors in grammar or punctuation.

☑ REVIEW CHECKLIST: Dangling and Misplaced Modifiers

- ☐ An *-ing* modifier consists of the present participle (the *-ing* form of the verb) along with the words it introduces. (See 24A.)
- ☐ An *-ed* modifier consists of the past participle (usually ending in *-d* or *-ed*) along with the words it introduces. (See 24B.)
- ☐ Correct a dangling modifier by supplying a word to which the dangling modifier can logically refer. (See 24C.)
- ☐ Avoid misplaced modifiers by placing modifiers as close as possible to the words they modify. (See 24D.)

UNIT REVIEW

Read the following student essay, which includes some common sentence problems. Revise any incorrect sentences to eliminate run-ons, sentence fragments, errors in subject-verb agreement, illogical shifts, and dangling and misplaced modifiers. The first sentence has been edited for you.

Helping Prisoners Go Straight

A cosmetology class in prison

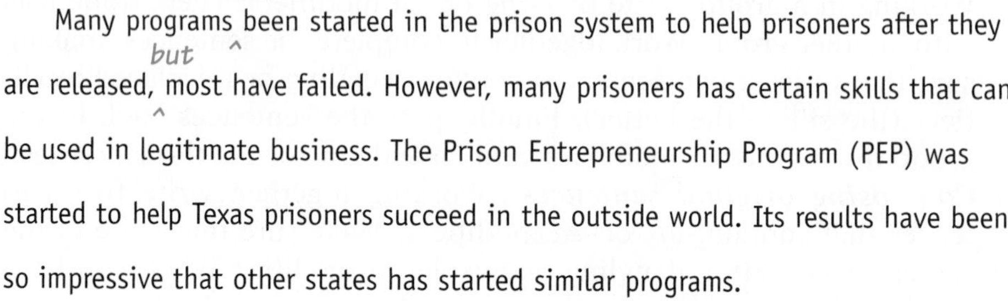

Many programs *have* been started in the prison system to help prisoners after they are released, *but* most have failed. However, many prisoners has certain skills that can be used in legitimate business. The Prison Entrepreneurship Program (PEP) was started to help Texas prisoners succeed in the outside world. Its results have been so impressive that other states has started similar programs.

The failures of American prisons are well known to anyone who pays attention to the news the costs are huge and growing fast. More than two million people are in U.S. prisons, the number of inmates are increasing. Few is trained for jobs in the outside world, however, each year more than 600,000 are freed. On the outside, many who have been released does not find it possible to find legitimate jobs. Or even places to live. The result being that within a few years, most are back in prison. Clearly, the system is not working.

At the same time, many people in jail has abilities when they are released that can help them succeed. Before going to prison, organizational skills were developed by many drug dealers that enabled them to oversee drug sales and manage their employees. These activities were illegal and harmful to society, but they required intelligence and the readiness to take chances. Skills that can be used in legal activities. Drug dealers know that you need to keep secrets from competitors. And about making a profit. They know why the product that they sell has to be better or cheaper than their competitors'. They understand distribution patterns and customer service. These are skills that any legitimate entrepreneur needs. In order to succeed.

Female inmates learn computer programs

The Prison Entrepreneurship Program was started in Dallas, Texas. To help prison inmates use their talents in legitimate businesses once they are paroled. While they are still in prison, inmates compete with one another to create the best business plans. Recruited to help them create these plans, inmates meet business owners and executives. These advisors also teach inmates how to raise money for their businesses. And serve as mentors. What has been the results? Inmates have started businesses that emphasize services. Such as repairing computers, power-washing buildings, selling used cars, and building home gyms. Of 212 inmates who have so far been released, 196 have legitimate jobs. When they left prison. Only 10 have gone back to prison.

A computer class in prison

PEP uses the skills that prison inmates already has, along with the interest and assistance of legitimate and successful businesspeople. It has been so successful that there is a waiting list of inmates. Who want to participate in PEP. California and Indiana have already followed Texas's example. And started similar programs of their own in their prisons. These programs offering hope to inmates and to society.

UNIT FIVE

Understanding Basic Grammar

CHAPTER 25

Verbs: Past Tense

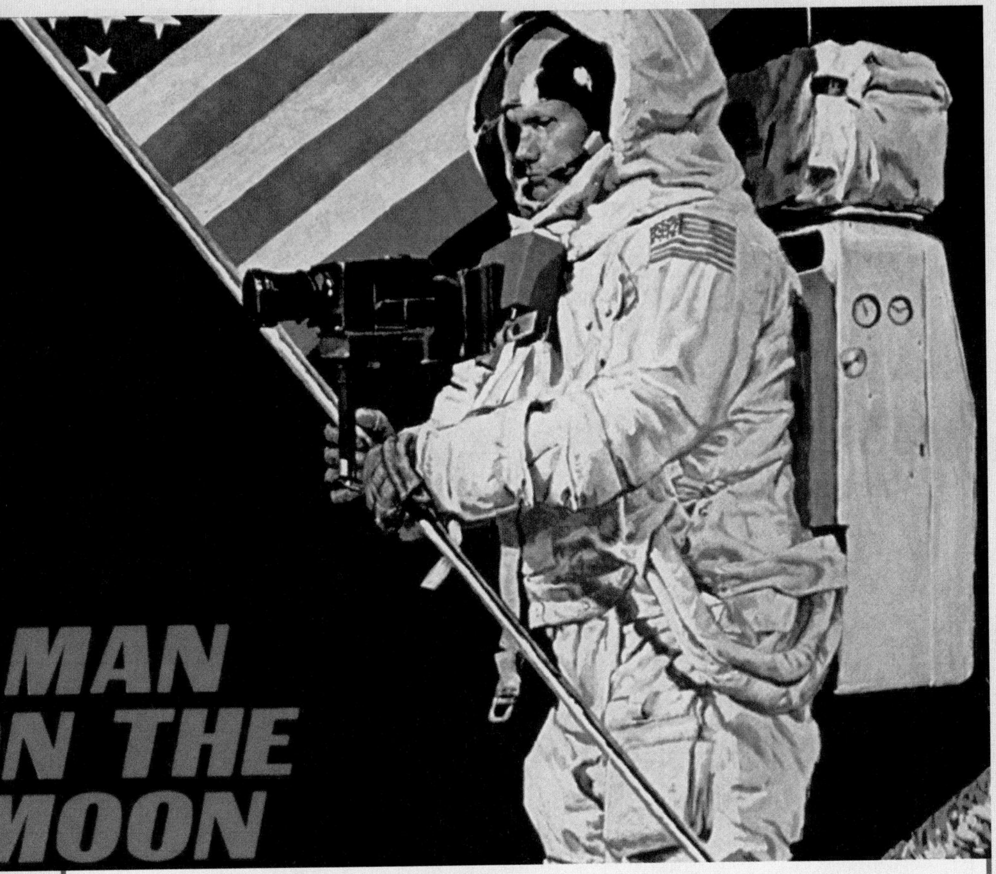

PREVIEW

In this chapter, you will learn

- to understand regular verbs in the past tense (25A)
- to understand irregular verbs in the past tense (25B)
- to deal with problem verbs in the past tense (25C and 25D)

• SEEING AND WRITING

The picture above shows astronaut Neil Armstrong planting the American flag on the moon in 1969. Look at the picture, and then select a newsworthy event in your life, and write a one-paragraph news story about it. Include a headline, and be sure to use the past tense.

▶ Word Power

memorable worth remembering

newsworthy worth reporting in the news

unique one of a kind

Verb tense indicates when an action or situation took place. The **past tense** indicates that an action or a situation happened in the past.

A Regular Verbs

Regular verbs form the past tense by adding *-d* or *-ed* to the **base form** of the verb (the present tense form of the verb that is used with *I*).

FOCUS Regular Verbs in the Past Tense

- Most regular verbs form the past tense by adding *-ed* to the base form of the verb.

  I edited my paper.

  Tia handed in her paper yesterday.

- Regular verbs that end in *-e* form the past tense by adding *-d*.

  He refused to take no for an answer.

  Last summer they biked through northern California.

- Regular verbs that end in *-y* form the past tense by changing the *y* to *i* and adding *-ed*.

  try tried
  vary varied

NOTE: All regular verbs use the same form for singular and plural in the past tense: *I cheered, They cheered*.

◆ PRACTICE 25-1

❖ **ON THE WEB**
For more practice understanding regular verbs in the past tense, visit **Exercise Central** *at bedford stmartins.com/foundations first.*

Some of the verbs in the following sentences are in the present tense, and some are in the past tense. First, underline the verb in each sentence. Then, on the line after each sentence, write *present* if the verb is present tense and *past* if the verb is past tense.

Examples

My grandparents lived with us after their retirement. past

Carol plays tennis every weekend. present

1. College students often watch daytime soap operas. ________
2. My brother believed in Santa Claus until he was eight. ________
3. Chung Ho and his family lived on a poultry farm in Korea for many years. ________
4. They decided to drive to Florida for spring vacation. ________
5. Jason received $5,000 from his aunt when she died. ________
6. I like to eat eggplant and sticky rice at my favorite restaurant. ________
7. Lee Harvey Oswald killed President John F. Kennedy in Dallas, Texas, in 1963. ________
8. Some people consider their wedding day to be the most important day of their lives. ________
9. Pink and red tulips bloomed everywhere in the garden. ________
10. General Robert E. Lee surrendered to General Ulysses S. Grant at Appomattox Court House on April 9, 1865. ________

◆ PRACTICE 25-2

Change the present tense verbs in the following passage to past tense. Cross out the present tense form of each underlined verb, and write the past tense form above it.

Example: Julio ~~tries~~ *tried* every year to get a green card.

(1) A native of Ecuador, he qualifies for the U.S. Green Card Lottery. (2) Hoping to win a permanent residence visa, he reapplies for the lottery every year. (3) He considers himself lucky to be eligible. (4) Lottery applicants need to be from an underrepresented country. (5) Because of the large number of Mexican immigrants in the United States, the American government rejects applications from Julio's Mexican friends. (6) Moreover, even people who qualify face disappointment. (7) Julio's chances to win remain slim. (8) Applicants also face the possibility of fraud. (9) Many companies try to scam applicants by charging them to apply for the lottery. (10) Nevertheless, Julio, along with thousands of others, hopes to win a green card.

B Irregular Verbs

Unlike regular verbs, **irregular verbs** do not form the past tense by adding *-d* or *-ed*. Instead, they use special irregular past tense forms that may look very different from their present tense forms.

The chart that follows lists the base forms and the past tense forms of the most common irregular verbs. (If you do not find a verb on this chart, look it up in a dictionary.)

Irregular Verbs in the Past Tense

Base Form	Past Tense	Base Form	Past Tense
awake	awoke	bet	bet
be	was, were	bite	bit
become	became	blow	blew
begin	began	break	broke
bring	brought	make	made
build	built	meet	met
buy	bought	pay	paid
catch	caught	quit	quit
choose	chose	read	read
come	came	ride	rode
cost	cost	ring	rang
cut	cut	rise	rose
dive	dove, dived	run	ran
do	did	say	said
draw	drew	see	saw
drink	drank	sell	sold
drive	drove	send	sent
eat	ate	set	set
fall	fell	shake	shook
feed	fed	shine	shone, shined
feel	felt	sing	sang
fight	fought	sit	sat
find	found	sleep	slept
fly	flew	speak	spoke
forgive	forgave	spend	spent
freeze	froze	spring	sprang
get	got	stand	stood
give	gave	steal	stole
go	went	stick	stuck
grow	grew	sting	stung
have	had	swear	swore
hear	heard	swim	swam
hide	hid	take	took
hold	held	teach	taught
hurt	hurt	tear	tore
keep	kept	tell	told
know	knew	think	thought

(continued on following page)

(continued from previous page)

Base Form	Past Tense	Base Form	Past Tense
lay (to place)	laid	throw	threw
lead	led	understand	understood
leave	left	wake	woke, waked
let	let	wear	wore
lie (to recline)	lay	win	won
light	lit	write	wrote
lose	lost		

◆ PRACTICE 25-3

Use the list of irregular verbs above to help you find the correct past tense forms of the irregular verb in parentheses. Then, write the correct form in the space provided.

Example: The defendant ___swore___ (swear) that he had never entered the room.

1. Alan ______________ (know) the answer even before the teacher finished asking the question.
2. I accidentally ______________ (leave) my cat behind when I moved out of my old apartment.
3. The river ______________ (freeze) early last year because it was unusually cold.
4. She ______________ (teach) her son to play the piano as soon as he was old enough to sit on the bench and reach the keys.
5. Huyn ______________ (find) a silver bracelet under her chair at the restaurant.
6. My father ______________ (hurt) his shoulder when he ______________ (throw) a football.
7. The hockey team ______________ (fight) hard, but they ______________ (lose) by one point.
8. Carmen ______________ (bring) paella to the potluck dinner.
9. They ______________ (light) candles when the power went out.
10. In 2006, Tiger Woods ______________ (win) ten tournaments, including the PGA Championship.

✣ **ON THE WEB**
For more practice understanding irregular verbs in the past tense, visit Exercise Central *at bedfordstmartins.com/foundationsfirst.*

◆ PRACTICE 25-4

In the following passage, fill in the correct past tense form of the irregular verb in parentheses. Refer to the list of irregular verbs on pages 342–43.

Example: After many years in the making, the Women's National Basketball Association (WNBA) finally ____got____ (get) its start in 1996.

(1) Former college star Sheryl Swoopes ______________ (become) the first player signed to a WNBA team. (2) Many people immediately ______________ (see) the financial possibilities of this new league, and corporations ______________ (pay) to sponsor the new teams. (3) Fans, especially young girls, ______________ (find) many women to admire. (4) Many people ______________ (buy) tickets to the games, and they ______________ (come) ready to cheer. (5) Unlike almost every other professional sport, women's professional basketball ______________ (draw) more female fans than male fans. (6) Many people appreciated how the WNBA ______________ (shake) up the sports establishment in this way. (7) The players ______________ (rise) to the challenges and ______________ (fight) hard to keep the WNBA going. (8) As a result, the league ______________ (go) from eight teams to sixteen, doubling in size in the first five years of its existence. (9) Some people ______________ (say) that the WNBA would fail. (10) However, the athletes and fans ______________ (know) how long women had been waiting for this opportunity.

C Problem Verbs: *Be*

The irregular verb *be* can cause problems for writers because it has two different past tense forms—a singular form and a plural form. The only way to make certain that you use these forms correctly is to memorize them.

Past Tense Forms of the Verb Be

	Singular	***Plural***
1st person	I was tired.	We were tired.
2nd person	You were tired.	You were tired.

3rd person	He was tired.	
	She was tired.	They were tired.
	It was tired.	

◆ PRACTICE 25-5

In each of the following sentences, circle the correct form of the verb *be*.

Example: The toy fire engine (was/were) surprisingly loud.

1. Jackie (was/were) unable to sleep after drinking coffee just before bedtime.
2. The plants (was/were) harmless to humans but poisonous to animals.
3. Lettuce (was/were) on sale at all the local supermarkets.
4. The most popular foreign language at my high school (was/were) Spanish.
5. Two department stores (was/were) closed three months after a new Wal-Mart opened nearby.
6. Gasoline prices (was/were) much higher this year than the year before.
7. When the four-year-old refused to sit down at the table, she (was/were) told to go to her room.
8. Ten men and seven women (was/were) in the computer class.
9. Matt (was/were) upset to find that someone had broken into his apartment and stolen his television set and computer.
10. After the snowstorm, the lost hikers (was/were) found uninjured.

❖ **ON THE WEB**
For more practice dealing with problem verbs in the past tense, visit Exercise Central *at bedfordstmartins.com/foundationsfirst.*

◆ PRACTICE 25-6

Edit the following passage for errors in the use of the verb *be*. Cross out any underlined verbs that are incorrect, and write the correct forms above them. If a verb form is correct, label it *C*.

Example: In 1947, the House Un-American Activities Committee (HUAC) began questioning people in the movie industry who ~~was~~ *were* suspected of being Communists.

(1) This investigation was one result of the fear of Communism that defined the Cold War between the United States and the Soviet Union.

(2) HUAC were concerned that Communists were using films to spread their ideas. (3) The committee thought that Hollywood were too important to ignore. (4) Many people in the Hollywood community was called to testify in front of HUAC. (5) The most famous group were the "Hollywood 10." (6) These ten people refused to answer questions about their politics, and each one were sent to prison. (7) Other suspected Communists in the film industry was blacklisted. (8) This meant that they were not allowed to work in the industry. (9) Some blacklisted screenwriters used false names and was able to continue making movies. (10) Fifty years later, after the end of the Cold War, the Screen Writers' Guild was able to add the writers' real names to the credits of the movies they wrote.

D Problem Verbs: *Can/Could* and *Will/Would*

The helping verbs *can/could* and *will/would* can cause problems for writers because their past tense forms are sometimes confused with their present tense forms.

Can/Could

Can, a present tense verb, means "is able to" or "are able to." *Could,* the past tense of *can,* means "was able to" or "were able to."

Students can use the copy machines in the library.

Columbus told the queen he could find a short route to India.

Could is also used to express a possibility or a wish.

The president wishes he could balance the budget.

Will/Would

Will, a present tense verb, talks about the future from the perspective of the present. *Would,* the past tense of *will,* talks about the future from the perspective of the past.

I will finish writing the report tomorrow.

Last week, I told my boss that I would work an extra shift today.

Would is also used to express a possibility or a wish.

If we moved to the country, we would be able to have a garden.

Felicia would like to buy a new car.

FOCUS ***Can/Could* and *Will/Would***

Can/could and *will/would* never change form, no matter what the subject is.

I can/he can/they can

I could/he could/they could

I will/he will/they will

I would/he would/they would

◆ PRACTICE 25-7

In each of the following sentences, circle the correct form of the helping verb.

Example: When I was a child, I (can, could) play for hours without getting tired.

1. Even though the car had a new battery, it (will, would) not start.
2. If it rains all day, the baseball game (will, would) have to be postponed.
3. Carlos (can, could) still play the piano better than anyone I know.
4. When the new library opens next year, it (will, would) have thirty computers.
5. Last Saturday, my friends (can, could) not visit me because the roads were too icy.
6. On the first day of class, the instructor told us that he (will, would) not take attendance.
7. I wish that I (can, could) speak another language.
8. Even if he ran in the marathon, he (will, would) not win.
9. Ben said that he (can, could) drive his sister to the train station.
10. Mary (will, would) like to graduate from college in four years.

◆ PRACTICE 25-8

In the following paragraph, circle the correct form of the helping verb from the choices in parentheses.

Example: In the 1970s, my father decided that his next car (will/would) get good gas mileage.

(1) Although everyone complains about the high cost of energy, people (can/could) do something about their energy use. (2) As the price of gasoline rises, drivers (will/would) have to pay more to fill up their vehicles. (3) If car owners switched from gas-guzzling SUVs to hybrid cars, they (will/would) save money and do something good for the environment. (4) Heating oil (can/could) also be a major expense during the winter. (5) Although no one (can/could) do anything about the weather, homeowners (can/could) lower their heating bills if they kept the thermostat turned down in the house. (6) During the energy crisis of the 1970s, people realized that they (will/would) save energy this way. (7) If every household took this step, the United States (will/would) lower its need for foreign oil. (8) Even changing a light bulb (can/could) make a difference. (9) A person who replaces a single light bulb with an energy-efficient bulb (will/would) not see a huge difference in the electric bill, but if everyone made this change, the United States (will/would) save a lot of electricity. (10) In the past, people made sacrifices to save energy, and Americans today (can/could) lower their energy use, too.

• REVISING AND EDITING

Look back at your response to the Seeing and Writing exercise on page 339. Underline every past tense verb you have used, and check to make sure you used the correct past tense form in each case. Then, cross out any incorrect forms, and write the correct past tense form of the verb above the line.

CHAPTER REVIEW

◆ EDITING PRACTICE

Read the following paragraph, which contains errors in past tense verb forms, and decide whether each of the underlined past tense verbs is correct. If the verb is correct, write *C* above it. If it is not, cross out the verb, and write the correct past tense form. The first two sentences have been corrected for you. (If necessary, consult the list of irregular verbs on pp. 342–43.)

Crazy Horse

Crazy Horse was the greatest Sioux leader. He was someone who ~~want~~ wanted to preserve Sioux traditions and ways of life. Along with other chiefs, such as Sitting Bull and Red Cloud, Crazy Horse resist the invasion of white settlers. For many years, he successfully defended the Black Hills and keeped them from U.S. military control. The American government want to move the Sioux to a reservation. However, Crazy Horse knew that the government could not be trusted, and he fight hard to keep his people on their land. Crazy Horse won many battles. His most famous victory were over General George Custer. In 1876, Crazy Horse meeted Custer at the Battle of Little Bighorn. Custer plan to surprise Sitting Bull at his camp next to the Little Bighorn River. Custer was not prepared for what he encounter, and Crazy Horse and Sitting Bull wipe out his entire unit. After defeating Custer, Crazy Horse continued to fight the U.S. Army. However, less than a year after the Battle of Little Bighorn, Crazy Horse surrender to the army. The Sioux finally agree to move to a reservation. Then, shortly after the army moved him and his people to a reservation, Crazy Horse were arrested. The army accuse him of planning a revolt, and once they had him in custody, they kill him. Many people thinked Crazy Horse was a hero because he defended his people and sticked to his beliefs. To honor him, a huge memorial was started in 1948. The Native Americans who commissioned the sculpture wanted everyone to know about their hero.

The battle between General Custer and Crazy Horse

The Crazy Horse memorial

◆ COLLABORATIVE ACTIVITIES

1. List ten verbs in the present tense. Then, exchange papers with another student, and write the past tense form of each verb beside the present tense form. Exchange papers again, and check the other student's work.
2. Work in a group of three or four students to choose ten verbs from the lists you made for activity 1. Work together to write a sentence for each of the verbs in the present tense. Then, exchange the sentences with another group, and ask them to rewrite the sentences in the past tense. When you have finished, check each other's work.
3. Working in a group, collaborate on a paragraph about an event that occurred in the past. First, write the paragraph in the present tense, as if the event were happening as you write. Then, exchange paragraphs with another group, and rewrite their paragraph by putting the verbs in the past tense wherever appropriate. When you get your group's paragraph back, check to make sure that all the past tense forms are correct.

4. ***Composing original sentences*** Working in a group, compose five sentences with past tense verbs. Make sure that the verb forms are correct. When you have finished, check your sentences again to correct any errors in grammar, punctuation, or spelling.

☑ REVIEW CHECKLIST: Verbs: Past Tense

- The past tense of a verb indicates that an action or situation happened in the past. (See 25A.)
- Regular verbs form the past tense by adding either *-d* or *-ed* to the base form of the verb. (See 25A.)
- Irregular verbs have irregular forms in the past tense. (See 25B.)
- *Be* is the only verb in English that has two different forms in the past tense—one for singular and one for plural. (See 25C.)
- *Could* is the past tense of *can*. *Would* is the past tense of *will*. (See 25D.)

Verbs: Past Participles

CHAPTER 26

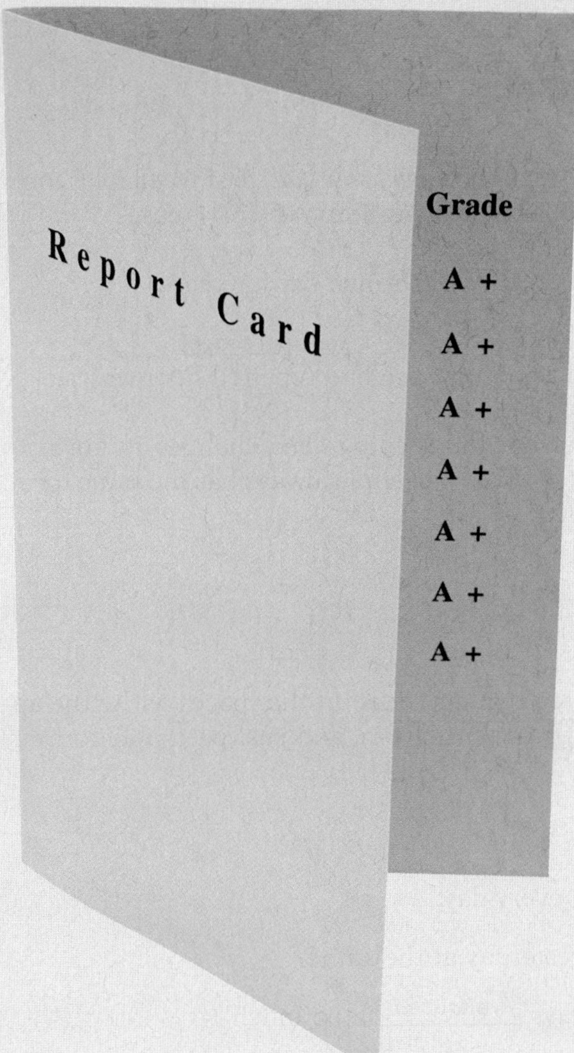

PREVIEW

In this chapter, you will learn

- to identify regular past participles (26A)
- to identify irregular past participles (26B)
- to use the present perfect tense (26C)
- to use the past perfect tense (26D)
- to use past participles as adjectives (26E)

• SEEING AND WRITING

The picture above shows a report card with all A+ grades. Look at the picture, and then write a paragraph about something you really wanted to achieve and finally did. Explain whether or not you now believe the goal you achieved was worth the struggle.

Word Power

crave to have a strong desire for something

envision to imagine

anticipate to look forward to

A Regular Past Participles

Every verb has a **past participle** form. The past participle form of a *regular verb* is the same as the past tense form. Both are formed by adding *-d* or *-ed* to the base form of the verb (the present tense form of the verb used with *I*).

PAST TENSE
He wondered.

PAST PARTICIPLE
He has wondered.

Combined with a helping verb, such as *has* or *had*, past participles form the **present perfect** (see 26C) and **past perfect** (see 26D) tenses.

HELPING VERB PAST PARTICIPLE
PRESENT PERFECT TENSE She has repaired her own car for years.

HELPING VERB PAST PARTICIPLE
PAST PERFECT TENSE She told him that she had repaired her own car.

In the examples above, note that the helping verb changes its form to agree with its subject but that the past participle always has the same form: *I have repaired/She has repaired*.

◆ PRACTICE 26-1

✣ **ON THE WEB**
For more practice identifying regular past participles, visit Exercise Central *at bedford stmartins.com/foundations first.*

Below are the base forms of ten regular verbs. In the spaces, write the appropriate present tense form, past tense form, and past participle form.

Example
shout

present: She ___shouts___ every day.

past: They ___shouted___ yesterday at the game.

past participle: I have always ___shouted___ too much.

1. agree

   present: He always __________ with me.

   past: We __________ yesterday.

   past participle: They had __________ before the summit meeting.

2. love

   present: She __________ her new iPod.

   past: You __________ those cupcakes last week.

   past participle: He has __________ her for years.

3. drop

present: He always __________ the ball.

past: I __________ that course last semester.

past participle: She has always __________ the children off at day care before work.

4. cry

present: The baby __________ every night.

past: He __________ when she left.

past participle: He had also __________ the night before.

5. work

present: It __________ every time.

past: I __________ the late shift last year.

past participle: You have __________ since you were fourteen years old.

◆ PRACTICE 26-2

Fill in the correct past participle form of each verb in parentheses.

Example: An energetic and engaging performer, Cuban singer Celia Cruz had ___*gained*___ (gain) the devotion of fans all over the world.

1. By the time she died in 2003, Celia Cruz had __________ (live) in the United States for more than forty years.
2. She had __________ (start) her career in Cuba, where she was one of her country's biggest stars.
3. She had __________ (escape) to the United States in 1959, fleeing the Communist regime in Cuba.
4. Cruz had always __________ (refuse) to return to Cuba as long as Castro was in power.
5. Over the years, her many recordings have __________ (help) to make her music popular in Europe as well as in the United States.
6. Because of her singing, many people around the world have __________ (learn) to love salsa music.
7. Her music has also __________ (inspire) many young Latina singers.

8. By the time of her death at the age of seventy-nine, Celia Cruz had __________ (record) more than seventy albums.
9. She had also __________ (earn) many awards, including five Grammys, two Latin Grammys, three honorary doctorates, and a National Medal of Arts.
10. For her many contributions to Latin music, she had also __________ (acquire) the title "The Queen of Salsa."

B Irregular Past Participles

Irregular verbs nearly always have irregular past participle forms. Irregular verbs do not form the past participle by adding *-d* or *-ed* to the base form of the verb.

Base Form	*Past Tense*	*Past Participle*
choose	chose	chosen
sing	sang	sung
wear	wore	worn

The following chart lists the base form, the past tense form, and the past participle of the most common irregular verbs. If you do not find a verb on this chart, look it up in a dictionary.

Irregular Past Participles

Base Form	**Past Tense**	**Past Participle**
awake	awoke	awoken
be (am, are)	was, were	been
beat	beat	beaten
become	became	become
begin	began	begun
bet	bet	bet
bite	bit	bitten
blow	blew	blown
break	broke	broken
bring	brought	brought
build	built	built
buy	bought	bought
catch	caught	caught
choose	chose	chosen
come	came	come

(continued on following page)

(continued from previous page)

Base Form	***Past Tense***	***Past Participle***
cost	cost	cost
cut	cut	cut
dive	dove, dived	dived
do	did	done
draw	drew	drawn
drink	drank	drunk
drive	drove	driven
eat	ate	eaten
fall	fell	fallen
feed	fed	fed
feel	felt	felt
fight	fought	fought
find	found	found
fly	flew	flown
forgive	forgave	forgiven
freeze	froze	frozen
get	got	got, gotten
give	gave	given
go	went	gone
grow	grew	grown
have	had	had
hear	heard	heard
hide	hid	hidden
hold	held	held
hurt	hurt	hurt
keep	kept	kept
know	knew	known
lay (to place)	laid	laid
lead	led	led
leave	left	left
let	let	let
lie (to recline)	lay	lain
light	lit	lit
lose	lost	lost
make	made	made
meet	met	met
pay	paid	paid
put	put	put
quit	quit	quit
read	read	read
ride	rode	ridden
ring	rang	rung
rise	rose	risen
run	ran	run
say	said	said
see	saw	seen

(continued on following page)

(continued from previous page)

Base Form	***Past Tense***	***Past Participle***
sell	sold	sold
send	sent	sent
set	set	set
shake	shook	shaken
shine	shone, shined	shone, shined
sing	sang	sung
sit	sat	sat
sleep	slept	slept
speak	spoke	spoken
spend	spent	spent
spring	sprang	sprung
stand	stood	stood
steal	stole	stolen
stick	stuck	stuck
sting	stung	stung
swear	swore	sworn
swim	swam	swum
take	took	taken
teach	taught	taught
tear	tore	torn
tell	told	told
think	thought	thought
throw	threw	thrown
understand	understood	understood
wake	woke, waked	woken, waked
wear	wore	worn
win	won	won
write	wrote	written

◆ PRACTICE 26-3

Below are the base forms of ten irregular verbs. In the spaces after each verb, write the appropriate present tense form, past tense form, and past participle form. If necessary, refer to the chart on pages 354–56.

✣ **ON THE WEB**
For more practice identifying irregular past participles, visit Exercise Central *at bedford stmartins.com/foundations first.*

Example
sleep

present: He ___sleeps___ late every Sunday morning.

past: Until she was three years old, she ___slept___ in a crib.

past participle: The dog has ___slept___ on our bed since he was a small puppy.

1. take

   present: She __________ cream in her coffee.

   past: The hospital emergency room __________ more patients than it could handle.

   past participle: It has __________ three months to straighten out my bills.

2. say

   present: Walter __________ he knows how to ski, but I'm not sure I believe him.

   past: The teacher __________ we had to write all our answers in complete sentences.

   past participle: Until this year, every graduation speaker had __________ that we graduates were the hope of the future.

3. spend

   present: I __________ more and more on gas every week.

   past: Last year, the United States __________ millions of dollars on AIDS prevention.

   past participle: Because they had __________ more than they earned for several years, they had to declare bankruptcy.

4. read

   present: She __________ three newspapers every day.

   past: She __________ in the paper that state legislators voted themselves a raise.

   past participle: He has already __________ most of the books for the course.

5. choose

   present: Every Sunday, the minister __________ a subject for the sermon.

   past: They __________ the best players for the All-Star team.

   past participle: He had __________ an engagement ring before he proposed, but his fiancée didn't like it.

◆ PRACTICE 26-4

Fill in the correct past participle form of each irregular verb in parentheses below. Refer to the chart on pages 354–56 as needed.

Example: The nation of Dubai, one of the United Arab Emirates, has ___*begun*___ (begin) a number of spectacular building projects during the past few years.

(1) As the price of oil has gone up, Dubai has __________ (receive) a great deal of oil money. (2) At the same time, many wealthy people have __________ (invest) in Dubai. (3) One way it has __________ (spend) much of this oil wealth is on construction. (4) In the past, Dubai had not __________ (allow) outsiders to invest in projects within the country. (5) Now, however, Dubai has __________ (let) foreigners invest. (6) One investment project has __________ (extend) Dubai's coastline past its original forty miles. (7) Developers have __________ (build) luxury homes and shopping malls in the new area. (8) In the Persian Gulf, builders have __________ (decide) to create artificial islands, some in the shape of palm trees. (9) They have __________ (plan) to spend $14 billion on this area, which will include expensive hotels. (10) The Crown Prince of Dubai has also __________ (say) that there will be a huge theme park called Dubailand.

C The Present Perfect Tense

The **present perfect tense** consists of the present tense of the helping verb *have* plus the past participle.

The Present Perfect Tense
(have or has + past participle)

Singular	***Plural***
I have gained.	We have gained.
You have gained.	You have gained.
He has gained.	They have gained.
She has gained.	
It has gained.	

Use the present perfect tense to indicate that an action or activity began in the past and continues into the present.

PRESENT PERFECT TENSE The Gallup poll has predicted elections since the 1930s. (The predicting began in the past and continues into the present.)

Use the present perfect tense to indicate that an action has just occurred.

PRESENT PERFECT TENSE I have just voted. (The voting has just occurred.)

◆ PRACTICE 26-5

In the following paragraph, form the present perfect tense by filling in the correct form of *have* and the correct past participle form of the verb in parentheses.

❖ **ON THE WEB**
For more practice using the present perfect tense, visit Exercise Central *at* bedford stmartins.com/foundations first.

Example: The invention of the cochlear implant ___has___ ___given___ (give) many deaf people the chance to get back some of their hearing.

(1) The cochlear implant, an electronic device that is surgically implanted in the inner ear, __________ __________ (be) available since the 1980s. (2) Although an implant cannot fully bring back a person's hearing, it __________ __________ (make) it easier for some people to function in the hearing world. (3) People who __________ __________ (choose) to get cochlear implants can usually hear well enough to use a telephone. (4) Children who get the implants early enough __________ __________ (be) able to learn to speak. (5) However, this device __________ __________ (cause) a heated debate within the deaf community. (6) Many deaf people __________ __________ (speak) out against cochlear implants. (7) They are proud of their deafness and feel that they __________ __________ (lead) full and satisfying lives using American Sign Language (ASL) as their main means of communication. (8) They think that cochlear implants __________ __________ (hurt) deaf culture. (9) As a result, although some people __________ __________ (welcome) cochlear implants, others have not. (10) The invention of this device __________ __________ (cause) more controversy than anyone ever thought possible.

◆ PRACTICE 26-6

Circle the appropriate verb tense (past tense or present perfect) from the choices in parentheses.

Example: Don Larsen (threw/has thrown) the ceremonial first pitch in the first game of the 2000 World Series.

(1) For more than a century, baseball fans (enjoyed/have enjoyed) talking about their favorite games. (2) One of the most famous games ever played (was/has been) the fifth game of the 1956 World Series. (3) The New York Yankees (played/have played) the Brooklyn Dodgers in the World Series that year. (4) In game five, the Yankees' Don Larsen (pitched/has pitched) a perfect game, allowing no hits and no runs. (5) People who (saw/has seen) that game agree that it was unforgettable. (6) Perfect games (were always/have always been) extremely rare. (7) Only a few pitchers ever (had/have had) a perfect game, and so far, no one other than Larsen ever (pitched/has pitched) a perfect game in the World Series. (8) The Yankees (won/have won) the 1956 World Series in seven games. (9) In 1957, the Brooklyn Dodgers (moved/have moved) to Los Angeles. (10) The 1956 World Series (was/has been) the last all–New York series until 2000, when the Mets (played/have played) the Yankees.

D The Past Perfect Tense

The **past perfect tense** consists of the past tense of the helping verb *have* plus the past participle.

The Past Perfect Tense
(*had + past participle*)

Singular	*Plural*
I had returned.	We had returned.
You had returned.	You had returned.
He had returned.	They had returned.
She had returned.	
It had returned.	

Use the past perfect tense to indicate that one past action occurred before another past action.

PAST PERFECT TENSE — The job applicant told (PAST) the receptionist that he had arrived (PAST PERFECT). (The job applicant arrived at the interview *before* he talked to the receptionist.)

◆ PRACTICE 26-7

Circle the appropriate verb tense (present perfect or past perfect) from the choices in parentheses.

Example: Many businesses today (have invested/had invested) in "detective" software to monitor their staff.

1. Before this software became available, many employers (have become/had become) convinced that their employees were not always working when they were online.
2. "Detective" software (has allowed/had allowed) companies to track the Web sites that their workers visit.
3. Originally, manufacturers of this software (have marketed/had marketed) their product mostly to businesses.
4. Now, it is widely available, and many people (have bought/had bought) this kind of software for their own personal use.
5. Previously, parents (have been/had been) unable to monitor what their children were doing online.
6. Now, using this "detective" technology, parents (have been/had been) tracking their young children's searches and even blocking some sites.
7. In addition, husbands and wives (have used/had used) this software to find out what their spouses were doing online.
8. Although this "detective" software (has taken/had taken) away some privacy, it also (has given/had given) us more control.
9. Nowadays, most people (have developed/had developed) a healthy suspicion of computers and are aware that others may be watching.
10. Those who (have hoped/had hoped) for complete privacy now realize that for better or for worse, they are never alone.

ON THE WEB
For more practice using the past perfect tense, visit Exercise Central *at bedfordstmartins.com/foundationsfirst.*

◆ PRACTICE 26-8

Fill in the appropriate tense (past tense or past perfect) of the verb in parentheses.

Example: In 1914, Sir Ernest Shackleton ___set___ (set) out with twenty-seven men to cross the Antarctic continent.

(1) No one ______________ (do) this before, and Shackleton ______________ (hope) to be the first. (2) However, he ______________ (fail) to reach his goal. (3) Early in the journey, his ship, called the *Endurance*, ______________ (run) into ice in the Weddell Sea. (4) The ice ______________ (destroy) the ship and ______________ (halt) the expedition. (5) Although Shackleton ______________ (plan) to end the journey on the other side of Antarctica, the team never even ______________ (make) it to the Antarctic continent. (6) After they ______________ (lose) the *Endurance*, the crew ______________ (have) only three small lifeboats. (7) They ______________ (spend) the next year trying to get back to their starting point. (8) Their difficult journey home through the dark, frozen sea ______________ (become) one of the greatest survival stories of all time. (9) Miraculously, by 1916, the entire crew ______________ (arrive) home safely. (10) None of them ______________ (die). (11) On earlier expeditions, Shackleton ______________ (show) himself to be an excellent leader; this time, he ______________ (prove) that he could lead a group safely through the most hostile territory on earth.

E Past Participles as Adjectives

In addition to functioning as verbs, past participles can function as **adjectives**, modifying nouns that follow them.

My aunt sells painted furniture.

I like fried chicken.

The past participle is also used as an adjective after a **linking verb**—such as *be*, *become*, or *seem*. A linking verb connects a subject to the word that describes it.

Mallory was surprised.

My roommate became depressed.

The applicant seemed qualified for the job.

◆ PRACTICE 26-9

The following paragraph contains errors in past participle forms used as adjectives. Cross out any underlined participle that is incorrect, and write the correct form above it. If the participle form is correct, label it *C*.

Example: For more than 150 years, the telegram was ~~use~~ used by people who wanted to send messages in the fastest way.

(1) The telegram was invented by Samuel F. B. Morse in 1844. (2) He created Morse Code, a system of dots and dashes that were transmit by skill operators. (3) Before the first transcontinental telegraph line was completed, the fastest way to send a message from New York to California was by Pony Express, which took about ten days. (4) With a telegram, that message could be receive almost immediately. (5) For many years, the Western Union Company, with its teams of 14,000 uniform messenger boys, was the most famous telegraph company. (6) At first, the dots and dashes of the Morse Code messages were wrote out by clerks. (7) In 1914, the teletype was create, allowing the Morse Code to be automatically decoded on a strip of ticker tape. (8) For many years, people received unexpect bad news by telegram, so they learned to fear a knock at the door by a Western Union messenger. (9) After World War II, long-distance telephone calls became easier and cheaper to make, and the telegram was needed less and less. (10) In 2001, the last telegram was deliver.

ON THE WEB
For more practice using past participles as adjectives, visit Exercise Central *at bedford stmartins.com/foundations first.*

● REVISING AND EDITING

Look back at your response to the Seeing and Writing exercise on page 351. Did you use the present perfect or past perfect tense? If so, underline the helping verbs and past participles. Then, check to make sure that you used these tenses correctly. Cross out any incorrect verb forms, and write your corrections above them.

CHAPTER REVIEW

◆ EDITING PRACTICE

Read the following paragraph, which contains errors in the use of past participles and in the use of the past, present perfect, and past perfect tenses. Decide whether each of the underlined verbs is correct. If it is correct, write *C* above it. If it is not, cross it out, and write in the correct verb form. The first sentence has been done for you.

The Boondocks

When *The Boondocks* started in 1997, Aaron McGruder, its creator, ~~have~~ had not yet graduated from college. McGruder wants to draw a comic strip that examined serious subjects, especially racial issues. Since *The Boondocks* begun, it had amused many people. It has also maked many others angry. Through the eyes of two African-American brothers who have moved from Chicago to an all-white suburb, *The Boondocks* has comment on many controversial topics. The comic strip had often criticized politicians and pop icons, including black entertainers. For example, one of the brothers, Huey, is name after Huey P. Newton, a black radical of the 1960s. Huey is often anger by ignorance of black issues, even among blacks themselves. He has disapprove of Secretary of State Condoleezza Rice and actor Cuba Gooding Jr. The other brother, Riley, is fascinated by the "thug life" that some rappers glamorize even though *The Boondocks* has condemn this lifestyle. The comic strip had been very successful. Starting in November 2005, an animated series featuring *The Boondocks* was showed on television. In 2006, the TV series was nominate by the NAACP Image Awards for the Most Outstanding Comedy Series.

The Boondocks *by Aaron McGruder*

◆ COLLABORATIVE ACTIVITIES

1. Form a group of four students. Working on your own, list five verbs on a sheet of paper. Pass the paper to the person next to you, and write the past tense after each verb on the sheet you receive. Then, pass the paper again; this time, add the past participle of each verb on the sheet you receive. Pass the paper one final time, and then check the work on the sheet you receive.
2. Working in the same group, choose five of the verbs from your papers in activity 1. Write a sentence for each verb. In each sentence, use the present perfect or past perfect tense, or use the past participle as an adjective.
3. Exchange your sentences from activity 2 with another group. Then, choose two of their sentences, and use them in a paragraph that contains at least three other verbs in the present perfect or past perfect tense.
4. ***Composing original sentences*** In a group of four students, work together to create five sentences that use the present perfect or past perfect tense or that use a past participle as an adjective. Be sure that you use the correct participle for each verb, that the verb tense is appropriate, and that the form of the verb in each sentence is correct. When you have finished, check your sentences to correct any errors in grammar, punctuation, or spelling.

☑ REVIEW CHECKLIST: Verbs: Past Participles

- ☐ The past participle form of a regular verb adds *-d* or *-ed* to the base form of the verb. (See 26A.)
- ☐ Irregular verbs usually have irregular past participles. (See 26B.)
- ☐ The present perfect tense consists of the present tense of *have* plus the past participle. It shows a continuing action, usually one that began in the past and continues into the present. (See 26C.)
- ☐ The past perfect tense consists of the past tense of *have* plus the past participle. It describes a past action that occurred before another past action. (See 26D.)
- ☐ The past participle can function as an adjective. (See 26E.)

CHAPTER
27 Nouns

PREVIEW

In this chapter, you will learn

- to identify nouns (27A)
- to recognize singular and plural nouns (27B)
- to form plural nouns (27C)

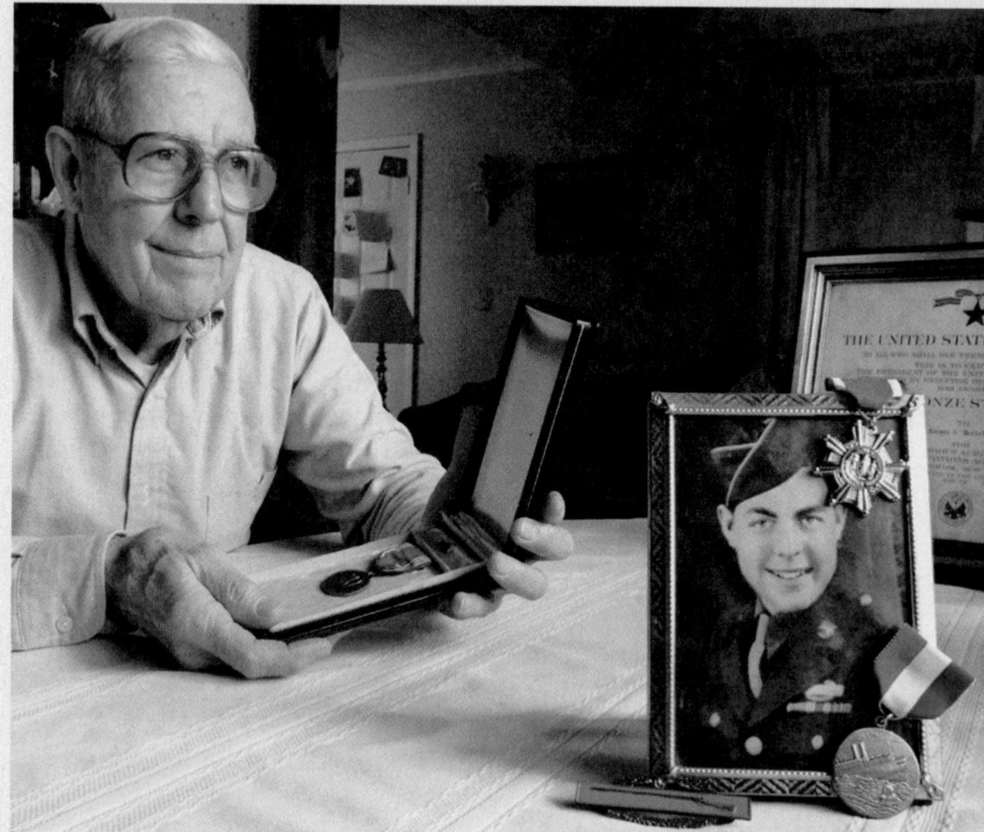

Word Power

memento a reminder of the past; a keepsake (the plural form is *mementos*)

memorabilia objects valued because of their link to historical events or culture

SEEING AND WRITING

The photo above shows a World War II veteran with his treasured wartime memorabilia. What objects do you treasure? Why? Look at the picture, and then write a paragraph in which you answer these questions.

A Nouns

A **noun** is a word that names a person (*actor, Denzel Washington*), an animal (*elephant, Babar*), a place (*city, Houston*), an object (*game, Monopoly*), or an idea (*theory, Darwinism*).

FOCUS Common and Proper Nouns

Most nouns, called **common nouns**, name general classes of people, places, or things. Common nouns begin with lowercase (not capital) letters.

prince holiday

Some nouns, called **proper nouns**, name particular people, places, or things. A proper noun always begins with a capital letter.

Prince Charming Memorial Day

◆ PRACTICE 27-1

In each of the following sentences, underline every noun. Label common nouns *C* and proper nouns *P*.

Example: Day of the Dead (P) is a holiday (C) celebrated in Mexico (P) and in other countries (C) in Latin America (C).

1. This holiday is celebrated every year to honor the spirits of the dead.
2. The celebration occurs in early November, just after people in the United States celebrate Halloween.
3. This holiday was started by the Aztecs, who held a similar ritual.
4. However, the holiday now has Christian as well as Indian traditions.
5. Today, people observe the Day of the Dead differently in different regions.
6. Usually, families visit the graves of their ancestors and bring them offerings of food.
7. In Mexico City, residents usually have a festival and decorate the town with skeletons and skulls made of papier-mâché.
8. For some people, this day is a religious occasion.

ON THE WEB
For more practice identifying nouns, visit Exercise Central *at bedfordstmartins.com/foundationsfirst.*

9. In many places, tourists come to watch the celebration.
10. Many Americans travel to Mexico to see the elaborate decorations and eat the traditional food.

B Recognizing Singular and Plural Nouns

A **singular noun** names one thing: *book, family*. A **plural noun** names more than one thing: *books, families*.

FOCUS Singular and Plural Nouns

Recognizing whether a noun is singular or plural is particularly important when a noun is the subject of a sentence. This is because subjects and verbs must always be in **agreement**: a singular subject takes a singular verb; a plural subject takes a plural verb.

SINGULAR The book sits on the shelf.

PLURAL The books sit on the shelf.

Because many plural nouns end in *-s*, you can often tell whether a noun is singular or plural by looking at its ending. However, many other nouns that end in *-s* are singular (*gas, series, focus*), and some plural nouns have special forms that do not end in *-s* (*men, women, children*).

Sometimes, a noun is introduced by a **determiner**, a word that specifically identifies the noun or limits its meaning (*this house*, not *that house*). In these cases, the determiner can tell you whether the noun is singular (*this house*) or plural (*these houses*).

Using Determiners with Nouns

Determiners That Introduce Singular Nouns	***Determiners That Introduce Plural Nouns***
a	all
an	both
another	few
each	many
every	most
one	several
that	these
this	those
	two, three, etc.

NOTE: *The* can introduce either a singular or a plural noun.

◆ PRACTICE 27-2

In the following sentences, fill in the blanks with appropriate singular or plural nouns.

Example: Both ___men___ applied for the same job.

1. He tried to rent an ________, but he couldn't find one big enough.
2. Each ________ that she called had tables available only at 6 p.m.
3. There were few ________ on the train.
4. She has always wanted to own a ________.
5. Those ________ can be steamed or boiled for fifteen minutes.
6. I can get along with most ________.
7. That ________ has never been away from home for more than one ________.
8. Every ________ in the audience stood up and cheered at the end of the speech.
9. Carmine went to three ________, but he couldn't find the book he wanted.
10. Another ________ substituted while Mr. Blaine was sick.

✣ **ON THE WEB**
For more practice regarding singular and plural nouns, visit Exercise Central *at bedfordstmartins.com/foundationsfirst.*

◆ PRACTICE 27-3

In the following sentences, singular and plural nouns that follow determiners are underlined. Decide whether the correct singular or plural form is used for each underlined noun. If the form is correct, write *C* above the noun. If it is incorrect, cross it out; then, write in the correct singular or plural noun form.

Example: How do you tell if a ~~nouns~~ noun is plural?

1. The Carolina Hurricanes won the Stanley Cup after hockey players were on strike for several <u>month</u>.
2. Many <u>student</u> do not have Internet access at home.
3. Not even Superman could break down that <u>door</u>.
4. Where did you find those <u>clip</u> of old Beatles concerts?
5. His family goes to the Indianapolis 500 every <u>years</u>.
6. Pittsburgh has very few <u>mornings</u> without fog.

7. Why did you bring me another burgers?

8. She has never been to that museums.

9. These math problem can be very challenging.

10. I have watched every episodes of *Lost*.

C Forming Plural Nouns

Some nouns form plurals in predictable ways; others do not.

Regular Noun Plurals

Most nouns add *-s* to form plurals. Other nouns form plurals with *-es*. For example, most nouns that end in *-o* add *-es* to form plurals. Other nouns, whose singular forms end in *-s*, *-ss*, *-sh*, *-ch*, *-x*, or *-z*, also add *-es* to form plurals. Some nouns that end in *-s* or *-z* double the *s* or *z* before adding *-es*.

Singular	*Plural*
chair	chairs
hero	heroes
campus	campuses
kiss	kisses
wish	wishes
bunch	bunches
box	boxes
quiz	quizzes

Irregular Noun Plurals

Some nouns form plurals in unusual ways.

- Some nouns have plural forms that are the same as their singular forms.

Singular	*Plural*
one fish	two fish
this species	these species
a series	several series

- Nouns ending in *-f* or *-fe* form plurals by changing the *f* to *v* and adding *-es* or *-s*.

Singular	*Plural*
each half	both halves
one life	nine lives
a thief	many thieves
that loaf	those loaves
the first shelf	several shelves

Exceptions to this rule include the words *roof* (plural *roofs*), *proof* (plural *proofs*), and *belief* (plural *beliefs*).

- Most nouns ending in *-y* form plurals by changing the *y* to *ie* and adding *-s*.

Singular	*Plural*
a new baby	more babies
one berry	many berries

Note, however, that when a vowel (*a*, *e*, *i*, *o*, or *u*) comes before the *y*, the noun has a regular plural form: *turkey* (plural *turkeys*), *day* (plural *days*).

- A **compound noun**—two or more nouns that function as a unit—generally forms the plural just as other nouns do: by adding *-s* at the end (*baby doll, baby dolls*). However, most hyphenated compound nouns form plurals by adding *-s* to the *first word* of the compound.

Singular	*Plural*
Ben's brother-in-law	Ben's two favorite brothers-in-law
a husband-to-be	all the husbands-to-be
one runner-up	many runners-up

- Other irregular plurals must be memorized.

Singular	*Plural*
that child	those children
a good man	a few good men
one woman	several women
my left foot	both feet
a wisdom tooth	my two front teeth

◆ PRACTICE 27-4

Next to each of the following singular nouns, write the plural form of the noun. Then, circle the irregular plurals. (If you are not sure of a word's plural form, check the dictionary. Irregular plurals will be listed there.)

ON THE WEB
For more practice forming plural nouns, visit Exercise Central *at bedfordstmartins .com/foundationsfirst.*

Example: hamburger hamburgers goose (geese)

1. lady-in-waiting ______
2. wolf ______
3. potato ______
4. band ______
5. bench ______
6. knife ______
7. calendar ______
8. boss ______
9. highway ______
10. sheep ______
11. cheese ______
12. bandit ______
13. enemy ______
14. cactus ______

15. calf ______________
16. mouse ______________
17. tax ______________
18. projector ______________
19. stomach ______________
20. fly ______________

◆ PRACTICE 27-5

Proofread the underlined nouns in the following paragraph, checking for correct singular or plural form. If a correction needs to be made, cross out the noun, and write the correct form above it. If the noun is correct, write *C* above it.

Example: Explorers from China sailed the ~~seas~~ (C) before Europeans began to circle the globe.

(1) Many people do not know that in the fifteenth century, Chinese explorers sailed to countrys in the Middle East and even in East Africa. (2) Nine huge sailing shippes made these voyages, with dozenz of others carrying supplys. (3) Over 27,000 mens guarded the fleet. (4) The Chinese travelers brought silks and porcelain with them. (5) They traded to get spicess and pearles for the Chinese royal family. (6) Between 1406 and 1433, the Chinese made several series of trading trips. (7) This was fifty yeares before the first European explorer sailed around the tip of Africa and before Columbus sailed to America. (8) At that time, the Chinese emperor-in-residences could have colonized the world and collected taxs from many other nations. (9) However, they had to spend money to defend themselves against their enemyes, so they had less money to pay for large ships. (10) Also, some traditional beliefs, such as the idea that it was wrong to travel abroad during the lifes of one's parents, ended the trading journies.

• REVISING AND EDITING

Look back at your response to the Seeing and Writing exercise on page 366. First, underline every noun. Then, check to be sure you have capitalized every proper noun and formed plurals correctly.

CHAPTER REVIEW

◆ EDITING PRACTICE

Read the following paragraph, which contains noun errors. Make any editing changes you think are necessary. The first sentence has been edited for you.

The Case for Home Schooling

More than a million ~~childrens~~ children are home schooled in the United ~~states~~ States today, and ~~parentes~~ parents have many different ~~reason~~ reasons for choosing home schooling. For one thing, most school now rely more heavily on standardized testing than they did in past yeares, and some parents disagree with this focus on test score. Also, for some minoritys, the lack of minority role modeles in traditional classrooms is a good reason to leave the public school system. By choosing home schooling, parents can choose the adults who will affect their children's lifes. Another reason why parents choose home schooling is to meet specific needs their children may have. For example, gifted children may not be getting the challenge they need, and students with learning disabilitys may not be getting enough extra help. When they are home schooled, children can get more individual attention and also pursue the activitys that interest them. Of course, home schooling is not an option for every families; there are minus as well as pluses. For example, few parent-to-bes imagine giving up their careeres to teach their children. However, some parents (usually woman) do. Also, because there is less socializing and less competition in a home environment, many people worry that home-schooled children will not be prepared for college or for the real world. However, there are many success story, and home schooling appears to be here to stay.

A parent homeschooling children

◆ COLLABORATIVE ACTIVITIES

1. Working in a group, complete the following chart by listing nouns related to each category, writing one noun on each line. If the noun is a proper noun, be sure to capitalize it. When you have completed the chart, work together to add to the chart the plural form of each singular noun and the singular form of each plural noun. (Use a different color pen, and write these forms beside the nouns.) If the noun has only one form, circle it.

Sports		*Politics*		*Television*		*College*		*Holidays*	
______	______	______	______	______	______	______	______	______	______
______	______	______	______	______	______	______	______	______	______
______	______	______	______	______	______	______	______	______	______
______	______	______	______	______	______	______	______	______	______
______	______	______	______	______	______	______	______	______	______
______	______	______	______	______	______	______	______	______	______
______	______	______	______	______	______	______	______	______	______

2. Continuing to work in the same group, write a sentence on a sheet of paper using one of the nouns from activity 1. Pass the paper to the person next to you; on the sheet you receive, write a related sentence, but use a different noun. Keep passing the sheets and adding sentences until you have a paragraph of at least six sentences on each page.
3. From the paragraphs composed in activity 2, choose the one that your group likes best, and work together to expand it. Then, exchange paragraphs with another group. Rewrite the other group's paragraph, substituting a noun from your chart for one of the nouns in each sentence the other group has written. Finally, read the paragraphs to the class, and choose the funniest revision.
4. ***Composing original sentences*** Working in a group, write five sentences. Make sure that you have used at least one proper noun, at least one determiner that introduces a singular noun, at least one determiner that introduces a plural noun, and at least two plural nouns with irregular plurals. Then, check the nouns carefully to be sure that the forms are correct. When you have finished, check your sentences again to correct any errors in grammar, punctuation, or spelling.

☑ REVIEW CHECKLIST: Nouns

- A noun is a word that names a person, an animal, a place, an object, or an idea. (See 27A.)
- A singular noun names one thing; a plural noun names more than one thing. (See 27B.)
- Most nouns add *-s* to form plurals. Some nouns have irregular plural forms. (See 27C.)

CHAPTER 28

Pronouns

PREVIEW

In this chapter, you will learn

- to identify pronouns and antecedents (28A)
- to solve special problems with pronoun-antecedent agreement (28B)
- to eliminate vague and unnecessary pronouns (28C)
- to understand pronoun case (28D)
- to solve special problems with pronoun case (28E)
- to identify reflexive and intensive pronouns (28F)

SEEING AND WRITING

The picture above shows a vanity license plate. If you had a vanity license plate, what would you want it to say? Why? Look at the picture, and then write a paragraph in which you answer these questions.

Word Power

vanity excessive pride in one's appearance or achievements

vanity plate a license plate that can be customized for an extra charge

A Identifying Pronouns

A **pronoun** is a word that refers to and takes the place of a noun or another pronoun.

> Evan was bored, so he decided to enlist in the Air Force and change his life.

In the sentence above, the pronouns *he* and *his* refer to and take the place of the noun *Evan*. Without pronouns, you would have to repeat the same nouns over and over again.

> Evan was bored, so Evan decided to enlist in the Air Force and change Evan's life.

Singular and Plural Pronouns

Pronouns, like nouns, can be singular or plural.

- Singular pronouns (*I*, *he*, *she*, *it*, *him*, *his*, *her*, and so on) always take the place of singular nouns or pronouns.

  > Julia forgot to pick up Max, so she went back to get him. (*She* takes the place of *Julia*; *him* takes the place of *Max*.)

- Plural pronouns (*we*, *they*, *our*, *their*, and so on) always take the place of plural nouns or pronouns.

  > Kyle and Mike took their little brother fishing. (*Their* takes the place of *Kyle and Mike*.)

Keep in mind that the pronoun *you* can be either singular or plural.

> When the fans met the rock star, they said, "We're crazy about you." The rock star replied, "I couldn't do it without you." (The first *you* is singular; it takes the place of *rock star*. The second *you* is plural; it takes the place of *fans*.)

◆ PRACTICE 28-1

In each of the following sentences, fill in a suitable pronoun.

Example: ___He___ ate twelve pancakes for breakfast.

1. ______ sold flowers on the street corner.
2. ______ was a very dull book.
3. ______ spent hours trying to get tickets to the game.
4. When the alarm rang, ______ turned it off.
5. The neighborhood is so quiet that ______ seems deserted.

ON THE WEB
For more practice identifying pronouns, visit Exercise Central *at bedfordstmartins .com/foundationsfirst.*

6. Derek, ______ should try out for the cross-country team.

7. The boy looked hungry, but ______ did not ask for any food.

8. The room is clean, children, but ______ forgot to make the beds.

9. Strangers turned away when ______ asked for help.

10. If Cathy had married Heathcliff, ______ might have been happy.

Pronoun-Antecedent Agreement

The word to which the pronoun refers is called its **antecedent**. In the following sentence, the noun *runner* is the antecedent of the pronoun *he*.

> The runner slowed down, but he did not stop.

A pronoun must always **agree** with its antecedent. If an antecedent is singular, the pronoun must also be singular. In the sentence above, the antecedent *runner* is singular, so the pronoun that refers to it (*he*) is also singular.

If the antecedent is plural, the pronoun must also be plural.

> The runners slowed down, but they did not stop.

Here, the antecedent *runners* is plural, so the pronoun that refers to it (*they*) is also plural.

◆ PRACTICE 28-2

In each of the following sentences, a pronoun is underlined. In the blank after each sentence, write the noun that is the antecedent of the underlined pronoun. Then, draw an arrow from the pronoun to its antecedent.

Example: When the kittens were awake, <u>they</u> were constantly eating.

kittens

1. The woman spoke out angrily before <u>she</u> left. ______

2. A frog's skin is so thin that <u>it</u> absorbs pesticides. ______

3. The hitchhiker put out <u>his</u> thumb. ______

4. Felicia won <u>her</u> first karaoke contest and took Friday off. ______

5. When the two lawyers started dating, <u>they</u> decided to stop working together. ______

6. Tino could not get <u>his</u> diploma without a foreign-language credit. ______

7. Esteban saw a film that <u>he</u> hated. ______

ON THE WEB
For more practice understanding pronoun-antecedent agreement, visit Exercise Central *at bedfordstmartins.com/foundationsfirst.*

8. Mr. and Mrs. McCoy almost missed their bus to Florida. ______________

9. Fries taste good, but they are not very nutritious. ______________

10. As Bob crossed the street, a truck narrowly missed him. ______________

◆ PRACTICE 28-3

In the following passage, circle the antecedent of each underlined pronoun. Then, draw an arrow from the pronoun to its antecedent.

Example: Americans are more dissatisfied with the public schools than they used to be.

(1) Some reformers think that if schools have to compete for students, they will be forced to improve. (2) A school voucher system is one way to introduce competition, and it is growing in popularity. (3) School vouchers allow parents to select a school—public or private—of their choice. (4) Some people support a voucher program because they think it will give children in poor and failing school districts the opportunity to get a high-quality education. (5) According to these people, the program would also force weak schools to close their doors. (6) Others, however, oppose the idea because it takes money away from public schools. (7) Washington, D.C., is testing a voucher program for its students. (8) Low-income students can receive up to $7,500 a year for tuition so that they can attend a private school. (9) So far, the parents and schools participating in the voucher program are pleased with it. (10) The parents say that their children are doing better in school and are more interested in going to college.

B Special Problems with Pronoun-Antecedent Agreement

Certain kinds of antecedents can cause problems for writers because they are not easy to identify as singular or plural.

Compound Antecedents

A **compound antecedent** consists of two or more words connected by *and* or *or*: *England and the United States*; *Japan or China*.

- Compound antecedents connected by *and* are always plural. They are always used with plural pronouns.

  England and the United States drafted soldiers into their armies.

- Compound antecedents connected by *or* may take a singular or a plural pronoun. The pronoun always agrees with the word that is closer to it.

  When will European nations or our own country use its [not *their*] resources to fight famine in Africa?

  When will our own country or European nations use their [not *its*] resources to fight famine in Africa?

◆ PRACTICE 28-4

In each of the following sentences, underline the compound antecedent, and circle the connecting word (*and* or *or*). Then, circle the appropriate pronoun in parentheses.

Example: Music fans and moviegoers are finding many reasons to put (its/their) faith in Queen Latifah.

(1) Her power and intelligence have made (its/their) mark on films, television, and music. (2) Her music speaks about the abuse or the lack of respect women receive and (its/their) effects on women's confidence. (3) Queen Latifah is unafraid of her own power and position and uses (it/them) to express her ideas. (4) Feminist issues and politics are never far from her mind, and (its/their) influence on her is clear. (5) In recent years, Queen Latifah has been less focused on music and more focused on movies and television and (its/their) opportunities. (6) On her own talk show, she was able to interview a celebrity guest or ordinary people and speak with (him or her/them) about many issues. (7) In addition, both *Cover Girl* cosmetics and Pizza Hut restaurants have featured Queen Latifah in (its/their) television commercials. (8) After four rap albums, she released an album of soul music and jazz standards, which offered (its/their) own special styles and arrangements. (9) Recently, her movies *Last Holiday* and *Beauty Shop* brought her praise because of (its/their) box office success. (10) Queen Latifah's beauty and independence are inspiring, and (it/they) will clearly take her far in her career.

ON THE WEB
For more practice solving special problems with pronoun-antecedent agreement, visit Exercise Central *at bedfordstmartins .com/foundationsfirst.*

Indefinite Pronoun Antecedents

Most pronouns refer to a specific person or thing. **Indefinite pronouns**, however, do not refer to any particular person or thing.

Most indefinite pronouns are singular.

Singular Indefinite Pronouns

another	either	neither	somebody
anybody	everybody	nobody	someone
anyone	everyone	no one	something
anything	everything	nothing	
each	much	one	

When the indefinite pronoun antecedent is singular, use a singular pronoun to refer to it.

Something was out of its usual place. (*Something* is singular, so it is used with the singular pronoun *its*.)

FOCUS Singular Indefinite Pronouns with *Of*

The singular indefinite pronouns *each*, *either*, *neither*, and *one* are often used in phrases with *of*—*each of*, *either of*, *neither of*, *one of*—followed by a plural noun (*each of the boys*). In such phrases, these indefinite pronoun antecedents are always singular and take singular pronouns.

Each of the games has its [not *their*] own rules.

A few indefinite pronouns are plural.

Plural Indefinite Pronouns

both	others
few	several
many	

When the indefinite pronoun antecedent is plural, use a plural pronoun to refer to it.

The whole group wanted to go swimming, but few had brought their bathing suits. (*Few* is plural, so it is used with the plural pronoun *their*.)

FOCUS **Using *His or Her* with Indefinite Pronouns**

Singular indefinite pronouns that refer to people—such as *anybody*, *anyone*, *everybody*, *everyone*, *somebody*, and *someone*—require a singular pronoun, such as *his*.

However, using the singular pronoun *his* in such cases suggests that the indefinite pronoun refers to a male. Using *his or her* is more accurate because the indefinite pronoun may refer to either a male or a female.

Everyone must revise his or her work.

When used over and over again, however, *he or she*, *him or her*, and *his or her* can create wordy, repetitive sentences. To avoid this problem, use a plural noun instead of the indefinite pronoun.

All students must revise their work.

◆ PRACTICE 28-5

Edit the following sentences for errors in pronoun-antecedent agreement. In some sentences, substitute *his or her* for *their* when the antecedent is singular and could refer to a person of either gender. In other sentences, replace the antecedent with a plural word or phrase.

Example: Everyone in the restaurant complained to ~~their~~ *his or her* waiter.

1. Someone left their key in the lock.
2. Each of the trees grows at their own rate.
3. Everyone on the platform missed their train.
4. Neither of the boys remembers their former home in Oregon.
5. Every telemarketer hated making their calls at dinnertime.
6. Either Sandra or Emily should sign their name here.
7. Anyone would love to give this toy to their children.
8. Neither of these chairs will look as good as they did before the fire.
9. Everyone must email their essays to the professor.
10. Each of us has our own cell phone.

◆ PRACTICE 28-6

In each of the following sentences, circle the indefinite pronouns. Then, circle the pronoun in parentheses that refers to the indefinite pronoun antecedent.

Example: Everyone who plays an ongoing character on the popular *CSI* television series uses (his or her/their) forensic skills to solve crimes.

1. Like the investigators on *CSI*, many forensic scientists work for the police, spending (his or her/their) time on crime detection.
2. Investigators started modern forensic science in the nineteenth century, when several used (his or her/their) knowledge of photography to identify repeat criminals.
3. Someone could be identified by (his or her/their) "mug shot," taken at a previous arrest.
4. Eventually, anyone who had (his or her/their) fingerprints on file with a police department could be traced.
5. The first murder solved by fingerprint identification involved two suspects in Argentina, and both were required to supply (his or her/their) fingerprints.
6. After the police matched one fingerprint with a bloody fingerprint found at the scene of the crime, one of the most notorious cases in Argentina came to (its/their) end.
7. When criminals violate the law, few can avoid leaving some evidence of (his or her/their) presence at the scene.
8. Neither the careless criminal nor the careful criminal can escape (his or her/their) punishment if there is a DNA match.
9. When we study the investigators on the *CSI* television shows, we notice that each specializes in (his or her/their) own area of forensics.
10. On the show, someone usually uses DNA analysis to solve (his or her/their) assigned crime.

Collective Noun Antecedents

Collective nouns are singular words (like *band* and *team*) that name a group of people or things. Because they are singular, collective noun antecedents are used with singular pronouns.

The band was very loud, but it was not very good.

In the sentence above, the collective noun *band* names a group of individual musicians, but it refers to them as a unit. Because *band* is singular, it is used with the singular pronoun *it*.

Frequently Used Collective Nouns

army	committee	government	pack
association	company	group	posse
band	crowd	jury	team
class	family	league	union
club	gang	mob	

◆ PRACTICE 28-7

In each of the following sentences, underline the antecedent. If the antecedent is a collective noun, write *coll* above it. Then, circle the correct pronoun in parentheses.

Example: The mob (coll) chased (its/their) victim.

1. A wolf pack sometimes tracks (its/their) prey for a long time.
2. Last night, our football team celebrated (its/their) first victory in two years.
3. The officers carried (its/their) guns all the time.
4. The committee holds (its/their) meeting on the first Friday of every month.
5. The gang displayed (its/their) colors proudly.
6. The crowd roared (its/their) encouragement to the runners.
7. The class applauded (its/their) teacher, Mr. Henry.
8. The posse made (its/their) way across the plains.
9. The jury gave (its/their) decision to the court clerk.
10. Some people move (its/their) hands rapidly while speaking.

◆ PRACTICE 28-8

Edit the following paragraph for correct pronoun-antecedent agreement. First, identify the antecedent of each underlined pronoun. (Some antecedents will be compounds, some will be indefinite pronouns, and some will be collective nouns.) Next, cross out any pronoun that does not agree with its antecedent, and write the correct form above it. If the pronoun is correct, label it *C*.

Example: Tiger Woods and Jerome Iginla have both won acclaim for ~~his~~ their athletic abilities.

(1) Golf and hockey are very different sports, but they have one thing in common: its players tend to be white. (2) In golf, though, this situation is changing, with one of the world's most popular golfers leaving their mark on the sport. (3) Tiger Woods is unique because no one has broken the records of their sport more often. (4) Woods and other nonwhite golfers are opening the sport to others who want to follow in his or her footsteps. (5) Because of these players, everyone has altered their view of what a golfer looks like. (6) Although hockey is still waiting for its own Tiger Woods, black players are now more common. (7) For example, in 2004, the Calgary Flames team introduced their right wing, Jerome Iginla, the first black hockey captain to play in the National Hockey League's Stanley Cup Finals. (8) Both American fans and Canadian fans have given Iginla his or her strong support. (9) On youth teams and in professional hockey, players like Iginla are becoming role models for their young followers. (10) In the future, either Iginla or the African-American hockey players who follow him should take his place among famous athletes of all races.

C Vague and Unnecessary Pronouns

Vague and unnecessary pronouns clutter up your writing. Eliminating them will make your writing clearer and easier for readers to follow.

Vague Pronouns

A pronoun should always refer to a specific antecedent. When a pronoun has no antecedent, it confuses readers. The pronouns *it* and *they* can be particularly troublesome.

VAGUE PRONOUN In the news report, they said city workers would strike. (Who said city workers would strike?)

VAGUE PRONOUN It says in today's paper that overcrowded prisons are a serious problem. (Who says overcrowded prisons are a problem?)

When you use *it* or *they* as the subject of a sentence, check carefully to be sure the pronoun refers to a specific antecedent in the sentence. If it does not, delete it, or replace it with a noun that communicates your meaning to readers.

REVISED The news report said city workers would strike.

REVISED An editorial in today's paper says that overcrowded prisons are a serious problem.

Unnecessary Pronouns

When a pronoun directly follows its antecedent, it is usually unnecessary.

UNNECESSARY PRONOUN The librarian, he recommended Toni Morrison's *Beloved*.

In the above sentence, the pronoun *he* serves no purpose. Readers do not need to be directed back to the pronoun's antecedent (the noun *librarian*) because it appears right before the pronoun. The pronoun should therefore be eliminated.

REVISED The librarian recommended Toni Morrison's *Beloved*.

◆ PRACTICE 28-9

The following sentences contain vague and unnecessary pronouns. Rewrite each sentence correctly on the lines below it.

Example: On the Web site, it claimed that a spaceship was following the comet.

The Web site claimed that a spaceship was following the comet.

ON THE WEB
For more practice eliminating vague and unnecessary pronouns, visit Exercise Central *at bedfordstmartins .com/foundationsfirst.*

1. In Canada, they have many sparsely populated areas.

2. My dog, he likes to play in water.

3. The video game that I bought, it broke almost immediately.

4. In the pamphlet, it explained how AIDS is transmitted.

5. Her granddaughter, she lives in another state.

6. On that game show, they know the answers to very difficult questions.

____

____

7. These apples, they were damaged in the hailstorm.

____

____

8. On the sidewalk, they were all watching the television in the store window.

____

____

9. The acrobat, he almost fell off the tightrope.

____

____

10. In her class, they do not review grammar.

____

____

D Pronoun Case

A **personal pronoun** refers to a particular person or thing. Personal pronouns change form according to their function in a sentence. Personal pronouns can be *subjective*, *objective*, or *possessive*.

Personal Pronouns

	Subjective Case	***Objective Case***	***Possessive Case***
singular forms	I	me	my, mine
	he	him	his
	she	her	her, hers
	it	it	its
plural forms	we	us	our, ours
	you	you	your, yours
	they	them	their, theirs
	who	whom	whose
	whoever	whomever	

Subjective Case

When a pronoun functions as a subject, it is in the **subjective case**.

She walked along the beach looking for seashells. (The pronoun *She* is the sentence's subject.)

Objective Case

When a pronoun functions as an object, it is in the **objective case**.

Walking along the beach, Lucia saw them. (The pronoun *them* is the direct object of the verb *saw*.)

Lucia brought him a seashell. (The pronoun *him* is the indirect object of the verb *brought*.)

Lucia gave some seashells to them. (The pronoun *them* is the object of the preposition *to*.)

FOCUS Objects

A **direct object** is a noun or pronoun that tells to whom or what the action of the verb is directed.

DIR OBJ
Lucia saw seashells. (What did Lucia see?)

DIR OBJ
Lucia saw them. (What did Lucia see?)

An **indirect object** is a noun or pronoun that tells to whom or for whom the verb's action was done.

IND OBJ
Lucia brought Greg a seashell. (For whom did Lucia bring a seashell?)

IND OBJ
Lucia brought him a seashell. (For whom did Lucia bring a seashell?)

A word or word group introduced by a preposition is called the **object of the preposition**. (See 15C.)

OBJ OF PREP
Lucia gave some seashells to Chris and Kelly. (To whom did Lucia give some seashells?)

OBJ OF PREP
Lucia gave some seashells to them. (To whom did Lucia give some seashells?)

Possessive Case

When a pronoun shows ownership, it is in the **possessive case**.

Tuan rode his bike to work. (The bike belongs to Tuan.)

Kate and Alex took their bikes, too. (The bikes belong to Kate and Alex.)

◆ PRACTICE 28-10

✣ **ON THE WEB**
For more practice understanding pronoun case, visit Exercise Central *at bedfordstmartins.com/ foundationsfirst.*

Above each of the underlined pronouns, indicate whether it is subjective (S), objective (O), or possessive (P).

Example: She gave me my first kiss.
(S over She, O over me, P over my)

1. He played basketball in his first two years of high school.
2. We asked her if she would share her umbrella with us.
3. For a moment, I couldn't remember my name.
4. It gave them great satisfaction to help others.
5. Is this drink mine or yours?
6. You must help me.
7. This is a gift from me to her.
8. The card says, "Happy birthday to you from all of us."
9. Their anniversary is next week, so we are having a party for them at our house.
10. Your car is better than ours or theirs.

◆ PRACTICE 28-11

Above each of the underlined objective case pronouns, indicate whether it is a direct object (DO), an indirect object (IO), or the object of a preposition (OP).

Example: My friends played a clever trick on me.
(OP over me)

1. The president gave him a special citation.
2. The package was sent to them by mistake.
3. The transit officer helped us when we got lost.
4. The band dedicated the last song to her.
5. The owner of the wallet rewarded him very generously.

6. All the attention embarrassed us.
7. I mailed you that check weeks ago.
8. The family always looks to her for the final answer.
9. The clerk handed me my change.
10. Stop tickling me.

E Special Problems with Pronoun Case

Pronouns in Compounds

Sometimes, a pronoun is linked to a noun or to another pronoun with *and* or *or* to form a **compound**.

The tutor and I met in the writing lab.

He and I worked to revise my paper.

To decide whether to use the subjective or objective case for a pronoun in a compound, follow the same rules you would apply for a pronoun that is not part of a compound.

- If the compound in which the pronoun appears is the subject of the sentence, use the subjective case.

  Kia and I [not *me*] like rap music.

  She and I [not *me*] went to a concert.

- If the compound in which the pronoun appears is a direct or indirect object or the object of a preposition, use the objective case.

  The personnel office sent my friend and me [not *I*] the application forms. (indirect object)

  There is a lot of competition between her and me [not *she and I*] for this job. (object of the preposition)

FOCUS Choosing Pronouns in Compounds

To determine which pronoun case to use in a compound that links a noun and a pronoun, rewrite the sentence with just the pronoun.

Kia and [*I* or *me*?] like rap music.

I like rap music. (not *Me like rap music.*)

Kia and I like rap music.

◆ PRACTICE 28-12

In each blank, write the correct form (subjective or objective) of the pronouns in parentheses.

❖ **ON THE WEB**
For more practice solving special problems with pronoun case, visit Exercise Central *at bedfordstmartins.com/foundationsfirst.*

Example: I told ___her___ (she/her) that I wouldn't be able to come to the wedding.

1. Michael's parents took __________ (he/him) to the emergency room three times last week.
2. The server brought fresh coffee for my father and __________ (I/me).
3. The dentist asked __________ (she/her) to come back in a week to make sure that the filling was secure.
4. Their parents gave __________ (they/them) five dollars for each A on their report cards.
5. My roommates and __________ (I/me) were asleep when the earthquake struck.
6. The judges chose __________ (she/her) as the contestant with the most talent.
7. Whenever __________ (he/him) and his wife get the chance, they go dancing.
8. Two dolphins were spotted by my brother and __________ (I/me).
9. Feeding __________ (they/them) was a problem because they wouldn't eat anything green.
10. While choosing a major, my friends and __________ (I/me) should consider what jobs will be available when we graduate.

Pronouns in Comparisons

Sometimes, a pronoun appears after the words *than* or *as* in a **comparison**.

Neil is hungrier than I.

Marriage changed Sonia as much as him.

To decide whether to use the subjective or objective case, write in the words needed to complete the comparison.

Neil is hungrier than I am.

Marriage changed Sonia as much as it changed him.

If the pronoun is a subject, use the subjective case.

Neil is hungrier than I [am].

If the pronoun is an object, use the objective case.

Marriage changed Sonia as much as [it changed] him.

FOCUS Choosing Pronouns in Comparisons

Sometimes the pronoun you choose can change the meaning of your sentence. For example, if you say, "She likes potato chips more than I," you mean that she likes potato chips more than you like potato chips.

She likes potato chips more than I [do].

If, however, you say, "She likes potato chips more than me," you mean that she likes potato chips more than she likes you.

She likes potato chips more than [she likes] me.

◆ PRACTICE 28-13

In each blank, write the correct form (subjective or objective) of the pronouns in parentheses. In brackets, add the word or words needed to complete the comparison.

Example: My sister is very unemotional; the movie affected me much more than *[it affected] her* (she/her).

1. No one could be less qualified than ______ (he/him).
2. Marisol worked as hard as ______ (he/him), but he took all the credit.
3. You eat much more than ______ (I/me), so how do you stay so thin?
4. David exercises as regularly as ______ (she/her).
5. A visit to the doctor could not frighten you more than ______ (I/me).
6. I play the piano better than ______ (they/them).
7. The trip to Florida cost you as much as ______ (we/us).
8. Doug has a much larger house than ______ (they/them).

9. Clarence pays you a higher hourly rate than ______________________ (she/her).

10. In these photos, you look as tired as ______________________ (we/us).

Who and *Whom*

Who is a pronoun that functions as a subject; *whom* is a pronoun that functions as an object. To determine whether to use *who* or *whom*, you need to know how the pronoun functions within the clause in which it appears.

- When the pronoun is the subject of the clause, use *who*.

  I wonder who teaches that course. (*Who* is the subject of the clause *who teaches that course*.)

- When the pronoun is the object, use *whom*.

  I wonder to whom the course will appeal. (*Whom* is the object of the preposition *to* in the clause *to whom the course will appeal*.)

  Mr. Brennan is the instructor whom we all like. (*Whom* is the direct object of the verb *like* in the clause *whom we all like*.)

FOCUS *Who* and *Whom*

In conversation, people often use *who* for both the subjective case (*I wonder who teaches that course*) and the objective case (*I wonder who this course will appeal to*.) Although this usage is acceptable in casual conversation, in college writing, you should always use *whom* for the objective case: *I wonder to whom this course will appeal.*

◆ PRACTICE 28-14

In each of the following sentences, circle the correct form of *who* or *whom* in parentheses.

Example: An athlete (who/whom) most people have heard of is Muhammad Ali.

1. Ali, (who/whom) was named Cassius Clay at his birth in 1942, in Louisville, Kentucky, changed his name after he became famous.
2. He was a professional heavyweight boxer (who/whom) was known as "The Greatest" for his amazing career.

3. In 1960, Ali, (who/whom) had been trained by Joe Elsby Martin Sr., in Louisville, won an Olympic gold medal in the light heavyweight division.
4. That same year, he boxed with the police chief of Fayetteville, West Virginia, against (who/whom) Ali won his first professional fight.
5. In his boxing matches, Ali, (who/whom) had extraordinary reflexes and footwork, avoided his opponents' blows.
6. When he was at his peak, Ali seemed to be a boxer for (who/whom) it was easy to win.
7. The former Cassius Clay, (who/whom) was a member of the Nation of Islam, changed his name because he said that it symbolized his slave ancestry.
8. At the height of his career, Ali, (who/whom) became famous for his refusal to serve in the U.S. Armed Forces in Vietnam, became a conscientious objector.
9. Because of his political views, Ali, for (who/whom) boxing was a profession, was not allowed to box in the United States for over three years, until the Supreme Court intervened.
10. Ali, (who/whom) was reinstated in 1970, then fought several well-known boxers, including Joe Frazier and George Foreman.

Word Power

conscientious guided by one's conscience; principled

conscientious objector someone who refuses to serve in the military for moral reasons

F Reflexive and Intensive Pronouns

Like other pronouns, *reflexive pronouns* and *intensive pronouns* always agree with their antecedents. Although these two kinds of pronouns have different functions, their forms are exactly the same.

Reflexive Pronouns

Reflexive pronouns always end in *-self* (singular) or *-selves* (plural). These pronouns indicate that people or things did something to themselves or for themselves.

Christina bought herself a new watch.

You need to pace yourself when you exercise.

Eliza and Jill made themselves a plate of nachos.

Intensive Pronouns

Intensive pronouns also end in *-self* or *-selves*. Unlike reflexive pronouns, however, they always appear directly after their antecedents. Intensive pronouns are used for emphasis.

I myself have a friend with an eating disorder.

The actor himself did all the dangerous stunts.

They themselves questioned their motives.

Reflexive and Intensive Pronouns

Singular Forms

Antecedent	*Reflexive or Intensive Pronoun*
I	myself
you	yourself
he	himself
she	herself
it	itself

Plural Forms

Antecedent	*Reflexive or Intensive Pronoun*
we	ourselves
you	yourselves
they	themselves

◆ PRACTICE 28-15

✣ **ON THE WEB**
For more practice identifying reflexive and intensive pronouns, visit Exercise Central *at bedfordstmartins .com/foundationsfirst.*

In each of the following sentences, fill in the correct reflexive or intensive pronoun.

Example: You two should take ___yourselves___ out for dinner to celebrate your anniversary.

1. She ______ had always walked to school, and she told her children they should do the same thing.
2. The legislators voted ______ a raise.
3. The cat curled ______ up on the bed and dozed off.
4. Einstein ______ could not have solved that problem.
5. After my haircut, I caught a frightening glimpse of ______ in the mirror.
6. My sister hates to weigh ______ at the doctor's office.
7. If you fall, pick ______ up and start over again.
8. You ______ told me that this material would not be on the final exam.

9. The toddlers covered ______________________ with mud before their mother could stop them.

10. They bought the property for thousands of dollars, but they tore down the house ______________________ almost immediately afterward.

REVISING AND EDITING

Look back at your response to the Seeing and Writing exercise on page 375. Underline every pronoun you have used, and check your work carefully to be sure that all your pronouns and antecedents agree. (Remember, singular pronouns must refer to singular antecedents, and plural pronouns must refer to plural antecedents.) Eliminate any vague or unnecessary pronouns. Finally, check to make sure you have used correct pronoun case.

CHAPTER REVIEW

EDITING PRACTICE

Read the following paragraph, which contains pronoun errors. Check for errors in pronoun case and pronoun-antecedent agreement as well as for any vague or unnecessary pronouns. Then, make any editing changes you think are necessary. The first error has been corrected for you.

School Schedules: Time for a New Tradition

American educators and parents are starting to see the advantages of a longer school day. ~~Every~~ ^All working ~~parent worries~~ ^parents worry about leaving their children at home alone after school. On the news every night, they talk about criminals, peer pressure, and drugs. Many parents, they feel guilty about having to be at work while their children are at home alone. Many employers and politicians whom have voted to increase funds for preschool programs have not yet done much to solve the problem of unsupervised older children. Recently, in a newspaper article it suggested a solution to this problem: a longer school day and school year. A school today still has their calendar set by the needs of nineteenth-century farm families. The school day ends at three o'clock because anyone living on a farm needs the time before dark to finish their chores. In most parts of the United States today,

A student doing his homework

however, they no longer need to schedule school around farming because very few children whom attend school live on working farms. A child should be in school while their parents are at work. A longer school day could keep young Americans safer, put his or her parents at ease, and perhaps even help American schools become more competitive. After all, Japanese, Korean, and Taiwanese students all spend many more hours in school than us. Maybe someday this will change, and the 180-day school-year calendar will seem to we Americans a foolish thing of the past.

◆ COLLABORATIVE ACTIVITIES

1. Working in a small group, choose a topic to write about. Then, write a sentence with a compound subject on a sheet of paper, and then pass your paper to the person on your left. On the paper you receive from the person on your right, write a new sentence that includes a pronoun that refers to the compound subject that student wrote, and then pass your sheet to the person on your left. On the next sheet you get, write a new sentence using *who* or *whom* to refer to the original compound subject. Repeat this process until each of you has a paragraph six to eight sentences long.
2. Choose the paragraph from activity 1 that your group likes best. Then, exchange paragraphs with another group. Check each other's work, making sure that pronoun case and pronoun-antecedent agreement are correct.
3. Create a test for another group in your class. Copy a paragraph from a book or magazine, adding errors in pronoun-antecedent agreement and pronoun case. Then, exchange paragraphs with a different group. Try to correct every error introduced in the other group's test paragraph.
4. ***Composing original sentences*** Working as a group, write five original sentences. Be sure to use at least one indefinite pronoun, at least one compound subject, and at least one comparison with a pronoun. Then, check pronoun case and pronoun-antecedent agreement carefully. When you have finished, check your sentences again to correct any errors in grammar, punctuation, or spelling.

☑ REVIEW CHECKLIST: Pronouns

- ☐ A pronoun is a word that refers to and takes the place of a noun or another pronoun. (See 28A.)
- ☐ The word to which a pronoun refers is called the pronoun's antecedent. (See 28A.)

(continued on following page)

(continued from previous page)

- Compound antecedents connected by *and* are plural and are used with plural pronouns. Compound antecedents connected by *or* may take singular or plural pronouns. (See 28B.)
- Most indefinite pronoun antecedents are singular. Therefore, they are used with singular pronouns. (See 28B.)
- Collective noun antecedents are singular and must be used with singular pronouns. (See 28B.)
- A pronoun should always refer to a specific antecedent. (See 28C.)
- When a pronoun directly follows its antecedent, it is usually unnecessary. (See 28C.)
- Personal pronouns can be in the subjective, objective, or possessive case. (See 28D.)
- Pronouns present special problems when they are used in compounds and comparisons. The pronouns *who* and *whom* also cause problems. (See 28E.)
- Reflexive pronouns and intensive pronouns must agree with their antecedents in person and number. (See 28F.)

CHAPTER 29

Adjectives and Adverbs

PREVIEW

In this chapter, you will learn

- to identify adjectives and adverbs (29A)
- to understand comparatives and superlatives (29B)
- to identify demonstrative adjectives (29C)

SEEING AND WRITING

The picture above shows people at a masquerade party. Look at the picture, and then write a paragraph in which you describe the costume you would wear to this party.

Word Power

masquerade (verb) to wear a mask or disguise; (noun) a costume party at which guests wear masks

A Identifying Adjectives and Adverbs

Adjectives and adverbs are words that modify—that is, describe or identify—other words. By using these modifying words, you can make your sentences more precise and more interesting.

Identifying Adjectives

An **adjective** answers the question *What kind? Which one?* or *How many?* Adjectives modify nouns or pronouns.

> The Spanish city of Madrid has exciting nightlife. (The adjective *Spanish* modifies the noun *city*; the adjective *exciting* modifies the noun *nightlife*.)
>
> It is lively because of its many clubs and tapas bars. (The adjective *lively* modifies the pronoun *it*.)

◆ PRACTICE 29-1

In each of the blanks in the following paragraph, write an adjective from the list below. Cross each adjective off the list as you use it. Be sure to choose an adjective that makes sense in each sentence.

Example: It is ___*unusual*___ for a group of famous writers to form a rock group.

talented	big	devoted	~~unusual~~
famous	rare	modest	successful
wild	tiny	diverse	

(1) The group called Rock Bottom Remainders is made up entirely of ______________ writers. (2) Its ______________ members include Amy Tan, Dave Barry, and Stephen King. (3) They play to raise money for charity, and they sometimes make ______________ fools of themselves in the process. (4) Amy Tan, for instance, will often wear a ______________ leather outfit when she is performing with the group. (5) Usually, she wears more ______________ clothes. (6) She does not get the chance to show her ______________ side too often. (7) The Rock Bottom Remainders' ______________ concerts take place only once or twice a year. (8) The band is ______________ at raising money because people want to see their favorite writers on stage. (9) Of course, nobody thinks that the writers are ______________ musicians. (10) Their ______________ fans come to see them because they love their writing.

ON THE WEB
For more practice identifying adjectives and adverbs, visit Exercise Central *at bedfordstmartins.com/foundationsfirst.*

Identifying Adverbs

An **adverb** answers the question *How? Why? When? Where?* or *To what extent?* Adverbs modify verbs, adjectives, or other adverbs.

The huge Doberman barked angrily. (The adverb *angrily* modifies the verb *barked*.)

Still, we felt quite safe. (The adverb *quite* modifies the adjective *safe*.)

Very slowly, we held out a big juicy steak. (The adverb *very* modifies the adverb *slowly*.)

◆ PRACTICE 29-2

In each of the blanks in the following paragraph, write an adverb from the list below. Cross each adverb off the list as you use it. Be sure to choose an adverb that makes sense in each sentence.

Example: I waited ___wearily___ for the train.

quickly	heavily	easily	unusually	uncomfortably
noisily	rudely	bravely	really	~~wearily~~

(1) The subway train screeched ____________ into the station. (2) The doors ____________ slid open, and departing passengers ____________ pushed their way out. (3) Entering passengers struggled ____________ to get through the narrow doors. (4) It was ____________ hot for April, and people were sweating ____________ in the steamy underground tunnel. (5) I stood jammed ____________ in the middle of the car, hoping I'd be able to wriggle out ____________ when I reached my stop. (6) What a ____________ great way to start the work day!

Telling Adjectives and Adverbs Apart

Many adverbs are formed when the ending *-ly* is added to an adjective.

Adjective	*Adverb*
bad	badly
nice	nicely
quick	quickly
quiet	quietly
real	really
slow	slowly

Because the adjective and adverb forms of the words in the list on page 400 are similar, you may sometimes be confused about which form to use in a sentence. Remember, adjectives modify nouns or pronouns; adverbs modify verbs, adjectives, or other adverbs.

ADJECTIVE Kim likes the slow dances. (*Slow* modifies the noun *dances*.)

ADVERB Kim likes to dance slowly. (*Slowly* modifies the verb *dance*.)

ADJECTIVE Mark Twain's real name was Samuel L. Clemens. (*Real* modifies the noun *name*.)

ADJECTIVE It was really generous of him to donate his time. (*Really* modifies the adjective *generous*.)

◆ PRACTICE 29-3

In the following passage, circle the correct form (adjective or adverb) from the choices in parentheses.

Example: India has a (real/really) productive film industry.

(1) Bollywood, as the Indian film industry is called, has been making movies for (near/nearly) seventy-five years. (2) It puts out more than a thousand movies every year, so its releases are even more (frequent/frequently) than Hollywood's. (3) However, Bollywood movies are made very (different/differently) from Hollywood ones. (4) They are often made (quick/quickly) and with a relatively small budget. (5) They also use musical numbers more (free/freely). (6) At least a half a dozen times per film, characters will (sudden/suddenly) begin songs or dances. (7) The songs themselves often become (wide/widely) known. (8) The plots of Bollywood movies often focus on romance or revenge, and the films always end (happy/happily). (9) Bollywood films are (real/really) popular in India. (10) More recently, Bollywood has also found an audience abroad, with the South Asian immigrant community in the United States showing a (particular/particularly) strong interest in these films. (11) In many large cities, Bollywood films are (regular/regularly) shown in movie theaters, and a musical about Bollywood, *Bombay Dreams*, ran on Broadway in 2004.

FOCUS *Good* and *Well*

Be careful not to confuse *good* and *well*. Unlike regular adjectives, whose adverb forms add the ending *-ly*, the adjective *good* is irregular. Its adverb form is *well*.

Remember, *good* is an adjective; *well* is an adverb. Use *good* to modify a noun or pronoun; use *well* to modify a verb, an adjective, or another adverb.

ADJECTIVE John Steinbeck was a good writer. (*Good* modifies the noun *writer*.)

ADVERB He wrote particularly well in the novel *The Grapes of Wrath*. (*Well* modifies the verb *wrote*.)

However, always use *well* when you are describing someone's health.

He wasn't at all *well* [not *good*] after his trip.

◆ PRACTICE 29-4

In the following passage, circle the correct form (*good* or *well*) in parentheses.

Example: Have Americans treated U.S. veterans (good/well) enough?

(1) Some U.S. veterans of twentieth-century wars were treated (good/well); others, unfortunately, were not. (2) In the 1940s, most American veterans of World War II came home to a (good/well) life. (3) No one doubted that these men and women had done a (good/well) thing by going to war. (4) The G.I. Bill ensured that many of them were able to get a (good/well) education. (5) In the strong postwar economy, (good/well) jobs were not difficult to find. (6) Unfortunately, things were not nearly as (good/well) for the veterans who returned from the Vietnam War. (7) Many Americans felt that the U.S. involvement in that war was not a (good/well) idea. (8) Some blamed the soldiers who had gone to Vietnam even though most of them had done their jobs as (good/well) as they could. (9) Rather than being (good/well) respected, the returning veterans were sometimes treated badly. (10) In addition, injured soldiers

often ended up in veterans' hospitals that were not (good/well) staffed. (11) By comparison, veterans of the two Gulf Wars have been (good/well) received when they returned home. (12) Even people who did not support the war did not take out their anger on the soldiers who fought so (good/well). (13) Still, veterans of today's wars must continue to deal with underfunded veterans' hospitals, and improvements in veteran care are much needed and (good/well) deserved. (14) No matter what the public may think of a war, it is important to treat veterans (good/well) when they return home.

B Comparatives and Superlatives

Adjectives and adverbs are sometimes used to compare two or more people or things.

The **comparative form** of an adjective or adverb compares *two* people or things. The **superlative form** of an adjective or adverb compares *more than two* people or things. Special forms of the adjectives and adverbs are used to indicate these comparisons.

ADJECTIVE These shoes are ugly.

COMPARATIVE The brown shoes are uglier than the black ones.

SUPERLATIVE The purple ones are the ugliest of all.

ADVERB Will you be able to get home soon?

COMPARATIVE I may not be home until midnight, but I will try to get there sooner.

SUPERLATIVE Unfortunately, the soonest I can leave work is 7:30.

NOTE: Some adverbs—such as *almost, very, somewhat, quite, extremely, rather,* and *moderately*—do not have comparative or superlative forms.

Forming Comparatives and Superlatives

Adjectives and adverbs form the comparative with *-er* or *more* and the superlative with *-est* or *most*.

Adjectives

- To form the comparative of a one-syllable adjective, add *-er*. To form the superlative of a one-syllable adjective, add *-est*.

young younger youngest

- To form the comparative of an adjective that has two or more syllables, use *more*. To form the superlative of an adjective that has two or more syllables, use *most*.

  beautiful more beautiful most beautiful

Adverbs

- To form the comparative of an adverb that ends in *-ly*, use *more*. To form the superlative of an adverb that ends in *-ly*, use *most*.

  slowly more slowly most slowly

- Some other adverbs form the comparative with *-er* and the superlative with *-est*.

  soon sooner soonest

Solving Special Problems with Comparatives and Superlatives

The following four rules will help you avoid errors with comparatives and superlatives.

1. Never use both *-er* and *more* to form the comparative.

   The comic could have been a lot funnier. (not *more funnier*)

2. Never use both *-est* and *most* to form the superlative.

   Scream was the scariest (not *most scariest*) movie I ever saw.

3. Never use the superlative when you are comparing only two things.

   Beth is the younger (not *youngest*) of the two sisters.

4. Never use the comparative when you are comparing more than two things.

   This is the worst (not *worse*) of my four part-time jobs.

ON THE WEB
For more practice understanding comparatives and superlatives, visit Exercise Central *at bedfordstmartins.com/foundationsfirst.*

◆ PRACTICE 29-5

In the blank at the right, fill in the comparative form of each adjective or adverb.

Examples

rich *richer*

embarrassed *more embarrassed*

1. strong ______
2. playful ______
3. quickly ______
4. traditional ______
5. neat ______
6. neatly ______

7. fair ______________________
8. mature ______________________
9. young ______________________
10. intense ______________________
11. blue ______________________
12. new ______________________
13. easy ______________________
14. easily ______________________
15. useful ______________________
16. poor ______________________
17. hard ______________________
18. gently ______________________
19. deep ______________________
20. lazy ______________________

◆ PRACTICE 29-6

In the blank at the right, fill in the superlative form of each adjective or adverb.

Example

rich *richest*

embarrassed *most embarrassed*

1. strong ______________________
2. playful ______________________
3. quickly ______________________
4. traditional ______________________
5. neat ______________________
6. neatly ______________________
7. fair ______________________
8. mature ______________________
9. young ______________________
10. intense ______________________
11. blue ______________________
12. new ______________________
13. easy ______________________
14. easily ______________________
15. useful ______________________
16. poor ______________________
17. hard ______________________
18. gently ______________________
19. deep ______________________
20. lazy ______________________

◆ PRACTICE 29-7

Fill in the correct comparative form of the word in parentheses.

Example: In 1961, the East German government erected the Berlin Wall to make it *harder* (hard) for residents of Communist East Berlin to travel to West Berlin.

1. Once East Germany started to build the Berlin Wall, it went up ______________ (quick) than anyone expected.

2. After the Wall was built, it became much ____________________ (difficult) for East Germans to escape even though many wanted to leave.
3. Originally, the Wall was made of barbed wire, but it was later replaced by ____________________ (strong) concrete.
4. The Wall stayed up for twenty-eight years but luckily did not stay up ____________________ (long).
5. When the Wall came down in 1989, people around the world saw ____________________ (clear) that Communist rule in East Germany would soon end.
6. In 1990, East Germany became part of the Federal Republic of Germany, and most people were ____________________ (happy).
7. Now, all Berliners could travel around their city ____________________ (free).
8. However, the eastern side of Berlin remained ____________________ (depressed) economically than the western side.
9. The population of East Germany was ____________________ (poor), and many of its residents did not have the money to travel to the western part of the country.
10. Differences between east and west still remain today despite ____________________ (free) movement between the two sides.

◆ PRACTICE 29-8

Fill in the correct superlative form of the word in parentheses.

Example: Sports fans must be the ___*most obsessive*___ (obsessive) people in the world.

(1) Today's extreme sports often seem to be designed to show which athlete is the ____________________ (crazy). (2) The human obsession with extremes is not new, however; records showing who could run the ____________________ (fast) or swim the ____________________ (far) go back more than a century. (3) Only the ____________________ (tiny) minority of people will ever compete well enough in any sport to approach a world record. (4) Anyone else who wants to be a record holder

must scan *Guinness World Records* to find the record he or she can break the ____________________ (easy). (5) Athletic ability is not the ____________________ (necessary) skill for many events listed in *Guinness World Records*. (6) One young man simply stayed awake for the ____________________ (long) period on record. (7) Another grew to the ____________________ (great) height seen in modern times. (8) Of course, his record would be one of the ____________________ (difficult) to break. (9) Growing hair and fingernails and peeling an apple will never be Olympic sports, but people have set some of the ____________________ (surprising) records in those events. (10) After looking through *Guinness World Records*, many people conclude that extreme sports are not, after all, the ____________________ (bizarre) obsession a person can have.

FOCUS *Good/Well* and *Bad/Badly*

The adjectives *good* and *bad* and their adverb forms, *well* and *badly*, are irregular. They do not form the comparative and superlative in the same way other adjectives and adverbs do. Because their forms are so irregular, you must memorize them.

Adjective	*Comparative Form*	*Superlative Form*
good	better	best
bad	worse	worst

Adverb	*Comparative Form*	*Superlative Form*
well	better	best
badly	worse	worst

◆ PRACTICE 29-9

Fill in the correct comparative or superlative form of *good*, *well*, *bad*, or *badly*.

Example: The ___best___ (good) guess is that poker may have originated in Persia, France, or Great Britain.

1. Poker may be one of the ____________________ (good) card games ever invented.

2. The game was carried all over the world by American soldiers, who often competed to see who were the _____________ (good) poker players.
3. After the World Series of Poker started in 1970, poker fans saw that if they were _____________ (good) players than their opponents, they could win a lot of money.
4. During the 1970s, new books on poker strategy helped fans play _____________ (well).
5. It seemed that even the _____________ (good) players could learn from the experts.
6. With online poker, those who played _____________ (badly) than their friends could play at home without embarrassing themselves.
7. With cameras that showed players' cards to the audience, TV poker shows became _____________ (good) for viewers.
8. Winning at poker requires skill, but even the _____________ (good) players need luck in order to win.
9. To a poker player, there is nothing _____________ (bad) than having good cards and losing to someone who is bluffing.
10. Some people fear that the increased popularity of poker is making gambling addictions _____________ (bad).

C Demonstrative Adjectives

Demonstrative adjectives do not describe other words. These adjectives—*this, that, these,* and *those*—simply identify particular nouns.

This and *that* identify singular nouns.

This book is much more interesting than that one.

These and *those* identify plural nouns.

These books are novels, but those books are biographies.

◆ PRACTICE 29-10

In the following paragraph, circle the correct form of the demonstrative adjective in parentheses.

Example: (That/Those) African-American musicians who came out of Detroit in the 1960s had a unique sound.

❖ **ON THE WEB**
For more practice identifying demonstrative adjectives, visit Exercise Central *at bedford stmartins.com/foundations first.*

(1) (That/Those) sound came to be known as Motown, after Motown Records, which in turn was named for Detroit, the "Motor City." (2) The sound was created by a powerful lead singer accompanied by (that/those) distinctive harmonizing backup vocals. (3) Some of the recording artists who sang in (this/these) style are Diana Ross and the Supremes, Gladys Knight and the Pips, and Smokey Robinson and the Miracles. (4) The names of (this/these) Motown groups often had two parts—the lead singer and the backup group. (5) (This/These) kind of group became famous under the direction of Motown Records owner Barry Gordy. (6) Many of (this/these) singers are still famous today. (7) Recently, some of (that/those) musicians who were not well known have gotten more attention. (8) In particular, the record company's in-house band, the Funk Brothers, has gotten credit for creating (that/those) recognizable Motown sound. (9) The 2002 movie *Standing in the Shadows of Motown* highlights the work of (this/these) band. (10) The band is also featured at the Motown Museum in Detroit, which is dedicated to preserving the memory of (this/these) group of extraordinary musicians.

REVISING AND EDITING

Look back at your response to the Seeing and Writing exercise on page 398. First, underline every adjective and adverb. Have you used any comparatives or superlatives? Any demonstrative adjectives? If so, check to be sure you have used the correct forms. Then, add or substitute descriptive words if necessary to make your writing more precise and more interesting.

CHAPTER REVIEW

EDITING PRACTICE

Read the following paragraph, which contains errors in the use of adjectives and adverbs. Make any changes necessary to correct adjectives that are incorrectly used instead of adverbs, adverbs that are incorrectly used instead of adjectives, errors in the use of comparatives and superlatives, and errors in the use of demonstrative adjectives. You may also add adjectives or adverbs that you feel would make the writer's ideas clearer or more specific. The first sentence has been edited for you.

Craigslist.com

Craigslist: A Web Site for the People

The Web site known as Craigslist provides ~~freely~~ free classified ads to people all over the world. Ordinary life situations are Craigslist's mainly focus. Someone who is looking for a job or an apartment can often find it quick on Craigslist. People can also sell or trade possessions. Sometimes, real sad people who have lost a beloved pet try to find it on Craigslist. Lonely people can even find partners on Craigslist. The popularly Web site, started in 1995 by Craig Newmark, was at first used only by San Francisco area residents. However, it expanded rapid to more than 150 cities on six continents. Craigslist has been amazing popular, providing the most greatest number of classified ads anywhere. Unlike more commercial sites, these site does not advertise, relying entirely on word-of-mouth. In general, people looking for jobs or apartments do not pay any fees. However, in a few cities, Craigslist charges users a reasonably fee to post job and real estate ads. There have been some problems with this site. For example, some people have claimed that the personal ads can be too sexual explicit. Also, Craigslist has been sued for letting users post apartment ads that discriminate against certain groups. Still, Craigslist has been real successful because its users trust it and find it usefully.

◆ COLLABORATIVE ACTIVITIES

1. Working on your own, write five simple sentences on a sheet of paper. Then, working in a group of three, pass your page to another student in your group. Add one adjective and one adverb to one of the sentences on the paper you receive. Keep passing the pages among the three of you until modifying words have been added to every sentence on each sheet. Then, working together, check to make sure all the adjectives and adverbs are used correctly.
2. Working in the same group, choose the most interesting sentence from each of the three pages. Work together to write a one- or two-paragraph story using all three of these sentences. When you have finished, try to add several more adjectives and adverbs to the story.
3. Exchange stories from activity 2 with another group. Then, rewrite the other group's story by changing every adjective and adverb you can find. Make the story as different from the original as you can. When you have finished, exchange the stories again, and make any necessary corrections.

4. ***Composing original sentences*** Working in a group of three, write five original sentences. Make sure each sentence contains at least one adverb and at least one adjective. In addition, include at least one comparative form of an adjective or adverb, at least one superlative form of an adjective or adverb, and at least one demonstrative adjective. Then, check the adjectives and adverbs carefully to be sure you have used them correctly. When you have finished, check your sentences again to correct any errors in grammar, punctuation, or spelling.

✓ REVIEW CHECKLIST: Adjectives and Adverbs

- Adjectives modify nouns or pronouns. (See 29A.)
- Adverbs modify verbs, adjectives, or other adverbs. (See 29A.)
- To compare two people or things, use the comparative form of an adjective or adverb. To compare more than two people or things, use the superlative form of an adjective or adverb. (See 29B.)
- Adjectives and adverbs form the comparative with *-er* or *more* and the superlative with *-est* or *most*. (See 29B.)
- The adjectives *good* and *bad* and their adverb forms, *well* and *badly*, have irregular comparative and superlative forms. (See 29B.)
- Demonstrative adjectives—*this*, *that*, *these*, and *those*—identify particular nouns. (See 29C.)

CHAPTER 30

Grammar and Usage Issues for ESL Writers

PREVIEW

In this chapter, you will learn

- to include subjects in sentences (30A)
- to avoid special problems with subjects (30B)
- to identify plural nouns (30C)
- to understand count and noncount nouns (30D)
- to use determiners with count and noncount nouns (30E)
- to understand articles (30F)
- to form negative statements and questions (30G)
- to indicate verb tense (30H)
- to recognize stative verbs (30I)
- to use modal auxiliaries (30J)
- to use gerunds (30K)
- to place modifiers in order (30L)
- to choose correct prepositions (30M)
- to use prepositions in familiar expressions (30N)
- to use prepositions in phrasal verbs (30O)

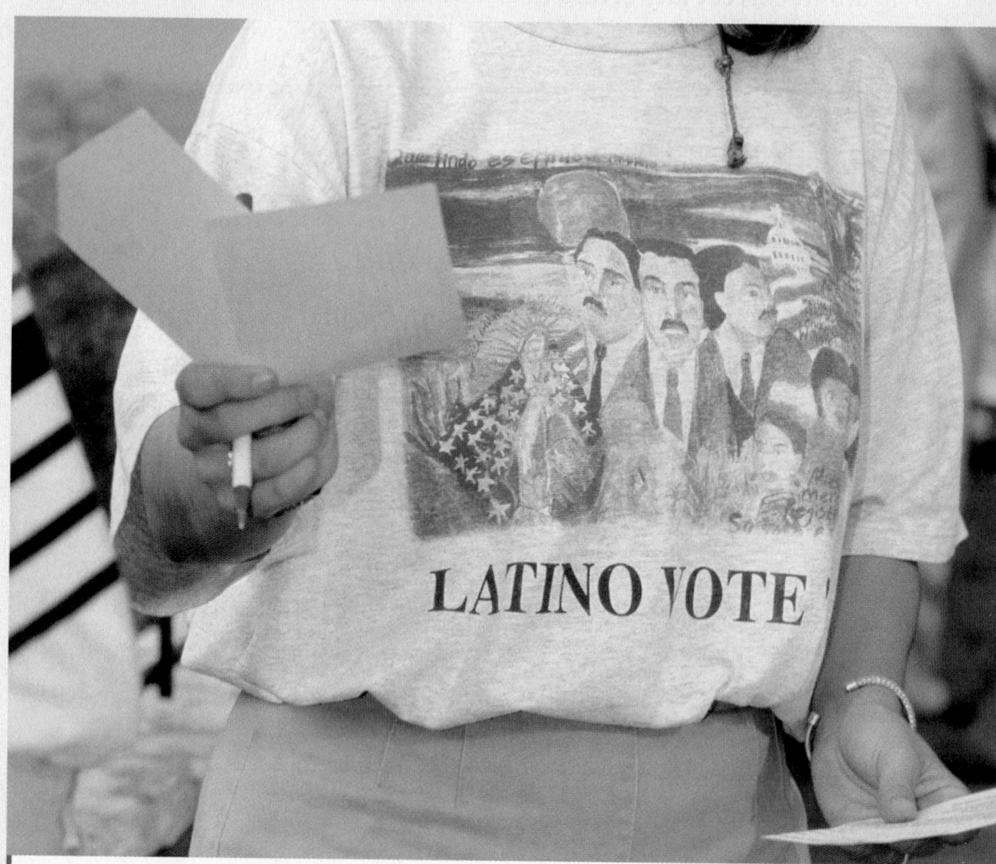

SEEING AND WRITING

The picture above shows an election worker handing out ballot information. Do you think U.S. ballots should be available in languages other than English? If not, why not? If so, what languages should be represented? Why? Look at the picture above, and then write a paragraph that answers these questions.

Word Power

ballot a written or printed paper on which voters indicate their choices in an election

Learning English as a second language involves more than just learning grammar. In fact, if you have been studying English as a second language, you may know more English grammar than many native speakers do. Still, you will need to learn conventions and rules that many native speakers already know. This chapter covers the grammar and usage issues that give nonnative speakers the most trouble.

A Subjects in Sentences

English requires that every sentence state its subject. In fact, every dependent clause must also have a subject.

INCORRECT My parents do not make much money although work hard. (Who works hard?)

CORRECT My parents do not make much money although they work hard.

English even requires a "dummy" subject to fill the subject position in sentences like this one.

It is hot here.

It is not correct to write just *Hot here* or *Is hot here*.

◆ PRACTICE 30-1

Each of the following sentences is missing the subject of a dependent or an independent clause. On the lines after each sentence, rewrite it, adding an appropriate subject.

Example: The essay was interesting even though had some errors.

The essay was interesting even though it had some errors.

1. Will rain all day tomorrow.

2. She was excited after answered a question in class.

3. Javier studied so that could become an American citizen.

ON THE WEB
For more practice including subjects in sentences, visit Exercise Central *at bedfordstmartins.com/foundationsfirst.*

4. Was not my fault.

5. Sofia watched television programs for children when was learning English.

6. Is a very difficult problem.

7. She waited until was sure they were gone.

8. He missed the bus because overslept that morning.

9. After Jean scored the winning goal, went out to celebrate with his friends.

10. Is quieter than usual in the library today.

B Special Problems with Subjects

Some languages commonly begin a sentence with a word or phrase that has no grammatical link to the sentence but that states clearly what the sentence is about. If you speak such a language, you might write a sentence like this one.

INCORRECT Career plan I am studying to be a computer scientist.

A sentence like this cannot occur in English. The phrase *career plan* cannot be a subject of this sentence because the sentence already includes a subject: the pronoun *I*, which agrees with the verb *am studying*. In addition, *career plan* is not connected to the rest of the sentence in any other way. One way to revise this sentence is to rewrite it so that *career plan* is the subject.

CORRECT My career plan is to become a computer scientist.

Another way to revise the sentence is simply to delete *career plan*.

CORRECT I am studying to become a computer scientist.

Standard English also does not permit a two-part subject in which the second part of the subject is a pronoun referring to the same person or thing as the first part.

INCORRECT My sister she is a cardiologist.

CORRECT My sister is a cardiologist.

When the real subject follows the verb and the normal subject position before the verb is empty, it must be filled by a "dummy" subject, such as *there*.

INCORRECT Are tall mountains in my country.

CORRECT There are tall mountains in my country.

◆ PRACTICE 30-2

The following sentences contain problems with subjects. Rewrite each sentence correctly on the lines provided. (Some of the sentences can be corrected in more than one way.)

Example: Are no roads in the middle of the jungle.

There are no roads in the middle of the jungle.

1. The old woman she sells candles in the shop downstairs.

____

____

2. Are six kinds of rice in the cupboard.

____

____

3. Dmitri he rides his bicycle ten miles every day.

____

____

ON THE WEB
For more practice avoiding special problems with subjects, visit **Exercise Central** *at bedfordstmartins.com/foundationsfirst.*

4. The doctor says is hope for my father.

5. My neighbor she watches my daughter in the evenings.

6. My former home I grew up in a village near the Indian Ocean.

7. My job it starts at six o'clock in the morning.

8. Plan for the future Mr. Esposito hopes to buy his own taxi someday.

9. The best thing in my life I feel lucky that my family is together again.

10. My brother's big problem at school he is afraid of his teacher.

C Plural Nouns

In English, most nouns add *-s* or *-es* to form plurals. Every time you use a noun, ask yourself whether you are talking about one item or more than one, and choose a singular or plural form accordingly. Consider this sentence.

> The books in both branches of the library are deteriorating.

The three nouns in this sentence are underlined: one is singular (*library*), and the other two are plural (*books, branches*). You might think that the word *both* is enough to indicate that *branch* is plural and that it is obvious that there would have to be more than one book in any branch of a library.

However, even if the sentence includes information that tells you that a noun is plural, you must always use a form of the noun that shows explicitly that it is plural.

◆ PRACTICE 30-3

In each of the following sentences, underline the plural nouns.

Example: Julia came from Argentina to the United States last year to work in the home of two lawyers.

1. Julia's new job has many challenges.
2. She does some cooking, and she takes care of the children while their parents are at work.
3. She takes English classes twice a week.
4. Julia was surprised when her American family invited all their relatives for Thanksgiving dinner.
5. She had never cooked for so many people.
6. The guests said that the vegetables were delicious.
7. Three women wore pants to the holiday meal.
8. Two families brought their young babies to the table.
9. The family dogs waited under the table in case any scraps were dropped on the floor.
10. When the meal was over, the men watched a football game on TV, and their wives helped Julia clean up.

ON THE WEB
For more practice identifying plural nouns, visit Exercise Central *at bedfordstmartins .com/foundationsfirst.*

D Count and Noncount Nouns

A **count noun** names one particular thing or a group of particular things: *a teacher, a panther, a bed, an ocean, a cloud*; *two teachers, five panthers, three beds, two oceans, fifteen clouds*. A **noncount noun**, however, names things that cannot be counted: *gold, cream, sand, blood, smoke*.

Count nouns usually have a singular form and a plural form: *cloud, clouds*. Noncount nouns usually have only a singular form: *smoke*. Note how the nouns *cloud* and *smoke* differ in terms of how they are used in sentences.

CORRECT The sky is full of clouds.

CORRECT The sky is full of smoke.

INCORRECT The sky is full of smokes.

CORRECT I see ten clouds in the distance.

CORRECT I see some smoke in the distance.

INCORRECT I see ten smokes in the distance.

In many cases, you can use either a count noun or a noncount noun to communicate the same idea.

Count	*Noncount*
people (plural of *person*)	furniture (not *furnitures*)
tables, chairs, beds	mail (not *mails*)
letters	equipment (not *equipments*)
supplies	information (not *informations*)
facts	

Some words can be either count or noncount, depending on the meaning intended.

COUNT Students in this course are expected to submit two papers.

NONCOUNT These artificial flowers are made of paper.

FOCUS Count and Noncount Nouns

Here are some general guidelines for using count and noncount nouns.

- Use a count noun to refer to a living animal, but use a noncount noun to refer to the food that comes from that animal.

  COUNT There are several live lobsters in the tank.

  NONCOUNT This restaurant specializes in lobster.

- If you use a noncount noun for a substance or class of things that can come in different varieties, you can often make that noun plural if you want to talk about those varieties.

  NONCOUNT Cheese is a rich source of calcium.

  COUNT Many different cheeses come from Italy.

- If you want to shift from a general concept to specific examples of it, you can often use a noncount noun as a count noun.

  NONCOUNT You have a great deal of talent.

  COUNT My talents do not include singing.

◆ PRACTICE 30-4

In each of the following sentences, identify the underlined word as a count or noncount noun. If it is a noncount noun, circle the *N* following the sentence, but do not write in the blank. If it is a count noun, circle the *C*, and then write the plural form of the noun in the blank.

Examples

She was filled with admiration for the turtle. (N) C ______

A seagull watched from a safe distance. N (C) seagulls

1. Rosa walked across the sand. N C ______
2. The moon shone brightly. N C ______
3. The moon was reflected in the water. N C ______
4. A sea turtle came out of the waves. N C ______
5. The turtle crawled slowly up the beach and dug a hole for her eggs. N C ______
6. A turtle egg feels like leather. N C ______
7. Rosa felt sympathy for the turtle. N C ______
8. An enemy could be nearby, waiting to attack the turtle or eat her eggs. N C ______
9. The enemy could even be a human being who likes to eat turtle. N C ______
10. Rosa sighed with relief when the turtle finished laying her eggs and swam away. N C ______

ON THE WEB
For more practice understanding count and noncount nouns, visit Exercise Central *at bedfordstmartins.com/foundationsfirst.*

E Determiners with Count and Noncount Nouns

Determiners are adjectives that *identify* rather than describe the nouns they modify. Determiners may also *quantify* nouns (that is, indicate an amount or a number). Determiners include the following words.

- Articles: *a, an, the*
- Demonstrative pronouns: *this, these, that, those*
- Possessive pronouns: *my, our, your, his, her, its, their*
- Possessive nouns: *Sheila's, my friend's,* and so on
- *Whose, which, what*
- *All, both, each, every, some, any, either, no, neither, many, most, much, a few, a little, few, little, several, enough*
- All numerals: *one, two,* and so on

When a determiner is accompanied by one or more other adjectives, the determiner always comes first. For example, in the phrase *my expensive new gold watch*, *my* is a determiner; you cannot put *expensive*, *new*, *gold*, or any other adjective before *my*.

A singular count noun must be accompanied by a determiner—for example, *my watch* or *the new gold watch*, not just *watch* or *new gold watch*. Noncount nouns and plural count nouns, however, sometimes have determiners but sometimes do not. *This honey is sweet* and *Honey is sweet* are both acceptable, as are *These berries are juicy* and *Berries are juicy*. (In each case, the meaning is different.) However, you cannot say *Berry is juicy*; say instead, *This berry is juicy*, *Every berry is juicy*, or *A berry is juicy*.

FOCUS Determiners

Some determiners can be used only with certain types of nouns.

- *This* and *that* can be used only with singular nouns (count or noncount): *this berry*, *that honey*.
- *These*, *those*, *a few*, *few*, *many*, *both*, and *several* can be used only with plural count nouns: *these berries*, *those apples*, *a few ideas*, *few people*, *many students*, *both sides*, *several directions*.
- *Much*, *little*, and *a little* can be used only with noncount nouns: *much affection*, *little time*, *a little honey*.
- *Some*, *enough*, *all*, and *most* can be used only with noncount or plural count nouns: *some honey*, *some berries*, *enough trouble*, *enough problems*; *all traffic*, *all roads*; *most money*, *most coins*.
- *A*, *an*, *every*, *each*, *either*, and *neither* can be used only with singular count nouns: *a berry*, *an elephant*, *every possibility*, *each citizen*; *either option*, *neither candidate*.

◆ PRACTICE 30-5

In each of the following sentences, underline the more appropriate choice from each pair of words or phrases in parentheses.

Example: There have been (many/much) different immigration laws in the United States.

1. (Few/Little) people know that American immigration laws have changed a great deal since the country started.
2. At first, (each/all) people could immigrate to the United States.
3. Between 1831 and 1840, (many/much) people came from Ireland to escape the famine in their country.
4. The Gold Rush of 1849 brought people from almost (every/enough) country in the world to California.

ON THE WEB
For more practice using determiners with count and noncount nouns, visit Exercise Central *at bedfordstmartins .com/foundationsfirst.*

5. Germans, French Canadians, Scandinavians, Italians, and Poles were (a few/a little) of the people who came to the United States in the nineteenth and early twentieth centuries.
6. The 1927 immigration law set quotas for immigrants from different countries, making it harder for (many/much) people to enter the United States.
7. (This/These) quotas kept many people from immigrating.
8. U.S. immigration policy made it impossible for (most/much) Jews to escape from Europe during the time of Hitler.
9. U.S. immigration laws now permit (some/each) family members of current U.S. citizens to enter the country.
10. Today, (many/much) immigrants live and work in the United States.

Word Power

quota a number of people or percentage of people designated as an upper limit

F Articles

The definite article *the* and the indefinite articles *a* and *an* are determiners that tell readers whether the noun that follows is one they can identify (*the book*) or one they cannot yet identify (*a book*).

Definite Articles

When the definite article *the* is used with a noun, the writer is saying to readers, "You can identify which particular thing or things I have in mind. The information you need to make that identification is available to you. Either you have it already, or I am about to supply it to you."

Readers can find the necessary information in the following ways.

- By looking at other information in the sentence

  Meet me at the corner of Main Street and Lafayette Road.

  In this example, *the* is used with the noun *corner* because other words in the sentence tell readers which particular corner the writer has in mind: the one located at Main and Lafayette.
- By looking at information in other sentences

  Aisha ordered a slice of pie and a cup of coffee. The pie was delicious. She asked for a second slice.

  Here, *the* is used before the word *pie* in the second sentence to indicate that it is the same pie identified in the first sentence. Notice, however, that the noun *slice* in the third sentence is preceded by an indefinite article (*a*) because it is not the same slice referred to in the first sentence. There is no information that identifies it specifically.

- By drawing on general knowledge

The earth revolves around the sun.

Here, *the* is used with the nouns *earth* and *sun* because readers are expected to know which particular things the writer is referring to.

Always use *the* rather than *a* or *an* in the following three situations.

1. Before the word *same*: *the same day*
2. Before the superlative form of an adjective: *the youngest son*
3. Before a number indicating order or sequence: *the third time*

Indefinite Articles

When an indefinite article is used with a noun, the writer is saying to readers, "I don't expect you to have enough information right now to identify a particular thing that I have in mind. I do expect you to recognize that I'm referring to only one item."

Consider the following sentences.

We need a table for our computer.

I have a folding table; maybe you can use that.

In the first sentence, the writer has no actual table in mind. Because the table is indefinite to the writer, it is clearly indefinite to the reader, so *a* is used, not *the*. The second sentence refers to an actual table, but because the writer does not expect the reader to be able to identify the table specifically, it is also used with *a* rather than *the*.

FOCUS Indefinite Articles

Unlike the definite article, the indefinite articles *a* and *an* occur only with singular count nouns. *A* is used when the next sound is a consonant, and *an* is used when the next sound is a vowel. In choosing *a* or *an*, pay attention to sounds rather than to spelling: *a house, a year, a union*, but *an hour, an uncle*.

No Article

Only noncount and plural count nouns can stand without articles: *butter, chocolate, cookies, strawberries* (but *a cookie* or *the strawberry*).

Nouns without articles can be used to make generalizations.

Infants need affection as well as food.

The absence of articles before the nouns *infants*, *affection*, and *food* indicates that this statement is not about particular infants, affection, or food but about infants, affection, and food in general. Remember not to use *the* in such sentences. In English, a sentence like The *infants need affection as well as food* can refer only to particular, identifiable infants and not to infants in general.

Articles with Proper Nouns

Proper nouns may be divided into two classes: names that take *the* and names that take no article.

- Names of people do not take articles: *Napoleon, Mahatma Gandhi.* However, if a name is used in the plural to refer to members of a family, it takes *the*: *the Clintons, the Kennedys.*
- Names of places that are plural in form usually take *the*: *the Andes, the United States.*
- Names of most places on land (cities, states, provinces, and countries) take no article: *Salt Lake City, Mississippi, Alberta, Japan.* Names of most bodies of water (rivers, seas, and oceans) take *the*: *the Mississippi, the Mediterranean, the Pacific.* However, names of lakes and bays do not take articles: *Lake Erie, San Francisco Bay.*
- Names of streets take no article: *Main Street.* Names of highways take *the*: *the Belt Parkway.* (Names of numbered highways, however, do not take *the*: for example, Route 80.)

◆ PRACTICE 30-6

In the following passage, decide whether each blank space needs a definite article (*the*), an indefinite article (*a* or *an*), or no article. If a definite or an indefinite article is needed, write it in the space provided. If no article is needed, leave the space blank.

ON THE WEB
For more practice understanding articles, visit **Exercise Central** *at bedfordstmartins.com/foundationsfirst.*

Example: Salma Hayek was born in __a__ little town in Veracruz, Mexico.

(1) ____ father of ____ actress Salma Hayek is of Lebanese descent, and her mother is of Spanish origin. (2) At ____ age of twelve, Salma's parents sent her away to ____ small boarding school in ____ state of Louisiana in ____ United States. (3) Salma was asked to leave that school after ____ brief stay because she was ____ rebellious girl. (4) After high school, Salma decided to move to ____ Mexico City to attend ____ large university. (5) ____ frustrated college student soon decided she wanted ____ career in acting. (6) Salma's parents did not like ____ idea of her becoming ____ actress. (7) Salma began performing in ____ variety of plays and ____ television commercials. (8) She finally became ____ star of ____ very popular telenovela in ____ Mexico. (9) In 1991, Salma

moved to ____ apartment in ____ California. (10) She had eighteen months of ____ English lessons before she got ____ big movie role. (11) Salma played ____ role of Mexican artist Frida Kahlo in ____ movie *Frida*. (12) Salma earned ____ nomination for ____ Academy Award as the best actress of 2003 and produced and performed in ____ television show *Ugly Betty*.

G Negative Statements and Questions

Negative Statements

To form a negative statement, add the word *not* directly after the first helping verb of the complete verb.

Global warming has been getting worse.

Global warming has not been getting worse.

When there is no helping verb, a form of the verb *do* must be inserted before *not*.

Automobile traffic contributes to pollution.

Automobile traffic does not contribute to pollution.

Remember that when *do* is used as a helping verb, the form of *do* used must match the tense and number of the original main verb. Note that in the negative statement above, the main verb loses its tense and appears in the base form (*contribute*, not *contributes*).

NOTE: If the main verb is *am, is, are, was,* or *were,* do not insert a form of *do* before *not*: *Harry was late*; *Harry was not late.*

Questions

To form a question, move the helping verb that follows the subject to the position directly before the subject.

The governor has tried to compromise.

Has the governor tried to compromise?

The governor has worked on the budget.

Has the governor worked on the budget?

A helping verb never comes before the subject if the subject is a question word (such as *who* or *which*) or contains a question word.

Who is talking to the governor?

Which bills have been vetoed by the governor?

As with negatives, when the verb does not include a helping verb, you must supply a form of *do*. To form a question, put *do* directly before the subject.

The governor works hard.

Does the governor work hard?

NOTE: If the main verb is a form of *be* (*am*, *is*, *are*, *was*, or *were*), do not insert a form of *do* before the verb. Instead, move the verb so it comes before the subject: *Harry was late*; *Was Harry late?*

◆ PRACTICE 30-7

Rewrite each of the following sentences in two ways: first, turn the sentence into a question; then, rewrite the original sentence as a negative statement.

Example: Moths are living in my closet.

Question: Are moths living in my closet?

Negative statement: Moths are not living in my closet.

1. The sparrows are searching for winter food.

   Question: ______________________

   Negative statement: ______________________

2. Wild raspberries grow all along these dirt roads.

   Question: ______________________

   Negative statement: ______________________

3. I answered her email immediately.

   Question: ______________________

   Negative statement: ______________________

4. Shiho felt sick after eating the pizza.

   Question: ______________________

   Negative statement: ______________________

5. The porcupine attacked my dog.

   Question: ______________________

   Negative statement: ______________________

6. Final exams will be given during the last week of school.

   Question: ______________________

   Negative statement: ______________________

ON THE WEB
For more practice forming negative statements and questions, visit Exercise Central *at bedfordstmartins .com/foundationsfirst.*

7. Gunnar saw the robbery at the convenience store.

   Question: ______________________________

   Negative statement: ______________________________

8. The telephone has been ringing all morning.

   Question: ______________________________

   Negative statement: ______________________________

9. He is working on the problem right now.

   Question: ______________________________

   Negative statement: ______________________________

10. She dropped the box of dishes on the concrete floor.

    Question: ______________________________

    Negative statement: ______________________________

H Verb Tense

In English, a verb's form indicates its **tense**—when the action referred to by the verb took place (for instance, in the past or in the present). Be sure to use the appropriate tense of the verb even if the time is obvious or if the sentence includes other indications of time (such as *two years ago* or *yesterday*).

INCORRECT Yesterday, I get a letter from my sister Yunpi.

CORRECT Yesterday, I got a letter from my sister Yunpi.

I Stative Verbs

Stative verbs usually tell us that someone or something is in a state that will not change, at least for a while.

Hiro knows American history very well.

Most English verbs show action, and these action verbs can be used in the progressive tenses. The **present progressive** tense consists of the present tense of *be* plus the present participle (*I am going*). The **past progressive** tense consists of the past tense of *be* plus the present participle (*I was going*). Stative verbs, however, are rarely used in the progressive tenses.

INCORRECT Hiro is knowing American history very well.

FOCUS Stative Verbs

Verbs that are stative often refer to mental states—for example, *know, understand, think, believe, want, like, love,* and *hate*. Other stative verbs include *be, have, need, own, belong, weigh, cost,* and *mean*. Certain verbs of sense perception, like *see* and *hear,* are also stative even though they can refer to momentary events rather than unchanging states.

Many verbs have more than one meaning, and some of these verbs are active with one meaning but stative with another. An example is the verb *weigh*.

ACTIVE The butcher is weighing the meat.

STATIVE The meat weighs three pounds.

In the first sentence above, the verb *weigh* means "to put on a scale;" it is active, not stative, as the use of the present progressive tense shows. In the second sentence, however, the same verb means "to have weight," so it is stative, not active. It would be incorrect to say, "The meat is weighing three pounds."

◆ PRACTICE 30-8

In each of the following sentences, circle the verb. Then, correct any problems with stative verbs by crossing out the incorrect verb tense and writing the correct verb tense above the line. If a sentence is correct, write *C* in the blank after the sentence.

Example: Ahmed ~~is wanting~~ (wants) to take advanced calculus next semester. ____

1. Ahmed is studying mathematics in college. ____
2. He is also knowing a lot about astronomy. ____
3. He is understanding the movements of planets and stars. ____
4. He was being president of the school's Astronomy Club last year. ____
5. Ahmed is working his way through school. ____
6. He is having a job at a gas station. ____
7. He is hating the boring work there. ____
8. Ahmed is needing the money for his tuition. ____
9. Little by little, he is earning enough to help his family. ____
10. Ahmed is knowing he has to keep his boring job for now. ____

ON THE WEB
For more practice recognizing stative verbs, visit Exercise Central *at bedfordstmartins .com/foundationsfirst.*

J Using Modal Auxiliaries

A **modal auxiliary** (such as *can, may, might,* or *must*) is a helping verb that is used with a sentence's main verb to express ability, possibility, necessity, intent, obligation, and so on. In the following sentence, *can* is the modal auxiliary, and *imagine* is the main verb.

I *can imagine* myself in medical school.

Modal auxiliaries usually intensify the main verb's meaning:

I *must study* as hard as I can.

You *ought to gain* some weight.

Modal Auxiliaries

can	ought to
could	shall
may	should
might	will
must	would

FOCUS Modal Auxiliaries

Modal auxiliaries can be used to do the following.

- Express physical ability

  I can walk faster than my brother.

- Express the possibility of something occurring

  He might get the job if his interview goes well.

- Express or request permission

  May I join you?

- Express necessity

  I must get to the airport on time.

- Express a suggestion or advice

  To be healthy, you should [or ought to] exercise and eat balanced meals.

(continued on following page)

(continued from previous page)

- Express intent

    I will try to study harder next time.

- Express a desire

    Would you please answer the door?

◆ PRACTICE 30-9

In the exercise below, circle the correct modal auxiliary.

Example: (May/Would) you help me complete the assignment?

1. It doesn't rain very often in Arizona, but today it looks as if it (can/might).
2. I know I (will/ought to) call my aunt on her birthday, but I always find an excuse.
3. Sarah (should/must) study for her English exam, but she is happier spending time with her friends.
4. John (can/would) be the best person to represent our class.
5. Since the close presidential election of 2000, many people now believe they (could/should) vote in every election.
6. All students (will/must) bring two pencils, a notebook, and a dictionary to class every day.
7. (Would/May) you show me the way to the post office?
8. I (could/should) not ask for more than my health, my family, and my job.
9. Do you think they (could/can) come back tomorrow to finish the painting job?
10. A dog (should/might) be a helpful companion for your disabled father.

K Gerunds

A **gerund** is a verb form ending in *-ing* that always acts as a noun.

> Reading the newspaper is one of my favorite things to do on Sundays.

Just like a noun, a gerund can be used as a subject, a direct object, a subject complement, or the object of a preposition.

FOCUS Gerunds

- A gerund can be the subject of a sentence.

  Playing soccer is one of my hobbies.

- A gerund can be a direct object.

  My brother influenced my playing.

- A gerund can be a subject complement.

  The most important thing is winning.

- A gerund can be the object of a preposition.

  The crowd cheered him for trying.

◆ PRACTICE 30-10

To complete the sentences below, fill in the blanks with the gerund form of the verb provided in parentheses.

Example: ___Typing___ (type) is a skill that every girl used to learn in high school.

1. ______________ (eat) five or six small meals throughout the day is healthier than eating two or three big meals.
2. In the winter, there is nothing better than ______________ (skate) outdoors on a frozen pond.
3. The household task I dread the most is ______________ (clean).
4. The fish avoided the net by ______________ (swim) faster.
5. ______________ (quit) is easier than achieving a goal.
6. Her parents praised her for ______________ (remember) their anniversary.
7. The job she enjoyed the most was ______________ (organize) the files.
8. I did not like his ______________ (sing).
9. For me, ______________ (cook) is a relaxing way to spend the evening.
10. The best way to prepare for the concert is by ______________ (practice).

L Placing Modifiers in Order

Adjectives and other modifiers that come before a noun usually follow a set order.

Required Order

- Determiners always come first in a series of adjectives: *these fragile glasses*. The determiners *all* or *both* always precede any other determiners: *all these glasses*.
- If one of the modifiers is a noun, it must come directly before the noun it modifies: *these wine glasses*.
- All other adjectives are placed between the determiners and the noun modifiers: *these fragile wine glasses*. If there are two or more of these adjectives, the following order is preferred.

Preferred Order

- Adjectives that show the writer's attitude generally precede adjectives that merely describe: *these lovely fragile wine glasses*.
- Adjectives that indicate size generally come early: *these lovely large fragile wine glasses*.

◆ PRACTICE 30-11

Arrange each group of modifiers in the correct order, and rewrite the complete phrase in the blank.

Example: (rubber, a, red, pretty) ball

a pretty red rubber ball

1. (family, old, a, pleasant) tradition

____

2. (some, disgusting, work) boots

____

3. (four, cute, Anita's) poodles

____

4. (three, the, circus, funny) clowns

____

5. (my, annoying, both) sisters

____

6. (son's, his, favorite, television) show

____

ON THE WEB
For more practice placing adjectives in order, visit Exercise Central *at bedfordstmartins.com/foundationsfirst.*

7. (a, wedding, delightful, outdoor) celebration

____

8. (cat, furry, ugly, this) toy

____

9. (birthday, a, wonderful, chocolate) cake

____

10. (traveling, all, these, banjo) players

____

M Choosing Prepositions

A **preposition** is a word that introduces a noun or pronoun and links it to other words in the sentence. The word the preposition introduces is called the object of the preposition.

A preposition and its object combine to form a **prepositional phrase**: *on the table, near the table, under the table*. Thus, prepositions show the precise relationships between words—for example, whether a book is *on, near*, or *under* a table.

> I thought I left the book on the table or somewhere near the table, but I found it under the table.

The prepositions *at, in*, and *on* sometimes cause problems for nonnative speakers of English. For example, to identify the location of a place or an event, you can use *at, in*, or *on*.

- The preposition *at* specifies an exact point in space or time.

  > Please leave the package with the janitor at 150 South Street.
  > I will pick it up at 7:30 tonight.

- Expanses of space or time are treated as containers and therefore require *in*.

  > Jean-Pierre went to school in the 1970s.

- *On* must be used in two cases: with names of streets (but not with exact addresses) and with days of the week or month.

  > We will move into our new office on 18th Street either on Monday or on March 12.

N Prepositions in Familiar Expressions

Many **idioms** (familiar expressions) end with prepositions. Learning to write clearly and **idiomatically**—following the conventions of written English—means learning which preposition is used in each expression.

Even native speakers of English sometimes have trouble choosing the correct preposition.

The sentences that follow illustrate idiomatic use of prepositions in various expressions. Note that sometimes different prepositions are used with the same word. For example, both *on* and *for* can be used with *wait* to form two different expressions with two different meanings: *He waited on their table; She waited for the bus.* Which preposition you choose depends on your meaning. (In the list that follows, pairs of similar expressions that end with different prepositions are bracketed.)

Prepositions in Familiar Expressions

Expression with Preposition	***Sample Sentence***
acquainted with	It took the family several weeks to become acquainted with the new neighbors.
addicted to	I think Abby is becoming addicted to pretzels.
[agree on (a plan or objective)	It is vital that all members of the school board agree on goals for the coming year.
agree to (a proposal)]	Striking workers finally agreed to the terms of management's offer.
[angry about or at (a situation)	Taxpayers are understandably angry about (or at) the deterioration of city recreation facilities.
angry with or at (a person)]	When the mayor refused to hire more police officers, his constituents became angry with (or at) him.
approve of	Amy's adviser approved of her decision to study in Guatemala.
bored with	Just when Michael was getting bored with his life, he met Sharon.
capable of	Dogs may be able to fetch and roll over, but they certainly are not capable of complex reasoning.
consist of	The deluxe fruit basket consisted of five pathetic pears, two tiny apples, a few limp bunches of grapes, and one lonely kiwi.
contrast with	Coach Headley's relaxed style contrasts sharply with Coach Morgan's more formal approach.
convenient for	The location of the new day-care center is convenient for many families.
deal with	Many parents and educators believe it is possible to deal with the special needs of autistic children in a regular classroom.
depend on	Children depend on their parents for emotional as well as financial support.

(continued on following page)

(continued from previous page)

Expression with Preposition	***Sample Sentence***
differ from (something else)	The music of Norah Jones differs from the music of Alicia Keys.
differ with (someone else)	I strongly differ with your interpretation of my dream about *The Wizard of Oz*.
emigrate from	My grandfather and his brother emigrated from the part of Russia that is now Ukraine.
grateful for (a favor)	If you can arrange an interview next week, I will be very grateful for your time and trouble.
grateful to (someone)	Jerry Garcia was always grateful to his loyal fans.
immigrate to	Many Cubans want to leave their country and immigrate to the United States.
impatient with	Keshia often gets impatient with her four younger brothers.
interested in	Diana, who was not very interested in the discussion of the Treaty of Versailles, stared out the window.
interfere with	Sometimes it is hard to resist the temptation to interfere with a friend's life.
meet with	I hope I can meet with you soon to discuss my research paper.
object to	The defense attorney objected to the prosecutor's treatment of the witness.
pleased with	Marta was very pleased with Eric's favorable critique of her speech.
protect against	Nobel Prize winner Linus Pauling believed that large doses of vitamin C could protect people against the common cold.
reason with	When a two-year-old is having a tantrum, it is nearly impossible to reason with her.
reply to	If no one replies to our ad within two weeks, we will advertise again.
responsible for	Parents are not responsible for the debts of their adult children.
similar to	The blood sample found at the crime scene was remarkably similar to one found in the suspect's residence.
specialize in	Dr. Casullo is a dentist who specializes in periodontal surgery.

(continued on following page)

(continued from previous page)

succeed in	Lisa hoped her MBA would help her succeed in a business career.
take advantage of	Some consumer laws are designed to prevent door-to-door salespeople from taking advantage of buyers.
wait for (something to happen)	Snow White slept while she waited for her prince to arrive.
wait on (in a restaurant)	We sat at the table for twenty minutes before someone waited on us.
worry about	Why worry about things you cannot change?

◆ PRACTICE 30-12

In the following passage, fill in each blank with the correct preposition.

Example: Naomi's family lives ___in___ a small house ___on___ Parsons Street.

(1) Naomi emigrated __________ Ghana when she was a teenager. (2) Her family settled __________ New Jersey, __________ the East Coast of the United States. (3) Naomi had studied English __________ Ghana, but she was not prepared for the kind of English spoken __________ the United States. (4) The other students __________ her class sometimes laughed __________ her pronunciation. (5) Still, she studied hard, and her high school teachers were pleased __________ her progress. (6) Naomi was interested __________ attending college and getting a nursing degree. (7) She knew that she was capable __________ doing well __________ college classes if she could continue to improve her English. (8) Before sending an application __________ a local college, Naomi met __________ an admissions officer to discuss her application. (9) Everyone __________ the admissions office was encouraging, and Naomi decided to take advantage __________ their offers to help her. (10) __________ April 12, Naomi's mother called her __________ her after-school job to tell her that the college had accepted her.

✣ **ON THE WEB**
For more practice using prepositions in familiar expressions, visit **Exercise Central** *at bedfordstmartins .com/foundationsfirst.*

O Prepositions in Phrasal Verbs

A **phrasal verb** consists of two words, a verb and a preposition, that are joined to form an idiomatic expression. Many phrasal verbs are **separable**. This means that a direct object can come between the verb and the preposition. However, some phrasal verbs are **inseparable**; that is, the preposition must always come immediately after the verb.

Separable Phrasal Verbs

In many cases, phrasal verbs may be split, with the direct object coming between the two parts of the verb. When the direct object is a noun, the second word of the phrasal verb can come either before or after the object.

In the sentence below, *turn off* is a phrasal verb. Because the object of the verb *turn off* is a noun (*printer*), the second word of the verb can come either before or after the verb's object.

CORRECT Please turn off the printer.

CORRECT Please turn the printer off.

When the object of a transitive verb is a pronoun, however, these two-word verbs must be split, and the pronoun must come between the two parts.

CORRECT Please turn it off.

INCORRECT Please turn off it.

Some Common Separable Phrasal Verbs

ask out	hang up	put back	think over
bring up	leave out	put off	throw away
call up	let in	put on	try out
carry out	let out	set aside	turn down
drop off	look over	shut off	turn off
fill out	make up	take down	wake up
give away	put away	take off	

Remember, when the object of the verb is a pronoun, these two-word verbs must be split, and the pronoun must come between the two parts: *take (it) down*, *put (it) on*, *let (it) out*, *make (it) up*, and so on.

Inseparable Phrasal Verbs

Some phrasal verbs, however, cannot be separated; that is, the preposition cannot be separated from the verb. This means that a direct object cannot come between the verb and the preposition.

CORRECT Please go over the manual carefully.

INCORRECT Please go the manual over carefully.

Notice that in the correct sentence above, the direct object (*manual*) comes right after the preposition (*over*).

Some Common Inseparable Phrasal Verbs

come across	run across	show up
get along	run into	stand by
go over	see to	

◆ PRACTICE 30-13

Consulting the lists of inseparable and separable phrasal verbs above, decide whether the preposition is placed correctly in each of the following sentences. If a sentence is correct, write **C** in the blank after the sentence. If it is not correct, edit the sentence.

ON THE WEB
For more practice using prepositions in phrasal verbs, visit Exercise Central *at bedfordstmartins.com/foundationsfirst.*

Example: Before she called the taxi, Chong looked up the phone number in the phone book. C

1. Chong had never traveled alone, and she wanted to try out it. ______
2. She planned to stay away for at least a week. ______
3. Chong went over her instructions for her family before she left on her trip. ______
4. On the kitchen counter, she left out a list of chores for her family to do while she was away. ______
5. She told her husband that the children had to get to school early on Friday and that he should wake up them at 6:30 a.m. ______
6. She warned him not to give to them in if they wanted to watch cartoons on Saturday morning. ______
7. When her husband and children asked how long she would be gone, Chong put off them. ______
8. Before she left, she collected some of her old clothes and gave away them. ______
9. She also dropped off her husband's shirts at the cleaners. ______
10. After three days, Chong missed her family so much that she called up them and said that she was coming home right away. ______

▶ **Word Power**

elector a qualified voter in an election

● REVISING AND EDITING

Look back at your response to the Seeing and Writing exercise on page 412. Review this chapter; then, make any necessary grammar and usage corrections to your writing. When you have finished, add any additional transitional words and phrases you need to make your ideas clear to your readers.

George Washington

CHAPTER REVIEW

◆ EDITING PRACTICE

Read the following paragraph, which contains errors in the use of subjects, articles and determiners, stative verbs, and idiomatic expressions containing prepositions. Look carefully at each underlined word or phrase. If it is not used correctly, cross it out and write the correct word or phrase above the line. If the underlined word or phrase is correct, write *C* above it. The first sentence has been edited for you.

John Quincy Adams

The Electoral College

Many Americans ~~are believing~~ *believe* that the winning candidate is the person who has gotten the most votes, but when an election is ~~being~~ very close, the candidate who gets the greatest number of votes may not win the presidency. The president is actually selected by the Electoral College, a group consisting with electors from every state. The Electoral College was created by the Continental Congress on 1787, before George Washington was elected president. Since those time, the United States has depended for the Electoral College to select the president. If the no candidate wins a majority of Electoral College votes, the House of Representatives decides the election. In 1824, John Quincy Adams was elected by the House of Representatives even though he had received only the third of the popular vote. Were two more elections in the nineteenth century in which the apparent winner lost in the Electoral College. At 1876, the Electoral College chose Rutherford B. Hayes, who had lost for Samuel Tilden in the popular vote. In 1888, Benjamin Harrison got fewer votes than Grover Cleveland, but Harrison got more electoral votes and became president. Americans become very interested with the Electoral College when an election is close. For example, in 2000 George W. Bush got more

George W. Bush

electoral votes and defeated Al Gore even though Gore won the popular vote. Most Americans think that every vote should be equally important in the democracy. Some people feel that the Electoral College system is not fair. Perhaps some twenty-first-century Congress will finally object on the system enough to try out a new one.

◆ COLLABORATIVE ACTIVITIES

1. Working in a group of three or four students, write down as many determiners as you can think of. Next, make a list of ten adjectives. Then, list ten nouns. Finally, combine the determiners and adjectives (in the correct order) in front of the nouns. Be as creative, original, and funny as you can. Choose your group's best phrase, and write it on the board.
2. Working in the same group, write ten sentences using the phrases you wrote in activity 1. Make sure that each sentence contains at least one prepositional phrase. Then, exchange sentences with another group. Look over the other group's sentences, and correct any errors you find.
3. Working in the same group, choose one sentence that your group wrote in activity 2. Then, write a short paragraph that begins with this sentence. Use as many specific, interesting nouns and prepositional phrases as you can, and include at least one phrasal verb. Finally, have one member of the group read the paragraph aloud to the class.
4. ***Composing original sentences*** Working in the same group, write five additional original sentences. Make sure that you use at least two plural nouns, at least one noncount noun, at least one negative statement or question, at least one stative verb, and at least one idiomatic expression with a preposition. Check the articles and prepositions carefully. When you have finished, check your sentences to correct any errors in grammar, punctuation, or spelling.

☑ REVIEW CHECKLIST: Grammar and Usage Issues for ESL Writers

- In almost all cases, English sentences must state their subjects. (See 30A and 30B.)
- In English, most nouns add *-s* to form plurals. Always use a form of the noun that indicates that it is plural. (See 30C.)
- English nouns may be count nouns or noncount nouns. A count noun names one particular thing or a group of particular things (*a teacher, oceans*). A noncount noun names something that cannot be counted (*gold, sand*). (See 30D.)
- Determiners are adjectives that identify rather than describe the nouns they modify. Determiners may also indicate amount or number. (See 30E.)

(continued on following page)

(continued from previous page)

- The definite article *the* and the indefinite articles *a* and *an* are determiners that indicate whether the noun that follows is one readers can identify (*the book*) or one they cannot yet identify (*a book*). (See 30F.)
- To form a negative statement, add the word *not* directly after the first helping verb of the complete verb. To form a question, move the helping verb that follows the subject to the position directly before the subject. (See 30G.)
- A verb's form must indicate when the action referred to by the verb took place. (See 30H.)
- Stative verbs indicate that someone or something is in a state that will not change, at least for a while. Stative verbs are rarely used in the progressive tenses. (See 30I.)
- A modal auxiliary is a helping verb that expresses ability, possibility, necessity, intent, obligation, and so on. (See 30J.)
- A gerund is a verb form ending in *-ing* that is always used as a noun. (See 30K.)
- Adjectives and other modifiers that come before a noun usually follow a set order. (See 30L.)
- The prepositions *at*, *in*, and *on* sometimes cause problems for nonnative speakers of English. (See 30M.)
- Many familiar expressions end with prepositions. (See 30N.)
- A phrasal verb consists of two words, a verb and a preposition, that are joined to form an idiomatic expression.

UNIT REVIEW

Read the following student essay, which includes some basic grammatical errors. Correct any errors you find in the use of the past tense, past participles, nouns, pronouns, adjectives, and adverbs. The first error has been corrected for you.

The Peace Corps: A Way to Give Back

Americans often say that they are interested in promoting world peace. In 1960, John F. Kennedy ~~has~~ had the idea that the U.S. government could give ordinary citizens a way to do just that. Beginning in 1961, Americans have had a chance to become Peace Corps volunteers. Why do people volunteer for the Peace Corps? First, they could travel. Second, they get valuable experience. Most important, they have the chance to help others.

First group of Peace Corps volunteers, 1961

One reason to join the Peace Corps is to travel. Members of the Peace Corps have been send all over the world by the U.S. government, which pays their costs. For example, the Peace Corps had had volunteers in the nation of Kazakhstan since 1993. Kazakhstan used to be a communist country. Now, the Peace Corps is helping the people of Kazakhstan to change to a free-market system and to practice democracy. Peace Corps volunteers always work close with ordinary people. Before they are sent to Kazakhstan or any other country, every volunteer studies the local language. During their stay, he or she eats the local food and participates in local activitys, such as village meetings and weddings. In some countries, members of the Peace Corps live with host families; in others, he or she lives alone in small huts. Running water and electricity may be available, or conditions may be more difficult. These are not typical tourist experiences; they are priceless opportunitys to learn about people in another part of the world.

Kazakhstan

Another reason to join the Peace Corps is to learn skills for the future. Living in another country is a life-changing experience. Young volunteers have to become more self-reliant, poised, and self-confident. Far from home, they learn to get along with many other people. They learn how to deal with frustration and to survive and thrive in a new environment. From the beginning, Peace Corps volunteers had became fluent in another language and familiar with another culture — skills that corporations and government value. If former Peace Corps members want to go to graduate school, he or she can get financial aid from many colleges. Thus, someone whom is thinking about the future may find that their Peace Corps experience is very valuable.

The most important reason to join the Peace Corps is to help others. Peace Corps volunteers can make especially important contributions in education and agriculture. In the developing world, many people have little education, yet they need to be well educate. Peace Corps volunteers not only teach academic subjects like English and math, but also provide vital health information. Volunteers can even teach a local resident to be teachers themselves. In this way, the volunteers' contributions can continue after they have return to the United States. Agriculture is another area where Peace Corps volunteers can make a real significant difference; after all, increasing the food supply is essential for many countries. Peace Corps volunteers also help with business skills, community development, and information technology. The Peace Corps makes it possible to work with individuals on projects that really contribute to positive change.

Peace Corps volunteer in Kazakhstan

Joining the Peace Corps offers several benefits. First, volunteers get to travel and live in a foreign country. Second, Peace Corps experience gives volunteers skills that can help them find rewarding employment. Third, and more important, is the opportunity for volunteers to do well. Often, young Americans want to "give something back" and share some of their advantages with others. They could do this by becoming Peace Corps volunteers.

UNIT SIX

Understanding Punctuation, Mechanics, and Spelling

CHAPTER 31

Using Commas

PREVIEW

In this chapter, you will learn

- to use commas in a series (31A)
- to use commas with introductory phrases and transitional words and phrases (31B)
- to use commas with appositives (31C)
- to use commas with nonrestrictive clauses (31D)
- to use commas in compound and complex sentences (31E)
- to use commas in dates and addresses (31F)

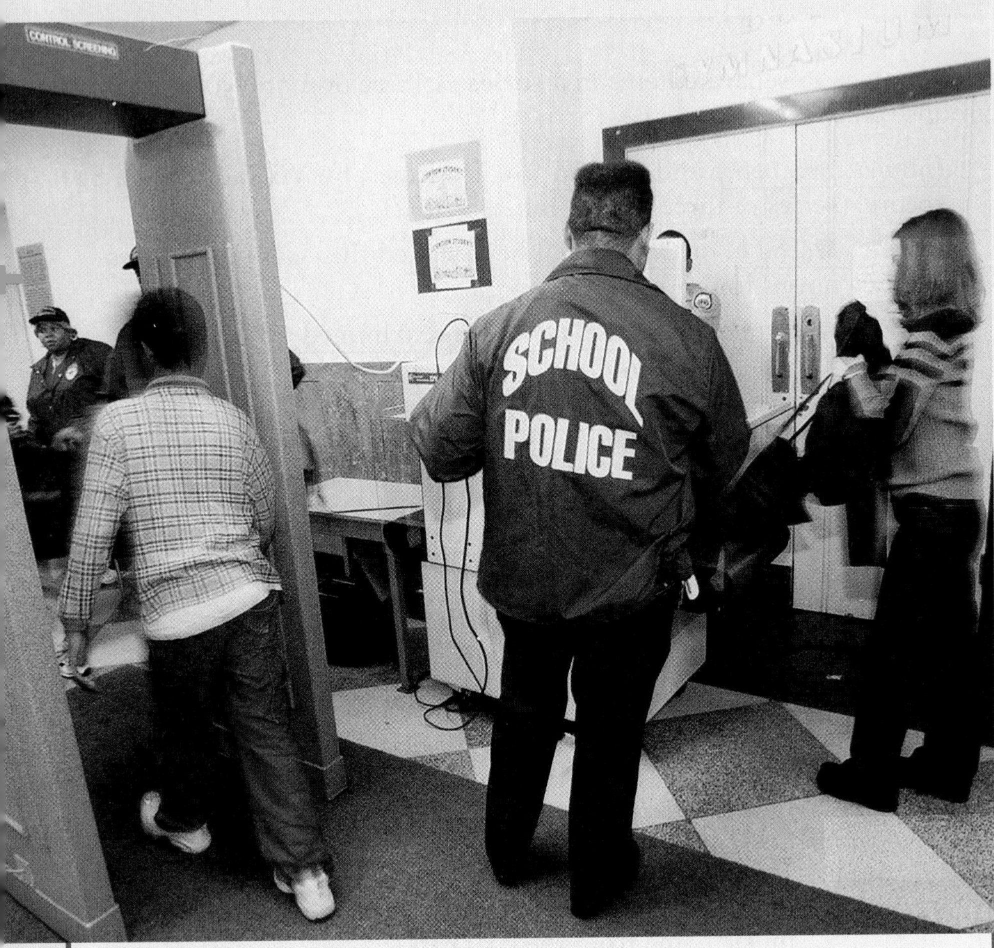

SEEING AND WRITING

The picture above shows a security checkpoint in a public high school. What kind of security do you think is needed in America's high schools? Why? Look at the picture, and then write a paragraph in which you answer these questions.

Word Power

surveillance the close observation of a person or a group of people, especially a person or group under suspicion

A **comma** is a punctuation mark that separates words or groups of words within sentences. In this way, commas help readers by keeping ideas distinct from one another. As you will learn in this chapter, commas also have several other uses.

A Commas in a Series

Use commas to separate items in a **series** of three or more words or word groups (phrases or clauses).

Hamlet, *Macbeth*, and *Othello* are tragedies by William Shakespeare. (series of three nouns linked by *and*)

Hamlet, *Macbeth*, or *Othello* will be assigned this semester. (series of three nouns linked by *or*)

Brian read *Hamlet*, started *Macbeth*, and skimmed *Othello*. (series of three phrases linked by *and*)

Hamlet is a tragedy, *Much Ado about Nothing* is a comedy, and *Richard III* is a history play. (series of three clauses linked by *and*)

FOCUS Using Commas in a Series

Newspapers and magazines usually leave out the comma before the coordinating conjunction in a series of three or more items. However, your writing is clearer when you use a comma before the coordinating conjunction (*and*, *or*, *but*, and so on) in this situation.

UNCLEAR The party had 200 guests, great food and rock music blaring from giant speakers. (Did food as well as music come from the speakers?)

CLEAR The party had 200 guests, great food, and rock music blaring from giant speakers.

◆ PRACTICE 31-1

Edit the following sentences for the correct use of commas in a series. If the sentence is correct, write *C* in the blank.

Example: We stowed our luggage, took our seats, and fastened our seat belts. ______

1. The street was crowded with buses cars and trucks. ______
2. The boys are either in the house, in the yard or at the park. ______

❖ **ON THE WEB**
For more practice using commas in a series, visit Exercise Central *at bedfordstmartins.com/foundationsfirst.*

3. *Star Wars*, *Alien*, and *Blade Runner* are classic science fiction movies. ______

4. Jo Ellen took a walk Roger cleaned the house and Phil went to the movies. ______

5. A good marriage requires patience, honesty and hard work. ______

6. Volunteers collected signatures accepted donations and answered phones. ______

7. We did not know whether to laugh, cry, or cheer. ______

8. Owls are good hunters because they are strong, quick and silent. ______

9. The kitchen is to the left the guest room is upstairs and the pool is out back. ______

10. This computer is fast, has plenty of memory, and comes with an extra-large monitor. ______

B Commas with Introductory Phrases and Transitional Words and Phrases

Introductory Phrases

Use a comma to set off an **introductory phrase** (a group of words that opens a sentence) from the rest of the sentence.

For best results, take this medicine with a full glass of water.
In case of fire, keep calm.
After the concert, we walked home through the park.

◆ PRACTICE 31-2

Edit the following sentences for the correct use of commas with introductory phrases. If the sentence is correct, write *C* in the blank.

Example: After school,^ Thieu went to soccer practice. ______

1. According to recent studies most parents of young children use the TV as a babysitter. ______

2. During the thunderstorm my dog hid under the bed and howled. ______

❖ **ON THE WEB**
For more practice using commas to set off introductory phrases, visit Exercise Central *at bedfordstmartins.com/ foundationsfirst.*

3. In Scandinavia, most people speak excellent English. ______
4. In nursing homes patients are sometimes given medication that makes them drowsy. ______
5. After the concert, my friends and I decided to drive to the beach. ______
6. Without a background in advanced algebra and calculus students will find college-level math courses difficult. ______
7. Due to an unexpected power failure, all the computers in the building shut down. ______
8. Between 1350 and 1451, half of Europe's population died of the plague. ______
9. To purchase a new home you have to consider whether you will be able to manage the mortgage payments. ______
10. In communities where property taxes are low the schools are sometimes inferior. ______

Transitional Words and Phrases

Use commas to set off **transitional words and phrases** whether they appear at the beginning, in the middle, or at the end of a sentence.

In fact, Scott Gomez grew up in Alaska.
He is, however, a center for the New Jersey Devils.
He plays for the NHL, of course.

FOCUS Using Commas in Direct Address

Always use commas to set off the name of a person (or an animal) whom you are addressing (speaking to directly). Use commas whether the name of the person addressed appears at the beginning, in the middle, or at the end of a sentence.

Spike, roll over and play dead.

Roll over, Spike, and play dead.

Roll over and play dead, Spike.

◆ PRACTICE 31-3

Edit the following sentences for the correct use of commas with transitional words and phrases and names of people being addressed. If the sentence is correct, write *C* in the blank.

Example: The Dallas Cowboys, surely, are one of football's most famous teams. ___C___

1. Bill how did you do on the test? ______
2. The plane unfortunately never got off the ground. ______
3. In addition, bottled water is quite expensive. ______
4. We wanted to make a good impression of course. ______
5. When you give your speech Jeanne be sure to speak clearly. ______
6. In fact even experienced professionals make mistakes. ______
7. The party consequently was a disaster. ______
8. How old are you, anyway? ______
9. Don't forget the key to the cabin Amber. ______
10. However no one knew what the outcome would be. ______
11. Furthermore the team had lost its best defensive player. ______
12. The mayor unfortunately was associated with a number of scandals. ______
13. What material will be on the test Dr. Chen? ______
14. No one can say, moreover, how the economy will change in the future. ______
15. Besides genetics is the next medical frontier. ______

ON THE WEB
For more practice using commas to set off transitional words and phrases, visit Exercise Central *at bedfordstmartins.com/foundationsfirst.*

◆ PRACTICE 31-4

Choose five items from the list of words and phrases provided, and then write three sentences for each—one with the transitional word or phrase at the beginning of the sentence, one with the transitional word or phrase in the middle, and one with the transitional word or phrase at the end.

Examples

In fact, some dinosaurs were highly intelligent creatures.

Some dinosaurs, in fact, were highly intelligent creatures.

Some dinosaurs were highly intelligent creatures, in fact.

after all	in contrast
as a result	in fact
at the same time	in other words
consequently	nevertheless
for example	subsequently
however	therefore
in addition	

1a. ______________________________

____

b. ______________________________

____

c. ______________________________

____

2a. ______________________________

____

b. ______________________________

____

c. ______________________________

____

3a. ______________________________

____

b. ______________________________

____

c. ______________________________

____

4a. ______________________________

____

b. ______________________________

____

c. ______________________________

____

5a. ______________________________

____

b. ____

____

c. ____

____

C Commas with Appositives

Use commas to set off an **appositive**, a word or word group that identifies, renames, or describes a noun or a pronoun.

> Luis Valdez, an award-winning playwright, wrote *Los Vendidos* and *Zoot Suit*. (*An award-winning playwright* is an appositive that describes the noun *Luis Valdez*.)
>
> The Cisco Kid rode in on his horse, a white stallion. (*A white stallion* is an appositive that describes the noun *horse*.)
>
> She, the star of the show, applauded the audience. (*The star of the show* is an appositive that identifies the pronoun *she*.)

FOCUS Using Commas with Appositives

An appositive can appear at the beginning, in the middle, or at the end of a sentence. Wherever it appears, it is always set off from the rest of the sentence by commas.

> A Native American writer, Sherman Alexie wrote the novel *Reservation Blues*.
>
> One of Alexie's poems, "Defending Walt Whitman," is about a basketball game.
>
> One of Alexie's books was made into a film, *Smoke Signals*.

◆ PRACTICE 31-5

Edit the following sentences for the correct use of commas to set off appositives. If the sentence is correct, write *C* in the blank.

Example: Hawaii's capital, Honolulu, is on the island of Oahu. ______

1. My mother Sandra Thomas used to work for the city. ______
2. Coca-Cola, a popular soft drink has been around for decades. ______

✣ **ON THE WEB**
For more practice using commas with appositives, visit Exercise Central *at bedfordstmartins.com/foundationsfirst.*

3. The convention is in Chicago my hometown. _______
4. A rookie he approached the suspect cautiously. _______
5. The world's tallest mountain Mount Everest is in Nepal. _______
6. Life on earth could not exist without our nearest star the sun. _______
7. Aloe a common houseplant, has medicinal value. _______
8. An excellent dancer, she won the competition easily. _______
9. Elvis Presley a white singer, was influenced by African-American music. _______
10. Adam Smith was a leading figure in economics the study of wealth and society. _______

D Commas with Nonrestrictive Clauses

> **Word Power**
> **restrict** to keep within limits
> **restrictive** limiting

Clauses can add information in a sentence. In some cases, you need to add commas to set off these clauses; in other cases, commas are not required.

- A **restrictive clause** contains information that is essential to a sentence's meaning. Restrictive clauses are *not* set off from the rest of the sentence by commas.

  The artist who was formerly known as Prince is now known as Prince again.

  In the above sentence, the clause *who was formerly known as Prince* supplies specific information that is essential to the idea the sentence is communicating. The clause tells readers which particular artist is now known as Prince again. Without the clause *who was formerly known as Prince*, the sentence does not communicate the same idea because it does not specify which particular artist is now once again known as Prince.

  The artist is now known as Prince again. (Which artist is known as Prince?)

- A **nonrestrictive clause** does *not* contain essential information. Nonrestrictive clauses *are* set off from the rest of the sentence by commas.

  Violent crime in our cities, which increased steadily for many years, is now decreasing.

  Here, the underlined clause provides extra information to help readers understand the sentence, but the sentence communicates the same point without this information.

  Violent crime in our cities is now decreasing.

FOCUS *Which, That,* and *Who*

- *Which* always introduces a nonrestrictive clause.

NONRESTRICTIVE Natural disasters, which can be terrifying, really appeal to movie audiences. (clause set off by commas)

- *That* always introduces a restrictive clause.

RESTRICTIVE They wanted to see the movie that had the best special effects. (no commas)

- *Who* can introduce either a restrictive or a nonrestrictive clause.

RESTRICTIVE Many people who watch *Oprah* have bought the books her book club recommends. (no commas)

NONRESTRICTIVE Wally Lamb, who wrote a novel recommended by Oprah's Book Club, saw his book become a best-seller. (clause set off by commas)

◆ PRACTICE 31-6

In each of the following sentences, decide whether the underlined clause is restrictive or nonrestrictive, and then add commas where necessary. If the sentence is correct, write *C* in the blank.

Examples

My boss, who loves fishing, has a picture of his boat in his office. ______

The train that derailed yesterday was empty. ___C___

1. Clocks that tick loudly can be irritating. ______
2. The reader who graded my essay gave me an A. ______
3. The camera which is automatic is easy to use. ______
4. Fish that live in polluted water are unsafe to eat. ______
5. The artist who painted this picture is famous for her landscapes. ______
6. Boxing which requires quick reflexes can be exciting to watch. ______
7. Rafael who finishes work at 5:30 met Carla for dinner at 7:00. ______
8. The Thai restaurant that opened last month is supposed to be excellent. ______

ON THE WEB
For more practice using commas to set off nonrestrictive clauses, visit Exercise Central *at bedfordstmartins.com/foundationsfirst.*

9. Gray wolves which many ranchers dislike are making a comeback in the West. ______

10. The Broadway star who has also appeared in films has many devoted fans. ______

◆ PRACTICE 31-7

Edit the sentences in the following paragraph so that commas set off all nonrestrictive clauses. (Remember, commas are *not* used to set off restrictive clauses.) If the sentence is correct, write *C* in the blank.

> **Example:** The Weavers Society, which is based in Guyana, runs an Internet business. ______

(1) Many people who live in developing countries have difficulty making a living. ______ (2) Modern technology which includes the Internet is changing that. ______ (3) In fact, businesses that use the Internet can reach customers around the world. ______ (4) For example, a group of women who live in Guyana recently started an Internet business. ______ (5) The women who call themselves the Weavers Society needed buyers for their products. ______ (6) These products which they make themselves are handwoven hammocks. ______ (7) A company, that sells satellite telephones, donated some phones to the weavers. ______ (8) The same company which also sells computers helped the women connect to the World Wide Web. ______ (9) The weavers who could find no customers in their own village soon sold many of their hammocks to customers in other regions. ______ (10) These women have changed the economy of a village that had long been in poverty. ______

◆ PRACTICE 31-8

Edit the sentences in the following paragraph so that commas set off all nonrestrictive clauses. If the sentence is correct, write *C* in the blank.

> **Example:** The Tenth Mountain Division, which is one of the U.S. Army's most famous units, was formed in the early 1940s. ______

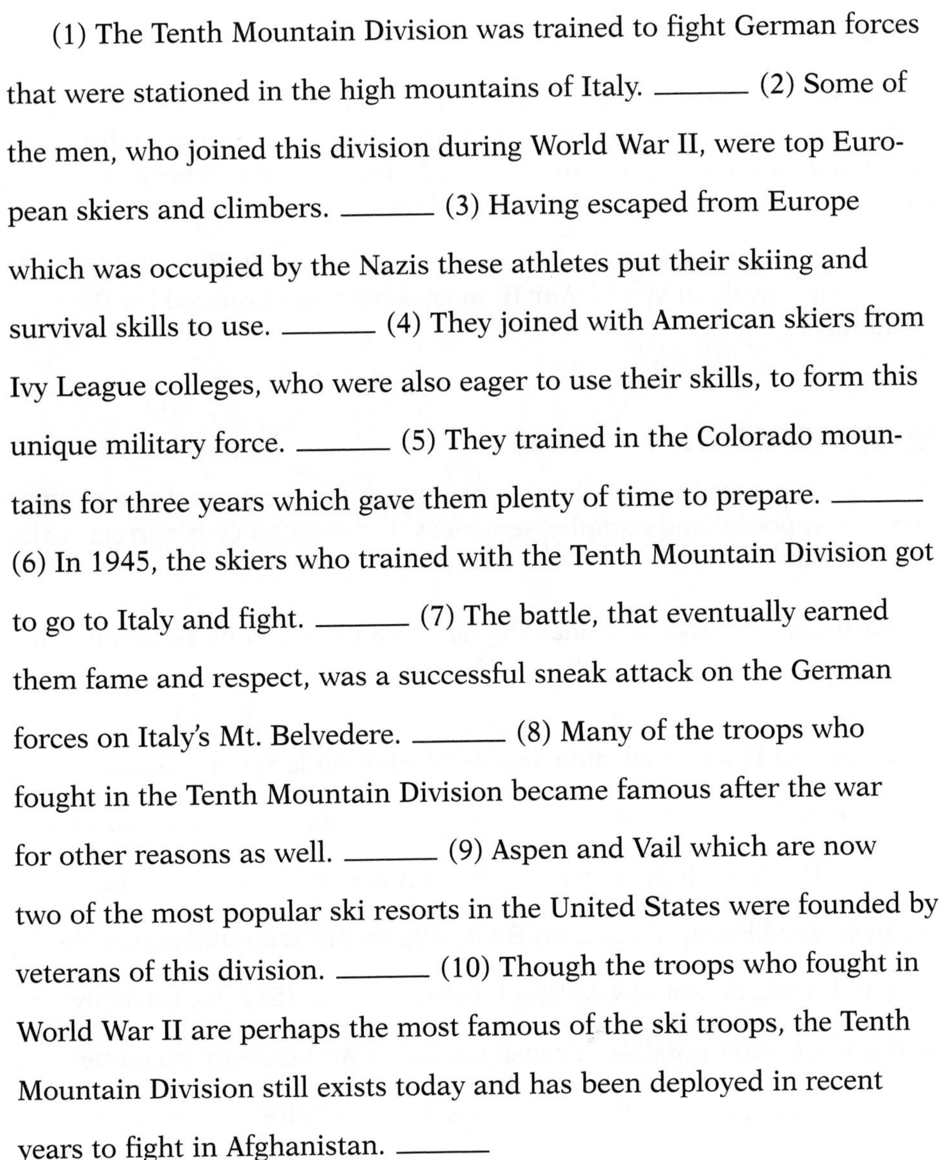

(1) The Tenth Mountain Division was trained to fight German forces that were stationed in the high mountains of Italy. ______ (2) Some of the men, who joined this division during World War II, were top European skiers and climbers. ______ (3) Having escaped from Europe which was occupied by the Nazis these athletes put their skiing and survival skills to use. ______ (4) They joined with American skiers from Ivy League colleges, who were also eager to use their skills, to form this unique military force. ______ (5) They trained in the Colorado mountains for three years which gave them plenty of time to prepare. ______ (6) In 1945, the skiers who trained with the Tenth Mountain Division got to go to Italy and fight. ______ (7) The battle, that eventually earned them fame and respect, was a successful sneak attack on the German forces on Italy's Mt. Belvedere. ______ (8) Many of the troops who fought in the Tenth Mountain Division became famous after the war for other reasons as well. ______ (9) Aspen and Vail which are now two of the most popular ski resorts in the United States were founded by veterans of this division. ______ (10) Though the troops who fought in World War II are perhaps the most famous of the ski troops, the Tenth Mountain Division still exists today and has been deployed in recent years to fight in Afghanistan. ______

E Commas in Compound and Complex Sentences

In Chapters 16 and 17, you learned how to use commas between the clauses in compound and complex sentences. Here is a brief review.

Compound Sentences

A **compound sentence** is made up of two or more independent clauses (simple sentences) joined by a coordinating conjunction (*and*, *or*, *nor*, *but*, *for*, *so*, *yet*), by a semicolon, or by a conjunctive adverb. When a coordinating conjunction joins two independent clauses, always use a comma before the coordinating conjunction.

Morocco is in North Africa, but Senegal is in West Africa.

Complex Sentences

A **complex sentence** is made up of an independent clause and one or more dependent clauses. The clauses are joined by a subordinating conjunction or a relative pronoun. Use a comma after the dependent clause when it comes *before* the independent clause.

> Although the African-American men called the Buffalo Soldiers fought bravely in World War II, most were never honored for their heroism.

✣ ON THE WEB
For more practice using commas in compound and complex sentences, visit **Exercise Central** *at bedford stmartins.com/foundations first.*

◆ PRACTICE 31-9

Edit the sentences in the following paragraph for the correct use of commas in compound and complex sentences. If the sentence is correct, write *C* in the blank.

Example: Alaska is a challenging place to live, so its residents must adapt. ______

(1) Alaska is a rugged state and its population is small. ______ (2) Travel there is difficult so people rely on airplanes for transportation. ______ (3) Although many people live in Alaska's cities many others live in small villages. ______ (4) Such villages are scattered across the state and roads do not always reach them. ______ (5) Also, travel by road is not always possible because the state's Arctic weather can be severe. ______ (6) Even though air travel is expensive it is the best option available in some places. ______ (7) Alaska's bush pilots use small planes because these planes can take off and land in tight spots. ______ (8) When a landing strip is not available a pilot may land on snow or even on open water. ______ (9) Most of Alaska's air passengers are locals, but visiting hunters and sightseers also fly with bush pilots. ______ (10) Until residents find a better means of transportation bush pilots will enjoy a brisk business in Alaska. ______

F Commas in Dates and Addresses

Dates

Use commas in dates to separate the name of the day from the month and to separate the number of the day from the year.

The first Christmas that Elena's son celebrated was Saturday, December 25, 1999.

When a date that includes commas falls in the middle of a sentence, place a comma after the date.

Saturday, December 25, 1999, was the first Christmas that Elena's son celebrated.

Addresses

Use commas in addresses to separate the street address from the city and to separate the city from the state or country.

The British prime minister lives at 10 Downing Street, London, England.

When an address that includes commas falls in the middle of a sentence, place a comma after the address.

The residence at 10 Downing Street, London, England, has been home for Winston Churchill and for Margaret Thatcher.

◆ PRACTICE 31-10

Edit the following sentences for the correct use of commas in dates and addresses. Add any missing commas, and cross out any unnecessary commas. If the sentence is correct, write *C* in the blank.

Examples

Atif was born on August 15,1965. ______

Islamabad,Pakistan,is near his hometown. ______

1. Atif is from Lahore Pakistan. ______
2. On March 12, 1995 his family arrived in the United States. ______
3. Their first home was at 2122 Kent Avenue Brooklyn New York. ______
4. Atif and his wife became citizens of the United States in December, 1999. ______
5. They wanted to move to Boston Massachusetts where Atif's cousins lived. ______
6. On Tuesday June 6 2000 the family moved to the Boston area. ______
7. Their new address was 14 Arden Street Allston Massachusetts. ______
8. Atif's daughters started school there on September 5. ______
9. The school is located at 212 Hope Street, Allston. ______
10. Atif's older daughter graduated from the sixth grade on Friday June 28 2002. ______

ON THE WEB
For more practice using commas in dates and addresses, visit Exercise Central *at bedfordstmartins .com/foundationsfirst.*

• REVISING AND EDITING

Look back at your response to the Seeing and Writing exercise on page 445. First, circle every comma in your writing. Then, review this chapter, and decide whether each comma you have used is necessary. If you find any unnecessary commas, cross them out. When you have finished, reread your work again to make sure you have not left out any necessary commas.

Elizabeth Cady Stanton speaking to women

A suffragist

CHAPTER REVIEW

◆ EDITING PRACTICE

Read the following paragraph, which contains some errors in the use of commas. Add commas where necessary between items in a series and with introductory phrases, transitional words or phrases, appositives, and nonrestrictive clauses. Cross out any unnecessary commas. The first sentence has been edited for you.

The Battles of Elizabeth Cady Stanton

In the 1880s, two human rights campaigns divided public opinion. One was abolition the movement to end slavery. The other was women's suffrage the movement to allow women to vote. Elizabeth Cady Stanton was an important figure in both struggles and she helped to bring about their success. Her work toward abolition which included lobbying Congress went on for more than twenty years. At the same time she wanted to improve the lives of women. Women, who had almost no legal rights were treated as the property of men. Cady Stanton believed women would never be equal to men, until they had the right to vote. Although the suffrage movement was an uphill fight she devoted herself to it for more than fifty years. She wrote to Congress spoke about women's rights, and published a newspaper called *The Revolution*. Elizabeth Cady Stanton's work which she did while raising seven children changed women's lives. Her important place in history therefore is well deserved.

◆ COLLABORATIVE ACTIVITIES

1. Working in a group of three or four students, list some of the specific dangers that high school students might be exposed to while in school.

Next, list security measures that high schools might take to protect students from these dangers. Once you have completed your lists, work together to write a paragraph that includes at least three dangers to high school students and three possible security measures. Finally, exchange paragraphs with another group. Check one another's paragraphs to be sure commas are used correctly.

2. Bring to class a textbook for one of your courses. Working with a partner, turn to a page in the textbook, and use a pencil to circle every comma on the page. Take turns explaining why each comma is necessary.
3. Working with a partner, take turns interviewing each other, and use the information you get as material for a brief biography of your partner. Find out when and where your partner was born, where he or she has lived, the schools he or she has attended, and so on. Then, write a paragraph that includes all the information you have gathered, being sure to include transitions where necessary. When you have finished, exchange papers with your partner. Check one another's papers to be sure commas are used correctly. Pay particular attention to commas in dates and addresses.
4. ***Composing original sentences*** Imagine that you are writing a handbook for middle-school students on the use of commas. Compose seven sample sentences to show the correct use of commas in each of the following situations.
   - in a series
   - to set off an introductory phrase
   - to set off a transitional word or phrase
   - to set off an appositive
   - to set off a nonrestrictive clause
   - in a compound sentence before a coordinating conjunction (*and*, *but*, *or*, and so on)
   - in a complex sentence that begins with a dependent clause

   When you have finished, check your sentences again to correct any errors in grammar, punctuation, or spelling.

REVIEW CHECKLIST:
Using Commas

- Use commas to separate elements in a series of three or more words or word groups. (See 31A.)
- Use commas to set off introductory phrases and transitional words and phrases. (See 31B.)
- Use commas to set off an appositive from the rest of the sentence. (See 31C.)
- Use commas to set off nonrestrictive clauses. (See 31D.)
- Use commas in compound and complex sentences. (See 31E.)
- Use commas to separate parts of dates and addresses. (See 31F.)

CHAPTER

32 Using Apostrophes

PREVIEW

In this chapter, you will learn

- to use apostrophes to form contractions (32A)
- to use apostrophes to form possessives (32B)
- to revise incorrect use of apostrophes (32C)

Word Power

tradition a custom handed down from generation to generation

traditional relating to tradition

SEEING AND WRITING

The picture above shows a female firefighter. Do you believe that men and women are equally qualified for all jobs, or do you think that some jobs should be "men's jobs" or "women's jobs"? Look at the picture, and then write a paragraph in which you explain your position.

An **apostrophe** is a punctuation mark that is used in two situations: to form a contraction and to form the possessive of a noun or an indefinite pronoun.

A Apostrophes in Contractions

A **contraction** is a word that uses an apostrophe to combine two words. The apostrophe takes the place of the letters that are left out.

I didn't [did not] understand the question.

It's [it is] sometimes hard to see the difference between right and wrong.

Frequently Used Contractions

I	+	am	=	I'm	could	+	not	=	couldn't
we	+	are	=	we're	do	+	not	=	don't
you	+	are	=	you're	does	+	not	=	doesn't
it	+	is	=	it's	will	+	not	=	won't
I	+	have	=	I've	should	+	not	=	shouldn't
I	+	will	=	I'll	would	+	not	=	wouldn't
there	+	is	=	there's	let	+	us	=	let's
is	+	not	=	isn't	that	+	is	=	that's
are	+	not	=	aren't	who	+	is	=	who's
can	+	not	=	can't					

◆ PRACTICE 32-1

Edit the following paragraph so that apostrophes are used correctly in contractions.

Example: Berea College in Kentucky ~~doesnt~~ doesn't require its students to pay tuition.

(1) This means that students from low-income families who cant pay for school can still get a college education. (2) In fact, Berea wont accept anyone who has the ability to pay. (3) The college wants only students who wouldnt otherwise be able to afford to attend a four-year college. (4) There arent many other colleges or universities that offer this kind of support. (5) Berea has made itself unique in other ways as well, in ways that other schools havent. (6) For example, the college has a community-service program thats very well respected. (7) Its not unusual for Berea students to spend many hours every week volunteering in their

ON THE WEB
For more practice using apostrophes to form contractions, visit Exercise Central *at bedfordstmartins .com/foundationsfirst.*

Appalachian community. (8) Theyre also all required to have on-campus jobs. (9) This school offers students a rare opportunity in an age where income tends to determine whos eligible for college and who isnt. (10) Its unfortunate that more schools havent decided to follow Berea's lead.

◆ PRACTICE 32-2

In each of the following sentences, add apostrophes to contractions, if needed, and edit to make sure all apostrophes are placed correctly. If a sentence is correct, write *C* in the blank.

Example: Some couples who ~~cant~~ can't have biological children have adopted children from other countries. ______

1. Its fairly common for couples to be infertile, but they dont have to give up on having a family; they might be able to adopt a child from a foreign country. ______
2. One out of five American couples can't have a biological child. ______
3. Modern reproduction technology cant help all couples; it does'nt work for everyone, and its very expensive. ______
4. Should'nt everyone have a chance to be a parent? ______
5. Some countries won't let foreigners adopt their children, but adoption is possible from other countries. ______
6. For example, there have been many adoptions of baby girls from China and Korea, where daughters arent always valued. ______
7. Its' really important for adoptive parents to know the laws of their child's native country. ______
8. State laws are important, too; for example, American parents whov'e traveled abroad to adopt may want to adopt the child again in their home state to be sure that the adoption is'nt illegal. ______
9. Theres one thing thats really important: a careful medical evaluation of the child to identify any serious health problems. ______
10. Often, parents don't care about all the red tape; they just want a child to love. ______

B Apostrophes in Possessives

Possessive forms of nouns and pronouns show ownership. Nouns (names of people, animals, places, objects, or ideas) and indefinite pronouns (words like *everyone* and *anything*) use apostrophes to show ownership.

Singular Nouns and Indefinite Pronouns

To form the possessive of singular nouns (including names), add an apostrophe plus an *s*.

The game's score [the score of the game] was very close.

Coach Nelson's goal [the goal of Coach Nelson] was to win.

Some singular nouns end in *-s*. Even if a singular noun already ends in *-s*, add an apostrophe plus an *s* to form the possessive.

The class's new computers were unpacked on Tuesday.

Carlos's computer crashed on Wednesday.

FOCUS Indefinite Pronouns

Indefinite pronouns—words like *everyone* and *anything*—form possessives in the same way singular nouns do: they add an apostrophe and an *s*.

Rodney was everyone's choice [the choice of everyone] for quarterback.

Plural Nouns

Most nouns form the plural by adding *-s*. To form the possessive of plural nouns (including names) that end in *-s*, add just an apostrophe. Do *not* add an apostrophe plus an *s*.

The two televisions' features [the features of the two televisions] were very different.

The Thompsons' house [the house of the Thompsons] is on the corner.

Some irregular plural nouns do not end in *-s*. If a plural noun does not end in *-s*, add an apostrophe plus an *s* to form the possessive.

The children's room is upstairs.

❖ **ON THE WEB**
For more practice using apostrophes to form possessives, visit Exercise Central *at bedfordstmartins .com/foundationsfirst.*

◆ PRACTICE 32-3

Rewrite the following groups of words, changing the singular noun or indefinite pronoun that follows *of* to the possessive form.

Example: the plot of the book ___*the book's plot*___

1. the owner of the shop ______________________
2. the pilot of the plane ______________________
3. the cat of my neighbor ______________________
4. the desk of the manager ______________________
5. the cell phone of Indira ______________________
6. the engine of the truck ______________________
7. the sister of Chris ______________________
8. the guess of anyone ______________________
9. the opinion of our class ______________________
10. the waiting room of the doctor ______________________

◆ PRACTICE 32-4

Rewrite the following groups of words, changing the plural noun that follows *of* to the possessive form.

Example: the rhythm of the dancers ___*the dancers' rhythm*___

1. the bags of the travelers ______________________
2. the quills of the porcupines ______________________
3. the faces of the women ______________________
4. the room of the children ______________________
5. the car of the ministers ______________________
6. the bills of the customers ______________________
7. the apartment of the Huangs ______________________
8. the voice of the people ______________________
9. the first meeting of the lawyers ______________________
10. the telephone number of the Tewars ______________________

◆ PRACTICE 32-5

In each of the following sentences, edit the underlined possessive forms (nouns and indefinite pronouns) so that apostrophes are used correctly. If a correction needs to be made, cross out the noun or indefinite pronoun, and write the correct form above it. If the possessive form is correct, write *C* above it.

Example: A ~~business'~~ *business's* success depends on the owner's *C* hard work and good luck.

1. In 1888, Lee Kee Lo opened a business in New Yorks Chinatown.
2. He became one of the neighborhoods' best-known grocers.
3. Lee's son, Harold, expanded his fathers' business.
4. He met many customer's financial needs, such as currency exchange.
5. Harold Lees' bank also filled business owners' requests for loans.
6. Then, Harolds' son Arthur changed the business' mission again.
7. He became the familys'—and Chinatowns'—first insurance agent.
8. If someones' property needed to be insured, Arthur Lee's agency took the job.
9. The insurance agencys' office is now run by Arthurs' children.
10. The Lee's business continues to operate in Lee Kee Lo's original storefront.

C Incorrect Use of Apostrophes

Watch out for the following problems with apostrophes.

- Do not confuse a plural noun (*girls*) with the singular possessive form of the noun (*girl's*). Do not use apostrophes to form noun plurals.

  In the following sentences, the nouns are plural, not possessive. Therefore, no apostrophes are used.

  Cats [not *cat's*] can be wonderful pets [not *pet's*].

  The Fords [not *Ford's*] went to Disney World.

- Never use apostrophes with possessive pronouns that end in *-s*.

Possessive Pronouns	*Incorrect Spelling*
hers	her's
its	it's
ours	our's
yours	your's
theirs	their's

- Do not confuse possessive pronouns with sound-alike contractions. Remember, possessive pronouns never include apostrophes.

Possessive Pronoun	*Contraction*
The dog licked its paw.	It's [it is] not fair.
This apartment is theirs.	There's [there is] the bus.
Whose turn is it?	Who's [who is] there?
Is this your hat?	You're [you are] absolutely right.

◆ PRACTICE 32-6

In each of the following sentences, circle the correct form (contraction or possessive pronoun) in parentheses.

✣ **ON THE WEB**
For more practice revising the incorrect use of apostrophes, visit **Exercise Central** *at bedfordstmartins.com/foundationsfirst.*

Example: This is (you're/your) last chance.

1. The elephant sprayed water from (it's/its) trunk.
2. (There's/Theirs) something wrong with this engine.
3. According to the newspaper, (it's/its) supposed to rain tomorrow.
4. The Guzmans say the yellow rake is (there's/theirs).
5. The building was restored to (it's/its) former beauty.
6. (Who's/Whose) in charge of refreshments?
7. Erica says (you're/your) an excellent softball player.
8. Does anyone know (who's/whose) sweater this is?
9. I never use that vase because (it's/its) an antique.
10. (You're/Your) suggestion was the best one presented at the meeting.

◆ PRACTICE 32-7

In each of the following sentences, check the underlined words to be sure apostrophes are used correctly. If a correction needs to be made, cross out the word, and write the correct version above it. If the noun or pronoun is correct, write *C* above it.

Example: Tulips grew along the garden's (C) edge, even in ~~it's~~ its shadiest spots.

1. Songs about lover's problems are always popular.
2. The worlds' population won't stop growing for some time.
3. Don't you think its a lovely evening?
4. Children are quick to say which toys are there's.

5. The committee reported it's findings in today's newsletter.
6. All the government agency's were closed.
7. Whose coming to your party?
8. If your such an expert, why can't you fix Lois' computer?
9. You'll need five hundred resident's signatures on you're petition.
10. Both of Henrys sister's made the dresses they're wearing.

◆ PRACTICE 32-8

Write an original sentence for each of the following possessive pronouns.

- its

____

____

- your

____

____

- theirs

____

____

Now, write a sentence for each of the following contractions.

- it's

____

____

- you're

____

____

- there's

____

____

When you have finished, check to make sure you have used apostrophes only in contractions, not in possessive pronouns.

◆ PRACTICE 32-9

Write a short paragraph that includes all these words: *it's*, *its*, *birds*, *bird's nest*.

____

____

____

____

____

____

● REVISING AND EDITING

Look back at your response to the Seeing and Writing exercise on page 460. First, circle every apostrophe in your writing. Then, review this chapter to make sure that all the apostrophes in your response are used correctly and that you have not forgotten any necessary apostrophes.

CHAPTER REVIEW

◆ EDITING PRACTICE

Read the following paragraph, which contains some errors in the use of apostrophes. Edit it to eliminate errors by crossing out incorrect words and writing corrections above them. (Note that this is an informal essay, so contractions are acceptable.) The first sentence has been edited for you.

Dolphins: People with Fins?

Tame ~~dolphin's~~ dolphins are a common sight at aquariums and water shows, where people are fascinated by the ~~creatures~~ creatures' friendly behavior. Many wild dolphins also seem comfortable around people. In some ways, the social pattern's of dolphins are'nt so different from our's. The dolphins mating pattern isn't just biological; its social as well. In fact, its like the human practice of dating. Dolphin family's also show some human traits. For example, young dolphins stay close to their mother's for several years. The mothers sometimes work together in group's to

guard their calves safety. One mother might even babysit for another while shes busy elsewhere. And the family bond does'nt end when the baby dolphins grow up. A mature dolphin may return to it's mothers side when the mother is giving birth to a new calf. Finally, dolphins seem to choose their friends the same way people do. Dolphins tend to spend time with other's of the same age and gender, and they may even have "best friends" who's company they enjoy. Male dolphins, especially, tend to have a couple of buddies their often found with. With so many things in common, its no wonder dolphins and humans get along so well.

◆ COLLABORATIVE ACTIVITIES

1. Working in a group of four and building on your responses to the Seeing and Writing exercise at the beginning of this chapter, think about how the definitions of "men's jobs" and "women's jobs" have changed in recent decades. Then, make two lists.

   - jobs that were once held only by men but are now also performed by women (such as firefighter)
   - jobs that were once held only by women but are now also performed by men (such as nurse)

2. Consulting the lists your group developed in activity 1, divide into pairs. One pair of students in each group should list reasons why there should be "men's jobs" and "women's jobs," and one pair should list reasons why both men and women should be able to do any sort of work they choose. Use possessive forms whenever possible—for example, *women's earnings* rather than *the earnings of women*. When you have finished, check the other pair's sentences for correct use of apostrophes.
3. Bring to class a book, magazine, or newspaper whose style is informal—for example, a popular novel, an entertainment magazine, or the sports section of a newspaper. Working in a group, circle every contraction you can find on one page of each publication. Then, replace each contraction with the words that combine to form it. Are your substitutions an improvement? (You may want to read a few paragraphs aloud before you reach a conclusion.)
4. ***Composing original sentences*** Work together with your group to write a total of seven original sentences. Three sentences should include contractions of a pronoun and a verb using an apostrophe (for example: *it's* = *it is*). Three sentences should use singular and plural nouns in the possessive form. One sentence should include an indefinite pronoun. When you have finished, check the sentences again to make sure you have no errors in grammar, punctuation, or spelling.

✓ REVIEW CHECKLIST: Using Apostrophes

- Use apostrophes to form contractions. (See 32A.)
- Use an apostrophe plus an *s* to form the possessive of singular nouns and indefinite pronouns. Even when a noun ends in *-s*, use an apostrophe plus an *s* to form the possessive. (See 32B.)
- Use an apostrophe alone to form the possessive of most plural nouns, including names. (See 32B.)
- Do not use apostrophes with plural nouns unless they are possessive. Do not use apostrophes with possessive pronouns. (See 32C.)

Using Other Punctuation Marks

CHAPTER

33

PREVIEW

In this chapter, you will learn

- to use semicolons (33A)
- to use colons (33B)
- to use dashes and parentheses (33C)

• SEEING AND WRITING

The picture above shows a child playing with a doll house. Look at the picture, and think about the toys you used to play with indoors when you were a child. Write a paragraph about some of your favorite indoor toys and games.

Word Power

recreation activity done for enjoyment when one is not working; play

pastime a pleasant activity that fills spare time

Punctuation marks are signals to your readers. They tell readers to slow down, to look ahead, or to pause. To write clear sentences, you need to use appropriate punctuation.

Every sentence ends with a punctuation mark—a period, a question mark, or an exclamation point.

- If a sentence is a statement, it ends with a **period**.

  Nine associate justices sit on the U.S. Supreme Court.

- If a sentence is a question, it ends with a **question mark**.

  Is there a woman on the Supreme Court?

- If a sentence is an exclamation, it ends with an **exclamation point**.

  That's incredible! I can't believe there's only one woman on the Supreme Court!

Other important punctuation marks are the **comma**, discussed in Chapter 31, and the **apostrophe**, discussed in Chapter 32. Four additional punctuation marks—*semicolons*, *colons*, *dashes*, and *parentheses*—are discussed and illustrated in the pages that follow.

A Semicolons

Use a **semicolon** to join two simple sentences (independent clauses) into one compound sentence.

Sandra Day O'Connor was the first woman to sit on the U.S. Supreme Court; Ruth Bader Ginsburg was the second.

FOCUS Semicolons

Never use a semicolon between a phrase and an independent clause. Use a comma instead.

INCORRECT I voted for the most qualified candidate; the Independent.

CORRECT I voted for the most qualified candidate, the Independent.

Never use a semicolon between a dependent clause and an independent clause. Use a comma instead.

INCORRECT When Christa was in high school; she had a pet iguana.

CORRECT When Christa was in high school, she had a pet iguana.

◆ PRACTICE 33-1

Each of the following sentences includes errors in the use of semicolons. Correct any errors you find. If a sentence is correct, write *C* on the line after the sentence.

Example: Telenovelas are popular Spanish-language television shows; the name comes from the Spanish words for "television" and "novel."

______

1. These shows are like American soap operas; but with several important differences. ______
2. American soap operas can run for many years, a telenovela runs for a limited time. ______
3. Like soap operas, telenovelas have complicated plots; the most popular plot is a poor woman who falls in love with a wealthy man. ______
4. Some telenovelas are set in colonial times other telenovelas deal with serious issues facing modern society. ______
5. The popularity of the telenovelas has caught the attention of American networks several plan to create telenovelas for American audiences. ______

B Colons

Colons are used to introduce quotations, explanations, clarifications, examples, and lists. A complete sentence must always come before the colon.

- Use a colon to introduce a quotation.

  The golden rule is very simple: "treat others as you would like to be treated."

- Use a colon to introduce an explanation, a clarification, or an example.

  Glenn finally conquered his greatest fear: arachnophobia, the fear of spiders.

- Use a colon to introduce a list.

  Aisha decided to accept the job for four reasons: stimulating work, great working conditions, competitive pay, and opportunity for advancement.

◆ PRACTICE 33-2

The following sentences include errors in the use of colons to introduce quotations, examples, lists, and so on. Correct any errors you find. (Remember that every colon must be preceded by a complete sentence.) If a sentence is correct, write *C* on the line after the sentence.

Example: Many people have stopped buying film for a simple reason: the growing use of digital cameras. ______

1. Digital cameras have several advantages: they do not need film, their files can be easily uploaded to the Internet, and their pictures can be viewed immediately. ______
2. Choosing the right digital camera requires: knowing what you will use the camera for. ______
3. The quality of a digital camera's image is measured in megapixels the higher the number, the better the image. ______
4. Cnet.com explains the challenge of choosing a camera's megapixels this way: "This is one of the trickiest questions in digital photography." ______
5. Web sites like cnet.com offer: helpful advice and guidance for new users. ______

C Dashes and Parentheses

Dashes and parentheses set words off from the rest of the sentence. In general, dashes call attention to the material that is set off, while parentheses do the opposite.

- Use **dashes** to enclose important information.

  Sophia wore her new shoes—espadrilles with four-inch wedges—to the picnic.

- Use **parentheses** to enclose information that is relatively unimportant.

  The whole family (even Uncle Oscar) attended the reunion.

◆ PRACTICE 33-3

Add dashes or parentheses to the following sentences where you think they are necessary to set off material from the rest of the sentence. Remember that dashes tend to emphasize the material they set off, while parentheses tend to de-emphasize the enclosed material.

Example: The lead singer of U2, "Bono"(Paul Hewson), is more than just an entertainer.

1. He was born in Dublin the capital of Ireland in 1960.
2. Violence in Northern Ireland which is still considered part of the United Kingdom influenced the band's song lyrics and inspired their anti-violence message.
3. As U2 became more popular selling over 50 million albums in the United States alone, Bono continued to voice his opinion on many of the world's problems.
4. Bono's organization, which is called Debt, AIDS, Trade, Africa DATA, focuses on solving the problems facing Africa.
5. He has traveled around the world speaking about the urgent need to provide economic assistance to Africa which owes countries such as the United States billions of dollars.

• REVISING AND EDITING

Look back at your response to the Seeing and Writing exercise on page 471. Try adding a quotation, example, or list to your paragraph. Be sure to introduce this new material with a colon, and make sure a complete sentence comes before the colon.

CHAPTER REVIEW

◆ EDITING PRACTICE

The following student paragraph includes errors in the use of semicolons, colons, dashes, and parentheses. (Some are used incorrectly; others have been omitted where they are needed.) Correct any errors you find. The first sentence has been corrected for you.

An Alligator for a Neighbor

The alligator is a popular symbol in Florida; the University of Florida even uses one as its mascot. However, alligators are: wild animals that can sometimes hurt humans. As we build our homes closer to animal habitats; we may find we have

Alligator

Woman, 74, fends off 9-foot-7 alligator

■ After being dragged into a canal, her quick thinking spares her from serious injury, officials say.

By TOM ZUCCO
Times Staff Writer

Darkness was settling in Wednesday evening, and Jane Keefer was getting in some last-minute gardening. She had her back to the freshwater canal behind her Sanibel home.

In an instant, the 74-year-old woman was grabbed by her left leg and pulled under the water by a 9-foot, 7-inch male alligator.

Keefer, 5-foot-5, instinctively fought back, a move that probably saved her life.

"She struck the alligator several times in the nose, and it let go," said Larry Gregory, an investigator with the Florida Fish and Wildlife Conservation Commission. "When she came back up, the gator tried to bite her again on her arm."

At that point, Keefer's husband, William, came running from their house and helped her out of the water.

Keefer was treated at HealthPark Medical Center and released.

"I'm doing fine," she said Thursday from her home. She declined to talk further about the attack. "I don't want to think about it."

The attack happened about 8:15 p.m. By 10:45 p.m., Gregory, two Sanibel police officers, and licensed Fish and Wildlife trappers John French of North Fort Myers and Tracey Hansen of Fort Myers captured the gator by tossing a piece of meat attached to a cord into the canal.

It took all five men to haul the

Please see GATOR 4B

an alligator for a neighbor. Human construction often forces alligators out of their natural habitat swamps and other wetlands. The destruction of their homes and hunting grounds means alligators must find shelter close to human habitats in parks, in golf ponds, or even in swimming pools. This means the animals come much closer to humans than they should. An alligator can seriously harm or even kill a human, but following a few rules should keep you safe if you encounter an alligator. The first rule is the most important leave the alligator alone. Most alligator attacks occur after people have tried to feed or touch the alligator. Second, stay away from alligator nests a mother will always fight to defend her young. If an alligator does attack you; try to strike it in its most vulnerable areas the eyes or nose. Hit the alligator on the nose to make it let go often, alligators open their jaws when hit on the snout. Any scrapes or bites from an alligator no matter how small should be immediately treated by a doctor. As we build closer to the alligator's natural habitat; we may have more encounters with these animals. For this reason: it is important to understand the challenges of having an alligator for a neighbor.

◆ COLLABORATIVE ACTIVITIES

1. Write five original compound sentences, each composed of two simple sentences connected with *and*. Exchange papers with another student, and edit each compound sentence so that it uses a semicolon instead of *and* to connect the independent clauses.
2. Compile three lists, each with three or four items (people, places, or things). Then, working in a group, compose a sentence that could introduce each of your lists. Use a colon after each introductory sentence.
3. ***Composing original sentences*** Working in a group, decide on a topic to write about. Next, compose a paragraph of six original sentences. Finally, add a quotation to one sentence and a list to another.

☑ REVIEW CHECKLIST: Using Other Punctuation Marks

- ☐ Use semicolons to separate two simple sentences (independent clauses). (See 33A.)
- ☐ Use colons to introduce quotations, explanations, clarifications, examples, and lists. (See 33B.)
- ☐ Use dashes and parentheses to set off material from the rest of the sentence. (See 33C.)

Understanding Mechanics

CHAPTER

34

PREVIEW

In this chapter, you will learn

- to capitalize proper nouns (34A)
- to punctuate direct quotations (34B)
- to set off titles (34C)
- to use hyphens (34D)

SEEING AND WRITING

The picture above shows Bugs Bunny facing his longtime enemy, Elmer Fudd. Look at the picture. Then, write a paragraph in which you describe your favorite cartoon or comic strip. Be sure to name the most important characters, and try to quote some dialogue that you remember.

Word Power

contemporary current; modern

classic something typical or traditional; an outstanding example of its kind

A Capitalizing Proper Nouns

A **proper noun** names a particular person, animal, place, object, or idea. Proper nouns are always capitalized. The list that follows explains and illustrates the rules for capitalizing proper nouns. It also includes some important exceptions to these rules.

- Always capitalize **names of races**, **ethnic groups**, **tribes**, **nationalities**, **languages**, and **religions**.

  The census data revealed a diverse community of Caucasians, African Americans, and Asian Americans, with a few Latino and Navajo residents. Native languages include English, Korean, and Spanish. Most people identified themselves as Catholic, Protestant, or Muslim.

- Capitalize **names of specific people** and **any titles that go along with those names**.

  President Vicente Fox led Mexico from 2000 until 2006.

  In general, do not capitalize titles that are used without a name.

  The student body president met with the dean.

- Capitalize **names of specific family members** and **their titles**.

  Cousin Matt and Cousin Susie are the children of Mom's brother, Uncle Bill.

  Do not capitalize words that identify family relationships, including those introduced by possessive pronouns.

  My cousins Matt and Susie are the children of my mother's brother Bill, who is my uncle.

- Capitalize **names of specific countries**, **cities**, **towns**, **bodies of water** (**lakes**, **rivers**, **oceans**), **streets**, and so on.

  The Liffey runs through Dublin.

  Do not capitalize words that identify unnamed places.

  The river runs through the city.

- Capitalize **names of specific geographical regions**.

  Louis L'Amour's novels are set in the American West.

  Do not capitalize such words when they refer to a direction.

  We got lost after we turned west off the freeway.

- Capitalize **names of specific buildings** and **monuments**.

  He drove past the Space Needle and toward Pike Place Market.

  Do not capitalize general references to buildings and monuments.

  He drove past the monument and toward the market.

- Capitalize **names of specific groups, clubs, teams,** and **associations.**

  Members of the Teamsters' Union worked at the Democratic Party convention, the Backstreet Boys concert, and the Sixers-Pacers game.

  Do not capitalize general references to groups of individuals.

  Members of the union worked at the party's convention, the rock group's concert, and the basketball teams' game.

- Capitalize **names of specific historical periods, events,** and **documents.**

  The Emancipation Proclamation was signed during the Civil War, not during Reconstruction.

  Do not capitalize general references to periods, events, or documents.

  The document was signed during the war, not during the post-war period.

- Capitalize **names of businesses, government agencies, schools,** and **other institutions.**

  Our local Burger King and McDonald's want to hire students from Lincoln High School and Brooklyn College.

  Do not capitalize nonspecific references to such institutions.

  Our local fast-food restaurants want to hire high school and college students.

- Capitalize **brand names.**

  Jan put on her Rollerblades and skated off to Xerox her paper.

  Do not capitalize general references to kinds of products.

  Jan put on her in-line skates and skated off to photocopy her paper.

- Capitalize **titles of specific academic courses.**

  Calvin registered for English 101 and Psychology 302.

  Do not capitalize names of general academic subject areas, except for proper nouns—for example, the name of a language or a country.

  Calvin registered for English and psychology.

- Capitalize **days of the week, months of the year,** and **holidays.**

  Christmas, Chanukah, and Kwanzaa all fall in December.

  Do not capitalize the names of the seasons (*summer, fall, winter, spring*).

  Christmas, Chanukah, and Kwanzaa all fall in the winter.

❖ **ON THE WEB**
For more practice capitalizing proper nouns, visit Exercise Central *at bedfordstmartins .com/foundationsfirst.*

◆ PRACTICE 34-1

Edit the following sentences, capitalizing letters and changing capitals to lowercase letters where necessary.

Example: Archaeologists study the Ojibwa at ~~m~~Mackinac State Historic Park in ~~m~~Michigan, a ~~S~~state where many members of the group live.

1. The Ojibwa are the largest native american group in north america.
2. Today, they live near the Great lakes in the united states and canada.
3. The Ojibwa migrated to the midwest from their original homes near the atlantic ocean.
4. Many modern Ojibwa live in the cities of Detroit and duluth and on rural Reservations.
5. Activist Winona LaDuke, who served as the Principal of an Ojibwa school, ran for Vice President on the green party ticket in 2000.

◆ PRACTICE 34-2

Write a sentence that includes each of the following pairs of words. Capitalize where necessary. Each sentence should be at least six or seven words long.

Example: valentine's day/holiday

Graham's least favorite holiday is Valentine's Day.

1. aunt mary/aunt

____

2. johnson's department store/store

____

3. reverend jackson/minister

____

B Punctuating Quotations

A **direct quotation** reproduces the *exact* words of a speaker or writer. Direct quotations are always placed within quotation marks. A direct quotation is usually accompanied by an **identifying tag**, a phrase that names the person being quoted. In the following sentences, the identifying tag is underlined.

Brian said, "I've decided to go to business school."

Tolstoy wrote, "Happy families are all alike; every unhappy family is unhappy in its own way."

When a quotation is a complete sentence, as it is in the two examples above, it begins with a capital letter and ends with end punctuation (a period, a question mark, or an exclamation point). When a quotation falls at the end of a sentence (as it does in the examples above), the period is placed *inside* the quotation marks. If the quotation is a question or an exclamation, the question mark or exclamation point is also placed *inside* the quotation marks.

Regis asked, "Is that your final answer?"

When the vampire attacked, Ted cried, "Help me!"

The rules for punctuating direct quotations with identifying tags are summarized below.

Identifying Tag at the Beginning

When the identifying tag comes before the quotation, it is followed by a comma.

Jamie announced, "I really need to cut up all my credit cards."

Identifying Tag at the End

When the identifying tag comes at the end of a sentence, it is followed by a period. A comma (or, sometimes, a question mark or exclamation point) inside the closing quotation marks separates the quotation from the identifying tag.

"I really need to cut up all my credit cards," Jamie announced.

"Do I really need to cut up all my credit cards?" asked Jamie.

Identifying Tag in the Middle

When the identifying tag comes in the middle of a quoted sentence, it is followed by a comma. The first part of the quotation is also followed by a comma, which is placed *inside* the quotation marks. Because the part of the quotation that follows the tag is not a new sentence, it does not begin with a capital letter.

"I'll cut up all my credit cards," Jamie promised, "and then I'll start over."

Identifying Tag between Two Sentences

When the identifying tag comes between two quoted sentences, it is followed by a period, and the second quoted sentence begins with a capital letter.

"Doing without credit cards will be good for me," Jamie decided. "Paying cash for everything will help me stick to my budget."

FOCUS Indirect Quotations

Be careful not to confuse direct and indirect quotations. A direct quotation reproduces someone's *exact* words, but an **indirect quotation** simply summarizes what was said or written.

Indirect quotations are **not** placed within quotation marks.

DIRECT QUOTATION Martin Luther King Jr. said, "I have a dream."

INDIRECT QUOTATION Martin Luther King Jr. said that he had a dream.

◆ PRACTICE 34-3

❖ **ON THE WEB**
For more practice punctuating direct quotations, visit **Exercise Central** *at bedfordstmartins.com/foundationsfirst.*

Rewrite each of the following sentences twice. In the first version, place the identifying tag at the end of the sentence. In the second version, place the identifying tag in the middle of the sentence. Be sure to check punctuation and capitalization carefully.

Example: Joe said, "The grapes don't taste as good as they look."

"The grapes don't taste as good as they look," Joe said.

"The grapes," Joe said, "don't taste as good as they look."

1. The senator promised, "I will do my best to defeat the new immigration bill."

2. The mayor announced, "Everyone should evacuate before the hurricane strikes."

3. Sunita said, "I wonder if we will ever have a woman president of the United States."

◆ PRACTICE 34-4

In the following sentences containing direct quotations, first underline the identifying tag. Then, punctuate the quotation correctly, adding capital letters where necessary.

Example: "Injustice anywhere," said Dr. Martin Luther King Jr., "is a threat to justice everywhere."

1. The guide announced whatever you do, don't leave the group.
2. Why does it always rain on my birthday Patrice asked.
3. Move along, everyone the officer shouted.
4. The game isn't over till it's over said baseball legend Yogi Berra.
5. If we get separated Paul asked where should I meet you?

C Setting Off Titles

Some titles are *italicized* (or underlined to indicate italics). Others are enclosed in quotation marks. In general, underline titles of books and other long works, and enclose titles of shorter works (stories, essays, poems, and so on) in quotation marks.

The following chart indicates which titles should be italicized and which should be enclosed in quotation marks.

Italicized Titles

Books: *The Joy Luck Club*
Newspapers: *Los Angeles Times*
Magazines: *People*, *Latina*
Record albums: *Motown Legends*
Long poems: *Paradise Lost*
Plays: *Our Town*, *Death of a Salesman*
Films: *Lord of the Rings*
Television and radio series: *Eyes on the Prize*

Titles in Quotation Marks

Book chapters: "Writing a Paragraph"
Short stories: "The Lottery"
Essays and articles: "Shooting an Elephant"
Short poems: "The Road Not Taken"
Songs: "The Star-Spangled Banner"
Individual episodes of television or radio series: "The Montgomery Bus Boycott" (episode of *Eyes on the Prize*)

❖ **ON THE WEB**
For more practice setting off titles of books, stories, and other works, visit Exercise Central *at bedfordstmartins .com/foundationsfirst.*

◆ PRACTICE 34-5

In each of the following sentences, underline or insert quotation marks around titles. (Remember that titles of books and other long works are underlined and that titles of stories, essays, and other shorter works are enclosed in quotation marks.)

> **Example:** <u>A Good Man Is Hard to Find</u>, a book of stories by Flannery O'Connor, includes "The Life You Save May Be Your Own" and "Good Country People."

1. The newsmagazine U.S. News and World Report featured a review of the movie made from the book The Da Vinci Code.
2. Norah Jones's first album, Come Away with Me, contained the award-winning song Come Away with Me.
3. The musical Wicked, based on the book The Wonderful Wizard of Oz, shows what might have happened before the events in the book.
4. The textbook Foundations First includes the chapter Understanding Mechanics.
5. Julia Child's best-selling cookbook Mastering the Art of French Cooking has a section called Kitchen Equipment and another section called Ingredients.

FOCUS Capitalizing Words in Titles

Capitalize the first letters of all important words in titles. Do not capitalize an **article** (*a*, *an*, or *the*), a **preposition** (*to*, *of*, *around*, and so on), or a **coordinating conjunction**—unless it is the first or last word of the title (<u>On</u> *the Road*; *No Way* <u>Out</u>).

◆ PRACTICE 34-6

Edit the following sentences, capitalizing letters where necessary in titles.

> **Example:** The movie ~~c~~C*harly* was based on the short story "~~f~~Flowers for ~~a~~Algernon."

1. Lucy's favorite novel is *for whom the bell tolls*.
2. Jack London's short story "to build a fire" is a classic.

3. Television cartoons created for adults include *the simpsons* and *king of the hill.*

4. The soundtrack for the movie *the matrix* features songs such as "ultrasonic sound" and "wake up."

5. The articles "stream of consciousness" and "school's out" in *wired* magazine focus on new technology.

D Hyphens

A hyphen has two uses: to divide a word at the end of a line, and to join words in compounds.

- Use a hyphen to divide a word at the end of a line. If you need to divide a word, divide it between syllables. Check your dictionary to see how a word is divided into syllables. (Never break a one-syllable word, no matter how long it is.)

  In the Natural History Museum, we saw a model of a stego-saurus, a huge dinosaur.

- Use a hyphen in a **compound word**—a word that is made up of two or more words. Many of these constructions join two words into compound adjectives that describe a noun in the sentence.

  The instructor recommended some problem-solving strategies.

  His long-awaited trip to India was about to begin.

◆ PRACTICE 34-7

In each of the following sentences, decide whether a hyphen is needed. If the sentence is correct, write *C* in the blank. If not, insert a hyphen where necessary.

Examples

Overcrowding can cause conflict among residents of fast-growing cities. ______

California is home to many diverse cultures. __C__

1. Our forward thinking boss is always coming up with new ways to improve sales. ______

2. Visitors to the National Zoo are usually most excited to see the panda bears. ______

3. People often argue about banning cigarettes in all pub lic places. ______

4. At the end of the semester, Cynthia sold her much-hated geology textbook back to the bookstore. ______

5. In February, many popular magazines are filled with Oscar related articles. ______

FOCUS Abbreviations

An **abbreviation** is a shortened form of a word. In college writing, it is acceptable to abbreviate the following.

- Titles—such as Mr., Ms., Dr., and Jr.—that are used along with names.
- a.m. and p.m. (also written A.M. and P.M.)
- BC and AD (in dates such as 43 BC)
- Names of organizations (NRA, CIA) and technical terms (DNA). Note that some abbreviations, called **acronyms**, are pronounced as words: AIDS, FEMA.

In college writing, it is *not* acceptable to abbreviate days of the week, months, names of streets and places, names of academic subjects, or titles that are not used along with names.

FOCUS Numbers

In college writing, most numbers are spelled out (*forty-five*) rather than written as **numerals** (*45*). However, numbers more than two words long are always written as numerals (*4,530*, not *four thousand five hundred thirty*).

In addition, you should use numerals in the following situations.

- Dates: January 20, 1976
- Addresses: 5023 Schuyler Street
- Exact times: 10:00 (If you use *o'clock*, spell out the number: *ten o'clock*)
- Percentages and decimals: 80% 8.2
- Divisions of books: Chapter 3 Act 4 Page 102 Paragraph 6

NOTE: Never begin a sentence with a numeral. Either use a spelled-out number, or reword the sentence so the numeral does not come at the beginning.

REVISING AND EDITING

Look back at your response to the Seeing and Writing exercise on page 477. Check your work carefully. Have you capitalized all proper nouns? Have you used quotation marks correctly to set off direct quotations? Have you punctuated direct quotations correctly? Have you underlined the title of the cartoon you chose to write about and used capital letters throughout? Edit where necessary to correct any errors in mechanics.

CHAPTER REVIEW

EDITING PRACTICE

Read the following paragraph, which contains errors in mechanics. Then, edit the passage to correct the errors. The first sentence has been edited for you.

Minority Actors in Hollywood

Until recently, minority actors had trouble finding work in ~~h~~Hollywood. Recently, however, there have been more opportunities for minority actors in american movies. 2 well known Asian-American actors are Sandra Oh, who was in the films "Sideways" and Under the Tuscan sun, and George Takei, who was in Star trek. In addition, Native-American actor Adam Beach appeared in the movies "Smoke signals" and "Windtalkers." Some minority actors have received academy award nominations, including Djimon Hounsou for "In America," Shohreh Aghdashloo for "House of Sand and Fog," and Don Cheadle for Hotel Rwanda. In 2002, two african-american actors won academy awards. Halle berry won for her performance in Monster's Ball, and Denzel washington won for his role in Training day. In her acceptance speech, berry said, This is for every faceless woman who now has a chance because the door tonight has been opened. In 2004, Jamie foxx won an academy Award for portraying ray charles in the movie Ray, and morgan Freeman won for his role in "Million dollar baby." As a result of these awards, more acting roles are likely to be available for minority actors in the future.

Jamie Foxx

Halle Berry

◆ COLLABORATIVE ACTIVITIES

1. Working in a small group, make a list of at least fifteen famous people, places, and historical or news events you have heard of or read about recently. Be sure to capitalize all proper nouns. Next, choose three of the items on your list, and work together to write a sentence about each person, place, or event, explaining why it is important. Then, exchange papers with another group. Check one another's papers to be sure capital letters are used correctly.
2. Imagine that you and the other members of your group are in charge of creating the American Entertainment Hall of Fame. Make lists of your favorite songs, movies, and television shows. When you have finished, choose one item from each person's list. Then, write a sentence explaining why that song, movie, or television show belongs in the American Entertainment Hall of Fame. When you have finished, exchange papers with another group. Check one another's papers to be sure capital letters, quotation marks, and underlining are used correctly.
3. Working in a group of four, choose two people in the group to take different positions on a topic such as the drinking age, gun safety, or required college courses. Next, have these two people present their views to the group. While the discussion is going on, each of the two remaining group members should record a few statements by each participant. After the discussion has ended, work together to write a paragraph that includes the viewpoints of both participants. Place all direct quotations within quotation marks, and include identifying tags that clearly indicate which person is speaking. When you have finished, exchange paragraphs with another group, and check each other's papers to be sure capital letters and quotation marks are used correctly and all quotations are punctuated correctly.
4. ***Composing original sentences*** Working in a group of four, write a five- or six-sentence paragraph about your city or neighborhood, capitalizing proper nouns to identify important places, public officials, schools, and landmarks. Include at least one direct quotation and one title of a local newspaper and an article in that paper. (The quotation and the article title can be made up.) Then, exchange paragraphs with another group. Check each other's work to be sure capitals and quotation marks are used correctly, and make sure all quotations are punctuated correctly. When you have finished, check your own group's paragraph again to make sure you have corrected any errors in grammar, punctuation, or spelling.

✓ REVIEW CHECKLIST: Understanding Mechanics

- Capitalize proper nouns. (See 34A.)
- Always place direct quotations within quotation marks. (See 34B.)

(continued on following page)

(continued from previous page)

- In titles, capitalize all important words, as well as the first and the last words. Use quotation marks or underline to set off titles. (See 34C.)
- Use hyphens to divide words at the end of a line and to join words in compounds. (See 34D.)
- Use abbreviations for titles used along with names, for names of organizations and technical terms, and in other conventional situations. (See 34D.)
- Spell out numbers that can be written in one or two words. Use numerals for numbers more than two words long. (See 34D.)

CHAPTER

35

Understanding Spelling

PREVIEW

In this chapter, you will learn

- to become a better speller (35A)
- to know when to use *ie* and *ei* (35B)
- to understand prefixes (35C)
- to understand suffixes (35D)

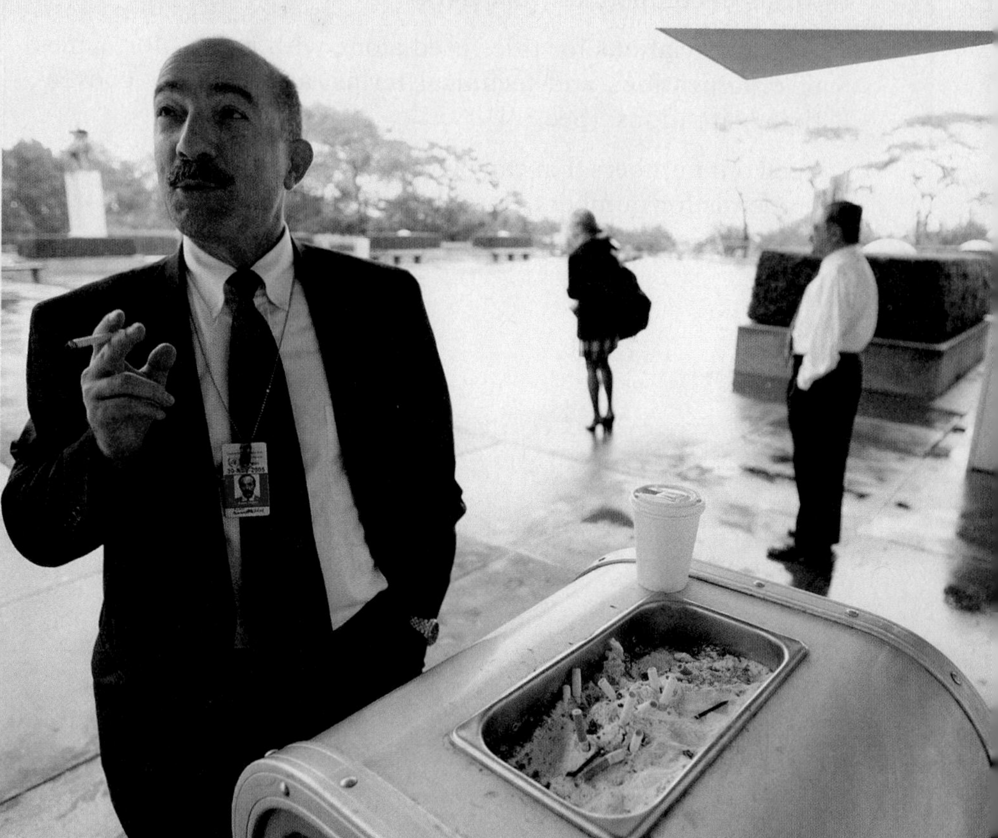

SEEING AND WRITING

The picture above shows a man smoking outside his place of work. Look at the picture, and then write a paragraph in which you discuss whether you think local, state, and federal governments are right to pass laws that prohibit smoking in public places.

Word Power

ban to forbid somebody from doing something

obligation a course of action demanded of a person by law or conscience

ostracize to exclude from a group

prohibit to forbid

A Becoming a Better Speller

Teachers and employers will expect you to be able to recognize and correct misspelled words. The following suggestions can help you become a better speller.

- *Use a spell checker.* Always use a spell checker if you are writing on a computer. It will identify and correct many typos and misspelled words. However, keep in mind that spell checkers will not identify some misspelled words—for example, some foreign words and proper nouns. In addition, they will not identify typos that create words (*form* instead of *from*) or words that you have used incorrectly (*there* for *their*). Because of these limitations, you still have to know how to spell—even if you do use a spell checker.
- *Use a dictionary.* As you proofread, circle words whose spellings you are not sure of. Look up these words in a dictionary to make sure they are spelled correctly.
- *Proofread carefully.* If spelling is your biggest problem, proofread first for misspellings. Then, go back and check for other errors. (You might try starting with the last sentence of your paper and reading backwards to the beginning. This strategy enables you to concentrate on one word at a time without being distracted by your paper's content.)
- *Keep a personal spelling list.* Write down all the words you misspell. Also keep a record of the words your spell checker highlights, and write down any misspelled words that your instructor identifies. (These will usually be circled or marked *sp.*)
- *Look for patterns in your misspellings.* Do you have trouble forming plurals? Do you misspell words with *ei* combinations? Once you have identified these problems, you can focus on eliminating them.
- *Learn the basic spelling rules.* Memorize the spelling rules outlined in this chapter. Each rule you learn can help you spell many words correctly.
- *Review commonly confused words.* Study the commonly confused words in Chapter 36. If any of these words give you trouble, add them to your personal spelling list.
- *Use memory cues.* Think of a memory cue that will help you remember how to spell each particularly troublesome word. For example, remembering that *definite* contains the word *finite* will help you remember that *definite* is spelled with an *i*, not an *a*.
- *Learn how to spell the most frequently misspelled words.* Study the words on the following list. If a word gives you trouble, add it to your personal spelling list.

Some Frequently Misspelled Words

across	all right	argument	becoming
address	a lot	beautiful	beginning

(continued on following page)

(continued from previous page)

believe	exercise	noticeable	roommate
benefit	experience	occasion	secretary
calendar	finally	occur	sentence
cannot	forty	occurred	separate
careful	fulfill	occurrences	speech
careless	generally	occurring	studying
cemetery	government	occurs	surprise
certain	grammar	personnel	tomato
crowded	harass	possible	tomatoes
definite	height	potato	truly
definitely	holiday	potatoes	until
dependent	integration	prejudice	usually
describe	intelligence	prescription	Wednesday
develop	interest	privilege	weird
disappoint	interfere	probably	window
early	judgment	professor	withhold
embarrass	loneliness	receive	woman
entrance	medicine	recognize	women
environment	minute	reference	writing
everything	necessary	restaurant	written

FOCUS Vowels and Consonants

Knowing which letters are vowels and which are consonants will help you understand the spelling rules presented in this chapter.

VOWELS *a, e, i, o, u*

CONSONANTS *b, c, d, f, g, h, j, k, l, m, n, p, q, r, s, t, v, w, x, z*

B *ie* and *ei*

Memorize this rule: *i* before *e*, except after *c*, or when *ei* sounds like *ay* (as it does in *neighbor* and *weigh*).

i *before* **e**	*except after* **c**	*or when* **ei** *is pronounced* **ay**
achieve	ceiling	eight
believe	conceive	freight
friend	deceive	neighbor
		weigh

FOCUS Exceptions to the "*i* before *e*" Rule

The exceptions to the "*i* before *e*" rule follow no pattern, so you must memorize them.

ancient	foreign	neither	society
caffeine	height	science	species
conscience	leisure	seize	weird
either			

◆ PRACTICE 35-1

In each of the following sentences, proofread the underlined words for correct spelling. If a correction needs to be made, cross out the incorrect word, and write the correct spelling above it. If the word is spelled correctly, write *C* above it.

Example: The winner of the college science [C] competition will ~~recieve~~ [receive] a full scholarship.

1. If you believe in yourself, you will find it easier to acheive your goals.
2. Sometimes an emergency can turn nieghbors into friends.
3. Niether one of these dresses fits, and the colors aren't flattering either.
4. The frieght charge depends on the wieght of the package.
5. In the future, people will have more leisure than we can conceive of.
6. The children could not control thier grief over the death of the dog.
7. The prosperous soceity of ancient Rome depended on the labor of slaves.
8. The hieght of the cieling was impressive.
9. A criminal may confess to releive a guilty conscience.
10. That unusual species of butterfly must have migrated here from a foriegn country.

ON THE WEB
For more practice deciding between ie *and* ei, *visit* Exercise Central *at bedfordstmartins.com/foundationsfirst.*

C Prefixes

A **prefix** is a group of letters added to the beginning of a word that changes the word's meaning. Adding a prefix to a word does not change the spelling of the original word.

dis + service = disservice
un + able = unable
co + operate = cooperate

pre + heat = preheat
un + natural = unnatural
over + rate = overrate

◆ PRACTICE 35-2

❖ **ON THE WEB**
For more practice understanding prefixes, visit Exercise Central *at bedfordstmartins.com/ foundationsfirst.*

Write in the blank the new word that results when the given prefix is added to each of the following words.

Example: pre + view = *preview*

1. un + easy = ______
2. dis + satisfied = ______
3. over + cook = ______
4. co + exist = ______
5. un + wind = ______
6. dis + respect = ______
7. under + pay = ______
8. non + sense = ______
9. pre + war = ______
10. tele + communications = ______

D Suffixes

A **suffix** is a group of letters added to the end of a word that changes the word's meaning or its part of speech. Adding a suffix to a word can change the spelling of the original word.

Words Ending in Silent *e*

A **silent *e*** is an *e* that is not pronounced. If a word ends with a silent *e*, drop the *e* if the suffix you are adding begins with a vowel.

Drop the *e*

hope + ing = hoping
continue + ous = continuous

dance + er = dancer
insure + able = insurable

Exceptions

change + able = changeable
notice + able = noticeable

courage + ous = courageous
replace + able = replaceable

Keep the *e* if the suffix begins with a consonant.

Keep the *e*

hope + ful = hopeful
excite + ment = excitement
bore + dom = boredom
same + ness = sameness

Exceptions

argue + ment = argument
judge + ment = judgment
true + ly = truly
nine + th = ninth

◆ PRACTICE 35-3

Write in the blank the new word that results when the given suffix is added to each of the following words.

Examples

decide + ing = deciding

lone + ly = lonely

1. adore + able = ________
2. definite + ly = ________
3. judge + ment = ________
4. care + ful = ________
5. whistle + ed = ________
6. invite + ation = ________
7. true + ly = ________
8. dine + ing = ________
9. insure + ance = ________
10. dedicate + ion = ________
11. sense + less = ________
12. disgrace + ful = ________
13. notice + able = ________
14. become + ing = ________
15. amuse + ment = ________
16. write + er = ________
17. imagine + ation = ________
18. place + ment = ________
19. microscope + ic = ________
20. simple + ly = ________

ON THE WEB
For more practice understanding suffixes, visit Exercise Central *at bedfordstmartins.com/foundationsfirst.*

Words Ending in *y*

When you add a suffix to a word that ends in *-y,* change the *y* to an *i* if the letter before the *y* is a consonant.

Change *y* to *i*

beauty + ful = beautiful
try + ed = tried
busy + ly = busily
friendly + er = friendlier

Exceptions

- Keep the *y* if the suffix starts with an *i*.

cry + ing = crying
baby + ish = babyish

- Keep the *y* when you add a suffix to some one-syllable words.

shy + er = shyer | dry + ness = dryness

- Keep the *y* if the letter before the *y* is a vowel.

Keep the *y*

annoy + ance = annoyance | enjoy + ment = enjoyment
play + ful = playful | display + ed = displayed

Exceptions

day + ly = daily | say + ed = said
gay + ly = gaily | pay + ed = paid

◆ PRACTICE 35-4

Write in the blank the new word that results when the given suffix is added to each of the following words.

Examples

cry + ed = *cried*

fry + ing = *frying*

employ + ment = *employment*

1. try + ing = ______
2. pay + ed = ______
3. noisy + ly = ______
4. buy + er = ______
5. destroy + ed = ______
6. annoy + ance = ______
7. dry + ness = ______
8. play + ful = ______
9. tiny + er = ______
10. happy + ness = ______
11. busy + ly = ______
12. marry + es = ______
13. reply + ed = ______
14. fifty + eth = ______
15. thirty + ish = ______
16. lonely + ness = ______
17. joy + ful = ______
18. spy + ed = ______
19. day + ly = ______
20. lively + hood = ______

Doubling the Final Consonant

When you add a suffix that begins with a vowel—for example, *-ed*, *-er*, or *-ing*—double the final consonant in the original word if you can answer "yes" to *both* these questions:

1. Do the last three letters of the word have a consonant-vowel-consonant pattern (cvc)?

2. Does the word have only one syllable (or place the stress on the last syllable)?

Final Consonant Doubled

cut	+	ing	=	cutting (cvc—one syllable)
bat	+	er	=	batter (cvc—one syllable)
pet	+	ed	=	petted (cvc—one syllable)
commit	+	ed	=	committed (cvc—stress is on last syllable)
occur	+	ing	=	occurring (cvc—stress is on last syllable)

Final Consonant Not Doubled

answer	+	ed	=	answered (cvc—stress is not on last syllable)
happen	+	ing	=	happening (cvc—stress is not on last syllable)
act	+	ing	=	acting (no cvc)

◆ PRACTICE 35-5

Write in the blank the new word that results when the given suffix is added to each of the following words.

Examples

hit + ing = *hitting*

slow + er = *slower*

1. shop + er = ____________
2. squeak + ing = ____________
3. prefer + ed = ____________
4. thin + est = ____________
5. climb + ed = ____________
6. wrap + ing = ____________
7. fair + est = ____________
8. regret + ed = ____________
9. begin + ing = ____________
10. star + ed = ____________
11. write + en = ____________
12. swim + er = ____________
13. appeal + ing = ____________
14. excel + ed = ____________
15. exist + ing = ____________
16. occur + ed = ____________
17. run + er = ____________
18. commit + ed = ____________
19. trap + er = ____________
20. occur + ence = ____________

● REVISING AND EDITING

Type your response to the Seeing and Writing exercise on page 490 if you have not already done so. Then, run a spell check. Did the computer pick up all the errors? Which did it identify? Which did it miss? Correct all the spelling errors in your Seeing and Writing exercise.

CHAPTER REVIEW

◆ EDITING PRACTICE

Read the following paragraph, which contains spelling errors. As you read, identify the words you think are misspelled. Then, check the list on pages 491–92. If you do not find them there, check a dictionary. Finally, cross out each incorrectly spelled word, and write the correct spelling above the line. The first error has been corrected for you.

Using hand gestures to show enthusiasm during a job interview

Maintaining eye contact during a job interview

Body Language

Body language is the gestures and facial expressions by which a person communicates with others. Body and facial ~~movments~~ movements can certanly tell alot about a person. In fact, some sceintists claim that body language comunicates more than speach does. Gestures, smiles, posture, eye contact, and even the position of a person's head, arms, and legs can all revele whether the person is honest or lying, interested or bored, defensive or coperative. Body language can be especialy important in a job interview. The first thing to remember is to maintain eye contact with the interviewer but not to stare. The point is to look intrested without harrassing the interviewer. Experts also say that it is alright to use hand gestures to show enthusiasm. Again, the trick is not to overdo it because this can make you seem agressive or just plain wierd. Another suprising recommendation is not to cross your arms. This can make you look stuborn. Finaly, at the end of the interview, give the interviewer a firm handshake. This shows that you are honest and trustworthy. These tips about body language can come in handy at a job interveiw. They can also help you acheive sucess in other situations as well.

◆ COLLABORATIVE ACTIVITIES

1. Working with a partner, test each other on the list of frequently misspelled words on pages 491–92. Then, make a list of the words you misspelled, and study these words, using flash cards and memory cues if necessary. Retake the test until you have learned all the misspelled words.
2. Create a personal spelling list, checking a dictionary for the correct spelling of each word. Then, try to identify patterns in your misspelling habits, and memorize the rules and exceptions that apply to your misspellings. Working with a partner, test each other on your problem words.

3. Work in a small group to create a spelling test for another group. The test can be a list of words, or it can be a paragraph in which you have intentionally misspelled some words. Correct the other group's test.
4. ***Composing original sentences*** Choose ten of the most troublesome words from your personal spelling list. Then, write a sentence using each word. When you have finished, exchange sentences with another student, and correct any errors in grammar, punctuation, or spelling.

☑ REVIEW CHECKLIST: Understanding Spelling

- Follow the steps to becoming a better speller. (See 35A.)
- *I* comes before *e*, except after *c* or in any *ay* sound, as in *neighbor* and *weigh*. (See 35B.)
- Adding a prefix to a word does not affect the word's spelling. (See 35C.)
- Adding a suffix to a word can change the word's spelling. (See 35D.)
- When a word ends with a silent *e*, drop the *e* if the suffix begins with a vowel. Keep the *e* if the suffix begins with a consonant. (See 35D.)
- When you add a suffix to a word that ends with a *-y*, change the *y* to an *i* if the letter before the *y* is a consonant. Keep the *y* if the letter before the *y* is a vowel. (See 35D.)
- When you add a suffix that begins with a vowel, double the final consonant in the original word if (1) the last three letters of the word have a consonant-vowel-consonant pattern (cvc), and (2) the word has one syllable, or the last syllable is stressed. (See 35D.)

CHAPTER 36

Learning Commonly Confused Words

PREVIEW

In this chapter, you will learn to distinguish words that are often confused.

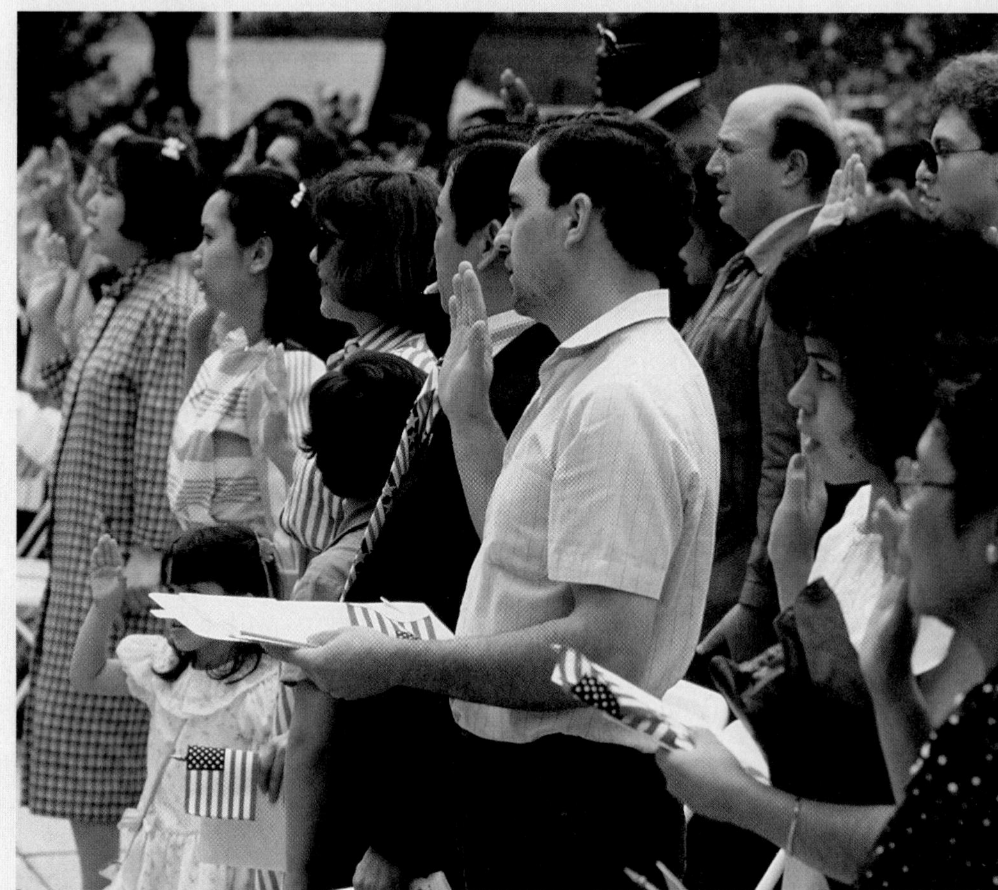

● SEEING AND WRITING

The picture above shows a group of people taking the oath of allegiance at a naturalization ceremony for new U.S. citizens. Look at the picture, and then write a paragraph in which you discuss what America means to you.

▶ **Word Power**

immigrant a person who comes to a country to permanently settle there

multicultural of or relating to many cultures

mobility the ability to move from one social group, class, or level to another

naturalization the process of becoming a citizen

Some English words cause spelling problems because they look or sound like other words. The following word pairs are often confused. Learning to distinguish them can help you become a better speller.

Accept/Except *Accept* means "to receive something." *Except* means "with the exception of."

"I accept your challenge," said Alexander Hamilton to Aaron Burr.

Everyone except Darryl visited the museum.

Affect/Effect *Affect* is a verb meaning "to influence." *Effect* is a noun meaning "result" and sometimes a verb meaning "to bring about."

Jodi's job could affect her grades.

Overexposure to sun can have a long-term effect on skin.

Commissioner Williams tried to effect changes in police procedure.

All ready/Already *All ready* means "completely prepared." *Already* means "previously, before."

Serge was all ready to take the history test.

Gina had already been to Italy.

Brake/Break *Brake* means "a device to slow or stop a vehicle." *Break* means "to smash" or "to detach."

Peter got into an accident because his foot slipped off the brake.

Babe Ruth bragged that no one would ever break his home-run record.

Buy/By *Buy* means "to purchase." *By* is a preposition meaning "close to" or "next to" or "by means of."

Tina wanted to buy a laptop.

He drove by but didn't stop.

He stayed by her side all the way to the hospital.

Malcolm X wanted "freedom by any means necessary."

◆ PRACTICE 36-1

Proofread the underlined words in the following sentences for correct spelling. If a correction needs to be made, cross out the incorrect word, and write the correct spelling above it. If the word is spelled correctly, write *C* above it.

Example: The ~~breaks~~ *brakes* on this car work well, except *C* on icy roads.

1. The sign in the shop read, "If you break anything, you have to buy it."
2. Brad was already for the beach except that he forgot his sunglasses.
3. Some medications effect concentration by causing drowsiness.
4. If we hope to affect change in our government, we have to except our obligation to vote.

ON THE WEB
For more practice identifying words that are often confused, visit Exercise Central *at bedfordstmartins.com/foundationsfirst.*

5. The college basketball player had already accepted an offer from a professional team by the end of his junior year.
6. Gervase plans to buy a car with antilock breaks.
7. Buy the way, I've all ready taken that course.
8. Mild stress, such as the excitement before a test, can effect a person in a positive way, whereas long-term stress usually has a negative affect.
9. The excited contestant was all ready to accept the prize money she had won.
10. Participating in sports can affect young people strongly and affect a change for the better in their ability to get along with others.

Conscience/Conscious *Conscience* refers to the part of the mind that urges a person to choose right over wrong. *Conscious* means "aware" or "deliberate."

After he cheated at cards, his conscience started to bother him.

As she walked through the woods, she became conscious of the hum of insects.

Elliott made a conscious decision to stop smoking.

Everyday/Every day *Everyday* is a single word that means "ordinary" or "common." *Every day* is two words that mean "occurring daily."

I Love Lucy was a successful comedy show because it appealed to everyday people.

Every day, Lucy and Ethel would find a new way to get into trouble.

Fine/Find *Fine* means "superior quality" or "a sum of money paid as a penalty." *Find* means "to locate."

He sang a fine solo at church last Sunday.

Demi had to pay a fine for speeding.

Some people still use a willow rod to find water.

Hear/Here *Hear* means "to perceive sound by ear." *Here* means "at or in this place."

I moved to the front so I could hear the speaker.

My great-grandfather came here in 1883.

Its/It's *Its* is the possessive form of *it*. *It's* is the contraction of *it is* or *it has*.

The airline canceled its flights because of the snow.

It's twelve o'clock, and we're late.

Ever since it's been in the accident, the car has rattled.

◆ PRACTICE 36-2

Proofread the underlined words in the following sentences for correct spelling. If a correction needs to be made, cross out the incorrect word, and write the correct spelling above it. If the word is spelled correctly, write *C* above it.

Example: Every day, we ~~fine~~ find new challenges to face.

1. Sarita became conscience of someone staring at her.
2. "Its been a long time since I've seen you here," Tony said.
3. Sarita smiled as she said, "Its a great place to here jazz."
4. Paul hated paying the fine for parking in a disabled spot, but his conscious bothered him more than losing the money.
5. Everyday, the dog eats it's dinner at precisely 12:00 noon.
6. As soon as a child becomes conscious of right and wrong, his or her conscience begins to develop.
7. This week, everyday has been fine weather.
8. You will fine an outstanding collection of American art right hear in the college museum.
9. The restaurant made a conscience effort to enforce it's "no smoking" policy.
10. The wind had stopped its roaring, but in my mind, I could still hear it.

Know/Knew/New/No *Know* means "to have an understanding of" or "to have fixed in the mind." *Knew* is the past tense form of the verb *know*. *New* means "recent or never used." *No* expresses a negative response.

I know there will be a lunar eclipse tonight.

He knew how to install a new light switch.

Is anything wrong? No.

Lie/Lay *Lie* means "to rest or recline." The past tense of *lie* is *lay*. *Lay* means "to put or place something down." The past tense of *lay* is *laid*.

Every Sunday, I lie in bed until noon.

They lay on the grass until it began to rain, and then they went home.

Tammy told Carl to lay his cards on the table.

Brooke and Cassia finally laid down their hockey sticks.

Loose/Lose *Loose* means "not fastened" or "not attached securely." *Lose* means "to misplace."

In the 1940s, many women wore loose-fitting pants.

Sometimes I lose my keys.

Mine/Mind *Mine* is a possessive pronoun that indicates ownership. *Mind* can be a noun meaning "human consciousness" or "intelligence" or a verb meaning "to obey" or "to attend to."

That red mountain bike is mine.

A mind is a terrible thing to waste.

"Mind your manners when you visit your grandmother," Dad said.

Passed/Past *Passed* is the past tense of the verb *pass*. It means "moved by" or "succeeded in." *Past* is a noun meaning "earlier than the present time."

The car that passed me must have been doing more than eighty miles an hour.

David finally passed his driving test.

The novel was set in the past.

Peace/Piece *Peace* means "the absence of war" or "calm." *Piece* means "a part of something."

The prime minister thought he had achieved peace with honor.

My peace of mind was destroyed when the flying saucer landed.

"Have a piece of cake," said Marie.

◆ PRACTICE 36-3

Proofread the underlined words in the following sentences for correct spelling. If a correction needs to be made, cross out the incorrect word, and write the correct spelling above it. If the word is spelled correctly, write *C* above it.

Example: Heads of state ~~no~~ know that peace C is hard to achieve.

1. Everyone was amazed when the troops lay down their weapons and went home in peace.
2. He new he should not eat another peace of candy, but he ate it anyway.
3. In the passed, it was more important to mine one's manners than it is today.
4. Jamal past his chemistry final with a high grade, as we knew he would.
5. I loose my way every time I drive to the mall.
6. The car passed us as if the driver did not no the speed limit.
7. Janet decided to lay on a lounge chair and enjoy the peace of the garden.
8. The violinist was able to finish playing the piece even though one string had come loose.

9. The new dog had to be trained not to lay on the couch.

10. The children were warned to mine the babysitter.

Plain/Plane *Plain* means "simple, not elaborate." *Plane* is the shortened form of *airplane*.

Sometimes the Amish are referred to as the plain people.

Chuck Yeager was the first person to fly a plane faster than the speed of sound.

Principal/Principle *Principal* means "first" or "highest" or "the head of a school." *Principle* means "a law or basic assumption."

She had the principal role in the movie.

I'll never forget the day the principal called me into his office.

It was against his principles to tell a lie.

Quiet/Quit/Quite *Quiet* means "free of noise" or "still." *Quit* means "to leave a job" or "to give up." *Quite* means "actually" or "very."

Jane looked forward to the quiet evenings at the lake.

Sammy quit his job and followed the girls into the parking lot.

"You haven't quite got the hang of it yet," she said.

After practicing all summer, Tamika got quite good at softball.

Raise/Rise As a verb, *raise* means "to elevate" or "to increase in size, quantity, or worth." The past tense of *raise* is *raised*. *Rise* means "to stand up" or "to move from a lower position to a higher position." The past tense of *rise* is *rose*. As a noun, *raise* means "an increase in salary."

Carlos raises his hand whenever the teacher asks for volunteers.

They raised the money for the down payment.

The fans rise every time their team scores a touchdown.

Sarah rose before dawn so she could see the sunrise.

Her boss gave her a raise.

Right/Write *Right* means "correct" or "the opposite of left." *Write* means "to form letters with a writing instrument."

If you turn right at the corner, you will be going in the right direction.

All students are required to write three short papers.

Sit/Set *Sit* means "to assume a sitting position." The past tense of *sit* is *sat*. *Set* means "to put down or place" or "to adjust something to a desired position." The past tense of *set* is *set*.

I usually sit in the front row at the movies.

They sat at the clinic waiting for their names to be called.

Every semester I set goals for myself.

Elizabeth set the mail down on the kitchen table and left for work.

Suppose/Supposed *Suppose* means "to consider" or "to assume." *Supposed* is both the past tense and the past participle of *suppose*. *Supposed* also means "expected" or "required." (Note that when *supposed* has this meaning, it is followed by *to*.)

Suppose researchers found a cure for AIDS tomorrow.

We supposed the movie would be over by ten o'clock.

You were supposed to finish a draft of the report by today.

◆ PRACTICE 36-4

Proofread the underlined words in the following sentences for correct spelling. If a correction needs to be made, cross out the incorrect word, and write the correct spelling above it. If the word is spelled correctly, write *C* above it.

Example: Everyone in the creative writing class was ~~suppose~~ supposed to write (C) a short autobiography.

1. You are supposed to raise from your seat when an older person enters the room.
2. The school board hasn't quite selected a new principle for the high school yet.
3. The dress Lindsay is making started out plane but is now quite fancy.
4. We watched as the plane raised slowly and disappeared in the clouds.
5. All she wanted was a quite place to set and think for a while.
6. I suppose I should sit this glass on a coaster so as not to damage the wood table.
7. Set the dial to the right level for the kind of fabric you are ironing.
8. Although Yuki was usually quiet, she spoke up to defend her principals.
9. Do you suppose Raoul will be chosen for the principle role in the play?
10. If the candidate cannot rise enough money, she will have to quite the race for mayor.

Their/There/They're *Their* is the possessive form of *they*. *There* means "at or in that place." *There* is also used in the phrases *there is* and *there are*. *They're* is a contraction meaning "they are."

Jane Addams helped poor people improve their living conditions.

I put the book over there.

There are three reasons why I will not eat meat.

They're the best volunteer firefighters I've ever seen.

Then/Than *Then* means "at that time" or "next in time." *Than* is used to introduce the second element in a comparison.

He was young and naive then, but now he knows better.

I went to the job interview and then stopped off for a burger.

My dog is smarter than your dog.

Threw/Through *Threw* is the past tense of *throw*. *Through* means "in one side and out the opposite side" or "finished."

Satchel Paige threw a baseball faster than ninety-five miles an hour.

It takes almost thirty minutes to go through the tunnel.

"I'm through," he said, storming out of the office.

To/Too/Two *To* means "in the direction of." *Too* means "also" or "more than enough." *Two* denotes the numeral 2.

During spring break, I am going to Disney World.

My roommates are coming too.

The microwave popcorn is too hot to eat.

"If we get rid of the tin man and the lion, the two of us can go to Oz," said the scarecrow to Dorothy.

Use/Used *Use* means "to put into service" or "to consume." *Used* is both the past tense and the past participle of *use*. *Used* also means "accustomed." (Note that when *used* has this meaning, it is followed by *to*.)

I use a soft cloth to clean my glasses.

"Hey! Who used all the hot water?" he yelled from the shower.

Mary had used all the firewood during the storm.

After living in Alaska for a year, they got used to the short winter days.

◆ PRACTICE 36-5

Proofread the underlined words in the following sentences for correct spelling. If a correction needs to be made, cross out the incorrect word, and write the correct spelling above it. If the word is spelled correctly, write *C* above it.

Example: *There* ~~Their~~ are at least *C* two good reasons not to rent that apartment.

1. It was hard to get use to the cold when they first came to New York from there home in Puerto Rico.

2. The shortstop threw the ball to second base, but it flew on through the air and landed in the bleachers.
3. I'm threw with the two of them and all they're nonsense!
4. Her blind date was more fun then she expected although it was too early to tell if she really liked him.
5. "They're used to staying up until nine," Mrs. Tsang told the babysitter.
6. Four-year-old Zachary got spaghetti sauce all over his face and than use his T-shirt to clean it off.
7. If they had known then what problems there car would have, they never would have bought it.
8. As a new teacher, Spencer use to feel tired at the end of the day.
9. Is there any reason to risk driving after drinking to much at a party?
10. I don't like the food at that restaurant, and it's two expensive too.

Weather/Whether *Weather* refers to the state of the atmosphere with respect to temperature, humidity, precipitation, and so on. *Whether* means "if it is so that; if the cause is that."

> The *Farmer's Almanac* says that the weather this winter will be severe.
>
> Whether or not this prediction will be correct is anyone's guess.

Where/Were/We're *Where* means "at or in what place." *Were* is the past tense of *are*. *We're* is a contraction meaning "we are."

> Where are you going, and where have you been?
>
> Charlie Chaplin and Mary Pickford were popular stars of silent movies.
>
> We're doing our back-to-school shopping early this year.

Whose/Who's *Whose* is the possessive form of *who*. *Who's* is a contraction meaning "who is" or "who has."

> My roommate asked, "Whose book is this?"
>
> "Who's there?" squealed the second little pig as he leaned against the door.
>
> "Who's been sleeping in my bed?" asked Goldilocks.

Your/You're *Your* is the possessive form of *you*. *You're* is a contraction meaning "you are."

> "You should have worn your running shoes," said the hare as he passed the tortoise.
>
> "You're too kind," replied the tortoise sarcastically.

◆ PRACTICE 36-6

Proofread the underlined words in the following sentences for correct spelling. If a correction needs to be made, cross out the incorrect word, and write the correct spelling above it. If the word is spelled correctly, write *C* above it.

Example: We're (C) not sure ~~weather~~ whether or not this is the right road to take.

1. "Whose going to the party," Tracey asked, "and whose car are we taking?"
2. Orlando, were we went on vacation, has good weather and great beaches.
3. "Your late for you're appointment," the receptionist said.
4. Someone who's had experience buying cameras can tell you whether or not to buy that one.
5. Where you surprised at the sudden change in the weather?
6. Do you know whose left this laptop were anyone might take it?
7. By the time your finished with school and work, your energy is all gone.
8. Whether you like it or not, no one is going to make you're decisions for you.
9. Who's car is parked in the spot were my car usually is?
10. Were you excited when you're letter to the editor was printed?

● REVISING AND EDITING

Look back at your response to the Seeing and Writing exercise on page 500. Make sure you have not misused any of the words listed in this chapter. If you are writing on a computer, use the Search or Find function to locate any words you think you might have misused.

CHAPTER REVIEW

◆ EDITING PRACTICE

Read the following paragraph, which contains errors in word use. Identify the words you think are used incorrectly, and then find them in this chapter or look them up in a dictionary. Finally, cross out each word that is used incorrectly, and write the correct word above the line. The first sentence has been done for you.

The Minimum Wage

As someone who has had minimum-wage jobs, I strongly believe in the ~~principal~~ *principle* of a living wage. How in good conscious can employers not pay workers enough to support themselves? Many employers say that rising the minimum wage would have a negative affect on there business. Small business owners think that the minimum wage is all ready to high. I do not agree with these arguments. A minimum wage is suppose too be enough to supply a person's basic needs. The present minimum wage, however, is not fair. I realize, however, that the definition of fair depends on whom your talking to. They're is also the question of weather the minimum hourly wage should be enough to support one person or an entire family. In the United States, about forty states have minimum-wage laws. The federal government first past a minimum-wage law in 1938. About eighty percent of all private industries are all ready covered by federal law. But to often, self-employed workers and employees of small businesses are not effected by this law. This is a complex problem that will not be easily layed to rest. As lawmakers try to fine a solution, they must except the idea that everyone needs a living wage.

◆ COLLABORATIVE ACTIVITIES

1. After completing the practice exercises in this chapter, make a list of the words that you found confusing, and study their meanings and the sample sentences. Then, have a partner quiz you on these words.
2. Working in a small group, choose one section of this chapter, and write a five-item test on the material it discusses. (Use the practices in this chapter as a model for your test.) Each of your sentences should contain one of the commonly confused words. When you have finished, exchange tests with another group, and take its test. Finally, correct the other group's work on your test.

3. Divide into two teams, and stage a spelling bee that covers the words in this chapter. Each team should prepare a list of twenty words and quiz the other, with students on the two teams alternating to try to spell each word. The team that spells the most words correctly is the winner.
4. ***Composing original sentences*** Working with a partner, choose the five commonly confused word pairs that give you the most trouble. Write sample sentences for the two words in each pair to illustrate the correct use of the commonly confused words.

   Examples

   1. Don't drop that vase or it will break.
   2. I hit the brake suddenly to avoid hitting the deer.

   When you have finished, check the sentences to correct any errors in grammar, punctuation, or spelling.

✓ REVIEW CHECKLIST: Learning Commonly Confused Words

- Memorize the differences between the most commonly confused words.

UNIT REVIEW

Read the following student essay, which includes errors in the use of punctuation, mechanics, and spelling. Correct any errors you find. The first sentence has been edited for you.

Helicopter Parents

Are your parents obsessed with ~~you're~~ *your* every ~~acheivement?~~ *achievement?* Do they dispare whenever you fail a test? Do you ever feel as if your never allowed to make an independent decision? If this sounds familiar you may be the child of helicopter parents. When we think of a helicopter we imagine a loud aircraft hovering overhead. Helicopter parents are parents, who hover over their children — watching every move protecting them from failure and pressuring them to succeed. Helicopter parents can have children of any age babies and toddlers, school-age children, and even college students.

Mother chauffeuring children

Pediatricians can sometimes identify helicopter parents' even before the children are born. These parents are very commited to having read everthing they can about how to create the best child posible. Hoping to improve the babys inteligence, they play tapes of classical music while its' still in the womb. Once the child is born, they read books about child development, and frantically call the pediatrician, whenever they think that their child isnt keeping up. In fact they expect their child to be much better than average. They drive their children to carefully chosen play dates; and by only educational toys.

Cartoon showing parents fighting in the stands at their children's soccer game

When their children go to school; helicopter parents interfear even more. They harrass alot of the teachers, questioning there judgements about testing and placment, and they are not shy about demanding, that there child have a different teacher or be placed in a more advanced class. Although all parents are encouraged to supervize their childrens' homework some helicopter parents actually sieze the homework and do it for them. The days when children could dissappear for long hours — playing or daydreaming — are long gone. Instead, children of helicopter parents are ferryed from school to piano lessons to soccer practice to gymnastics. If their on a team that looses, they get a trophy anyway.

Once there children go to college, helicopter parents can be nightmares for administrator's. They show up at college ocasions that are intended for the students not the parents. They accompany their children through registration and complain when a certian class is closed. When a child has an arguement with a roomate, helicopter parents demand a new one and they call the proffessor when they're child gets a low grade. Because these children have never used an alarm clock (Mom used to get them up every morning), the parents call everyday to make sure that their getting ready for class. These students have little chance to learn the coping skills they need. Sue shellenbarger says in the july 29 2005 Wall street journal Online, Some of these hovering parents, whose numbers have been rising for several years, are unwittingly undermining their children's chances of success.

A parent helping his child move to college

Its clear that good parenting involves a careful balance between concern for the childs' well being, and the need to let go. Every child needs the freedom to make mistakes. Helicopter parents do not allow there children too have this important freedom. The dangers are that the children will never learn how to make their own decitions and that they will feel to much pressure to meet their parents expectations. Good parents need to care deeply about their children but they also need to know when its' time to let go.

UNIT SEVEN

Learning College Reading Skills

CHAPTER 37

Readings for Writers

The following eighteen essays by student and professional writers are designed to give you interesting material to read, react to, think critically about, discuss, and write about. Each essay is accompanied by a short introduction that tells you something about the reading and its author. Definitions of some of the words used in the essay appear in **Word Power** boxes in the margins.

Following each essay are four **Thinking about the Reading** discussion questions, some of which can be done collaboratively. (These are marked in the text with a star.) With your instructor's permission, you can discuss your responses to these questions with other students and then share them with the class. Three **Writing Practice** assignments also follow each essay.

As you read each of these essays, you should **highlight** and **annotate** it to help you understand what you are reading. (Highlighting and annotating are discussed in Chapter 2.) Then, reread the essays more carefully in preparation for class discussion and for writing.

37

TRIGGER-HAPPY BIRTHDAY

Kiku Adatto

Cultural historian and Harvard lecturer Kiku Adatto is writing a book about how childhood is changing in modern America. In this essay, she describes her own experience with paintball birthday parties for children and questions whether they are appropriate for twelve-year-olds like her son.

> **Word Power**
> **missive** a letter or message
> **liability** a financial and legal responsibility; a debt that must be paid

Some months ago, my twelve-year-old son received a brightly colored invitation to a friend's birthday party, which was being held someplace called Boston Paintball. A few days later, I received a more somber missive: "This is a Release of Liability—read before signing." 1

A couple of clauses stood out. No. 1: "The risk of injury from the activity and weaponry involved in paintball is significant, including the potential for permanent disability and death." No. 4: "I, for myself and on behalf of my heirs, assigns, personal representatives and next of kin, *hereby release . . . the American Paintball League (A.P.L.), Boston Paintball . . . with respect to any and all injury, disability, death. . . .*" 2

Welcome to today's birthday party. And by the way, if your kid is killed at the party, it's not our fault. Call me an old-fashioned mother, but I just couldn't sign. Apparently, all the other parents did, however; my son's friends told him that everyone had a great time. 3

I decided to visit Boston Paintball to check it out. Located in an old converted warehouse, the place was teeming with white suburban boys. Over at one end, I found another birthday party, for a kid named Max and 10 or so friends. 4

With their parents' help, the kids were putting on safety gear—chest protectors, neck guards and "Star Wars"–style masks. "It's fun," said Max's mom encouragingly, "like a video game." Then a referee held up a paintball gun (which looked like a real semiautomatic) and shot off a few rounds. The boys quickly lined up to get their weapons. 5

> **Word Power**
> **orientation** a meeting in which participants are introduced to a new situation, such as a new school, job, or other activity
> **sporadic** infrequent; happening from time to time
> **adrenaline** a hormone that produces a rush of energy and excitement when a person is in danger

Next came the safety orientation. "First rule: don't lift off the masks on the field. We shoot balls at 100 miles an hour. Lift a mask, you'll lose an eye. Second rule: on the field, no shooting point-blank. No taking hostages. No using dead guys as shields. No hitting with fists or with gun butts." Max's dad snapped a few photos and handed out the ammunition. 6

The referee gave the signal, and the game began. 7

But nothing happened. The boys huddled behind the bunkers. Eventually some of them poked their heads out; sporadic shots were fired. A few brave souls ventured into the open. 8

I was watching with the other parents from behind a window in the viewing area. Suddenly a paintball bullet hit the window with a dull thud. I started back. My adrenaline was pumping, but my mind said, "Trust the plexiglass." More bullets splattered the window. It sounded like real gunfire. "Hey, it looks like one of the kids is shooting at us," joked one of the mothers. We all laughed. And moved back from the window. 9

There was a release of tension after the first game. Max appeared in the lobby flushed and jubilant. "It was awesome," he said. "I hit someone." Max's parents laid out pizza. Spirits were high. "I killed a person," a boy said as he downed a Coke. 10

While they ate, I visited the gift shop. Along the back wall were racks of paintball guns—all looking like assault weapons—from the Sniper II at $249.99 to the Express Pro Autococker at $749.99. Even without these souvenirs, paintball is pricey: $29 for kids ($39 for adults), with numerous extra fees. A birthday party for ten boys with pizza can run $450. 11

Back at Max's party, one boy was pressing a cold Coke can against a welt. I asked Max's mom about the cost. "Max has contributed a hundred bucks of his birthday money to help pay for the party," she said fondly. Suddenly she spotted a welt on another boy's chin. "Oh, my God. How did that happen?" She turned back to me. "He's a little warrior," she said. 12

When paintball was invented nineteen years ago in New Hampshire, it was played by adults who focused less on simulated violence than on self-reliant survival. Today, it is reportedly a billion-dollar business in North America alone, with outdoor theme parks featuring mock Vietcong villages and bases named the Rambo Hotel. It's a business that proudly markets itself as an all-purpose sport: the Boston Paintball Web site said it was great for "stress relief, confidence, company outings, morale boosting" and, of course, "birthdays." 13

Some of the mothers in attendance that day said that paintball is no different from the war games their brothers played a generation ago. I disagree. True, when I was a kid, my friends and I spun violent fantasies, some (like cowboys and Indians) as troubling as the new high-tech games. But there were differences. We didn't pay for admission. The guns weren't lethal. We used our imaginations. And our parents didn't open the paper several times a year to read about kids firing guns in school. 14

Word Power
lethal capable of killing

As I was pulling out of the paintball parking lot, the attendant, a guy in his forties, asked if I had played. I said no. "I don't think it's good, kids and paintball," he said. "They don't realize that they can hurt somebody with those guns." 15

Well I'm with the parking-lot attendant. And as for the contract, I still couldn't sign. 16

Thinking about the Reading

1. In the Release of Liability, what does Boston Paintball say it will *not* be responsible for?
2. Why does Boston Paintball want parents to sign this Release of Liability? Why does Adatto refuse to sign?
3. Compare Adatto's reaction to the paintball game she watches with the reaction of Max's parents. How are their reactions different?
*4. According to Adatto, how is paintball different from the war games children played in the past? Do you agree with her?

Writing Practice

1. Imagine that you are the parent of a twelve-year-old boy who has just been invited to a paintball party. Would you sign the Release of Liability and allow him to participate? Explain your decision.
2. The author seems to make a connection between the violent game of paintball, which is played with weapons that look like real semiautomatics, and the problem of "kids firing guns in school" (paragraph 14).

Do you agree or disagree that paintball might encourage violent behavior in real life? Give reasons for your answer.

3. Why do you think paintball is popular among both children and adults? Do you agree that violent games fulfill a useful function in society, such as preventing real-life violence or relieving stress and building confidence, as the Boston Paintball people claim? Explain your position.

DON'T HANG UP, THAT'S MY MOM CALLING

Bobbi Buchanan

Telemarketers' sales calls often interrupt our already hectic lives. Bobbi Buchanan's article reminds us that there is a real, and sometimes familiar, person on the other end of every telemarketing call. Buchanan, whose writing has appeared in the *New York Times* and the *Louisville Review*, is the editor of the online journal *New Southerner*.

1 The next time an annoying sales call interrupts your dinner, think of my 71-year-old mother, LaVerne, who works as a part-time telemarketer to supplement her Social Security income. To those Americans who have signed up for the new national do-not-call list, my mother is a pest, a nuisance, an invader of privacy. To others, she's just another anonymous voice on the other end of the line. But to those who know her, she's someone struggling to make a buck, to feed herself and pay her utilities—someone who personifies the great American way.

2 In our family, we think of my mother as a pillar of strength. She's survived two heart surgeries and lung cancer. She stayed at home her whole life to raise the seven of us kids. She entered the job market unskilled and physically limited after my father's death in 1998, which ended his pension benefits.

3 Telemarketing is a viable option for my mother and the more than six million other Americans who work in the industry. According to the American Teleservices Association, the telemarketing work force is mostly women; 26 percent are single mothers. More than 60 percent are minorities; about 5 percent are disabled; 95 percent are not college graduates; more than 30 percent have been on welfare or public assistance. This is clearly a job for those used to hardship.

> **Word Power**
> **viable** able to survive; capable of success

4 Interestingly enough, the federal list exempts calls from politicians, pollsters, and charities, and companies that have existing business relationships with customers can keep calling. Put this in perspective. Are they not the bulk of your annoying calls? Telemarketing giants won't be as affected by the list but smaller businesses that rely on this less costly means of sales will. The giants will resort to other, more expensive forms of advertisement and pass those costs along to you, the consumer.

> **Word Power**
> **exempts** frees from an obligation that others are subject to

5 My mother doesn't blame people for wanting to be placed on the do-not-call list. She doesn't argue the fairness of its existence or take offense when potential clients cut her off in mid-sentence. All her parenting experience has made her impervious to rude behavior and snide remarks, and she is not discouraged by hang-ups or busy signals. What worries my mother is that she doesn't know whether she can do anything else at her age. As it is, sales are down and her paycheck is shrinking.

> **Word Power**
> **impervious** impossible to affect

6 So when the phone rings at your house during dinnertime and you can't resist picking it up, relax, breathe deeply and take a silent oath to be polite. Try these three painless words: "No, thank you."

7 Think of the caller this way: a hard-working, first-generation American; the daughter of a Pittsburgh steelworker; a survivor of the Great Depression; the widow of a World War II veteran; a mother of seven, grandmother of eight, great-grandmother of three. It's my mother calling.

Thinking about the Reading

1. What does Buchanan want readers to know about her mother? Be as specific as you can.
2. In paragraph 3, Buchanan says that telemarketing is "clearly a job for those used to hardship." What does she mean?
3. What is Buchanan's objection to the national do-not-call list? Do you agree with her?

*4. What was your opinion of telemarketers before you read this essay? Did the essay change your mind in any way?

Writing Practice

1. Write a letter to Buchanan arguing that although telemarketers may be nice people who need the income, they are still annoying invaders of our privacy.
2. What do you think can be done to achieve a compromise between telemarketers' need for employment and our desire not to be bothered by their calls? Suggest some ways to make such calls less annoying.
3. Imagine you have just accepted a job as a telemarketer, and your friends are critical of your decision. Respond to their criticisms, explaining why you took the job and what you hope to get out of it.

TORTILLAS

José Antonio Burciaga

José Antonio Burciaga was born in El Paso, Texas, in 1940, and his Chicano identity is the main subject of his poems, stories, and essays. In this essay, he explores his childhood memories—as well as the cultural significance—of tortillas. Tortillas, thin, round, griddle cakes made of cornmeal, are a staple of Mexican cooking.

My earliest memory of *tortillas* is my *Mamá* telling me not to play with them. I had bitten eyeholes in one and was wearing it as a mask at the dinner table. 1

As a child, I also used *tortillas* as hand warmers on cold days, and my family claims that I owe my career as an artist to my early experiments with *tortillas*. According to them, my clowning around helped me develop a strong artistic foundation. I'm not so sure, though. Sometimes I wore a *tortilla* on my head, like a *yarmulke*, and yet I never had any great urge to convert from Catholicism to Judaism. But who knows? They may be right. 2

For Mexicans over the centuries, the *tortilla* has served as the spoon and the fork, the plate and the napkin. *Tortillas* originated before the Mayan civilizations, perhaps predating Europe's wheat bread. According to Mayan mythology, the great god Quetzalcoatl, realizing that the red ants knew the secret of using maize as food, transformed himself into a black ant, infiltrated the colony of red ants, and absconded with a grain of corn. (Is it any wonder that to this day, black ants and red ants do not get along?) Quetzalcoatl then put maize on the lips of the first man and woman, Oxomoco and Cipactonal, so that they would become strong. Maize festivals are still celebrated by many Indian cultures of the Americas. 3

> **Word Power**
> **maize** corn
> **absconded** left quickly and secretly to avoid punishment

When I was growing up in El Paso, *tortillas* were part of my daily life. I used to visit a *tortilla* factory in an ancient adobe building near the open *mercado* in Ciudad Juárez. As I approached, I could hear the rhythmic slapping of the *masa* as the skilled vendors outside the factory formed it into balls and patted them into perfectly round corn cakes between the palms of their hands. The wonderful aroma and the speed with which the women counted so many dozens of *tortillas* out of warm wicker baskets still linger in my mind. Watching them at work convinced me that the most handsome and *deliciosas tortillas* are handmade. Although machines are faster, they can never adequately replace generation-to-generation experience. There's no place in the factory assembly line for the tender slaps that give each *tortilla* character. The best thing that can be said about mass-producing *tortillas* is that it makes it possible for many people to enjoy them. 4

In the *mercado* where my mother shopped, we frequently bought *taquitos de nopalitos*, small tacos filled with diced cactus, onions, tomatoes, and *jalapeños*. Our friend Don Toribio showed us how to make delicious, crunchy *taquitos* with dried, salted pumpkin seeds. When you had no money for the filling, a poor man's *taco* could be made by placing a warm *tortilla* on the left palm, applying a sprinkle of salt, then rolling the *tortilla* up quickly with the fingertips of the right hand. My own kids put peanut butter and jelly on *tortillas*, which I think is truly bicultural. And speaking of fast foods for kids, nothing beats a *quesadilla*, a *tortilla* grilled-cheese sandwich. 5

Depending on what you intend to use them for, *tortillas* may be made in various ways. Even a run-of-the-mill *tortilla* is more than a flat corn cake. A skillfully cooked homemade *tortilla* has a bottom and a top; the top skin forms a pocket in which you put the filling that folds your *tortilla* into a taco. Paper-thin *tortillas* are used specifically for *flautas*, a type of taco that is filled, rolled, and then fried until crisp. The name *flauta* means *flute*, which probably refers to the Mayan bamboo flute; however, the only sound that comes from an edible *flauta* is a delicious crunch that is music to the palate. In México *flautas* are sometimes made as long as two feet and then cut into manageable segments. The opposite of *flautas* is *gorditas*, meaning *little fat ones*. These are very thick small *tortillas*. 6

The versatility of *tortillas* and corn does not end here. Besides being tasty and nourishing, they have spiritual and artistic qualities as well. The Tarahumara Indians of Chihuahua, for example, concocted a corn-based beer called *tesgüino*, which their descendants still make today. And everyone has read about the woman in New Mexico who was cooking her husband a *tortilla* one morning when the image of Jesus Christ miraculously appeared on it. Before they knew what was happening, the man's breakfast had become a local shrine. 7

> **Word Power**
>
> **versatility** the ability to do many things well
>
> **concocted** mixed various ingredients together

Then there is *tortilla* art. Various Chicano artists throughout the Southwest have, when short of materials or just in a whimsical mood, used a dry *tortilla* as a small, round canvas. And a few years back, at the height of the Chicano movement, a priest in Arizona got into trouble with the Church after he was discovered celebrating mass using a *tortilla* as the host. All of which only goes to show that while the *tortilla* may be a lowly corn cake, when the necessity arises, it can reach unexpected distinction. 8

Thinking about the Reading

1. In one sentence, define *tortilla*.
2. List some of the uses for tortillas that Burciaga identifies.
3. What exactly does the tortilla mean to Burciaga? Why are tortillas so important to him?
*4. What food in your culture represents for you what the tortilla represents for Burciaga?

Writing Practice

1. Write about another food that you think is as versatile as tortillas are. Use your imagination to identify as many unusual uses for this food as you can.
2. Write an essay about the foods that you consider to be typically American. Define each food, and explain what makes it "American."
3. Imagine you have met someone who knows nothing about your family's culture. Explain the different ethnic foods eaten in your household. Include information about when and where these foods are eaten and why they are important to your family.

EMIL'S BIG CHANCE LEAVES ME UNEASY

Tricia Capistrano

In this essay, Tricia Capistrano tells about taking her son to the Philippines to audition for commercials. Although she hopes that her light-skinned son's success will help someday to pay for his education, she is also critical of the commercials. Capistrano believes that the commercials' exclusive use of light-skinned actors reinforces both racism and self-hatred.

Brad Pitt and Angelina Jolie may have the most popular baby in the world right now, but I do not envy them. I had my taste of celebrity when I took my infant son on a trip to the Philippines two years ago. I walked away from him for a moment at a baby-goods store in Manila and when I returned, he was surrounded by four women in their 20s who were ogling him. "He is so cute!" they said. "So fair-skinned!" Whether we were in the mall or at church, people would gather around to look at his face. 1

> **Word Power**
> **ogling** staring at

My son is mestizo, of mixed race. My husband is Caucasian with ancestors from Sweden and Slovakia. I am a brown-skinned woman from the Philippines, where many people I know have a fascination with the lighter skinned—probably because our islands were invaded so many times by whites who tried to convince us that they were better and more beautiful than us. We were under Spain's rule for nearly 400 years, the United States' for almost 50. As a result, skin-whitening products fly off the pharmacy shelves. 2

"Any plans to move back here?" my relatives ask when I visit. 3

"I'll send Emil when he is a teenager so he can become a matinee idol and fund our retirement," I joke. Most of the country's famous actors are of mixed race, and the teen actors who are on their way up don't have to be talented, just fair-skinned and preferably of Spanish, American or Chinese descent. 4

I started to reconsider my response several months ago after my husband and I read that by the time our son goes to college in 16 years, his education will cost about $500,000. When we visited my parents last January, I asked my friends in the advertising industry if I could bring my son by their offices to take some test shots. I wondered if he could land a commercial for diapers, cereal or maybe ice cream. 5

By the time I got the number of an agent, I had started to second-guess my idea. I realized that I was going to be part of the system that can sometimes make us dark-skinned people believe that we are inferior. I do not want Filipino children who look like me to feel bad about themselves. When I was a kid, my grandmother would get upset whenever I told her that I'd be spending the afternoon swimming in my cousin's pool, because it meant that my skin would get darker than it already was. My mom, whose nose I acquired, has one of the widest among her brothers and sisters. She taught me to pinch the bridge daily so that the arch would be higher, like my cousins'. Most of her girlfriends got blond highlights and nose jobs as soon as they received their first paychecks, almost as a rite of passage. 6

> **Word Power**
> **second-guess** to reconsider a decision

As a teenager, I tried to hang out with the mestizas, because I wanted to be popular like them. It was only when I was 22 years old and moved to New York, where people of different colors, beliefs and sexual orientations 7 are embraced, that I learned to appreciate my brown skin, wide nose, straight, black hair and five-foot stature. Because of the self-confidence I saw in the people I met, I found everyone—in the subway, on the street, in restaurants—beautiful.

When some of my friends in Manila express disappointment that their children are not as light-skinned as Emil, I tell them it doesn't matter. And for a long time, I've been content with my decision to scrap my plans for Emil to be on the airwaves. I felt I was doing my share for my brown brothers and sisters. 8

Then, on one of the first warm days this spring, Emil and I went to the playground with our half-Irish, half-Polish neighbor, Julia, and her son. While we were watching the kids play, I joked that I was going to send Emil to the Philippines to be on TV. "Oh, that would be great!" she said earnestly. She told me that as a little girl she had been in a series of Kodak commercials in the 1970s, ads I remember seeing during episodes of "Three's Company." Julia's parents were working class, so it was the only way they could afford to pay for her college education. 9

Once again, I'm tempted to call that agent. After all, I am sure other fair-skinned children are being chosen to appear in Philippine commercials even as I write this. I know my boycott is just an anecdote in the world's bigger drama. The real stage is in my decolonized mind. If my son ever lands a part on TV because of his color, do I want to be the one who has cast him? 10

> **Word Power**
> **boycott** (noun) a refusal to participate
> **decolonized** freed from dependency

Thinking about the Reading

1. Capistrano faces a **dilemma**, a choice between two or more equally unappealing options. What does she see as her two options? What arguments does she offer for each option?
2. Why does Capistrano's son attract so much attention in Manila? How does she account for his appeal?
3. In paragraphs 6 and 7, Capistrano remembers some of her own childhood experiences. How do you think these experiences might explain the decision she finally makes about her son?

*4. What do you think Capistrano should do? Why?

Writing Practice

1. Write an editorial for a college newspaper in the Philippines. In your editorial, argue that Capistrano owes it to her fellow Filipinos not to let her son make TV commercials.
2. Write about a time when you faced a **dilemma**. What options did you have? Which option did you choose, and why? Do you see this decision as the right one?
3. Do you think the people you see in television commercials look like the people you see every day? How are they like your relatives, friends, and neighbors? How are they different? Do you think advertisers should select actors who look more like "real people"? Why or why not?

DELUSIONS OF GRANDEUR

Henry Louis Gates Jr.

An award-winning writer and critic, Henry Louis Gates Jr. is currently the W. E. B. Du Bois Professor of the Humanities at Harvard. In the following essay, first published in *Sports Illustrated* in 1991, he attempts to awaken black youth from their dreams of basketball stardom. He encourages them, instead, to focus on education, where a more realistic chance of success awaits them.

Standing at the bar of an all-black VFW post in my hometown of Piedmont, W. Va., I offered five dollars to anyone who could tell me how many African-American professional athletes were at work today. There are 35 million African-Americans, I said. 1

"Ten million!" yelled one intrepid soul, too far into his cups. 2

"No way . . . more like 500,000," said another. 3

> **Word Power**
> **intrepid** brave

"You mean *all* professional sports," someone interjected, "including golf and tennis, but not counting the brothers from Puerto Rico?" Everyone laughed. 4

"Fifty thousand, minimum," was another guess. 5

Here are the facts: 6

There are 1,200 black professional athletes in the U.S.
There are 12 times more black lawyers than black athletes.
There are 2½ times more black dentists than black athletes.
There are 15 times more black doctors than black athletes.

Nobody in my local VFW believed these statistics; in fact, few people would believe them if they weren't reading them in the pages of *Sports Illustrated*. In spite of these statistics, too many African-American youngsters still believe that they have a much better chance of becoming another Magic Johnson or Michael Jordan than they do of matching the achievements of Baltimore Mayor Kurt Schmoke or neurosurgeon Dr. Benjamin Carson, both of whom, like Johnson and Jordan, are black. 7

In reality, an African-American youngster has about as much chance of becoming a professional athlete as he or she does of winning the lottery. The tragedy for our people, however, is that few of us accept that truth. 8

Let me confess that I love sports. Like most black people of my generation—I'm 40—I was raised to revere the great black athletic heroes, and I never tired of listening to the stories of triumph and defeat that, for blacks, amount to a collective epic much like those of the ancient Greeks: Joe Louis's demolition of Max Schmeling; Satchel Paige's dazzling repertoire of pitches; Jesse Owens's in-your-face performance in Hitler's 1936 Olympics; Willie Mays's over-the-shoulder basket catch; Jackie Robinson's quiet strength when assaulted by racist taunts; and a thousand other grand tales. 9

> **Word Power**
> **revere** to regard with respect and awe
> **epic** a long poem celebrating heroic acts

Nevertheless, the blind pursuit of attainment in sports is having a devastating effect on our people. Imbued with a belief that our principal avenue to fame and profit is through sport, and seduced by a win-at-any-cost system that corrupts even elementary school students, far too many black kids treat basketball courts and football fields as if they were classrooms in an alternative school system. "O.K., I flunked English," a young athlete will say. "But I got an A plus in slam-dunking." 10

> **Word Power**
> **imbued** thoroughly influenced

The failure of our public schools to educate athletes is part and parcel of the schools' failure to educate almost everyone. A recent survey of the Philadelphia school system, for example, stated that "more than half of all students in the third, fifth and eighth grades cannot perform minimum math and language tasks." One in four middle school students in that city fails to pass to the next grade each year. It is a sad truth that such statistics are repeated in cities throughout the nation. Young athletes—particularly young black athletes—are especially ill-served. Many of them are functionally illiterate, yet they are passed along from year to year for the greater glory of good old Hometown High. We should not be surprised to learn, then, that only 26.6% of black athletes at the collegiate level earn their degrees. For every successful educated black professional athlete, there are thousands of dead and wounded. Yet young blacks continue to aspire to careers as athletes, and it's no wonder why; when the University of North Carolina recently commissioned a sculptor to create archetypes of its student body, guess which ethnic group was selected to represent athletes? 11

▶ **Word Power**
archetypes models
prevailed upon persuaded
shirked avoided responsibility
earmark to set aside for a particular purpose

Those relatively few black athletes who do make it in the professional ranks must be prevailed upon to play a significant role in the education of all of our young people, athlete and nonathlete alike. While some have done so, many others have shirked their social obligations: to earmark small percentages of their incomes for the United Negro College Fund; to appear on television for educational purposes rather than merely to sell sneakers; to let children know the message that becoming a lawyer, a teacher or a doctor does more good for our people than winning the Super Bowl; and to form productive liaisons with educators to help forge solutions to the many ills that beset the black community. These are merely a few modest proposals. 12

A similar burden falls upon successful blacks in all walks of life. Each of us must strive to make our young people understand the realities. Tell them to cheer Bo Jackson but to emulate novelist Toni Morrison or businessman Reginald Lewis or historian John Hope Franklin or Spelman College president Johnetta Cole—the list is long. 13

▶ **Word Power**
emulate to imitate

Of course, society as a whole bears responsibility as well. Until colleges stop using young blacks as cannon fodder in the big-business wars of so-called nonprofessional sports, until training a young black's mind becomes as important as training his or her body, we will continue to perpetuate a system akin to that of the Roman gladiators, sacrificing a class of people for the entertainment of the mob. 14

Thinking about the Reading

1. What do you think this essay's title means? According to Gates, what "delusions" do many young African Americans have?
2. Reread paragraph 10, where Gates explains why he sees African Americans' drive to succeed in sports as a problem. In your own words, summarize his argument.

*3. What does Gates think the schools should do to solve the problem he identifies? What does he think black athletes should do? What does he think must be done by other successful blacks?

*4. *Cannon fodder* is a term that usually refers to soldiers who are likely to be injured or killed in combat. What do you think Gates means when he says that colleges use young African-American men as "cannon fodder" (paragraph 14)?

Writing Practice

1. Imagine you are making a speech to a group of teenage boys. Try to explain the information in paragraph 6 in terms they can understand, and use this information to convince your audience how important it is for them to stay in school.
2. When you were a child, what did you want to be when you grew up? How did your goals change as you grew up? Why?
3. Young people's heroes are often celebrities in sports and the arts. What do young people admire about such celebrities? What do they envy? Do you think having such individuals as role models helps or hurts young people?

37

AT THE HEART OF A HISTORIC MOVEMENT

John Hartmire

As executive director of the National Farmworker Ministry, John Hartmire's father worked closely with Cesar Chavez to fight for social justice for farmworkers. However, his father's dedication to the cause meant that he was absent for most of Hartmire's childhood. In this essay, Hartmire discusses what it is like to make a personal sacrifice for a social cause.

1 When my friend's daughter asked me if I knew anything about the man her school was named after, I had to admit that I did. I told her that in California there are at least twenty-six other schools, seventeen streets, seven parks, and ten scholarships named after Cesar Chavez. Not only that, I said, I once hit a ground ball through his legs during a softball game, and I watched his two dogs corner my sister's rabbit and, quite literally, scare it to death. I used to curse his name to the sun gods while I marched through one sweltering valley or another knowing my friends were at the beach staring at Carrie Carbajal and her newest bikini.

2 During those years I wasn't always sure of how I felt about the man, but I did believe Cesar Chavez was larger than life. The impact he had on my family was at once enriching and debilitating. He was everywhere. Like smoke and cobwebs, he filled the corners of my family's life. We moved to California from New York in 1961 when my father was named executive director of the National Farmworker Ministry, and for the next thirty-plus years our lives were defined by Cesar and the United Farm Workers.

> **Word Power**
> **debilitate** to take away the strength of something or someone
> **viable** able to survive; capable of success

3 During those years my father was gone a lot, traveling with, or for, Cesar. I "understood" because the struggle to organize farmworkers into a viable union was the work of a lifetime, and people would constantly tell me how much they admired what Dad was doing. Hearing it made me proud. It also made me lonely. He organized the clergy to stand up for the union, went to jail defying court injunctions, and was gone from our house for days on end, coming home, my mother likes to say, only for clean underwear. It was my father who fed the small piece of bread to Cesar ending his historic twenty-five-day fast in 1968. It's no wonder Dad missed my first Little League home run.

4 The experience of growing up in the heart of a historic movement has long been the stuff of great discussions around our dinner table. The memories are both vibrant and difficult. There were times when Cesar and the union seemed to be more important to my father than I was, or my mother was, or my brothers and sister were. It is not an easy suspicion to grow up with, or to reconcile as an adult.

5 While my friends surfed, I was dragged to marches in the Coachella and San Joaquin valleys. I was taken out of school to attend union meetings and rallies that interested me even less than geometry class. I spent time in supermarket parking lots reluctantly passing out leaflets and urging shoppers not to buy nonunion grapes and lettuce. I used to miss Sunday-afternoon NFL telecasts to canvass neighborhoods with my father. Since my dad wanted his family to be a part of his life, I marched and slept and ate and played with Cesar Chavez's kids. When we grew older his son, Paul, and I would drink beer together and wonder out loud how our lives would have been different had our fathers been plumbers or bus drivers.

But our fathers were fighting to do something that had never been done before. Their battle to secure basic rights for migrant workers evolved into a moral struggle that captured the nation's attention. I saw it all, from the union's grape strike in 1965, to the signing of the first contracts five years later, to the political power gained then lost because, for Cesar, running a union was never as natural as orchestrating a social movement. 6

> **Word Power**
> **orchestrate** to arrange

My father and Cesar parted company four years before Chavez died in 1993. Chavez, sixty-six at the time of his death, father of eight, grandfather of twenty-seven, leader of thousands, a Hispanic icon who transcended race, left the world a better place than he found it. He did it with the help of a great many good people, and the sacrifice of their families, many of whom believed in his cause but didn't always understand what he was asking of, or taking from, them. 7

> **Word Power**
> **transcend** to be greater than; to go beyond

So as students here attend Cesar Chavez Elementary School, as families picnic in a Sacramento park named after him and public employees opt to take off March 31 in honor of his birthday, I try to remember Cesar Chavez for what he was—a quiet man, the father of friends, a man intricately bound with my family—and not what he took from my childhood. Namely, my father. I still wrestle with the cost of my father's commitment, understanding that social change does not come without sacrifice. I just wonder if the price has to be so damn high. 8

Do I truly know Cesar Chavez? I suppose not. He was like a boat being driven by some internal squall, a disturbance he himself didn't always understand, and that carried millions right along with him, some of us kicking and screaming. 9

Thinking about the Reading

1. When he was a child, why did Hartmire "curse [Cesar Chavez's] name to the sun gods" (paragraph 1)? Do you think he still feels bitterness about his childhood? If so, at whom is this bitterness directed?
2. In paragraph 2, Hartmire says that Chavez was "larger than life. The impact he had on my family was at once enriching and debilitating. He was everywhere." What does he mean?

*3. In paragraph 5, Hartmire says that he and Paul Chavez used to try to imagine how their lives might have been different if their fathers had been "plumbers or bus drivers." How do you think their lives would have been different?

4. How has Hartmire's opinion of Chavez changed over the years? Has his opinion of his father also changed?

Writing Practice

1. What historical or political figure was "larger than life" for your family? Write an essay explaining the impact that this person had on you.
2. Who is your greatest living hero? Write an essay explaining this person's contributions to society. (If you like, you may write your essay as a recommendation for an award, addressing your remarks to the awards committee.)
3. If your middle school or high school was named after a person, write an article for the school newspaper in which you explain why this individual deserves (or does not deserve) this honor.

AMERICA, STAND UP FOR JUSTICE AND DECENCY

Macarena Hernández

Born in Texas to migrant Mexican workers, Macarena Hernández is an editorial columnist for the *Dallas Morning News*. In this article, she reports on the dangers that undocumented immigrants often face. She also suggests changes to help reduce this kind of violence and suffering.

On the last night of September, while they slept after a long day of work in the fields, six men were beaten to death with aluminum bats. One was shot in the head. Among the victims, a father and son killed in the same battered trailer. 1

The killers demanded money as they broke their bones. 2

The victims were all Mexican farm workers living in rundown trailer parks spread across two counties in southern Georgia. They had earned the money the killers were after by sweating their days on cotton and peanut farms or building chicken coops—the kind of jobs you couldn't pay Americans enough to do. 3

In a few hours, the killers hit four trailers. In one, they raped a woman and shot her husband in the head, traumatizing their three small children, who were present. In others, they left at least a half-dozen men wounded. Some are still in the hospital with shattered bones, including broken wrists from trying to protect their faces from the bats. 4

> **Word Power**
> **reverberated** had a prolonged or continuing effect

The news of the killings in Georgia reverberated outside Tift and Colquitt counties, but it didn't cling to national headlines like you would expect with such a bloodbath. Two weeks later, residents are still afraid the attackers will come back, even though the Georgia Bureau of Investigation has arrested six suspects and charged them with the slayings. 5

> **Word Power**
> **pushcart** a light cart pushed by hand

Across the country, assaults on immigrants are common and happen at a much higher rate than reported. Two years ago in Grand Prairie, a pushcart ice cream vendor was shot to death and robbed. Seven months later, another one met the same fate in West Oak Cliff. In March, at a Far North Dallas apartment complex, two thieves raped and killed a 20-year-old woman. They slit her husband's throat. 6

In Dallas, attacks against immigrants are one reason individual robberies have gone up in the last five years. Authorities call undocumented immigrants "ready-made victims." Without proper documentation to open bank accounts, many resort to stashing their sweat-soaked earnings under mattresses, in kitchen cabinets, in their socks or boots. If they are robbed, many don't call police for fear of deportation or because, back home, cops aren't trusted, anyway. 7

> **Word Power**
> **lenient** not harsh or strict

Some solutions are simple and concrete, such as making it easier for immigrants to establish bank accounts. Wells Fargo and Bank of America are among the banks that require only a Mexican consulate–issued ID card to open an account; others require documentation many immigrants lack. If there was ever a reason for adopting the more lenient policy, this is it. 8

More globally, horrors like these demand that a nation descended from immigrants take a hard look at the ways we think and speak about these most recent arrivals. 9

When Paul Johnson, the mayor of Tifton, where three of the four attacks took place, responded by flying the Mexican flag at City Hall, some 10 residents complained. "I did that as an expression of sorrow for the Hispanic community," he told reporters. "For those who were offended, I apologize, but I think it was the right thing to do."

Were the complainers angrier about the red, white, and green Mexican flag fluttering in the Georgia air than they were about the horrific murders? Do they watch Fox's *The O'Reilly Factor*, where the anchor and the callers constantly point to the southern border as the birth of all America's ills? (Sample comment: "Each one of those people is a biological weapon.") 11

It is one thing to want to secure the borders and another to preach hate, to talk of human beings as ailments. Taken literally, such rhetoric gives criminals like those in southern Georgia license to kill; it gives others permission to look the other way. In this heightened anti-immigrant climate, what Mr. Johnson did was not only a welcome gesture, but a brave one, too. 12

There are those who will want to gloss over the deaths of these six men because they are "criminals" and "lawbreakers," in this country illegally. But regardless of where you stand on the immigration reform debate, you can't stand for the senseless death of the vulnerable. 13

We should all be outraged. We must demand justice. Or else the real criminals here will win. 14

Word Power

ailments illnesses

rhetoric elaborate, insincere, or pretentious language

gloss to skim

vulnerable (noun) those who are likely to be victims of physical or emotional injury

Thinking about the Reading

1. What specific events inspired Hernández to write this article? Why do you think she wrote it?
*2. What other events does Hernández mention? How are they like the events that occurred in the trailer parks in Georgia?
3. According to Hernández, "Authorities call undocumented immigrants 'ready-made victims'" (paragraph 7). Why? What solutions does she suggest for this problem?
4. How does Hernández believe the nation should respond to the incidents she discusses?

Writing Practice

1. Write a letter to Paul Johnson, the mayor of Tifton, telling him what you think of his decision to fly the Mexican flag at City Hall.
2. What, if anything, do you think needs to be done to "secure the border" between the United States and Mexico?
3. In addition to Hernández's suggestions in paragraph 8, what do you think can be done to protect undocumented immigrants from crimes like the ones she describes?

37

ORANGE CRUSH

Yiyun Li

At twenty-four, Yiyun Li moved from Beijing, China, to the United States to study biology. Before long, however, she transferred to the Iowa Writers' Workshop, where she wrote a collection of stories, *A Thousand Years of Good Prayers*. In the following article, she recalls her childhood desire for a trendy Western drink that her family in China could not afford.

During the winter in Beijing, where I grew up, we always had orange and tangerine peels drying on our heater. Oranges were not cheap. My father, who believed that thrift was one of the best virtues, saved the dried peels in a jar; when we had a cough or cold, he would boil them until the water took on a bitter taste and a pale yellow cast, like the color of water drizzling out of a rusty faucet. It was the best cure for colds, he insisted. 1

I did not know then that I would do the same for my own children, preferring nature's provision over those orange- and pink- and purple-colored medicines. I just felt ashamed, especially when he packed it in my lunch for the annual field trip, where other children brought colorful flavored fruit drinks—made with "chemicals," my father insisted. 2

> **Word Power**
> **provision** something that is supplied

The year I turned 16, a new product caught my eye. Fruit Treasure, as Tang was named for the Chinese market, instantly won everyone's heart. Imagine real oranges condensed into a fine powder! Equally seductive was the TV commercial, which gave us a glimpse of a life that most families, including mine, could hardly afford. The kitchen was spacious and brightly lighted, whereas ours was a small cube—but at least we had one; half the people we knew cooked in the hallways of their apartment buildings, where every family's dinner was on display and their financial states assessed by the number of meals with meat they ate every week. The family on TV was beautiful, all three of them with healthy complexions and toothy, carefree smiles (the young parents I saw on my bus ride to school were those who had to leave at 6 or even earlier in the morning for the two-hour commute and who had to carry their children, half-asleep and often screaming, with them because the only child care they could afford was that provided by their employers). 3

> **Word Power**
> **assessed** measured

The drink itself, steaming hot in an expensive-looking mug that was held between the child's mittened hands, was a vivid orange. The mother talked to the audience as if she were our best friend: "During the cold winter, we need to pay more attention to the health of our family," she said. "That's why I give my husband and my child hot Fruit Treasure for extra warmth and vitamins." The drink's temperature was the only Chinese aspect of the commercial; iced drinks were considered unhealthful and believed to induce stomach disease. 4

> **Word Power**
> **induce** to cause; to bring about

As if the images were not persuasive enough, near the end of the ad an authoritative voice informed us that Tang was the only fruit drink used by NASA for its astronauts—the exact information my father needed to prove his theory that all orange-flavored drinks other than our orange-peel water were made of suspicious chemicals. 5

Until this point, all commercials were short and boring, with catchy phrases like "Our Product Is Loved by People Around the World" flashing on screen. The Tang ad was a revolution in itself: the lifestyle it represented—a more healthful and richer one, a Western luxury—was just 6 starting to become legitimate in China as it was beginning to embrace the West and its capitalism.

Even though Tang was the most expensive fruit drink available, its sales soared. A simple bottle cost 17 yuan, a month's worth of lunch money. A boxed set of two became a status hostess gift. Even the sturdy glass containers that the powder came in were coveted. People used them as tea mugs, the orange label still on, a sign that you could afford the modern American drink. Even my mother had an empty Tang bottle with a snug orange nylon net over it, a present from one of her fellow schoolteachers. She carried it from the office to the classroom and back again as if our family had also consumed a full bottle. 7

> **Word Power**
> **coveted** desired

The truth was, our family had never tasted Tang. Just think of how many oranges we could buy with the money spent on a bottle, my father reasoned. His resistance sent me into a long adolescent melancholy. I was ashamed by our lack of style and our life, with its taste of orange-peel water. I could not wait until I grew up and could have my own Tang-filled life. 8

> **Word Power**
> **melancholy** sadness; depression

To add to my agony, our neighbor's son brought over his first girlfriend, for whom he had just bought a bottle of Tang. He was five years older and a college sophomore; we had nothing in common and had not spoken more than 10 sentences. But this didn't stop me from having a painful crush on him. The beautiful girlfriend opened the Tang in our flat and insisted that we all try it. When it was my turn to scoop some into a glass of water, the fine orange powder almost choked me to tears. It was the first time I had drunk Tang, and the taste was not like real oranges but stronger, as if it were made of the essence of all the oranges I had ever eaten. This would be the love I would seek, a boy unlike my father, a boy who would not blink to buy a bottle of Tang for me. I looked at the beautiful girlfriend and wished to replace her. 9

My agony and jealousy did not last long, however. Two months later the beautiful girlfriend left the boy for an older and richer man. Soon after, the boy's mother came to visit and was still outraged about the Tang. "What a waste of money on someone who didn't become his wife!" she said. 10

"That's how it goes with young people," my mother said. "Once he has a wife, he'll have a better brain and won't throw his money away." 11

"True. He's just like his father. When he courted me, he once invited me to an expensive restaurant and ordered two fish for me. After we were married, he wouldn't even allow two fish for the whole family for one meal!" 12

That was the end of my desire for a Tangy life. I realized that every dream ended with this bland, ordinary existence, where a prince would one day become a man who boiled orange peels for his family. I had not thought about the boy much until I moved to America 10 years later and discovered Tang in a grocery store. It was just how I remembered it—fine powder in a sturdy bottle—but its glamour had lost its gloss because, alas, it was neither expensive nor trendy. To think that all the dreams of my youth were once contained in this commercial drink! I picked up a bottle and then returned it to the shelf. 13

Thinking about the Reading

1. What does Tang represent for Li and for her family and friends? Why do you think they find it so appealing?
2. The drink Li discusses, called Tang in the United States, is called Fruit Treasure in China. Why? What might these two different names suggest to consumers?

*3. What products do you think hold the same fascination for children today that Tang held for Li? Why?

4. What does Li learn from her family's experiences with Tang?

Writing Practice

1. Write about a food that was considered a luxury in your family when you were growing up. Tell about some of the special occasions on which your family ate this special food.
2. In paragraphs 3 through 6, Li discusses the TV commercials for Tang that were shown in China. Think about commercials you have seen that make fairly ordinary products seem glamorous or desirable, and write about how these commercials persuade consumers to buy the products.
3. Part of the appeal of Tang to Li was the fact that it was "exotic" and foreign. What products from other countries have this kind of appeal for you? Why do you think these products are more appealing than familiar American products?

BEFORE AIR CONDITIONING

Arthur Miller

The late Pulitzer Prize–winner Arthur Miller is considered one of America's greatest playwrights. His dramas *Death of a Salesman*, *All My Sons*, and *The Crucible* are classics of the modern theater. In the following essay, Miller recalls his life in New York City in the days before modern air conditioning.

Exactly what year it was I can no longer recall—probably 1927 or '28—there was an extraordinarily hot September, which hung on even after school had started and we were back from our Rockaway Beach bungalow. Every window in New York was open, and on the streets venders manning little carts chopped ice and sprinkled colored sugar over mounds of it for a couple of pennies. We kids would jump onto the back steps of the slow-moving, horse-drawn ice wagons and steal a chip or two; the ice smelled vaguely of manure but cooled palm and tongue. 1

People on West 110th Street, where I lived, were a little too bourgeois to sit out on their fire escapes, but around the corner on 111th and farther uptown mattresses were put out as night fell, and whole families lay on those iron balconies in their underwear. 2

> **Word Power**
> **bourgeois** middle-class and proper in attitudes

Even through the nights, the pall of heat never broke. With a couple of other kids, I would go across 110th to the park and walk among the hundreds of people, singles and families, who slept on the grass, next to their big alarm clocks, which set up a mild cacophony of the seconds passing, one clock's ticks syncopating with another's. Babies cried in the darkness, men's deep voices murmured, and a woman let out an occasional high laugh beside the lake. I can recall only white people spread out on the grass; Harlem began above 116th Street then. 3

Later on, in the Depression thirties, the summers seemed even hotter. Out West, it was the time of the red sun and the dust storms, when whole desiccated farms blew away and sent the Okies,[1] whom Steinbeck immortalized, out on their desperate treks toward the Pacific. My father had a small coat factory on Thirty-ninth Street then, with about a dozen men working sewing machines. Just to watch them handling thick woolen winter coats in that heat was, for me, a torture. The cutters were on piecework, paid by the number of seams they finished, so their lunch break was short—fifteen or twenty minutes. They brought their own food: bunches of radishes, a tomato perhaps, cucumbers, and a jar of thick sour cream, which went into a bowl they kept under the machines. A small loaf of pumpernickel also materialized, which they tore apart and used as a spoon to scoop up the cream and vegetables. 4

> **Word Power**
> **desiccated** dried-up
> **immortalize** to make famous forever
> **trek** a difficult journey

The men sweated a lot in those lofts, and I remember one worker who had a peculiar way of dripping. He was a tiny fellow, who disdained scissors, and, at the end of a seam, always bit off the thread instead of cutting it, so that inch-long strands stuck to his lower lip, and by the end of the day he had a multicolored beard. His sweat poured onto those thread ends and dripped down onto the cloth, which he was constantly blotting with a rag. 5

> **Word Power**
> **disdained** looked down on; despised

1. Oklahoma farmers forced to abandon their farms during the dust storms of the 1930s; subject of the 1939 Pulitzer Prize–winning novel *The Grapes of Wrath* by John Steinbeck.

Given the heat, people smelled, of course, but some smelled a lot worse than others. One cutter in my father's shop was a horse in this respect, and my father, who normally had no sense of smell—no one understood why—claimed that he could smell this man and would address him only from a distance. In order to make as much money as possible, this fellow would start work at half past five in the morning and continue until midnight. He owned Bronx apartment houses and land in Florida and Jersey, and seemed half mad with greed. He had a powerful physique, a very straight spine, a tangle of hair, and a black shadow on his cheeks. He snorted like a horse as he pushed through the cutting machine, following his patterns through some eighteen layers of winter-coat material. One late afternoon, he blinked his eyes hard against the burning sweat as he held down the material with his left hand and pressed the vertical, razor-sharp reciprocating blade with his right. The blade sliced through his index finger at the second joint. Angrily refusing to go to the hospital, he ran tap water over the stump, wrapped his hand in a towel, and went right on cutting, snorting, and stinking. When the blood began to show through the towel's bunched layers, my father pulled the plug on the machine and ordered him to the hospital. But he was back at work the next morning, and worked right through the day and into the evening, as usual, piling up his apartment houses. 6

Word Power

physique the structure or form of a person's body

There were still elevated trains then, along Second, Third, Sixth, and Ninth Avenues, and many of the cars were wooden, with windows that opened. Broadway had open trolleys with no side walls, in which you at least caught the breeze, hot though it was, so that desperate people, unable to endure their apartments, would simply pay a nickel and ride around aimlessly for a couple of hours to cool off. As for Coney Island on weekends, block after block of beach was so jammed with people that it was barely possible to find a space to sit or to put down your book or your hot dog. 7

My first direct contact with an air conditioner came only in the sixties, when I was living in the Chelsea Hotel. The so-called management sent up a machine on casters, which rather aimlessly cooled and sometimes heated the air, relying, as it did, on pitchers of water that one had to pour into it. On the initial filling, it would spray water all over the room, so one had to face it toward the bathroom rather than the bed. 8

A South African gentleman once told me that New York in August was hotter than any place he knew in Africa, yet people here dressed for a northern city. He had wanted to wear shorts but feared that he would be arrested for indecent exposure. 9

High heat created irrational solutions: linen suits that collapsed into deep wrinkles when one bent an arm or a knee, and men's straw hats as stiff as matzohs,[2] which, like some kind of hard yellow flower, bloomed annually all over the city on a certain sacred date—June 1 or so. Those hats dug deep pink creases around men's foreheads, and the wrinkled suits, which were supposedly cooler, had to be pulled down and up and sideways to make room for the body within. 10

The city in summer floated in a daze that moved otherwise sensible people to repeat endlessly the brainless greeting "Hot enough for ya? Ha-ha!" It was like the final joke before the meltdown of the world in a pool of sweat. 11

2. Large, flat, crisp bread eaten during the Jewish holiday of Passover.

Thinking about the Reading

1. The opening paragraphs describe how poor people coped with extreme heat in the 1920s. Was Miller's family poor? Which details in the essay supply the answer to this question?
*2. Why do you suppose New York businessmen in the 1920s wore suits instead of cooler, more comfortable clothes? How has men's summer business wear changed since the days Miller writes about?
3. Why do you think Miller focuses on the man in his father's factory who smelled like a horse? How does Miller feel about this man? Which details reveal his attitude?
4. Why do you think Miller decided to write about life before air conditioning? Does he accomplish his purpose?

Writing Practice

1. Write a description of a day when you had to live without a modern convenience, such as a refrigerator, a computer, or electricity. How did you cope? As an alternative, imagine a day in your life without one of these conveniences, and write about how your life would be affected.
2. Write a description of your workplace. Include descriptions of one or two particular coworkers.
3. Write about a time when you were physically uncomfortable—hot, cold, exhausted, or in pain or discomfort. What caused this situation? What ended it?

37

THE LAST GENERATION TO LIVE ON THE EDGE

Robb Moretti

Is our culture becoming obsessed with protecting children from everyday life? Robb Moretti reminds us that there was a time when children had more fun—even though they lived more dangerous lives than they do today.

> **Word Power**
> **malign** to make harmful statements about someone or something

> **Word Power**
> **diligence** attentive care

My parents are part of what has been labeled the Greatest Generation. I hail from a great generation as well. That's because my peers and I, the oft-maligned baby boomers,[1] came before seat belts, bike helmets, and all things plastic protected children from the hazards of everyday life. We were the last Americans to grow up without a childproof safety net. 1

I know that many of today's protective gadgets prevent kids from getting seriously injured. Looking back, I sometimes wonder how my friends and I survived childhood at all. But I believe that we experienced a kind of freedom that children who came after us have not. 2

I was born in November 1954 and whisked from the hospital during a violent California rainstorm, not in a car seat but in my mother's arms. Since our car didn't have seat belts, we drove commando. 3

As a baby, I was tucked into my crib without a padded bumper guard or a machine that soothed me to sleep with amplified sounds of the ocean. Baby pictures show me smiling while I stuck my big head through the wooden bars. At night my mother swaddled me in warm pajamas—the non-flame-retardant kind. 4

Once I could walk, I was free to roam around the house under the watchful eye of my parents. Unfortunately, their diligence couldn't prevent every mishap. My mom still tells the story of how I learned not to play with electricity by sticking my toy into an open light socket. When my parents needed peace and quiet, they didn't put me in front of the television to watch a "Baby Einstein" video; they plopped me in a chair to watch my mom do housework or cook. 5

My dad drove a monstrous Chrysler that had a rear window ledge large enough to provide a comfortable sleeping area during long drives. As a five-year-old, I loved lying on that ledge, staring at the sky or the stars while we roared down the new California freeways. I was a projectile object waiting to happen! Riding in the front didn't improve my odds much: whenever the car came to an abrupt stop, my mother or father would fling an arm across my chest to keep me from going airborne. 6

During my grade-school years, my mother would often leave my younger sister and me in the car, keys in the ignition and doors unlocked, while she went shopping. When we got home, I would run out to join my friends, with the only rule being to get home by dark. My parents weren't terrified if I was out of their sight. In fact, they enjoyed the silence. 7

Playing at the park was a high-risk adventure for my friends and me. The jungle gym was a heavy gray apparatus with metal bars, screws, and hooks. On a hot day the metallic surface of the sliding board would burn our behinds. A great afternoon at the park usually meant coming home with blisters on our hands, a bump or two on the melon, and the obligatory skinned knee. 8

1. The generation born between 1946 and 1964.

I rode my red Schwinn Stingray without wearing a bike helmet; my Davy Crockett cap protected me from serious head injury. Although I did not have the benefit of a crossing guard at the blind intersection I had to traverse to get to school, I was sure the snapping sound made by the baseball cards stuck in my spokes alerted the oncoming traffic to my presence. 9

Every school day my mother packed my Jetsons lunchbox with a tunafish sandwich, which we found out later often contained high levels of mercury and a dolphin or two. Also stuffed in my lunchbox was a pint of whole chocolate milk and a package of Hostess Twinkies or cupcakes. 10

Despite our high-fat, high-sugar diets, my friends and I were not out of shape. Maybe that was because we worked so hard in phys-ed class every day. Occasionally our teacher pushed us so far that some poor kid would throw up his lunch. 11

In the afternoons we all played in a school-sponsored baseball league. We didn't wear plastic batting helmets or cups, and we hit pitched balls instead of hitting off a plastic tee. Worst of all, we received trophies or medals only if our team won the championship. 12

Last February, Americans were captivated by the skeleton event at the 2002 Winter Olympics. But thirty-five years earlier, my junior-high friends and I had invented our own version of the sport. We'd roar down steep Bay Area streets on a flexible sled with wheels instead of runners. Like the Olympians, we held our chins just inches above the ground. You don't see kids today with two false front teeth nearly as often as you did in 1967. 13

We baby boomers may not have weathered the Depression or stormed the beaches at Normandy. But we were the last generation to live on the edge and, I believe, to have fun! 14

Thinking about the Reading

1. What examples does Moretti give to support his claim that his generation lived "on the edge" (paragraph 14)?
2. How were Moretti's childhood experiences different from those of today's children? How do you explain those differences?
3. Do you agree with Moretti that his life "on the edge" was worth the risk, or do you believe that the dangers of his generation's behavior outweighed the benefits?

*4. How were Moretti's childhood experiences like and unlike your own? Do you think he is correct in saying that his generation was "the last generation to live on the edge" (paragraph 14)?

Writing Practice

1. Explain in what sense you lived "on the edge" when you were a child—and in what sense you did not.
2. What risks do you experience as part of your adult life? Do you see these risks as necessary? Do you seek them out? Do you think you live "on the edge"?
3. Do you believe today's parents are overprotective? Do you think children should be given fewer rules? Write a letter to the editor of a parenting magazine in which you support your position with examples from your own experience.

37

WHY WE NEED ANIMAL EXPERIMENTATION

Thuy Nguyen

Student writer Thuy Nguyen argues that animal experimentation is necessary to improve medical technology and thus to save human lives. As you read her essay, note the specific examples she supplies to support her points.

1 With our advanced medical technology today, medicine has helped save many lives. The advances in medical technology that have saved these lives, for the most part, have been developed from animal experimentation. However, some people have claimed that animal experimentation is cruel and should not be continued. In my opinion, because medical research is so dependent on it, animal experimentation should be continued. It provides preventive measures to protect humans against getting diseases, helps discover cures and treatments for diseases, and helps surgeons to perfect the surgical techniques that are needed to save human lives.

2 First of all, animal experimentation provides preventive measures to protect humans from getting diseases. With the help of medical research on animals, scientists have found useful applications of vaccines to prevent many diseases. For example, the vaccines for polio, typhoid, diphtheria, tetanus, tuberculosis, measles, mumps, and rubella were all developed through animal experimentation. In addition, the principle of sterilization came out of Pasteur's[1] discovery, through animal experimentation, that microbes cause diseases. As a result, nowadays, medical professionals know that it is extremely important to sterilize medical tools such as gloves and syringes in order to keep them bacteria-free and to prevent patients from getting infections. Also, from experiments on rats, the connection between smoking and lung cancer was conclusively proved. This led many people to quit smoking and avoid getting cancer.

> **Word Power**
> **sterilization** the process of making something free of germs
> **microbe** a germ

3 Besides leading to preventive measures, animal experimentation also leads to the discovery of cures and treatments for many diseases. For instance, it has helped with the treatment of diabetic patients who are in need of insulin. Through experiments on cows and pigs, researchers have found the usefulness of cows' and pigs' insulin for treating diabetes. In addition, many drugs discovered through animal tests have been proven to cure ill patients. For example, a number of antibiotics, such as penicillin and sulfonamides, which were found from animal experimentation, help cure many infections. Also, many antihypertension medicines, which were developed in experiments on cats, help control blood pressure in hypertensive patients. Similarly, anticancer drugs were developed from tests on rats and dogs.

> **Word Power**
> **hypertensive** having high blood pressure

4 Besides providing preventive measures to protect humans from getting diseases and helping discover cures and treatments for many diseases, animal experimentation also helps surgeons to perfect the surgical techniques needed to save human lives. Surgeons have always been searching for better techniques to make surgery safer and more effective for their patients. One good way to perfect these techniques is to practice them on animals. From experiments on cats, researchers have found suturing techniques for transplants. Similarly, techniques for open heart surgery were

> **Word Power**
> **suture** to use fiber to close up wounds or to connect two parts of the body

1. Louis Pasteur (1822–1895) was a French chemist.

perfected through many years of animal experimentation. Animal research programs have also helped surgeons to refine their techniques for kidney dialysis needed by patients with kidney failure.

Animal experimentation should be continued because it provides pre- 5
ventive measures to protect humans against diseases, helps to discover cures and treatments for diseases, and helps surgeons to perfect their surgical techniques. Therefore, animal experimentation is vital for the medical research that saves human lives.

Thinking about the Reading

1. What are the three points Thuy Nguyen makes to develop her argument that animal experimentation is essential to medical research?
2. What does the first paragraph of this essay accomplish? Where does Thuy first state each of her reasons for continuing animal experimentation? Where does she support each of these points? What does the last paragraph achieve?

*3. Are the examples Thuy presents convincing? Does she present enough support? Do any of the following elements appear in this essay?

- An explanation of what animal experimentation means
- Expert opinions on the subject of animal experimentation
- A response to possible arguments *against* Thuy's point of view

If not, how would the addition of these elements improve the essay?

*4. Do you agree with Thuy's position on animal experimentation? What objections do you have? Try to support your position with facts and examples from your reading and experience.

Writing Practice

1. Revise Thuy's essay to give it more personal appeal for readers. For example, try adding one or two paragraphs about specific people who could be helped by animal experimentation.
2. Write an editorial that takes a position *against* the use of animal experimentation. Consider some of the following points made by opponents of animal experimentation.
   - The same medical results could be obtained by means other than animal experimentation.
   - Some animal experimentation is not necessary and could be eliminated.
   - Animal experimentation is not humane.
3. Choose an issue that is important to you, and write an essay supporting your position on that issue. Use facts and examples from your reading and experience to support your point of view.

37

HOW TO STOP A CAR WITH NO BRAKES

Joshua Piven and David Borgenicht

In this instructional essay from *The Worst-Case Scenario Handbook*, Joshua Piven and David Borgenicht explain how to avoid catastrophe in a car with no brakes. Piven and Borgenicht are the authors of the best-selling book *The Worst-Case Scenario Handbook* (1999), whose success sparked a series of *Worst-Case Scenario* books as well as a reality television show.

1. Begin pumping the brake pedal and keep pumping it. You may be able to build up enough pressure in the braking system to slow down a bit, or even stop completely. If you have anti-lock brakes, you do not normally pump them—but if your brakes have failed, this may work. 1

2. Do not panic—relax and steer the car smoothly. Cars will often safely corner at speeds much higher than you realize or are used to driving. The rear of the car may slip; steer evenly, being careful not to over-correct. 2

3. Shift the car into the lowest gear possible and let the engine and transmission slow you down. 3

4. Pull the emergency brake—but not too hard. Pulling too hard on the emergency brake will cause the rear wheels to lock, and the car to spin around. Use even, constant pressure. In most cars, the emergency brake (also known as the hand brake or parking brake) is cable operated and serves as a fail-safe brake that should still work even when the rest of the braking system has failed. The car should slow down and, in combination with the lower gear, will eventually stop. 4

5. If you are running out of room, try a "bootlegger's turn." Yank the emergency brake hard while turning the wheel a quarter turn in either direction—whichever is safer. This will make the car spin 180 degrees. If you were heading downhill, this spin will head you back uphill, allowing you to slow down. 5

6. If you have room, swerve the car back and forth across the road. Making hard turns at each side of the road will decrease your speed even more. 6

7. If you come up behind another car, use it to help you stop. Blow your horn, flash your lights, and try to get the driver's attention. If you hit 7

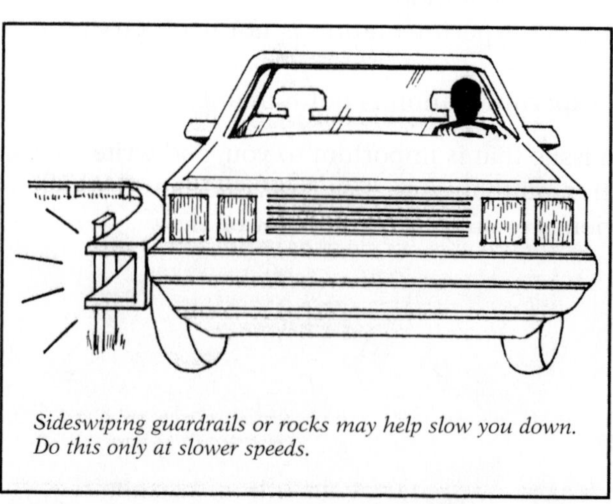

Sideswiping guardrails or rocks may help slow you down. Do this only at slower speeds.

the car, be sure to hit it square, bumper to bumper, so you do not knock the other car off the road. This is an extremely dangerous maneuver: It works best if the vehicle in front of you is larger than yours—a bus or truck is ideal—and if both vehicles are traveling at similar speeds. You do not want to crash into a much slower-moving or stopped vehicle, however.

8 8. Look for something to help stop you. A flat or uphill road that intersects with the road you are on, a field, or a fence will slow you further but not stop you suddenly. Scraping the side of your car against a guardrail is another option. Avoid trees and wooden telephone poles: They do not yield as readily.

9 9. Do not attempt to sideswipe oncoming cars.

10 10. If none of the above steps has enabled you to stop and you are about to go over a cliff, try to hit something that will slow you down before you go over. This strategy will also leave a clue to others that someone has gone over the edge. But since very few cliffs are sheer drops, you may fall just several feet and then stop.

Word Power
readily easily

Word Power
sheer steep; almost vertical

Thinking about the Reading

1. Because the steps in the process that Piven and Borgenicht outline are numbered, they do not include transitions to indicate the order of the steps or the relationship between one step and the next. Can you suggest some transitional words and phrases that could be added?
2. What warnings and reminders do the writers include? Do you think they need additional cautions to guide readers?
3. Do you think the picture in this essay is necessary? Can you suggest other pictures that might be more effective?

*4. Do you think the writers should have omitted step number 10? Why or why not?

Writing Practice

1. Write an introduction and a conclusion for "How to Stop a Car with No Brakes."
2. List ten steps that would help readers survive a different difficult or dangerous situation. Then, expand the items on your list into an essay, adding an introduction and a conclusion.
3. Write an essay directed at an urban audience in which you explain a process that is familiar to residents of rural areas. Or, write an essay for a rural audience in which you explain a process that is familiar to city dwellers.

37

THE LITTLE PRETZEL LADY

Sara Price

For some children, adult responsibility comes early in life. Student writer Sara Price recounts her experience as a ten-year-old working a Saturday job with her brother. For three years, to help their financially strapped family, Sara and her brother sold pretzels in a local shopping center.

When I was ten years old, selling pretzels at the corner of a shopping center was not my favorite weekend activity. Unfortunately, however, I had no alternative. My father had recently been injured on the job, and we had been experiencing severe financial difficulties. His disability payments and my mother's salary were not enough to support four children and my grandparents. When my parents could not pay our monthly mortgage, the bank threatened to take our house. 1

Knowing we had to find jobs to help, my older brother and I asked the local soft pretzel dealer to give us work on Saturdays. At first he refused, saying we were too young. But we simply would not take no for an answer because our parents desperately needed financial help. When we persisted, the pretzel dealer agreed to let us start the next week. In return for his kindness, my brother and I agreed to work faithfully for the next three years. 2

> **Word Power**
> **persist** to continue to do something despite setbacks

On the first Saturday morning, my brother and I reported promptly to our positions in front of the Cool-Rite appliance shop at the Academy Plaza shopping center. When Tom, our dealer, arrived with three hundred pretzels, he set up the stand and gave us instructions to sell each pretzel for a quarter, and five for a dollar. Then, Tom wished us luck and said he would be back later to pick up the table and the money. The arrangement with him was that we would get one-third of the total sales. 3

On that first Saturday, after selling our three hundred pretzels, my brother and I earned ten dollars each. (We also received a two-dollar tip from a friendly man who bought fifteen pretzels.) Our first day was considered a good one because we sold out by 4 p.m. However, the days that followed were not always as smooth as the first. When the weather was bad, meaning rain or snow, sales decreased; there were times when we had to stay as late as 7 p.m. until the last pretzel was sold. 4

To my regular customers, I was the little pretzel lady. But to my classmates, I was the target of humiliation. My worst nightmare came true when they found out that I ran a pretzel stand. Many of the boys made fun of me by calling out nasty names and harassing me for free pretzels. It was extremely embarrassing to see them walk by and stare while I stood like a helpless beggar on the street. I came to dread weekends and hate the sight of pretzels. But I was determined not to give up because I had a family that needed support and a three-year promise to fulfill. With that in mind, I continued to work. 5

Although winter was the best season for sales, I especially disliked standing in the teeth-chattering cold. I still remember that stinging feeling when the harsh wind blew against my cheeks. In order to survive the hours of shivering, I usually wore two or three pairs of socks and extra-thick clothing. Many times, I felt like a lonesome, leafless tree rooted to one spot and unable to escape from the bitter cold of winter. 6

The worst incident of my pretzel career occurred when I was selling alone because my brother was sick. A pair of teenage boys came up to the stand, called me offensive names, and squirted mustard all over the pretzels. My instant reaction was total shock, and before I could do anything else, they quickly ran away. A few minutes later, I discarded the pretzels, desperately fighting back the tears. I felt helpless and angry because I could not understand their actions. 7

> **Word Power**
> **offensive** hurtful; disagreeable; unpleasant

The three years seemed like forever, but finally they were over. Even though selling pretzels on the street was the worst job I ever had, I was grateful for it. The money I earned each Saturday accumulated over the three years and helped my family. Selling pretzels also taught me many important values, such as responsibility, teamwork, independence, and appreciation for hard-earned money. Today, as I pass the pretzel vendors on my way to school, I think of a time not too long ago when I was the little pretzel lady. 8

> **Word Power**
> **accumulate** to gather or pile up little by little

Thinking about the Reading

1. What emotions did you experience as you read "The Little Pretzel Lady"? Which parts of the essay caused these emotions?
2. Children are often cruel to one another. What do you think caused the cruelty that Sara Price experienced?
3. Sara says that she sometimes felt like "a lonesome, leafless tree rooted to one spot and unable to escape from the bitter cold of winter" (paragraph 6). Explain how this image suits Sara's situation.
*4. Do you think that Sara's experience as a "pretzel lady" was more hurtful than beneficial to her? Give reasons to support your answer.

Writing Practice

1. Write about a time in your childhood when you were teased or bullied by other children.
2. Write about the "little pretzel lady" and her experiences from the point of view of a clerk in the Cool-Rite appliance shop who watches the two children sell pretzels every Saturday.
3. Write about an experience you had at work that made you like or dislike your job. Be sure to include details about the workplace, your job responsibilities, the other people involved in the situation, and any conversations you remember.

THE DOG ATE MY DISK, AND OTHER TALES OF WOE

Carolyn Foster Segal

Carolyn Foster Segal, associate professor of English at Cedar Crest College in Pennsylvania, has heard practically every student excuse for handing in late papers. In this humorous essay, she divides student excuses into categories. This article appeared in *The Chronicle of Higher Education*, a periodical for college teachers.

> **Word Power**
> **woe** sadness
> **feline** (noun) a member of the cat family; (adjective) catlike

Taped to the door of my office is a cartoon that features a cat explaining to his feline teacher, "The dog ate my homework." It is intended as a gently humorous reminder to my students that I will not accept excuses for late work, and it, like the lengthy warning on my syllabus, has had absolutely no effect. With a show of energy and creativity that would be admirable if applied to the (missing) assignments in question, my students persist, week after week, semester after semester, year after year, in offering excuses about why their work is not ready. Those reasons fall into several broad categories: the family, the best friend, the evils of dorm life, the evils of technology, and the totally bizarre. 1

> **Word Power**
> **veracity** truthfulness

The Family The death of the grandfather/grandmother is, of course, the grandmother of all excuses. What heartless teacher would dare to question a student's grief or veracity? What heartless student would lie, wishing death on a revered family member, just to avoid a deadline? Creative students may win extra extensions (and days off) with a little careful planning and fuller plot development, as in the sequence of "My grandfather/grandmother is sick"; "Now my grandfather/grandmother is in the hospital"; and finally, "We could all see it coming—my grandfather/grandmother is dead." 2

> **Word Power**
> **conjure up** to bring to mind

Another favorite excuse is "the family emergency," which (always) goes like this: "There was an emergency at home, and I had to help my family." It's a lovely sentiment, one that conjures up images of Louisa May Alcott's little women rushing off with baskets of food and copies of *Pilgrim's Progress*, but I do not understand why anyone would turn to my most irresponsible students in times of trouble. 3

The Best Friend This heartwarming concern for others extends beyond the family to friends, as in, "My best friend was up all night and I had to (a) stay up with her in the dorm, (b) drive her to the hospital, or (c) drive to her college because (1) her boyfriend broke up with her, (2) she was throwing up blood [no one catches a cold anymore; everyone throws up blood], or (3) her grandfather/grandmother died." 4

> **Word Power**
> **adjunct** an instructor at a college or university who is not a permanent staff member; any temporary employee

At one private university where I worked as an adjunct, I heard an interesting spin that incorporated the motifs of both best friend and dead relative: "My best friend's mother killed herself." One has to admire the cleverness here: A mysterious woman in the prime of her life has allegedly committed suicide, and no professor can prove otherwise! And I admit I was moved, until finally I had to point out to my students that it was amazing how the simple act of my assigning a topic for a paper seemed to drive large numbers of otherwise happy and healthy middle-aged women to their deaths. I was careful to make that point during an off week, during which no deaths were reported. 5

The Evils of Dorm Life These stories are usually fairly predictable; almost always feature the evil roommate or hallmate, with my student in 6 the role of the innocent victim; and can be summed up as follows: My roommate, who is a horrible person, likes to party, and I, who am a good person, cannot concentrate on my work when he or she is partying. Variations include stories about the two people next door who were running around and crying loudly last night because (a) one of them had boyfriend/girlfriend problems; (b) one of them was throwing up blood; or (c) someone, somewhere, died. A friend of mine in graduate school had a student who claimed that his roommate attacked him with a hammer. That, in fact, was a true story; it came out in court when the bad roommate was tried for killing his grandfather.

The Evils of Technology The computer age has revolutionized the 7
student story, inspiring almost as many new excuses as it has Internet businesses. Here are just a few electronically enhanced explanations:

- The computer wouldn't let me save my work.
- The printer wouldn't print.
- The printer wouldn't print this disk.
- The printer wouldn't give me time to proofread.
- The printer made a black line run through all my words, and I know you can't read this, but do you still want it, or wait, here, take my disk. File name? I don't know what you mean.
- I swear I attached it.
- It's my roommate's computer, and she usually helps me, but she had to go to the hospital because she was throwing up blood.
- I did write to the newsgroup, but all my messages came back to me.
- I just found out that all my other newsgroup messages came up under a different name. I just want you to know that its really me who wrote all those messages, you can tel which ones our mine because I didnt use the spelcheck! But it was yours truely :) Anyway, just in case you missed those messages or dont belief its my writting. I'll repeat what I sad: I thought the last movie we watched in clas was borring.

The Totally Bizarre I call the first story "The Pennsylvania Chain 8
Saw Episode." A commuter student called to explain why she had missed my morning class. She had gotten up early so that she would be wide awake for class. Having a bit of extra time, she walked outside to see her neighbor, who was cutting some wood. She called out to him, and he waved back to her with the saw. Wouldn't you know it, the safety catch wasn't on or was broken, and the blade flew right out of the saw and across his lawn and over her fence and across her yard and severed a tendon in her right hand. So she was calling me from the hospital, where she was waiting for surgery. Luckily, she reassured me, she had remembered to bring her paper and a stamped envelope (in a plastic bag, to avoid bloodstains) along with her in the ambulance, and a nurse was mailing everything to me even as we spoke.

That wasn't her first absence. In fact, this student had missed most of 9
the class meetings, and I had already recommended that she withdraw from the course. Now I suggested again that it might be best if she dropped the class. I didn't harp on the absences (what if even some of this story were true?). I did mention that she would need time to recuperate and that making up so much missed work might be difficult. "Oh, no," she said, "I can't drop this course. I had been planning to go on to medical school and become a surgeon, but since I won't be able to operate because

Word Power
harp on to repeat over and over again

of my accident, I'll have to major in English, and this course is more important than ever to me." She did come to the next class, wearing—as evidence of her recent trauma—a bedraggled Ace bandage on her left hand.

You may be thinking that nothing could top that excuse, but in fact I 10
have one more story, provided by the same student, who sent me a letter to explain why her final assignment would be late. While recuperating from her surgery, she had begun corresponding on the Internet with a man who lived in Germany. After a one-week, whirlwind Web romance, they had agreed to meet in Rome, to rendezvous (her phrase) at the papal Easter Mass. Regrettably, the time of her flight made it impossible for her to attend class, but she trusted that I—just this once—would accept late work if the pope wrote a note.

Word Power

rendezvous (verb) to meet at a prearranged place and time; (noun) a meeting of this kind

Thinking about the Reading

1. What categories of excuses does Segal identify? Can you think of others she does not mention?

*2. **Sarcastic** remarks mean the opposite of what they say and are usually meant to mock or poke fun at someone or something. In what ways does Segal use sarcasm? Give some examples.

*3. Do you think this essay is funny? Do you find it offensive in any way? Explain.

4. Would you be interested in reading a serious essay on Segal's topic? Why or why not?

Writing Practice

1. Write about the strangest excuse you have ever been given by someone for not doing something he or she was supposed to do. Explain the circumstances of this excuse in a humorous manner.
2. Discuss one of the following topics (or a similar topic of your own choice).
   - Ways to turn down a date
   - Types of behavior by a baby, child, or pet
   - Types of students at your school
3. Write a letter to Carolyn Foster Segal explaining why your English paper will be late. Admit that you have read her essay about various categories of student excuses, but insist that *your* excuse is true.

TAKE-OUT RESTAURANT

Kimsohn Tang

In this essay, student writer Kimsohn Tang examines the life of her Uncle Meng, the owner of a Chinese take-out restaurant. As Kim describes the stresses and risks of this demanding job, she asks whether the money he makes is worth the problems that Uncle Meng faces.

My Uncle Meng owns the New Phoenix Take-Out Restaurant at the corner of Main Street and Landfair Avenue in North Philadelphia, a dangerous place. Words of profanity and various kinds of graffiti are written on the wall outside his restaurant. On his windows are black bars just like those on the windows of prisons. Inside his take-out, bulletproof glass separates the customers' area from the workers' area. Every day, Uncle Meng works in his restaurant with his wife and a cook. He must prepare the food, carry it to the cooking area, take orders, run back and forth to get things, cook the food, and satisfy his customers. Although he earns a decent salary, his job not only takes him away from his family but is also stressful, hard, and dangerous. 1

> **Word Power**
> **profanity** offensive language

Uncle Meng works long hours, from 11 a.m. to midnight. He is constantly working. Even before he opens the restaurant, he has to prepare the food by getting the raw food from the wholesaler, marinating and putting bread crumbs on fifty pounds of chicken, coloring rice, making soup, and carrying heavy pots and pans of food to the cooking area. After he opens the take-out, the customers come in, and now Uncle Meng has to take orders; cook the food; put the food in containers, place sodas, drinks and food in bags; and hand the customers the bags through the little hole in the bulletproof glass. Throughout the day and into the night, Uncle Meng continues to work. Even at midnight, after the take-out is closed, his work is not finished because he has to clean up the place. 2

> **Word Power**
> **wholesaler** a person who sells large amounts of a product to stores or individuals, who then resell it
> **marinate** to let meat, fish, or vegetables soak in a sauce to make them more flavorful or tender

Because of his long working hours, Uncle Meng has little time to spend with his family, especially his two children, a sixteen-year-old daughter and a thirteen-year-old son. Most of his time is spent in his restaurant. The only time he is free is on Sunday, when the restaurant is closed; this is the only time he and his family actually spend together. On regular school days, if he has time, Uncle Meng brings his children to and from school; otherwise, his sister or one of his other relatives takes them. When his children get home, they stay in their apartment above the take-out and only come down once in a while. Because Uncle Meng is so busy, he does not even have time to help his children with their homework. 3

Having little time to spend with his family is not the worst thing about his job; the stress from customers is even worse. Customers will yell out, "Man, where's my food? Why is it taking so long? I can't wait all day, you know!" Uncle Meng must have a lot of patience with the customers and not yell back at them. If the customers complain about getting different food from what they have ordered, Uncle Meng has to calm them down and make another dish for them. In addition, the customers are always asking for various things, such as more forks, spoons, or napkins, which is hard for Uncle Meng to handle. When a customer has a question pertaining to a dish on the menu, Uncle Meng also has to explain what ingredients are in the dish. He has to satisfy the customers and give them what they want, or else they will give him more trouble. 4

> **Word Power**
> **pertaining to** relating to or having to do with

Uncle Meng's working conditions are the worst aspect of his job. Because the cooking area is always hot, Uncle Meng is never comfortable. The working area is also a dangerous place to be in; if he is not cautious while frying, he can get burns from the splattering oil. Lifting heavy pans while stir-frying, which requires a great amount of strength, causes Uncle Meng a lot of pain in his arms and wrists. In addition, because he has to stand on his feet all day and run all over the take-out to get food, he often gets pains in his legs. By the time the take-out is closed, Uncle Meng is always exhausted. 5

Uncle Meng works long hard hours at difficult, physical labor. Although the take-out brings in a lot of money, it is a stressful and risky environment. Money is worthless compared to family and health. Even though money can buy many things, it cannot buy strong family relationships or good health. Working in a take-out, therefore, is not a desirable job. 6

Thinking about the Reading

1. According to Kimsohn Tang, how do job stresses harm Uncle Meng's health? Give examples.
2. In what ways is Uncle Meng's job dangerous? Consider both the working conditions at the restaurant and the neighborhood in which it is located.
3. How does Uncle Meng's job affect his family life? Give examples.

*4. Why do you think Tang chose to write about her Uncle Meng? What does she think of her uncle's way of life?

Writing Practice

1. Imagine that you are Uncle Meng's teenage son or daughter. Write a letter to your father telling him how you feel about the sacrifices he is making by working at the restaurant.
2. Have you ever worked at a job that was stressful or dangerous? Give examples of the stresses and dangers and the effect they had on you. If you have never held a job that fits this description, write about a friend's or relative's job.
3. Tang states, "Money is worthless compared to family and health" (paragraph 6). Explain why you agree or disagree with this statement. Give examples from your own experience and observation of the world to support your position.

A "GOOD" AMERICAN CITIZEN

Linda S. Wallace

What is patriotism, and how should we demonstrate it? In this article, media consultant and former journalist Linda Wallace uses the controversy surrounding the war in Iraq to explore the role of dissent in the American system of government.

Recently, I passed an antiwar protest in Center City Philadelphia, a mix of young and old, office workers and students, patting drums to the rhythm of their rap. A moment later, a pickup truck filled with guys clad in bluejeans drove by, waving the American flag and yelling, "Go, America!" Passers-by cringed as they tensely viewed the scene and caught a glimpse of the hundred police officers monitoring the drama from across the street. 1

This "we versus we" conflict is uncomfortable. Even U.S. leaders seem more focused on middle ground rather than finding ways to disagree more productively. But there is a critical conversation America has yet to have with itself. And with the ongoing dissension over the war with Iraq, it appears that now is the perfect time. 2

Definitions of what qualifies as national loyalty have always shifted as American society has diversified and matured. A person who is viewed by many as a troublemaker, such as Dr. Martin Luther King Jr., just might end up an honored U.S. hero. 3

So what defines a patriot, exactly? Is it a person who supports the government through right and wrong in a war or a crisis or the person who disagrees loudly and engages in lawful protest? Are those who push us all to conform and unite as one country the folks who most love this nation, or is it those who embrace differences and challenge fellow citizens' assumptions in order to reorder society and find hidden flaws? 4

> **Word Power**
>
> **patriot** someone who loves and supports his or her country

There is no national handbook—at least not yet—that details how to be a good American. Some would prefer a manual filled with "dos" and "don'ts" to point to and say, "I'm the real deal, and you are the pretender." 5

So it seems for the moment, each person is left to follow his or her own set of personal rules regarding patriotism, even though those lists are bound to disagree. The first few rules on my own list are simple: 6

1. Vote in every federal, state, and local election even when you can't find one candidate you like.
2. Learn the names of elected officials, and email them periodically to offer insight. (Most of mine are white, and I am African American.)
3. Attend community or council meetings, and stay abreast of public policy and key issues by reading newspapers, listening to the radio, or watching the evening TV news.
4. Model the behavior you want to see in others: Put democratic principles into practice by challenging bias and discrimination in everyday life.

The next rules, which came with wisdom and experience, require a bit more effort and resolve:

5. Respect the rights of other Americans to disagree with you.
6. Accept that your point of view is not the only legitimate perspective.
7. Tolerate dissent.

As I watch American commentators condemn fellow citizens for expressing views contrary to the government, it saddens me. Some people see conformity and unity as building blocks of strength, but I tend to view them as indicators that fear or intimidation is stifling helpful dissent. I am like the CEO who prefers to identify the drawbacks before launching a new product rather than wait until after it hits the stores. The country that is able to identify the weakness of its own arguments, and make strategic adjustments, is more likely to win over its opponents. 7

> **Word Power**
> **dissent** a difference of opinion; a disagreement

Some Americans will look at these scenes of antiwar protesters standing off against those who support the war effort and shake their heads. They may see a nation in turmoil, but I see a country with the will and savvy to tolerate dissent. Those who think that the opinion of the majority is somehow sacred might wish to revisit history. Our Founding Fathers decided to create a republic instead of a democracy because many feared the majority would not, could not, rule without eventually becoming oppressive and unfair. 8

> **Word Power**
> **savvy** practical knowledge

Wisely, they opted for a republic, once described by John Adams as "an empire of laws, not of men." Therefore, the protection of the laws that safeguard liberty and free expression is more critical to us than any national consensus ever will be. 9

> **Word Power**
> **consensus** a position reached by group agreement

The law protects free speech, and those who seek to silence protesters in the name of patriotism might remember these words that Thomas Jefferson wrote in 1815: 10

> Difference of opinion leads to enquiry, and enquiry to truth; and that, I am sure, is the ultimate and sincere object of us both. We both value too much the freedom of opinion sanctioned by our Constitution, not to cherish its exercise even where in opposition to ourselves.

If we decide that sincere patriots are those who rally behind the government, then we have suppressed the law and sidestepped principles in order to gain a temporary accord. That's not only unpatriotic; it's downright dangerous. 11

Thinking about the Reading

1. What is the "critical conversation" that Wallace believes "America has yet to have with itself" (paragraph 2)?
*2. In paragraph 4, Wallace asks a series of questions. Answer those questions.
*3. How does Wallace define a patriot? Do you agree with her definition? Do you agree with all seven of her rules?
4. Why does Wallace begin her essay by describing an antiwar protest? How does she use this protest to support her position?

Writing Practice

1. Using the seven rules that Wallace lists in paragraph 6 as a starting point, write a pamphlet *in your own words* for middle-school students (or for new American citizens). Call your pamphlet "How to Be a Good American Citizen." (If you like, you may add rules of your own to Wallace's list.)

2. Choose one of Wallace's seven rules, and write about an incident you witnessed or experienced to illustrate the importance of the rule.
3. Choose an issue on which you and a friend, parent, or coworker strongly disagree. Interview the person whose position differs from yours, and then express your support for his or her position.

THE ONLINE ALTERNATIVE

Marc Williams

As more and more schools offer online courses, students must think carefully about the costs and benefits of enrolling in them. In the following essay, student writer Marc Williams compares and contrasts an online class and a traditional class.

Last semester, my friend Jason and I decided to sign up for a course called Twentieth-Century African-American Literature. We were both interested in the course's subject, and we thought we could study for exams together, share our notes, and maybe even buy just one set of books. When the course schedule came out, I realized I had a problem. The course was scheduled for Monday, Wednesday, and Friday at noon—a convenient time for Jason but impossible for me because I was working the lunch shift in the cafeteria. When I told my advisor my problem, she had an idea: she suggested that I take the course online. This seemed like a good idea, so I signed up. However, when Jason and I compared notes at the end of the semester, I realized that online learning was not for me. 1

> **Word Power**
> **online** connected to the Internet

In some ways, the two courses were a lot alike. For example, Jason and I had the same teacher and the same writing assignments. We had to read the same short stories, plays, poems, and articles, as well as *Invisible Man*, a novel by Ralph Ellison. The course materials were posted on the course's Web site for both traditional and online students. And, of course, we would both take exams (although mine would be given in the campus testing center, not given in class). According to the course syllabus (also the same), our final grades would depend on the same thing: papers, exams, and class participation. Also, we both got three credits for the course. Despite these similarities, the two courses were very different from day one. 2

On the first day of his class, Jason met the instructor and the other students taking the course. The students talked about other literature classes they had taken, works by African-American writers they had read, and their experiences with writing papers about literature. They also asked questions about the syllabus and the course materials. My introduction to the course was different. The instructor emailed me information about how the online course would work. She set up a bulletin board on Blackboard, and students in the class could introduce themselves there and tell why they were taking the course. (This bulletin board would stay up all term so we could talk informally about the class if we wanted to.) So, the first thing I did was log on and write a little bit about myself. Then, I read what other students had written. Although it was possible to chat with other students, I didn't want to take the time. 3

> **Word Power**
> **log on** to identify oneself on a computer by entering a username and password

> **Word Power**
> **posted** entered information online

As the semester continued, I realized that the two courses were run very differently. In Jason's class, the instructor gave short lectures about various writers and works and provided historical background when necessary. She also answered questions as they came up and helped move the class discussion along. In my course, the instructor posted a lecture every week, along with a set of questions. Our assignment was to read the lecture material and email her our answers to the questions. Class "discussion" was also different. In Jason's class, students exchanged ideas in person. In my class, everything happened online. The teacher posted questions for online discussion, and then the students in the class would all log on at a prearranged time and have a discussion about the posted ques- 4 tions. We could also ask questions about the assigned readings during this time.

Contact with the instructor was also different. For Jason, contact was whatever he wanted it to be. He could email the instructor, drop in or call during her office hours, or schedule an appointment. For online students, contact was more limited. Although we could set up face-to-face conferences, this wasn't encouraged. So, I was limited to emailing and to phone calls during the two hours a week that were set aside for online students. When I needed face-to-face help with my papers, I went to the Writing Center. 5

The hardest thing for me to get used to was the lack of real interaction with other students. Jason set up study groups with other students. In class, they watched and discussed a DVD of Alice Walker's short story "Everyday Use," acted out scenes from *A Raisin in the Sun*, read Yusef Komunyakaa's poetry out loud, and critiqued drafts of other students' papers. Although some of these things were also possible in my online class, it just wasn't the same. Arranging an online discussion with other students in real time was hard because of our different school and work schedules. We could watch films on our own, but we couldn't all discuss the film together right after we saw it. And I missed the chance to see other students' physical reactions and expressions and hear their voices. 6

At the end of the semester, when Jason and I talked about our classes, it was easy for me to see the positive side of my online course. The most important advantage was convenience. Instead of having to attend classes during specific hours each week, I could log on whenever I had time. Still, I didn't feel I got as much out of my course as Jason got out of his. In regular classes, when I have something to say, I raise my hand and say it, and I get instant feedback from other students and from the instructor. In the online class, I usually had to wait to get an email reply to a posting. I also missed being able to drop by the instructor's office to talk about a problem. Most of all, I missed the chance to get to know other students in the class by working with them in study groups, collaborating with them on projects, or talking to them informally outside of class. For me, taking the online class was definitely worth it because this was the only way I could take the class at all. But I don't think I'll do it again. 7

Thinking about the Reading

1. Where does Marc Williams discuss the *similarities* between online and traditional courses?
2. List the differences Marc identifies between online and traditional courses.
3. What advantages does Marc's course have over Jason's more traditional course? What disadvantages does Marc identify?

*4. Can you think of advantages of online courses that Marc doesn't mention? Can you think of additional disadvantages?

Writing Practice

1. Write an email to Marc's instructor suggesting ways to improve her online course.
2. Imagine that the writing course you are now taking were conducted online. How would it be different?
3. Interview a few students who have taken online courses, and write a summary of their views on the advantages and disadvantages of this kind of learning.

THE TRANSACTION

William Zinsser

William Zinsser has written many articles and books on improving writing and study skills. He has also had a long career as a professional newspaper and magazine writer, drama and film critic, and author of nonfiction books on subjects ranging from jazz to baseball. This excerpt is from his book *On Writing Well: An Informal Guide to Writing Nonfiction*.

Word Power
transaction an exchange or transfer of goods, services, or money; an exchange of thoughts and feelings

A school in Connecticut once held "a day devoted to the arts," and I was asked if I would come and talk about writing as a vocation. When I arrived, I found that a second speaker had been invited—Dr. Brock (as I'll call him), a surgeon who had recently begun to write and had sold some stories to magazines. He was going to talk about writing as an avocation. That made us a panel, and we sat down to face a crowd of students, teachers, and parents, all eager to learn the secrets of our glamorous work. 1

Word Power
vocation an occupation; regular employment
avocation a hobby or interest pursued for enjoyment rather than money

Dr. Brock was dressed in a bright red jacket, looking vaguely bohemian, as authors are supposed to look, and the first question went to him. What was it like to be a writer? 2

Word Power
arduous difficult and tiring

He said it was tremendous fun. Coming home from an arduous day at the hospital, he would go straight to his yellow pad and write his tensions away. The words just flowed. It was easy. I then said that writing wasn't easy and it wasn't fun. It was hard and lonely, and the words seldom just flowed. 3

Next, Dr. Brock was asked if it was important to rewrite. Absolutely not, he said. "Let it all hang out," he told us, and whatever form the sentences take will reflect the writer at his most natural. I then said that rewriting is the essence of writing. I pointed out that professional writers rewrite their sentences over and over and then rewrite what they have rewritten. 4

"What do you do on days when it isn't going well?" Dr. Brock was asked. He said he just stopped writing and put the work aside for a day when it would go better. I then said that the professional writer must establish a daily schedule and stick to it. I said that writing is a craft, not an art, and that the man who runs away from his craft because he lacks inspiration is fooling himself. He is also going broke. 5

"What if you're feeling depressed or unhappy?" a student asked. "Won't that affect your writing?" 6

Probably it will, Dr. Brock replied. Go fishing. Take a walk. Probably it won't, I said. If your job is to write every day, you learn to do it like any other job. 7

A student asked if we found it useful to circulate in the literary world. Dr. Brock said he was greatly enjoying his new life as a man of letters, and he told several stories of being taken to lunch by his publisher and his agent at Manhattan restaurants where writers and editors gather. I said that professional writers are solitary drudges who seldom see other writers. 8

Word Power
symbolism the use of a symbol (something that stands for something else) in a work of art or literature

"Do you put symbolism in your writing?" a student asked me. 9

"Not if I can help it," I replied. I have an unbroken record of missing the deeper meaning in any story, play, or movie, and as for dance and mime, I have never had any idea of what is being conveyed. 10

"I *love* symbols!" Dr. Brock exclaimed, and he described with gusto the joys of weaving them through his work. 11

So the morning went, and it was a revelation to all of us. At the end, Dr. Brock told me he was enormously interested in my answers—it had never occurred to him that writing could be hard. I told him I was just as interested in *his* answers—it had never occurred to me that writing could be easy. Maybe I should take up surgery on the side. 12

Word Power
gusto enthusiasm; lively enjoyment

As for the students, anyone might think we left them bewildered. But in fact, we probably gave them a broader glimpse of the writing process than if only one of us had talked. For there isn't any "right" way to do such personal work. There are all kinds of writers and all kinds of methods, and any method that helps you to say what you want to say is the right method for you. Some people write by day, others by night. Some people need silence, others turn on the radio. Some write by hand, some by word processor, some by talking into a tape recorder. Some people write their first draft in one long burst and then revise; others can't write the second paragraph until they have fiddled endlessly with the first. 13

But all of them are vulnerable and all of them are tense. They are driven by a compulsion to put some part of themselves on paper, and yet they don't just write what comes naturally. They sit down to commit an act of literature, and the self who emerges on paper is far stiffer than the person who sat down to write. The problem is to find the real man or woman behind all the tension. 14

Ultimately, the product that any writer has to sell is not the subject being written about, but who he or she is. I often find myself reading with interest about a topic I never thought would interest me—some scientific quest, perhaps. What holds me is the enthusiasm of the writer for his field. How was he drawn into it? What emotional baggage did he bring along? How did it change his life? It's not necessary to want to spend a year alone at Walden Pond[1] to become deeply involved with a writer who did. 15

This is the personal transaction that's at the heart of good nonfiction writing. Out of it come two of the most important qualities that this book will go in search of: humanity and warmth. Good writing has an aliveness that keeps the reader reading from one paragraph to the next, and it's not a question of gimmicks to "personalize" the author. It's a question of using the English language in a way that will achieve the greatest strength and the least clutter. 16

Can such principles be taught? Maybe not. But most of them can be learned. 17

Thinking about the Reading

1. Why do you think Zinsser chose to use an interview format to compare and contrast his own writing methods and experiences with those of Dr. Brock?
2. What is Zinsser's purpose in comparing his views on the writing process with those of Dr. Brock? In what ways does he suggest that his work and methods are superior to those of the doctor?

1. The place where Henry David Thoreau (1817–1862), an American writer, naturalist, and political activist, lived for two years in a cabin he built himself. He wrote about the experience in his most famous book, *Walden*.

3. Zinsser claims that "rewriting is the essence of writing" (paragraph 4). Use your own experience to support or challenge this statement.

*4. Zinsser says that the writer's ability to draw the reader into his subject is the "personal transaction" (paragraph 16) or exchange between two people that, according to Zinsser, makes writing come alive. Consider the essays in this chapter that you have read. Which of the topics did not really interest you until you were drawn in by the writer's personal view of the topic?

Writing Practice

1. Imagine that you have been asked some of the same questions as Zinsser and Dr. Brock—but about your own experience as a college student. How would you respond? Be sure to include answers to the following questions: What is it like to be a student? What do you do when schoolwork or classes are not going well? Does being depressed or unhappy affect your performance in the classroom? How?
2. In paragraph 13, Zinsser writes, "There are all kinds of writers and all kinds of methods." Describe the kind of writer you are. Do you find writing easy, as Dr. Brock does, or difficult, as Zinsser does? What methods do you use to come up with ideas or to get through a particularly difficult assignment? Do you use any of the methods that Zinsser describes in paragraph 13?
3. Zinsser claims that the most successful pieces of writing are produced when the writer really cares about his or her subject. Try to identify three or four topics that interest you—for example, a book, a sport, a famous person, a political opinion, or a religious belief. Try to explain why each of these topics interests you.

APPENDIX

A

Building Word Power

Building a vocabulary is an important part of your education. Knowing what words mean and how to use them can help you become a better reader and a better writer. As you have worked your way through *Foundations First*, you have encountered one or more Word Power boxes in each chapter. At this point, you may know the meanings of many of these words, and you have probably used some of them in writing or speaking. By continuing to use these and other new words, you can further expand your vocabulary.

FOCUS Using Context to Build Word Power

You can often figure out what a word means by studying its **context**, the words that surround it. For example, consider the following paragraph:

> Do I truly know Cesar Chavez? I suppose not. He was like a boat being driven by some internal squall, a disturbance he himself didn't always understand, and that carried millions right along with him, some of us kicking and screaming. (John Hartmire, "At the Heart of a Historic Movement")

If you did not know the meaning of the word *squall* (a short, sudden windstorm), you might be able to figure it out by its context. For example, the paragraph as a whole compares Chavez to a boat, and placement of the word *driven* suggests a force that blows the boat around. The *disturbance* ("some internal squall, a disturbance . . .") makes it clear that a squall is a disturbance, and the rest of the paragraph indicates that the disturbance was powerful enough to affect millions of people. So, even though the paragraph does not explicitly define a squall as a windstorm, the word's context suggests that a squall is a powerful disturbance.

1 Using a Dictionary

One of the best ways to improve your vocabulary is to get into the habit of using a dictionary to help you understand what new words mean and how to use them in your writing. A **dictionary** is an alphabetical list of the words in a language. However, a good dictionary is more than just a collection of words. In addition to showing how to spell and pronounce a word and what its most common meanings are, a dictionary can give you a great deal of other information.

A typical dictionary entry appears below.

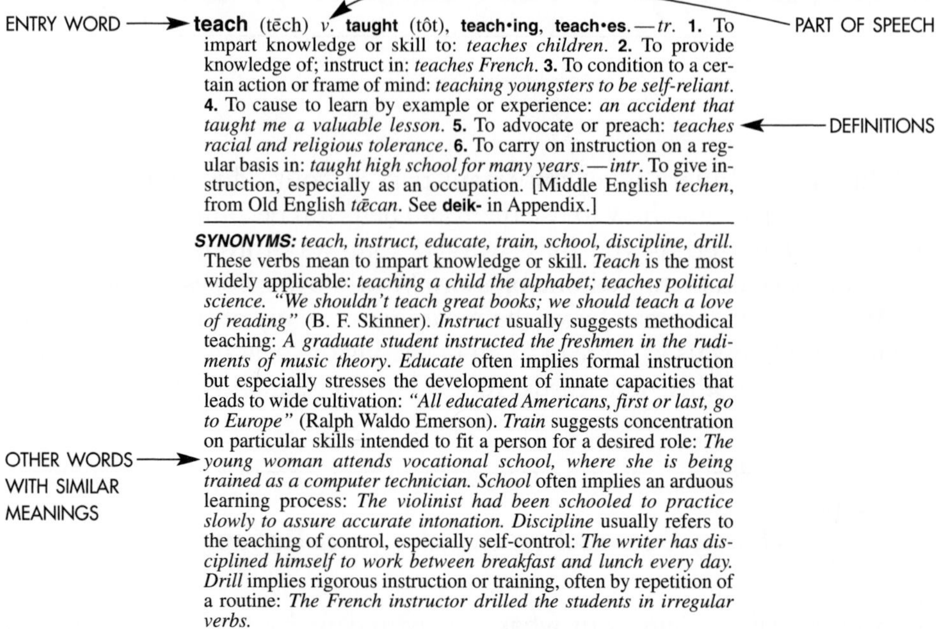
ENTRY WORD → **teach** (tēch) *v.* **taught** (tôt), **teach•ing, teach•es.** —*tr.* **1.** To impart knowledge or skill to: *teaches children.* **2.** To provide knowledge of; instruct in: *teaches French.* **3.** To condition to a certain action or frame of mind: *teaching youngsters to be self-reliant.* **4.** To cause to learn by example or experience: *an accident that taught me a valuable lesson.* **5.** To advocate or preach: *teaches racial and religious tolerance.* **6.** To carry on instruction on a regular basis in: *taught high school for many years.* —*intr.* To give instruction, especially as an occupation. [Middle English *techen,* from Old English *tǣcan.* See **deik-** in Appendix.] ← PART OF SPEECH; ← DEFINITIONS

SYNONYMS: *teach, instruct, educate, train, school, discipline, drill.* These verbs mean to impart knowledge or skill. *Teach* is the most widely applicable: *teaching a child the alphabet; teaches political science. "We shouldn't teach great books; we should teach a love of reading"* (B. F. Skinner). *Instruct* usually suggests methodical teaching: *A graduate student instructed the freshmen in the rudiments of music theory. Educate* often implies formal instruction but especially stresses the development of innate capacities that leads to wide cultivation: *"All educated Americans, first or last, go to Europe"* (Ralph Waldo Emerson). *Train* suggests concentration on particular skills intended to fit a person for a desired role: *The young woman attends vocational school, where she is being trained as a computer technician. School* often implies an arduous learning process: *The violinist had been schooled to practice slowly to assure accurate intonation. Discipline* usually refers to the teaching of control, especially self-control: *The writer has disciplined himself to work between breakfast and lunch every day. Drill* implies rigorous instruction or training, often by repetition of a routine: *The French instructor drilled the students in irregular verbs.* ← OTHER WORDS WITH SIMILAR MEANINGS

A dictionary entry can also explain the history of the word and provide **usage notes** that discuss changing or disputed uses of the word.

The pages that follow list (in alphabetical order) and define all the words that appear in Word Power boxes in *Foundations First*. You can use this list as a minidictionary to help you incorporate these words into your written and spoken vocabulary.

Following the list are several pages on which you can create a personal vocabulary list, your own list of new words (and their definitions) that you encounter in your reading. Space has been provided for you to write an original sentence for each word so you can remember how it is used.

Finally, exercises at the end of this appendix will give you additional practice in using the Word Power feature in *Foundations First*.

2 Word Power List

This alphabetical list includes all the words, along with their definitions, that appear in the Word Power boxes throughout *Foundations First*.

abacus an ancient instrument for making mathematical calculations

absconded left quickly and hid

accumulate to gather or pile up little by little

adjunct an instructor at a college or university who is not a permanent staff member; any temporary employee

adrenaline a hormone that produces a rush of energy and excitement when a person is in danger

adversity difficulty

affectionate loving

ailment an illness

alienated emotionally withdrawn or unresponsive

altercation a loud quarrel

annotate to make explanatory notes on a page

anticipate to look forward to

apathetic feeling or showing a lack of interest

apathy a lack of interest

archetypes models

arduous difficult and tiring

assessed measured

avocation a hobby or interest pursued for personal enjoyment rather than for money

ballot a piece of paper on which voters indicate their choices in an election

ban to forbid somebody from doing something

bodega small grocery store specializing in Hispanic products

bourgeois middle-class and proper in attitudes

boycott (noun) a refusal to participate

brawl a noisy fight

cautious careful

classic something typical or traditional; an outstanding example of its kind

commission to place an order for something

commitment devotion or dedication

conceited self-important

concern a reason to worry

conclusion the end or the finish

concocted mixed various ingredients together

conflict a disagreement or clash

conjure up to bring to mind

conscientious guided by one's conscience; principled

conscientious objector someone who refuses to serve in the military for moral reasons

consensus a position reached by group agreement

consistently regularly; steadily

contemporary current; modern

coordinating being equal in importance, rank, or degree

courageous brave

coveted desired

crave to have a strong desire for something

daring bold

debilitate to take away the strength of something or someone

decolonized freed from dependency

dependent relying on another for support

desiccated dried-up

determined firm; strong-minded

die-casting a process of forcing very hot metal into a mold

dilemma a situation that requires a choice between two or more equally unappealing alternatives

diligence attentive care

disdained looked down on; despised

dissent a difference of opinion; a disagreement

diverge to separate and go in different directions

dry goods fabrics and clothing

earmark to set aside for a particular purpose

elector a qualified voter in an election

empower to give power or confidence

emulate to imitate

envision to imagine

epic a long poem celebrating heroic acts

estranged separated from someone else by feelings of hostility or indifference

evaluating judging the value, quality, or importance of something

exaggerate to overstate

excessive extreme

exempts frees from an obligation that others are subject to

exotic foreign; unusual

extemporaneous prepared, but performed without the help of notes

feline (noun) a member of the cat family; (adjective) catlike

ferocious fierce

foolhardy reckless

fused melded together

gender sex (male or female)

generation a group of individuals born at about the same time

genome a complete set of chromosomes and its associated genes; DNA

gloss to skim

grate a framework of metal bars

gusto enthusiasm; lively enjoyment

hardware tools; nails, hinges, and the like

harp on to repeat over and over again

heritage something passed down from previous generations

highlight to mark a page to emphasize important details

humble modest

hypertensive having high blood pressure

imbued thoroughly influenced

immigrant a person who comes to a country to permanently settle there

immortalize to make famous forever

imperialism the act of one country taking over the land or government of another

impervious impossible to affect

improvise to make do with available materials; to invent with little or no preparation

indefensible hard to defend

independent free from the influence of others

induce to cause; to bring about

institution a well-known person, place, or thing

intimidating threatening

intrepid brave

invincible unbeatable

kiosk a small structure used to sell merchandise

lectern a stand or desk with a slanted top that supports a speaker's notes

lenient not harsh or strict

lethal capable of killing

liability a financial and legal responsibility; a debt that must be paid

log on to identify oneself on a computer by entering a username and password

maize corn

malign to make harmful statements about someone or something

marinate to let meat, fish, or vegetables soak in a sauce to make them more flavorful or tender

marooned stranded

masquerade (verb) to wear a mask or disguise; (noun) a costume party at which guests wear masks

mature full-grown

melancholy sadness; depression

mellow to gain wisdom and tolerance with age

memento a reminder of the past; a keepsake (the plural form is *mementos*)

memorabilia items kept as souvenirs

memorable worth remembering

mentor a wise and trusted teacher or advisor

microbe a germ

migrate to move from one region to another

missive a letter or message

mobility the ability to move from one social group, class, or level to another

monument a structure built as a memorial

morale willingness to perform a task

multicultural of or relating to many cultures

naturalization the process of becoming a citizen

networking interacting with others to share information

newsworthy worth reporting in the news

obligation a course of action demanded of a person by law or conscience

observer someone who watches attentively

offensive hurtful; disagreeable; unpleasant

ogling staring at

online connected to the Internet

orchestrate to arrange

orient to adjust

orientation adjustment to a new environment; a meeting in which participants are introduced to a new situation, such as a new school, job, or other activity

ostracize to exclude from a group

pandemic an epidemic that affects many people over a wide area

parity equality in power or value

pastime a pleasant activity that fills spare time

patriot someone who loves and supports his or her country

persist to continue to do something despite setbacks

perspective a view or an outlook; the ability to see things as they are

pertaining to relating to or having to do with

physique the structure or form of a person's body

posted entered information online

prevailed upon persuaded

priority an important or urgent goal

priorities things considered more important than others

produce fruits and vegetables

profanity offensive language

prohibit to forbid

provision something that is supplied

public service a service performed for the benefit of the public

pushcart a light cart pushed by hand

quaint old-fashioned

qualifications skills, knowledge, or experience

quota a number of people or percentage of people designated as an upper limit

raw materials natural resources such as wood, water, and carbon that can be made into other useful things

readily easily

recreation activity done for enjoyment when one is not working; play

renaissance a rebirth or revival

rendezvous (verb) to meet at a prearranged place and time; (noun) a meeting of this kind

restrict to keep within limits

restrictive limiting

reverberated had a prolonged or continuing effect

revere to regard with respect and awe

rhetoric elaborate, insincere, or pretentious language

rigor a hardship or difficulty

role model a person who serves as a model of behavior

savvy practical knowledge

second-guess to reconsider a decision

self-esteem pride in oneself; self-respect; self-worth

sentimental overly romantic

sheer steep; almost vertical

shirked avoided responsibility

shrine a place at which respects are paid to a person who has died

skepticism a doubtful or questioning attitude

sophisticated experienced and refined

spectacle a public performance or exhibition; an unusual sight

splice a connection made by joining two ends

sporadic infrequent; happening from time to time

sterilization the process of making something free of germs

subsidize to give financial support to a project

surveillance the close observation of a person or a group, especially a person or group under suspicion

suture to use fiber to close up wounds or to connect two parts of the body

syllabus an outline or summary of a course's main points (the plural form is *syllabi*)

symbol a thing that represents something else

symbolism the use of a symbol (something that stands for something else) in a work of art or literature

timid shy, nervous

tradition a behavior or custom handed down from generation to generation

traditional relating to tradition

transaction an exchange or a transfer of goods, services, or money; an exchange of thoughts and feelings

transcend to be greater than; to go beyond

trek a difficult journey

trudge to walk with effort, to plod

unanticipated not expected

undermine to weaken support for something

unique one of a kind

unwarranted unnecessary

vanity excessive pride in one's appearance or achievements

vanity plate a license plate that can be customized for an extra charge

veracity truthfulness

versatility the ability to do many things well

viable able to survive; capable of success

vocation an occupation; regular employment

vulnerable (noun) those who are likely to be victims of physical or emotional injury

wholesaler a person who sells large amounts of a product to stores or individuals, who then resell it

woe sadness

3 Your Personal Vocabulary List

On the facing page, start a list of new words you come across in your reading. Write down a brief definition of each word, and then use it in a sentence. Continue this list in your journal.

Example

Word: memento Definition: a reminder of the past

Sentence: I kept a seashell as a memento of our vacation at the beach.

Word: ______ Definition: ______

Sentence: ______

Word: ______ Definition: ______

Sentence: ______

Word: ______ Definition: ______

Sentence: ______

Word: ______ Definition: ______

Sentence: ______

Word: ______ Definition: ______

Sentence: ______

Word: ______ Definition: ______

Sentence: ______

APPENDIX

B Strategies for Workplace Success

Looking for a job requires that you understand your goals, look for job leads in the right places, learn about companies and organizations that might employ you, and—most important—learn how to sell yourself.

1 Defining Your Goals

Before you look for a job, you should determine how much time you can devote to work and what you hope to gain from the experience.

1. ***Determine how much time you have.*** How many hours do you think you need to work? How many hours a week *can* you work while still in school? Are those hours distributed throughout the week, or are they all grouped in one or two days? Can you work during regular business hours, or will you need to work evenings?
2. ***Consider unpaid work.*** If you can afford to take an unpaid internship, you can gain the experience you need to get a paying position later on. In addition to exploring existing internships, you can create your own internship by offering to work at an organization without pay so that you can gain experience.

2 Learning about Job Openings

Once you define your goals, you should look for a job in an organized way. The strategies below will help you get the most out of your search.

1. ***Check your college placement office.*** Placement offices generally list both part-time and full-time jobs as well as short-term and temporary positions.
2. ***Scan newspaper and Web listings.*** Many people find jobs through classified advertisements in newspapers or on Web sites. Web sites called **job boards** also post listings and invite job seekers to post their résumés (see B4 for a sample résumé). Here are two of the most popular job boards.

   - Monster Board: www.monster.com
   - The Job Resource: www.thejobresource.com

3. ***Network.*** **Networking** involves telling instructors, friends, and relatives about your goals and qualifications and finding out who may have helpful information for you.
4. ***Keep your eyes open.*** Many jobs are never advertised. Some small businesses, for example, rely on word of mouth, signs put in store windows, or flyers posted on campus or community bulletin boards.

3 Marketing Yourself

Once you have found a job you want to apply for, you have to market yourself to a prospective employer.

1. ***Prepare your résumé.*** The résumé that you spend hours perfecting usually gets no more than a one-minute review. To increase your résumé's chance of generating interest, you should include most of the following items:
   - **Objective** or **Goal** to indicate which position you are suited for
   - **Education** and **Experience** to demonstrate your qualifications
   - **Special Skills** to illustrate how you are different from others who are applying for the job
   - **Activities, Achievements, Honors, Leadership,** and **Interests** to highlight your accomplishments
   - **References** to support what you have written about yourself

   NOTE: Be prepared to update your résumé on a regular basis as your experiences and objectives change. (See B4 for a sample résumé.)
2. ***Prepare a cover letter.*** Don't simply repeat in the cover letter what your résumé already says. Instead, use the cover letter to make yourself stand out. Show what you know about the organization's needs, and tell how you can benefit the organization. If possible, address your letter to a specific individual rather than to a general audience such as "To Whom It May Concern." (See B4 for a sample cover letter.)
3. ***Prepare for an interview.*** Interviews may take place in person or by phone; they may occur on campus or in an employer's office. The interviewer wants to see if you are suited for the job and if you can answer his or her questions.

FOCUS Interviews: Frequently Asked Questions

Go into an interview prepared to answer the following frequently asked questions.

- Can you tell me about yourself?
- Where do you see yourself in five years?
- How do you respond to criticism?

(continued on following page)

(continued from previous page)

- What accomplishment are you most proud of?
- What is your greatest strength? What is your greatest weakness?
- Why did you choose your school? What did you like about it? What did you not like?
- What do you know about our organization?
- Are you willing to relocate or travel?

At the interview, dress appropriately, make eye contact, demonstrate professional behavior (arrive on time, do not smoke, and so on), and sell yourself.

Speak slowly, answer the interviewer's questions fully, and illustrate your points with specific examples from your previous job experiences. If the interviewer asks you a difficult question, take time to think of an answer; don't just say the first thing that comes to your mind. At the end of the interview, thank the interviewer.

4. ***Write a follow-up letter.*** A strong follow-up letter will make a favorable impression on a potential employer (see B4 for a sample follow-up letter). If you want to expand on an answer that you gave in the interview, this is your chance.

4 Sample Job-Application Materials

An important part of applying for a job is putting together an effective résumé and writing letters of application and follow-up letters. The following examples were written by a student who was applying for a full-time position in the field of hotel management.

Rolando J. Matta

School
321 Topland Avenue
Johnson City, NY 13790
607-737-1111
rjmatta@fhcc.edu

Home
6543 Lincoln Street, 6D
Chicago, IL 60666
312-787-5555
rjmatta@hotmail.com

Include relevant contact information

OBJECTIVE Associate innkeeper position in the Chicago area

EDUCATION Fox Hollow Community College,
Johnson City, NY 13790
Major: Hospitality Management
Expected date of graduation: June 2006
GPA of 3.4 on a 4.0 scale

Omit GPA if under 3.0

Major courses (partial list)
Hotel and Restaurant Accounting
Hotel-Restaurant Organization and Management
Food Purchasing
Principles of Food Preparation
Executive Housekeeping
Hotel Front-Office Operations
Hospitality Law

EXPERIENCE **Hospitality Internship,**
Grande Hotel, New York, NY
May 2005 to August 2005
- Rotated through Front Desk, Housekeeping, and Room Service departments in hands-on and supervisory positions
- Participated in weekly question-and-answer sessions with key managers
- Reported on satisfaction of American Bar Association conventioneers
- Researched cost savings on gifts for returning guests

Assistant to Meetings Supervisor,
VIP Executive Suites, Binghamton, NY
August 2004 to May 2005
- Coordinated and reviewed setup and breakdown of furniture and refreshments for all meeting rooms
- Communicated with Audiovisual Department
- Reviewed all billing against contracts
- Scheduled appointments for prospective clients with supervisor

Use boldface and bullets to highlight important information

OTHER SKILLS Proficiency with MS Office, the Internet; bilingual (English/Spanish)

ACTIVITIES Travel in Europe and Latin America; summer cooking classes in New York

REFERENCES Available on request

Sample Résumé

Include your address and the date

321 Topland Avenue
Johnson City, NY 13790
607-737-1111
rjmatta@fhcc.edu

April 1, 2006

Include the name and address of the person you are writing to

Ms. Jennifer T. White
Manager
Rotunda Hotel and Sports Club
88990 Airport Highway
Chicago, IL 60677

Write to a specific person → Dear Ms. White:

Mr. Luigi Cuenca of the Grande Hotel in New York, where I worked last summer, told me that you are looking for a management assistant. I believe my experience at the Grande Hotel and elsewhere has prepared me for this position.

Tell what you know about the organization and what you can bring to it → Since the Rotunda is at O'Hare Airport, I know that many of your guests stay there because of last-minute flight cancellations. For this reason, my experience in responding to frustrated travelers will be of use to you. In addition, I have been reading about the services that hotels in Europe offer to business travelers. I would like to have the opportunity to implement some of these services in the United States.

Politely indicate your availability for an interview → I have enclosed my résumé, and I look forward to talking with you. I will be available for an interview anytime after my final exams on May 30.

Sincerely,

Sign above your typed name → *Rolando J. Matta*

Rolando J. Matta

Sample Cover Letter

321 Topland Avenue
Johnson City, NY 13790
607-737-1111
rjmatta@fhcc.edu

June 10, 2006

Ms. Jennifer T. White
Manager
Rotunda Hotel and Sports Club
88990 Airport Highway
Chicago, IL 60677

Dear Ms. White:

Thank you for meeting with me earlier today. I appreciated the opportunity to speak with you. I especially enjoyed hearing how the Rotunda is similar to the Grande Hotel in New York City. ← Thank the interviewer

The Web site for the hotel in Sydney that we discussed is http://www.medusa.com.au. On this Web site, you will find photos of the wall units in each room. These units not only make an attractive appearance, but they also save space in the closet and in the mini-kitchen. ← Provide supplementary information

I am extremely interested in joining your staff and feel certain that I could contribute much to your organization. ← State your enthusiasm directly and briefly

Sincerely,

Rolando J. Matta

Rolando J. Matta

Sample Follow-up Letter after an Interview

Answers to Odd-Numbered Exercises

Chapter 15

◆ **PRACTICE 15-2, page 205**

Answers: **1.** Simple subject: clocks; complete subject: Alarm clocks **3.** Simple subject: consumers; complete subject: consumers **5.** Simple subject: sleepers; complete subject: Heavy sleepers **7.** Simple subject: Times; complete subject: Times **9.** Simple subject: people; complete subject: Few people

◆ **PRACTICE 15-4, page 206**

Answers: **1.** P **3.** P **5.** S **7.** P **9.** S

◆ **PRACTICE 15-5, page 207**

Answers: **1.** memorial; singular **3.** people; plural **5.** men and women; plural **7.** man; singular **9.** Spouses, children, parents, and friends; plural

◆ **PRACTICE 15-6, page 208**

Answers: **1.** Subject: People; prepositional phrase: about these puzzles **3.** Subject: puzzle; prepositional phrase: of nine 3 x 3 squares **5.** Subject: number; prepositional phrase: in each column, each row, and each 3 x 3 square **7.** Subjects: "givens"; prepositional phrase: of an individual puzzle **9.** Subject: solvers; prepositional phrase: of these puzzles

◆ **PRACTICE 15-7, page 209**

Answers: **1.** traveled **3.** advertised **5.** packed; joined **7.** wrote **9.** see

◆ **PRACTICE 15-9, page 210**

Answers: **1.** are; linking verb **3.** are; linking verb **5.** appeal; action verb **7.** appear; linking verb **9.** are; linking verb

◆ **PRACTICE 15-10, page 211**

Answers: **1.** Subject: The night; linking verb: grew; descriptive word: cold **3.** Subject: George W. Bush; linking verb: became; descriptive phrase: the forty-third president of the United States **5.** Subject: Many people; linking verb: were; descriptive phrase: outraged at the mayor's announcement **7.** Subject: The fans; linking verb: appeared; descriptive phrase: upset by their team's defeat **9.** Subject: Charlie; linking verb: got; descriptive word: sick

◆ **PRACTICE 15-11, page 212**

Answers: **1.** Helping verb: may; main verb: risk **3.** Helping verbs: has been; main verb: thinking **5.** Helping verbs: could have; main verb: been **7.** Helping verb: have; main verb: wondered **9.** Helping verb: has; main verb: loved

Chapter 16

◆ **PRACTICE 16-1, page 216**

Answers: **1.** [Speech is silver], *but* [silence is golden]. **3.** [The house was dark], *so* [he didn't ring the doorbell]. **5.** [They will not surrender], *and* [they will not agree to a cease-fire]. **7.** [She has lived in California for years], *yet* [she remembers her childhood in Kansas very clearly]. **9.** [Melody dropped French], *and* [then she added Italian].

◆ **PRACTICE 16-2, page 218**

Answers: **1.** nor **3.** so **5.** and **7.** and **9.** but/yet

◆ **PRACTICE 16-3, page 218**

Answers: **1.** and **3.** nor **5.** or **7.** so **9.** so

◆ **PRACTICE 16-5, page 220**

Possible answers: Americans love the freedom and independence of driving a car, and they also love movies. Not surprisingly, the United States was the home of the very first drive-in movie theater. The first drive-in opened in New Jersey in 1934, and the second one, Shankweiler's Drive-In in Orefield, Pennsylvania, opened the same year.

Today, the very first drive-in no longer exists, nor is there a single drive-in theater remaining in the entire state of New Jersey. However, Shankweiler's is still open for business, so fans of drive-ins can still go there. Shankweiler's Drive-In still has the in-car speakers that moviegoers used to hang in their car windows, but they are rarely used. Instead, drive-in visitors simply turn on the car radio to hear the movie sound, for Shankweiler's broadcasts movie soundtracks on FM stereo. Anyone with a car, a love of movies, and a sense of history should make a trip to Shankweiler's Drive-In.

◆ PRACTICE 16-6, page 221

Possible answers: Many young children want their own cell phones, but it can be difficult for them to convince their parents that a cell phone is a necessity. Some parents think cell phones are too expensive, and they don't want to pay the bills. Other parents feel that cell phones are just status symbols. Meanwhile, wireless companies are designing more cell phones with children and teens in mind, for they see the youth market as very important. More and more parents are giving in, and they are buying cell phones for their children. After all, parents want the security of knowing their children can be reached. Cell phone companies realize that parents are anxious about their children's safety, so they are beginning to add features that allow parents to track a child's location. Children do not like this invasion of their privacy, but parents find such features hard to resist. The cell phone conflict may seem new, yet it is just another example of the age-old battle between protective parents and their independent children.

◆ PRACTICE 16-10, page 226

Answers: **1.** Most of these tiny schools are in isolated rural areas; that is, they exist in places far from towns with larger school systems. **3.** Most one-room schools have only one teacher and a few students; therefore, one room is all they need. **5.** These days, declining population is the reason most one-room schools close; in other words, the town does not have enough students to make operating the school worthwhile. **7.** Supporters of one-room schools see many benefits; for example, students in these schools get more individual attention from their teachers. **9.** One-room schools also give a town's residents a sense of community and tradition; therefore, many towns fight hard to keep their schools.

◆ PRACTICE 16-11, page 227

Possible answers: **1.** Most of these shrines honor the victims of car accidents; therefore, it makes sense to have memorials along the roadways. **3.** A shrine is sometimes just a simple white cross; however, people often add flowers, photos, toys, or teddy bears. **5.** The shrines can create obstacles for snowplows and lawnmowers; in addition, they can distract curious drivers. **7.** This seems to be a sensible compromise; still, it does not address one essential issue. **9.** Most states do not enforce their regulations about temporary memorials; for instance, some memorials remain beside roads for many months.

Chapter 17

◆ PRACTICE 17-3, page 236

Answers: **1.** Correct **3.** They could practice their moves because they were not afraid to break the law. **5.** Now that skateboarding is more popular, skating gear has become very fashionable. **7.** Correct **9.** Correct

◆ PRACTICE 17-4, page 237

Possible answers: **1.** Although many Westerners rarely think about problems in Africa, the lack of money for medical supplies should concern everyone. **3.** When an outbreak of Ebola virus appeared in northern Uganda in 2000, doctors and nurses did not have disinfectants and latex gloves. **5.** Because the Ebola virus makes a patient bleed heavily, medical workers without gloves are in danger. **7.** The virus is named for the Ebola River in Zaire because it first appeared there in human beings. **9.** Even though a doctor and several nurses died of the Ebola virus, more than half of the patients survived.

◆ PRACTICE 17-6, page 239

Answers: **1.** Dependent clause: *which* lasts five days; modifies: holiday **3.** Dependent clause: *that* contain saffron, almonds, butter, and milk; modifies: cakes **5.** Dependent clause: *that* stand for the banishing of ignorance and darkness; modifies: candles **7.** Dependent clause: *who* is said to have rescued sixteen thousand daughters of gods and saints from a demon king; modifies: Krishna **9.** Dependent clause: *which* is associated with legends about mountains; modifies: day

◆ PRACTICE 17-7, page 240

Possible answers: **1.** In the nineteenth century, American whalers, who had very dangerous jobs, sailed around the world to hunt whales. **3.** Today, U.S. laws protect several whale species that are considered to be in danger of extinction. **5.** Whale hunting is the focus of a disagreement between the United States and Japan, which have different ideas about whaling. **7.** Some of the whales killed in the Japanese hunt, which include minke whales, Bryde's whales, and sperm whales, are considered by the U.S. government to be endangered. **9.** The U.S. government argues that the Japanese whale hunt is not for research, but for businesses that want whale meat to sell to restaurants.

Chapter 18

◆ PRACTICE 18-1, page 245

Possible answers: **1.** Since the 1940s, stock car racing has grown into a multi-billion-dollar sport. **3.** Originally, the association raced "stock cars"—unmodified Fords and Chevys. **5.** Correct **7.** However, stock cars are still inspected according to strict rules. **9.** Correct

◆ **PRACTICE 18-2, page 246**

Possible answers: **1.** Correct **3.** For security reasons, experts recommend using a combination of letters and numbers. **5.** Correct **7.** In fact, seventy-one percent told theirs to the interviewer in exchange for a chocolate bar. **9.** Surprisingly, the most popular password of all is not a familiar name like "Jenny" or "Lakers" or "Spot." **11.** Correct

◆ **PRACTICE 18-3, page 248**

Possible answers: The founder of Meetup.com wanted more people to meet in person because he wanted people to really get to know one another. People were not meeting other people face-to-face; they were spending all their time on the Internet. Meetup.com was designed to solve this problem. People can search for groups by interest, or they can browse groups located nearby. Any group can schedule meetings, and groups may list contact information to allow members to meet in person. The site became very popular during the 2004 presidential election when political groups used it to coordinate rallies. Today, some groups attract people with very specific interests; for example, there is a group for almost every breed of dog. Other groups welcome people with varied interests, so Meetup.com provides ways for all kinds of people to meet.

◆ **PRACTICE 18-4, page 249**

Possible answers: **1.** Stephen Colbert, a comedian, hosts *The Colbert Report*. **3.** Always sold out, Duke basketball games are loud and exciting. **5.** Holding the winning ticket, the ten coworkers won the lottery.

◆ **PRACTICE 18-5, page 250**

Possible answers: **1.** Rebecca fed the elephants, watered the lemurs, and then talked to the children. **3.** America's favorite sports are basketball, baseball, and football. **5.** A ripe cantaloupe smells sweet, looks orange, and sounds hollow.

◆ **PRACTICE 18-6, page 251**

Possible answers: **1.** simmering heat of a Cuban cigar factory **3.** rumbling and buzzing of machinery **5.** Juan Julian, an elegant man in a sharply pressed white linen suit **7.** *Anna Karenina*, Tolstoy's novel about doomed Russian lovers **9.** harsh, frozen; nineteenth-century Russia

◆ **PRACTICE 18-9, page 254**

Possible answers: **1.** Immigrants and their supporters stayed away from work, school, and shopping to send a message to Washington. **3.** The proposed laws would make it much harder for illegal immigrants to live in the United States. **5.** Participation in the protest varied from state to state. **7.** Some groups organized counter-demonstrations. **9.** We do not yet know how these protests will affect future immigration laws.

◆ **PRACTICE 18-10, page 255**

Possible answers: **1.** A few years ago, antibacterial cleaning products were introduced throughout the American market. **3.** The ads try to make people afraid of the germs in their homes. **5.** When the ads first appeared, frightened people immediately began buying antibacterial soap to kill off the invisible germs. **7.** However, new research suggests that antibacterial products may actually kill good germs. **9.** Scientists have warned that children who grow up in germ-free homes may get sick from normally harmless bacteria.

◆ **PRACTICE 18-11, page 256**

Possible answers: **1.** Many Americans get their energy from a morning cup of coffee. **3.** In fact, there are more designer coffees than you can imagine. **5.** Others have sweet, intense flavors, such as hazelnut, vanilla, and raspberry. **7.** Some designer coffees even combine all three elements—exotic beans, strong flavors, and milk—to create a memorable taste. **9.** In fact, Seattle, the home of the Starbucks chain, even took a chance and tried to tax designer coffees.

Chapter 19

◆ **PRACTICE 19-1, page 260**

Answers: **1.** sudden; unexpected; destructive **3.** lie down; take a nap **5.** expanded the parking lot; added a deli counter **7.** a bath; a story; a lullaby **9.** A beautiful voice; acting ability

◆ **PRACTICE 19-2, page 261**

Answers: **1.** Hundreds of people wanted to be on a game show that required them to live on an island, catch their own food, and have no contact with the outside world. **3.** Parallel **5.** The contestants held their breath underwater, rowed a canoe, and ate rats and caterpillars. **7.** Each week, the television audience saw one person win a contest and another person get voted off the island. **9.** Parallel

◆ **PRACTICE 19-3, page 263**

Answers: **1.** Most countries have a standard greeting: a handshake, a series of kisses, a hug, a bow, or a nod of the head. **3.** Most Americans greet each other with a handshake, a cheek kiss, a wave, or a hug. **5.** A greeting often depends on people's ages, their genders, and the situation. **7.** Businesspeople are often more comfortable shaking hands with each other than kissing each other. **9.** An unexpected kiss can result not only in bumped noses but also in great embarrassment.

Chapter 20

◆ **PRACTICE 20-1, page 272**

Answers: **1.** run-on **3.** run-on **5.** run-on **7.** run-on **9.** correct

◆ **PRACTICE 20-2, page 273**

Answers: **1.** correct **3.** fused sentence **5.** fused sentence **7.** correct **9.** comma splice

◆ **PRACTICE 20-3, page 275**

Answers: **1.** Parker Brothers turned down Darrow's first offer to sell Monopoly. The company has now sold over 200 million games. **3.** Monopoly was recently updated. The company asked the public to vote on possible new settings for the game. **5.** The old version of Monopoly had railroads on the board. The new version of the game has airports instead.

◆ **PRACTICE 20-4, page 275**

Possible answers: **1.** A company pays a fee, and a TV or movie character uses its product onscreen. **3.** Car companies want to show off a new model, but how do they reach their audience? **5.** Many people ignore commercials, but with product placement, advertisers' messages are hard to miss.

◆ **PRACTICE 20-5, page 276**

Answers: **1.** Caffeine is the primary ingredient in most energy drinks; this chemical stimulates the central nervous system and increases alertness. **3.** Advertisements for energy drinks stress this boost of energy; Red Bull uses the slogan "Red Bull gives you wings." **5.** Some scientists worry about the dangers of consuming energy drinks; studies have so far not shown any serious negative effects.

◆ **PRACTICE 20-6, page 277**

Answers: **1.** Geisel wrote many of his books as poetry; in addition, he illustrated most of his own books. **3.** *The Cat in the Hat* uses about 220 different words; in contrast, *Green Eggs and Ham* uses only 50 words. **5.** Geisel died in 1991; however, "Dr. Seuss" lives on in books, in movies, in cartoons, and even in a Broadway musical called *Seussical*.

◆ **PRACTICE 20-7, page 279**

Possible answers: **1.** Flatbread is bread that is flat; usually, it does not contain yeast. **3.** The tortilla is a Mexican flatbread; tortillas are made of corn or wheat. **5.** Italians eat focaccia, but when they put cheese on a focaccia, it becomes a pizza. **7.** Indian cooking has several kinds of flatbreads, and all of them are delicious. **9.** Fifty years ago, most people ate only the flatbreads from their native lands; today, flatbreads are becoming popular all over the world.

◆ **PRACTICE 20-8, page 280**

Possible answers: **1.** As text messaging has become more popular, people have found more reasons to text. **3.** School administrators who need to get in touch with parents quickly are also using text messaging. **5.** People who are not always near a computer can still send and receive mail on their cell phones. **7.** In fact, because students may text each other during tests, schools are starting to ban cell phones. **9.** If users subscribe to the appropriate service, they can receive sports scores, weather reports, and stock prices as text messages.

◆ **PRACTICE 20-9, page 280**

Possible answers: **1.** For years, Wangari Maathai has successfully fought for peace, prosperity, and democracy in Kenya; she received the Nobel Peace Prize in 2004. **3.** Kenya was developing fast, and the disappearance of the forests was causing many problems for the people. **5.** When Maathai saw poor women suffering because of the reckless development, she encouraged them to plant trees. **7.** Maathai, who is a political activist as well as a biology professor and tree-planter, has also promoted democracy and human rights in Kenya. **9.** In 2002, she was elected to Kenya's parliament; she now serves as an assistant environmental minister.

Chapter 21

◆ **PRACTICE 21-2, page 288**

Answers: **1.** Fragment **3.** Fragment **5.** Fragment **7.** Correct **9.** Fragment

Rewrite: According to some users of lip balm, this product is addictive. The purpose of lip balm is to keep the lips from getting chapped. Can people become dependent on lip balm? Some users say yes. However, the makers of lip balm strongly disagree. They say it is completely safe.

◆ **PRACTICE 21-3, page 288**

Answers: **1.** Fragment **3.** Correct **5.** Fragment **7.** Fragment **9.** Fragment

Rewrite: The main characters in most animated movies nowadays have the voices of celebrities. Producers want stars in a film to bring in a bigger audience and to increase the movie's chances of success. Generally, famous names do not matter to children but are important to adults. For instance, fans of Willem Dafoe and Ellen DeGeneres did not go to see *Finding Nemo* to watch cartoon fish but to hear their favorite actors' voices. All in all, celebrity voices help make animated films more popular.

◆ **PRACTICE 21-5, page 291**

Answers: **1.** Correct **3.** Correct **5.** Fragment **7.** Fragment **9.** Fragment **11.** Fragment

Rewrite: Frida Kahlo is known to many for her marriage to fellow artist Diego Rivera, a mural painter. She is also famous for her many self-portraits. In these portraits, Kahlo is usually dressed up in colorful clothes. In her portraits, she is adorned with jewelry and flowers. The scenes that surround her are often exotic, with a dreamlike atmosphere. Kahlo's paintings express the reality of her own life, a life of great beauty and great pain.

◆ **PRACTICE 21-6, page 292**

Answers: **1.** Correct **3.** Correct **5.** Fragment **7.** Fragment **9.** Correct

Rewrite: To this day, the eruption of Krakatoa remains one of the worst disasters in recorded history. Nearly forty thousand people died. The eruption caused tsunamis, giant tidal waves one hundred feet high. In addition, the force of the eruption caused changes in climate around the world. Writer Simon Winchester researched this disaster. In 2003, he published a best-selling book, *Krakatoa: The Day the World Exploded*.

Chapter 22

◆ PRACTICE 22-1, page 303

Answers: **1.** know **3.** remain **5.** taste **7.** produces **9.** continue

◆ PRACTICE 22-2, page 304

Answers: **1.** seems **3.** roars **5.** stand **7.** honors **9.** provides

◆ PRACTICE 22-3, page 305

Answers: **1.** is **3.** are **5.** is

◆ PRACTICE 22-4, page 306

Answers: **1.** has **3.** have **5.** have

◆ PRACTICE 22-5, page 306

Answers: **1.** do **3.** does **5.** do

◆ PRACTICE 22-6, page 306

Answers: **1.** is **3.** has, are **5.** does, has **7.** is **9.** does **11.** do, are **13.** do **15.** have **17.** does **19.** has

◆ PRACTICE 22-7, page 308

Answers: **1.** are **3.** choose **5.** are **7.** make **9.** struggle

◆ PRACTICE 22-8, page 309

Answers: **1.** Prepositional phrase: of one of China's cities; subject: resident; verb: goes **3.** Prepositional phrase: with a huge, heavy frame; subject: bicycle; verb: has **5.** Prepositional phrase: of China; subject: economy; verb: is **7.** Prepositional phrase: with a long commute; subject: worker; verb: does **9.** Prepositional phrase: under age thirty; subject: people; verb: do

◆ PRACTICE 22-9, page 310

Answers: **1.** has **3.** makes **5.** choose **7.** is **9.** inspires

◆ PRACTICE 22-10, page 311

Answers: **1.** Subject: program; verb: is **3.** Subject: dormitory; verb: is **5.** Subject: tests; verb: are **7.** Subject: people; verb: are **9.** Subject: student; verb: does

Chapter 23

◆ PRACTICE 23-1, page 316

Answers: **1.** Verbs: worked, go; correction: *go* becomes *went* **3.** Verbs: told, eats; correction: *eats* becomes *ate* **5.** Verbs: saved, shelters; correction: *shelters* becomes *sheltered* **7.** Verbs: wanted, became; correct **9.** Verbs: came, build; correction: *build* becomes *built*

◆ PRACTICE 23-2, page 318

Answers: **1.** Some people may decide not to buy a Toyota because they can buy a similar Hyundai for less money. **3.** Correct **5.** Correct **7.** The instructor informed his students that they should proofread carefully. **9.** Correct

◆ PRACTICE 23-3, page 319

Answers: **1.** Anna ordered the sandwich special, and Dave ordered the chef's salad. **3.** In 1910, Luther Gulick founded Camp Fire Girls, and the organization still exists today. **5.** The Kingdom of Lesotho does have a king, but the Prime Minister governs the country. **7.** Soldiers and hunters wear camouflage so that they blend in with their surroundings. **9.** The lawyers discussed a settlement, but the defendant refused it.

Chapter 24

◆ PRACTICE 24-1, page 324

Answers: **1.** Present participle modifier: Surfing the Web; modifies: Ada **3.** Present participle modifier: Sampling the appetizers; modifies: I **5.** Present participle modifier: Wanting to keep some open space downtown; modifies: planners **7.** Present participle modifier: Explaining the significance of the architecture at Machu Picchu; modifies: guide **9.** Present participle modifier: wishing him luck; modifies: parents

◆ PRACTICE 24-3, page 326

Answers: **1.** Past participle modifier: Seated in the fifth row; modifies: I **3.** Past participle modifier: fascinated by bugs; modifies: Georgia **5.** Past participle modifier: delayed by rain; modifies: game **7.** Past participle modifier: Forced to increase the price of stamps; modifies: U.S. Postal Service **9.** Past participle modifier: produced on an assembly line; modifies: furniture

◆ PRACTICE 24-5, page 328

Possible answers: **1.** Coming home from a long day of mowing lawns, Allison thought an ice cream cone sounded perfect. **3.** Convinced by friends to leave her current job, Janelle found a new job in two weeks. **5.** Working full-time at the coffee shop, I did not always finish my homework. **7.** Raised in Florida, Alessandra thought the winters in Michigan seemed harsh. **9.** Prepared for an afternoon at the game, she did not expect the rain.

◆ PRACTICE 24-6, page 330

Possible answers: **1.** The angry bull with a ring in his nose threw every rodeo rider. **3.** Blushing furiously, Henry quickly closed the bathroom door. **5.** A car kept in a garage is not likely to be damaged by rust. **7.** With enthusiasm, a bartender served strong drinks. **9.** A white limousine waited as the director, blowing kisses, came out of the restaurant.

Chapter 25

◆ **PRACTICE 25-1, page 340**

Answers: **1.** Verb: watch; present **3.** Verb: lived; past **5.** Verb: received; past **7.** Verb: killed; past **9.** Verb: bloomed; past

◆ **PRACTICE 25-2, page 341**

Answers: **1.** qualified **3.** considered **5.** rejected **7.** remained **9.** tried

◆ **PRACTICE 25-3, page 343**

Answers: **1.** knew **3.** froze **5.** found **7.** fought; lost **9.** lit

◆ **PRACTICE 25-4, page 344**

Answers: **1.** became **3.** found **5.** drew **7.** rose; fought **9.** said

◆ **PRACTICE 25-5, page 345**

Answers: **1.** was **3.** was **5.** were **7.** was **9.** was

◆ **PRACTICE 25-6, page 345**

Answers: **1.** Correct **3.** was **5.** was **7.** were **9.** were

◆ **PRACTICE 25-7, page 347**

Answers: **1.** would **3.** can **5.** could **7.** could **9.** could

◆ **PRACTICE 25-8, page 347**

Answers: **1.** can **3.** would **5.** can; could **7.** would **9.** will; would

Chapter 26

◆ **PRACTICE 26-1, page 352**

Answers: **1.** Present: agrees; past: agreed; past participle: agreed **3.** Present: drops; past: dropped; past participle: dropped **5.** Present: works; past: worked; past participle: worked

◆ **PRACTICE 26-2, page 353**

Answers: **1.** lived **3.** escaped **5.** helped **7.** inspired **9.** earned

◆ **PRACTICE 26-3, page 356**

Answers: **1.** Present: takes; past: took; past participle: taken **3.** Present: spend; past: spent; past participle: spent **5.** Present: chooses; past: chose; past participle: chosen

◆ **PRACTICE 26-4, page 358**

Answers: **1.** received **3.** spent **5.** let **7.** built **9.** planned

◆ **PRACTICE 26-5, page 359**

Answers: **1.** has been **3.** have chosen **5.** has caused **7.** have led **9.** have welcomed

◆ **PRACTICE 26-6, page 360**

Answers: **1.** have enjoyed **3.** played **5.** saw **7.** have had; has pitched **9.** moved

◆ **PRACTICE 26-7, page 361**

Answers: **1.** had become **3.** had marketed **5.** had been **7.** have used **9.** have developed

◆ **PRACTICE 26-8, page 362**

Answers: **1.** had done; hoped **3.** ran **5.** had planned; made **7.** spent **9.** had arrived **11.** had shown; proved

◆ **PRACTICE 26-9, page 363**

Answers: **1.** Correct **3.** Correct **5.** uniformed **7.** created **9.** Correct

Chapter 27

◆ **PRACTICE 27-1, page 367**

Answers: **1.** holiday (common); year (common); spirits (common); dead (common) **3.** holiday (common); Aztecs (proper); ritual (common) **5.** people (common); Day of the Dead (proper); regions (common) **7.** Mexico City (proper); residents (common); festival (common); town (common); skeletons (common); skulls (common); papier-mâché (common) **9.** places (common); tourists (common); celebration (common)

◆ **PRACTICE 27-2, page 369**

Possible answers: **1.** apartment **3.** passengers **5.** potatoes **7.** child; night **9.** libraries

◆ **PRACTICE 27-3, page 369**

Answers: **1.** months **3.** Correct **5.** year **7.** burger **9.** problems

◆ **PRACTICE 27-4, page 371**

Answers: **1.** ladies-in-waiting (irregular) **3.** potatoes **5.** benches **7.** calendars **9.** highways **11.** cheeses **13.** enemies (irregular) **15.** calves (irregular) **17.** taxes **19.** stomachs

◆ **PRACTICE 27-5, page 372**

Answers: **1.** Correct; countries **3.** men **5.** spices; pearls **7.** years **9.** enemies

Chapter 28

◆ **PRACTICE 28-1, page 376**

Possible answers: **1.** She **3.** We **5.** it **7.** he **9.** we

◆ **PRACTICE 28-2, page 377**

Answers: **1.** woman **3.** hitchhiker **5.** lawyers **7.** Esteban **9.** Fries

◆ **PRACTICE 28-3, page 378**

Answers: **1.** schools **3.** parents **5.** schools **7.** Washington, D.C. **9.** program

◆ **PRACTICE 28-4, page 379**

Answers: **1.** Compound antecedent: Her power and intelligence; connecting word: and; pronoun: their **3.** Compound antecedent: power and position; connecting word: and; pronoun: them **5.** Compound antecedent: movies and television; connecting word: and; pronoun: their **7.** Compound antecedent: Cover Girl cosmetics and Pizza Hut restaurants; connecting word: and; pronoun: their **9.** Compound antecedent: *Last Holiday* and *Beauty Shop*; connecting word: and; pronoun: their

◆ **PRACTICE 28-5, page 381**

Possible answers: **1.** Someone left his or her key in the lock. **3.** All the people on the platform missed their train. **5.** All of the telemarketers hated making their calls at dinnertime. **7.** Anyone would love to give this toy to his or her children. **9.** All of the students must email their essays to the professor.

◆ **PRACTICE 28-6, page 381**

Answers: **1.** Indefinite pronoun antecedent: many; pronoun: their **3.** Indefinite pronoun antecedent: Someone; pronoun: his or her **5.** Indefinite pronoun antecedent: both; pronoun: their **7.** Indefinite pronoun antecedent: few; pronoun: their **9.** Indefinite pronoun antecedent: each; pronoun: his or her

◆ **PRACTICE 28-7, page 383**

Answers: **1.** Antecedent: pack (collective); pronoun: its **3.** Antecedent: officers; pronoun: their **5.** Antecedent: gang (collective); pronoun: its **7.** Antecedent: class (collective); pronoun: its **9.** Antecedent: jury (collective); pronoun: its

◆ **PRACTICE 28-8, page 383**

Answers: **1.** Correct; their **3.** his or her **5.** his or her **7.** its **9.** Correct

◆ **PRACTICE 28-9, page 385**

Answers: **1.** Canada has many sparsely populated areas. **3.** The video game that I bought broke almost immediately. **5.** Her granddaughter lives in another state. **7.** These apples were damaged in the hailstorm. **9.** The acrobat almost fell off the tightrope.

◆ **PRACTICE 28-10, page 388**

Answers: **1.** He (subjective); his (possessive) **3.** I (subjective); my (possessive) **5.** mine (possessive); yours (possessive) **7.** me (objective); her (objective) **9.** Their (possessive); we (subjective); them (objective); our (possessive)

◆ **PRACTICE 28-11, page 388**

Answers: **1.** him (indirect object) **3.** us (direct object) **5.** him (direct object) **7.** you (indirect object) **9.** me (indirect object)

◆ **PRACTICE 28-12, page 390**

Answers: **1.** him **3.** her **5.** I **7.** he **9.** them

◆ **PRACTICE 28-13, page 391**

Answers: **1.** he [is] **3.** I [eat] **5.** [it frightens] me **7.** [it cost] us **9.** [he pays] her

◆ **PRACTICE 28-14, page 392**

Answers: **1.** who **3.** who **5.** who **7.** who **9.** whom

◆ **PRACTICE 28-15, page 394**

Answers: **1.** herself **3.** itself **5.** myself **7.** yourself [or yourselves] **9.** themselves

Chapter 29

◆ **PRACTICE 29-1, page 399**

Answers: **1.** famous **3.** big **5.** modest **7.** rare **9.** talented

◆ **PRACTICE 29-2, page 400**

Answers: **1.** noisily **3.** bravely **5.** uncomfortably; quickly

◆ **PRACTICE 29-3, page 401**

Answers: **1.** nearly **3.** differently **5.** freely **7.** widely **9.** really **11.** regularly

◆ **PRACTICE 29-4, page 402**

Answers: **1.** well **3.** good **5.** good **7.** good **9.** well **11.** well **13.** well

◆ **PRACTICE 29-5, page 404**

Answers: **1.** stronger **3.** more quickly **5.** neater **7.** fairer **9.** younger **11.** bluer **13.** easier **15.** more useful **17.** harder **19.** deeper

◆ **PRACTICE 29-6, page 405**

Answers: **1.** strongest **3.** most quickly **5.** neatest **7.** fairest **9.** youngest **11.** bluest **13.** easiest **15.** most useful **17.** hardest **19.** deepest

◆ **PRACTICE 29-7, page 405**

Answers: **1.** more quickly **3.** stronger **5.** more clearly **7.** more freely **9.** poorer

◆ **PRACTICE 29-8, page 406**

Answers: **1.** craziest **3.** tiniest **5.** most necessary **7.** greatest **9.** most surprising

◆ **PRACTICE 29-9, page 407**

Answers: **1.** best **3.** better **5.** best **7.** better **9.** worse

◆ **PRACTICE 29-10, page 408**

Answers: **1.** That **3.** this **5.** This **7.** those **9.** this

Chapter 30

◆ PRACTICE 30-1, page 413

Answers: **1.** It will rain all day tomorrow. **3.** Javier studied so that he could become an American citizen. **5.** Sofia watched television programs for children when she was learning English. **7.** She waited until she was sure they were gone. **9.** After Jean scored the winning goal, he went out to celebrate with his friends.

◆ PRACTICE 30-2, page 415

Answers: **1.** The old woman sells candles in the shop downstairs. **3.** Dmitri rides his bicycle ten miles every day. **5.** My neighbor watches my daughter in the evenings. **7.** My job starts at six o'clock in the morning. **9.** The best thing in my life is that my family is together again. OR I feel lucky that my family is together again.

◆ PRACTICE 30-3, page 417

Answers: **1.** challenges **3.** classes **5.** people **7.** women; pants **9.** dogs; scraps

◆ PRACTICE 30-4, page 419

Answers: **1.** Noncount **3.** Noncount **5.** Count; beaches **7.** Noncount **9.** Noncount

◆ PRACTICE 30-5, page 420

Answers: **1.** Few **3.** many **5.** a few **7.** These **9.** some

◆ PRACTICE 30-6, page 423

Answers: **1.** The; the **3.** a; a **5.** The; a **7.** a; no article **9.** an; no article **11.** the; the

◆ PRACTICE 30-7, page 425

Answers: **1.** Question: Are the sparrows searching for winter food? Negative statement: The sparrows are not searching for winter food. **3.** Question: Did I answer her email immediately? Negative statement: I did not answer her email immediately. **5.** Question: Did the porcupine attack my dog? Negative statement: The porcupine did not attack my dog. **7.** Question: Did Gunnar see the robbery at the convenience store? Negative statement: Gunnar did not see the robbery at the convenience store. **9.** Question: Is he working on the problem right now? Negative statement: He is not working on the problem right now.

◆ PRACTICE 30-8, page 427

Answers: **1.** Verb: is studying (Correct) **3.** Verb: is understanding (understands) **5.** Verb: is working (Correct) **7.** Verb: is hating (hates) **9.** Verb: is earning (Correct)

◆ PRACTICE 30-9, page 429

Answers: **1.** might **3.** should **5.** should **7.** Would **9.** can

◆ PRACTICE 30-10, page 430

Answers: **1.** Eating **3.** cleaning **5.** Quitting **7.** organizing **9.** cooking

◆ PRACTICE 30-11, page 431

Answers: **1.** a pleasant old family tradition **3.** Anita's four cute poodles **5.** both my annoying sisters **7.** a delightful outdoor wedding celebration **9.** a wonderful chocolate birthday cake

◆ PRACTICE 30-12, page 435

Answers: **1.** from **3.** in; in **5.** with **7.** of; in **9.** in; of

◆ PRACTICE 30-13, page 437

Answers: **1.** Chong had never traveled alone, and she wanted to try it out. **3.** Correct **5.** She told her husband that the children had to get to school early on Friday and that he should wake them up at 6:30 a.m. **7.** When her husband and children asked how long she would be gone, Chong put them off. **9.** Correct.

Chapter 31

◆ PRACTICE 31-1, page 446

Answers: **1.** The street was crowded with buses, cars, and trucks. **3.** Correct **5.** A good marriage requires patience, honesty, and hard work. **7.** Correct **9.** The kitchen is to the left, the guest room is upstairs, and the pool is out back.

◆ PRACTICE 31-2, page 447

Answers: **1.** According to recent studies, most parents of young children use the TV as a babysitter. **3.** Correct **5.** Correct **7.** Correct **9.** To purchase a new home, you have to consider whether you will be able to manage the mortgage payments.

◆ PRACTICE 31-3, page 449

Answers: **1.** Bill, how did you do on the test? **3.** Correct **5.** When you give your speech, Jeanne, be sure to speak clearly. **7.** The party, consequently, was a disaster. **9.** Don't forget the key to the cabin, Amber. **11.** Furthermore, the team had lost its best defensive player. **13.** What material will be on the test, Dr. Chen? **15.** Besides, genetics is the next medical frontier.

◆ PRACTICE 31-5, page 451

Answers: **1.** My mother, Sandra Thomas, used to work for the city. **3.** The convention is in Chicago, my hometown. **5.** The world's tallest mountain, Mount Everest, is in Nepal. **7.** Aloe, a common houseplant, has medicinal value. **9.** Elvis Presley, a white singer, was influenced by African-American music.

◆ PRACTICE 31-6, page 453

Answers: **1.** Correct **3.** The camera, which is automatic, is easy to use. **5.** Correct **7.** Rafael, who finishes work at 5:30, met Carla for dinner at 7:00. **9.** Gray wolves, which many ranchers dislike, are making a comeback in the West.

◆ PRACTICE 31-7, page 454

Answers: **1.** Correct **3.** Correct **5.** The women, who call themselves the Weavers Society, needed buyers for their products. **7.** A company that sells satellite telephones donated some phones to the weavers. **9.** The weavers, who could find no customers in their own village, soon sold many of their hammocks to customers in other regions.

◆ PRACTICE 31-8, page 454

Answers: **1.** Correct **3.** Having escaped from Europe, which was occupied by the Nazis, these athletes put their skiing and survival skills to use. **5.** They trained in the Colorado mountains for three years, which gave them plenty of time to prepare. **7.** The battle that eventually earned them fame and respect was a successful sneak attack on the German forces on Italy's Mt. Belvedere. **9.** Aspen and Vail, which are now two of the most popular ski resorts in the United States, were founded by veterans of this division.

◆ PRACTICE 31-9, page 456

Answers: **1.** Alaska is a rugged state, and its population is small. **3.** Although many people live in Alaska's cities, many others live in small villages. **5.** Correct **7.** Correct **9.** Correct

◆ PRACTICE 31-10, page 457

Answers: **1.** Atif is from Lahore, Pakistan. **3.** Their first home was at 2122 Kent Avenue, Brooklyn, New York. **5.** They wanted to move to Boston, Massachusetts, where Atif's cousins lived. **7.** Their new address was 14 Arden Street, Allston, Massachusetts. **9.** Correct

Chapter 32

◆ PRACTICE 32-1, page 461

Answers: **1.** This means that students from low-income families who can't pay for school can still get a college education. **3.** The college wants only students who wouldn't otherwise be able to afford to attend a four-year college. **5.** Berea has made itself unique in other ways as well, in ways that other schools haven't. **7.** It's not unusual for Berea students to spend many hours every week volunteering in their Appalachian community. **9.** The school offers students a rare opportunity in an age when income tends to determine who's eligible for college and who isn't.

◆ PRACTICE 32-2, page 462

Answers: **1.** It's fairly common for couples to be infertile, but they don't have to give up on having a family; they might be able to adopt a child from a foreign country. **3.** Modern reproduction technology can't help all couples; it doesn't work for everyone, and it's very expensive. **5.** Correct **7.** It's really important for adoptive parents to know the laws of their child's native country. **9.** There's one thing that's really important: a careful medical evaluation of the child to identify any serious health problems.

◆ PRACTICE 32-3, page 464

Answers: **1.** the shop's owner **3.** my neighbor's cat **5.** Indira's cell phone **7.** Chris's sister **9.** our class's opinion

◆ PRACTICE 32-4, page 464

Answers: **1.** the travelers' bags **3.** the women's faces **5.** the ministers' car **7.** the Huangs' apartment **9.** the lawyers' first meeting

◆ PRACTICE 32-5, page 464

Answers: **1.** New York's **3.** Correct; father's **5.** Harold Lee's; Correct **7.** family's; Chinatown's **9.** agency's; Arthur's

◆ PRACTICE 32-6, page 466

Answers: **1.** its **3.** it's **5.** its **7.** you're **9.** it's

◆ PRACTICE 32-7, page 466

Answers: **1.** lovers' **3.** Correct; it's **5.** its; Correct **7.** Who's **9.** Correct; residents'; your

Chapter 33

◆ PRACTICE 33-1, page 473

Answers: **1.** These shows are like American soap operas but with several important differences. **3.** Correct **5.** The popularity of the telenovelas has caught the attention of American networks; several plan to create telenovelas for American audiences.

◆ PRACTICE 33-2, page 474

Answers: **1.** Correct. **3.** The quality of a digital camera's image is measured in megapixels: the higher the number, the better the image. **5.** Web sites like cnet.com offer helpful advice and guidance for new users.

◆ PRACTICE 33-3, page 474

Possible answers: **1.** He was born in Dublin (the capital of Ireland) in 1960. **3.** As U2 became more popular (selling over 50 million albums in the United States alone), Bono continued to voice his opinion on many of the world's problems. **5.** He has traveled around the world speaking about the urgent need to provide economic assistance to Africa (which owes countries such as the United States billions of dollars).

Chapter 34

◆ **PRACTICE 34-1, page 480**

Answers: **1.** The Ojibwa are the largest Native American group in North America. **3.** The Ojibwa migrated to the Midwest from their original homes near the Atlantic Ocean. **5.** Activist Winona LaDuke, who served as the principal of an Ojibwa school, ran for vice president on the Green Party ticket in 2000.

◆ **PRACTICE 34-3, page 482**

Answers: **1.** "I will do my best to defeat the new immigration bill," the senator promised. "I will do my best," the senator promised, "to defeat the new immigration bill." **3.** "I wonder if we will ever have a woman president of the United States," Sunita said. "I wonder," Sunita said, "if we will ever have a woman president of the United States."

◆ **PRACTICE 34-4, page 483**

Answers: **1.** *The guide announced*, "Whatever you do, don't leave the group." **3.** "Move along, everyone!" *the officer shouted.* **5.** "If we get separated," *Paul asked,* "where should I meet you?"

◆ **PRACTICE 34-5, page 484**

Answers: **1.** The newsmagazine *U.S. News and World Report* featured a review of the movie made from the book *The Da Vinci Code*. **3.** The musical *Wicked*, based on the book *The Wizard of Oz*, shows what might have happened before the events in the book. **5.** Julia Child's best-selling cookbook *Mastering the Art of French Cooking* has a section called "Kitchen Equipment" and another section called "Ingredients."

◆ **PRACTICE 34-6, page 484**

Answers: **1.** Lucy's favorite novel is *For Whom the Bell Tolls*. **3.** Television cartoons created for adults include *The Simpsons* and *King of the Hill*. **5.** The articles "Stream of Consciousness" and "School's Out" in *Wired* magazine focus on new technology.

◆ **PRACTICE 34-7, page 485**

Answers: **1.** Our forward-thinking boss is always coming up with new ways to improve sales. **3.** People often argue about banning cigarettes in all pub-lic places. **5.** In February, many popular magazines are filled with Oscar-related articles.

Chapter 35

◆ **PRACTICE 35-1, page 493**

Answers: **1.** Correct; achieve **3.** Neither; Correct **5.** Correct; Correct **7.** society; Correct **9.** relieve; Correct

◆ **PRACTICE 35-2, page 494**

Answers: **1.** uneasy **3.** overcook **5.** unwind **7.** underpay **9.** prewar

◆ **PRACTICE 35-3, page 495**

Answers: **1.** adorable **3.** judgment **5.** whistled **7.** truly **9.** insurance **11.** senseless **13.** noticeable **15.** amusement **17.** imagination **19.** microscopic

◆ **PRACTICE 35-4, page 496**

Answers: **1.** trying **3.** noisily **5.** destroyed **7.** dryness **9.** tinier **11.** busily **13.** replied **15.** thirtyish **17.** joyful **19.** daily

◆ **PRACTICE 35-5, page 497**

Answers: **1.** shopper **3.** preferred **5.** climbed **7.** fairest **9.** beginning **11.** written **13.** appealing **15.** existing **17.** runner **19.** trapper

Chapter 36

◆ **PRACTICE 36-1, page 501**

Answers: **1.** Correct; Correct **3.** affect; Correct **5.** Correct; Correct **7.** By; already **9.** Correct; Correct

◆ **PRACTICE 36-2, page 503**

Answers: **1.** conscious **3.** It's; hear **5.** Every day; its **7.** every day; Correct **9.** conscious; its

◆ **PRACTICE 36-3, page 504**

Answers: **1.** laid; Correct **3.** past; mind **5.** lose **7.** lie; Correct **9.** Correct; lie

◆ **PRACTICE 36-4, page 506**

Answers: **1.** Correct; rise **3.** plain; Correct **5.** quiet; site **7.** Correct; Correct **9.** Correct; principal

◆ **PRACTICE 36-5, page 507**

Answers: **1.** used; their **3.** through; Correct; their **5.** Correct; Correct **7.** Correct; their **9.** Correct; too

◆ **PRACTICE 36-6, page 509**

Answers: **1.** Who's; Correct **3.** You're; your **5.** Were; Correct **7.** you're; Correct **9.** Whose; where

Acknowledgments

Picture acknowledgments

3, Jenny Pouech; 21 (top), Google homepage image © Google Inc.; 21 (bottom), © 2006, Yahoo! Inc.; 26, Gary Conner/Index Stock Imagery, Inc.; 27, © 2001, Tropicana Products, Inc.; 28, The Metropolitan Museum of Art, Catharine Lorillard Wolfe Collection, Wolfe Fund, 1906. (06.1234) Photograph © 1995, The Metropolitan Museum of Art; 43, Michael Bryant/*Philadelphia Inquirer*; 45, U.S. Environmental Protection Agency; 51, Bob Daemmrich Photography, Inc.; 71, Lee Snider/The Image Works; 90 (top), AP/Wide World Images; 90 (center), © 2007 eBay Inc. All rights reserved.; 90 (bottom), David Graham/AP; 92, Bettmann/CORBIS; 100, Steve Skjold/PhotoEdit; 101, Mike Watson Images/SuperStock; 109, Elizabeth Barakah Hodges/SuperStock; 110, Richard Cummins/CORBIS; 119, Visions of America, LLC/Alamy; 120, David Bentley/CORBIS; 129, Chuck Savage/CORBIS; 130, Getty Images; 139, David Young-Wolff/PhotoEdit; 140, Jerzyworks/Masterfile; 152 (left), Mark Sherman/Grant Heilman Photography; 152 (right), Fabian Bimmer/AP Images; 153, Ian Shaw/Alamy; 162 (top), Columbia Pictures/Photofest; 162 (center), Warner Bros., courtesy Everett Collection; 162 (bottom), Everett Collection; 163, Roberto Schmidt/AFP/Getty Images; 172 (top left), Alistair Berg/Photonica/Getty Images; 172 (top right), David Young-Wolff/Photographer's Choice/Getty Images; 172 (bottom right), Ken Chernus/Photodisc Red/Getty Images; 172 (bottom left), Jeff Greenberg/PhotoEdit; 173, Columbia Pictures/Photofest; 183 Getty Images; 184, Lou Requena/AP Images; 197, Plush Studios/Bill Reitzel/Blend Images/Getty Images; 203, Michael Newman/PhotoEdit; 213 (top), AP Images; 213 (bottom), Library of Congress; 215, Zefa/CORBIS; 229 (top), MTV/Photofest; 229 (bottom), ThinkFilm, courtesy Everett Collection; 233, Dave Nagel/The Image Bank/Getty Images; 242 (top), Jeff Greenberg/PhotoEdit; 242 (bottom), David Young-Wolff/PhotoEdit; 244, Judy Gelles; 257 (top), Dennis MacDonald/age fotostock; 257 (bottom), John Giustina/Iconica/Getty Images; 259, Charles Gupton Photography; 265 (top), Bettmann/CORBIS; 265 (bottom), Bettmann/CORBIS; 267 (top), Spencer Grant/PhotoEdit; 267 (bottom), National Archives; 268, Jeff Greenberg/PhotoEdit; 271, Scott Houston/Sygma/CORBIS; 282, Nocturno Estudio/age fotostock; 283, The Kobal Collection; 285, Joe Raedle/Getty Images; 300, Ricco/Maresca Gallery/Art Resource, NY; 301, Myrleen Ferguson Cate/PhotoEdit; 302, John Elk III; 312, Bobby Yip/REUTERS; 313 (top), Alan Schein Photography/CORBIS; 313 (bottom), Tony Freeman/PhotoEdit; 315, John Barry/Syracuse Newspapers/The Image Works; 320, From PERSEPOLIS: THE STORY OF A CHILDHOOD by Marjane Satrapi, translated by Mattias Ripa & Blake Ferris, Translation copyright © by L'Association, Paris, France. Used by permission of Pantheon Books, a division of Random House.; 321 (top), V for Vendetta™ and © 1990 DC Comics. All Rights Reserved. Used with Permission.; 321 (bottom), Stu Forster/Getty Images; 323, Mitch Diamond/Index Stock Imagery, Inc.; 332 (top), Mireille Vautier/The Art Archive; 332 (center), Getty Images; 332 (bottom), William Gottlieb/CORBIS; 334 (top), Ric Feld/AP Images; 334 (bottom), Getty Images; 335, Shane Young/The New York Times/Redux; 337, Time Life Photos/Getty Images; 349 (top), Stapleton Collection/Bridgeman Art Library; 349 (bottom), Index Stock Imagery, Inc.; 351, C Squared Studios/Photodisc Green/Getty Images; 364, BOONDOCKS © 2004 Aaron McGruder. Dist. By UNIVERSAL PRESS SYNDICATE. Reprinted with permission. All rights reserved.; 366, Syracuse Newspapers/The Image Works; 373, James Marshall/The Image Works; 375, CORBIS; 395, Scholastic Studio 10/Index Stock Imagery, Inc.; 410, Bob Daemmrich/The Image Works; 412, Bob Daemmrich/The Image Works; 438 (top), Library of Congress; 438 (center), Library of Congress; 438 (bottom), Brooks Craft/CORBIS; 441 (top), AP Images; 441 (bottom), CIA-The World Factbook; 442, Tass/Sovfoto; 445, Dan Loh/AP Images; 458 (top), Bettmann/CORBIS; 458 (bottom), Bettmann/CORBIS; 460, Grantpix/Photo Researchers, Inc.; 468, Volvox/Index Stock Imagery, Inc.; 471, Ken Sherman/Graphistock/Jupiterimages; 476 (top), Creatas/age fotostock; 476 (bottom), © St. Petersburg Times 2004; 477, Warner Bros./Photofest; 487 (top), Getty Images; 487 (bottom), Kevin Winter/Getty Images; 490, AP Images; 498 (top), Bob

Daemmrich/The Image Works; 498 (bottom), Jeff Dunn/Index Stock Imagery, Inc.; 500, George B. Jones III/Photo Researchers, Inc.; 510, Seth Perlman/AP Images; 512 (top), Barry Austin Photography/Riser/Getty Images; 512 (bottom), Kirk Anderson; 513, Bob Daemmrich/The Image Works.

Text acknowledgments

Kiku Adatto. "Trigger-Happy Birthday." From *The New York Times*. Copyright © The New York Times Company. Reprinted by permission.

American Heritage Dictionary of the English Language, Third Edition. Entries "teach," "frying pan," "tax," "sneak." Copyright © 1996 by Houghton Mifflin Company. Reprinted by permission from *The American Heritage Dictionary of the English Language*, Third Edition.

Bobbi Buchanan. "Don't Hang Up, That's My Mom Calling." From *The New York Times*, December 8, 2003. Copyright © 2003 The New York Times Company. Reprinted by permission.

José Antonio Burciaga. "Tortillas." Reprinted with permission.

Tricia Capistrano. "Emil's Big Chance Leaves Me Uneasy." First published in *Newsweek*, June 19, 2006. Copyright © 2006 Tricia Capistrano. Reprinted with permission of the author.

Henry Louis Gates Jr. "Delusions of Grandeur." Originally published in *Sports Illustrated*. Copyright © 1991 by Dr. Henry Louis Gates, Jr. Reprinted with the permission of the author.

Ray Hanania. "One of the Bad Guys?" Originally published in *Newsweek*, November 2, 1998. Copyright © 1998 Ray Hanania. Reprinted with permission of the author.

John Hartmire. "At the Heart of a Historic Movement." From *Newsweek*, July 24, 2000, p. 12. Copyright © 2000 Newsweek, Inc. Reprinted with permission. All rights reserved.

Macarena Hernández. "America, Stand Up for Justice and Decency." From the *Dallas Morning News*, October 15, 2005. Copyright © 2005 Dallas Morning News. Reprinted with permission of the Dallas Morning News.

Yiyun Li. "Orange Crush." From *The New York Times Magazine*, January 22, 2006. Copyright © 2006 by The New York Times Company. Reprinted by permission.

Arthur Miller. "Before Air Conditioning." Copyright © Arthur Miller. Reprinted with permission of International Creative Management, Inc.

Robb Moretti. "The Last Generation to Live on the Edge." From *Newsweek*, August 5, 2002. Copyright © 2002 Newsweek, Inc. Reprinted with permission. All rights reserved.

Joshua Piven and David Borgenicht. "How to Stop a Car with No Brakes" (including line art). From *Worst-Case Scenario Survival Handbook: Travel* by Joshua Piven and David Borgenicht. Copyright © 2001 by book soup publishing, inc. Used with permission of Chronicle Books LLC, San Francisco. Visit www.chroniclebooks.com.

Lucie Prinz. "Say Something." Originally published in *Atlantic Monthly*, October 1996. Copyright © 1996 Lucie Prinz. Reprinted with permission of the author.

Carolyn Foster Segal. "The Dog Ate My Disk, and Other Tales of Woe." Originally published in *The Chronicle of Higher Education*. Copyright © Carolyn Foster Segal. Reprinted with permission of the author.

Susan Snyder and Kristin E. Holmes. "Philadelphia students get a scholarship guarantee." From the *Philadelphia Inquirer*, October 1, 2003. Copyright © 2003 Philadelphia Inquirer. Reprinted by permission of the publisher.

Linda S. Wallace. "A 'Good' American Citizen." Originally published in *The Christian Science Monitor*, April 1, 2003, p. 11. Copyright © 2003 by Linda S. Wallace. Reprinted with permission of the author.

William Zinsser. "The Transaction." From *On Writing Well*, Seventh (30th Anniversary) edition by William Zinsser. Copyright © 1976, 1980, 1985, 1988, 1990, 1944, 1998, 2001, 2006 by William K. Zinsser. Reprinted by permission of the author.

Index

Note: Page numbers in **bold** type indicate pages where terms are defined.

Index of Rhetorical Patterns

Correction Symbols

This chart lists symbols that many instructors use to point out writing problems in student papers. Next to each problem is the chapter or section of *Foundations First* where you can find help with that problem. If your instructor uses different symbols from those shown here, write them in the space provided.

YOUR INSTRUCTOR'S SYMBOL	STANDARD SYMBOL	PROBLEM
________	*adj*	problem with use of adjective 29A
________	*adv*	problem with use of adverb 29A
________	*agr*	agreement problem (subject-verb) 22
________		agreement problem (pronoun-antecedent) 28A–B
________	*apos*	apostrophe missing or used incorrectly 32
________	*awk*	awkward sentence structure 23, 24
________	*cap*	capital letter needed 34A
________	*case*	problem with pronoun case 28D–E
________	*cliché*	cliché 18E
________	*coh*	lack of paragraph coherence 4C
________	*combine*	combine sentences 16, 21B
________	*cs*	comma splice 20
________	*d*	diction (poor word choice) 18C
________	*dev*	lack of paragraph development 4B
________	*frag*	sentence fragment 21
________	*fs*	fused sentence 20
________	*ital*	italics or underlining needed 34C
________	*lc*	lower case; capital letter not needed 34A
________	*para* or ¶	indent new paragraph 3A
________	*pass*	overuse of passive voice 23C
________	*prep*	nonstandard use of preposition 30M–O
________	*ref*	pronoun reference not specific 28B
________	*ro*	run-on 20
________	*shift*	illogical shift 23
________	*sp*	incorrect spelling 35
________	*tense*	problem with verb tense 25, 26
________	*thesis*	thesis unclear or not stated 14D
________	*trans*	transition needed 4C
________	*unity*	paragraph not unified 4A
________	*w*	wordy, not concise 18D
________	//	problem with parallelism 19
________	(,)	problem with comma use 31
________	(;)	problem with semicolon use 33A
________	(“ ”)	problem with quotation marks 34B
________	⁀‿	close up space
________	^	insert
________	ℓ	delete
________	∼	reversed letters or words
________	*X*	obvious error
________	✓	good point, well put